Intermediate Microeconomics with Applications

INTERNATIONAL EDITION

International Edition

Intermediate Micro-economics with Applications

Aroop K. Mahanty UNIVERSITY OF NORTHERN COLORADO

Academic Press NEW YORK SAN FRANCISCO LONDON
A Subsidiary of Harcourt Brace Jovanovich, Publishers

International Edition
Cover Photo by Dan Lenore

ACADEMIC PRESS, INC.
111 Fifth Avenue, New York, New York 10003

United Kingdom Edition published by
ACADEMIC PRESS, INC. (LONDON) LTD.
24/28 Oval Road, London NW1 7DX

ISBN: 0-12-465160-7
Library of Congress Catalog Card Number: 78-73965
PRINTED IN THE UNITED STATES OF AMERICA

To my mother and father

CONTENTS

PREFACE

This book was written with the premise that there are better methods to show the practicality and excitement of microeconomics than through widgets and indifference curves for meat and potatoes. It essentially grew out of a class in microeconomics and one in managerial economics accompanied by the lack of a totally satisfying textbook. I have written this book as I would teach my classes. It is a culmination of my efforts to share with my students and colleagues some of the ideas and innovations that I have used very effectively in the past eleven years.

I have included many applications—both hypothesized and from actual empirical models—in each chapter. Some topics thought solely to be in the domain of business or operations research are included in separate chapters. These include linear programming, decisions under uncertainty, and cash flow analysis. Individual chapters are also devoted to the discussion of profits, revenue, and the economics of regulation.

One of the best ways to motivate students is to ask questions which are thought provoking as well as interesting. To that end I have included many exercises at the end of each chapter. There is also a current list of references following each chapter.

Mathematics and graphs are included only when they reinforce a point. All diagrams are very clear and explanations accompany each graph, obviating the need of referring to the text. Because footnotes are distracting, only those considered absolutely necessary are included. A detailed set of appendices containing advanced material or descriptions of quantitative methods appears at the end of the book. I have also included a comprehensive glossary of terms.

Since portions of each chapter may be deleted without any loss in continuity, this text can be used for several courses. My colleagues will find the book suitable either for economics or business majors at the undergraduate level, or as an introductory book for exploratory graduate courses in business administration, or other areas requiring knowledge of price theory. I have included material that is contained in all the leading microeconomics books, however, the emphases are different. There is much of the gospel according to Mahanty between the covers, and I hope that I prove to be half as good an evangelist as my predecessors.

My dissertation contained a very simple acknowledgement—"To Him, to her, and to them." I think I will be a little more specific this time. It is not easy to recognize all the ways in which a person has been helpful to a project, so if I leave anyone out it is simply because I am human and not because I intended to omit the person from my list.

I owe a tremendous debt to my wife, Pauletta Jane, and my three beautiful children, Radhika Linda, Devika Mae, and Daniel Ranjeet. Although they do not admit it, there is no doubt that they bore a heavy burden during the time I was so engrossed with the manuscript. My wife even took up long distance jogging and is now one of the city's better runners.

Thanks are due to all the wonderfully patient people at Academic Press and the team of experts who guided me throughout the entire project. I would like to thank Miss Malmalida and Miss Manikuku who typed more than a thousand pages of economics material. Finally, I am grateful to all the Mahantys, the Willigs, the Kaczynskis, the Otises, and the Christensens who stood behind me in solid support.

Greeley, Colorado   **Aroop K. Mahanty**
October 1979

Chapter One Chapter One Chapter One

INTRODUCTION TO MICROECONOMICS

Microeconomics is the detailed economic analysis of individual components of a society. Just as a microscope focuses attention on one cell at a time, microeconomics tends to magnify the workings of the individual economic entities in a disaggregated environment. The theories of microeconomics help us understand the economic motivations of buyers, sellers, and governments. They attempt to provide answers to such questions as: Why have coffee prices risen so much? What purpose does the minimum wage have? Why do the OPEC nations wield so much power?

Almost all economic issues involve the resolution of human wants in the face of relatively scarce amounts of resources. Economic units such as consumers and producers must make choices and select the most desirable of the available alternatives. For example, General Motors has a limited quantity of resources. It must decide whether to produce the Corvette, the Corvair, the Monte Carlo, or all three. The correct quantities of each type must be produced in order to realize profits and a good share of the market. Frequently, the objectives of one group may be in direct conflict with those of another. The wage earners, for instance, consistently demand higher wages in order to increase their standard of living, whereas the firms that employ them are very reluctant to grant excessive pay increases because such an act would decrease the profits of the companies. Yet unless wages are increased the labor force may refuse to work. On the other hand, if the companies do grant substantial wage increases, all other things remaining equal, the prices of the products must rise. Most often, once this happens, fewer units of the higher-priced products can be sold which, in effect, may also cause the firms to cut back on hiring. Employees prefer high wages to low ones and at the same time they prefer to pay low prices as consumers.

A SIMPLE MICROECONOMIC MODEL

Every introductory economics class employs a *production-possibilities curve* to bring out the scarcity–choice dilemma faced by an economic society. We will assume that a particular system can produce food and clothing and that it has only two resources, land and labor, in limited quantities. If the methods of production for both items do not change and no other extraordinary changes occur, the economy should be able to produce various combinations of food and clothing. When we plot these combinations of the two goods, we obtain the production-possibilities frontier shown in Figure 1-1a.

You might recall, from your experience in an introductory course in economics, that the study of economics attempted to raise three basic questions concerning consumption, production, and distribution: (1) what, (2) how, and (3) for whom? Thus, with reference to our production-possibilities curve for food and clothing, since only certain combinations of food/clothing were possible, the system's economic agents must choose the appropriate combinations of the two items for production and consumption. Suppose the economy is operating at point *A* at the beginning. Why point *A*? Presumably the consumers expressed certain demands for the two items by way of the market,

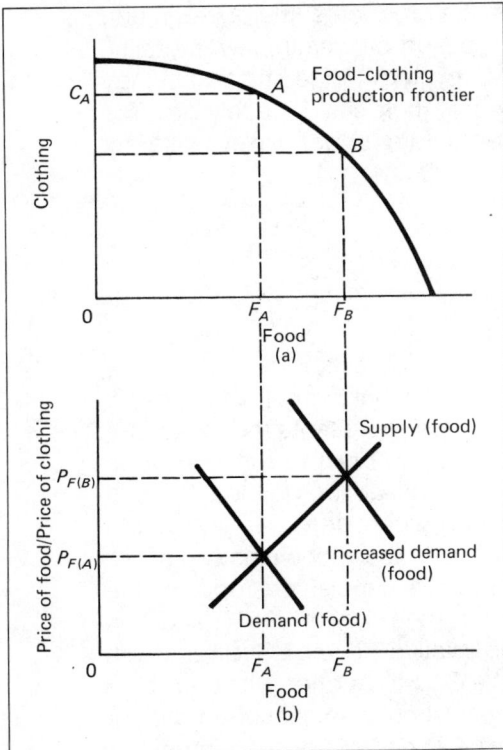

Food-clothing production frontier

(a)

Clothing

Food

Supply (food)

Increased demand (food)

Demand (food)

Food

(b)

FIGURE 1-1
(a) shows the economy's ability to produce food and clothing with all its available resources. In a free market with properly operating demand and supply forces, the food and clothing markets will be at equilibrium when the demand and supply are equal. Thus, initially the economy is at point A on the production-possibilities curve, producing C_A of clothing and F_A of food. This quantity is also being demanded, as shown by one of the markets (food) depicted in (b). At the relative price of (food/clothing) $P_{F(A)}$, the demand and supply in the food industry are equal. If there is a subsequent increase in the demand for food, the production point would move to B and more resources would be allocated to food production and away from clothing. The new higher demand would cause the relative price of food and quantity produced to rise. Such changes would be true if the economy was at, and continued to operate at, full employment. All points along the production boundary of (a) are full-employment points provided all resources are being fully utilized in the most efficient manner consistent with perfect competition.

and the producers reacted by offering the correct amounts of food and clothing at prices which permitted the markets to be in equilibrium. The initial equilibrium is shown for the food industry in Figure 1-1b.

Now suppose that people's tastes changed so that they demanded more food and less clothing. Increased demand for food, other factors remaining equal, would pull up its price and cause suppliers to allocate more resources to food production. We would now have a new equilibrium in the food industry with more being produced and consumed at higher prices. You can understand why the price of clothing would fall in such a "free market" and less clothing would be produced (supplied). A lower demand for clothing would be equated to a smaller quantity supplied at a lower price.

The analysis just concluded illustrates a very simple microeconomic model. It answers part of the set of economic questions: What should be produced? Generally speaking, only those goods and services that are in demand are produced, because not only do they yield profits to the producers but they also bring forth *utility* or happiness to the consumers. Naturally, this model is only valid under the circumstances described and may not operate that way under other conditions. For instance, resources engaged in clothing production may not be mobile enough to be diverted to food production; or the government may enact certain restrictions in consumption or production which would preclude the operations of point B. Economic decisions are made within an environment influenced by the consumers, the producers, the government, the political process, and nature. Constraints posed by wealth, law, morality, religion, ethics, and the environment as well as by knowledge and technology affect these decisions. Microeconomic models help us in analyzing the economic behavior of each of the above factors under many different circumstances.

MICROECONOMICS AND THE THEORY OF PRICE

Microeconomics is often referred to as *price theory*. Ordinarily, the discussions in microeconomics center around the "prices" of the many economic goods and services. We normally assume that every product has a price, be it in terms of money, time, or yams. Price represents the value of a good in terms of other goods, and more accurately, such a price is referred to as a *relative price*. However, since the majority of transactions in today's world are conducted with money, and since money can be converted into goods and vice versa, the dollar may be used as a common denominator in the measurement of prices in the United States just as we can use the rupee as the indicator in India. Thus, if a Cadillac has a market price of $8000 and this textbook sells for $20, we may state that the relative price of Cadillacs with respect to textbooks would be 400:1, or that the Cadillac's price was 400 times that of the textbook and therefore 400 textbooks should be exchangeable for one Cadillac. In a barter economy, where money does not play an important part, presumably the employers pay the employees in kind and even under those circumstances a set of "prices" is possible. But such a system would hardly be conducive to economic growth or consumer satisfaction. Life is complicated enough without having to be paid for in textbooks and tires.

Prices may also reflect the cost or sacrifice incurred in the production of a good. We often speak of paying a "very high price" when we change jobs, for example. In order to produce a higher income, we may move to an unattractive location, and if the higher income at the new location does not adequately compensate for the undesirable elements of that location, we will indeed have paid a high price for moving. Taxes are essentially the price we pay for public goods, and congestion and pollution are the price of progress.

Just as *macroeconomics* emphasizes the aggregate values of the nation's income, employment, and the price level, *microeconomics* emphasizes the price and quantity relationship prevailing in each segment of the complex economic system. This is not to say that the microeconomic models cannot or do not handle other variables in addition to price and quantity, for they do. This textbook, as well as the literature in economics, amply demonstrates that microeconomic models are fully capable of analyzing a multitude of variables in arriving at certain predictable behavioral patterns of the economic entities. Although we keep models of macroeconomics separate from those in microeconomics, the latter is absolutely essential to the understanding of the former. In the end, the microeconomic tools are utilized toward the understanding of the macroeconomic process. For example, we can explain demand–pull inflation without the use of the conventional supply–demand analysis.

NORMATIVE AND POSITIVE MICROECONOMICS

Economics is not a pure science like physics or chemistry. Not only are the many experiments in economics observed under (at best) highly *uncontrolled laboratory conditions,* but the subject matter itself is highly *interdisciplinary.* In addition, the theories concerning economic behavior often incorporate a certain amount of *value judgement.* The Law of Gravity can be proved time after time just as we can always validate Newton's First Law without substantially different results. The many "laws" of economics are based on certain observed or assumed human behavior. But, generally speaking, economics is quite logical and hence the many theorems pertaining to producers, consumers, the government, and society are logically quite consistent, though they may not all be empirically provable. Economics as a discipline is tied closely to sociology, anthropology, psychology, and several other behavioral as well as hard sciences. With the increased use of quantitative techniques and computers, economics is also becoming more sophisticated and more empirical in nature. Keeping the "dual" nature of economics in mind, we define two points of view adopted in economics, including microeconomics. The *normative* view refers to the questions concerning *what ought to be.* For example, should the government provide free medical care to everyone? On the other hand, *positive* economics reflects on *what is.* A positivist might ask: Do firms maximize profits? In the models that we will discuss, you will encounter both points of view and that is often what makes microeconomics so exciting.

ASSUMPTIONS AND MICROECONOMICS

There are so many variables that affect economic behavior that it is almost impossible to analyze each and every one of them without confusing the main issue. Consequently, microeconomic models focus attention on the most important or salient factors. This keeps the models from becoming unduly cumbersome. When the lesser variables are deliberately kept out of the discussion, they are not just assumed away as so many people think. On the contrary, they are allowed to remain on the sidelines and are only *assumed* to be constant for the *time being.* Analysts can allow as many variables to vary as they see fit, but often the close scrutiny of some factors is more important than the broad examination of all variables. For example, in the analysis of longevity, the main factors to be considered should be the person's diet, exercise habits, the working and living atmosphere, hereditary information, general health, and perhaps income. We need not delve into the effects of smog in Chicago or, for that matter, the impact of fewer days of snow, if trips to the Windy City are infrequent, even though we know these factors are likely to have *some* effect on longevity.

When the economist holds all other factors constant, a *ceteris paribus assumption* is being made. Unless otherwise mentioned, we shall continue to make this assumption throughout our models. This assumption is not unlike the assumptions of *standard temperature and pressure* (STP) employed in experiments in the physical sciences. For example, the density of water is 62.4 pounds per cubic foot only at STP. If either the temperature or the pressure were other than standard, the density would be different and adjustments would have to be made accordingly. The same reasoning applies to ceteris paribus assumptions.

Suppose the demand for gasoline is assumed to be a function of many variables, some of which are

a. the price per gallon;
b. the number of licensed drivers;
c. the income of users;
d. the distance traversed by users;
e. the number of cars in the community;
f. the extent of car pooling arrangements; and
g. the average gasoline consumption of vehicles.

Only the main variables are being considered in this model and no attempt is being made to quantify the relationship as yet. But we could reasonably state that *if* all the variables above except one were assumed to be constant, *then* the impact of a change in that variable could be understood. For example, all other things remaining equal, if the number of people living and driving in the community increased, the demand for gasoline would rise. This does not by any means say that the other factors do remain constant, but *if they did,* the previous statement regarding higher demand could be quite true. To make the model a little more complete, let us assume that as the number of drivers increases, more car pooling arrangements are made. This development could decrease the demand for gasoline and offset the former increase, leaving the quantity demanded the same as before.

A BRIEF REVIEW OF SUPPLY AND DEMAND

Practically all microeconomic models begin and end with supply and demand analysis. This fundamental model helps explain many economic phenomena. We will employ the usual price–quantity version to review the concepts and subsequently use somewhat more elaborate models with a demand–supply theme.

Demand represents the *willingness* and *ability* to acquire goods and services at various prices. There are many factors that affect a consumer's demand for a product. For example, the demand for a particular make of vehicle would be influenced by its price, the income of the buyers, the looks of the car, the prices of other cars, and the fuel and mechanical efficiency of the motor, as well as the price of gasoline. There may also be other variables. But if all factors except the price of the automobile are assumed to be constant, the quantity demanded usually tends to vary inversely with the price. That is to say, *ceteris paribus,* the lower the price of the product, the higher the quantity demanded by the consumers. This inverse relationship of quantity to price is sometimes known as the *Law of Demand.*

Supply, on the other hand, represents the producers' willingness and ability to *offer* the goods and services at various prices. Some variables that may affect the supply of a product may include the number of producers, the quantity and quality of resources, the cost of production, and the firms' objectives, as well as the price of the product. Again, all other factors remaining equal, we may generalize by observing that larger quantities would be offered (supplied) at higher prices than at lower ones. The *Law of Supply* corresponds to the direct or positive relationship of quantity supplied to the price.

Both the supply and demand forces do change in the market place. For instance, even if the price of a particular product does not change, more units may be demanded due to an increase in the number of buyers. The greater the number of sick people, the higher the demand for health care. Similarly, the supply of a product may also change. In the area of health care, if more doctors open up practices in a given community, or if more health care organizations are open for the public, the supply of health care increases. These changes in demand and supply would eventually have some effect on the price, although no price change is necessary to bring about such changes. Not all products conform to the conventional laws of demand and supply. Furthermore, we cannot analyze all types of markets using this simple model.

Let us suppose that the industry for elementary school teachers is such that we can use the supply and demand model. Generally speaking, the "product" being considered has to be homogeneous or highly standardized before we can use the supply and demand model. In Figure 1-2 we draw the familiar demand and supply functions. The price along the vertical axis shows the various possible annual salaries for teachers, and the horizontal axis measures the number of teachers. The demand schedule is shown to be negatively sloped, in keeping with our assumptions. Similarly, the supply curve is shown as a positively sloped line. The teachers' market is said to be in equilibrium when the demand for teachers equals the supply. This occurs at an

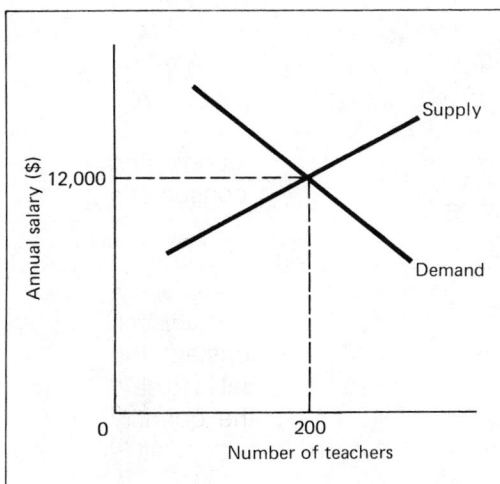

FIGURE 1-2
The most general models in microeconomics assume that the quantity demanded varies inversely with price while the quantity supplied varies positively with the price of the product. The diagram shows that at an annual salary (price) of $12,000, the demand for teachers would exactly equal the supply of 200 teachers. Such a price is said to "clear" the market. At prices above this equilibrium price, supply will exceed demand and prices below $12,000 will bring about excess demand. In most cases, excess supply forces price down, while excess demand pushes it up.

annual salary of $12,000. The graph suggests that only when the salary offered by the school district equals $12,000 will the number of teachers seeking jobs equal the number that the district would hire at that pay. According to our example, 200 teachers would be employed.

The market equilibrium process is fairly simple. At higher than $12,000, the employer would tend to hire fewer teachers, although more than 200 teachers would be looking for jobs. If the free market is operating, the excess supply of teachers would bring the pay down—that is, the school district could afford to hire more teachers without offering them the higher wage. As the salary for teachers falls, some teachers prefer not to supply themselves. Eventually, at $12,000 per year, the district is able to attract 200 teachers. Those teachers who *would have worked* for the district at higher pay, are either *voluntarily unemployed* or are working in some other capacity. We could very easily reason out the tendencies of the market forces at a salary of less than $12,000. If the salary were less than $12,000, the demand for teachers would exceed the supply and, in essence, cause a shortage. In a free market environment, such excess demand would cause the salary (price) to rise and attract more teachers and, again at $12,000, the demand for teachers would equal the supply of teachers. In general, excess supply causes prices to fall and excess demand pulls up prices. However, there are exceptions to the rule.

Suppose the school district has a salary budget of $4.6 million. Then the "demand" for teachers would be made up of all combinations of salary and the number of teachers that amount to an expenditure equal to the available budget. A few of the combinations are shown in Table 1-1.

Suppose further that the supply of teachers is such that any number up to a maximum of 400 can be hired at an annual wage of $12,500. In addition, let us assume that the school district must hire a minimum of 350 teachers in order to staff the schools. How many teachers would be hired by the district?

We will use Figure 1-3 to illustrate the various conditions. First of all, the demand for teachers in this case is a special category, in that all the products of salary and the number of teachers must equal a constant, namely $4.6 million. Strictly speaking, it is more correct to call such a demand function a *constant-expenditure function*, although the curve is a demand function of sorts because it tells us what the quantity demanded at each price would be. When the salary is plotted against the number of teachers that should be hired,

TABLE 1-1

Salary per year	Number hired	Expenditures
$18,000	256	$4.6 million
15,000	307	$4.6 million
14,000	329	$4.6 million
13,000	354	$4.6 million
12,000	383	$4.6 million
10,000	460	$4.6 million
9,000	511	$4.6 million

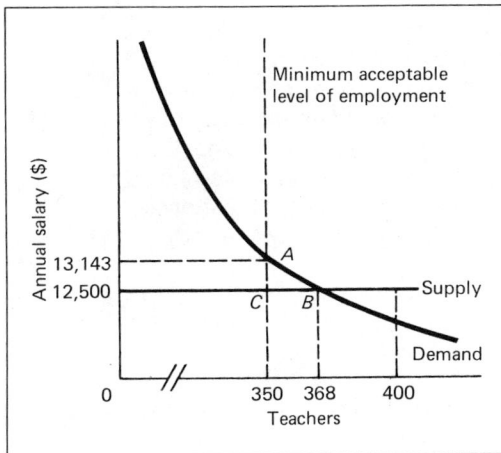

FIGURE 1-3
The school administrator's employment budget is limited to $4.6 million per year and he must hire a minimum of 350 teachers. All combinations of teachers and corresponding salaries that constitute an expenditure of $4.6 million form the administrator's "demand." As the diagram shows, teachers are willing to work for $12,500 per year. For the total money available, the administrator could hire as many as 368 teachers. However, he can hire as few as 350 teachers and pay them $13,143—$643 more than what they would have been willing to accept and possibly bring about higher morale among his faculty. It is generally believed that high morale among workers contributes toward high productivity. Alternatively, the administrator can spend part of the $4.6 million by hiring 350 teachers at $12,500 per year and spend the rest to employ 35 teachers' aids at $6500 per year. As an economist, the administrator should weigh the benefits and costs of all the options.

a *rectangular hyperbola* emerges. Such curves are utilized in many economic models. The special characteristic of such a hyperbola is that no matter which point we pick, the values along the vertical and horizontal axes, when multiplied, always yield a constant and in our case the constant equals $4.6 million. The supply of teachers is a horizontal line drawn at $12,500 which stops at 400 due to the supply limitations. The other dotted vertical line drawn at 350 teachers shows the minimum number of teachers the school district must employ. The price–quantity combination would then fall in the area bound by the three lines—the demand curve, the supply curve, and the minimum-of-350 constraint.

If the free market is allowed to take its course, the equilibrium salary would be at $12,500, and for $4.6 million the school district could hire 368 teachers. On the other hand, the $4.6 million could be spent on only 350 teachers with each teacher receiving $13,143. The extra $643 per year could conceivably add to high employee morale and therefore, perhaps, to productivity. If the school district has 14,720 pupils and it hires 350 teachers, the student/teacher ratio will be about 42:1. However, if 368 teachers are hired, the student/teacher ratio will drop to 40:1. Is it better to (a) have fewer teachers with a higher student/teacher ratio, and a better salary; or (b) hire 368 teachers and reduce the load per teacher to 40:1; or (c) hire the 350 teachers at $12,500 each and use the remaining $225,000 to hire 35 teachers' aids at $6500 per year? It is difficult to give a simple answer to such a complex question. Microeconomics offers tools for a thorough examination of such situations. In the above illustration, we could also consider the cost associated with necessary classrooms as well as constraints imposed by classroom space. We will have ample opportunity to examine some involved models in Chapter 9.

APPLICATIONS

1 . The International Money Market

Unlike our ancestors, who traded clam shells, beads, and shrunken heads for goods and services, we use flat money as a medium of exchange. In each country we need money that is acceptable by the merchants of that country. So long as we remain in the U.S., Polish zlotys are of very little use. However, zlotys would be very useful if we were to travel in Poland. If there was a demand for products made in Poland, there would be a demand for zlotys. People possessing convertible currency could exchange their money for equivalent amounts of Polish money. Foreign currencies are also referred to as *foreign exchange* and the ratio of exchange between one type of money and another is called the *foreign exchange rate*.

The exchange rate is the price of foreign money. Thus, if the U.S. dollar exchanges for 2 deutsche marks (DM), the "price" of each deutsche mark is $0.50. At one time, the exchange rates for currencies in the free world were set by agreement which came to be known as the Bretton Woods System or the International Monetary Fund (IMF) Plan. Each nation was expected to take appropriate action to maintain the agreed upon exchange rates. Let us use this framework to explain the market in foreign exchange.

Americans wishing to import West German goods and services and to invest in German securities (denominated in deutsche marks) would need deutsche marks. This would give rise to the demand for German money. If the American currency is acceptable to the Germans, they would exchange their money for the U.S. dollar at the prevailing exchange rate. Germans wishing to acquire dollars exchange deutsche marks for the American currency and, in effect, create the supply of German money available to the Americans. The demand for deutsche marks interacts with the supply of deutsche marks and brings about an equilibrium exchange rate as illustrated in Figure 1-4. In this particular situation, the exchange rate to the Americans is $0.50 to the deutsche mark and a total of $1 million is being exchanged for 2 million deutsche marks. It follows that the exchange rate for the Germans equals 2 deutsche marks per dollar.

The demand and supply curves for deutsche marks exhibit the familiar shapes previously encountered, with one exception—part of the supply of deutsche marks is "backward bending." Such behavior is not surprising because the amount of deutsche marks offered at each exchange rate is a reflection of the amount of U.S. dollars demanded by Germans at those exchange rates. The higher the exchange rate is for the Germans, the less dollars they will demand, and in most cases they will be willing to supply less deutsche marks in exchange for dollars. By the same token, the higher the rate is for the Germans, the lower it is for the Americans. Table 1-2 shows the various quantities of the two currencies that are being supplied and demanded at each exchange rate, and also brings out the reason for the backward-bending phenomenon.

Both Figure 1-4 and Table 1-2 indicate that the equilibrium exchange rate is $0.50/DM for the Americans and DM2/$ for the Germans. This rate will prevail under strictly free market conditions provided that all the characteristics of perfect competition are present. Now let us suppose that the various governments decide to maintain the price of the dollar at a level corresponding to DM4. To "peg" the exchange rate at DM4/$ or $0.25/DM, either the demand for dollars has to increase or the supply of deutsche marks has to increase or both. If the monetary authorities stand ready to buy dollars at DM4 apiece and sell deutsche marks at $0.25 per unit,

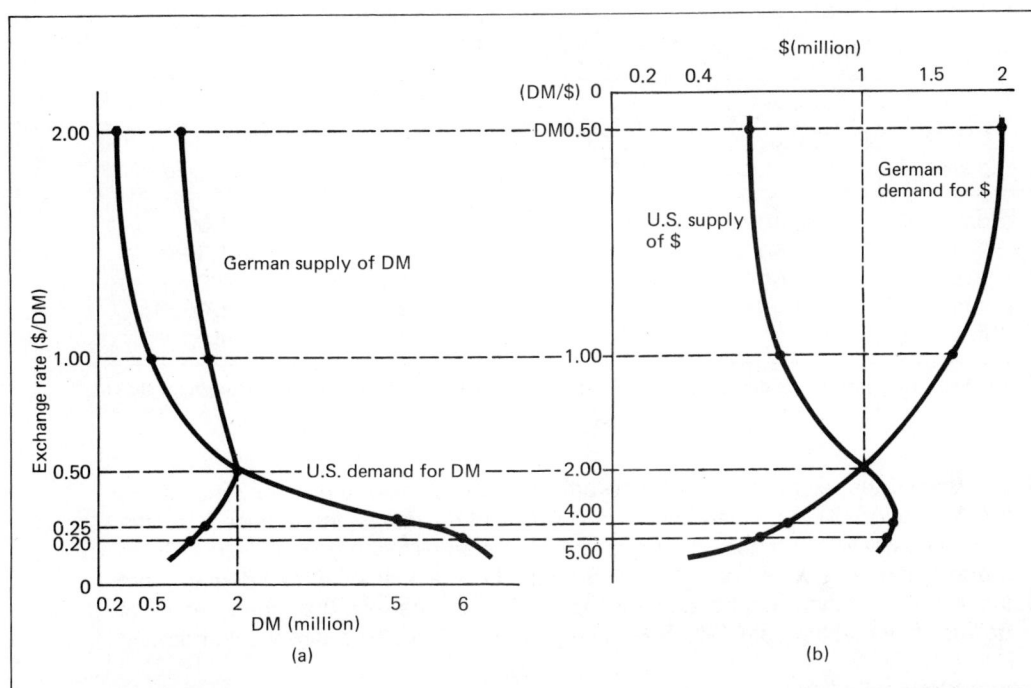

FIGURE 1-4

Americans demand foreign currency in order to carry out the transactions that require foreign money. Since U.S. dollars may be exchanged for foreign currency, all such foreign money is broadly referred to as *foreign exchange* and the ratio exchange between currencies is called the exchange rate. (a) shows the U.S. demand for German deutsche marks (DM) at various "prices" (exchange rates). The act of demanding DM constitutes an act of supplying U.S. dollars. Similarly, when Germans demand U.S. dollars, they in effect supply DM. It is for this reason that the foreign currency supply curves are sometimes referred to as *reciprocal supply* curves. (b) contains the supply and demand in the U.S. dollar market and this graph is purposely inverted to reflect that the U.S. and German exchange rates are reciprocals of each other. In this particular instance, both foreign currency markets are at equilibrium. The exchange rate to the Americans is $0.50/DM, which makes the rate to Germans DM2/$. The Americans purchase DM2 million and spend $1 million, which becomes the supply to the Germans, who purchase a like quantity of U.S. dollars by expending DM2 million. It can be shown that the exchange rates would change if either the demand or supply functions shifted appropriately. For example, if the autonomous demand for deutsche marks increases, the rate to the Americans would rise and fall for the Germans.

Figure 1-5, the demand for dollars on the part of the monetary authorities is horizontal at DM4, just as the supply of deutsche marks is virtually unlimited at $0.25.

the market price has no choice but to adjust to the artificially maintained rates. Such a rate variation could be brought about by the purchase of dollars with deutsche marks. The very act of buying (demanding) dollars constitutes an increase in the supply of deutsche marks, and when a sufficient number of deutsche marks have been spent and the demand for dollars has risen appropriately, the exchange rate would rise to DM4/$ for the Germans and fall to $0.25/DM for the Americans. Such changes would discourage sales of American products to Germans while inducing Americans to incur larger expenditures on German goods and services. As shown in

TABLE 1-2
DEMAND AND SUPPLY IN THE FOREIGN EXCHANGE MARKET[a]

(1) Dollars per DM	(2) DMs demanded[b]	(3)=(1)×(2) Dollars spent (supplied)[b]	(4)=1/(1) DM per dollar	(5) Dollars demanded[b]	(6)=(4)×(5) DMs spent (supplied)[b]
$2.00	0.20	$0.40	DM0.50	$2.00	DM1.00
1.00	0.50	0.50	1.00	1.50	1.50
0.50	2.00	1.00	2.00	1.00	2.00
0.25	5.00	1.25	4.00	0.40	1.60
0.20	6.00	1.20	5.00	0.20	1.00

[a]When the various figures representing the demand and supply figures are plotted in a graph, we obtain the diagrams shown in Figure 1-4.
[b]Amounts are in millions.

Should the exchange rate be so artificially maintained, the two countries are likely to suffer some imbalance in their *balance of payments,* in the sense that the autonomously inspired demand for dollars will not equal the supply of dollars. Since the exchange rate would now be higher for the Germans, the German demand (not including the central bank's demand) for dollars will be less than the quantity of dollars offered at that rate. With reference to Table 1-2, the Germans would demand

FIGURE 1-5
Prior to the intervention of the governments, the exchange rate for the Americans was $0.50/DM and to the Germans DM2/$. The "pegging" process involves the buying and/or selling of certain currencies to bring about a particular exchange rate other than the one that would prevail under natural market forces of supply and demand. Here we see that the central banks of governments are "selling" deutsche marks at a price of $0.25/DM, which is tantamount to "buying" U.S. dollars at a price of DM4/$. This forces the exchange rate down for the Americans but up for the Germans. In the situation illustrated, the U.S. dollar "'appreciates" while the German currency "depreciates." In effect, DM3.4 million at $0.25/DM were supplied to equate demand with supply at the artificial rate. This amounted to official dollar demand of 0.85 million at DM4/$.

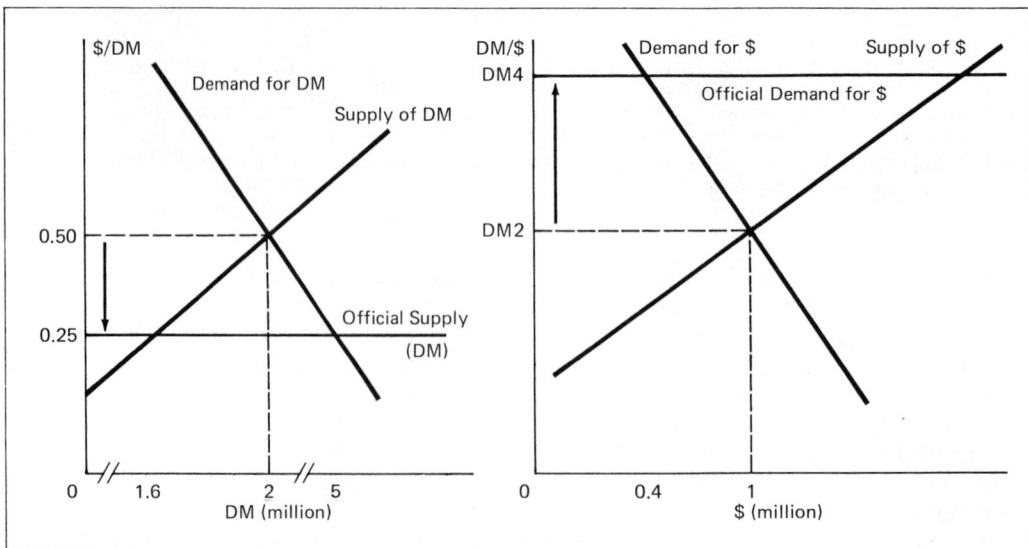

only $0.40 million, whereas the Americans (excluding the central bank) would offer $1.25 million. In essence, the Americans would spend $1.25 million and, since the Germans would not demand a smaller quantity of dollars ($0.40 million), the German central bank has to purchase the difference of $0.85 million with DM3.4 million. To express it a little differently, the Americans would be willing and able to spend DM5 million on German goods and services, whereas the Germans would expend only DM1.6 million on American products. This would lead to a deficit in the U.S. balance of payments equal to DM3.4 million or $0.85 million. By contrast, the German balance of payments would show a surplus by a like amount.

We need not elaborate upon the effects of such deficits or surpluses at this point except to mention some of the probable results of the pegging action. For one thing, American goods would become more expensive to Germans, leading to lower sales. This, in turn, may cause a reduction in income and employment in those industries which catered to foreigners. Since deficits in the balance of payments cause people to lose confidence in the currency of a country, other nations may not desire to hold dollars in their currency reserves. A decline in the demand for dollars may put downward pressures on its price to lower the rate below DM4/$, requiring even greater involvement by the central banks. Such intervention by banks usually affects the country's domestic money supply growth, and quite conceivably the banks may be forced to change the growth of the money supply in the "wrong" direction, creating other problems. Compounding such problems could be the effects on domestic rates of inflation and employment in the foreign (Germany included) countries affected by variations in exchange rates. If economies operating at close to full employment experience a boost in their exports due to changing exchange rates, their inflation rate would be aggravated. Rising exports mean higher levels of national income and, generally, higher demand for imports. Such increases in demand for imports could very well adversely affect a country's trading partners.

This brief discussion of the market forces in the foreign exchanges helps explain the fluctuations in a country's balance-of-payments position. It also shows why and how a country's currency is subject to certain pressures that would, in the absence of governmental support, lead to either appreciation or depreciation of a country's currency. Such a model could also be utilized to analyze the probable effects of exchange rate variations on a nation's employment, inflation, and interest rates. In the above illustration, the deficit in the U.S. balance of payments (or surplus in the German balance of payments) could be eliminated (at least partially) by relinquishing all supports for the dollar. Under a regime of freely fluctuating rates, the demand and supply forces would bring about a true market equilibrium in all currency markets which, in effect, would imply the absence of deficits and surpluses.

Volumes can be written about the policy instruments used by nations to correct chronic balance-of-payments problems and there are many notable references in the field of international finance. Our aim was to use a simple supply–demand model to illustrate the working of a market.

2. The Shortage of Nurses

There seems to be a perennial shortage of nurses in the United States. A shortage implies that the number of nurses demanded at a particular wage rate exceeds the number of nurses willing to work at that pay. Using the basic supply–demand model we might conclude that such an excess demand for nurses would increase the wage rate in order to equate demand with supply. Why isn't the market bringing about equilibrium?

Figure 1-6 shows the supply and demand to be at equilibrium during 1968 at a wage level of $40 per day with the employment level standing at 3.2 million. When the demand for health care services increased in 1972, the demand for nurses increased at all levels of pay. At the wage rate of $40, 3.8 million nurses were being demanded but only 3.2 million were being supplied. Let us assume that this shortage raised pay rates to $45 per day and brought about a supply of 3.3 million but also decreased the quantity demanded to 3.7 million, creating a shortage of 0.4 million. The new market equilibrium rate needs to be $50 in order to equate demand with supply at an employment level of 3.6 million. As long as wage rates are "sticky" in an upward direction, the market does not respond fast enough to bring about the equilibrium wage. In the health care industry, the wages offered to nurses rise much more slowly than is consistent with rising demands, and as long as the wages are somewhat rigid in adjusting to market forces, the demand will continue to be higher than supply. Thus, despite the forces of supply and demand, there would be a 0.4 million shortage of nurses at a pay rate of $45 per day.

FIGURE 1-6

The graph shows the effects of "sticky" wages in certain industries. Initially the demand and supply in the nursing industry was at equilibrium in 1968 at a wage of $40 per day, and 3.2 million nurses were employed in the health care industry. As the demand for nurses increased in 1972, the industry could not adjust rapidly enough to accomodate larger numbers of nurses due to the upward rigidity of wages in the industry. As long as wages remained at $40 per day, the increase in demand created a temporary shortage of 0.6 million nurses. Eventually wages rose to $45 per day, but this wage was still not high enough to equate the supply with the demand. At a wage of $45 per day, we see that there is still a shortage of 0.4 million nurses. Only at a wage of $50 per day will the demand for nurses be equal to the supply. This illustrates why there might be perennial shortages in some industries despite rising demand.

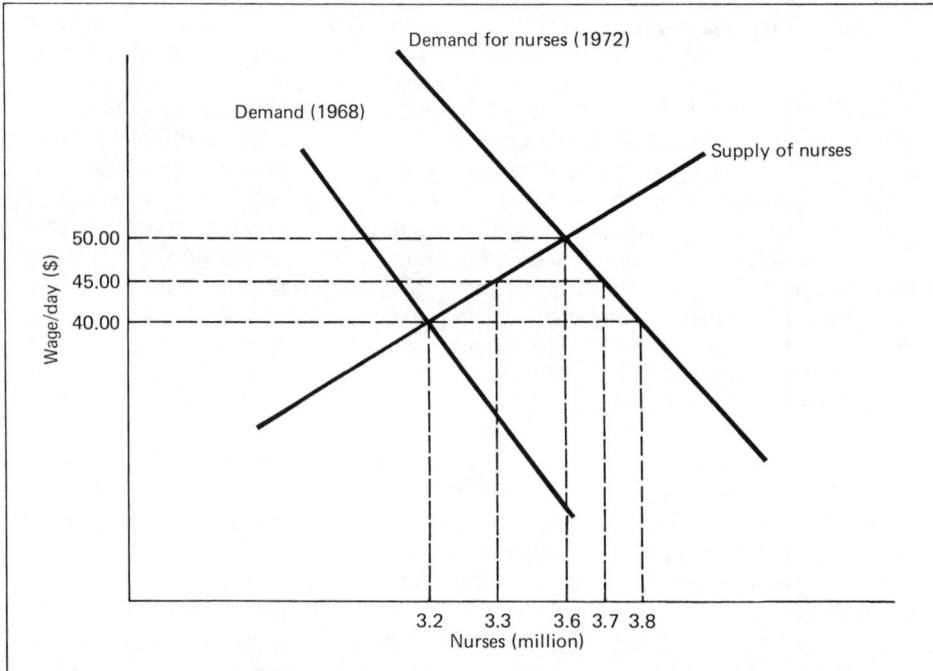

3. Scalping

As we all know, "scalping" refers to the practice of reselling admission tickets to theaters and sports events at prices above the official level charged by the issuer. As long as the scalper is able to sell the tickets at the price or prices of his choosing, we can assume that demanders are willing and able to pay such prices. Consider the diagram of Figure 1-7. The "official" supply of tickets to the Denver Broncos' game is shown to be at a price of $20, with a maximum supply of 10,000 tickets. If there is an adequate demand for such tickets as shown, all tickets can be sold at that price. How is it then possible for the scalper to charge $25 per ticket?

Suppose the scalper spends the necessary time and incurs the discomfort of standing in line in order to purchase 200 tickets at the legal price of $20. By so doing he "preempts" the supply of 2% of the total available. Those that are able buy the remaining 9,800 tickets. Since the box office will now be closed to the 200 buyers who would have bought the tickets at the $20 price, the scalper may have a ready market at higher prices. The demand for tickets indicates that any price along the demand curve is available for that corresponding quantity. Thus, if the 200 frustrated

FIGURE 1-7
The "scalper" profits by preempting a certain number of tickets to a football game. The maximum number of tickets available is shown as 10,000, which may be bought at the legal price of $20.00 each. If the scalper buys 200 tickets at this price and is able to sell them at a higher price, the difference in revenues less his "cost" would constitute his profits. The diagram shows that the 200 tickets can be sold at prices ranging from $20 to $45 and more, since there are buyers who would be willing to pay this price rather than go without the ticket, as shown by the negatively sloping demand curve. Even if there were a law regarding the maximum number of tickets a person could purchase, the scalper could employ others to buy the tickets for him, in which case the final sale price to the 200 ticket buyers would be more.

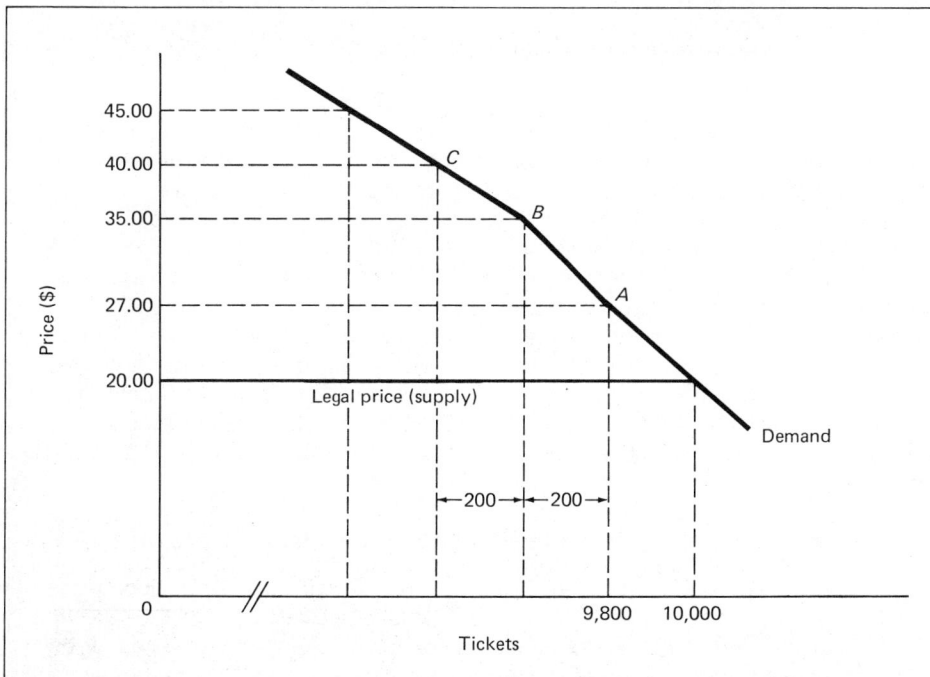

football fans' demand lies along segment *AB,* they would be willing to pay a price in the range of $27–$35. If their demand corresponds to segment *BC,* they would be willing to pay prices in the range $35–$40 in order to see the game. So if the profiteer (entrepreneur) sells the tickets at $25 each, he should have no trouble in clearing the market. His gross income in this event would amount to $1000. If this sum is considered adequate for the trouble of obtaining the 200 tickets, presumably the scalper would be acting in a rational manner. What if the authorities limited ticket sales to a maximum of 10 per person? Would that discourage scalping? Not necessarily. On the contrary, scalping could go on as before but at perhaps substantially higher prices. All the scalper has to do is to engage the services of 19 assistants, each of whom would be required to purchase 10 tickets. Collectively, the scalper would now have the 200 tickets as before. However, since he has to pay for the work done by his employees, in order to retain his original level of profits, he might have to charge higher prices for the tickets. For example, if each of the helpers was paid $40, the scalper's cost would rise by $760. This sum could be spread over the 200 tickets so that each ticket would now sell for $28.80 or even $30. Since there are people willing to pay 50% or more above the normal price, the scalper will be successful in his scheme. The limit on ticket purchasing did not abate scalping—it only pushed up prices.

SUGGESTED APPLICATIONS

1. The "Hog Cycle"

Farmers who raise hogs do not have perfect information about the hog prices in the future. They usually base their forecast on historical knowledge of costs, prices, demand, supply, and anticipated values of the significant variables based on current developments. The supply and demand model may be used to show the fluctuations in the prices of hogs in a dynamic setting.

2. The Market for Used Cars

Many car buyers wait for the new models to come out before buying a new car, either a new car from the latest vintage or a new car from the previous year. Since the overall supply of cars increases with the introduction of the latest models, why don't the prices of the cars, and particularly used cars, decline at such times? One explanation is that there are actually two markets that compete with each other—the market for used cars and that for brand new cars. If the prices of the new cars are substantially high, many people prefer to hold onto their existing vehicles instead of trading them in. By the same token, those who were waiting for a new car and would have bought one if the price had been reasonable, will abstain from purchasing a new car and will look instead for a good used automobile. These two reactions not only decrease the supply of used cars but also increase their demand. The result is that used car prices remain at high levels.

3. Why Does the College Bookstore Buy Used Textbooks?

In essence, the college bookstore is a scalper. It buys currently required used textbooks from impoverished students at a price often no more than 20% of the market value. Used textbooks (of the same edition) are perfect substitutes for new ones and are sometimes like new. Most students probably do not care whether they use a new or a used textbook, and would prefer a used one at $12 to a new one at $15.95. The bookstores generally receive about 20% of the retail price as their portion of revenues. Thus, if the bookstore can purchase used texts for about $4 and sell them for $12, it will clear $8 per book. On the other hand, the sale of a new textbook will yield only about $3.20. Naturally, not all students buy used books, nor are there sufficient numbers available for all. A student-organized bookstore can probably cut into the bookstore's profits by offering $5 for the used books and selling them for $11. Here, too, we can use the basic supply and demand model to illustrate the workings of the market.

EXERCISES

1. Chapter 1 basically deals with the fundamentals of supply, demand, and equilibrium. When equilibrium price and quantity are determined in this manner, the market is said to be operating under *perfect competition*, a concept to be discussed in more detail later. State what would happen to market equilibrium price and quantity under each of the following situations *ceteris paribus*.
    a. Demand for the product increases.
    b. Supply decreases.
    c. Demand and supply increase by different amounts.
    d. Demand increases by a greater amount than supply.
    e. Demand decreases.
    f. Demand and supply decrease.
    g. Supply decreases by a greater amount than demand.
    h. Demand increases and supply decreases.
    i. Demand decreases while supply increases.

2. Using a price–quantity graph, *draw* these situations from Exercise 1 above.
    a. Assuming the supply curve is horizontal.
    b. Assuming that the demand curve is horizontal.
    c. Situations (f) and (g).

3. Demand for money is positively related to income and negatively related to interest rates. Can you explain the relationship of savings to the two variables, interest and income? Suppose the supply of money was predominantly made up of savings. Draw a diagram of the supply schedule as a function of interest rates and one for the demand for money on the same graph. What will we have determined via this process?

4. With reference to Exercise 3 above, cite reasons why interest rates rose during the early part of 1976, fell during the early part of 1977, and started to rise during the last part of 1977. (This applies to the United States in general and you are asked to provide some of the reasons that may have contributed to the interest rate behavior.)

5. Is it appropriate to use supply and demand phenomena to explain the price behavior in the hand calculator market? Why or why not? Use a model to show how prices of various brands have continuously fallen over the past decade and provide reasons for such changes using suitable graphical analysis.

6. Farmers who raise pigs take a period of several months to get the animals ready for the market. Since most of the farmers individually decide on the size of the herd, the total supply of pigs in the market is unpredictable ahead of time. Consequently the price of pigs in the future is a function of the quantity supplied at the time. Assuming the

demand for pigs at any given time is reasonably steady, deduce what would happen to hog prices during the coming year if:
  a. farmers received very high prices for hogs this year;
  b. farmers received extremely low prices this year;
  c. there is an anticipated shortage of pig feed for next year;
  d. there is an anticipated shortage of beef next year;
  e. turkey and chicken growers are expected to take a year's holiday next year;
  f. ham is expected to be more popular than ever in the future;
  g. many pig growers want to quit this year;
  h. many pig growers want to quit next year.

7. Using demand and supply analysis, explain how the "futures" market operates.

8. "The lumber industry prospers on catastrophes, bad weather, rail car shortages, strikes, and acts of nature." Agree or disagree with this quotation, explaining your reasons with reference to recent developments in the lumber, building, and furniture industries. (The quotation is taken from a 1950 issue of *The Wall Street Journal*.)

9. The U.S. steel producers contend that iron and steel scrap is a scarce natural resource that should be conserved for domestic use in case of a military emergency. The scrap dealers, arguing that there is no prospect for a shortage of scrap as long as the steel mills continue to operate below capacity, vigorously oppose restrictions on exports. Show why the lifting of export restrictions would change the price of scrap. In which direction? Would the argument for stiffening export restrictions be stronger if the American mills were operating at capacity? Why or why not?

10. What might happen to the demand for public transportation if:
  a. the price per gallon of gasoline rose to $1.20?
  b. many downtown parking lots were placed "off limits"?
  c. toll booths were set up along each major street for private cars?
  d. automobile insurance rates varied positively and much more progressively with miles driven?
  e. more and fancier modes of public transportation were provided?
  f. the public vehicles ran more frequently and made more convenient stops?
  g. private automobile ownership was taxed very heavily?
  h. special lanes along the roads were reserved for public vehicles that did not require any stoppages?
  i. streamlined "bullet" trains were designed to travel at speeds of 100–150 mph with conveniently located stations?

11. Determine the equilibrium price, quantity, the total amount expended (by consumers), and revenues received (by suppliers) in each of the following cases.

a.

Demanders' (Q)					Suppliers' (Q)			
A	B	C	D	Price	E	F	G	H
2	3	1	0	$98	9	14	10	16
4	5	4	5	94	7	9	8	12
6	5	6	8	86	5	6	5	9
8	7	8	10	72	3	4	3	7
10	9	12	11	66	1	2	3	4
12	10	16	11	53	0	1	1	2

b. Demand: $Q_d = 100 - 2P$; supply: $Q_s = 50 + \frac{1}{2}P$
c. Demand: $P = \$5$; supply: $Q_s = 1 + 200P$
d. Demand: $Q_d = 100 - \frac{1}{2}P$; supply: $P = \$20$
e. Demand: $Q_d = 1000$; supply: $P = \$7.50$

12. Use the graph of Figure 1-8 to answer the following questions dealing with U.S. agricultural policy.
   a. What are the equilibrium P and Q in this wheat market?
   b. If, at the equilibrium quantity, we assume that the cost of growing and selling wheat is $3.00 per unit, what is the net income to the growers?
   c. What quantity of wheat should be supplied for a return of $5.50 per unit? $6.00 per unit? $2.25 per unit?
   d. If the government is willing to buy any amount of wheat at $5.50 per unit, how many units of wheat should be supplied? What will be the effective equilibrium price and quantity?
   e. With reference to part (d), will there be a shortage or surplus as far as the private buyers are concerned? How many units? If there is a storage cost involved, assume that it costs $0.25 to store each unit of wheat. What will be the total cost of buying and storing the amount that was produced at the guaranteed price but not bought by the consumers?
   f. Suppose the government guarantees a price of $5.50 per unit to the suppliers and sells the entire output at market prices compatible with such volume. What will be the price to the consumers? What will be the amount of subsidy per unit of wheat to the farmer? What will be the total cost of such a subsidy program? (Ignore all "other" costs.)
   g. Suppose the government paid the farmer $1.00 per unit *not to grow* wheat (compared to the equilibrium volume of part (b)) in order to raise the price of wheat to $5.50 per unit. If at this volume the cost of producing wheat is $2.50 per unit, will the farmers adjust quantity to receive more net income or will they prefer the completely free market devoid of government intervention? (Disregard the farmers' personal feelings for the government bureaucrat!)

13. Answer the questions that follow with respect to Figure 1-9.
   a. When the demand and supply functions are represented by D and S:

FIGURE 1-8

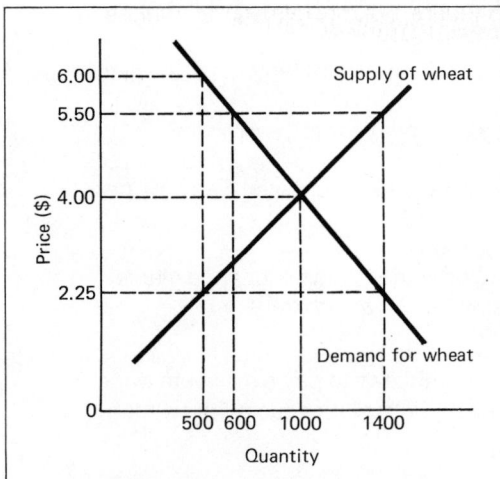

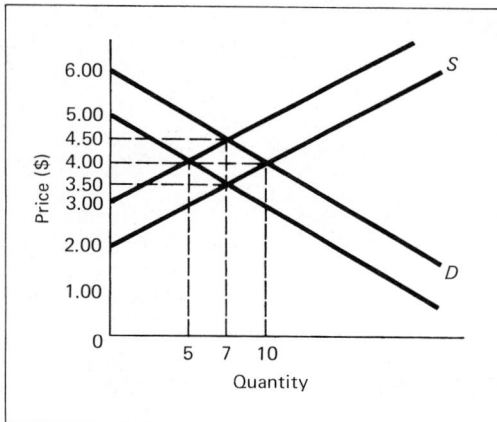

FIGURE 1-9

Equilibrium price: $_____, equilibrium quantity_____.
  b. Assume now that a tax of $1 per unit is levied on sellers:
     Quantity now exchanged will equal _____ and the price to the buyer inclusive of
     the tax will be $_____. The price to the seller net-of-tax will be $_____. In effect,
     the consumers pay _____ percent of the tax and the suppliers absorb _____
     percent of the tax.
  c. Assume now that a tax of $1 per unit is levied on buyers:
     Equilibrium market price will be $_____ and the price to the consumer including
     the tax will be $_____. The quantity bought now will be _____ units and the price
     received by the seller will be $_____.

14. Compare the effects of a "price ceiling" with those of subsidized supply. Use
graphs to explain your answer.

15. Compare the effects of a "price floor" with those of taxed supply. Supplement your
answer with the use of proper demand and supply diagrams.

16. Speculators purchase commodities such as wheat in order to sell them at more
favorable prices. Assume that speculators purchase wheat in 1978 and sell in 1979.
Answer the following questions with reference to Figure 1-10, neglecting any further
effects of speculative buying in 1979.
  a. Use an asterisk (*) to indicate the demand and supply in 1978 and 1979 which
     include the effects of speculation. Explain.
  b. Did such speculation help stabilize wheat prices from year to year? How?
  c. How much gross profit did the speculators make?
  d. What was their real profit if the cost of the money that they borrowed was 10% per
     annum and the cost of storage was 40¢ per bushel?
  e. Could the speculators just as easily have lost money? How?
  f. Could the above model be applied to speculation in the foreign exchange market?
     (Speculation in the foreign exchange market is known as *arbitrage*.)

17.
  a. (See Figure 1-11a.) Suppose all employers were required to pay a minimum wage
     of $3.80 per hour. Would there be unemployment in this labor sector? How many

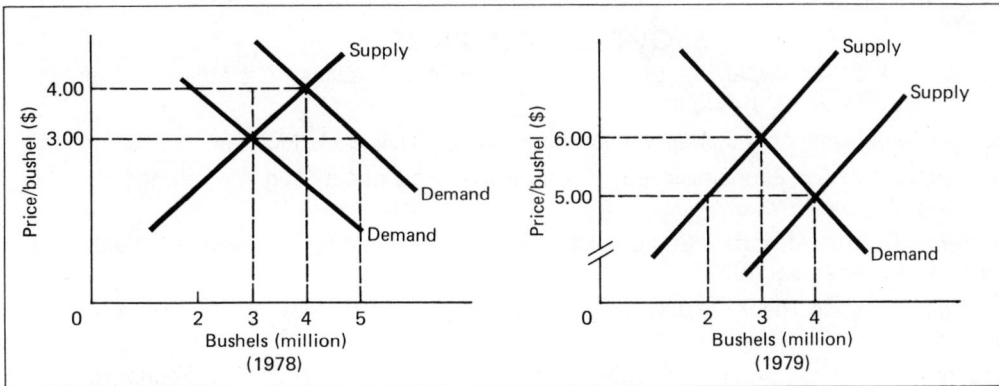

FIGURE 1-10

people would be hired? At what wage would the employers hire 110 people? If we wish 110 people to be employed, how much subsidy per person per hour should the employers receive? What would be the weekly cost to the government? (Assume a 40-hour week.) What is the equilibrium wage?

b. (See Figure 1-11b.) Assume that a law was passed which forbade landlords to charge any more than $150 per month per rental unit. Would there be a surplus or shortage of rental units? At what monthly rent would the owners of units be willing to provide accomodation for 200 renters? How many dollars of subsidy must the landlord receive in order to supply 200 units? What is the total cost to the government per month?

FIGURE 1-11

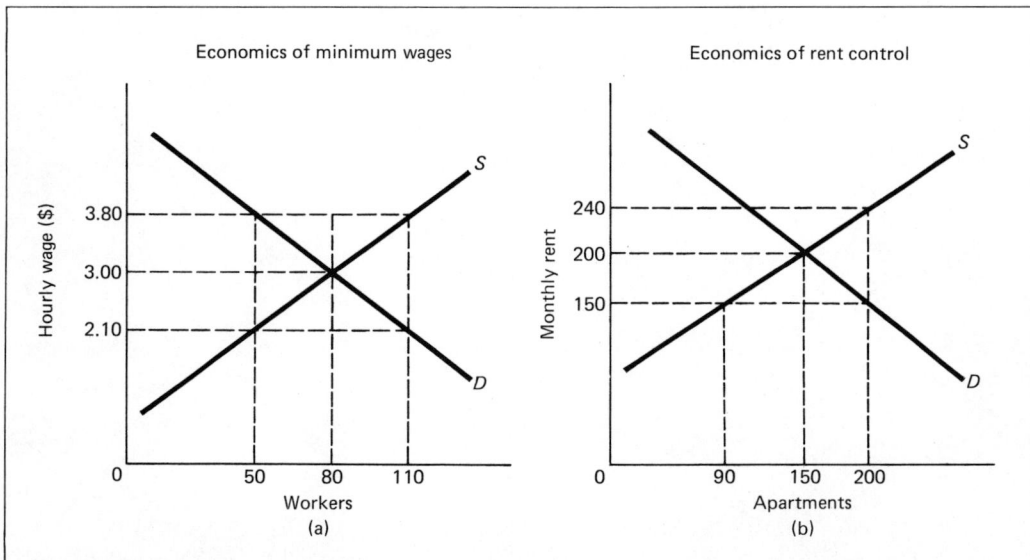

SUGGESTED READINGS

Blomqvist, A. S. "Small Cars, Large Cars, and the Price of Gasoline." *Canadian Journal of Economics,* Volume II, August 1978.

Dahl, D., and Hammond, J. *Market and Price Analysis.* New York: McGraw-Hill, 1976.

Gordon, S. "Should Economists Pay Attention to Philosophers?" *Journal of Political Economy,* August 1978.

Heerema, D. "The Artist as a Source of Economic Understanding." *Journal of Cultural Economics,* December 1977.

Hirshleifer, J. *Price Theory and Applications.* Englewood Cliffs, New Jersey: Prentice-Hall, 1976.

Kagann, S. "Major Journals in Economics: A User Study." *Journal of Economic Literature,* September 1978.

Layard, W. *Microeconomics.* New York: McGraw-Hill, 1979.

Lowes, B. "Economics and the Modern Business Enterprise." *Business Economics,* September 1978.

Nicholson, W. *Intermediate Microeconomics and Its Applications.* Hinsdale, Illinois: The Dryden Press, 1979.

Stigler, G. *The Theory of Price.* New York: MacMillan, 1957.

Chapter Two Chapter Two Chapter Two

UTILITY AND PREFERENCE

Decision makers usually have certain objectives in mind when they choose a particular course of action. For example, sellers and producers of goods have profits foremost in their minds, and as such their behavior is consistent with the profit motive. Similarly, the government presumably has societal welfare in mind when it elects to enforce transportation laws. What do consumers want? Consumers consume in order to satisfy their needs and they normally select those goods and services which satisfy their needs and wants the most. That is, normal and rational consumers are expected to consume those combinations of goods and services within their reach that satisfy them the most, with respect to the future or the immediate present. In economics, we use the term *utility* to suggest the notion of happiness, want satisfaction, and well being. Conceivably, the economic and rational person behaves in a manner which will maximize utility.

UTILITY AND RATIONALITY

We often refer to humans as rational animals. As a general rule, our actions are systematic and purposive and are taken in order to realize our goals. Although no strict hedonistic connotations are necessarily associated with rational behavior, we may generally assume that people prefer to increase pleasure and avoid pain wherever possible. Occasionally, the desire for present satisfaction may be in conflict with the attainment of pleasure or utility in the future. Rational consumers, theoretically, calculate the benefits and costs of their actions and eventually choose the utility-maximizing combination of actions. For example, it is reasonably certain that heavy smokers will contract lung cancer sometime during their lives. If Sue Schulze enjoys smoking, despite her knowledge of the probable danger of cancer, and makes no attempt to reduce her consumption of cigarettes, she presumably prefers to enjoy her moments today even though she may suffer unhappiness at some future date. Under these circumstances, we can state that the *discounted present value of her unhappiness* is far less than the present value of unhappiness which would result if she were not to smoke. From a utility point of view, Sue's action is perfectly rational. On the other hand, if wealth or earnings are more important and Sue knows that her capacity to earn will be reduced due to the potential health hazards of smoking and she continues to smoke, we can perhaps say that she is acting in an irrational fashion.

The Measurement of Utility

Most people agree that it is very difficult to *measure* utility. If we could measure utility, it would then be a simple matter to test the accuracy of the utility-maximization hypothesis. It is sufficient at this point to recognize that ordinarily a rational decision maker prefers the more satisfying alternative to the one that yields a lesser amount of utility. After all, why would someone choose to be unhappy or less happy than possible?

Economists carry out utility analysis by two different approaches—the *ordinal utility* method and the *cardinal utility* approach. In the first, consumers must be able to rank their preferences. For example, under this method, the decision maker must be able to compare two alternatives, *A* and *B*, and be able to decide whether *A* is better than, as good as, or worse than *B*. The cardinal utility method of consumer analysis assumes that the consumer will be able to attach certain absolute values to the alternatives. These values need not be measurable themselves as long as the person is subjectively able to assign certain discernible values to the many choices. It should not be hard to understand why economists prefer to use the ordinal utility measurement approach in their models. It will be seen that, in the end, the two approaches have quite a bit in common, and the cardinal utility method supplements the ordinal utility approach in our understanding of the theory of utility.

The Utility Function.

The *utility function* describes a person's tastes or preferences. Just as a mathematical function shows the relationship among variables, the utility function relates the person's utility to the quantity and quality of goods and services that he or she consumes. We can generalize by stating the utility function as

$$U = f(X, Y, Z). \tag{1}$$

In equation (1), *U* represents the amount of utility, and *X, Y,* and *Z* correspond to the various quantities as well as the qualitative attributes of the many goods and services that would affect our happiness should we choose to consume them. For example, a utility function may relate satisfaction to the various amounts of money (income), leisure, and mountain scenery. Generally speaking, economic *goods* are those that, when consumed, add to our utility. On the other hand, those qualities or goods that reduce our well being are sometimes referred to as economic *bads*. We could say that bads create *disutility* while goods bring forth utility. A decrease in disutility is tantamount to an increase in utility. Where possible, economic man seeks out utility-generating alternatives and avoids those that yield disutility. There are situations, however, where we must consume a bad in order to maximize our utility. For example, we must tolerate some disutility from smog, congestion, and pollution while we commute to work in order to earn income to acquire the more satisfying goods and services.

The (Single Commodity) Cardinal
Utility Function

Suppose we have an instrument that can actually measure satisfaction. It is likely that sometime in the future we could determine the exact amount of utility or disutility offered by a particular alternative via the use of electrodes taped to various parts of the body. Then the various impulses emanating from the brain would be indicative of the levels of utility experienced by the subject.

There would be some difficulties with such a procedure, since the subject being experimented on may have different feelings at different times affected by the events preceding such experiments. In that case, the magnitude of the impulses responding to identical situations over the period of the experiment would tend to vary and confuse the accuracy of the measurements. Conceptually speaking, there is no harm done in assuming that such a machine exists and is able to measure the utility generated from the consumption of apples.

In Figure 2-1, we graphically portray a person's utility as a function of the number of apples consumed while all other factors are held constant. This person's ceteris paribus utility function may be simply described as

$$U = f\left(\frac{A}{X, Y, Z}\right) \tag{2}$$

Equation (2) tells us that utility will vary with the quantity of apples A under the given conditions $X, Y,$ and $Z,$ where these conditions include the quantity and quality of other goods, the person's background, the environment surrounding consumption, and other associated factors. The graph indicates that this person likes apples under the circumstances, since utility U is shown to be rising, to a point, with an increase in the consumption of apples. Instead of assigning certain units of measurement to utility (such as utils) we will simply use the cardinal numbers as indicators—the higher the number, the greater the utility.

Technically speaking, the utility function of Figure 2-1 is *increasing at a decreasing rate* up to five apples. Utility is maximum when the consumer eats five apples. Beyond five apples the utility actually declines, which means that satisfaction actually decreases if the consumer eats any more than five apples. The change in utility resulting from an additional apple (or from a one unit change in consumption) is called *marginal utility.* For example, in our illustration, zero apples corresponds to a utility level of 0. As the consumer eats the very first apple, the utility rises to 9. Since the change in utility from the consumption of 1 apple equals 9, the marginal utility of the first apple is 9. The total utility rises to 15 with the consumption of the second apple. Thus the marginal utility of the second apple is 6. Theoretically, the marginal value of a function indicates the geometric value of the *slope* of the function at a point. The slope of a function is indicated by the value of the inclination of the tangent, and is sometimes referred to as the rise-over-the-run value. In the case of the utility function under consideration, the marginal utility MU of an apple may be described as

$$MU = \frac{\Delta U}{\Delta A} \tag{3}$$

Equation (3) can accomodate the definition of marginal utility for changes in utility resulting from the change in the quantity of apples consumed other than one unit. Thus, if the utility levels for 10 and 12 units were to be 100 and 106, respectively, the marginal utility in that range would equal $(106-100)/(12-10),$ or $6/2 = 3.$

Figure 2-1 contains the diagram of the MU function drawn below the U

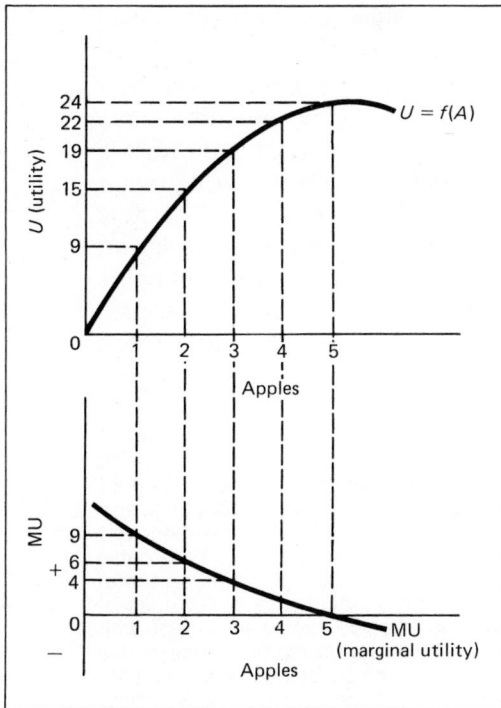

FIGURE 2-1
Marginal utility is defined as the change in total utility resulting from a one-unit change in consumption—or, more generally, MU = $\Delta U/\Delta Q$. In our illustration, the utility or satisfaction U is derived from the consumption of apples A. The cardinal utility function $U = f(A)$ is shown in the upper portion of the figure and utility is shown to be increasing at a decreasing rate. The lower diagram shows the values of the marginal utility MU of apples at various points of apple consumption. Since utility increases at a decreasing rate, the marginal utility declines, and is also so indicated by the progressively smaller slope of the utility function. The slope of a function is generally indicated by the value of the corresponding marginal function. Maximum utility occurs with five apples and, accordingly, the slope of the total utility function is zero where $A = 5$. The MU of apples is also zero where $A = 5$.

function. The MU values are positive to the fifth apple and negative beyond that point. Since the U value is maximum when $A = 5$, the slope of the utility function is zero at that point. The MU function is shown to attain a zero value accordingly. It was also mentioned that utility decreases after the fifth apple. A decrease in utility is equivalent to *negative* marginal utility. Our consumer obviously dislikes the sixth apple, as well as the seventh and the eighth. It is not very difficult to imagine someone getting sick from eating too many apples. So long as the utility function is increasing at a decreasing rate, the MU will continue to decline. If the function possesses a maximum, it will occur where the marginal utility equals zero. The analysis of apples suggests that, all other factors remaining equal, consumers may be persuaded to eat five apples at most, for that number would maximize their utility. Put differently, if apples were 20¢ each and consumers had sufficient income and considered the apples to be worthwhile relative to some other goods that they could purchase, they would spend a dollar to buy the apples.

So far we have assumed that the consumer's utility varies as shown provided we hold all other factors constant. To illustrate a related phenomenon, suppose we present him with a pound of cheese before he commences to eat the apples. Would the utility function and, for that matter, his utility be any different from the one shown in Figure 2-1? Since many people enjoy eating apples and cheese together, we could theorize that the apple eater's utility would be greater with cheese than in its absence. Conceivably, a person could eat more apples in conjunction with cheese than in isolation.

Figure 2-2 illustrates the probable effects of various quantities of cheese given to a person who also likes apples. The original utility function (no cheese) is labelled U, while the others, labelled U_1, U_2, and U_3, correspond to the utility functions accompanied by the amounts of cheese indicated. We have purposely drawn the utility function to reflect diminishing marginal utility. It is quite clear that the consumer's utility would be successively higher with greater amounts of cheese, as long as he doesn't eat too much cheese. His utility is greatest when he consumes two pounds of cheese and eight apples, as shown by utility function U_2 and a utility value of 38. Originally, he chose five apples without cheese in order to maximize his utility. If he continues to eat five apples along with one pound of cheese, his utility equals 28, or four more than when

FIGURE 2-2
The singe-commodity utility function measures or indicates the utility of consumption of one commodity under the usual ceteris paribus conditions. In this situation, utility is affected by the quantity of apples, while other factors are held constant. However, should some of the other variables be allowed to change, the utility from apples would change even though the quantity of apples consumed may not have. Thus, if consumers are given certain quantities of cheese, their utility from apple consumption would be greater than before. The additional utility from other sources is referred to as the *incremental utility*. For example, with reference to the figure, consumers would receive 24 units of satisfaction with five apples alone and 28 units if they had one pound of cheese to go with the apples. In such an instance, the incremental utility of the one pound of cheese, when $A = 5$, would equal 4 units. This incremental utility is shown as U. Since marginal utility, when it is positive, and incremental utility can both increase a consumer's utility, important economic implications about resource allocation can appear in such analyses.

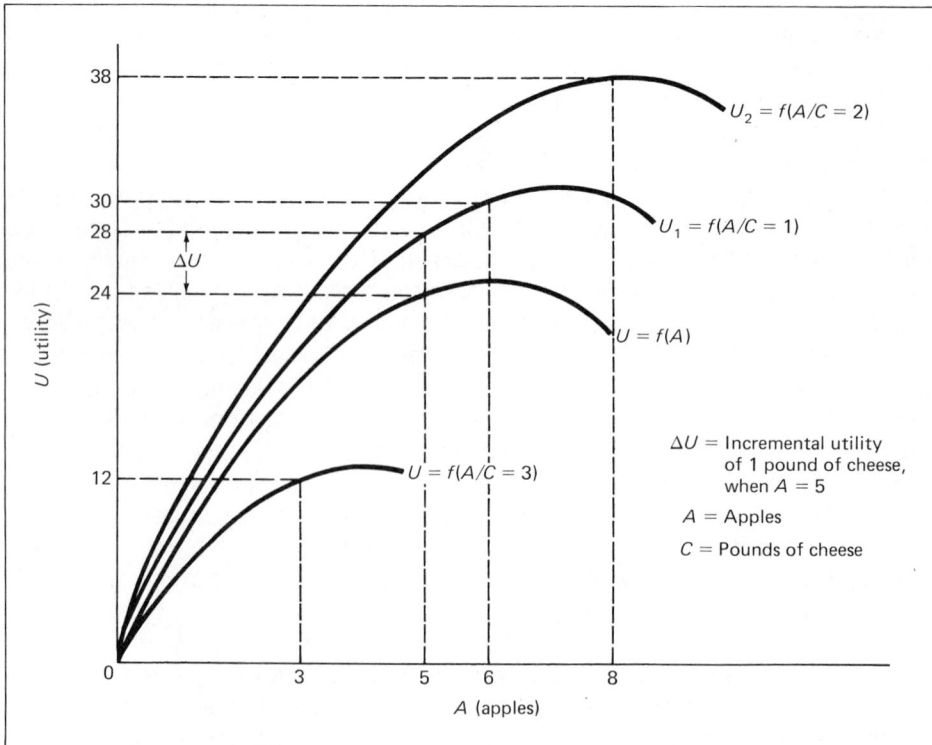

he consumes five apples without cheese. The additional utility obtained due to the cheese is termed the *incremental utility*. The notion of incremental is somewhat different than the idea of marginal. Whereas the marginal utility of apple consumption measures the change in utility resulting from apple consumption, incremental utility refers to the change in utility brought about by other factors. Alternatively, if the number of apples eaten is held constant, the change in utility due to a change in consumption of one unit of cheese may be termed the marginal utility of cheese. The lowest utility function depicts utility levels corresponding to various quantities of apples accompanied by the consumption of three pounds of cheese, suggesting that the overall level of utility is much less than before. Why?

Before we embark upon other matters concerning utility, the following summary is in order.

For a *ceteris paribus* utility function

$$U_A = f[A/(X, Y, Z)],$$

Marginal utility of $A = MU_A = \dfrac{\Delta U}{\Delta A}$;

Total utility of $A = U_A = \displaystyle\sum^{n} MU_{A_i}$;

Incremental utility $= \Delta U = \dfrac{\Delta U}{\Delta X \text{ or } \Delta Y \text{ or } \Delta Z}$;

Cardinal utility indicates *absolute* degree of utility;

Ordinal utility measurement uses *relative* degree of satisfaction.

So far we have assumed that marginal utility of a given product will decline with increasing consumption. This axiom is more often true than not. People discuss this phenomenon by referring to it as "diminishing returns" without going into the specifics of marginal utility. For example if you sit through three hours of fancy iceskating of the variety offered by Icecapades or Ice Follies, you will run into diminishing marginal utility offered by each additional performance as the hours wear on. The same thing applies to clothing—an extra new shirt added to your wardrobe after the first forty will not add much to your overall utility. The author continues to receive shirts on his birthdays, Father's Day, and Christmas!

The assumption of declining marginal utility fits most cases quite well and as such many economists refer to this phenomenon as the "law" of diminishing marginal utility. However certain situations call for other than diminishing marginal utility functions. For example, consider a school administrator in charge of the activities of a school district. Let her utility be largely a function of the number of teachers under her jurisdiction. We have assumed that her utility will vary linearly with the number of teachers. If the linear utility function is valid, the administrator's utility will continuously increase by constant amounts due to each additional teacher employed. Presumably, in the administrator's opinion, one teacher is as good as another and the greater the number of teachers, other factors remaining equal, the greater the quality of education and perhaps the higher the reputation of the administration. This, however, may not be absolutely true in reality, since eventually too many teachers relative to the number of pupils and/or the other complementary facilities could contribute to an overall chaos and lack of productivity. As in the case of the apples and cheese, an excessive number of teachers may very well shift the administrator's utility function downward, suggesting the disutility created by the situation. Figure 2-3 illustrates the linear utility function and the associated marginal utility function. Why is the MU horizontal?

Figure 2-4 contains the utility functions of two students, Jekyl and Hyde, who are enrolled in an economics course. No attempt is made to actually compare the utilities derived by the gentlemen, since the amount of utility derived from economics lectures is not measurable, and even if it were we couldn't truly say whether Jekyl was as happy as Hyde under identical circumstances. For that matter, neither could Jekyl or Hyde. In the figure, the vertical axis simply indicates the level of happiness experienced by each person *as judged by him.* Consequently, even if the utility functions show equal utility, it would be meaningless to say that both people are equally satisfied. Economists agree that *interpersonal utility comparisons* at best provide educated opinions as opposed to scientifically verifiable conclusions.

Jekyl is interested enough in economics to achieve increasing utility with greater amounts of time spent in listening to lectures, whereas Hyde's utility declines with time. Since Jekyl's utility function is linear and positive, his marginal utility is also positive but constant in contrast to his colleague's marginal utility, which is negative. We see another set of utility functions labeled U'_J and U'_H in the same graph. What could have caused a change in these functions? Jekyl's function is increasing at an increasing rate, while Hyde's remains constant. Perhaps a new teacher has taken over a class and

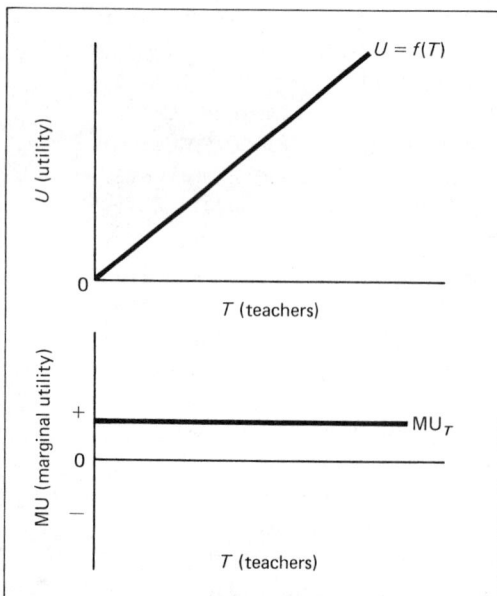

FIGURE 2-3
The administrator's utility function is deliberately drawn in linear fashion to indicate that her utility U, which is governed by the number of teachers T, varies positively and proportionately with T. The assumption is that as far as she is concerned, one teacher is as good as another, although we know this is not strictly true in all cases. However, *if* the utility function is a straight line, the slope of the function is constant and as such the marginal utility of each additional teacher is also constant. The constant marginal utility is shown as a horizontal line in the lower portion of the diagram.

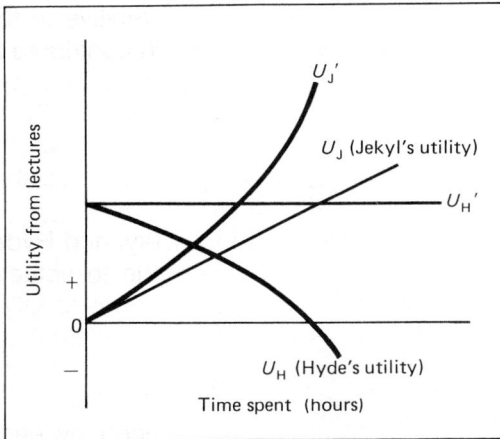

FIGURE 2-4
Utility functions come in all shapes and sizes, just as people do. To illustrate the variety that exists in cardinal utility functions, we have drawn the original utility functions for two college students, Jekyl and Hyde, as U_J and U_H. U_J depicts a constant marginal utility condition—Jekyl's utility increases at a constant rate with time spent at lectures. Hyde, however, apparently does not receive any satisfaction from lectures, since the utility level *decreases* with time. Declining utility means *negative marginal utility.* For some reason, the utility functions for both persons have subsequently changed to the new forms U'_J and U'_H, and both the new functions suggest that our gentlemen are now receiving more utility from the lectures than they did previously. Hyde's utility function indicates that his utility level is constant regardless of the amount of time spent at lectures—his marginal utility is zero, whereas it used to be negative. Someone like Hyde is better off staying at home. Jekyl, on the other hand, is experiencing increasing marginal utility, and this is further borne out by his utility function, which is now increasing at an increasing rate. Although no reason for the change in utility functions is being offered here, it is possible that a better textbook or a more inspiring teacher could affect the utility functions as suggested.

made the lectures more interesting. It is also conceivable that the class is using a better textbook which has greater appeal to the students. Under the circumstances, each person is receiving a greater amount of utility than he did before. Jekyl's marginal utility is increasing with time, while Hyde's is zero, which is still higher than negative marginal utility. We have used utility analysis to bring out the behavior of economics students. Could we use similar analysis in discussing the utility of marriage, having children, acquiring stocks, or going on trips?

Does income provide utility? Most people tend to say yes. But the answer may not always be affirmative if we pause to think about the sacrifices made in the process of acquiring income. A rational person would elect to chase after an extra dollar's income if and only if the sacrifice involved does not exceed a dollar. Using the notion of utility and marginal utility we may hypothesize that the marginal utility of the dollars at low levels of income is probably higher than the marginal utility received at higher incomes. Most of our needs are barely met when we have just sufficient income to come up to the poverty line. Let this minimum be about $8000 per year. As we earn more income, our utility increases because the extra income permits us to rise above the subsistence

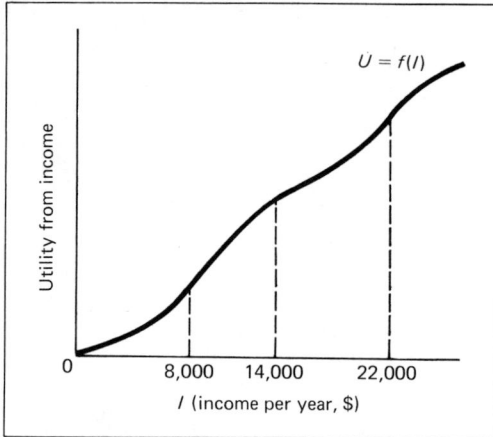

FIGURE 2-5
It is generally believed that income has certain peculiar utility characteristics. Instead of yielding either constant, increasing, or declining marginal utility, additional income presumably provides all three types. It is suggested that a person will receive increasing marginal utility from additional income to the point where he meets all his basic needs, such as an income level of $8000. After the first $8000 he receives utility from additional income, but the utility function in the range $8000–14,000 is subject to diminishing marginal utility because his valuation of the extra $6000 is not as high as the first $8000. The extra income beyond the $14,000 is capable of yielding increasing marginal utility, because a person earning that much income is probably under a lot of financial and social pressure, and hence every dollar means that much more to him. Again, after he is earning $22,000, he receives declining marginal utility from additional income for similar reasons.

level. But since the basic needs have been met at a level of $8000, it is conceivable that the additional income's marginal utility is not as high as that of the first $8000.

In Figure 2-5, you see that the utility function for a person changes at different rates at the many levels of income. In the $0–8000 range, the function is increasing at an increasing rate in keeping with our assumptions of rising marginal utility. From $8000 to $14,000, the function is increasing at a decreasing rate, implying that while the extra income is desirable, it is not as welcome as the first $8000. Furthermore, the person being analyzed is probably devoting more time and effort in earning the extra $6000 and incurring some loss in utility from the reduced amounts of leisure. In the next range of income, the utility function again rises at an increasing rate, signifying increasing marginal utility derived from the additional $8000. Quite conceivably, our person's tastes have adjusted to the new wealth and he probably feels that he is well on his way to the top. In addition there may be certain social pressure on him to keep up with the Martinezes. Additional dollars are not only necessary but highly desirable. After the $22,000, marginal utility presumably declines. This income is very satisfying and the extra money, although desirable, is not really necessary. A rational person will attempt to acquire the extra income, since it would increase his utility, provided no constraints are placed on him. We know, however, that sooner or later he has to stop because of the many limitations brought about by his time, skills, family obligations, and other market forces.

UTILITY MAXIMIZATION UNDER CONSTRAINTS

The Equimarginal Principle

We have discussed the basic theory of utility maximization in a cardinal utility environment without any constraints. Realistically speaking, the decision maker faces certain constraints or limitations posed by such factors as income, prices of goods and services, and the scarce amount of other resources. How do people maximize utility in view of the constraints or if they acquire more than one product? We will illustrate the basis for utility-maximizing allocation of resources with the help of an example and Figure 2-6.

Assume that Gilda has a maximum of 14 hours available to work either in her regular job or in moonlighting. Let us further suppose that she is free to

FIGURE 2-6
Whenever possible the marginal values received from alternative uses should be equal to each other in order to maximize total value from all sources. This principle is referred to as the *equimarginal principle* and sometimes as the *Second Law of Gossen.* In the diagram here we see that Gilda has a total time of 14 hours that she is free to allocate toward her regular job and her "second" job. Both jobs provide diminishing (but positive) marginal utility. Because maximum total utility occurs where the marginal utility from each job is equal, Gilda should spend 10 hours at her regular job and the remaining time moonlighting. The area under the MU function measures the total utility. Gilda's total utility from both occupations is shown by the area of the polygon *MVKZNM.*

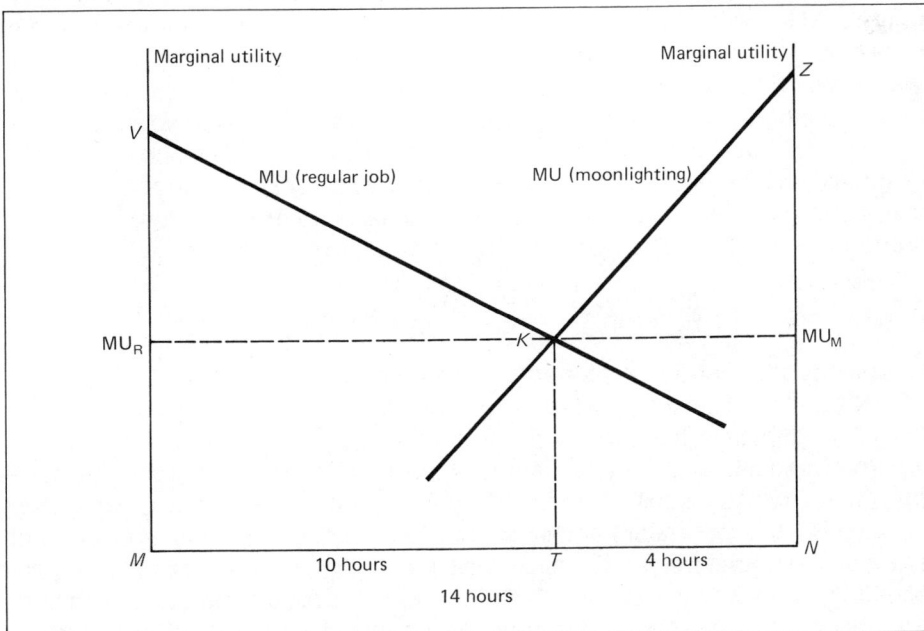

choose the number of hours at either job. Income from both occupations provides income and hence utility. If income's marginal utility is assumed to be subject to the so-called "law" of diminishing returns, the marginal utility from the hours spent at either job should decline. Figure 2-6 shows the total time available by the distance MN, where M is the origin for measuring time allocated to the regular work, which is measured in a left-to-right direction. The remaining time, presumably to be spent in moonlighting, is measured from right to left, with the origin located at point N. The two marginal utility functions reflect the presence of diminshing marginal utility, which may come about due to circumstances governing the employment conditions at both places of work. For example, Gilda's customary employment may be as an assistant banker while her avocation as a dance instructor is at Studio 80 (a discotheque). Just because she receives tremendous enjoyment at the disco or because she is paid an extremely high salary at the bank, there is no reason to assume that she would spend her entire time making money or dancing to flickering lights. How much time she devotes to either job will depend on the marginal utility derived from time spent at each.

You will agree that Gilda maximizes her total utility by allocating 10 hours to her regular job and the remaining 4 to moonlighting. Since the marginal utility from either type of work declines, "too much" time spent on one may yield very little marginal benefit while precluding higher levels of utility that could have been obtained from the other job. To the right of the 10-hour point (T), the MU of the regular work falls below the MU of moonlighting. For example, if Gilda works 11 hours at the regular job, the MU of the 11th hour would be less than the MU that could be obtained by allocating that hour to moonlighting. Similarly, spending more than 4 hours at the second job would be uneconomical, since the extra hour beyond the fourth would provide less additional utility than could be obtained by devoting the time to the regular occupation. In terms of geometry, the *total combined utility* from both jobs is given by the area under the relevant portions of the two MU functions. Thus, the area $MVKZNM$ measures the value of total utility. You will recall from earlier discussions that total utility is equal to the sum of the individual marginal utilities and this sum is graphically demonstrated by the use of areas. No other allocation of time would yield a larger area. Thus, in order to maximize utility from more than one source, under constraint, Gilda has to observe the following:

a. MU (Regular job) = MU (Moonlighting).
b. Time (Regular job) + Time (Moonlighting) = 14 hours.

Condition (a) is generally referred to as the *equimarginal principle*.

Now we will incorporate the role of income into the analysis of this important principle. If a person has a limited amount of income, the prices of the many goods and services impose the limits to the quantities of these products that the consumer may purchase. Suppose a particular family allocates $1300 per month among three utility-producing goods: housing and entertainment, children's education, and travel. Figure 2-7 shows the original allocation at points H_1, E_1, and T_1 for a combined total of $1300 per month. When you compare the three graphs, notice that under the original allocation

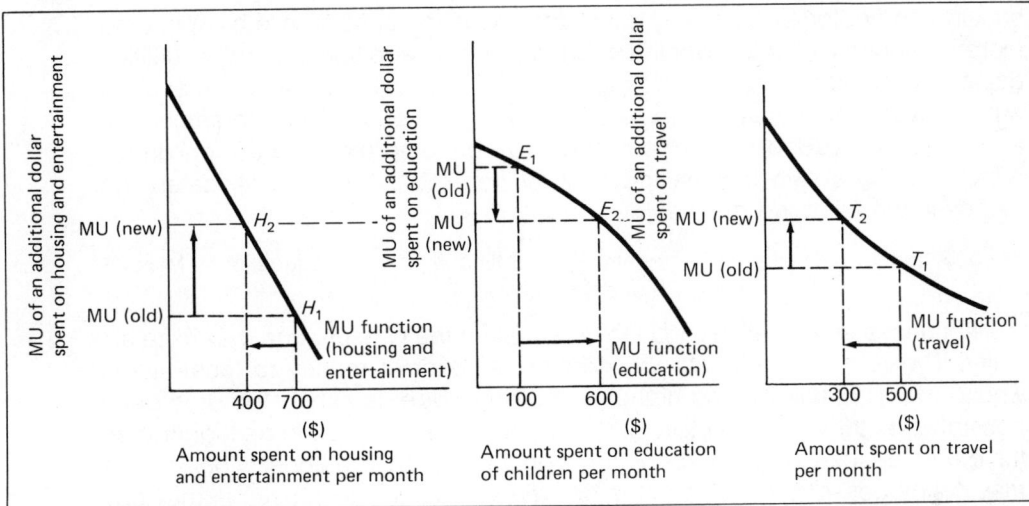

FIGURE 2-7
The *equimarginal principle,* sometimes called the *Second Law of Gossen,* suggests that specific amounts of resources will yield the maximum total effectiveness if the resources are allocated so that the marginal effectiveness of each alternative is equal. Thus, in terms of utility maximization, a given amount of income will bring forth the greatest amount of utility if it is allocated among the many alternative uses in a manner which satisfies the equation:

$$\frac{MU_A}{P_A} = \frac{MU_B}{P_B} = \frac{MU_C}{P_C} = \cdots \frac{MU_n}{P_n}$$

In the situation above, the consumer derives the maximum benefit (utility) from his income by allocating his income among entertainment, travel, and education so that *the marginal utility of each is equal per dollar.*

plan the marginal utility of the last dollar spent on children's education is the highest and that of housing and entertainment is the lowest. Because the principle of diminishing marginal utility is assumed to be operating here, the MU curves decline with extra expenditure. Consequently, if less is spent on a particular commodity, that item's MU should increase. If we spend less on those items whose MU is low, their MU will increase; if we spend more on the items whose MU is high, their MU will decline. If more money is spent on education, say $500 more, the new point for education will correspond to point E_2. At an expenditure level of $600, the MU of education will be less than before as shown by "MU-new." But, if the consumer does not have any more than $1300 the extra $500 for education has to come from the other items that he also consumes, namely, housing and entertainment and travel. If he cuts back on housing and entertainment and travel, the MUs in these areas will rise. Suppose he reduces expenditures on housing and entertainment by $300. This puts him at point H_2 on the MU function for housing and entertainment and similarly the new point for travel is at T_2 for a reduction of $200 on travel.

The three graphs of Figure 2-7 suggest that the cuts in housing and entertainment as well as travel amount to $500, which is the additional amount spent on the children's education. Furthermore, by cutting expenditures on housing and entertainment and travel, their MUs increased while by spending more on education its MU declined. But as long as additional marginal utilities gained are higher than the corresponding marginal utilities lost, the total utility will increase. The consumer reduced his utility in housing and entertainment and travel but added much more utility by spending more on the children's education. To obtain the maximum utility from his $1300, he allocated the money in the following manner.

MU of $ spent on housing and entertainment = MU of $ spent on education = MU of $ spent on travel

It is not necessary for all the MUs to be equal for the consumer to maximize his utility. The rule is to allocate the greatest amount of money to those items whose marginal utility is the highest until the budget is. exhausted. It is quite possible that the marginal utility of some goods will continue to be higher than the others despite greater expenditures on the former. The equality of the MUs may not be possible for some of the following reasons. The consumer may buy only one good—the one that yields the greatest MU. The consumer may be obliged to buy some of the other goods; or a minimum quantity of some of the other goods may be necessary to provide the first good with such high utility. In most cases, however, the equimarginal principle applies and is a very useful device in areas other than utility analysis.

THE INCOME–PRICE BUDGET CONSTRAINT AND UTILITY MAXIMIZATION

In addition to income and other constraints, the prices of the various goods and services also create a limitation for the consumer. Assume that you have a fixed amount of income $M with which to purchase quantities of the two products A and B with prices P_A and P_B, respectively, which provide utility. Since all money income must be spent on A and B, the *budget constraint* due to $M may be written as

$$P_A A + P_B B = M$$

which states that expenditures on A ($P_A A$) plus the expenditures on B ($P_B B$) must add to the total amount available (M). Thus the marginal utility per dollar spent on A is the marginal utility of a unit of A divided by its price. For example, if the second unit of A provides 10 units of marginal utility and A's price is $5, then the $5 spent in the acquisition of the second unit of A would yield 10 units of additional utility, which is equivalent to 2 units of marginal utility per dollar. If diminishing marginal utility is also assumed, the marginal utility per dollar from additional units of A should decline. Consequently, if A and B are both subject to diminishing returns and their prices are held constant, you will maximize your total utility by allocating $M among A and B so that the marginal utility per dollar for each commodity is equal, or

$$\frac{MU_A}{P_A} = \frac{MU_B}{P_B}$$

As an illustration, suppose the prices and income are: $P_A = \$5$, $P_B = \$8$, and $M = \$55$. Let the utility function of the purchaser be such that the utility obtained from one item is completely *independent* of the amounts purchased of the other. Table 2-1 reproduces the various conditions described. Under the circumstances described, many combinations of the purchase of A and B satisfy the equimarginal condition. However, due to the limitations of the budget, not all conditions are *feasible* and neither are all combinations equally desirable. For example, if we buy five of A we will spend $25 and the MU_A per dollar will equal 3. In order to obtain the same MU per dollar from B we will have to purchase seven units of B for $56. This combination of five As and seven Bs is out of the question because we have only $55. The combination is definitely desirable but not feasible. If we choose one of A and hence only six of B, the combination will be feasible, but we will not have spent all of the money. We will be depriving ourselves of some potential utility. Furthermore, the MU_A/P_A of the first A will not be equal to the MU_B/P_B of the sixth B. Thus, this combination is feasible but certainly not desirable. We are looking for a combination of A and B so that we will exhaust the entire $55 and also make sure that the equimarginal principle holds. Such a combination, under the circumstances, will be desirable and feasible and will yield the maximum utility from the available amount of money. The reader can verify that if we choose three As and five Bs, we will obtain the "best" combination of A and B, or what is also referred to as the *utility-maximizing bundle* and sometimes a *balanced bundle* of A and B. The total expenditures in this case would be $15 for A and $40 for B, and the sum of the total utilities would equal 370, which, in effect, is the sum of all the individual marginal utilities. How will changing price(s) and amounts of money available affect the choice of bundles?

If the price of one of the goods falls, then the MU/P will increase and we will tend to buy more of this good until the MU/P ratios are equal again. Similarly, if more money is made available, we are likely to purchase more of all goods until the MU/P ratios are equal and the total amount of money is spent. Money itself is also subject to the laws of utility as postulated before. Therefore, we can

TABLE 2-1
MARGINAL UTILITY AND CONSTRAINED UTILITY MAXIMIZATION

Units of A purchased	Utility of A	Marginal utility—A	$\dfrac{MU_A}{P_A}$	Units of B purchased	Utility of B	Marginal utility—B	$\dfrac{MU_B}{P_B}$
1	35	35	7	1	72	72	9
2	65	30	6	2	136	64	8
3	90	25	5	3	192	56	7
4	110	20	4	4	240	48	6
5	125	15	3	5	280	40	5
6	135	10	2	6	312	32	4
7	140	5	1	7	336	24	3
8	135	−5	−1	8	352	16	2
9	125	−10	−2	9	360	8	1
10	110	−15	−3	10	340	−20	−2.5

generally summarize by stating that for N goods and $\$M$, the consumer will be at *equilibrium,* that is, will be maximizing utility via the equation:

$$\frac{MU_A}{P_A} = \frac{MU_B}{P_B} = \cdots = \cdots = \frac{MU_N}{P_N} = \frac{MU_M}{P_M} \qquad (4)$$

Equation (4) is the *consumer equilibrium equation.* If the price of A falls, the left side of the equation will get larger. If diminishing marginal utility is present, more As bought will tend to lower the ratio. It is also possible that more Bs will be bought because the lower price of A will release money for B, and it is equally likely that less Bs will be bought since that tends to increase the ratio MU_B/P_B. The last term of equation (4) will also go up because the ratio will increase due to a fall in the general price level, that is, the *real* quantity of money will rise if the price level (price of money) goes down. In the end, the ratios (MU/P) for all goods including M will again be equal.

The analysis just concluded brings out the implications of the equimarginal utility-maximization principle in the face of variations in the prices of the goods, in income, or in some combination of prices and income. For instance, what would happen to the utility-maximizing bundle if the price of A rose while that of B fell and the consumer's income declined? Without specific information on the values of the variables, the utility function, as well as the amounts of change, there is no way we can conclude that the consumer will buy more or less of certain items. As an example, if the price of all meats decreases and the cost of entertainment increases, while your income falls, will you buy more beef and less entertainment? Such issues are discussed when we attempt to use other tools specifically reserved for *multicommodity utility functions.* Although income and money may have been used synonymously, money as a commodity has a different meaning from money as income. The consumer equilibrium condition described earlier does not make any attempt to distinguish one interpretation from another. For example, persons may hold money for its own sake (known as the Liquidity Preference Schedule) or because it is a store of purchasing power. An increase in the quantity of money does not automatically imply an increase in income and vice versa.

APPLICATIONS

1. Income Taxation and Sacrifice

The following is an example of the application of utility analysis in the area of income taxation.

Let us assume that all consumers have similar tastes and preferences and possess the same utility function for income as shown in Figure 2-8. Suppose we have two classes of people, the rich and the poor, with the former's income at R_1 and the latter's at P_1, so that the rich enjoy a utility level of U_{R_1} and the poor U_{P_1}. If we impose income taxes so that each class of people pay a "fair" share by undergoing equal proportional amounts of sacrifice, we will be comparing the loss of utility relative to income for each group. The sacrifice is measured by the ratio of the change in utility arising from the income tax to the amount of income. If the poor pay a tax

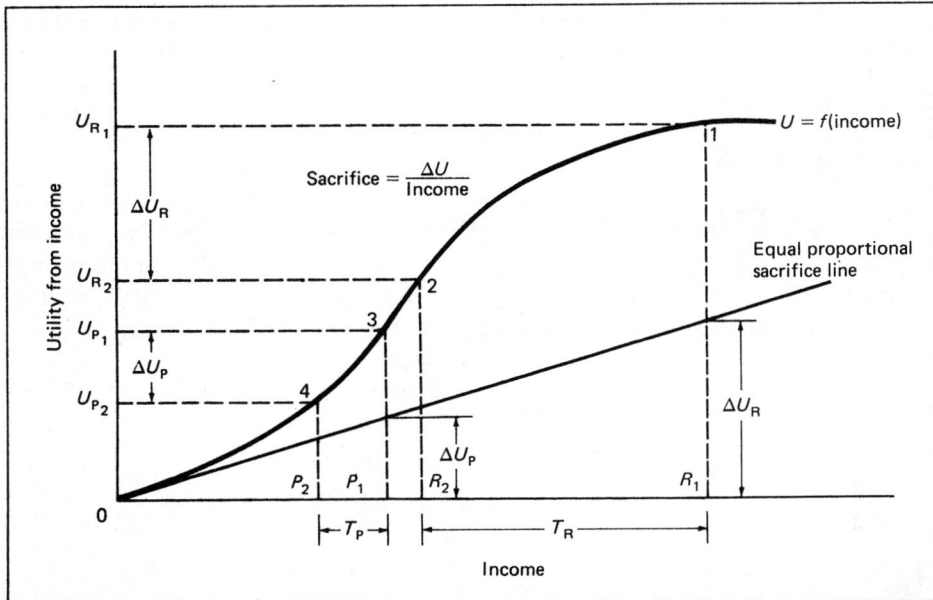

FIGURE 2-8
The utility function shown above relates the loss of well being associated with an income tax. Most people agree that under the current system of income taxes in many countries, despite the progressive nature of income tax rates, some people pay a proportionately heavier penalty than others. It is perhaps more equitable to have every taxpayer pay the right amount of taxes, which makes the *proportional sacrifice* for all taxpayers equal. This proportion is defined as the ratio of utility lost to the level of before-tax income. Thus, if we have two groups of people, say the rich (with income R_1) and the poor (with income P_1), each should pay taxes in an amount where the ratio of the utility lost by the rich, ΔU_R to their income R_1 equals $\Delta U_P/P_1$. The radius vector from the origin labelled the *equal proportional line* (whose tangent angle measures the sacrifice) suggests that the rich should pay T_R and the poor T_P in income taxes. After the income tax, the rich will move from 1 to 2 and the poor from 3 to 4 on the utility function. This is just an illustration of the application of the cardinal utility function to the revision of the income tax structure. It probably will be very difficult to ascertain the real shape of the utility functions for groups, if such group functions exist.

in the amount equal to T_P, their income after taxes will be P_2. The utility loss is ΔU_P. If we divide this ΔU_P by the original income we will obtain the sacrifice made by the poor, which is shown by the straight line labelled *equal proportional sacrifice line* and whose slope (or angle) shows the ratio of ΔU_P to P_1, or the sacrifice rate for the poor. The ΔU_P shown for this line is the same as the ΔU_P taken from the utility function. So that the rich may also undergo an equal proportional sacrifice, the income tax must be high enough so that the loss in utility of the rich as compared to their income is in the same proportion as the loss in utility of the poor compared to their income. This means that the tax to the rich T_R is such that $\Delta U_R/R_1=\Delta U_P/P_1$. This puts their after tax income at R_2. Here, too, we see that the ratio of ΔU_R to R_1 subtends the same angle as does ΔU_P to P_1 and both points lie along the equal proportional sacrifice line. The graph points out that the rich have to pay a larger amount of taxes as compared to the poor, so that the sacrifices made by both groups are *relatively equal*. This argument is used in part to explain the existence of the *progressive income tax structure* of the United States and many other countries. In absolute terms, the loss of utility to the rich is far greater than the loss of utility faced by the poor, that is, $\Delta U_R > \Delta U_P$, but, relatively speaking, each group sacrifices equal proportional utility as compared to earning power. Presumably this is a fair way of taxing income, although it may seem highly unequitable to many—especially the rich. Would the analysis just concluded be any different if we require both groups to pay *equal percentages of income* as income tax?

2. Utility Functions of Gamblers and Pessimists

So far we have theorized about the possible shapes of the utility functions for various individuals or groups under many different circumstances. Can we use microeconomic logic to suggest the shapes of the utility functions for gamblers (risk takers), pessimists (risk avoiders), and risk-neutral people?

Suppose you are asked to participate in a game where the entry fee is $1 but the prize is $2. The game is played by the usual coin-tossing method, where if you guess the outcome correctly you win the extra $1. If you are the gambling type, your marginal utility of the gain is much greater than the marginal disutility (loss in utility) from the loss of your money, and if that is the case, a rational person will gamble. Since the expected value* of the game is zero, the gambler must have a utility function which rises at an increasing rate, that is, the MU of additional dollars of income (due to winnings) is very high and rises progressively with income.

In like manner we may deduce that the utility function for a pessimist is such that the marginal utility of additional income due to possible winnings is less than the potential loss in utility due to losses. Accordingly, the utility function is drawn to reflect the diminishing marginal utility of income.

You can verify that the utility function for a risk-neutral person is linear under identical circumstances. The three suggested shapes are shown in Figure 2-9.

---

*Expected value is defined as the sum of each outcome times its probability of occurrence. Thus, in the coin-tossing example, the probability of each outcome (head, tail) is ½. Since the outcome will be either $1 or −$1, the expected value of the game is EV = ($1 × 0.50) + (−$1 × 0.50) = $0.00. The expected value concept is discussed in more detail in Chapter 14 which deals with uncertainty.

EXERCISES

1. Define and briefly explain the following.
   a. Utility.
   b. Cardinal utility.
   c. Utility function.
   d. Marginal utility.
   e. Incremental utility.
   f. The Second Law of Gossen (equimarginal principle).
   g. Rationality.
   h. Consumer equilibrium.
   i. Increasing at a decreasing rate.

2. Draw hypothetical utility functions reflecting cardinal utility as a function of the following:
   a. Number of children.
   b. Amount of savings.

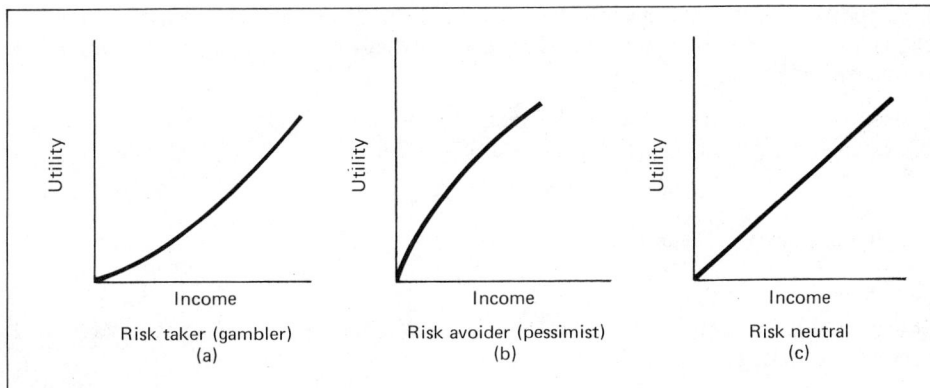

FIGURE 2-9
Panels (a–c) illustrate the probable shapes for the ordinal utility functions associated with gambling for different personalities. The gambler is one who is somewhat optimistic about the outcome of a gamble. Consequently, his expected gains and the utility derived from such gain, outweigh the potential disutility of an adverse outcome. The utility function for such a person shows that utility from gambling increases at an increasing rate and results in the shape shown by (a). The person characterized by (b) is a risk avoider, because the utility from gambling increases at a decreasing rate. If she wins, the additional utility will not be that much, but if she loses, the loss in utility will be quite high. Finally, the person whose utility function is shown in (c), is neither a gambler nor a risk avoider. In this case, the utility from gambling increases at a constant rate, implying constant marginal utility from each dollar gambled. This person will gamble, if and only if, the game is "fair".

   c. Weekly trips to Hawaii (from the mainland).
   d. Number of curtain calls.
   e. Number of journal articles published.
   f. Number of criminal cases won.
   g. Number of "affairs".
   h. Number of As received at college.

3. Suggest a change in one of the "other" variables that was previously held constant, which would (i) increase total utility and (ii) decrease total utility for each of the functions (a)–(h) of Exercise 2.

4. Indicate whether the following utility functions $U = f(X)$ are subject to increasing, diminishing, or constant marginal utility. Explain your answer.

   a. $U = 2X$
   b. $U = 10X^2$
   c. $U = 100\sqrt{X}$
   d. $U = 1000/X$

5. Suppose the marginal utility functions for three goods X, Y, and Z are, respectively,

$$MU_X = 100 - 2X$$
$$MU_Y = 20$$
$$MU_Z = 10 + Z$$

Identify the total utility functions as either *increasing at an increasing rate* or *increasing at a constant rate*, or describe it with other appropriate words.

6. Suppose the marginal utilities of A, B, and C are 10, 6, and 3, respectively. If the prices are A = \$5, B = \$2, and C = \$1.50, which product is economically most valuable? Explain.

7. Assume that you have \$1000 with which to take trips (*T*) and to go out to restaurants (*R*). Each *T* costs \$160 and each *R* costs \$20. If the marginal utility of travel is

$$MU_T = 80 - 2T$$

and that of eating at restaurants is

$$MU_R = 50 - R$$

what should be the optimal values of *T* and *R*? (Hint: Use the equimarginal principle and observe the budget constraint.)

8. Does money (as opposed to income) have any utility? Explain the difference in the two concepts.

9. The so-called Law of Demand suggests that the quantity demanded of a good varies inversely with its price. Can you use cardinal marginal utility analysis to supplement the reasoning behind the law?

10. Many people contend that the discussion of utility is useless since it is an abstract concept. State, and give reasons for, your opinion.

11. Name some (at least three) activities in which you engage that do not affect your utility (happiness), or those that you do without seeking some sort of utility.

12. Cite some examples where a person's consumption point is beyond her maximum utility point and where she now receives negative marginal utility. Is such behavior rational?

13. What sort of utility functions do you suppose habitual murderers possess?

SUGGESTED READINGS

Holahan, W., and Perlman, R. "Taxpayer Preferences and the Choice of Efficient Transfer Systems." *Southern Economic Journal,* July 1978.

Keller W., and Hartog, J. "Income Tax Rates and Proportional Sacrifice." *Public Finance,* 1977.

Maskin, E. "A Theorem on Utilitarianism." *Review of Economic Studies,* February 1978.

McCain, R. "Reflections on the Cultivation of Taste." *Journal of Cultural Economics,* Volume 3, No. 1, June 1978.

McKean, J., and Diemer, J. "The Assessment of Community Preference: A Methodology and Case Study." *Land Economics,* May 1978.

Rosen, H. "An Approach to the Study of Income, Utility and Horizontal Equity." *Quarterly Journal of Economics,* May 1978.

Chapter Three Chapter Three Chapter Three

UTILITY AND INDIFFERENCE ANALYSIS

MULTICOMMODITY UTILITY FUNCTION

We have already been exposed to some of the subtleties of the consumer decision-making process by way of the cardinal utility functions of Chapter 2. To bring out the basic notion of utility, we employed a utility function depicting a single variable, such as cheese or income. In reality, however, people consume or wish to consume a variety of goods and services. Their utility is affected by the quantities and qualities of all such goods and services in conjunction with other circumstances governing the situation. Furthermore, whereas the single-commodity cardinal utility function analyzed the effect of changes in that commodity, or the impact of changes of another product, it did not provide us with any understanding of the *interrelationship* among the many goods composing the consumption bundle. We did, however, discover that the utility from one good is affected by the presence of other goods and that the rational utility-maximizing consumer tends to allocate resources (income, time, and energy) in a manner suggested by the equimarginal principle. In this section we will use a utility function which depicts the consumer's satisfaction from several goods.

Let us assume that our utility is governed by the quantities of X and Y in our possession. If both X and Y yield satisfaction, the utility function may be simply expressed as

$$U = f(X, Y). \tag{1}$$

Equation (1) suggests that utility U will vary with the amounts of X and Y, and other factors which have been left out for the purposes of clarity. If X and Y are economic *goods,* an increase in the quantity of either should increase U. The above utility function, in essence, describes our preferences or tastes for the goods and services from which we choose certain combinations in keeping with our constraints. For example, if X represents longevity and Y income, it may be presumed that to a point we will prefer more longevity for a given income or more income for a given longevity, or greater longevity accompanied by higher income to combinations which provide lesser amounts of either. This is probably not true in all instances, because a very long life span may bring with it many miseries associated with old age; however, old age is more tolerable with adequate income than in its absence.

Ordinal Utility

Recall that cardinal utility analysis requires us to use certain values to designate the levels of utility experienced by the decision maker. It was also mentioned that while such an analysis is logically consistent, it does have certain drawbacks. *Ordinal* utility analysis, fortunately, does not necessitate the measurement of utility in absolute terms. With this method, the decision maker is expected to be able to *rank* preferences. For example, when asked to compare the utility of bundle A to that of bundle B, the decision maker should be able to discern whether combination A is more satisfying than B. If it is, and the consumer is rational, she will place A at a higher rank than B. On the other hand, should both A and B be equally satisfying, the consumer will be indifferent. Almost all of us can certainly identify those combinations of goods and services that please or aggravate us to varying degrees and rank them according to our preferences. As mentioned before, the difficulty arises when we attempt to measure others' utility, unless, of course, the other person has made public her likes and dislikes. Perhaps that is why parents have their children write letters to Santa Claus.

Indifference Curves

We may like two combinations of goods by different amounts, but there is also a possibility that we may like either bundle equally well, in which event, we should be *indifferent* between the two choices. If we use a two-variable utility function, such as $U = f(X,Y)$, and can obtain all combinations of X and Y that provide equal utility and join these points on a XY plane, we will obtain an *indifference curve*. Since there are different levels of satisfaction, indifference curves may be used to show a person's tastes by the ranking of these curves. Thus, combinations of X and Y that yield more utility to the consumer are ranked higher than those that provide lesser degrees of satisfaction. Each indifference curve shows us the combinations of goods that provide a *specific level of satisfaction.*

We will use the glass box of Figure 3-1 to illustrate our basic model. In this figure, the cheese-shaped hunk sitting atop the square box represents a consumer's utility function. The amount of X good is being measured horizontally along the surface *HIJL* and the amount of Y is measured at right angles to the X axis, also on the same top surface of the box. The consumer's utility is changing along the U axis, or in a direction perpendicular to the *HIJL* plane, that is, the height above the *HIJL* plane depicts the amount of utility, and the higher the point above the plane the greater the amount of utility. As you can see, there are many points on the surface of the utility function that are at equal height above the box top—*HIJL*. For example, if we assume that points A and B both lie at equal heights above *HIJL,* then we can say that either point is equally satisfying to the consumer, since the utility at each point is equal. If we locate other points, such as A and B, that are also as high above the *HIJL* plane, we would, in effect, be drawing contour lines showing equal utility (instead of equal elevation, as in geography). Since our consumer receives identical amounts of utility at points A, B, and other such points, she will be *indifferent* among them, all other things remaining equal. When such points as A, B, and others that also yield the same amount of utility (and hence lie at the same height above the plane *HIJL*) are joined by a smooth line, the resulting line is called an *indifference curve.*

As shown in Figure 3-1, the indifference curve AB yields a level of utility indicated as U_1. Thus, both combinations shown by A and B as well as all points in this curve on the surface of the cheese provide a utility level U_1. In a similar manner, we can draw other indifference curves that lie either higher or lower than AB which yield greater or lesser satisfaction than U_1. For example, the indifference curve EF is "higher" than AB and hence offers a greater level of

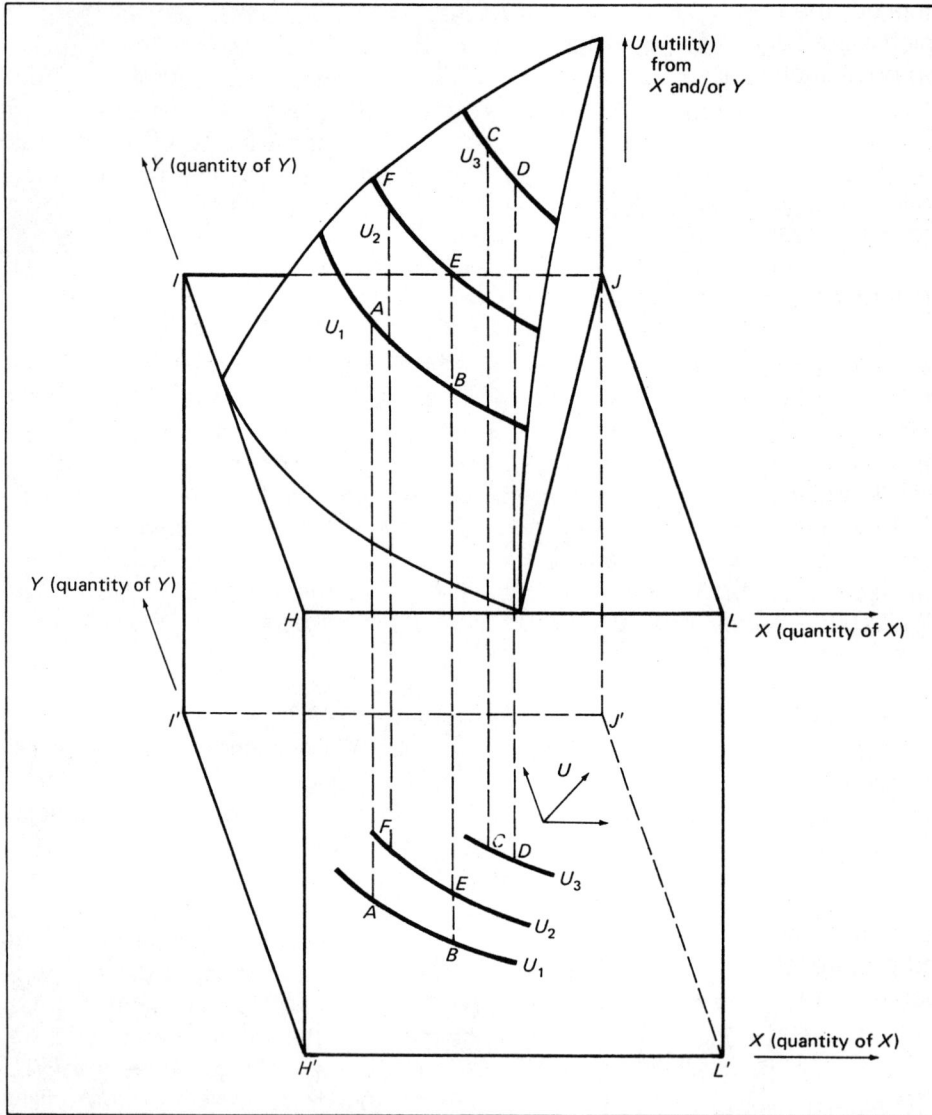

FIGURE 3-1
The utility hill and indifference curves.

satisfaction than *AB;* therefore, utility level U_2 is greater than level U_1 and along the same lines U_3 (indifference curve *CD*) is "better" than *EF*. What we are saying is that a consumer will always prefer higher to lower indifference curves, and in our particular model with only the three curves shown she will prefer *CD* to *EF* and *EF* to *AB*, because $U_3 > U_2 > U_1$. We may also generalize that because U_2 is preferred over U_1 and U_3 is preferred to U_2, then U_3 will certainly be preferred to U_1. Any action that permits the consumer to move "higher" along the surface of the utility hill will be very welcome and if there are no constraints imposed, the consumer will try to reach the peak of this particular mountain which will in our case maximize satisfaction. As can be seen, if the consumer is at a point such as A, utility will increase if she moves laterally (more X), or in a direction 90 degrees to the X axis along the HIJL (more Y), or at an angle (more of both X and Y), because she will succeed in getting onto a higher indifference curve by any of these movements. There are an infinite number of such indifference curves suggesting infinite possibilities of combinations X and Y and hence many levels of utility.

If we shine a flashlight through the transparent cheese we will see the indifference curves as shown on a plane labelled H'I'J'L', which represents the bottom of the square glass box. Consequently, if we choose not to utilize three-dimensional models, we can show the utility function via this *indifference map* drawn as a two-dimensional figure on the bottom surface. Here the origin is located at H' and the quantities of X and Y are measured along the X and Y axes, but the utility level is shown by the position of the indifference curve relative to the origin. You can see how the indifference curves from the three-dimensional model have been drawn to reflect their relative "heights" or utilities. As before, the curves that are farther to the right or above represent greater levels of utility because they correspond to higher points on the utility hill, and accordingly the level of utility changes in the directions shown by the three arrows. The arrows indicate that utility can increase due to more X or more Y or both, as long as the points so located are higher or to the right. Here, too, we see that $U_3 > U_2 > U_1$. In the models to follow, we shall use such indifference maps to carry out our discussions about consumer and utility behavior.

Basic Properties of Indifference Curves

Indifference curves collectively represent a person's or institution's tastes and preferences. They are drawn under a specific set of assumptions and as such may not all look alike for different people or tastes. For that matter, not all indifferences are "well behaved." Given below are some important observations concerning indifference curves.

a. Any point along a given indifference curve represents a unique level of satisfaction.
b. "Higher" indifference curves represent greater levels of satisfaction.
c. A consumer can *rank* his preferences via indifference curves, that is, the *measurement* of satisfaction is not required. *Ordinal* indicators designate superior or inferior bundles.
d. Indifference curves may not intersect.
e. The indifference map containing all the curves represents the utility function of the decision-maker.
f. Indifference curves may be linear, nonlinear, positively sloped, negatively sloped, rectangular, or just points.

Figure 3-2 shows an indifference curve for a particular individual whose

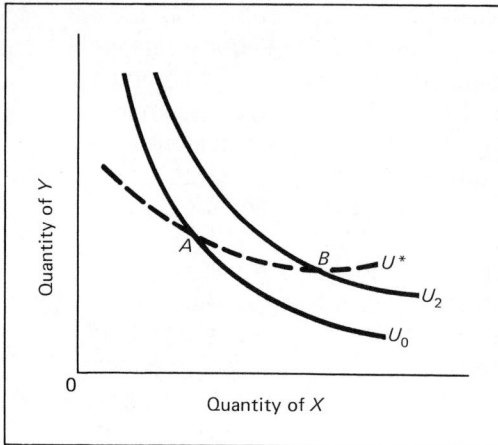

FIGURE 3-2
The indifference curves labelled U_0 and U_2, as well as the one shown as U^*, depict diminishing marginal rates of substitution. Because indifference curves may not intersect, the dotted curve represents either a different time or set of circumstances, or simply another utility function. Thus, even though at points A and B the two types of indifference curves intersect and therefore possess identical combinations of the two goods, there is no reason to believe that point B is as satisfying for U^* as it is for U_2. Theoretically, as far as U^* is concerned, points A and B are equally satisfying, while for the utility function ($U_0 \cdots U_2$), B is certainly superior to point A. A great deal of caution should be exercised in the comparison of different tastes or utilities under varying circumstances.

possession of X and Y is shown as point A on curve U_0, and the curve labelled U_2 is a higher indifference curve showing a greater level of utility. The dotted indifference curve labelled U^* purposely intersects with U_0 at point A and violates property (d), that is, indifference curves may not intersect. To the right of point A, U^* is superior to U_0; to the left of point A, U^* is inferior to U_0; and at point A, U^* is as good as U_0. Since an indifference curve such as U_0 is supposed to show a unique level of satisfaction, it cannot simultaneously be better than, worse than, and equal to U^*. For consistency, the other indifference curves will have to be drawn so they do not intersect each other and U_2 will have to be consistent and more desirable than U_0. It is possible, however, that indifference curves such as U^* may belong to *another utility function* which is superimposed on this one. The level of satisfaction offered by U^* cannot be measured on a comparative basis with U_0, including point A. In other words, we are in no position to say whether the person behind U^* and operating at point A is more or less, or even as, happy as the person associated with U_0, who is also at point A. Different people have different likes and dislikes and *interpersonal utility comparison* is usually meaningless. It is true, however, that persons possessing U^* at A will be equally happy at point B, which lies on U^*, but a person with U_0 will certainly be happier at point B (and utility level U_2) than he was at point A. Even then we cannot say for sure whether U^* for one person is any different from U_2 for another—we never know how happy we are. Two persons with identical utility functions are *supposed* to be equally happy with equal bundles of goods, but who knows for sure? How do we measure happiness? Indifference curves and associated models allow us to show the concept of the level of well being and permit us to rank the preferences for a given situation. The problem of interpersonal utility comparison will become more evident when we take up matters relating to society—is there such a thing as a *societal indifference curve*?

The indifference curves drawn so far depict negatively sloped, nonlinear, and convex-to-the-origin lines. Such shapes are usually referred to as "normal"

FIGURE 3-3
The diagram here depicts a very well-known phenomenon in utility analysis called the *principle of diminishing marginal rate of substitution* or the "*law*" *of diminishing marginal valuation.* The idea basically suggests that when a consumer is offered combinations such as *A, B, C,* and *D,* he is indifferent among them. However, as he has more of one type of vacation days and less of the other, he tends to value the rare good more than the abundant one. Thus, as he has more and more days in Miami, in order to remain as happy as he was before, he is willing to give up progressively fewer days in Aspen and vice versa. The more days spent in Aspen, the less their value at the margin as compared to the value of days not spent in Miami. This willingness to trade progressively smaller quantities of one good in exchange for additional units of the other in order to remain on the same indifference curve is called the principle of diminishing marginal rate of substitution. The so-called "law" of diminishing marginal utility in the theory of cardinal utility is equivalent to the concept of diminishing marginal rate of substitution in ordinal utility analysis.

or "well-behaved" indifference curves for a variety of reasons that can be explained with the aid of Figure 3-3. As was mentioned before under property (f), the indifference curves can take on any shape and these shapes are governed by the nature of the variables under discussion as well as by the specific assumptions. Not all indifference curves look like those in Figure 3-2.

Suppose you can spend a few days in Miami (M), a few days in Aspen (A), or both. Your utility from this vacation is written as $U = f(A, M)$. Figure 3-3 shows the various combinations of days spent in Miami and Aspen that will yield the same degree of satisfaction. We have chosen four such combinations—A, B, C, and D to draw the indifference curve U_0. Point A means eight days in Miami *and* one day in Aspen. Point B, which is as satisfying as point A, gives us five days in Miami and two days in Aspen. Because the satisfaction for both combinations is equal, you are willing to *trade* three days in Miami for one day in Aspen between points A and B. Now let us go to point C. Point C gives us yet another additional day in Aspen as compared to point B, but it also means two fewer days in Miami. Between points B and C you are willing to give up two days of Miami for an extra day at Aspen. Similarly, in going to point D you are willing to give up only one day in Miami for an additional day in Aspen. If this is true, then as you have more and more days in Aspen, you are willing to give up fewer days in Miami. This can mean only one thing. As you have more and more days in Aspen, the days in the beautiful Colorado town become less satisfying, because you are willing to trade fewer days in Miami for each additional day in Aspen.

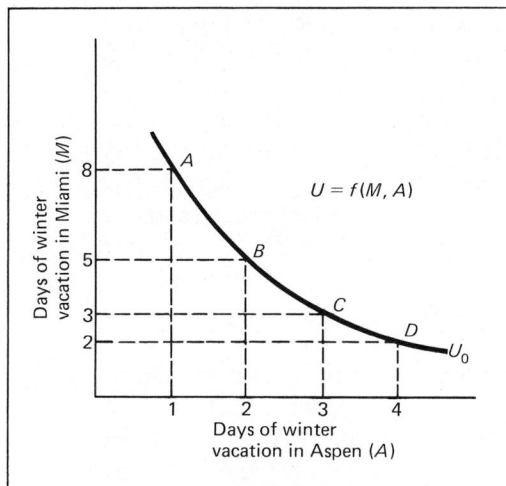

The Marginal Rate of Substitution

With reference to our illustration about vacationing in Miami or Aspen, the number of Miami vacation days that you are willing to give up to have an extra day in Aspen and be equally satisfied is called the *marginal rate of substitution* (MRS). This number indicates a consumer's relative valuation of one additional unit of a good in terms of the other goods. For whatever reason, the more you have of good X the less valuable it is. Likewise, the less you have of Y, the more precious it becomes. Consequently, as we move along a given indifference curve and find that the consumer is willing to give up increasingly smaller quantities of one good in exchange for extra units of the other, we infer that the larger the amount of a particular good, the less its marginal valuation by the consumer. This principle is sometimes referred to as the *law of diminishing marginal valuation* and is accompanied by declining values of the marginal rate of substitution. The basic postulate of diminishing marginal rate of substitution is *equivalent* to the principle of diminishing marginal utility discussed earlier.

The indifference curve of Figure 3-3 is deliberately drawn to reflect the decline of MRS. As we move down to the right along U_0, Miami vacation days appear more precious and Aspen holidays less satisfying. A declining MRS contributes to the *convexity* of indifference curves. If we work back from D toward A, the same result is obtained with reference to additional days in Miami. In going from point D to point C, you are willing to trade a day in Aspen for an extra day in Miami. However, in the range $C–B$, you will sacrifice a day in Aspen if you can have *two* extra days in Miami, which again suggests that the value of the additional days in Miami (in place of Aspen) declines at the margin. As long as MRS declines in either direction and the products are substitutable to some degree, the indifference curves are bound to be convex to the origin (convex from below) and negatively inclined. Such curves are also described as being "well behaved" or "normal."

Not all indifference curves have to be downward sloping. In our case involving vacation days in Miami or Aspen, the M and A are considered *substitutes* and hence more of M means less of A and vice versa, although the *degree of substitutability* of M for A or A for M varies between the points. If substitutability is absent or different we will have different types of indifference curves. With reference to Figure 3-3, it is understood that you prefer more Miami days *and* Aspen days to any of the present combinations shown by A, B, C, and D, that is, all points above U_0 are preferred to points along U_0, although not all such points may be feasible due to *constraints* imposed by your budget, the prices of vacation days, and available time.

Reconciliation of Cardinal and Ordinal Analysis

Both the cardinal and the ordinal methods may be used in the analysis of consumer behavior. The first relies on absolute values of utility under certain given conditions, while the second incorporates relative judgments of a consumer. Cardinal utility uses the so-called "law" of diminishing marginal

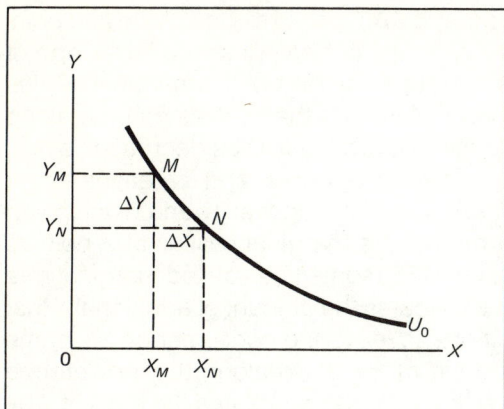

FIGURE 3-4
An indifference curve.

utility to analyze consumer equilibrium. The indifference curve technique employs the principle of diminishing marginal rate of substitution. You will recognize that both points of view are important and that they complement each other quite well.

Figure 3-4 illustrates one indifference curve yielding a U_0 level of utility. Since M and N on this curve are equally satisfying points, the consumption bundle representing Y_M and X_M is just as good as Y_N and X_N. In moving from M to N, if we give up ΔY we will be equally happy at point N by obtaining ΔX in the place of the lost Y's. From this we can say that the utility lost due to ΔY is exactly equal to the utility gained from the ΔX. The utility of the ΔY given up must equal the marginal utility of each Y times the amount ΔY. The utility of the ΔX should equal the marginal utility of the new X's times ΔX.* This can be stated in the following manner:

$$\therefore \text{ change in utility along this curve} = 0$$
$$\therefore \Delta U \text{ of } Y\text{'s given up} = \Delta U \text{ of new } X\text{'s}$$

or

$$(MU_Y)(\Delta Y) = (MU_X)(\Delta X)$$

or

$$\frac{\Delta Y}{\Delta X} = \frac{(MU_X)}{(MU_Y)}$$

The expression $\Delta Y/\Delta X$ is, in effect, the slope of U_0 between points M and N. Since the utility curve is not a straight line, it is not quite correct to assume that the slope given by $\Delta Y/\Delta X$ is constant for all points in the segment MN, but for

*Since U is constant along a given indifference curve, $dU = 0$. But $U = f(X,Y)$ and the marginal utilities of X and Y are, respectively, $\partial U/\partial X$ and $\partial U/\partial Y$. Using the differential dU we may say $dU = (\partial U/\partial X)\, dX + (\partial U/\partial Y)dY = 0$ or $(dY/dX) = -(\partial U/\partial X)\,/\,(\partial U/\partial Y) = -MU_X/MU_Y$. Because we are measuring absolute magnitudes the minus sign is allowed to drop. The dY/dX is the slope of the curve and is called the MRS—$\Delta Y/\Delta X$ approaches dY/dX if the change in X and Y are very small.

our purposes it is sufficient to assume that $\Delta Y/\Delta X$ measures the slope at a point along the indifference curve by allowing $\Delta Y/\Delta X$ to be very small. This slope of the indifference curve, or $\Delta Y/\Delta X$, also measures the ratio of the marginal utilities of Y and X at that point, and these marginal utilities themselves change along the entire indifference curve. The ratio of the marginal utilities decreases as we move down and to the right along the indifference curve, and increases as we move up and to the left, which is in keeping with the convexity and diminishing marginal utility assumptions. Such a ratio of the marginal utilities at a point is called the *marginal rate of substitution* or MRS (sometimes called marginal rate of commodity substitute or MRCS) and indicates the amount of additional Y that can be replaced by an additional unit of X to leave the consumer on the same level of satisfaction. More correctly, if we move down along the indifference curve acquiring more X and hence less Y, the $\Delta Y/\Delta X$ measures the MRS of Y by X. If we move up and possess more Y and fewer X's we will be measuring the replacement ability of the Y's for X. Consequently, the former MRS is a *reciprocal* of the latter. For example, if one additional apple can take the place of two bananas, then one banana can take the place of half an apple, or 2:1 = 1/(½).

We may define the geometric slope of the indifference curve as the ratio of the change in the vertical distance to that of a change in the horizontal, or what is commonly referred to as the rise over the run or, as in our case, Y/X. To summarize, let us state that the slope of an indifference curve at a point is measured by the $\Delta Y/\Delta X$ at that point and this slope equals the *absolute* ratio of the marginal utilities of the two goods at that point. The slope is called the MRS. Figure 3-5 shows that we have drawn a *tangent* to the indifference curve at point T and hence the slope of this tangent line reflects the slope of the indifference curve at point T. The MRS at that point is equivalent to the ratio MU_X/MU_Y.

Before going any further, let us recapitulate some of the discussions pertaining to single-commodity utility functions and multiple-commodity utility analysis with the aid of Figure 3-6. The upper panel of this figure shows an

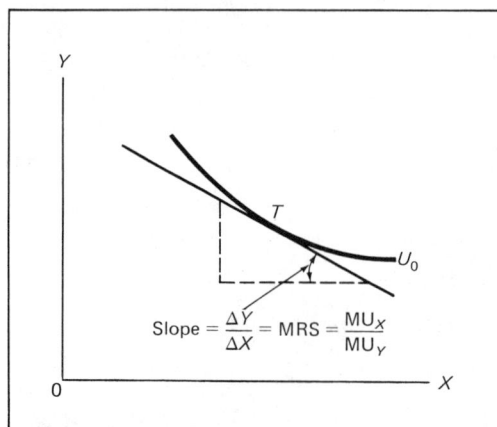

FIGURE 3-5
The marginal rate of substitution.

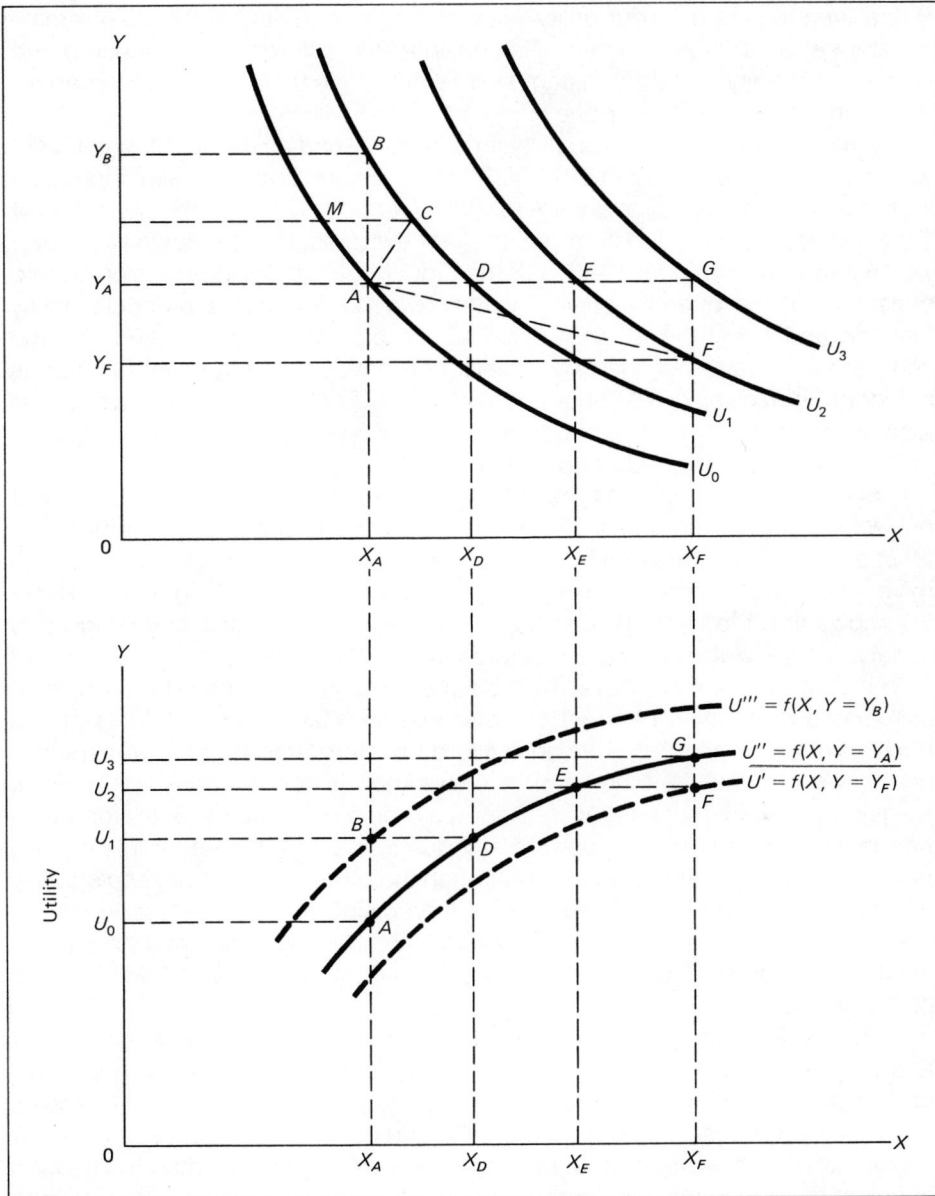

FIGURE 3-6
The lower diagram shows the derivation of the single commodity utility function from the indifference map shown above it. It shows the utility levels from the consumption of X while the quantity of Y is held constant at various levels.

indifference map derived from a utility hill. Points M and A yield utility level U_0, points B, C, and D provide U_1, points E and F are on U_2 and, lastly, point G is on U_3. Level U_3 is higher than U_2, which in turn is preferred to U_1 and so on. If we move from point A to D, then to E, and finally to G, we will be increasing the consumption of only one good, namely X, while the quantity of Y is held constant at level Y_A. Utility will increase. On the other hand, if we move from A to

B and then to *C* and *D*, our utility will increase from U_0 to U_1 and then remain constant at U_1. This phenomenon is shown a little differently by the use of the single-commodity (*Y* held constant at different levels but *X* allowed to change) utility function in the lower panel.

When we have Y_A of *Y*, our utility function is *U″* and as we acquire more *X*'s, we trace out the utility function *ADEG,* which shows that our utility increases with more *X* from level U_0 at point *A* to level U_3 at point *G*. When the quantities of *Y* are varied, our utility function "shifts"—for example, it shifts down with fewer *Y*'s (Y_F) and up with more *Y*'s (Y_B). If the amount of *Y* in our possession is held constant but the quantity of *X* is varied, we move *along* a particular utility function and enjoy the level of utility shown along the vertical axis. As you compare the graphs of the two panels, you notice that the utility function is subject to diminishing marginal returns (utility). Furthermore, the lower panel also shows that *B* and *D* yield equal utility (U_1), as do *E* and $F(U_2)$, but *B* is on utility function *U‴*, *D* on *U″*, and *F* on *U'*.

We have examined two types of nonlinear indifference curves—those that are convex to the origin and those that are concave to the origin. If the utility function is such that the indifference curves come out as straight lines, we will have indifference maps as shown by the two panels (c), (d) of Figure 3-7. Panel (c) shows that the two types of aspirin, Bayer's and the ordinary drug store variety, are considered to be substitutes by the consumer, but for every one of Bayer given up we must have 1½ tablets of the ordinary type. The utility level associated with a mild headache shows that two Bayer aspirin tablets are as good as three of the others, which is not to be interpreted as if Bayer aspirin is certainly superior to the other aspirin. All we know is how the *consumer feels*. It is quite possible that Bayer aspirin may be more effective in removing headaches faster or by a larger amount due to the ingredients, or it is equally possible that Bayer aspirin is no better than the other kind, but *psychologically* the consumer finds them more potent. Advertising may cause consumers to think in this manner. Panel (d) contains another situation involving linear indifference curves. Indifference curves of (a) illustrate increasing MRS, those of (b) diminishing MRS.

Figures 3-8a and 3-8b illustrate the consumer's utility functions for martinis and bicycles, respectively. In the case of the martini, suppose our consumer prefers a combination of four parts vodka to one part vermouth. Level U_1 shows one martini composed of four parts vodka and one part vermouth, whereas U_2 shows two martinis with double the amounts of vodka and vermouth. The ratio of vodka to vermouth is still four to one. Since our consumer does not like any other combination of vodka and vermouth except four to one, and since he prefers more martinis to fewer martinis (up to a point!), his utility function is composed of single points and the level of utility increases along the path $U_1U_2U_3$. All other combinations that do not fall along this path are inferior because they involve the "wrong" proportions of the two ingredients and cause disutility. We realize that even if the consumer proceeds along the maximum utility path he will eventually run into negative marginal utility from additional martinis, hence the (?) beyond the U_3 point. Such a point is determined by our consumer's propensity to absorb alcohol, and by other conditions. This is a

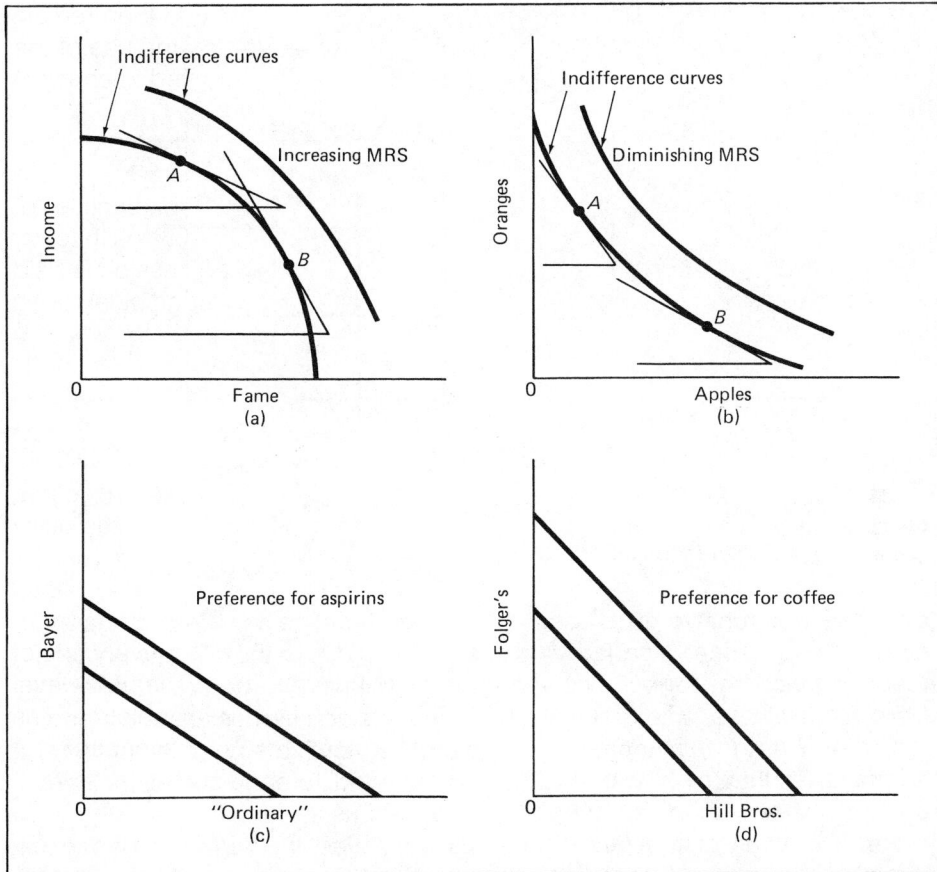

FIGURE 3-7
The "normal" shape of the indifference curve in (b) is drawn adjacent to different types of curves shown in (a). The first indicates a decreasing marginal rate of substitution. As we move away from point A toward point B in (b), the absolute value of the curve decreases. By contrast, as we move from point A to point B, the absolute value of the slope of the indifference curve increases and suggests progressively rising MRS. Although indifference curves of type (b) are generally considered to be most acceptable, the types shown in (a) cannot be entirely ruled out.

case where there is *zero substitutability* between vodka and vermouth—vodka and vermouth are *perfect complements* only at a ratio of four to one.

Figure 3-8b illustrates a similar example. The utility from bicycles increases with more *complete* bicycles. Thus one frame and two wheels yield the level of utility denoted by U_1 and two frames along with four wheels provide two bicycles and hence U_2. But there is a difference between martini indifference curves and bicycle indifference curves. We have shown that one frame plus two wheels will yield as much satisfaction as one frame and four wheels. That is to say, the extra two wheels neither add to nor subtract from the consumer's utility level, as opposed to the martini case, where too much vermouth or too much vodka will actually cause disutility. In reality, a consumer

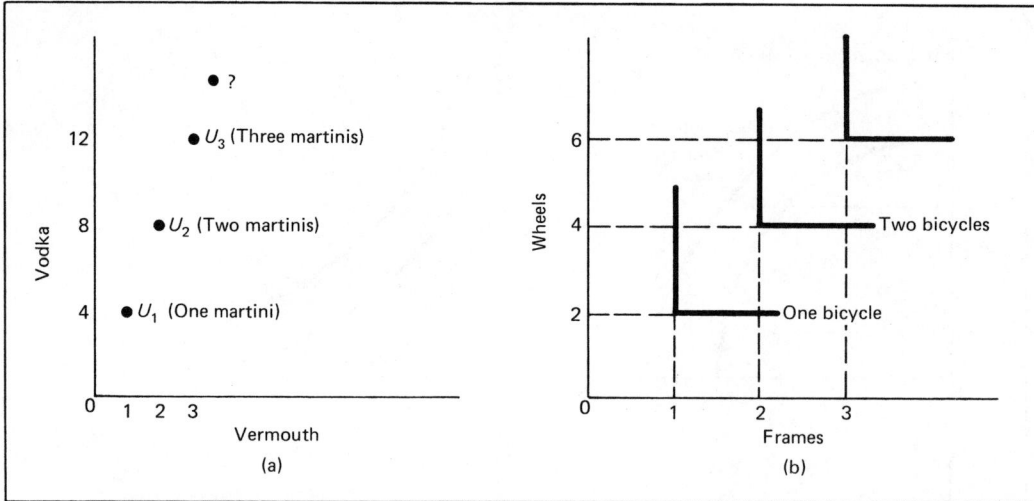

FIGURE 3-8
Some unique indifference curves.

may very well receive extra satisfaction from the extra wheels (as spares) or she might even receive negative utility from them due to the nuisance of storing them, in which case the indifference curves will have to be drawn differently. Here, too, we have indicated that wheels in pairs and frames are complements but not exactly in the manner that vodka and vermouth are complements. Other commodities that might yield such rectangular indifference curves include left and right shoes, shoes and shoe laces, and pens and refills.

Other types of indifference curves employed in many microeconomic models are shown in Figure 3-9. These curves are positively inclined and are nonlinear for the sake of illustration. Leisure is a precious and desirable good which yields utility. Income also provides utility. In order to consume leisure from a given amount of time, we must sacrifice work; and in order to earn income, we must sacrifice leisure. As illustrated, work turns out to be a *bad* and income and leisure are *goods*. This is not necessarily true, however, because work itself also yields utility a la the Protestant Work Ethic. We will elaborate on this in a separate model.

In Figure 3-9, the total time available is 0–T and utility increases vertically but decreases if we move horizontally. This makes sense. If income produces utility as leisure does, then more income and leisure plus a given amount of work will be preferred to less income and leisure and more work and, accordingly, U_3 is greater than U_2, which is greater than U_1. The amount of leisure consumed is measured from T to the left toward 0. The assumptions for this model depend on the existence of many combinations of work and income that yield equal satisfaction. For example, if a person is indifferent between 30 hours of work and $300 of income and 35 hours of work and $400 of income, the two combinations will appear on the same indifference curve; furthermore, the curves will be positively inclined with increasingly larger slopes at higher levels of income and work because of the existence of the very fundamental

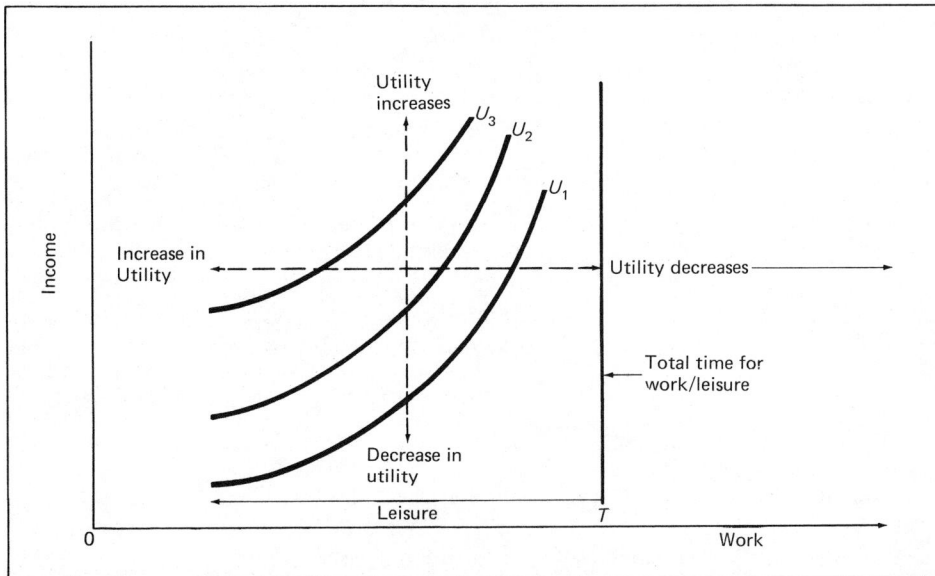

FIGURE 3-9
This utility function or indifference map suggests that income is a "good" and work is a "bad"—that is goods bring satisfaction, and bads produce disutility. Consequently, when the consumer has more income and no more work, her utility increases. On the other hand, if she works more, but has no more income, her utility decreases. It is possible for her to stay on a given indifference curve by receiving more income for more work, or less income for less work. Because the total time available to a consumer is limited, time not devoted to work is reserved for leisure. Thus, time allocated to work is measured from the left to the right, and leisure consumed from right to left. Total available time is shown by distance $0-T$.

law of diminishing marginal utility of income. Thus the extra 5 hours of work will produce $100 of extra income, whereas the previous 30 hours produced $300. Because our consumer suffers from diminishing marginal utility of income, the extra 5 hours of work will have to be purchased by relatively "cheap and low-worth" dollars. Because these last additional dollars do not produce as much satisfaction as the first dollars, we will have to pay more of them to obtain work from our consumer. In effect, the last 5 hours are compensated at the rate of $20 per hour. The more a person works the less leisure he has, but also the more income he has. More income implies progressively lower marginal utility of income and progressively higher marginal utility of leisure (or progressively higher *marginal disutility* of work). As was mentioned before, work itself may be rewarding and may be instrumental in offsetting the decline in marginal utility. Consider the case of the workaholic who is married to his job. How would you depict the indifference curves for such a personality?

There will be more about the various types of indifference curves later, but at this point it is sufficient to summarize by stating that indifference curves show preferences of individuals or decision makers. Such curves are drawn from utility functions. Any combination taken from a given indifference curve represents as much satisfaction as another point on the same indifference

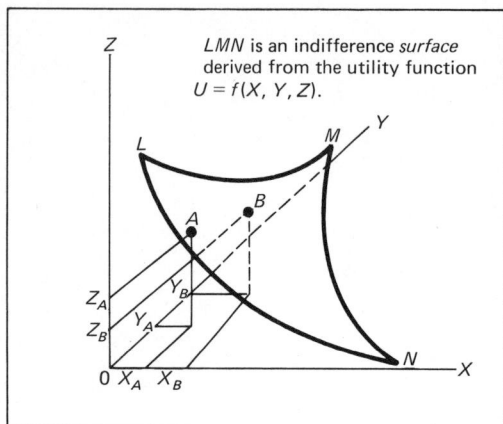

LMN is an indifference *surface* derived from the utility function $U = f(X, Y, Z)$.

FIGURE 3-10
We generally use a utility function that is a function of two variables as a matter of convenience. Theoretically, a utility function depicts the person's utility as a function of any number of variables. The figure here shows how a utility function $U = f(X, Y, Z)$ of three variables might look when drawn in the XYZ space. Whereas the utility function of X and Y yielded two-dimensional indifference curves, the three-variable model suggests that the indifference map will be composed of indifference surfaces.

curve. Indifference curves may be linear or nonlinear. They may be points or rectangles. They can be represented by convex as well as concave lines which may have a negative, positive, zero, or infinite slope.

The absolute value of the slope of an indifference curve is called the MRS. This slope shows the rate of trade-off between the two commodities in question, which will leave the consumer as well off as he was before the trade. If diminishing marginal utility is present, the indifference curves may very well be convex to the origin. It is possible that the utility function is such that many types of indifference curves may result for a single utility function or indifference map. As long as we observe the basic properties of indifference curves and are consistent about our assumptions, such an indifference map is not impossible. Figure 3-10 illustrates the case of the utility function U, which is affected by three goods—*X, Y, and Z*. In this case, the function will yield three-dimensional indifference surfaces, such as *LMN*.

THE BUDGET CONSTRAINT OR THE ISOCOST FUNCTION

Earlier it was mentioned that certain constraints affect the consumer's choice of goods and services that she purchases. Among such constraints, consumer *income* imposes a major limitation. If the consumer's income is limited to a budget, then the choice of goods that can be purchased in various combinations is also limited, because the individual must allocate her budget among the many goods, and the quantities of these goods that may be purchased are governed by their prices. So if a consumer has an income constraint and the prices of the goods are given, is there such a thing as an optimal bundle?

Suppose you have $100 at your disposal and the prices of going camping and skiing are $10 and $20 per day, respectively. Since your budget is limited to $100, you can have ten days of camping, which will leave no money for skiing. On the other hand, you can spend the entire $100 by going skiing for five days, but then camping is out. Of course, you can go camping and skiing

TABLE 3-1
CONSUMPTION POSSIBILITIES FOR A LIMITED BUDGET

Budget = $100
Price $_{camping}$ = $10   Price$_{skiing}$ = $20

Days of camping (C)	Amount spent on C:E_c	Days of skiing (S)	Amount spent on S:E_s	Total Amount spent on C, S:E
10	$100	0	$ 0	$100
8	80	1	20	100
6	60	2	40	100
4	40	3	60	100
2	20	4	80	100
0	0	5	100	100

for the same amount of money, too. The various *consumption possibilities* are shown in Table 3-1. Which is the "best" combination? Obviously the one that you like the most or that maximizes your utility. Total expenditures for the problem described equals E, or $100, and this in turn must equal the amounts spent on camping and skiing. Since the expenditure on a particular product equals the price of that product times the quantity of that product bought, we may say $E_c = P_c \times C$, $E_s = P_s \times S$, and $E = E_c + E_s$. The picture of the *budget constraint* or the *consumption possibilities* line is drawn in Figure 3-11. All points on or within this line are possible as far as consumption is concerned.

If we plot the various points representing the combinations of C and S that require exactly $100 of expenditure, the budget line will evolve and such a line will be straight, because the prices of the two types of vacation are being held at a ratio of 1:2—that is, one day of skiing not purchased will permit us to obtain two days of camping. The graph shows that a maximum of 10 days of camping is possible if we choose not to go skiing, or five days of skiing provided no camping is desired. In between these two extreme points we find the other intermediate points, or combinations of skiing and camping that can be bought with a limited budget of $100. The absolute value of the slope of this budget line is 1:2 for the reasons explained. Somewhere along this line lies the optimal

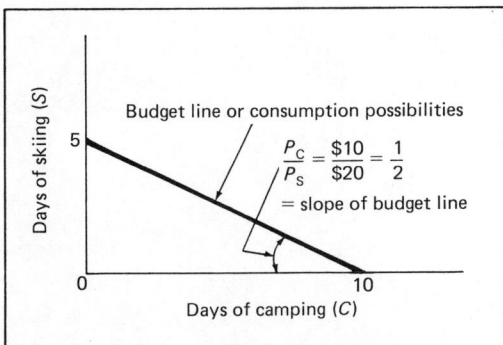

FIGURE 3-11
Consumption possibilities with a budget constraint.

combination of the two types of vacation, that is, the combination that maximizes utility for the available budget.

We have used the skiing–camping example to illustrate the concept of a budget line. We will now describe the general model. If a consumer has $\$E$ at his disposal to buy X and Y, and the prices of X and Y are P_X and P_Y, respectively, then $E = P_X X + P_Y Y$. This is the *budget equation.* Such an equation is also called an *isocost* line. The prefix "iso" means "equal," and since all points along a given budget line are equally costly, the name is appropriate. The maximum quantity of X that can be bought is E/P_X and, similarly, the maximum quantity of Y (that is, no X) equals E/P_Y. These two quantities are denoted by X_{max} and Y_{max}, respectively. When we connect these two end points we obtain our budget line. As you can see from Figure 3-12 the slope of this line equals Y_{max}/X_{max} or $(E/P_Y)/(Ep/_X)$ which equals P_X/P_Y. This is further illustrated in Figure 3-12.

The |slope| of the budget line = rise/run, or $Y_{max}/X_{max} = E/P_Y \div E/P_X = E/P_y \times P_x/E = P_x/P_y$. Since the line is straight, we may alternatively wish to express its equation via the *intercept–slope form* (see the Appendix to Chapter 1 at the end of the book). In this manner, the equation for the budget line changes from $E = P_x X + P_y Y$ to $Y = E/P_y - (P_x/P_y) X$, where E/P_y is the vertical intercept and $-P_x/P_y$ is the *negative* slope of the budget line.

The previous analysis was based on *constant money* or *nominal* income and *constant prices* of the goods. How will the budget line change if the price of one good changes while the money income is held constant? For the purposes of illustration, let us assume that the two goods are bread and potatoes, respectively, as shown in Figure 3-13a. If the price of bread increases, but the price of potatoes remains the same, our budget can buy fewer loaves of bread, and in their place, the same quantity of potatoes. This will cause the entire budget line to *rotate* to the left with P_{max} as the center of radius. The new isocost line will be shown as the solid line, whereas the old line was the dotted line. How will you draw the budget line to indicate a decrease in the price of potatoes without any corresponding change in the price of bread? Incidentally, since the price of bread increased and the price of potatoes did not change, the bread price is *relatively* higher, and as such the price ratio (or *price relative*) P_B/P_P is greater than before, which is shown by the steeper angle

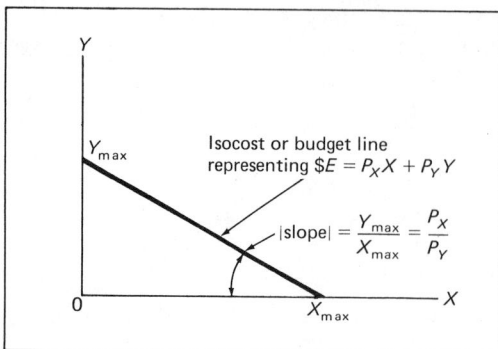

FIGURE 3-12
The isocost function.

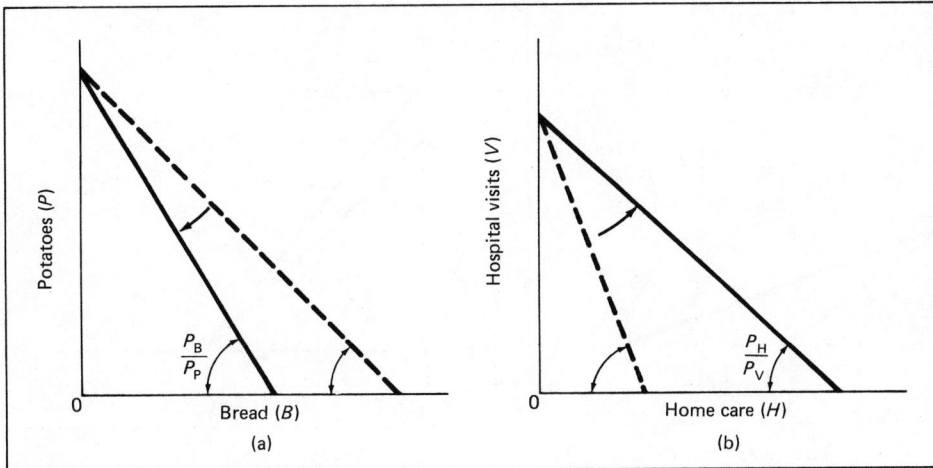

FIGURE 3-13
Impact of changing prices on the isocost line.

of the budget or isocost line. Note that the total amount of money involved for this steeper isocost line is still the same, except that bread is more expensive. The reader can verify that the graph in Figure 3-13b indicates a decrease in the price of home medical care.

A few quick arithmetical examples to illustrate budget constraints are shown below. Case 1 deals with an isocast analysis of books and vacations, and the expenditures on bourbon and whiskey are analyzed in Case 2.

Case 1

Budget = $250. Price of vacation days = $25/day. Price of books = $12.50.

We may state that the total cost of going on vacation and obtaining books (from the book clubs) may not exceed $250 (see Figure 3-14). We write the budget or isocost C equation as

$$C = 25V + 12.5B$$

which in slope–intercept form becomes $V = (C/25) - (12.5/25)B$, where $(C/25)$ represents the maximum number of vacation days possible (10) and (12.5)/(25) the price ratio of books to vacation days. The budget line will have a vertical intercept (along the V axis) of 10 and a slope of $-\frac{1}{2}$ and everywhere along this line the sum of $250 will be spent. The maximum amount of books (no vacation days) will equal 20. This is shown as the horizontal intercept of the budget line. If the price of books drops to $6.25 per book, and the cost of vacations stays the same, the budget line will rotate upwards to show that we may now purchase as many as 40 books for the same budget of $250, which is twice the original maximum because prices are halved. The price ratio is half as big now, causing the budget line to have a shallower slope and, more

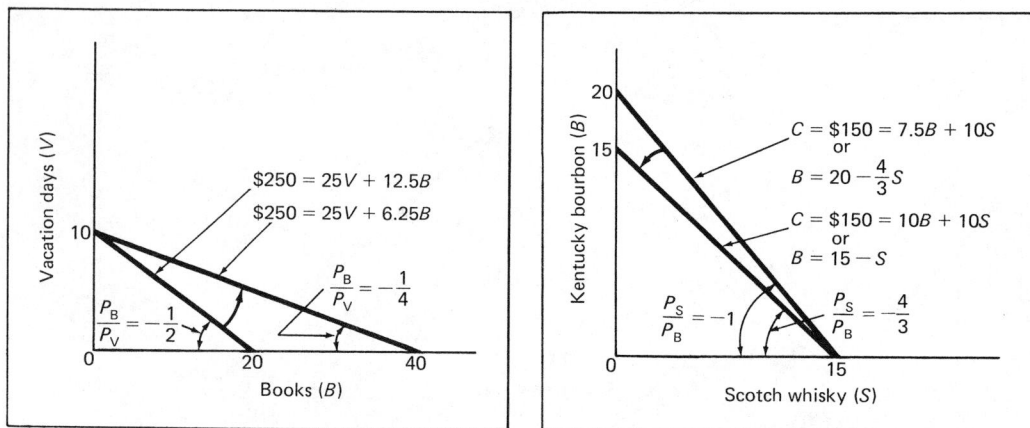

FIGURE 3-14, FIGURE 3-15

Figures 3-14 and 3-15 illustrate isocost or budget lines and the effect of changing prices on the slopes and intercepts of these functions. In Figure 3-14, the consumer has a budget of $250, and the price per book (B) is $12.50, while the cost of a day of vacation (V) is $25. Thus, the conditions are described by the line drawn from 10 on the V axis to 20 on the B axis. When the price of books falls to $6.25, *ceteris paribus,* the isocost line rotates outward and the new B intercept occurs at 40. In Figure 3-15, the consumer has a budget of $150, and the original prices of bourbon (B) and whiskey (W) are $7.50 and $10, respectively. This condition allows us to draw the budget line from 20 on the vertical axis to 15 on the horizontal. When the price of B increases to $10, the consumer can buy less B than before. Hence the new budget line with identical prices for B and W, is drawn from 15 of B to 15 of W.

specifically, a slope of $-\frac{1}{4}$. The new C equation will read as $C = 25V + 6.25B$ or, alternatively, $V = 10 - (6.25/25)B = 10 - \frac{1}{4}B$.

Case 2

Suppose you have a budget of $150 for purchasing bourbon and whiskey (see Figure 3-15). Assume the price per bottle of whiskey (S) is $10 and that for bourbon (B) is $7.50. Write the budget equation for B/S and change it to reflect the price increase of bourbon to $10 a bottle without any other accompanying changes.

Before the price change takes place we can buy 15 bottles of whiskey or 20 bottles of bourbon if we want just one or the other. This gives us the budget equation $C = 7.5B + 10S$, or $B = (C/7.5) - (10/7.5)S$, which equals $B = 20 - (4/3)S$. This equation is shown by the line (in Figure 3-15) which starts at 20 on the B axis and drops down to 15 on the S axis indicating the price ratio of 4:3 of whiskey to bourbon. After the price of bourbon increases to $10, the price ratio will be $10:$10 or 1:1, and only 15 bottles of bourbon may now be acquired. This causes the isocost line to rotate downwards and indicates that the relative price of bourbon is now higher (or that of whiskey lower), making the angle of the budget line flatter, so that the new inclination is $-1:1$. The budget equation now becomes $B = 15 - (1:1)S$ or simply $B = 15 - S$, which may also be written as $150 = 10B + 10S$.

A few more variations in the isocost line due to changes in the relative

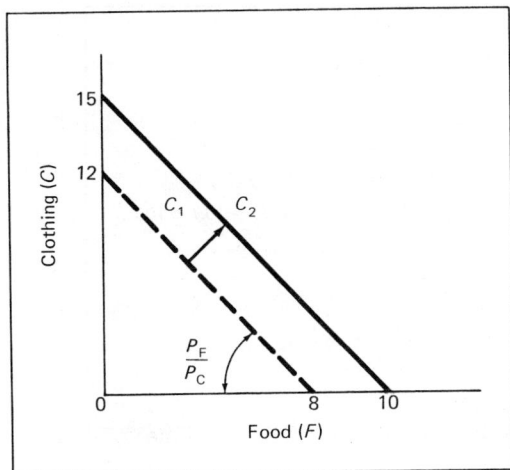

FIGURE 3-16
Impact of higher income or lower prices on budget line.

prices of goods or available income (budget) or both will be discussed with the use of Figures 3-16 and 3-17.

Figure 3-16 shows the isocost or budget line shifted outwards in a *parallel* position. Since the slopes of C_1 and C_2 are the same, the *relative price* (ratio) of P_F/P_C is still the same. Such a parallel shift comes about if more money is available to the consumer even if the prices of food and clothing do not change. The graph indicates that 25% more income will enable the consumer to purchase 25% of either food or clothing. So if the original prices of food and clothing are, respectively, $6 and $4, and the consumer has $48, she can buy a maximum of 8 food or a maximum of 12 clothing. Now suppose the consumer has an extra 25% income, so that her new income is $60. If the price of food and clothing do not change, the consumer can now purchase a maximum of 10 food or 15 clothing. The relative price of the two goods has remained the same, that is, the P_F/P_C = 6/4 or 1.5:1. Can the isocost line shift in the manner suggested even if the consumer's *money* income does not change? The answer is yes. If the price of each good falls, the same income will buy more F and C. If the price of food drops to $4.80 and that of clothing to $3.20—which means that both products' price falls by the same percentage (or 20%), the same $48 will enable the consumer to consume from C_2. In this case, the consumer's *real income* will have risen but her money income will have stayed the same. Occasionally we call real income by the name *purchasing power*. In the first case the consumer's money income increases to $60 and thereby increases her real income as well (because prices stay the same), and in the second case the real income alone increases while the money income stays constant, and prices of both goods are lower than before. Because the prices of both food and clothing drop by the same percentage, the relative prices of F and C still stay as before and hence the new budget line C_2 has the same slope as C_1. Shifts as shown in Figure 3-16 may come about due to falling prices, rising income, or a combination of both. Is the consumer better off with C_2 than C_1?

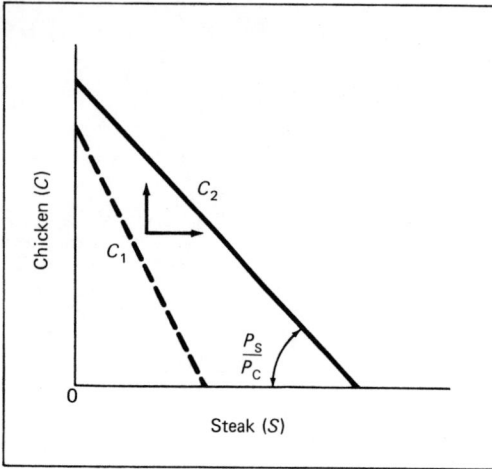

FIGURE 3-17
Effect of rising prices or falling income on budget line.

Figure 3-17 again shows a shift outward of the budget line, but this time the new and old line are *not parallel*. The solid line C_2 has a smaller slope, reflecting a lower relative price of steak (S) to chicken (C), which means that the relative price of steaks (compared to the price of chicken) is smaller. Since the budget line has shifted out, we know that *either* both prices have fallen and no additional income is available *or* the relative price ratio has changed and income has also increased, or a combination of both factors. We must realize that falling prices may be accompanied by rising income and rising prices may be accompanied by falling incomes. The final result depends on the amounts of proportional changes, the direction of such changes, the change in income, and the direction of such a change. For instance, will C_2 appear as drawn if income increases but the price of C and S increases, too?

Instead of employing two goods, we can also make use of a single commodity to explain the budget line considerations. Suppose we have one good, X. Then the available income can be allocated between X and all other (or non-X) goods. Since income can purchase X as well as non-X goods, we measure income on the vertical axis (see Figure 3-18). Let the income of the consumer be I_1 and the price of X be P_X. The price in this case is measured by the inclination of the budget line or I_1/X_{max}. If the price of X is \$10 and I_1 = \$1,000, X_{max} will equal 100. If the consumer does not have any X but only income, he will be at point I_1, and if he spends all his income on X he will be at X_{max}. At point A he buys Q_A of X and spends (P_XQ_A) of his income, which equals P_XZA. But the price of X can also be expressed by the ratio (I_1Z/ZA), because this is the same angle as the inclination of the budget line. Thus the income spent by the consumer in the acquisition of Q_A of X equals $(I_1Z/ZA)(ZA) = I_1Z$. This proves that the amount spent on X is measured from the I_1 point *down*. At point A the consumer will have spent I_1Z for X and have $0Z$ of income left which can be spent for other goods. Similarly, at point B of the budget line the consumer will have a bundle represented by Q_B of X and an income of OT, that is he will have spent amount I_1T on X and have OT amount of income left over. The two levels of expenditures at A and B are shown by E_A and E_B, respectively.

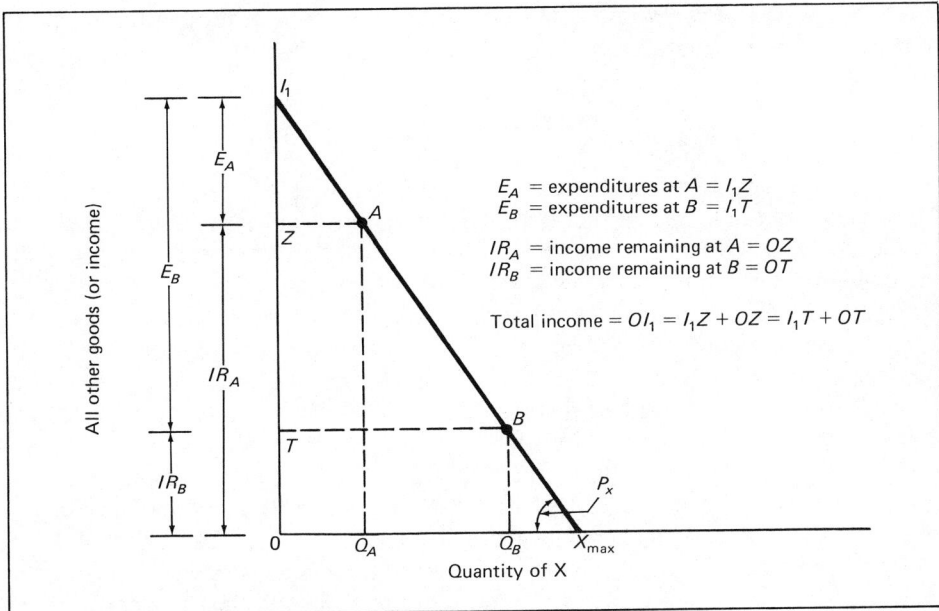

E_A = expenditures at $A = I_1Z$
E_B = expenditures at $B = I_1T$

IR_A = income remaining at $A = OZ$
IR_B = income remaining at $B = OT$

Total income = $OI_1 = I_1Z + OZ = I_1T + OT$

FIGURE 3-18
Expenditures and the isocost function.

Figure 3-19 illustrates the situation where the price of X is not constant but varies with quantities purchased. Thus, to quantity X_1 the price is P_1; beyond X_1 and including quantity X_2 the price is P_2, and beyond X_2 the price equals P_3. Since the angle of the budget line is getting steeper with larger quantities, we may assume that latter units are being sold at a higher price than the former ones, so long as we maintain the shape drawn in Figure 3-19a. Such pricing is

FIGURE 3-19
Budget lines with variable prices.

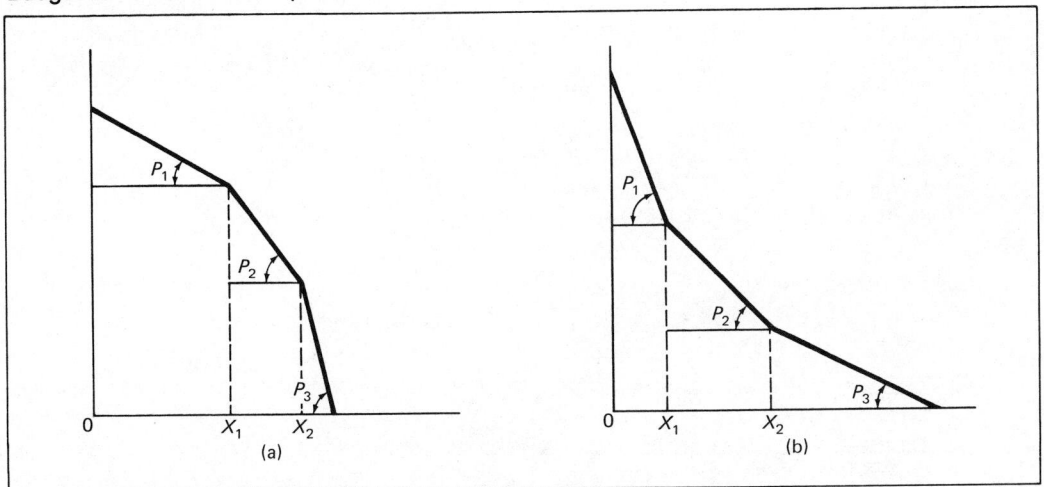

often encountered in the case of *marginal cost pricing,* a topic which will be covered in detail much later. How is Figure 3-19b different?

THE CONSUMER "OPTIMUM"

We have discussed utility functions and budget (or isocost) lines separately. Now we combine both ideas to arrive at the consumer equilibrium process. In Figure 3-20 the indifference map is shown along with the budget line. If consumers are rational, they will want to maximize their utility for the available budget. We cannot go beyond the budget line as much as we would like to. As long as the prices of X and Y—as well as money income—are held fixed, we must operate at a point on the isocost line *AB.* At points C and D our utility level is U_1. Points above D and C are superior. Thus, we will continue to progress to higher indifference curves by approaching point E, which is also on our budget line. If we go too far down (toward D) past E, our utility will decrease, and the same is true if we go too far up to the left (past E) toward C. At point E, our utility is highest and this point occurs where the budget line *touches* the *highest indifference curve.* In this case the indifference curves are convex to the origin and hence the budget line becomes *tangent* to the indifference curve depicting utility level U_3. At such a point of tangency the slopes of the indifference curve and the budget line are equal. The slope of the first, as we have discussed, provides us with the MRS, or the marginal rate of substitution, which is also the ratio of the marginal utilities of the two goods—X and Y in this situation. The slope of the budget line gives us the ratio of the prices of the two goods, or P_X/P_Y. At this point of tangency, then, MRS = P_X/P_Y, or MU_X/MU_Y = P_X/P_Y. This expression gives us the conditions for consumer equilibrium under a budget constraint. The *constrained optimization* as discussed may also be stated as:

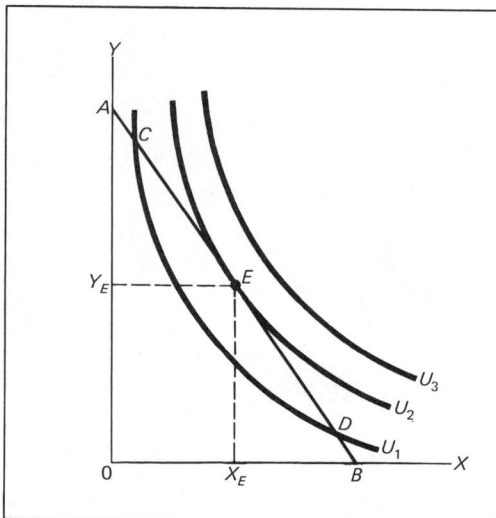

FIGURE 3-20
Consumer equilibrium and utility maximization.

$$\frac{MU_x}{MU_y} = \frac{P_x}{P_Y} \qquad \text{Tangency condition} \qquad (1)$$

$$XP_x + YP_Y = C \qquad \text{Budget constraint (\$C)} \qquad (2)$$

Condition (1) may also be represented as $MU_x/P_x = MU_Y/P_Y$, an expression discussed in connection with the single-commodity utility function. For the many-goods case the general conditions for consumer equilibrium (if tangencies exist) may be stated as:

$$\frac{MU_x}{P_x} = \frac{MU_Y}{P_Y} = \cdots = \frac{MU_z}{P_z} \qquad (3)$$

$$P_x X + P_Y Y + \cdots + P_z Z = \$C \qquad (4)$$

In plain English, expression (3) states that the consumers will maximize their utility if they allocate their income so that the marginal utility per dollar expended on each good is equal.

What if the slope of the budget line cannot be equated to the slope of the indifference curve due to the absence of convexity? Figure 3-21 shows some cases of consumer optimization where the indifference curves are not of the "normal" variety.

CONSUMER EQUILIBRIUM WITH CHANGES IN INCOME AND PRICES

How does the consumer react to changing prices and incomes? We have already seen how the budget line is affected via such changes, but the impact of such changes should be analyzed in light of the consumer's preferences. Such models with associated changes form the backbone of theory of consumer behavior and have many wide applications in a variety of fields and disciplines. Let us start with a change in the price of a single good and a fixed amount of money income. In Figure 3-22, the consumer is originally at point A maximizing the utility level as shown in (a). He is constrained by the budget, so utility level U_2 is the maximum. Figure 3-22b shows the old budget line as a dotted line. Since the price of meat declines, the budget line swings outward, indicating a lower price (via a shallower slope) and the new consumer optimum occurs at point B, which also yields a higher level of satisfaction, namely U_3. The consumer purchases more meat and also spends more of his income than before (point A). His utility has increased and he is now on a new isocost line that shows an increase in real income as far as meat is concerned, even though his money income is still the same. Accordingly, the budget line shifts only along the meat axis and remains steady along the income axis.

With reference to Figure 3-22, the consumer originally had $100 in income and the price of meat was $2.00 per pound, which made him choose 26 pounds of meat, leaving him with $48 in income (for other goods, if necessary). After the price drops to $1.00 per pound, the consumer chooses to buy 62

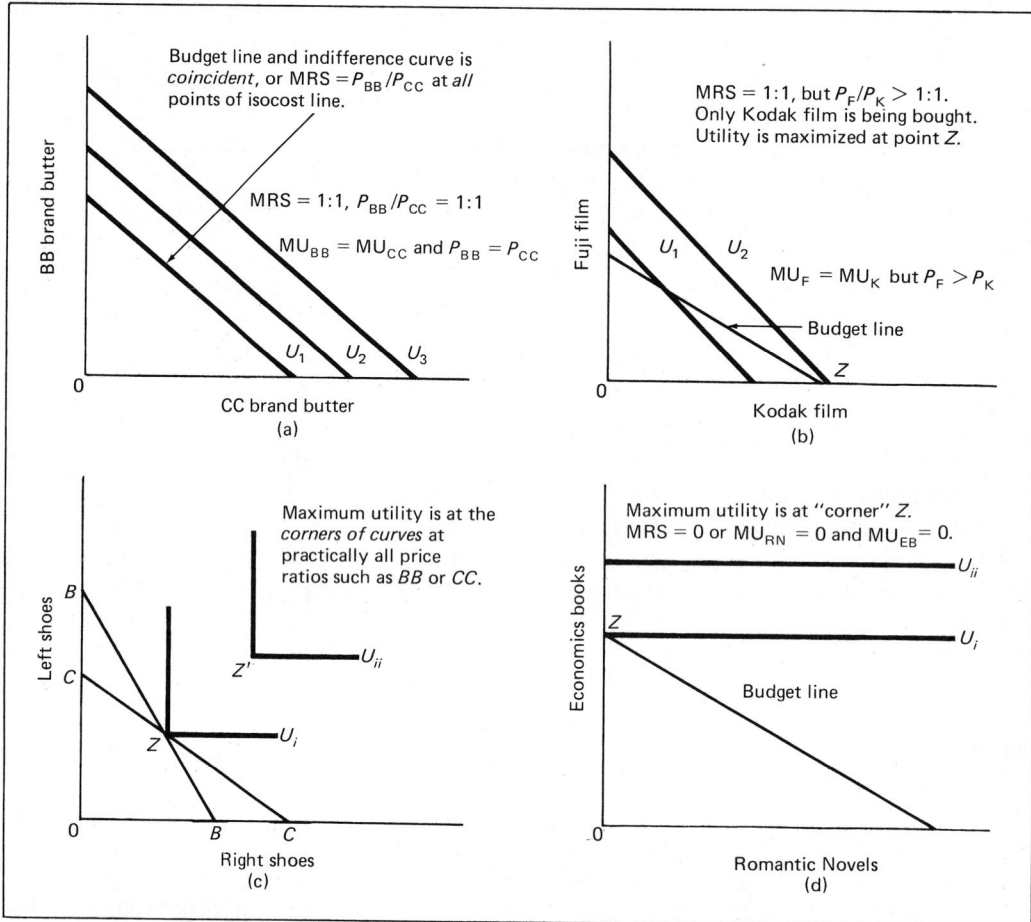

FIGURE 3-21

It was mentioned earlier that in some instances the indifference curves may not come out to be of the normal convex variety. Panels (a)–(d) suggest certain other shapes. Diagram (a) shows that the two brands of butter are *perfect substitutes,* while panel (c) indicates the shoes to be *perfect complements.* Panel (b) again suggests perfect substitutability, while (d) shows that utility is derived from economics books alone. Given the various price ratios shown by the budget lines in each case, the consumer may always buy a particular good, buy the goods in a unique ratio, or be completely indifferent among combinations available to him.

pounds of meat, spending $62.00 and keeping $38.00 of income for other purposes. Such behavior basically corroborates our discussion of demand— that is, all other factors remaining equal, the consumer will demand a greater quantity at lower prices. Here "all other factors" include, but are not limited to, the prices of other goods, the consumer's income, and his preference or taste. For instance, it is quite conceivable that while the price of meat drops the consumer's tastes change in favor of fish, so that he ends up buying much less meat than before. Such changes have the effect of reshaping his indifference curves so that points of tangency lie much more to the left than before.

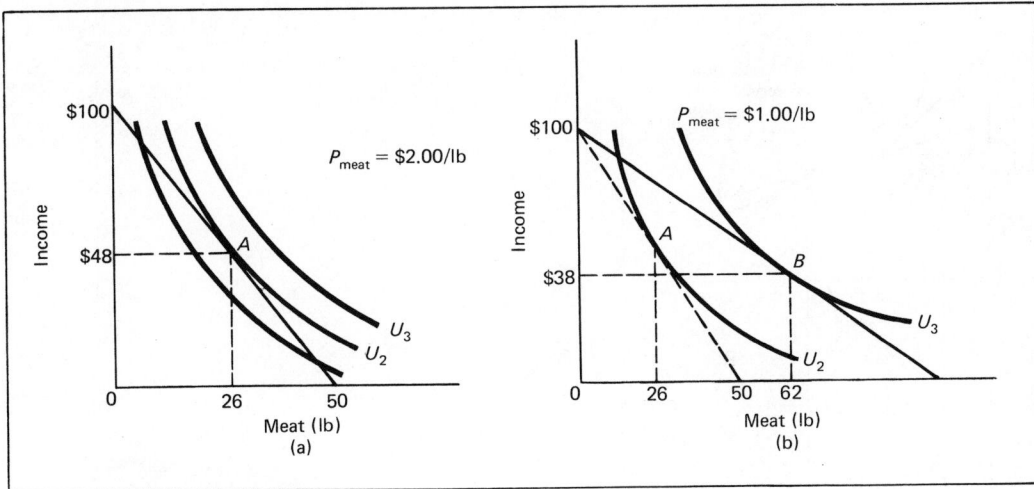

FIGURE 3-22
Utility maximization and falling prices.

UTILITY AND CONSUMER DEMAND—THE PRICE-CONSUMPTION LOCUS

Indifference analysis' primary contribution is toward demand theory. With adequate information regarding the important variables, we can use a utility function to obtain a demand function.

If the consumer's income is held constant and all other factors remain equal, different prices will lead the consumer (in most cases) to obtain different quantities of a product. If we can ascertain these quantities that correspond to the many different prices we will be able to obtain a demand curve for a consumer of a particular good.

Figure 3-23 is basically self-explanatory. Part (a) shows the various points of equilibrium for a fixed budget I_1 with many prices, such as P_1, P_2, and P_3. The consumer maximizes utility along the path traced out by the various points, where the indifference curves are tangent to the various budget lines. Such a path obtained by connecting the points of consumer equilibrium is called the *price-induced consumption locus* because the various quantities are induced via price changes alone. The corresponding quantities are labelled Q_1, Q_2, and Q_3.

Figure 3-23b shows the derivation of the demand curve from part (a). Whereas in part (a) the prices are shown as angles of the budget lines, in this graph they are shown as absolute values and measured along the vertical axis. Thus at a price of P_1 the consumer is at utility level U_1 and consumes quantity O_1. This point is located as point 1 on the demand curve of (b). At a lower price level, such as P_2, we see the consumer choosing quantity Q_2, and this point is taken down to the middle graph and designated as point 2, which forms a second point on the conventional demand curve. If we take enough equilibrium points by changing prices but holding money income constant we will obtain

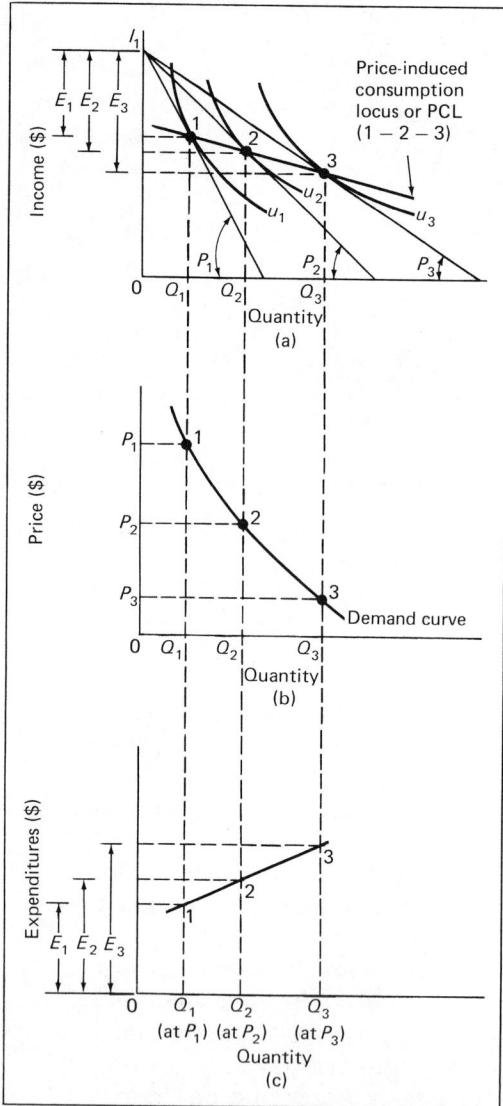

FIGURE 3-23

(a) $u_3 > u_2 > u_1$; $P_3 < P_2 < P_1$; money income is constant and $= I_1$. As price declines from P_1 to P_2 and then to P_3 the consumer moves from point 1 to point 2 and then to point 3 along the PCL. Utility increases from u_1 to u_2 and then to u_3. (b) As price falls, the quantity demanded increases along path 1–2–3 on the demand curve. (c) As price falls and quantity demanded increases, expenditures increase from E_1 to E_2 to E_3. The percentage increase in quantity is greater than the percentage decrease in price—expenditures increase. *Demand is price-elastic* because E varies inversely with price.

$P_1 Q_1 = E_1$, $P_2 Q_2 = E_2$, and $P_3 Q_3 = E_3$.

the demand curve as shown. The demand curve thus derived is comparable to the demand curve discussed earlier. The PCL is *not* the demand curve—the points along this line show the various consumer equilibrium points of maximum utility on an indifference map. The demand curve may be derived from the PCL.

Price Elasticity of Demand

Although we will discuss demand in the next chapter, a rather important concept of economics needs to be reviewed at this point. In theorizing consumer demand behavior, we wonder what effects changes in variables bring about on the demand for a particular good or service. For example, since price is an important factor in the consumer decision process, does a change in price of a product affect the quantity purchased? And if it does, how much? The response of the change in quantity to the change in price is described by the *price elasticity of demand*. Necessarily, the change in quantity demanded due to a price change will depend on all the other factors, including the person's utility function (indifference map).

The price elasticity of demand is more precisely defined as the ratio of the percentage change in quantity demanded to the percentage change in price, all other things remaining equal; or the price elasticity of demand, e_p = (% Δ in Q) ÷ (% Δ in P). Such a value will usually be a negative number, since Q usually varies inversely with P. For example, if house prices fall by 10% and this in turn leads to a 20% increase in house sales, the price elasticity of demand will be -2. For the discussion that follows, we will consider only the absolute value of e_p; that is, we will be concerned with the *magnitude* of the relative change.

Expenditures on an item can be computed by multiplying the price of the product by the quantity bought at that price. Thus, expenditures $E = PQ$. As price falls, quantity increases, and the product of a lower price, albeit a larger quantity, may yield either a larger, equal, or smaller value for expenditures depending on the relative changes of P and Q. If the percentage change in Q exceeds the percentage change in P, the e_p value will exceed one. Furthermore, if e_p is greater than one, E will change in the same direction as Q. Thus, for an increase in price, as long as e_p exceeds 1, E will decline; for a decrease in price, E will increase. Whenever the absolute value of e_p exceeds one, demand is said to be *price-elastic. Under conditions of elastic demand, E varies inversely with P.*

Figure 3-23c relates the quantity (and price) to the level of expenditures (PQ). In Figure 3-23a, at a price of P_1 the expenditures are indicated as E_1, and this amount is now transferred to part (b) and corresponds to quantity Q_1. Similarly, the other levels of expenditures corresponding to the different prices that we have chosen are also plotted against their respective quantities and such points trace out the 1–2–3 path shown as a positively inclined line. If you recall from our discussion of demand elasticity, expenditures vary inversely with price in the case of elastic demand. We have obviously shown the case of elastic demand, since lower prices bring forth larger levels of expenditures. At P_1 the expenditures are E_1, price falls to P_2, quantity demanded increases to Q_2, and expenditures increase to E_2. This makes the PCL negatively inclined. *In general, PCLs with negative slopes indicate that demand is elastic,* that is, a downward-sloping PCL is indicative of elastic demand. The PCL is derived by changing prices but holding other factors (e.g., income) constant. The demand curve derivation makes the same assumptions.

Figure 3-24 illustrates the shapes of the PCL in the case of *inelastic* and *unit elastic* demand. Again, we know that *in the case of inelastic demand* the *expenditures vary directly or positively with price,* and *in the case of unit elasticity, the expenditures do not change with price.* Consequently, we will expect that if demand is inelastic and price is allowed to decrease, expenditures will decrease, too. This results in an upward-sloping PCL, indicating that

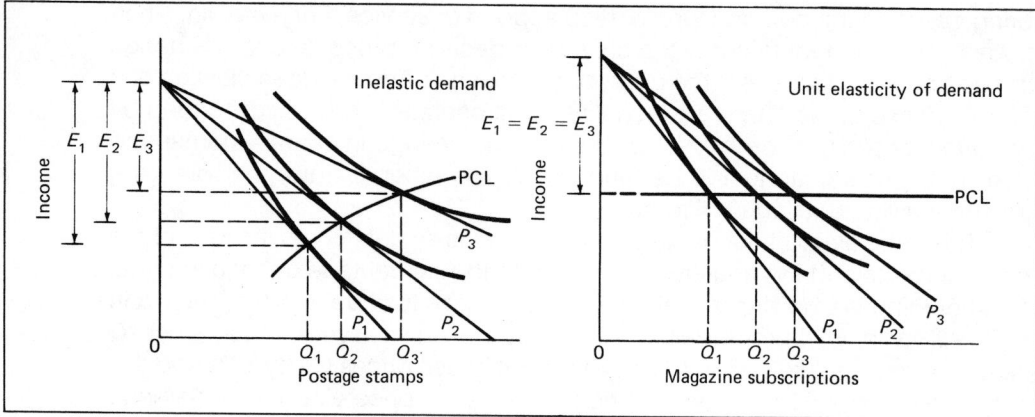

FIGURE 3-24
Price consumption loci for goods with inelastic demand and unit elasticity of demand.

the E values are lower at lower prices compared to those at higher price levels. Figure 3-24b shows that the PCL is horizontal at all price levels and this is consistent with the properties of unit elasticity of demand, which maintain that expenditures remain constant at levels of price and corresponding quantity. Since E is constant at all points, the PCL has to be horizontal.

The Income-Consumption Locus

Just as price changes lead to various points for the consumer along the PCL path, income changes alone, without accompanying price variations, also induce different quantities. If the income of the consumer changes but the price of the product does not change, the budget line will shift to a parallel position—outwards for price cuts and inwards for price increases. Figure 3-25

FIGURE 3-25
Income consumption loci for normal and superior goods.

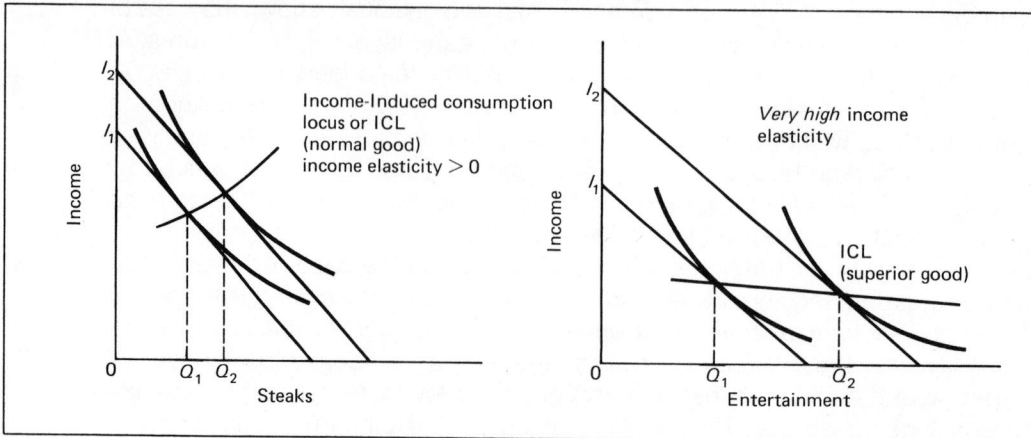

illustrates the equilibrium points for two levels of money income designated as I_1 and I_2. The locus of such tangency points is called the *income-induced consumption* locus or ICL. The greater the sensitivity of quantity demanded to income, the greater the change in quantity demanded and the flatter the ICL. For instance, in Figure 3-25, the demand for steaks increases as income increases, but because the income elasticity of steaks is assumed to be quite high, the larger quantities of steaks demanded come from small changes in income. If the ICL is positively sloped the goods are considered to be *normal*. If the ICL is downward-sloping (not backward bending) the good is called *superior*—a good which is *very sensitive* to income. Consequently, the indifference map for the consumption of entertainment is that of a superior good.

Income Elasticity of Demand

Chapter 4 contains a detailed analysis of demand and its associated elasticities. We will merely introduce another elasticity concept as it relates to consumer utility. The income elasticity of demand compares the relative sensitivity of demand to changes in income, all other factors remaining equal. In keeping with tradition, the income elasticity of demand is defined as the ratio of the percentage change in quantity demanded to the percentage change in income. We can write this definition of income elasticity as

$$e_I = \%\Delta \text{ in } Q \div \%\Delta \text{ in } I$$

Just as the price-consumption locus (PCL) indicates a good's price elasticity, the income-consumption locus (ICL) sheds light on the income elasticity of demand. Products with very high income elasticity of demand possess a steep negatively inclined ICL, and those that have very low elasticity yield a steep positively inclined ICL. In the extreme cases, a vertical ICL indicates zero income elasticity, while a backward-bending ICL suggests that a product is inferior or has negative income elasticity.

The Substitution and Income Effects

When the price of a good changes, the consumer purchases different quantities of the good, quantities that are consistent with her utility function. In demand theory, such changes come about due to two fundamental economic effects—the *substitution effect* and the *real income effect*. The first refers to the willingness of the consumer to substitute relatively less expensive goods for those that are dearer. For example, if the price of X declines, ceteris paribus, the consumer tends to maximize utility by purchasing larger quantities of X, even though it means buying either the same or different amounts of the other goods. Theoretically, a price decline permits the consumer to move along the PCL to a point which yields more utility. Technically speaking, the substitution effect is the change in quantity resulting from a price change, such that the new quantity in combination with the other goods yields as much utility as before.

In Figure 3-26, the consumer initially has an income of I_1 and maximizes her utility at point A by consuming Q_A units of X. Her utility level is indicated by U_0. If prices fall to level P_2 and nothing else happens, she will move to point C and obtain satisfaction level U_2. The new quantity Q_C will reflect a total change of $(Q_C - Q_A)$ units. Suppose we make it possible for the consumer to move to point B. Since point B is also on U_0, the consumer should be as happy at point B as she was at A. Point B will be optimum if the consumer is provided with a lower income and a lower price. We have drawn a dotted line parallel to the initial budget line which is tangent to U_0 at point B. This line (a fictitious budget line equivalent to income I_2 and price P_2), suggests that the consumer will be just as well off with the lower price P_2 as with P_1, if she also has the lower income, I_2. Consequently, the movement from point A to point B along the original indifference curve U_0 is called the substitution effect. You may say that, in order to leave the consumer at the former level of utility (U_0), a lower price

FIGURE 3-26
When the price of a good changes, all other things remaining equal, quantity generally varies inversely with price. In the diagram below we see a decline in price. Originally the consumer has an income of I_1 and the price level stands at P_1, and the consumer maximizes utility by operating at point A, the utility at that point being U_0. If price decreases to P_2, the consumer moves to point C. The movement from A to C can be broken down into two distinct effects—the *substitution effect* and the *real income effect*. The first effect is the additional quantity that the consumer will buy if she has less income along with the lower price in order to remain as well off as she was—that is, on indifference curve U_0. If the consumer has income of I_2 and pays price P_2, the budget constraint will be shown by the dotted line and she will be at point B. The quantity $(Q_B - Q_A)$ is known as the substitution effect. In moving from point B to point C, it seems that the dotted budget line has shifted outwards, a movement equivalent to an increase in income. Thus quantity $(Q_C - Q_B)$ is known as the real income effect. The consumer's money income does not change, however, her "real" income does. The two effects can also be worked out for price increases.

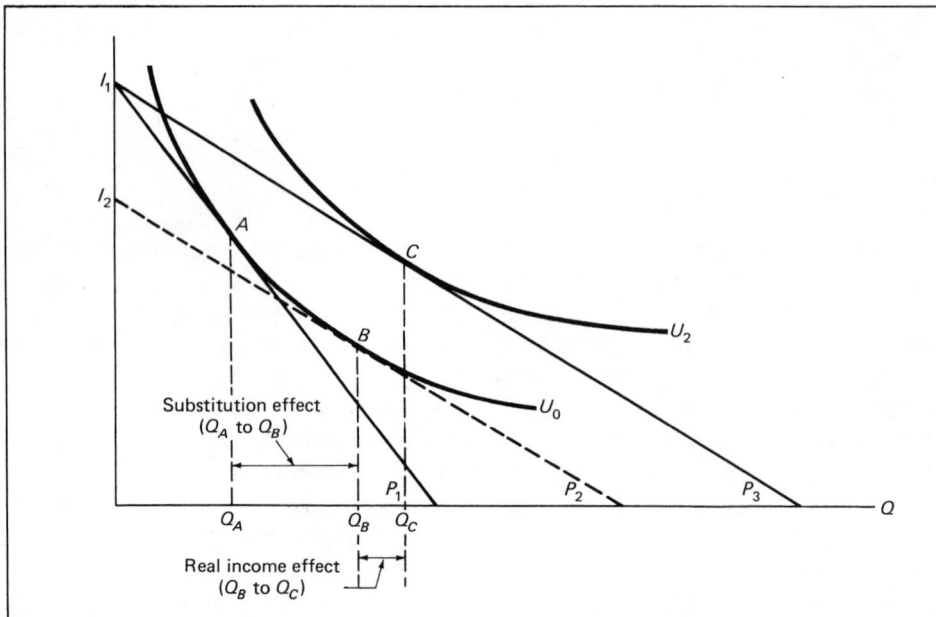

must accompany a lower level of income. The additional quantity of X that the consumer purchases at the lower price when confronted with the lower income and the same satisfaction she had at point A, is the substitution effect or quantity (Q_B-Q_A).

But the consumer's income has not changed—only the price has. Whenever prices fall, the same money income can purchase larger quantities of goods and services, that is, the consumer's *real income* increases. Consequently, if the consumer is at point B, movement to point C will be tantamount to an increase in income, since the budget line will have shifted out to a parallel position. The consumer will then have purchased additional quantities of X in the amount (Q_C-Q_B). This quantity change due to changes in the real income is called the *income* or *real income effect* of a price change.

Thus the total change in quantity due to a price change alone adds up to quantity (Q_C-Q_A), of which quantity (Q_B-Q_A) is due to the substitution effect and quantity (Q_C-Q_B) is accounted for by the income effect. *The substitution effect involves movement along the original indifference curve, whereas real income effect puts the consumer on a different indifference curve.*

APPLICATIONS

1. Public Policy on Gasoline

We will make use of Figure 3-27 and its indifference map to illustrate the place of utility analysis in the public sector as it applies to the policies that affect gasoline consumption.

Initially the consumer has I_1 of money income and pays P_1 for gasoline and operates at point 1 on the indifference curve U_0. If the government wants him to consume quanity Q_2 of gasoline without affecting his level of utility, they should effect a higher income (I_2) and higher prices (P_2). To raise prices the government taxes the gasoline, and to provide more income it withholds less income taxes. This puts the consumer at point 2. What is the cost to the government?

If he is given the higher income and prices remain at P_1, the consumer will have to spend amount $I_2- X$ in order to purchase quantity Q_2, but, in effect, he spends amount I_2-Z or an extra $XZ=(4-2)$ due to higher prices. This extra goes to the government in the form of tax revenues. Since the consumer is given an additional income of I_2-I_1, the net cost to government will be the difference between this amount and the amount of taxes collected from the consumer, or $(I_2-I_1)-(XZ) = ZT$ or $2-5$.

The discussion illustrates that if the consumers are to be left as well off as before, the government can possibly bring about reduced consumption of gasoline *at a cost*. The reader can verify (using the same figure and the light dotted lines) that if the government does not care about the utility of the consumer, it can very well bring about reduced consumption of gasoline (down to Q_2) at price P_2 by giving him an additional income of only (I^*-I_1) at *zero cost* (monetarily speaking), but the consumer will end up at a lower level of utility, namely, on U_{00}.

2. Keeping the Employees Happy

Suppose you own a grocery store and you want to spend a *specific amount* of money on your only employee. You may spend it on her by giving her groceries at a reduced

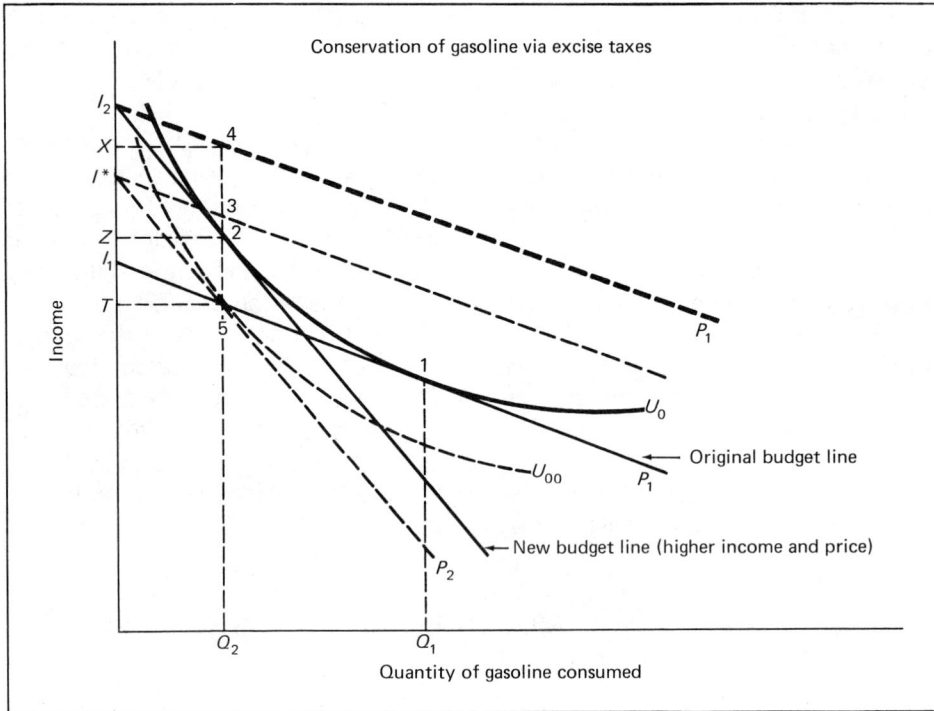

FIGURE 3-27
The graph suggests the possible effects of tax policy on the consumption of gasoline. Originally the consumer is at point 1 enjoying utility level U_0 consuming Q_1 gallons of gasoline per time period. If the government can somehow persuade the consumer to move left and up along this indifference curve, less gasoline will be consumed. The consumer should not be any less happy at point 2, since it lies on indifference curve U_0. If the new budget constraint is tangent at point 2, the consumer will be just as happy as he was at point 1 and such a budget could come about if the price of gasoline increased while the consumer's income also increased appropriately. Suppose the government transfers income to the consumer by the amount I_1-I_2. If the lower prices prevail, the consumer will have spent only amount I_2-X to purchase Q_2 gallons of gasoline, but due to the tax on gasoline he pays a total of I_2-Z, the indifference $X-Z$ being the tax revenue to the government. However, since the government also gives the consumer more income by the amount I_2-I_1, the *net cost* to government is $(I_2-I_1) - (X-Z)$, $(4-5) - (4-2)$, or $(2-5)$, which equals ZT.

price, by giving her free groceries, or by giving her cash. Which one will she prefer? Which policy do you prefer? Refer to Figure 3-28 for the following discussion.

Let the employee have an original income of I_1 and let her consume groceries by the amount Q_1, for which she pays the retail price as shown. This retail price is the same for all grocery stores, and the original budget line for the employee is line I_1L and the utility maximization point is at point 1. Assume that you wish to spend a total of I_2I_1. If you give this amount of income to your employee, her budget line will shift so that she will operate at point 2 on indifference curve U_2. Such a movement will increase her utility and have her consume a greater quantity of groceries at retail prices, and the relevant budget line will be I_2B. If you allow the employee to purchase the groceries *at cost* but do not give her any income, her budget line will be I_1K and the flatter line will reflect the lower price. This arrangement will put the employee at

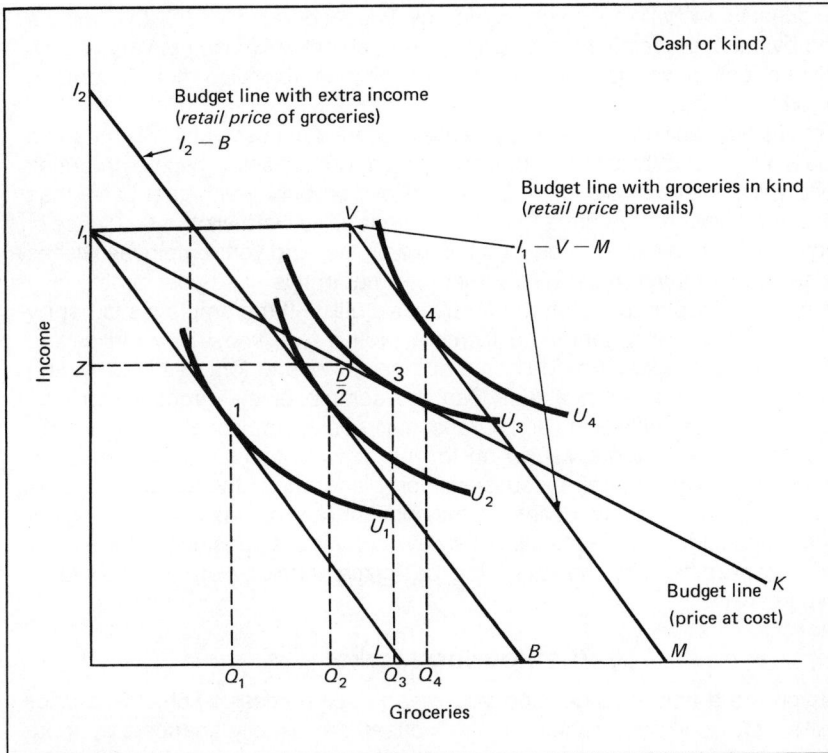

FIGURE 3-28
The employee's tastes are such that they are maximizing utility at point 1. If the employer wishes to spend only a specific amount of money for employee welfare, he can do so by giving the employee cash, lowering the price of groceries, or by giving groceries. If the employer pays more in cash, the employee's income will rise to I_2 and will be on utility level U_2. If the employer lowers the price of groceries that the employee buys such that the cost of subsidy equals $I_1 - I_2$, she will be on U_3 at point 3. Should the employee be given a certain amount of groceries whose cost (to the employer) is also $I_1 - I_2$, her budget will be shown by line $I_1 - V - M$ and she will maximize utility at point 4. Since the employee values the groceries given to her at the retail price, the budget line reflects the old price at point 1 and the horizontal "shift" occurs due to the subsidy in kind. Since point 4 yields the most utility, the employee will prefer a gift of groceries to the other two suggested means of increasing utility. The employer should also like this method, since, for his money, this method yields the maximum happiness for his employee.

point 3 on indifference curve U_3 and she will consume quantity Q_3 in groceries. The interesting part of this arrangement is that the employee pays the *entire amount* for her groceries because she pays the employer the full cost of such groceries, and hence the employer does not spend a dime! The employee is very happy because her utility level is at U_3 and to her the *perceived* benefits due to the lower price equal amount $3L$ (the savings due to price at cost.) Lastly, you can give your employee groceries whose value in terms of cost to you equal amount $I_2 I_1$. At cost, $I_2 I_1$ will buy $ZD = (I_1 V)$ quantity of groceries which, if given to the employee, will have the effect of shifting her budget line to the right by this amount. It will then slope downwards at an angle suggesting the retail price of groceries. Her relevant isocost or budget line will now be I_1-V-M. She will operate at point 4 with utility level U_4, consuming quantity Q_4, of which quantity I_1V will be given to her by you and quantity (Q_4-I_1V) will be purchased by her at the retail price. Such an arrangement will make her very happy, for she will not only have more groceries at her disposal but also more income to spend on other goods.

You may prefer selling your employee the groceries at cost which will mean no cost to you but higher utility to the employee or you may even sell her some groceries *below cost* which will involve some expenditure by you but even higher utility than before for the employee. You have to consider your utility vis-à-vis the employee's. Presumably you wish to minimize cost (maximize profits) and your employee wishes to maximize utility, but you must also remember that in this case your profits may have a very direct dependence on the employee's utility. If the employee is happy she may work harder and contribute to more profits. You know how the saying goes—"Mi casa—su casa!" Why do some companies spend fortunes in providing "fringe benefits" for their employees? Can the sample of the grocery store be extended to other areas where the employees may receive additional compensation in either cash or kind? Before we go on to one or two other areas it should be remembered that the foregoing discussion took place under the assumptions as shown by the shapes and locations of the indifference curves. We should not automatically conclude that the results will always come out as postulated if we draw the utility function differently; however, the basic methodology of such problems remains as shown.

3. The Housing Market

Suppose you are a home builder and you wish to sell homes at $60,000, a price which will satisfy your profit requirements. Houses are usually financed by mortgages available through the many lending institutions. In this particular situation you will finance the mortgage for a period of 30 years, and you feel that such mortgage money ought to be worth 10% interest. For the purpose of convenience we will assume that no down payment is required on the part of the home buyer. Are there many combinations of the price of house and the mortgage lending rate that will yield the 10% rate that you wish to obtain? In other words, can we use the concept of the equal-yield curve to arrive at a certain market strategy? As long as a particular combination of price–interest rate yields over 10% over the 30 years, the house seller (you) ought to be indifferent between such a combination and all other comparable combinations.

In order to explore this further, we have to go through the mechanics of interest rate calculations. To illustrate, suppose you agree to sell the house to a customer who promises to pay you the entire amount of the purchase price at the end of 30 years. How much should he pay you, including interest? The final sum payable by the house buyer would include the original price of the house—say $60,000—and the accumulated interest on this sum. If interest compounds at the rate of 10% a year, the sum due at the end of one year will be $66,000. But the sum is actually going to be due at the end of 30 years, which will amount to $60,000 $(1 + 0.10)^{30}$ or $60,000(17.45) = \$1.047000$ million—the interest alone will amount to $987,000. To obtain such figures, we employ Tables 3-2 and 3-3, which are adapted from standard calculations practiced in financial management courses and are available in any handbook for managers. The symbols used are as follows.

P = the original amount or principal financed
F = the future amount including interest
A = the annual amount including interest.

TABLE 3-2

n	$\frac{F}{P}$ [a]	$\frac{P}{F}$ [b]	$\frac{A}{F}$ [c]	$\frac{A}{P}$ [d]	$\frac{F}{A}$ [e]	$\frac{P}{A}$ [f]
			$i = 10\%$			
1	1.100	0.9091	1.00000	1.10000	1.000	0.909
2	1.210	0.8264	0.47619	0.57619	2.100	1.736
3	1.331	0.7513	0.30211	0.40211	3.310	2.487
4	1.464	0.6830	0.21547	0.31547	4.641	3.170
5	1.611	0.6209	0.16380	0.26380	6.105	3.791
6	1.772	0.5645	0.12961	0.22961	7.716	4.355
7	1.949	0.5132	0.10541	0.20541	9.487	4.868
8	2.144	0.4665	0.08744	0.18744	11.436	5.335
9	2.358	0.4241	0.07364	0.17364	13.579	5.759
10	2.594	0.3855	0.06275	0.16275	15.937	6.144
11	2.853	0.3505	0.05396	0.15396	18.531	6.495
12	3.138	0.3186	0.04676	0.14676	21.384	6.814
13	3.452	0.2897	0.04078	0.14078	24.523	7.103
14	3.797	0.2633	0.03575	0.13575	27.975	7.367
15	4.177	0.2394	0.03147	0.13147	31.772	7.606
16	4.595	0.2176	0.02782	0.12782	35.950	7.824
17	5.054	0.1978	0.02466	0.12466	40.545	8.022
18	5.560	0.1799	0.02193	0.12193	45.599	8.201
19	6.116	0.1635	0.01955	0.11955	51.159	8.365
20	6.727	0.1486	0.01746	0.11746	57.275	8.514
21	7.400	0.1351	0.01562	0.11562	64.002	8.649
22	8.140	0.1228	0.01401	0.11401	71.403	8.772
23	8.954	0.1117	0.01257	0.11257	79.543	8.883
24	9.850	0.1015	0.01130	0.11130	88.497	8.985
25	10.835	0.0923	0.01017	0.11017	98.347	9.077
26	11.918	0.0839	0.00916	0.10916	109.182	9.161
27	13.110	0.0763	0.00826	0.10826	121.100	9.237
28	14.421	0.0693	0.00745	0.10745	134.210	9.307
29	15.863	0.0630	0.00673	0.10673	148.631	9.370
30	17.449	0.0573	0.00608	0.10608	164.494	9.427
31	19.194	0.0521	0.00550	0.10550	181.943	9.479
32	21.114	0.0474	0.00497	0.10497	201.138	9.526
33	23.225	0.0431	0.00450	0.10450	222.252	9.569
34	25.548	0.0391	0.00407	0.10407	245.477	9.609
35	28.102	0.0356	0.00369	0.10369	271.024	9.644

F = future value; P = present value; A = annual value.
[a] F/P—compound amount factor for single payment.
[b] P/F—present worth factor for single payment.
[c] A/F—sinking fund factor for uniform series of payments.
[d] F/A—compound amount factor for uniform series of payments.
[e] A/P—capital recovery factor.
[f] P/A—present worth factor for uniform series of payments.

TABLE 3-3

n	$\dfrac{F}{P}$	$\dfrac{P}{F}$	$\dfrac{A}{F}$	$\dfrac{A}{P}$	$\dfrac{F}{A}$	$\dfrac{P}{A}$
			(a) $i = 8\%$			
1	1.080	0.9259	1.00000	1.08000	1.000	0.926
2	1.166	0.8573	0.48077	0.56077	2.080	1.783
3	1.260	0.7938	0.30803	0.38803	3.246	2.577
4	1.360	0.7350	0.22192	0.30192	4.506	3.312
5	1.469	0.6806	0.17046	0.25046	5.867	3.993
6	1.587	0.6302	0.13632	0.21632	7.336	4.623
7	1.714	0.5835	0.11207	0.19207	8.923	5.206
8	1.851	0.5403	0.09401	0.17401	10.637	5.747
9	1.999	0.5002	0.08008	0.16008	12.488	6.247
10	2.159	0.4632	0.06903	0.14903	14.487	6.710
11	2.332	0.4289	0.06008	0.14008	16.645	7.139
12	2.518	0.3971	0.05270	0.13270	18.977	7.536
13	2.720	0.3677	0.04652	0.12652	21.495	7.904
14	2.937	0.3405	0.04130	0.12130	24.215	8.244
15	3.172	0.3152	0.03683	0.11683	27.152	8.559
16	3.426	0.2919	0.03298	0.11298	30.324	8.851
17	3.700	0.2703	0.02963	0.10963	33.750	9.122
18	3.996	0.2502	0.02670	0.10670	37.450	9.372
19	4.316	0.2317	0.02413	0.10413	41.446	9.604
20	4.661	0.2145	0.02185	0.10185	45.762	9.818
21	5.034	0.1987	0.01983	0.09983	50.423	10.017
22	5.437	0.1839	0.01803	0.09803	55.457	10.201
23	5.871	0.1703	0.01642	0.09642	60.893	10.371
24	6.341	0.1577	0.01498	0.09498	66.765	10.529
25	6.848	0.1460	0.01368	0.09368	73.106	10.675
26	7.396	0.1352	0.01251	0.09251	79.954	10.810
27	7.988	0.1252	0.01145	0.09145	87.351	10.935
28	8.627	0.1159	0.01049	0.09049	95.339	11.051
29	9.317	0.1073	0.00962	0.08962	103.966	11.158
30	10.063	0.0994	0.00883	0.08883	113.283	11.258
31	10.868	0.0920	0.00811	0.08811	123.346	11.350
32	11.737	0.0852	0.00745	0.08745	134.214	11.435
33	12.676	0.0789	0.00685	0.08685	145.951	11.514
34	13.690	0.0730	0.00630	0.08630	158.627	11.587
35	14.785	0.0676	0.00580	0.08580	172.317	11.655

TABLE 3-3 *continued*

			(b) $i = 6\%$			
n	$\dfrac{F}{P}$	$\dfrac{P}{F}$	$\dfrac{A}{F}$	$\dfrac{A}{P}$	$\dfrac{F}{A}$	$\dfrac{P}{A}$
1	1.060	0.9434	1.00000	1.06000	1.000	0.943
2	1.124	0.8900	0.48544	0.54544	2.060	1.833
3	1.191	0.8396	0.31411	0.37411	3.184	2.673
4	1.262	0.7921	0.22859	0.28859	4.375	3.465
5	1.338	0.7473	0.17740	0.23740	5.637	4.212
6	1.419	0.7050	0.14336	0.20336	6.975	4.917
7	1.504	0.6651	0.11914	0.17914	8.394	5.582
8	1.594	0.6274	0.10104	0.16104	9.897	6.210
9	1.689	0.5919	0.08702	0.14702	11.491	6.802
10	1.791	0.5584	0.07587	0.13587	13.181	7.360
11	1.898	0.5268	0.06679	0.12679	14.972	7.887
12	2.012	0.4970	0.05928	0.11928	16.870	8.384
13	2.133	0.4688	0.05296	0.11296	18.882	8.853
14	2.261	0.4423	0.04758	0.10758	21.015	9.295
15	2.397	0.4173	0.04296	0.10296	23.276	9.712
16	2.540	0.3936	0.03895	0.09895	25.673	10.106
17	2.693	0.3714	0.03544	0.09544	28.213	10.477
18	2.854	0.3503	0.03236	0.09236	30.906	10.828
19	3.026	0.3305	0.02962	0.08962	33.760	11.158
20	3.207	0.3118	0.02718	0.08718	36.786	11.470
21	3.400	0.2942	0.02500	0.08500	39.993	11.764
22	3.604	0.2775	0.02305	0.08305	43.392	12.042
23	3.820	0.2618	0.02128	0.08128	46.996	12.303
24	4.049	0.2470	0.01968	0.07968	50.816	12.550
25	4.292	0.2330	0.01823	0.07823	54.865	12.783
26	4.549	0.2198	0.01690	0.07690	59.156	13.003
27	4.822	0.2074	0.01570	0.07570	63.706	13.211
28	5.112	0.1956	0.01459	0.07459	68.528	13.406
29	5.418	0.1846	0.01358	0.07358	73.640	13.591
30	5.743	0.1741	0.01265	0.07265	79.058	13.765
31	6.088	0.1643	0.01179	0.07179	84.802	13.929
32	6.453	0.1550	0.01100	0.07100	90.890	14.084
33	6.841	0.1462	0.01027	0.07027	97.343	14.230
34	7.251	0.1379	0.00960	0.06960	104.184	14.368
35	7.686	0.1301	0.00897	0.06897	111.435	14.498

For the example just discussed, we wish to compute the future amount at the end of 30 years at 10% interest if the price of the house is $60,000. To find the future value F we proceed as follows.

$$F = \frac{F}{P} P$$

The (F/P) is referred to as the *compound amount factor* which, when multiplied by the price of the house or P, will yield the future (F) accumulated sum to be paid at the end of 30 years. Looking at Table 3-2, we see that the first column shows the (F/P) factors for 10%. Under the column labelled n we go down to where $n = 30$ and read across under the (F/P) column—the number is 17.449 or 17.45. The future sum payable by the house buyer then becomes

$$F = (17.45)\,(\$60,000) = \$1,047,000.00$$

Now let us suppose that you wish to sell the house for $60,000 but agree to let the buyer pay for it through annual installments over a 30-year period. What will be the annual amount? Here we want the annual amount, or A, for a P of $60,000 at 10%. As before, we utilize Table 3-2 but this time we go to the column labelled (A/P), called the *capital recovery factor*. When (A/P) is multiplied by P we obtain A, or

$$\frac{A}{P} P = A$$

For $n = 30$, the (A/P) at 10% equals 0.10608. The annual amount payable by the house buyer then becomes

$$A = \frac{A}{P} P = (0.10608)\,(\$60,000)$$

$$= \$6364.80/\text{year for 30 years}$$

This is to say that receiving $6364.80 per year for 30 years on a $60,000 house is like earning a 10% rate of return on money. Now that we understand the use of the interest rate tables (or time-value-of-money tables) we will attempt to incorporate their use into a form of indifference analysis.

How high will the initial price of the house need to be so that a person paying only 8% on the mortgage will end up paying $6364.80 per year for 30 years? We realize that the price has to be more than $60,000 so that the higher price will help offset the lower interest rate in order to yield the same annual payments. Now we will use Table 3-3 to compute the house price. The problem here is to determine P from a known A value. The factor we need is the (P/A) which, when multiplied by A, gives us P, or $(P/A)\,(A) = P$. For $n = 30$ and $i = 8\%$, the (P/A) factor (known as the *present worth factor for a uniform series*) equals 11.26. The price of the house, or P, is then

$$P = \frac{P}{A} A = (11.26)\,(\$6364.80)$$

$$= \$71,667.65$$

The calculation shows us that the person paying $71,667.65 for the house and paying back the mortgage at an interest rate of 8% will have to pay $6364.80 per year for 30 years, which will be economically equivalent (from the seller's point of view) to paying 10% on a $60,000/30 year mortgage. In other words, you, the seller, will be making the 10% return from the sale of the house by charging a price of $71,667.65 and lending the money at 8%, or charging $60,000 and loaning money at 10%. Other combinations can also be worked out so that different house prices can be matched with corresponding interest rates so that the annual payment will remain at $6,364.80, amounting to a monthly payment of approximately $531. One other combination, the one corresponding to an interest rate of 6%, is also being provided for illustration. The (P/A) factor for 30 years at an interest rate of 6% is 13.765, as shown in Table 3-3b. When we take this factor and multiply it by $6364.80, we obtain the appropriate price, or

$$P = \frac{P}{A}A = (13.765)(\$6364.80)$$

$$= \$87,611.47$$

If the house price is $87,611.47 and the corresponding rate for money is 6%, the house buyer will have to make an annual payment of $6364.80 for 30 years, again yielding a 10% return for the $60,000 house. Since the three combinations of P and i yield the same annual payment for a $60,000 home, they should be equally liked by the seller. We can call the locus of all such points on a P–i map an *equal-satisfaction* (indifference) *curve*. The locus for this particular set of circumstances is illustrated in Figure 3-29. The cost of money or the interest rate on the mortgage is measured (in percentages) along the bottom or horizontal axis and the house price to the buyer is shown along the vertical axis. The three combinations calculated above are shown as points 1, 2, and 3, respectively. If we calculate more points they will reflect a trade-off between the house price and the corresponding interest rate. For example, a house price of, say, $65,000 might correspond to an interest rate of about 9%. The locus of points 1–2–3 is labeled as an equal-satisfaction curve or an indifference curve. We can see that higher curves will be associated with higher prices and higher interest rates and will certainly be preferred to ones at the lower end of the scale, but even though the higher curves are more liked by the seller they may not be available due to a lack of demand from home buyers. Different home buyers have different utility functions and some are more sensitive to interest rates, whereas others are more sensitive to the house price itself. The task of the home seller then is to charge different prices and hence different interest rates to the various types of consumers in keeping with their tastes. People who are reluctant to pay high interest

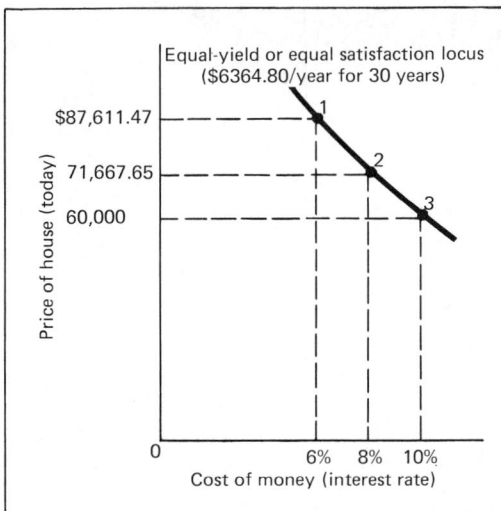

FIGURE 3-29
Present Value of $6364.80/year at 10% = $60,000.00; present value of $6364.80/year at 8% = $71,667.65; present value of $6364.80/year at 6% = $87,611.47.

costs may be persuaded to buy the house at a higher price, albeit a lower interest rate, and those that prefer lower-priced houses may very well be willing to pay a higher interest rate. It makes a difference whether the consumer is in the high or low income tax bracket. Because interest costs on home purchase are tax deductible, one consumer may very well elect the lower-price but higher interest combination. Furthermore, people receive different levels of utility by paying high or low prices for their homes. It is conceivable that one person may be very happy to pay $87,612 for his home so that he may brag about his conspicuous consumption. A second person may be willing to pay only $60,000 for such a home because he may have a different set of values. But we must realize that all three types of consumers (corresponding to preferences 1,2, and 3, respectively) end up paying the same equivalent amount of money and the seller receives 10% for his $60,000 home. Everyone is happy.

You are probably quite aware that the seller may very well vary the house price, the amount of the down payment, the cost of money, and the duration of the loan to achieve various results. The consumers, however, are free to choose the combination of variables that will produce the utility-maximizing bundle. Some may opt to put down large down payments for an expensive home and borrow the mortgage from a bank; others may elect to have the home seller finance them on his terms as long as the monthly payments are affordable. Just as the seller can come up with his equal-yield (and hence equal utility) curve, the buyer can also be indifferent among many combinations of price, interest rate, and down payment. We can employ such an analysis in a variety of similar instances—as long as there is room for trade-offs, there is room for indifference analysis.

EXERCISES

1. Define the following.
   a. Ordinal utility.
   b. Utility function.
   c. Marginal rate of substitution.
   d. Real income effect.
   e. Substitution effect.
   f. The PCL and the ICL.
   g. Price elasticity of demand.
   h. Income elasticity of demand.
   i. Budget constraint.
   j. Equimarginal principle.
   k. Marginal utility.

2. Draw an indifference map for a rational individual such that the indifference curves show a diminishing marginal rate of substitution between the two goods X and Y. If we hold Y constant and move along in a horizontal fashion, what will we be measuring? What will we obtain if we move vertically at a given level of X? How do your answers relate to MRS? Explain.

3. Draw indifference maps which indiate an individual's taste for the following pairs of goods.
   a. Potatoes and bread.
   b. Meat and potatoes.
   c. Toothpaste and bread.
   d. Sex and whisky.

e. Education and travel.
f. Pollution and congestion.
g. Income and pollution.
h. Income taxes and sales taxes.
i. Work and leisure.
j. Shirts and ties.
k. Present income and future income.
l. Consumption and savings.
m. Piety and wealth.
n. Food and clothing.
o. Being alone and dating.

4. Draw an indifference map indicating a "saturation point." Is such a point conceivable or ever likely to be?

5. Explain the "substitution effect" of a price increase. Illustrate the substitution and income effects of a price increase using suitable diagrams.

6. Suppose you wish the average individual to consume a given product in larger quantities. The greater consumption can be brought about by lower prices and higher income to the buyer. Which method will you recommend as the least costly, assuming that you have to pay for the cost of the price and income subsidy?

7. Assume indifference curves of the "normal" variety. Measuring income along the vertical axis and X along the other, "prove" the following propositons.
 a. If the government wishes to collect a specific amount of revenues by either an income or an excise tax, the consumer will most likely prefer the income tax.
 b. If the government wishes the consumption of X reduced to a specific quantity, it will end up collecting larger revenues if it imposes an income tax as opposed to an excise tax.
 c. If the government desires to raise the consumer's utility to a certain level, consumption will be greater if the price of X is subsidized than if the consumer is given more income.
 d. If the government wishes to encourage the consumption of X to a certain level, it will be less costly if the price is subsidized than if the consumer is given more income.

8. Show how the government can increase the consumption of a particular product by a mix of income tax–excise tax policy. (Hint: The two types of taxes should move in opposite directions, that is, a reduction in excise tax can be thought of as a price subsidy.)

9. Assume that the following is known.

Income	Price	Quantity	Utility
$1000	$12	60	U_1
1000	10	90	U_2
800	10	70	U_1

The consumer's income is $1000 and utility level U_2 is higher than level U_1. Answer the following questions with reference to the above table.
 a. At a price of $12, how many units will the consumer buy?
 b. When the price falls to $10, how many more does he buy?

c. What two combinations of income and price will leave the consumer equally well off?

d. If the consumer has to pay a price of $10 as opposed to $12, what income will leave her as well off as she was with $1000 of income and the $12 price?

e. How many units of consumption are due to the substitution effect? The real income effect?

f. Calculate the value of the price elasticity of demand between the prices of $12 and $10.

g. What are the consumer's expenditures at the two price levels? Is your answer consistent with the value of the price elasticity in (f)?

h. Is there any indication that the indifference curves are convex to the origin? Explain.

10. Suppose a person's utility function is represented by the following forms.

a. $U = MA$

b. $U = X + Y$

c. $U = I^2 L$

d. $U = \dfrac{X}{\sqrt{Y}}$

In each of the above functions, U represents the utility level and the other variables correspond to the goods and services entering into the utility function. Plot an indifference curve for each function for $U = 100$ and calculate two values for MRS associated with each indifference curve. Which of the functions exhibits the basic "law" of diminishing marginal rate of substitution?

11. Explain the following statement. "While the assumption of diminishing marginal utility may imply the existence of diminishing marginal rate of substitution, convex indifference curves do not necessarily suggest the presence of diminishing marginal utility."

12. Draw budget constraints or isocost curves for the following situations.

a. Budget = $100, $P_X = \$20$, $P_Y = \$10$
b. Budget = $300, $P_X = 2$, $P_Y = \$30$
c. Budget = $C, $P_X = \$M$, $P_Y = \$N$
d. Budget = $500, $P_X = \frac{1}{2}$, $P_Y = \$50$

13. Suppose the price of $I = \$10$ and the price of $L = \$5$ and the budget is limited to $100. Determine the utility-maximizing combination of I and L that the consumer will buy for the utility function given in (c) of Problem 10. (Both I and L must be integers.)

14. Match the indifference maps (a)–(e) of Figure 3-30 with the characteristics described (i)–(iv); $U_4 > U_3 > U_2 > U_1$.

i. Loves sex but dislikes food _____.
ii. Dislikes movies and theatres _____.
iii. Likes sex but is unaffected by food _____.
iv. Likes food but is indifferent to amount of sex _____.

15. Either support or refute this statement and explain your position: "For maximization of utility, the consumer should always choose that combination of X and Y which maximizes the value of the sum of the quantities."

16. Suppose an individual's utility function is such that for a given set of prices and income, utility is maximum when the product of the quantities is also maximum. Let the consumer have a budget of $100 per month and let the prices of whisky and cigarettes

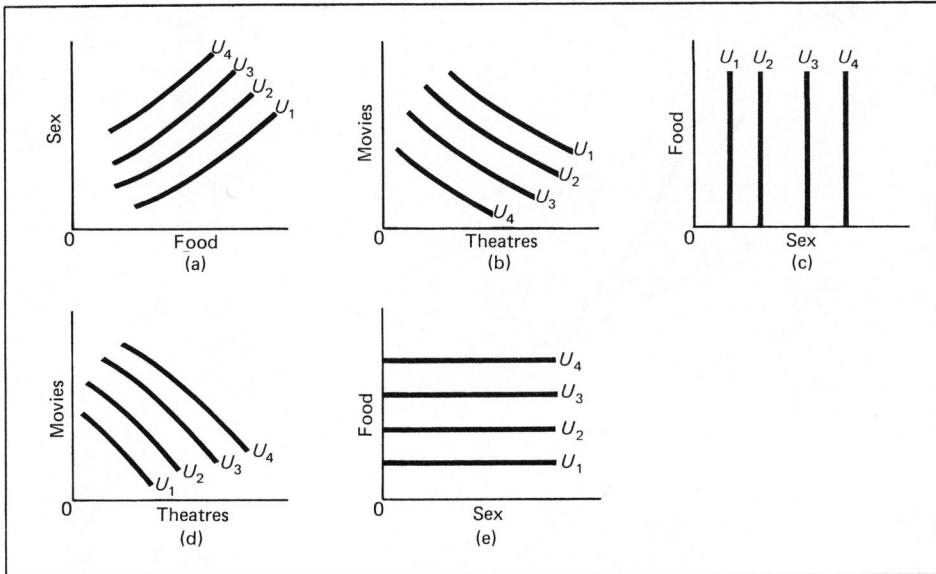

FIGURE 3-30

be $1.00 per bottle and $0.50 per package, respectively. It can be shown that utility will be maximum if the consumer buys 50 bottles of whisky and 100 packages of cigarettes. However, the consumer's health counselor, Dr. Holiday, recommends that the consumer drink no more than 20 bottles of whisky per month. In view of the circumstances,

a. What will be the "next best" consumption bundle?
b. Should the consumer be willing to give his wife $10 if she agrees not to squeal for such a consideration?
c. Will he be better off by bribing the doctor—with five bottles of whisky—who then will remove the drinking constraint?

17. From the information provided in Figure 3-31, complete the following (assume that the consumer is originally at point A).

a. Price of X at point A = _____.
b. Income remaining at point A = _____.

FIGURE 3-31

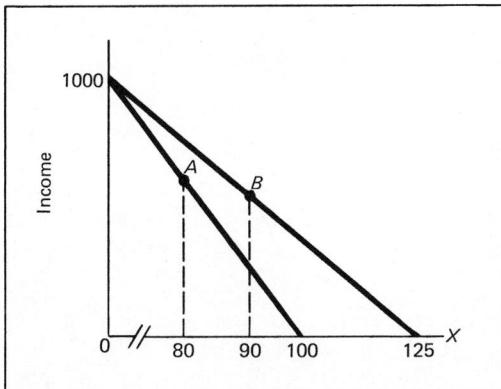

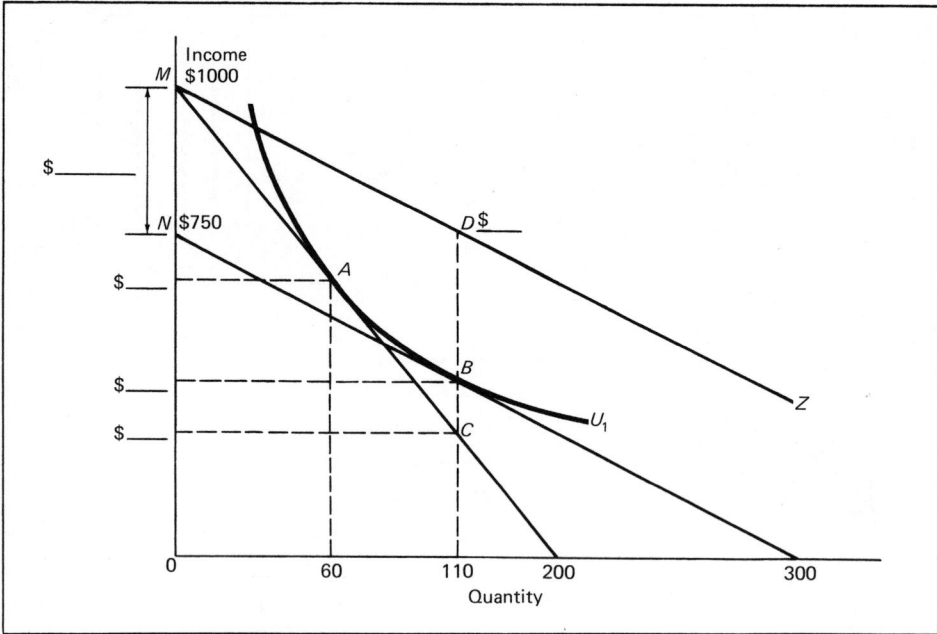

FIGURE 3-32

c. Price at point B = _____.
d. Income remaining at point B = _____.
e. Demand elasticity = _____.

18. Draw the budget constraint for an income of $100 and the price of X such that the price declines $1/unit for each ten additional units bought. Price for the first 10 units = $10/unit.

19. The consumer is originally at point A (see Figure 3-32).
Her income = $_____ and the price of the product = $_____ per unit.

If we want her to consume 110 units of the product and be just as "well off" as before, the money income should be $_____ and the price per unit should be $_____.

If the consumer buys 110 units at this lower price, she will spend a total of $_____ and will have $_____ remaining. To buy the 110 units at the original price she will have to spend $_____.

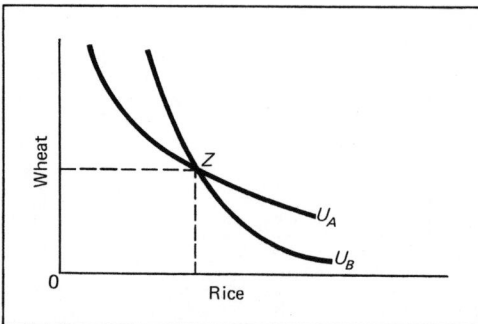

FIGURE 3-33

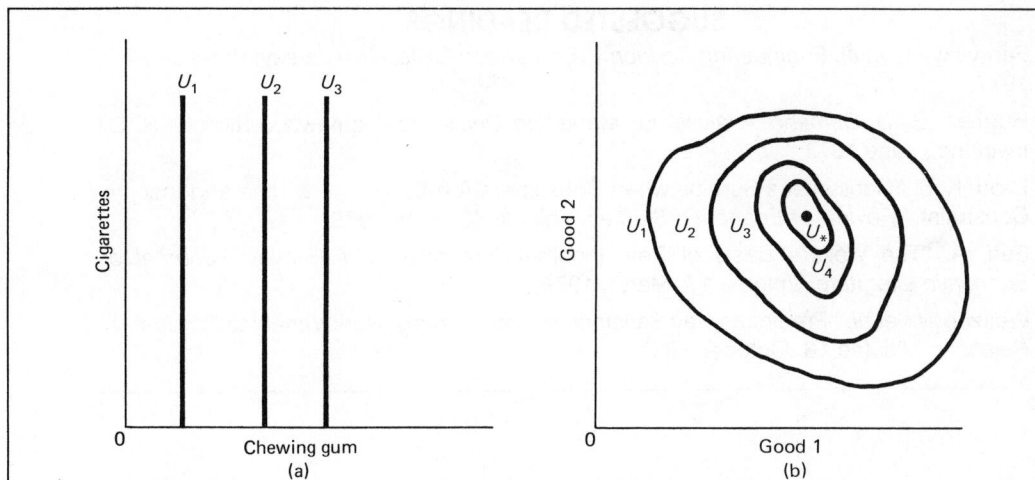

FIGURE 3-34

If the government reduces the consumer's income and reduces the price of the product such that the consumption point is at *B*, the utility level will be _____. The amount of income tax will equal distance _____ or $_____. The difference between what the consumer spends to buy the 110 units and the amount she will have to pay at the original price = $_____, which is the cost of subsidy to the government. However, part of this subsidy cost will be offset by the collection of income taxes. In the graph, the cost of subsidy is shown by *distance* _____ out of which *distance* _____ represents the amount of income tax. The net cost to government is shown by *distance*_____. The value of the subsidy = $_____ and the income taxes equal $_____, and consequently the net cost to the government = $_____.

20. Suppose there are two individuals, *A* and *B*, with the indifference curves as shown in Figure 3-33. Originally each person has an identical bundle of wheat and rice, shown by point *Z*.
   a. May we assume that each person is equally happy?
   b. Who likes what best?
   c. If each person can exchange some of the less desirable commodity, show that both persons will be better off.
   d. Prove that for maximum total utility of *A* and *B*, exchange should continue until the MRS for both is equal.

21. Draw indifference curves for the following products.
   a. an *inferior good* (quantity varies inversely with income)
   b. a *Giffen good* (quantity varies positively with price), but the higher the price, the lower the utility
   c. a *snob good* (quantity varies positively with price), but the higher the price, the higher the utility.

22. What can you say about a person's tastes from the two indifference maps (a) and (b) in Figure 3-34. (Assume that $U_4 > U_3 > U_2 > U_1$, etc.)

23. Show how indifference analysis can be used to explain the theory of population.

SUGGESTED READINGS

Fabrycky, J., *et al. Engineering Economy.* Englewood Cliffs, New Jersey: Prentice-Hall, 1977.

Hughes, G. D. *Demand Analysis for Marketing Decisions.* Homewood, Illinois: R. D. Irwin Inc., June 1973.

Lyon, K. S. "Consumer's Surplus when Consumers Are Subject to a Time and Income Constraint." *Review of Economic Studies,* Volume 45, June 1978.

Sen, A. "The Welfare Basis of Real Income Comparisons: A Survey." *Journal of Economic Literature,* Volume 17, March 1979.

Weitzel, W., *et al.* "Predicting Pay Satisfaction from Nonpay Work Variables." *Industrial Relations,* Volume 16, October 1977.

Chapter Four Chapter Four Chapter Four

THE THEORY OF DEMAND

The demand for a good or service may be thought of as the *willingness* and *ability* of the consumer to acquire the product under the prevailing circumstances. For example, your demand for education at a college or university will be influenced by the conditions surrounding college attendance. The factors that affect your decision to go to college, in effect, will test your willingness and ability to "demand" higher education. Thus, high tuition rates may deprive you of the ability to go to college, although you may be perfectly willing to do so. Generally speaking, you are a demander, if you are willing and able to buy the product.

DEMAND FUNCTIONS

You will recall from earlier discussions that a function relates the dependent variable to the independent ones. The utility function shows the dependence of utility on the various quantities and qualities of goods and services consumed. Similarly, a demand function relates the demand for a product to the many associated variables that influence demand. There are many types of demand functions and we shall examine a few widely used types in this section.

The Multivariate Demand Function

Since the demand for any product is affected by many variables, the comprehensive demand function includes as many variables as possible or necessary. A demand function so formulated is a *multivariate* (meaning many variables) *demand function*. Suppose we wish to discuss the demand for a particular brand of small car, say the Volkswagen Rabbit. We will use a generalized *additive* and multivariate function to introduce certain properties of demand. Equation (1) is additive because the terms have been added (or substracted):

$$D_R = K - aP_R + bP_S + cP_G + dA_R - eA_S + fY + gN \tag{1}$$

where

D_R = quantity of Rabbits demanded per time period
P_R = price of Rabbits
P_S = price of Subarus
P_G = price of gasoline per gallon
A_R = amount of advertising by Rabbit
A_S = advertising by Subaru
Y = average income of potential buyers
N = total number in driving population
$K, a, b, \ldots, g$ = constants

For the time being we will only examine the *signs* and *magnitudes* of the variables that affect the demand for Rabbits and subsequently analyze the economics of demand theory.

Equation (1) suggests that the quantity of Rabbits demanded varies inversely with two variables, P_R and A_S and positively with all others. The minus sign before a variable denotes that the dependent variable is negatively related to this variable, while a positive sign indicates a direct relationship. Thus, the higher the value of P_R and A_S, the smaller the quantity of Rabbits demanded. This makes sense. The higher the price of the car, the less the quantity bought, and the more advertising by a competitor, the less demand for Rabbits. The coefficients in front of the variables also tell us the magnitude of the impact of that variable. Thus, if the number shown by a is large, the quantity of Rabbits demanded will be greatly influenced by its price. The demand for Rabbits is further related to the other variables shown. For example, it is reasonable to assume that as the price of gasoline rises, the demand for Rabbits as well as other similar economy cars will increase. Hence the demand for Rabbits is positively, or directly, related to P_G. The constant K is simply a "catchall" factor that helps account for all the other components of demand that help explain the demand for Rabbits.

The generalized model of equation (1) is simply an illustration of a particular type of demand function. No attempt was made to include all possible variables that affect the demand for Rabbits. The real empirical form for such a demand function may be much more complex or even much simpler. There are many techniques available today that permit us to attempt to measure the demand for products. The subject matter of *econometrics* is largely involved with the measurement, interpretation, and empirical verification of economic phenomena. At the moment we are interested only in understanding the economic logic of such a demand function.

DEMAND VARIABLES

We can use the basic framework of equation (1) to relate demand to several important variables. Although many variables enter into the demand for a product, some of the more effective ones are the price of the product; the relative price of *substitutes;* the price of *complements;* the *income* of buyers; the *number* of buyers; the *actions* of *competitors, institutions, government* policy; and certain other *demographic* as well as *psychological* factors.

We already know that the quantity demanded of a product varies inversely with its price. But the price of a substitute also affects demand. For example, if the price of Subarus declines, in all probability there will be a decrease in the demand for Rabbits; or, if the price of government bonds falls and their yield is increased, it is entirely possible that there will be less demand for other types of outlets for savings and personal investment such as stocks and industrial bonds. *In general, the demand for a product varies directly with the price of substitutes.*

Complements are those items which are normally consumed or bought along with the product in question. If the demand for a product rises, the demand for the complementary goods and services also increases. Thus, when the price of pizza falls, the demand for beer increases, presumably because people drink beer with their pizza. In our example of the demand for Rabbits, however, gasoline is a complement to the car. Since the Rabbit's appeal is largely in its fuel economy, a higher gasoline price will make the purchase of Rabbits that much more attractive. Consequently, the relationship between the demand for Rabbits and the price of gasoline is positive, whereas normally we would expect it to be negative in the case of complements. In the case of the price of pizza versus the demand for beer, the relationship is negative. *Again, most often, the demand for a good varies inversely with the price of complements*.

The *income* of buyers, or for that matter the income of the nation, indicates the general economic health, and therefore the probable demand for certain products. Since income provides the consumer with the ability to purchase (demand) the goods and services that satisfy his needs, it is generally agreed that the higher the level of income, the greater the level of demand. However, there are occasional exceptions to every rule. It is usually true that beyond some level of income the demand for certain products may actually decline instead of increase. This happens presumably because wealthier individuals or groups find certain products below the standards to which they are accustomed. For example, when your income rises, you choose to consume "better" brands of certain products and reduce the purchase of the less attractive or less appealing ones. Since you can afford the better class of goods and services, the others that you used to consume become "*inferior*" by comparison. Would a Madison Avenue executive wear Jacque Pennay's suits, if he could afford the Society Brand? *In most cases,* it is true that the *demand for a good is positively related to income*.

The number of buyers as well as population characteristics influence demand. Greater numbers usually generate large demand, provided the population's tastes and desires are compatible with the product's intended usefulness. Varying backgrounds of consumers may lead to such wide dispersal of demand among so many different substitutes that demand for no one item will be very large. However, you will agree that the demand for hotel and motel rooms will be significantly higher during conventions than in their absence, just as the demand for airline tickets is very high during Thanksgiving and Christmas as compared to the middle of July.

If we are discussing the demand for a particular make of a product, it is necessary to include the effects of the actions of competitors. Thus, if Subaru decides to offer "free" airconditioners in their cars, will the Rabbit's demand be affected? Most likely. It is not so much what competitors do that affects demand as the changes in quantity and quality of other options available to the consumer. Since we are discussing the demand for Rabbits, we use the competitor's action as an influencing variable.

Naturally, governments play a very central role in the case of demand for certain commodities. For example, if the government convinces you that Rabbits cause cancer, you will probably look for a different brand of car; or, if the American dollar is devalued by the government, Rabbits will cost more and you may be persuaded to make alternate arrangements.

Psychological factors as well as other attributes possessed by the product influence demand. For example, the Rabbit may be so designed as to appeal to a person's masculinity. Or you may consider the Rabbit "cute." Product designers spend a good amount of resources to explore the many possible advantages associated with little known psychological factors. In addition to the psychological variables, the ethnic or cultural background of the buyers also affects demand. A good Hindu will not buy a car that has good cowhide seat covers!

Institutions, particularly financial ones, exert a good deal of influence on the demand for many goods and services. For example, low interest rates on loans offered by the banks can encourage the sale of homes, while effective advertising by the producers can also increase demand substantially. Note, however, that the demand for Rabbits varies inversely with the quantity of advertising by Subaru. Why?

The Price–Quantity Demand Function

Although the preceding discussion suggests that many variables affect demand, one of the more significant variables is the price of the product. Because the majority of microeconomics models use price-related phenomena, it is essential that we discuss the price–quantity demand function. When all other variables are assumed to be constant, the quantity demanded varies inversely with the price of the good. This basic concept is the "law" of demand. Thus, if we allow the price of Rabbits to fall, and hold the other variables constant, we will expect more Rabbits to be demanded.

Figure 4-1 summarizes the derivation of the price demand curve from an indifference map. Here we see that the consumer's income and taste are given by the budget constraint and the set of indifference curves. Initially the consumer is maximizing utility at point A and purchasing X_A units of X. When the price of X falls, the consumer moves along the PCL (price-induced consumption locus) to points B, C, and D. When quantities at the points A, B, C, and D are transferred to a price–quantity plane, we have the demand for product X as a function of its price, ceteris paribus.

The demand curve D_X tells us that the quantity demanded will increase with price cuts and decrease with price hikes. *The movement will be strictly along the demand curve.* However, if one of the "other" factors is allowed to change, then it is entirely possible that the demand curve will "shift" to a new position, indicating a change in demand. Thus, demand D_X^2 corresponds to a larger amount of demand than demand D_X. For example, if the income of the buyers increases, the demand for X will tend to increase even if the price of X does not change. Generalizing what was said before, we may say that whenever price alone changes, the consumer moves along the given demand curve in keeping with the law of demand. But, if other factors are allowed to vary, the demand is no longer the same and usually the consumer moves to a different point on a new demand function.

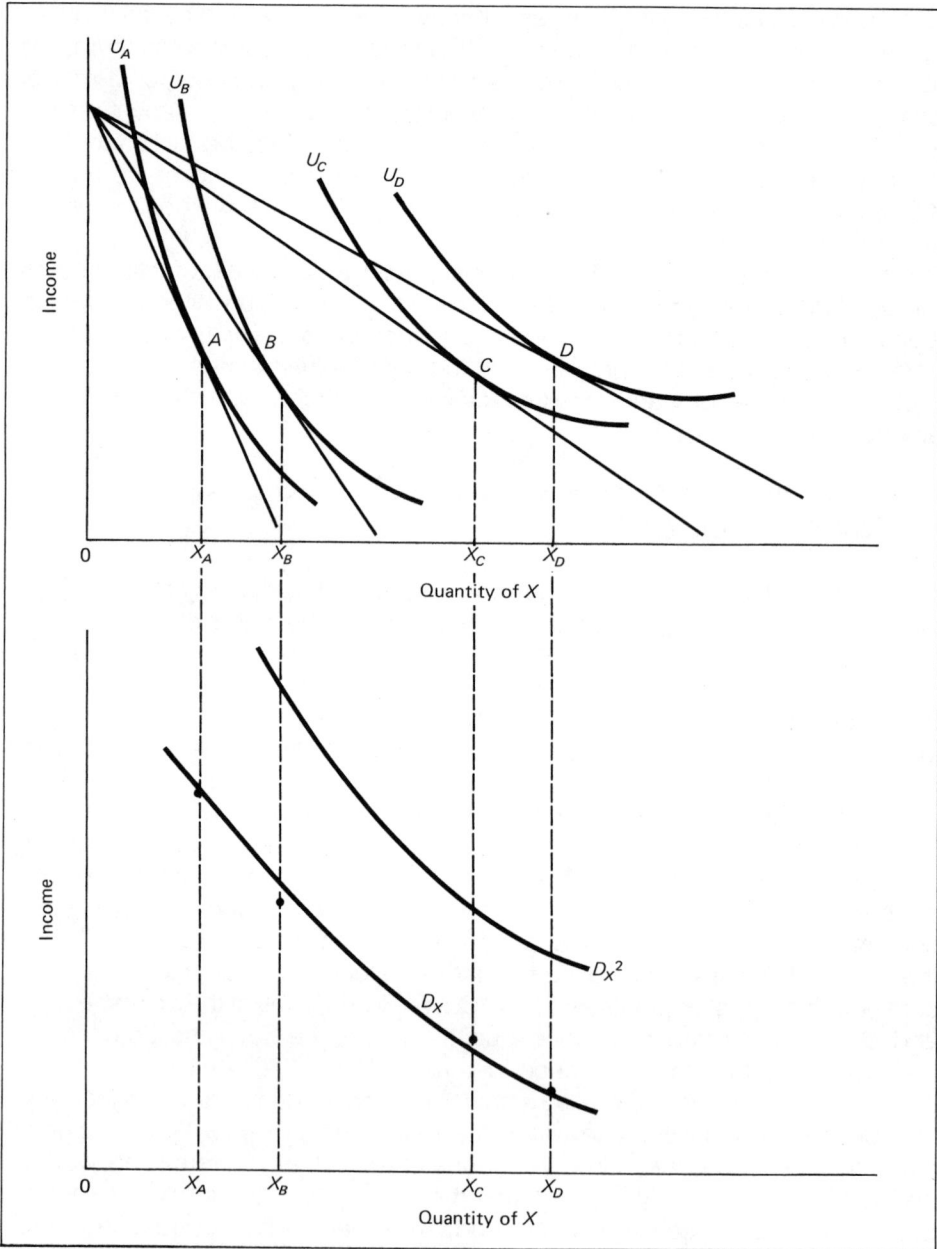

FIGURE 4-1
The derivation of demand curves from utility functions was studied in Chapter 3. This figure illustrates how we may obtain the price–quantity, ceteris paribus, demand function for X. In the upper panel we see the consumer maximizing utility at various points along the price-induced consumption locus, $ABCD$. When the corresponding quantities due to the price changes are plotted in a separate graph, as shown in the lower part of the figure, the demand for X emerges and is labelled D_X. The other demand for X, D_X^2, shows an increase in demand due to changes in "other" factors. If the price of the product changes, the consumer moves along the original demand curve. If other variables change, the demand function shifts. D_X^2, for example, indicates an increase in demand.

ELASTICITY OF DEMAND

Since demand is affected by many variables, it is important to consider the response of quantity to changes in these variables. For example, is the quantity of table salt demanded very sensitive to its price? Having knowledge of the sensitivity of demand to the many variables is essential to the understanding or predicting of consumer demand behavior.

In economics, we use the *elasticity of demand* to indicate the relative sensitivity of demand to the change in a particular variable. Thus, the *price elasticity of demand* tells us how responsive demand is to the change in the price of the product. In general, the elasticity of demand with respect to a particular variable *measures the ratio of the relative change in quantity demanded to the relative change in the variable under question.* Price elasticity of demand, for example, compares the percentage change in the quantity of a product to the percentage change in the variable that brought about the change in demand. Because all elasticity values end up as numbers, they are sometimes referred to as *elasticity coefficients.*

Price Elasticity of Demand

The price elasticity of demand is the ratio of the percentage change in quantity demanded to the percentage change in price of the product, all other factors remaining equal. Why do we use percentages instead of the actual absolute values? One of the reasons is that when measured in percentages, the changes are more meaningful. For example, if you are told that house prices have increased by $1000, you really wouldn't know whether the increase is substantial or insignificant. The $1000 increase is a paltry 1% change for $100,000 homes, but a hefty 20% for a house that sold for $5000; or, the measurement of body temperature is rather nonsensical unless we have a basis for comparison. Think how simple it would be to measure the relative amount of fever if the normal temperature were 100°F!

Despite heavy objections from mathematicians, we will denote elasticity with the letter e and, more specifically, we will use e_p for the price elasticity of demand. Thus, we may define the price elasticity of demand as

$$e_P = \frac{\text{Percentage change in } Q}{\text{Percentage change in } P}$$

The e_p is called the *price-elasticity coefficient.* A value of -2 for this coefficient is interpreted as meaning a 1% change in price leads to a 2% change in the quantity demanded. Because the coefficient is negative, it is indicative of the negative relationship of quantity to price. The larger the value of this coefficient, the greater the response of quantity demanded to price changes. A product whose demand is not very sensitive to price will not exhibit large changes in quantitites demanded when prices change. The fundamental concept of the price-elasticity of demand should be thoroughly understood, since it has many useful applications.

Price elasticity of demand is defined as the ratio of the two percentages, or

$$e_P = \frac{\%\Delta Q}{\%\Delta P} \qquad\qquad (2)$$

The percentages are computed by comparing the change of value to the original value. If prices fall from $1 a pound of ground beef to 90¢ a pound, the change will be 10¢ per pound; but the *relative* change in price will be 10¢ in $1 or 100¢, which will amount to 10%. So we can express the elasticity formula as

$$e_P = \frac{\%\text{ change in quantity}}{\%\text{ change in price}} = \frac{\Delta Q/Q}{\Delta P/P}$$

$$= \frac{\Delta Q}{\Delta P} \times \frac{P}{Q}$$

$$= \frac{(P/Q)}{\Delta P/\Delta Q} = \frac{(\text{price/quantity})}{\text{slope of demand function}} \qquad\qquad (3)$$

Equation (3) is the *point elasticity of demand.*

Figure 4-2 shows a linear demand function. Because the demand curve is a straight line, its slope is always constant. Slope in this formulation shows the ratio of the vertical to the horizontal, or $\Delta P/\Delta Q$. Using the elasticity expression $e_p = (\text{price/quantity})/\text{slope}$, we see that the elasticity value changes with changing prices because price changes cause quantity to change. The higher the price, the lower the quantity and hence the larger the *negative* value of the elasticity coefficient. The lower the price, the higher the quantity and the smaller the negative value of the price elasticity of demand. As we move down the demand curve of Figure 4-2, we can see that its slope does not change but the ratio P/Q does; in fact, it gets smaller. If we disregard the sign of the elasticity coefficient and only analyze the *absolute value,* such a value will be very high at high prices and low at low prices for the reasons explained above.

The way the demand curve is drawn it is evident that its slope is −2 or, more precisely, −80:40. The figure also indicates that each two dollar cut in price increases quantity demanded by one more unit. At a price of $60 the quantity demanded is 10, because at a price of $80 the demand is zero. Using

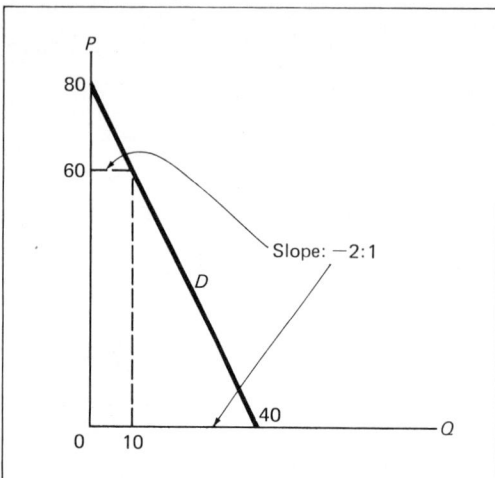

FIGURE 4-2
Elasticity versus slope of demand function.

our definition of elasticity, we can determine the value at this point as being equal to $(60/10)/-2 = -3$ or, in absolute terms, 3.

Arc and Exact Elasticities of Demand

So far we have defined the elasticity of demand as the ratio of the percentage change in quantity demanded to the percentage change in price, without specifying the direction of the change in price. In measuring the value of elasticities, the answers may differ depending on whether we are evaluating price increases or price decreases. To alleviate certain problems, there are alternative methods of computing the price elasticities.

Suppose a portion of the price–quantity demand is as shown.

Price	Quantity Demanded
$10	100 units
8	140 units

In calculating the elasticity of demand between the two prices we compute the percentage changes as before. However, the values of the coefficient will be different depending on whether we are talking about price increases or price reductions. If we calculate the elasticity value for a price decrease, then the price of $10 and quantity of 100 will have to be treated as the original values and a price of $8 and quantity of 140 will be the subsequent values. In this case, the percentage changes in price and quantity will be relative to the original values which constitute the bases for comparison. The percentage change in quantity will be a 40% increase caused by a 20% decrease in price. The elasticity of demand will then be -2.

Will we obtain identical values for e_p if we specify that prices increase from $8 to $10? The $8 figure will now be the original value, or the base, and the 140 units will form the base for the computation of the relative changes. Here the percentage decrease in quantity from 140 to 100 units will be 40 in 140, or 28.57%, whereas the price increase from $8 to $10 will constitute an increase of $2 in $8, or 25%. The price elasticity of demand in going from $8 to $10 will be the ratio of -28.75% to 25% or -1.14. The two elasticity values are substantially different. To avoid such discrepancies which result from the use of different bases we employ the arc-elasticity method which, in effect, uses an *average base* for the prices and quantities by determining the *midpoints* between the "old" and "new" values. To illustrate:

	Price	Quantity demanded	
	$10	100	
Average price:	9	120	Average quantity
	8	140	

The percentage changes are now calculated with the use of these average figures. Thus, the percentage change in quantity will be 40/120, or the change in quantity over the average quantity and the percentage change in price will amount to $2 in $9. The elasticity coefficient then turns out to be (40/120) ÷ (2/9) = 1.5 regardless of the direction of change in price. The number 1.5 is the absolute value of the arc-price elasticity of demand and realistically should be expressed as −1.5, since quantity varies inversely with price. The formula for arc-elasticity of demand with respect to price changes becomes

$$e_{\text{p-arc}} = \frac{\dfrac{Q_2 - Q_1}{(Q_2 + Q_1)/2}}{\dfrac{P_2 - P_1}{(P_2 + P_1)/2}}$$

which reduces to

$$\frac{(Q_2 - Q_1)/(Q_2 + Q_1)}{(P_2 - P_1)/(P_2 + P_1)}$$

Economists also use another variation for the measurement of price-elasticity of demand, which they maintain provides us with a more *exact* value. The so-called "exact" method for elasticity computations when two prices and two quantities are involved uses the *smaller* of the two prices as well as the *smaller* of the two quantities as the bases. We will use the same. demand schedule as before to illustrate this method.

Price	Quantity demanded
$10	100 units
8	140 units

Here the actual changes are $2 and 40 units for price and quantity, respectively. The base for quantity will be 100 units since it is the smaller of the two quantities and the base for the price will be $8, since it is the smaller of the two prices. The price elasticity of demand then becomes

$$|e_p| = \frac{40/100}{2/8} = \frac{40\%}{25\%} = 1.6$$

in *absolute* terms.

So we now have four values for the elasticity coefficient for the same two sets of price and quantity. We have −2 for price decreases, −1.14 for price increases, −1.5 via the arc method, and finally −1.6 if we use the exact method. Any one of the methods is valid depending on the circumstances surrounding the problem. When in doubt, use either the arc or the exact method unless otherwise specified.

Regardless of which method we use, the problem is limited to the correct choice of the bases for price and quantity. To summarize our discussion we will list the methods once more.

In general the price elasticity of demand $= \dfrac{\text{\% change in quantity}}{\text{\% change in price}}$

Point–elasticity method: elasticity $= \dfrac{\text{price/quantity}}{\text{slope of demand function}}$

Arc-elasticity method: elasticity $= \dfrac{\text{(difference of quantities)/(sum of quantities)}}{\text{(difference of prices)/(sum of prices)}}$

Exact-elasticity method: elasticity $= \dfrac{\text{(difference of quantities)/(smaller quantity)}}{\text{(difference of prices)/(smaller price)}}$

The presence or absence of price elasticity is determined by the value of the elasticity coefficient, and its absolute value will be used to explain the following guidelines. Demand is considered to be price-elastic if

$$|e_p| > 1$$

price-inelastic if

$$|e_p| < 1$$

Demand is considered *elastic* if the proportionate change in quantity exceeds the proportionate change in price, for then and only then will $|e_p|$ exceed one. Products whose quantities do not respond much to price changes will exhibit *inelastic* demand, because the quantity change measured in percentages will be less than the corresponding percentage change in price. In rare situations, where the percentage changes in quantity and price are equal, demand is *unit-elastic,* because the $|e_p|$ will equal one.

DETERMINANTS OF PRICE ELASTICITY

The price elasticity affects the quantity demanded resulting from a price change. Some products such as common table salt tend to have low price elasticity. It is unlikely that we will buy much more salt if its price falls, nor will we buy any less if its price rises by reasonable amounts. Other likely products with basically inelastic demand are rubber bands, gasoline for subsistence, first-class postage stamps, minimum required health care, and required microeconomic textbooks! Some items with fairly elastic demand might include expensive color TV sets, ski vacations, 14-speed bicycles, brand-X soap, detergent, and supplementary reference books in microeconomics. In general, the determinants of elasticity are mainly:

a. the number of substitutes for the product;
b. the percentage of the budget spent on the item;
c. the number of different uses served by the product;
d. the type of product (luxury versus necessity); and
e. The time period under discussion (long run versus short run).

The greater the number of substitutes available for a product, the more likely quantity will change following price changes, because consumers can readily substitute this product for the others or switch from the other substitutes to this one. For example, if the price of Sony Trinitrons drops from $563 to $481, it is conceivable that some potential users of Zenith will buy the Sony and others in the market for a new TV set will probably consider the Sony a good buy (or substitute) as compared to other brands in its price range. Demand for transportation via the personal automobile might be highly inelastic, because the average American does not believe there are suitable substitutes for it within the relevant range. Consequently, even if such transportation becomes more costly—via the higher price of gasoline, automobile excise taxes, and increased toll charges—the average use of the auto for transportation may not decline substantially.

Normally we spend a very small percentage of our budget or income on the purchase of rubber bands, paper clips, and table salt. But we spend a porportionately larger amount on housing, food, clothing, and entertainment. So when the prices of the items that involve a small percentage of the budget change, there is likely to be negligible change in the quantities of these items consumed. The amount spent does not cause a big dent in our income. On the other hand, if the price of ski vacations increases, we might have to be content with buying new furniture or watching more television on a relatively cheaper but new substitute; or, if the interest rate on new mortgages goes up, the monthly payments under ordinary circumstances will rise also and probably discourage some would-be home owners.

The different number of uses that a product can be put to can also influence the elasticity of demand. For instance, margarine is used not only for cooking but also in baking bread and cookies and as a bread spread. If the price of margarine changes, the quantities used will probably change and this, in turn, will cause demand to be quite elastic.*

We have discussed price elasticity in terms of slopes at some length. In reality, the demand curves for certain products might exhibit the shape postulated in Figure 4-3. Here we see the demand for gasoline for use in automobile transportation as having a variety of slopes and elasticities. It seems that the maximum demand occurs at a price of $0.18 or less per gallon. As the price rises from 18¢ to 30¢ a gallon, the quantity demanded is affected appreciably, but little change occurs in the range of 30–55¢. At prices of 55–95¢ per gallon demand is virtually unchanged, implying that some minimum level of gasoline will be demanded regardless of its price. If the price rises above 95¢ a gallon some reduction in quantity demanded will take place and above $1.10 the quantity demanded will not fall appreciably because some users will continue to use a certain amount of gasoline irrespective of its price. The

*We must be careful in the evaluation of elasticity. Arm and Hammer baking soda has many uses around the house, and precisely because of this reason demand might be quite *inelastic*. Conceivably the householder might be willing to put up with the new price even though it may be higher than before, in order to have the convenience of a good-for-all-occasions panacea. Table salt serves another good example. It, too, has many alternative uses. Such an unusual property coupled with the lack of substitutes provides for a rather price-inelastic demand. We must remember that all the determinants of elasticity discussed above do not necessarily operate in the same direction. For example, in the case of table salt, very few substitutes make demand inelastic, whereas many uses should make demand more elastic. It is the net effect that is important.

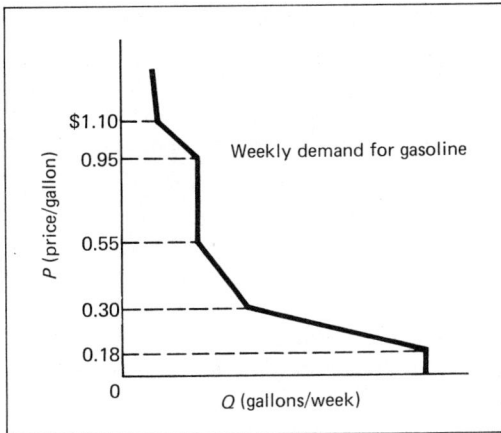

FIGURE 4-3
Although we draw smooth demand curves for purposes of discussion, in reality the demand functions might have very peculiar shapes. The figure reveals the varying degrees of response of gasoline demand to the price. For example, the quantity of gasoline demanded is more sensitive to its price in the range 0.18–0.30 as compared to the price range 0.55–0.95. The greater the response of quantity to price, the higher the price elasticity of demand.

demand for gasoline as illustrated serves to bring out the problem faced by decision makers in government who wish to discourage gasoline consumption via price increases. Even if price rises from 55¢ to 95¢ a gallon, the consumption of gasoline will not drop substantially—it will end up causing hardship on the very poor who have to have that certain amount of gasoline in order to commute to work.

It makes a difference for elasticity discussions whether the time period during which the price change takes place is brief or relatively long. Generally speaking, the *short-run time period* is defined as that length of time during which the consumers may not, cannot, and will not change their consumption habits despite price changes. Gasoline prices provide a good illustration. When the price of gasoline starts to rise, many users cannot afford to consume any less in the short run because they have no alternate arrangement for transportation. Furthermore, to many the increased price of gasoline is of small concern over the short run.

The "long run" on the other hand, allows considerable changes in quantity to take place. The United States is already planning for the long-run reduction of gasoline consumption by enacting various policies such as taxation of gas-guzzling automobiles, promotion of public transportation, and taxation of gasoline. In the long run the consumers themselves may find alternatives to using their own cars all the time. The rise of "car-pooling" or the increased usage of public transportation facilities illustrates the changeover from earlier traditions. In the long run there may also be more substitutes that the consumers may choose from. Thus the steps to produce economically feasible electric and solar cars have brought much encouragement from the private and public sectors and have altered the purchase decision of many car buyers of the future. Smaller cars or fuel-efficient vehicles are in big demand and, not surprisingly, command high prices. The use of motorcycles and "mopeds" is increasing.

In general, keeping in mind the exceptions, the caveats, and the contribution of "net effects," we may state: The larger the number of available substitutes for a product, the larger the percentage of income devoted to its purchase; the greater the number of uses it provides, the less absolute its necessity for "survival;" and the longer the time period under contemplation, the more price-elastic its demand.

Elasticity versus Slope of Demand Function

Many students of economics are guilty of equating elasticity with "flatness" of a demand curve. While this may be true in some instances, judging elasticity from the inclination of a demand curve is quite erroneous. Flatter demand curves are not necessarily more elastic. Regardless of the flatness or the steepness of the demand curve, it is the ratio of the relative changes of quantity and price that determines the value of price elasticity.

Take, for example, the two demand curves D_1 and D_2 shown in Figure 4-4. The two prices on D_1 are \$40 and \$30 and the corresponding quantities are 5 and 10, respectively. A price reduction from \$40 to \$30 constitutes a 25% change, while the quantity demanded increases by 100%. However, for identical price changes, D_2 indicates that the quantity demanded will change from 20 to 30 units, or show an increase of only 50%. Thus, computed very simply, the price elasticity of demand for D_1 will have an absolute value of 4, while D_2's elasticity will be only 2. If we had used the flatness test, D_2 would have been more elastic, although the opposite is true.

CONSUMER EXPENDITURES AND PRICE ELASTICITY

Usually the quantities purchased differ with price. Does the consumer spend equal amounts for such purchases or substantially different ones when

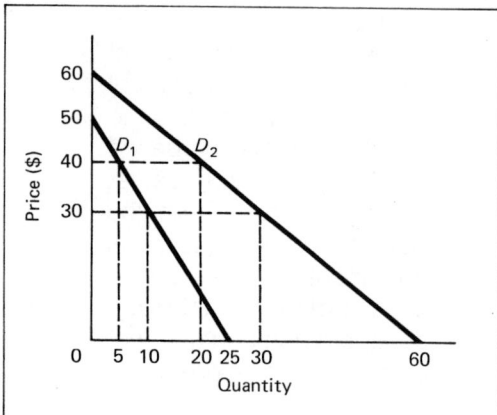

FIGURE 4-4
There is occasionally a misconception that the "flatter" the demand function, the more elastic it is. Here we see that demand curve D_2 is flatter than demand function D_1. When you examine the percentage changes in quantity and price, however, demand D_1 is more price elastic than demand D_2.

prices change? The value of the price elasticity of demand will reveal the relationship of expenditures to prices. Expenditures on a good are expressed by the product of the price per unit and the quantities of the units demanded. Thus,

$$\text{expenditures or } E = P \times Q \tag{4}$$

Equation (4) tells us that E will change if P and Q change. We know that as P changes Q will, too, but in the opposite direction. If price is reduced, the quantity demanded will increase. If Q increases by a larger percentage than P decreases, E will have to increase. If demand is price elastic, that is, if $|e_p|$ is greater than one, the percentage change in Q will exceed the percentage change in P and a price reduction will lead to an increase in expenditures. *When demand is price elastic, P and E move in opposite directions.* The increase in quantity will more than offset the decrease in price, causing E to increase. This "law" also holds if we consider price increases.

The left-hand diagram of Figure 4-5(a) shows the price–quantity relationship of the demand for shoes. At a price of $80 the quantity demanded is 2000 pairs; at a price of $64 the demand is 50% more. The price reduction in moving from point A to point B is less than the corresponding increase in quantity demanded when price and quantity are expressed as percentages. This is indicative of elastic demand. When demand is elastic a price reduction leads to greater expenditures, and this is shown via the *price expenditure* line of the figure to the right. At the higher price $160,000 was being spent, but this quantity increases to $192,000 at a lower price. To show the inverse relationship of expenditures to price we move from point C to point D.

Figure 4-5(b) shows the case of inelastic demand. Here the percentage change in quantity is less than the percentage change in price. When demand is inelastic, a price reduction brings about lower expenditures. Again at a price of $80 the expenditures amount to $160,000, but at a lower price of $64 the total expenditures are $153,600. *The expenditures vary positively, or directly, with price if the demand is price inelastic.*

When price elasticity of demand equals unity, the expenditures are unaffected by price changes.

CROSS-PRICE ELASTICITY OF DEMAND

Normally we measure the price elasticity of demand for a product with respect to its own price. The elasticity which compares the demand for one product to the price of a related product is known as the *cross-price elasticity of demand*. The definition of this elasticity is very similar to the price elasticity already discussed and the methodology of measurement applies here, too. If we determine the degree of substitutability of X for Y via this method, we can compare the percentage change in the demand for X to the percentage change in the price of Y. The cross-price elasticity of demand with respect to the P_y in equation form is

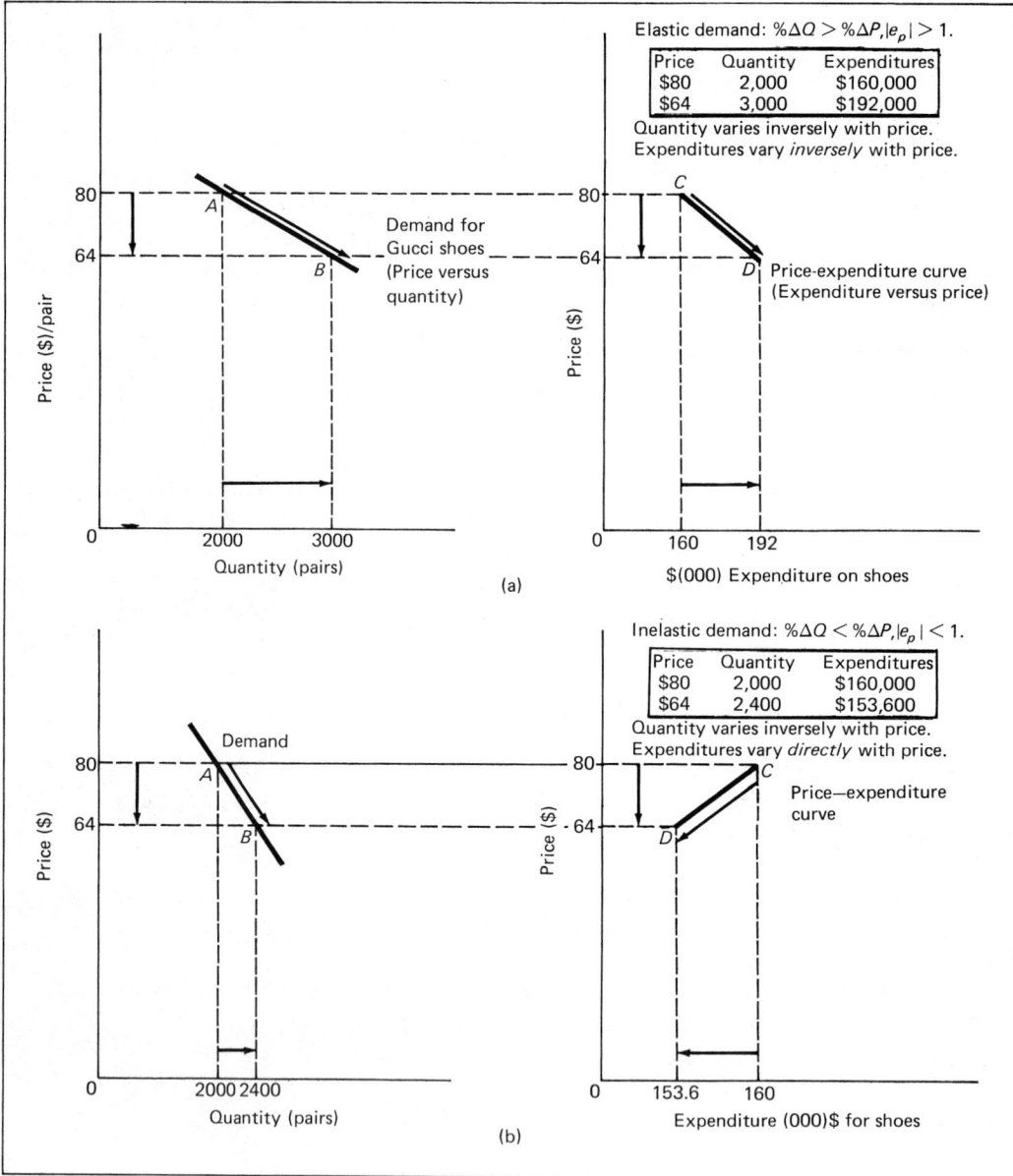

FIGURE 4-5
When demand is elastic, expenditures vary inversely with price, and when demand is inelastic, expenditures vary positively with price. Thus, in (a), the demand for Gucci shoes is shown to be price elastic, and hence when price falls, expenditures on shoes increase. In (b), demand is shown to be inelastic, and therefore as price falls, expenditures on shoes also decline.

$$\frac{e_X}{P_Y} = \frac{\text{\% change in quantity of } X \text{ demanded}}{\text{\% change in the price of } Y}$$

The result will be greater than 0 if the products are substitutes. You can see why *this elasticity is positive for substitutes* because an *increase* in the price of Y leads to an *increase* in the demand for X. The demand for X varies *positively* with the price of substitute Y. The larger the value of e_X/P_Y, the greater the change in the demand for X arising out of changes in P_Y. In general, the *cross-price elasticity of demand among complements is usually negative.*

INCOME ELASTICITY OF DEMAND

The income of the buyers provides the ability to demand goods and services. Some products exhibit close association with the levels of income, whereas the demands for many items are remotely dependent on income. The demand for luxury items, such as expensive, famous French champagne, may very well be dependent on income but the demand for table salt may not. The sensitivity of demand to income is the *income-elasticity of demand.* The larger the value of this coefficient, the greater the response of quantity demanded to changes in income. Those products whose demand responds positively with income are *normal goods,* and those products which respond by extraordinary amounts are *superior* or, according to some, *ultrasuperior.* If a 1% increase in income leads to 20% additional demand, the income elasticity of demand will be 20 and this item presumably will be classified as being ultrasuperior, whereas if the same 1% increase in income leads to only 1½% additional demand, we will call it a case of the normal good. As before, the income elasticity coefficient is derived by dividing the percentage change in quantity by the percentage change in income, and will normally be a positive number.

Occasionally, however, the quantity demanded will vary inversely with income—that is, the quantity demanded will *decrease* as income increases. Such products are termed *inferior* goods, and possess negative income elasticity. An example might be the demand for swimming facilities at a public or municipal pool. As the incomes of the users rise above a certain level, their demand for such pool usage might decrease because they now have the ability to own and use their own private pools or conceivably have the tendency to use the pools operated by private clubs or organizations; or the demand for coach-class airplane tickets might vary inversely with the income of regular travelers because they will now prefer to fly in first-class comfort and consider the coach style travel as an inferior substitute relative to their present income. Ground beef demand is a good illustration of product inferiority. If we plot a demand curve showing quantity versus income, we will derive an *income–quantity* (as opposed to price–quantity) *demand curve* which is also called an *Engel curve.*

Income elasticity of demand compares the relative change of quantity demanded to relative changes in income. We can compute the size of the coefficient if the values of the quantities and income are readily available. In the

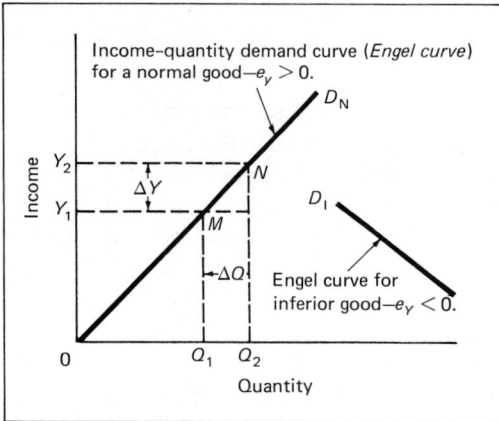

Income–quantity demand curve (*Engel curve*) for a normal good—$e_y > 0$.

D_N

Y_2

ΔY

Y_1

N

D_I

M

ΔQ

Engel curve for inferior good—$e_y < 0$.

Income

Q_1 Q_2

Quantity

FIGURE 4-6
An Engel curve is an income–quantity demand curve. If the product is *normal,* quantity demanded, *ceteris paribus,* varies positively with income, and if it is *inferior,* quantity varies negatively with income. Demand D_N represents a normal good, because the quantity increases as income increases. Demand D_I shows an inferior good since the quantity decreases as income increases. Both D_N and D_I are Engel curves.

absence of numbers, we can still judge the elasticity via the graphical method. We will employ the graph of Figure 4-6 to explain this method. The elasticity e_y is defined as % change in Q ÷ % change in Y, or

$$e_y = \frac{\Delta Q/Q_1}{\Delta Y/Y_1} = \frac{Y_1/Q_1}{\Delta Y/\Delta Q} = \frac{\text{(original income)/(original quantity)}}{\text{slope of Engel curve}}$$

If the consumer was originally at point M and subsequently moves to point N, the changes in income and quantity will be (Y_2-Y_1) and (Q_2-Q_1), respectively, and the expression for e_y will be

$$\frac{Y_1/Q_1}{(Y_2 - Y_1)/(Q_2 - Q_1)} = \frac{Y_1/Q_1}{\Delta Y/\Delta Q}$$

Because $Y_1/Q_1 = \Delta Y/\Delta Q$, as long as the Engel curve is linear and emanates from the origin, $e_y = 1$.

Not all Engel curves are positively sloped, nor are they always linear starting from the origin. The Engel curves for *inferior goods,* or those goods whose consumption declines at higher incomes, are negatively inclined, as shown in Figure 4-6. These goods have *negative income elasticity.* Figure 4-7 illustrates the Engel curves for two goods—(a) food and (b) entertainment. The demand for food is, in general, such that increases in income bring about correspondingly smaller additional increments of demand. Consequently, the income–quantity demand curve for food shows that demand increases at a decreasing rate. By our earlier definition of elasticity, the value of the coefficient at point Z will be $Y_1/Q_1 \div ZQ_1/TQ_1$, or the slope given by angle n ÷ the slope subtended by angle m. Thus the income elasticity of demand at point Z is less than one. You can verify that for entertainment, the income elasticity of demand at point Z in (b) $(n° > m°)$ is greater than one. Here we see that Q increases with Y at an increasing rate. Conceivably, unlike food demand, consumers usually consume and demand more entertainment at higher levels of income. Food is a necessity, whereas some type (or certain quantity) of entertainment is not. Entertainment is *income elastic* in demand, whereas food demand is usually

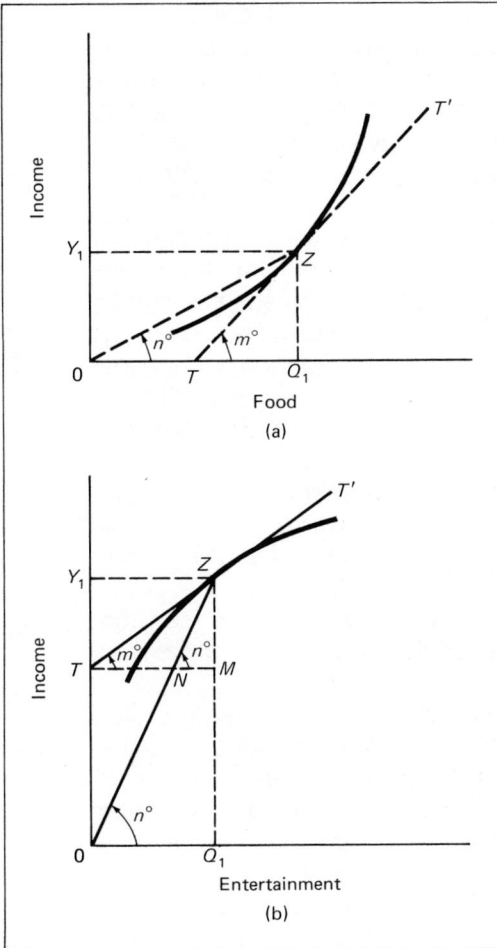

FIGURE 4-7
The income elasticity of demand at a point on
the income–quantity demand function is the
ratio of the slope of a line from the origin to that
point to the slope of the tangent drawn at that
point. Thus, in (a), this ratio at Z equals
$(ZQ_1/OQ_1)/(ZQ_1/TQ_1)$, or TQ_1/OQ_1, whose value
is less than 1. Similarly, the income elasticity of
demand at point Z in (b) is greater than 1.

rather *income inelastic,* and some type of food may even turn inferior at
sufficiently high income levels. As a rule, the greater the price elasticity, the
greater the income elasticity. This will be linked to the derivation of the
relationship between these two types of elasticities.

SOME OTHER ELASTICITIES

Institutional factors or variables necessarily affect the demand for a
product. Such considerations as the political climate, the income distribution
patterns of the consumers, the level of development of the infra-structure, the
social mores, the education–literacy level, government policies, and the
financial system should also be analyzed in the study of demand. There is no
specific type of elasticity that measures the relationship of demand to such
institutional variables. Each one will have to be examined separately. For

example, if the money supply growth rate for the economy increases and brings down the interest rates and increases credit availability, investment by businesses and spending by consumers will probably increase. Changes in investment demand due to changes in interest rates are analyzed by the *interest elasticity of investment demand,* and changes in demand for consumption due to more credit can be explained via the *credit elasticity of consumption demand.*

The number of buyers and the magnitude of demand usually go hand in hand. Unless we have information about the compositon of the population, we cannot say what types of goods will be demanded or how large such demands might be. Something like the demand for gasoline will certainly be positively related to the number of people driving cars, so that if immigration occurs, the demand for gasoline—at least, for a while—will increase. It is quite possible that some inhabitants, who are intolerant of big populations or crowded cities, will leave, thereby reducing their part of gasoline demand; or, consider the case where the demographers point out the increased tendency to have larger families—this will eventually increase the demand for housing. The elasticity relating demand to the number of consumers involved is the *population elasticity of demand.* The demand for made-to-order $132,000 Rolls Royces is probably not very population elastic, whereas the demand for sewage treatment facilities in a city probably is. What about the demand for fire and police protection?

Advertising plays a significant role in persuading the consumer to prefer one type of product over another. It also provides certain knowledge to the buyers. It is reasonable to assume, then, that the quantity and quality of advertising on behalf of a particular brand of margarine will have a certain influence on the consumer. The *advertising elasticity of demand* measures the response or sensitivity of demand to advertising, the elasticity coefficient being the ratio of the percentage change in quantity to the percentage change in the amount of advertising. Usually this number will be positive, showing that demand responds positively with advertising.

Finally, we come to a very important section of demand theory, namely that which concerns the attributes or qualitative features of a product. The demand for a product will most definitely be influenced by the many qualities it possesses. One person might prefer 100% nylon fabrics to 100% cotton ones because the first make him *feel good.* The author avoids wearing pure wool but accepts a gift of a Pendleton shirt given to him on his birthday by his wife! Some people strongly prefer round tables to square ones. Demand, then, will vary according to the quality and quantity of attributes, and even here we can conceptually discuss various elasticities. For instance, if the durability of a particular make of refrigerator goes up, it is quite possible that the demand for such a brand of refrigerator will also increase.

It should have become clear by now that there are as many types of elasticities as there are variables, and we have discussed a few of the salient ones. Any coefficient of elasticity (of demand) measures the ratio of percentage change in quantity demanded to the percentage change in a particular variable. As a summary of elasticity discussions, we have reproduced some of the basic demand elasticities in the coefficient form below. You are encouraged to investigate and formulate the many other types of elasticities of demand, including the income-tax elasticity of tithes!

$$\text{Price elasticity of demand: } E_p = \frac{\% \text{ change in } Q_x}{\% \text{ change in } P_x}$$

$$\text{Advertising elasticity: } E_a = \frac{\% \text{ change in } Q_x}{\% \text{ change in } A_x}$$

$$\text{Income elasticity: } E_y = \frac{\% \text{ change in } Q_x}{\% \text{ change in } Y}$$

$$\text{Population elasticity: } E_n = \frac{\% \text{ change in } Q_x}{\% \text{ change in } N}$$

$$\text{Cross-price elasticity: } E_{c_y} = \frac{\% \text{ change in } Q_x}{\% \text{ change in } P_y}$$

$$\text{Cross-advertising elasticity: } E_{a_y} = \frac{\% \text{ change in } Q_x}{\% \text{ change in } A_y}$$

$$\text{Elasticity of substitution: } \frac{E_x}{y} = \frac{\% \text{ change in } Q_x}{\% \text{ change in } Q_y}$$

$$\text{Market share elasticity: } E_m = \frac{\% \text{ change in market share of } X}{\% \text{ change in the price of } X}$$

COMMENTS

Demand analysis focuses attention on the determinants of demand as they influence consumer behavior. Although there are almost an infinite number of variables that influence a consumer's demand and, therefore, his decision to buy a product, several factors are more important than others. Generally speaking, prices and incomes play the dominant roles.

Demand functions indicate the general relationship of demand to the many variables that affect demand. From the all-inclusive demand functions, we can extract the ceteris-paribus demand curves, which relate quantity to either price or income or both. We can also use the indifference map to obtain a person's price–quantity or income–quantity demand functions from the PCL and ICL, respectively.

The elasticities of demand show the response of demand to each of the variables. Again, there are theoretically as many types of elasticities as there are variables. However, in most microeconomic discussions some play more important roles than others. Among the most widely used elasticities are the price, income, cross-price advertising, and population elasticities.

Demand theory suggests certain modes of behavior as predicted by the many models and their accompanying assumptions. Most of them are quite logical and highly straightforward. A good understanding of the theory of demand helps the decision makers in both the private and public sectors in formulating policies.

APPLICATIONS

1. Would You Buy a Car from This Man?

Because we have been discussing many variables that affect demand, a word about advertising is in order. It has been recognized that successful advertising brings forth additional demand and, furthermore, the success of the advertisement depends on its quality. In Figure 4-8a we show the presumed demand for the Continental Mark V by using three different movie and TV personalities. According to the three advertising–quantity curves shown, presumably Douglas Fairbanks, Jr., has the most appeal to potential buyers. Perhaps the "older swingers" and the *nouveau riche* like Fairbanks' style. Ricardo Montalban has somewhat less appeal than Fairbanks. We are using the graphs only to illustrate the concept of advertising elasticity of demand. We do not mean to suggest that Ricardo Montalban has any less *savoire faire* than the former screen hero of the *Prisoner of Zenda.* Conceivably, Montalban would be more effective in advertising a Cordoba. Again, by the same token, Red Foxx may have considerable influence on the buyers, but in our illustration has no effect. The two upward-sloping curves indicate that the demand for Continentals, influenced by additional advertising, increases at a decreasing rate. Why? We may conclude by saying that the demand for Continentals is more advertisement elastic when Fairbanks advertises as opposed to Montalban. Apparently, the elasticity coefficient with respect to advertising done by Foxx is zero. You will recognize that the success of an advertising campaign also depends on the amount of advertising expenditures in various media in addition to expenditures incurred by hiring different personalities. Thus a dollar of advertisement in the local newspaper might bring better results than an equal amount of advertising via radio.

Figure 4-8b tells a similar story. Steve McQueen, "Chips" Estrada, or Robert (Baretta) Blake will do more for motorcycle sales than Elton John. The way we have shown the relationships, too much advertisement by John may actually contribute to

---

FIGURE 4-8
Both (a) and (b) illustrate the probable effects of advertising on the demand for cars and motorcycles, all other factors remaining equal. In (a) we see that the sale of Continentals will be more influenced by Fairbanks and Montalban than by Foxx. As far as motorcycles are concerned, when they are endorsed by someone like McQueen, "Baretta," or "Chips" Estrada, their sales will be more influenced than by advertisements showing Elton John.

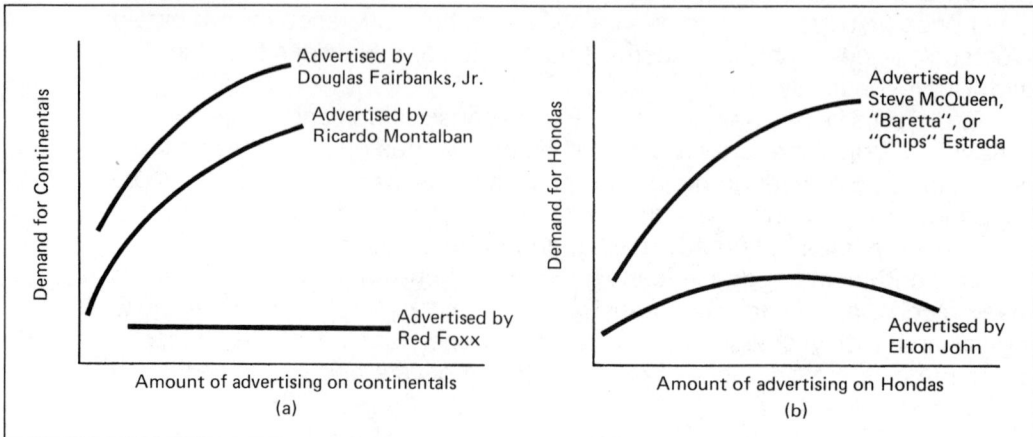

a declining demand for Hondas. This illustration is merely to expose advertising sensitivity of demand and in no way reflects the actual cause–effect behavior. The actual market conditions that affect elasticity and demand will have to be examined by experts in the field of advertising and Madison Avenue techniques. The Honda Corporation would pay the firm to use the "right" combination of advertising expenditures, media, and personalities to attract additional demand for its product. Does successful advertising make the price elasticity of demand higher or lower?

2. The Demand for Ground Beef

Figure 4-9 brings together various income elasticity considerations. As you can see, certain portions of this income-quantity demand curve are positively sloped and other sections are either negatively inclined (backward bending) or perfectly vertical. The product being analyzed is the ordinary variety (60% meat–40% ?) of ground beef. At an income level of Y_1, the consumer demands Q_1 amount of beef. If income rises to Y_2, the demand will increase to Q_2, making it a normal good in this range and, accordingly, e_y will be positive. Between the income levels of Y_2 and Y_3 the demand level does not change and, consequently, $e_y = 0$. Ground beef is considered *absolutely income inelastic* in this income range—presumably, the consumer is buying as much ground beef as she likes because she now has sufficient income. If income rises above Y_3 to Y_4, consumption of ground beef will be reduced because more of other cuts of meat will be bought instead of it, making ground beef an inferior product—this makes $e_y < 0$, or negative. Beyond Y_4 to Y_5, the consumption of ground beef is stabilized at quantity Q_4, indicating that no matter how high the income, the consumer will still like some amount of ground beef. Even the late John Paul Getty ate hamburgers once in a while, although it was served under glass. Why does the Engel curve start to move up to the right beyond income level Y_5? That is anybody's guess, but the author's is that if the consumer becomes that wealthy, maybe she can afford to feed ground beef to her St. Bernard!

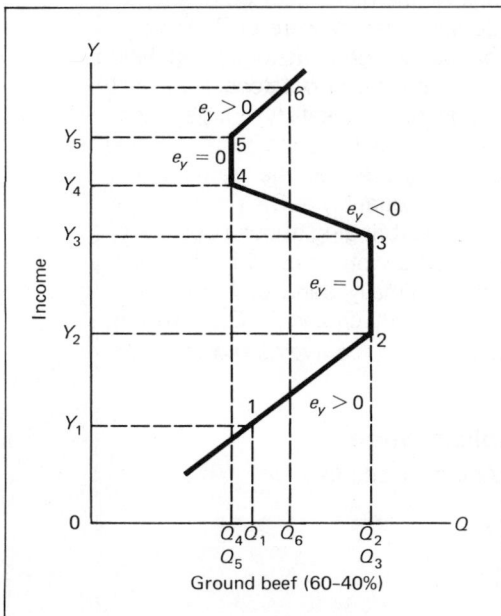

FIGURE 4-9
Income–quantity demand curve or the Engel curve for ground beef.

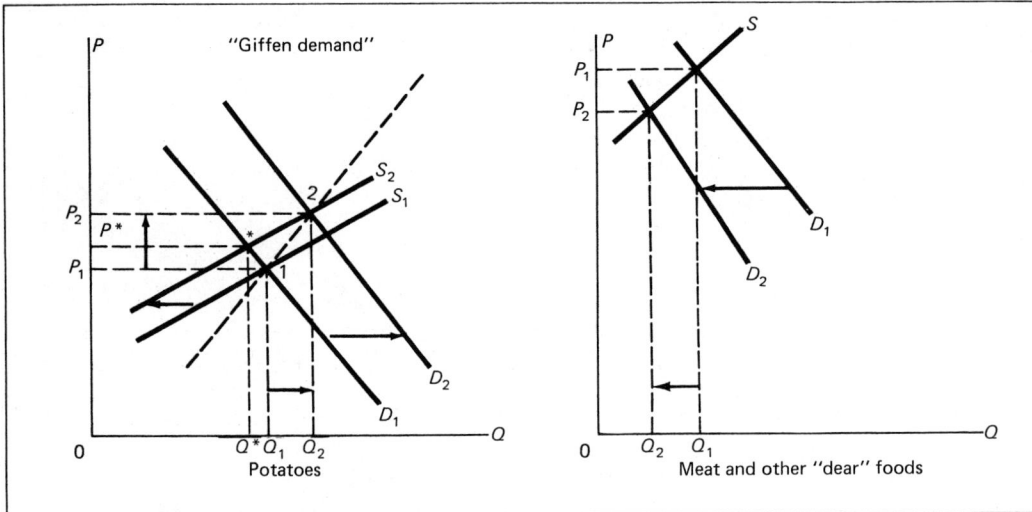

FIGURE 4-10
The "Giffen effect."

3. The Giffen Effect

A peculiar phenomenon observed in the market is the "Giffen effect." This refers to the "perverse" behavior of quantity changes to price changes—namely, the quantities bought vary *positively* with price. We might then conclude that such behavior invalidates the basic Law of Demand. This is not so, if we refer to Figure 4-10 in the case of demand for potatoes as observed by Mr. Giffen a long time ago in Ireland. During this time the average income of the Irish peasantry was abysmally low and because potatoes were relatively inexpensive, the diet consisted of a large amount of potatoes. Initially, the equilibrium price and quantity were at P_1 and Q_1, respectively. Due to natural hazards, the supply of potatoes decreased, forcing their price up to P^*, allowing the average Irish citizen to afford fewer potatoes. Because fewer potatoes in conjunction with the other foods did not satisfy hunger, and because potatoes were still *relatively* inexpensive, the Irish began to buy more potatoes, even at their higher price. Such behavior increased the demand for potatoes to D_2 and the price was stabilized at P_2 and the quantity at Q_2. You can see why the demand for meat and other foods had to decline, bringing about a decline in their price to P_2 and quantity to Q_2. In essence, the Law of Demand is still valid because the demand curves for potatoes are still "normally behaved." What Mr. Giffen observed was a series of market equilibria such as P_1–Q_1 and P_2–Q_2. If we join these two points, we will obtain an upward-sloping "demand" curve as shown by the dotted line labeled "Giffen demand."

4. The Demand For Adidas Shoes

Suppose researchers indicate the demand for Adidas shoes as

$$D_{Ad.} = 10,000 - 200P_{Ad} + 100P_{Puma} - 500P_{Te}$$

$$+ 50A_{Ad} - 100A_{Puma} + 300Y + 0.2N,$$

where

P_{Ad} = price of a pair of Adidas shoes = \$30.00;

P_{Puma} = price of a pair of shoes made by a competitor = $28.00;
P_{Te} = price of tennis equipment and memberships at clubs = $20.00;
A_{Ad} = amount (and quality) of advertising by Adidas = $2000.00;
A_{Puma} = amount (and quality) of advertising by Puma = $3200.00;
Y = average income of the community = $10,000.00;
N = potential number of tennis-shoe users = 6000.

If we substitute all the known values into the demand equation, we will come up with the quantity of Adidas shoes that will be demanded under the existing conditions. Notice that many of the variables are introduced without much regard to the time frame or the units of measurement. For example, it might not make too much sense to assign $20 as the price of "tennis equipment and club membership." There are sophisticated methods of model building and *econometrics* which take care of such problems. It is more important for us to understand the concepts at this time. Thus, the total Ad will equal 2.778 million pairs. If we want an ordinary demand curve that shows demand as a function of price, all other things remaining equal, all we need to do is to substitute the values for all the variables except the price of Adidas shoes. The demand function will then look like

$$Ad = 2.784m - 200P_{Ad}. \tag{5}$$

Similarly, we can also derive an income-quantity demand curve which will look something like

$$Ad = (constant) = 300Y \tag{6}$$

Equation (5) tells us that, all other things remaining equal, the quantity of Adidas shoes demanded will vary negatively with its price. Equation (6) shows us the positive relationship of Ad to Y if all other things are assumed to be constant.

5. Conspicuous Consumption Demand

Actually, there are situations where the quantities of a good bought in the market may rise with price increases. These goods are normally very expensive and presumably are of "very high quality." Consequently, the buyers associate price with quality and some buyers prefer to buy the item if and only if the price is high enough, for example, the market for aspirin. Many people buy Bayer aspirin at $2.50 per hundred as compared to the drugstore-brand-name type at $0.50 per hundred, and there are yet others who will not buy a particular brand of aspirin unless the price is at least $3.75 per hundred. It is conceivable that more new buyers will enter the market at very high prices even though many would-be buyers drop out because of very high prices. If there is a net increase in the quantity demanded at successively higher price, we will, in fact, have a market demand curve for a particular brand of aspirin which will be positively inclined. Usually such commodities are labelled as *Veblen goods,* named after the American social scientist Thorstein Veblen, famous for his book *The Theory of the Leisure Class* which describes American society of the early twentieth century. The demand for a good possessing such characteristics is shown in Figure 4-11. Veblen also gave us the term *conspicuous consumption,* which basically describes consumer behavior as described above, although buying high-priced aspirin does not constitute such an act of "conspicuous" consumption. But consider the case of the handmade and custom-designed $132,000 Stutz Blackhawk automobile. In such a market only those buyers who wish to be among the chosen few will enter the market to obtain such a vehicle, if and only if the price is high enough. Riding around in such an automobile allows consumers to impress those around them and presumably yields them a great deal of satisfaction.

FIGURE 4-11
The "Veblen effect."

Expensive, name-brand photographic equipment probably exhibits such behavior, as do a limited edition Rolls Royce and demand for education at very exclusive and expensive colleges.

EXERCISES

1. *Define* the following terms.
   a. Income–quantity demand curve.
   b. Engel curve.
   c. Price-expenditure curve.
   d. Giffen effect.
   e. Veblen effect.
   f. Snob effect.
   g. Bandwagon effect.
   h. Income and substitution effect.
   i. Diminishing marginal utility.
   j. Point price elasticity of demand.
   k. Inferior good.
   l. Income elasticity of demand.
   m. Price-elastic demand.
   n. Price-inelastic demand.

2. The *balance of trade* is defined as the value of exports less the value of imports or, more succinctly, the difference between receipts and expenditures in international trade. Suppose a country has a trade deficit, i.e., expenditures on foreign products exceed receipts from sale to the foreigners. Let us further assume that the demand for imports is fairly price elastic ($|e|>1$) and the foreign demand for products (exports) is price inelastic ($|e|<1$). Will devaluation of the country's currency widen the gap or reduce the deficit? (Assume ceteris paribus.) Why is devaluation used under conditions of trade deficits?

3. Write hypothetical demand functions for the following goods and services, indicating the appropriate relationship between demand and each variable using the symbols (+), (−) and (?). Explain your choice of variables.

a. Education at a private (four-year) college.
b. Health spa facilities for a small town.
c. Baby-sitters during the morning–afternoon hours.
d. Public transportation.
e. Life insurance.
f. Medical specialists.
g. Health care.
h. Tennis courts.
i. Chinese restaurants.
j. Duplicating service.
k. Economists.
l. Sociologists.
m. Anthropologists.
n. Men's clothing store.
o. Solar energy.
p. Government bonds.
q. Foreign currency.

4. Suppose the following is true for a particular segment of the population composed of 20 million families.
    a. Average annual income: $6500/family.
    b. Average annual consumption of meat: 200 pounds.
    c. Average price per pound of meat: $1.10.
Let us assume that the government wants to provide adequate nutrition to the needy families so that each family is able to afford 250 pounds of meat per year. This can be done either by subsidizing the price of meat or by transferring income to the families. The government's estimate of the elasticities of demand for meat are as follows.
    a. Price elasticity of demand = −0.80.
    b. Income elasticity of demand = 10.
Compute the *explicit* cost of each program separately (explicit in the sense that the other costs, including costs of administration, are to be neglected).

   Suppose it is known that the *implicit* cost of the price-subsidy program is $12 million and that of the income transfer program $3 million. What will be the true economic difference between the costs of the programs?

5. Very recently, a bill proposing the increase in prices of socially undesirable products via excise taxes was introduced by a very young congressman. The idea was to discourage consumption of such items. His proposal was opposed by an elderly senator on the grounds that such a tax would be ineffective in the short run, and he argued thus: "When the tax is imposed, prices will rise and consumers will demand less. When the demand is less, the prices will fall and hence a tax will not be successful in raising prices and maintaining them at the higher level." What is your opinion about the arguments offered by the two legislators?

6. Is the demand for all breakfast foods any different from the demand for a particular brand of cold cereal? How?

7. How does the practice of "scalping" affect the elasticity of demand for tickets? Is "scalping" a service? Explain.

8. Will the demand for new cars be affected by the supply of used ones? Will the supply of used cars be affected by the demand for new cars? Explain how each will be influenced by the other and the associated effects on the prices, quantities, and other services for new and old cars.

9. Using the fundamentals of behavior associated with elasticities, cite examples of two products in each case that are most likely to respond heavily to the demand variable indicated below.
   a. Price.
   b. Income.
   c. Advertising.
   d. Public pressure.
   e. Population growth.
   f. Technological improvements.
   g. Urbanization.
   h. Interest rates.
   i. Currency exchange rate fluctuations.
   j. Punishment.
   k. Reward.
   l. Threat.

10. Suppose there are two producers of men's suits (brand X and brand Y). The initial conditions are as follows.

	X	Y
Price:	$200	$180
Volume:	20,000	15,000

Price-elasticity of demand for $X = -1.5$ and the price elasticity of demand for $Y = -1.4$; the cross price elasticity of demand for X with respect to the price of $Y = 2.1$ and the cross price elasticity of demand for Y with respect to the price of $X = 1.00$.

   Assume now that Y lowers its price by $20. What should be the new price of X so that it will continue to sell the same number of suits?

11. Is the demand for public transportation in a city like Denver, Colorado price elastic? How about a city like Cucamonga, California? Anchorage, Alaska? Bombay, India? Explain.

12. Despite monetary punishment (fines) the 55 mph speed limit continues to go unheeded. Does this indicate that the desire to travel fast (demand for speeding) is quite elastic with respect to (probable) fines? Can you suggest other variables that might influence the decision to speed such that they may be changed via public policy in order to preserve the legal speed limit?

13. Car manufacturers give "rebates" to persuade the consumers to buy new cars. Do such rebates constitute an income increase for the buyer or a price reduction of the car? Explain.

14. Suppose we live in a world of two commodities, X and Y. All consumers buy X and Y and there is no hoarding. Furthermore, X and Y are considered to be substitutes. Prove that the product of the price elasticities of demand for X and Y must equal the product of the cross elasticities of demand.

15. Is the price elasticity of demand affected by income? In what manner?

16. Describe whether the cross price elasticity of demand for the first product with respect to the price of the second is positive, negative, or uncertain, and whether such an elasticity is large or small. Do the same by reversing the roles of the first and the second products. (Assume that the price of the second product always rises.)
   a. Tennis shoes and tennis clubs.

  b. Tennis club memberships and health spas.
  c. Vegas and Pintos.
  d. American Express and Diners Club credit cards.
  e. Honda 750 and Honda Express 50.
  f. Education at Harvard and at Yale.
  g. Chain saws made by Montgomery Ward and by Sears.
  h. RCA and Sony color TVs.
  i. Chinese and "regular" restaurants.
  j. Chinese and Mexican restaurants.
  k. Economics and biology courses on campus.
  l. Economics courses and textbooks.
  m. *American Economic Review* and *Eastern Economic Review*.
  n. Theft and burglary insurance and public protection.
  o. Private and public schools.
  p. Imperial margarine and Butternut coffee.
  q. Motorcycle helmets and motorcycles.
  r. Men's suits and ties.
  s. Automobiles and gasoline.
  t. Pornographic reading material and prostitution.
  u. Sucaryl and xyletol.
  v. Sugar and sucaryl.
  w. Cigarettes and chewing tobacco.
  x. Microeconomics texts by Mahanty and by Zilchheifer.
  y. Ground beef and steak.
  z. Savings and government bonds.
 aa. Egg rolls and chewing gum.
 bb. Bermuda grass and Astroturf.
 cc. Dogs and pet rocks.
 dd. Doctors and medical technicians.
 ee. Laetril and radiation therapy (for cancer).
  ff. Wigs and professional hair care.
 gg. Miami and Aspen vacations during winter.
 hh. Veal and steak.
  ii. Coffee and tea.
  jj. Bread and butter.

17. Draw representative demand (price–quantity) curves for the following goods and services and explain the rationale for the shapes you have chosen.
  a. Men's haircuts.
  b. $1.95 "bestsellers."
  c. Car rentals from Hertz.
  d. Courses in automotive mechanics.
  e. Private downtown parking lots.
  f. A commercial bank's services in a large town.
  g. Robbery, theft, and murder.
  h. Hard drugs.
  i. Pornographic reading material.
  j. Pornographic movies.
  k. Palmreading.
  l. Motorcycles.
  m. Electrical energy.
  n. Solar energy.
  o. Nuclear energy.

    p. Geothermal energy.
    q. Concerts.
    r. Cable television.
    s. Preschools for 2–4 year olds.
    t. Food stamps.
    u. Government bonds.
    v. Corporate stocks.
    w. Life insurance.
    x. "Facelifts" via plastic surgery.
    y. Silicone implant and similar surgery.
    z. Admissions to San Diego Zoo.

18. Sketch the *income–quantity* demand curves for the above. (Practice makes perfect!)

19. Explain "price flexibility" as opposed to price elasticity (as explained in the appendix to this chapter at the end of the book).

20. What would be some of the impacts on demand (for many goods and services) if the water table fell. Limit your discussion to a particular area, such as California.

21. If optometrists are given greater privileges that only opthalmologists now possess, will the demand for eye care be affected? How?

22. The U.S. government is demanding more and more from the American automobile manufacturers in the way of increased fuel efficiency and reduced pollutants emission. Will such demands have any affect on the demand for U.S. cars? Foreign cars? Explain.

23. How do Nielsen ratings affect the demand for TV shows in general and each major station?

SUGGESTED READINGS

Al-Janabi, A. "The Determinants of Long-Term Demand for OPEC Oil." *Journal of Energy and Development,* Volume 3, Spring 1978.

Arnott, R. "The Reduced Form Price Elasticity of Housing." *Journal of Urban Economics,* Volume 5, July 1978.

Boonekamp, C. "Inflation, Hedging and the Demand for Money." *American Economic Review,* Volume 68, September 1978.

Gum, R., and Martin, W. "Problems and Solutions in Estimating the Demand for and Value of Rural Outdoor Recreation." *American Journal of Agricultural Economics,* Volume 57, November 1975.

Hogarty, T., and Elzinga, K. "The Demand for Beer." *The Review of Economics and Statistics,* May 1972.

Parkman, A. "Simultaneous Legal and Illegal Demand for Prescription Drugs." *Nebraska Journal of Economics and Business,* Volume 17, Summer 1978.

Seade, J. "Consumers's Surplus and Linearity of Engel Curves." *Economic Journal,* September 1978.

Straszheim, M. "Airline Demand Functions in the North Atlantic and Their Pricing Implications." *Journal of Transportation and Economic Policy,* Volume 12, May 1978.

Working, F. "What Do Statistical Demand Curves Show?" *The Quarterly Journal of Economics,* February 1927.

Chapter Five

REVENUE ANALYSIS

The producer derives income and profits from the sale of goods and services to the consumer. That which is an expenditure to the buyer is *revenue* to the seller. For example, if you buy 20 redheaded woodpecker scalps for $200, the seller's revenue is $200. Revenue should not be confused with profit, which is the residual income to the producer or seller after the costs of production and selling expenses are subtracted from sales revenue.

Chapter 4 dealt with the theories associated with consumer behavior as they affect the demand for goods and services. Demand, in turn, is influenced by utility considerations discussed in Chapter 3. In this chapter we shall analyze the role of revenues. Revenues affect the producer's profits (or losses) and therefore (presumably) utility.

TOTAL, MARGINAL, AND INCREMENTAL REVENUE

Total revenue, or simply *revenue,* is the amount of sales receipts obtained from the buyers. This figure is obtained by multiplying the price of the product by the quantity of units of the product purchased at that price. Thus, total revenue (TR), or simply revenue (*R*), is the product of price (*P*) and quantity (*Q*), or

$$TR = P \times Q \qquad (1)$$

Equation (1) states that total revenue (TR) varies directly with *P* and *Q,* all other factors remaining equal. That is, if we can increase *P* without affecting *Q*, TR will increase; and if somehow *Q* can be increased while *P* remains constant, TR will also rise. However, we must not forget the inverse relationship between price and quantity. We know that if *P* rises, *Q* will fall and the effect on total revenue will depend on the relative changes of price and quantity.

Marginal revenue is the change in revenue associated with the change in the sale of 1 unit. For example, if the total revenue of 20 units is $200 and that of 21 units is $210, the marginal revenue of the 21st unit is $10. In general, marginal revenue (MR) is the rate of change of total revenue with respect to the change in quantity, or,

$$MR = \frac{\text{Change in total revenue}}{\text{Change in quantity}} = \frac{\Delta TR}{\Delta Q} \qquad (2)$$

From a graphical standpoint, the marginal revenue is the value of the tangent drawn to the total revenue function—that is, the value of the slope of the total revenue function indicates the value of the marginal revenue.

Total revenue changes when the price is altered, because the quantity demanded is inversely related to the price. However, the seller can also induce larger sales by policies other than changing prices. For example, even if price is left at the original level, more revenues can conceivably be obtained through better promotional tactics, advertising, or product variation. The change in total revenue associated with the change in another variable (instead of price), is *incremental revenue* (IR). Thus, if the firm is able to increase its revenue by

$20,000 by spending an additional $1000 on advertising, the incremental revenue from each additional advertising dollar will be $20. We can state incremental revenue by equation (3):

$$IR = \frac{\text{Change in revenue}}{\text{Change in variable}} \tag{3}$$

It should be understood that the increased revenue due to the additional advertising may have resulted from higher demand for the product, and greater demand enables the seller to sell a larger quantity at a higher price.

Another measurement of revenue is *average revenue*. Average revenue is the ratio of total revenue to total quantity and, in most cases, is no different from the price of the product. However, there are situations where the use of the average revenue is more meaningful than price, especially where all consumers do not pay the same price. For example, if in-state students pay $600 in tuition while the out-of-state students are required to pay $1000, the (roughly) average revenue per student is $800. Equations (4) and (5) bring out the difference between the two concepts of average revenue (AR).

$$AR = \frac{\text{Total revenue}}{\text{Total quantity}} = \frac{PQ}{Q} = P \tag{4}$$

or

$$AR = \frac{\text{Sum of different TR}}{\text{Sum of quantity}} = \frac{P_1 Q_1 + P_2 Q_2 + \cdots}{Q_1 + Q_2}$$

$$= \frac{\Sigma R_i}{\Sigma Q_i} \tag{5}$$

Equation (4) is valid when all buyers pay the same price P, whereas it is more correct to use equation (5) when different consumers pay different prices.

Finally, we can also obtain total revenue by summing the marginal revenue of each unit sold. Since the marginal revenue is the change in revenue resulting from the sale of an additional unit, the sum of all such marginal revenues equals total revenue. Thus, equation (6) shows the relationship of total revenue to marginal revenue by using the information contained in equation (2):

$$TR = \Sigma MR_i \tag{6}$$

Equation (6), in turn, allows us to express average revenue as equation (7):

$$AR = \frac{\text{Total revenue}}{\text{Total quantity}} = \frac{\text{Sum of marginal revenue}}{\text{Total quantity}}$$

$$= \frac{\Sigma MR_i}{Q} \tag{7}$$

REVENUE AND DEMAND

The basic law of demand suggests an inverse relationship of price to quantity. Suppose the price–quantity demand curve is linear and of the form $Q = 10 - P$. Table 5-1 shows the various values of price, quantity, total revenue, marginal revenue, and average revenue.

TABLE 5-1

Price	Quantity	Total revenue = PQ	Marginal revenue = $\Delta TR/\Delta Q$	Average revenue = TR/Q
$10	0	$ 0		$0
9	1	9	$9/1 = $9	$9/1 = 9
8	2	16	7/1 = 7	16/2 = 8
7	3	21	5/1 = 5	21/3 = 7
6	4	24	3/1 = 3	24/4 = 6
5	5	25	1/1 = 1	25/5 = 5
4	6	24	−1/1 = −1	24/6 = 4

Table 5-1 reveals the basic relationship of total revenue and marginal revenue to price and quantity. When price is lowered, quantity demanded increases. Since the demand function chosen is linear and possesses a slope of −1, each one-dollar reduction in price leads to one additional unit demanded. Total revenues increase due to price reductions, to a point. At a price of $5, the quantity is five units and total revenue equals $25. Any price below $5, although capable of increasing the quantity demanded, yields less revenue, just as prices above $5 produce less than $25 in total revenue.

Marginal revenue is calculated by dividing the difference in total revenue by the difference in total quantity. Thus, at a price of $8, the quantity is 2 and the total revenue is $16. At a price of $7, the quantity increases to 3 and the total revenue to $21. The marginal revenue in this price range, therefore, equals ($21−$16)/(3−2), or $5. The last column, labelled average revenue, records the ratio of total revenue to quantity and in this case the average revenue and the price are the same.

It might be of interest to note that for a linear demand function, the rate of descent of the marginal revenue is twice that of the demand function. Thus, while the demand schedule shows that for each additional unit the price must fall by $1, the marginal revenue column indicates that for each additional unit sold, the marginal revenue declines by $2. This phenomenon is not always true, but is generally so for linear demand functions under ordinary conditions.

Figure 5-1 illustrates the general relationship of all the revenue functions to each other. The upper portion of the diagram shows a continuous and linear demand function of the type discussed in Table 5-1. The associated marginal revenue curve is also linear and lies below the demand curve so that its negative inclination is twice that of the demand curve. In essence, linear marginal revenue functions bisect the base. The lower figure shows the total revenue function and because total revenue may either rise or fall due to price changes, the function is nonlinear. For linear demand functions, the corresponding total revenues appear as shown. This parabolic function is symmetrical—that is, the left and right halves of the total revenue function generated by a linear demand function are identical.

We mentioned earlier that the marginal revenue reflects the value of the slope of the total revenue function. In Figure 5-1, the slope of the total revenue

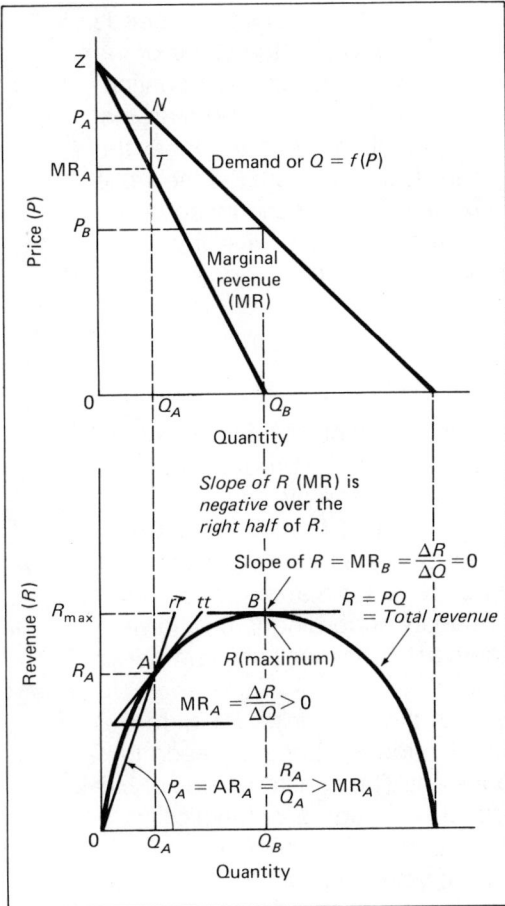

FIGURE 5-1
Each demand function has a unique set of marginal and total revenue functions associated with it. The upper diagram contains a conventional linear demand curve and the corresponding marginal revenue function. The lower diagram shows the revenue function derived from the given demand line. The maximum value for the parabolic revenue function occurs where its slope is zero. The marginal revenue indicates the slope of the revenue function. The average revenue, or price in this case, is the ratio of revenue to quantity, and its value can be measured by the slope of a line drawn from the origin. Thus, at point A on the R function, the slope shown by tt has a smaller value than the slope of the line rr drawn from the origin. Consequently, price at quantity Q_A exceeds the marginal revenue at that quantity. You will find that price will exceed marginal revenue at all positive quantities.

function is positive to quantity Q_B and equals zero at such a quantity. Furthermore, the positive slope's value decreases with quantity. Consequently, we can say that the total revenue increases at a decreasing rate. Because total revenue decreases past quantity Q_B, the maximum total revenues occur at quantity Q_B and, accordingly, the slope of the function is zero. The upper diagram is in agreement with our observations because the marginal revenue function also attains zero value at quantity Q_B. At price P_A, total revenue is less than maximum, although price P_A is higher than price P_B.

Point A on the total revenue function has two lines drawn through it—one as a tangent marked tt and the other from the origin labelled rr. A tangent measures the slope (and hence marginal values) of a function at a point, and a ray from the origin measures the average value of a function. Because the angle subtended by rr is greater than that formed by tt, the average revenue exceeds the marginal revenue. In this particular situation, average revenue is the same as price. Thus, price exceeds marginal revenue. We can see this from the upper portion of the diagram of Figure 5-1. In general, when the total

Revenue analysis
126

revenue (R) increases at a decreasing rate, price (P) at any quantity exceeds the marginal revenue (MR). Maximum revenue occurs where the slope of the function reaches zero, unless, of course, the revenue function rises continuously with quantity. Lastly, since the total revenue is the sum of the marginal revenues of the individual units for a continuous function, the area under the marginal revenue curve also equals total revenue. Thus, in Figure 5-1 the value of the area under the MR function to quantity Q_A (area $OZTQ_A$) should equal the area OP_ANQ_A (price × quantity) and both the areas should have the same value as total revenue TR_A. As long as the marginal revenue is positive, the total revenue will increase.

REVENUE WITH CONSTANT PRICE

The total revenue function, as well as the corresponding marginal revenue, are not the same as that shown in Figure 5-1 if the price of the product happens to be constant at all levels of output. For example, when we discuss the theory of perfect competition, we assume that each individual firm in the industry charges the same price—the price determined by the interaction of industry demand and supply. If that is so, producers accept the market price as the only price available to them and adjust their quantity according to this "given" price. Under such circumstances, the producers are free to sell any number of units at the market price.

When the price is constant, revenue rises at a constant rate. Figure 5-2 illustrates the case of revenues with a constant price P_0. Because each unit sold adds to P_0, the price equals MR and is constant. The constant value of MR ($= P_0$) is shown by the horizontal line. The total revenue, or R function, is a straight line. In keeping with the geometry, the slope of the R function is constant and equal to MR (or P_0) and the average value of R or AR (price) also has the same value at each point, because the line drawn from the origin coincides with the R function and this line has a constant slope equal to P_0 (or MR) at each and every volume of sales.

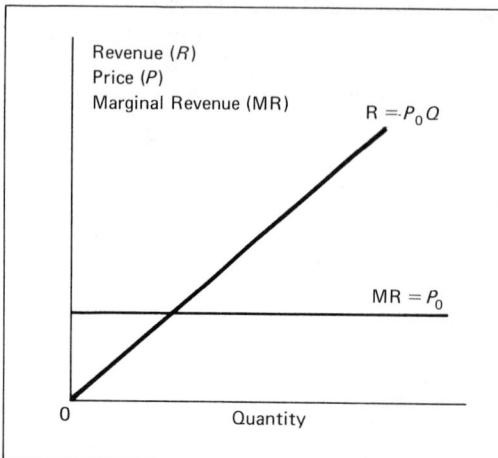

Revenue (R)
Price (P)
Marginal Revenue (MR)

$R = P_0 Q$

$MR = P_0$

0   Quantity

FIGURE 5-2
When the price is given or fixed, the total revenue (R) function is linear. Therefore, the marginal revenue is also linear and constant at a value which equals the price of the product. Here we see that the price is P_0, which makes R equal to $P_0 Q$. Because the change in revenue associated with a one-unit change in quantity is precisely P_0, P_0 and marginal revenue (MR) are one and the same.

REVENUES WHEN PRICE VARIES
WITH QUANTITY PURCHASED

Occasionally firms find it profitable to charge different prices for different quantities bought. The case of "quantity discount" pricing fits this description. For example, consider the following offer: $10 per unit for 1–100 units bought; $9 per unit for the *following* 100 units bought; and $8 per unit for the third 100 units bought. Because the firm is charging $10 per unit for the first 100 units, the revenue function will increase at the rate of $10 per unit to the first one hundred units. In Figure 5-3 this quantity is shown as quantity Q_1. Beyond quantity Q_1 the price decreases to $9 for the following 100 units, and hence the revenue function rises at a rate of only $9 per unit sold, a situation described by a flatter R function drawn from point 1. Similarly, after 200 units have been sold, the line becomes still flatter to reflect the $8 price for units beyond the first 200. Because price and marginal revenue are equal and constant over each range of quantities, they have been drawn as horizontal lines. Thus P_1 (MR_1) corresponds to $10, P_2(MR_2) equals $9, and P_3(MR_3) equals $8.

FIGURE 5-3
When the price of each incremental *block* or *range* of quantity declines at larger volumes, the revenue function has many kinks corresponding to points of price changes. Thus, up to quantity Q_1(100), the price of the product is P_1, and accordingly the marginal revenue is horizontal at a level equal to P_1. Quantities above Q_1, but no more than Q_2(200) sell for P_2, which is less than P_1. Similarly, when quantity lies above 200 but no more than 300, the price drops to P_3. Because the price is not uniform over total quantity sold, we can obtain an "average price" or average revenue by drawing a line from the origin and measuring the value of its slope. For example, at quantity Q_2, the average revenue (AR) is shown by the value of the slope of line AR_2. In this particular case, the value of AR_2 will equal $[(P_1Q_1) + (P_2)(Q_2-Q_1)]/Q_2$.

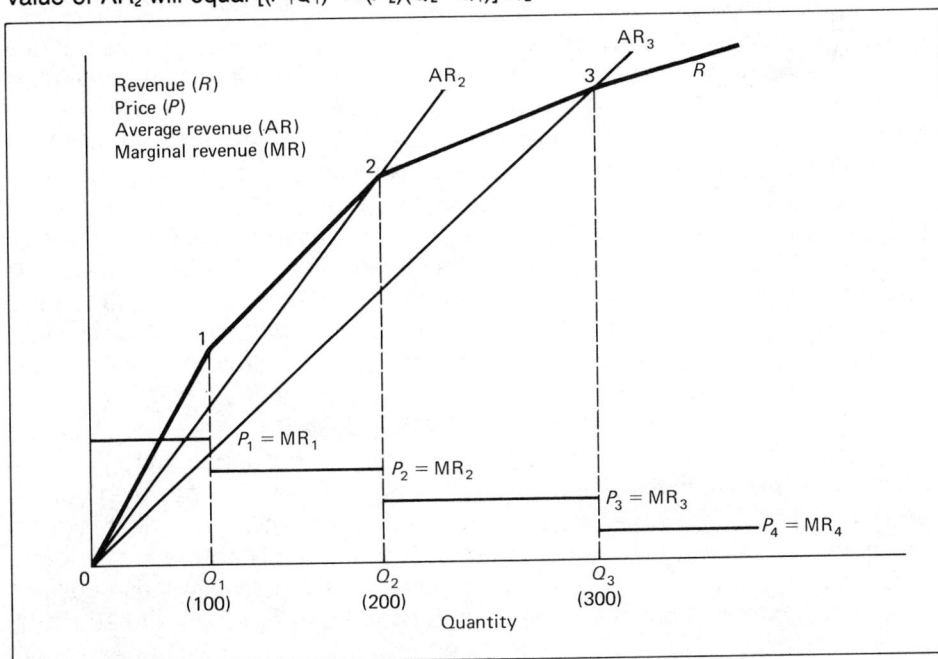

What sort of average revenue (AR) does the firm receive from such tactics? Are AR and MR equal? Here the AR = R/Q and does not equal price because there is no unique price. Consequently, the AR line is drawn from the origin to indicate an average value. For example, the average revenue to the firm at point 2 ($Q = 200$) is indicated by the slope of the line labelled AR_2. This slope amounts to $9.50, or the average revenue (average price) per unit is $9.50. This amount is arrived at by dividing the total revenue from the sale of the first 200 units by 200, or by dividing $ (10 × 100) + $ (9 × 100) = $1900 by 200. Similarly, the AR at point 3 (AR_3) is the value of the angle subtended by line AR_3, which appears to be parallel to the segment 1–2 of the R function. The value of the slope of portion 1–2 is $9 and the value of the angle made by line AR_3 equals [$ (10 × 100) + $ (9 × 100) + $ (8 × 100)]/300, or $2700/300 = $9. Other values of AR can be computed in a similar manner either arithmetically or geometrically.

REVENUES AND MULTIPART TARIFFS

Automobile rental companies are notorious for charging prices that are referred to as "multipart tariffs". The price of the rental is composed of essentially two parts—one part is charged for the days the car is rented and the other part is based on the number of miles the car is driven. Thus the charges are based on time and distance. The revenues to the company then come from both time and mileage. Strange as it may seem, the car rental companies receive a greater part of their revenues from the distance component than they do from the time part.

Figure 5-4 shows the revenue (R) functions for car rentals on a day/mile basis. The miles are shown along the horizontal axis, while the charges per day are measured along the vertical. Thus revenue line R_1 measures the revenues from a one-day rental, R_2 for a two-day rental, and so on. The revenue line has a positive slope equal to the per-mile charge. Thus if the standard rate is $20 per day and 20¢ per mile, the revenue function will start at $20 (no mileage) for a one-day rental and increase by 20¢ for each mile traveled. For a one-day rental that covers 100 miles, the total charges will come to $40. Suppose R_1 represents the one-day and R_2 the two-day rental. If the mileage charge is 30¢ per mile and the daily rate is $10, the total revenues to the company for a distance of 100 miles and a one-day rental will also be $40. This revenue line is shown by the dotted line labeled R_t. And if there are no time charges but only distance rates of 40¢ per mile, the total revenues to the company will also be $40 for a one-day rental. This is shown by the (dotted) revenue line R_m. From the graph, we can see that for a one-day rental and distances more than 100 miles, the revenues to the firm are maximum with R_m—that is, no time charges and only distance charges at the rate of 40¢ per mile. The next highest revenues accrue with R_t, or a daily rate of $10 and a mileage rate of 30¢ per mile. Often the consumer is neither willing nor able to calculate these costs in order to choose the best combination, and some rates appear more economical. Psychologically speaking, the $10 per day and 30¢ per mile appears more

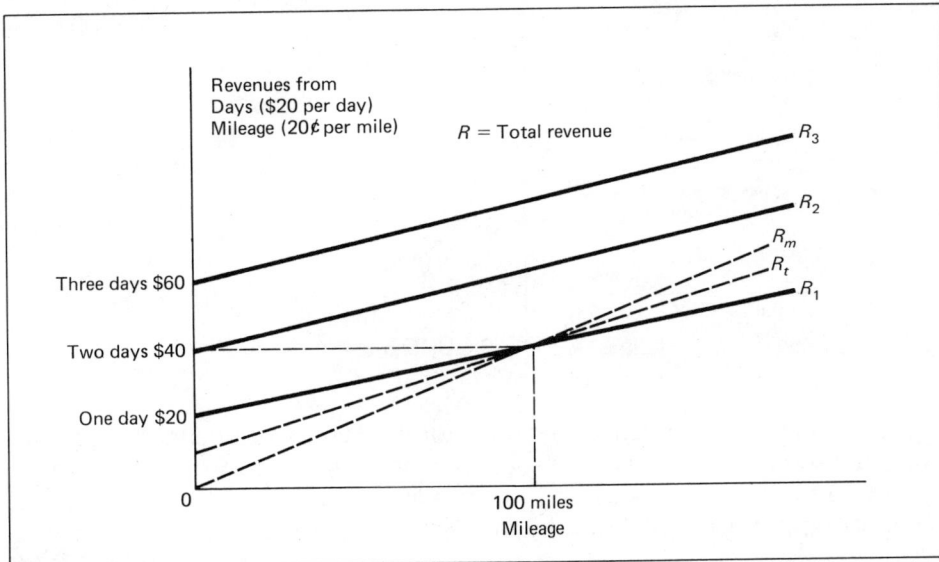

FIGURE 5-4
The revenues to companies that charge multipart tariffs, consist of more than one part. For example, in the situation of car rentals, part of the charges to the customer is based on time, and the other part comes from distance. In the diagram, distance is measured along the horizontal axis, and hence the revenue from mileage varies with distance, and is shown by the revenue line R_m. If the company charges a daily and a mileage rate, the revenue function will be like the one shown by R_t. Because R_m and R_t meet at a distance of 100 miles, the revenue to the company is the same for either rate. R_t starts above the origin and is flatter than R_m, while R_m is steeper but starts at the origin. As explained in the text, and shown in the figure, both rates produce $40 in revenue.

attractive than the $20 a day and 20¢ a mile and, in fact, is more economical for distances less than 100 miles for a one-day rental. But for distances greater than 100 miles, the $20-20¢ price is more economical.

REVENUES AND DISCOUNTS

Adding to the confusion and enticement are a host of so-called "discounts" that are offered on rentals. Examine the possibilities below and select the one you consider to be the most economical rate for a one-day/200-mile rental:

a. $10/day and 30¢/mile—discount of 15%.
b. $20/day and 20¢/mile—discount of 10%.
c. $00/day and 40¢/mile—discount of 25%.

When computed, the total charges for the three rates come to $59.50, $54.00, and $60.00, respectively. Some consumers may prefer the $10/30¢/15% combination because it seems cheaper. Revenues to the company are greater if the renters choose the 40¢ per mile deal, but it is unlikely that many will. The effect of a flat discount on time and distance charge is to shift the revenue

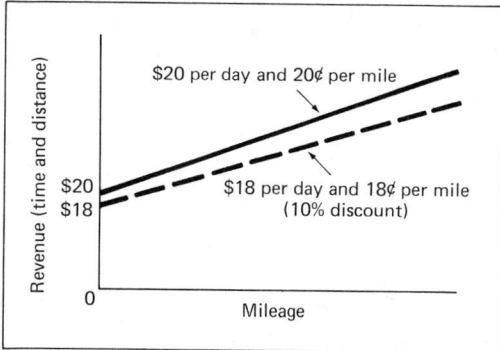

FIGURE 5-5

function down and decrease its slope. For the $20 per day and 20¢ per mile rate, a discount of 10% will, in effect, lower the daily rate by $2 and the mileage rate by 2¢. Thus, the discounted revenue line will start at $18 and rise at the rate of 18¢ per mile, as shown by the dotted line of Figure 5-5.

REVENUES FROM MULTIPLE MARKETS

Most firms have more than one market. Markets are categorized according to some common feature present in the buyers in a particular market. Thus, there can be different markets based on geographic location, sex, age, race, wealth, occupation, and time. For example, commercial banks view the demand for loans as originating from several sources—the market made up of borrowers desiring automobile loans, the market composed of businessmen requiring inventory loans, and the market where the demanders desire loans for holiday travel. Because the bank's money has competing uses among all the available alternatives, the profit-seeking bank should allocate its funds in a manner consistent with revenue-maximization* principles. Although the interest income varies positively with the amount of loans, so does the cost of processing them. A profit-maximizing institution need not lend out all its available funds, because some funds may have better alternative uses when compared to the cost of such loans.

Suppose a firm has two markets, 1 and 2, and has to sell a specified quantity Q_{1+2} between these two markets. We place the two MRs "back-to-back" in Figure 5-6. The origin for the MRs is at point 0. The quantity sold in market 1 is measured from right to left and the quantity sold in market 2 is measured from left to right. The quantity to be sold is shown as a solid line labelled Q_{1+2} at the upper right corner of the graph. This amount, Q_{1+2}, is wedged between the two MR lines until it just touches either marginal revenue

---

*We are assuming that for the situation described, maximum revenues equate to maximum profits. This is true if and only if the total costs to the bank are fixed. Thus, with costs entirely fixed, maximum revenues would imply maximum profits. When the bank has several markets, it can obtain the maximum total revenue if it allocates the chosen amount of funds in a manner suggested by the equimarginal principle.

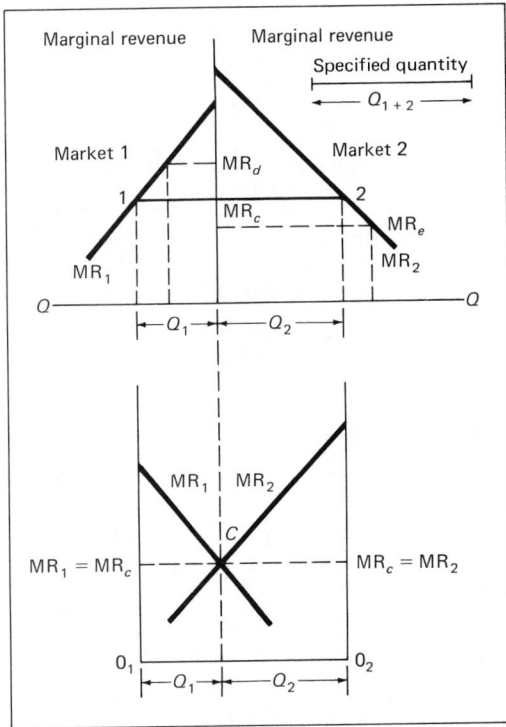

FIGURE 5-6
This figure shows how a firm may maximize total joint revenues from multiple markets. If the firm has a specific quantity of output that it wishes to sell in two markets, it will obtain the maximum sum of the revenues by allocating the output between the markets so that the marginal revenue of the last unit sold in each market is equal to the marginal revenue of the last unit in every other market. Thus, the total quantity (Q_1+Q_2) is distributed to make MR_1 equal to MR_2. Both graphs illustrate the *equimarginal* principle.

function. When this happens, the marginal revenue in each market is equal because the vertical distance which measures marginal revenue is the same for both MR_1 and MR_2 at point 1 for the first and point 2 for the second. Let us call this value MR_c. The graph shows that when quantity Q_1 is sold in market 1, the marginal revenue from this market (MR_1) is just as great as the marginal revenue from market 2 when quantity Q_2 is sold. You can verify from the graph that the sum of Q_1 and Q_2 has to equal the specified quantity Q_{1+2}. If the firm allocates fewer than Q_1 units to market 1 and, therefore, more units to market 2, the marginal revenue from 1 will equal MR_d, and MR_2 will equal MR_e, and the firm will lose revenues by selling too many in market 2 (MR_e) and not enough in market 1 (MR_d). The lower section of Figure 5-6 illustrates the maximization principle with the use of the *equimarginal principle* discussed before.

REVENUES FROM COMPETING PRODUCTS

Many firms produce a variety of merchandise such that the many items "compete" with one another in more than one way. For example, a cigarette manufacturer makes more than one brand. Not only do these brands compete against one another, but they also compete for the available resources of the firm. Thus brand A competes with brand B in the marketplace, but it will also

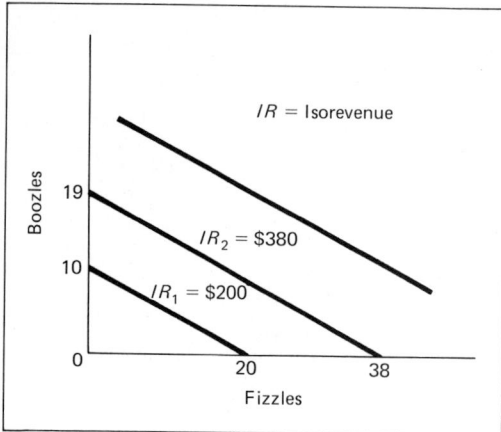

FIGURE 5-7
If the prices of Fizzles (*F*) and Boozles (*B*) are known and constant, the revenue to the company will be the sum of the revenues received from the sale of both *F* and *B*. Many combinations of *F* and *B* can provide a specific amount of revenue to the firm. An isorevenue line contains all combinations of *F* and *B* that produce a given amount of revenue, and under the circumstances described is linear. Isorevenue lines associated with higher revenues lie farther out than those which represent smaller values.

compete with brand B in the context of scarce resources. A book publisher may publish several books in microeconomics. These books will compete with one another in the market as well as within the publishing company. In general, when more of one is produced and sold, less of others may be produced and sold. Consequently, the products become "competing" products. If the price of each type of product is known, then the revenue from the sale of that product can be computed from the volume of sales. If we consider two products, then more revenues from one will imply less revenue from the other.

Figure 5-7 shows a firm producing Boozles and Fizzles. If the price of each Boozle is $20 and each Fizzle $10, then the revenue from one Boozle equals the revenue from two Fizzles. If we plot all combinations of Boozles and Fizzles that yield a specified amount of revenue, we will, in effect, be drawing an "isorevenue" line. Three isorevenue lines have been drawn in Figure 5-7. The trade-off between revenues from the sale of Boozles and revenue from the sale of Fizzles is shown by the negatively inclined isorevenue (IR) lines having slopes with an absolute value of 1:2. Ten Boozles or twenty Fizzles bring in revenues of $200. Similarly, IR_2 shows a revenue of $380 from a variety of combinations of sale of Boozles and Fizzles. If the constraints due to resources are also shown, then we will be in a position to pick the "best" combination of Boozles and Fizzles, a subject which will be covered in Chapter 8: Linear Programming.

"NET" REVENUES: COMMISSIONS, TRANSPORTATION COSTS, AND TAXES

In some instances, the firm may not receive the entire portion of sales revenues. For example, if the firm must pay commissions on sales, the firm's "net" revenues are the revenues reduced by the amount paid out in commissions. Take this textbook, for example. If the retail price is $14.95 and the author receives a royalty of 10% (of sales revenue), and the bookstore a discount of 20%, then the "net price" received by the publisher is only 70% of the retail price, or $10.47 per book. As such, the book publishing company will use this price for planning and decision making. Whenever there are such commissions or royalties that must be paid by the firm, all the relevant functions are lowered by the specified percentage. Thus, in the case of the book company, all the functions will drop by 30% of their value at each point, as is shown by the dotted lines in Figure 5-8.

Some firms have markets that are located in many geographical areas. As such, the firm usually has to pay transportation costs for selling its products in distant markets. In calculating the revenues from such markets, the firm should plan on receiving only revenues net of transportation costs for the units. For example, if the firm has two markets, one at home (no transportation cost) and one abroad, and if the transportation cost per unit of merchandise sold abroad is $ t, then the "net" marginal revenue of the distant market is the original MR less $ t for each additional unit sold. The net MR is shown as the MR line that has *shifted down* by the amount of the transportation cost of each unit as shown in Figure 5-9. Although the net price is also less than the actual price charged, the demand curve does not shift down. If the demand curve were to shift down (or inwards) it would mean that there had been a reduction in demand for one reason or another. The diagram shows that the price of the product is $12 and the MR is $8, but the MR_{net} is only $3.00 if transportation cost per unit is $5.00. The effects of excise taxes on revenues may be handled in a similar manner.

REVENUES AND "JOINT" PRODUCTS

Joint products are those that are produced "jointly" or as by-products. Thus, in the production of gasoline the refineries also produce natural gas, oil, and other petroleum products. The lumber industry not only produces lumber by the board-foot but also automatically produces sawdust (for particle-board manufacture) and tree bark shingles (for roofing). Whenever a firm produces such joint products it receives revenues from the main product as well as the by-product. Consequently, the revenues from the sales of such products are essentially *the sum of the revenues derived from each type of product*. For example, the meat processor who slaughters cattle and produces beef also happens to produce hides and other byproducts that also have markets and hence constitute sources of revenue. We must bear in mind, however, that the firm is interested in selling the appropriate quantities of the byproducts so that the byproducts actually contribute to revenue in a positive manner. It is unprofitable for a meat processor to slaughter too many cattle in order to have many hides, for the excess supply of beef might reduce the profits on beef although the hide sales might bring in more profits. Because beef is the main product, the firm concentrates on the right amount of cattle to slaughter for

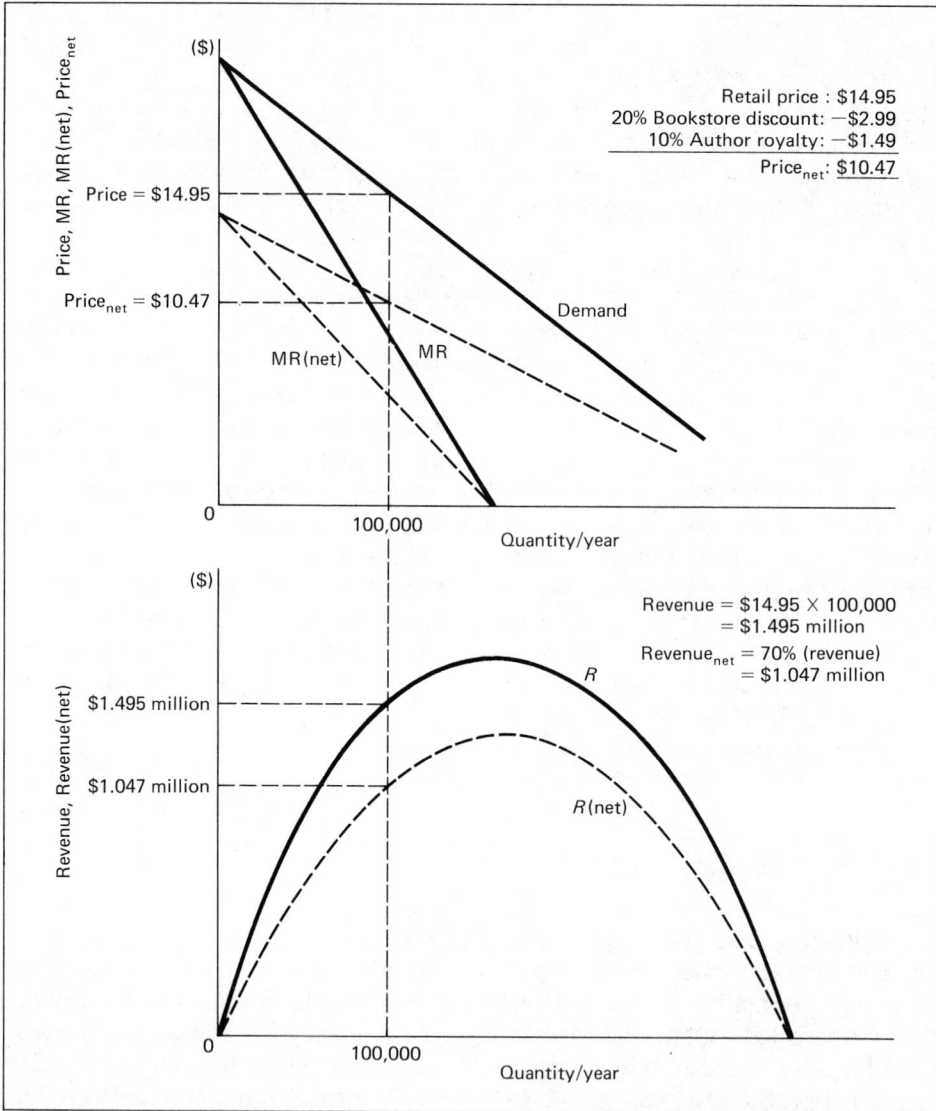

FIGURE 5-8
When the firm offers a discount as a percentage of the price, the *net price* received by the firm is less than the selling price. The book company not only offers a discount to the book store, but it also pays a royalty to the author. A retail price of $14.95 per book brings only $10.47 to the firm after discounts and royalties. Such discounts or royalties or commissions reduce the marginal revenue and the total revenue to the firm. However, it is important to recognize that the firm uses these "adjusted" figures for making decisions, since only those figures constitute true revenue to the firm.

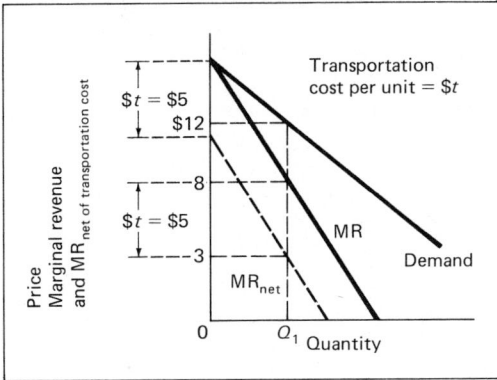

FIGURE 5-9
A firm incurring transportation costs faces a similar situation as the firm offering discounts on its products. Thus, even though the selling price of the item at Q_1 is $12, and the marginal revenue at that quantity is $8, a transportation cost of $5 per unit will reduce the MR to $3. The firm uses this adjusted marginal revenue (MR_{net}) to make decisions about markets which involve excessive transportation costs.

profits to be highest from beef sales; the hides that come about because of the slaughtering are then sold for the "best" price—that is, the price that yields the maximum revenue from hides. At times it may be necessary to sacrifice a few hides by destroying them rather than selling them at a very depressed price.

Figure 5-10 illustrates the basic procedure of demand "summation" involved in such joint product cases. The demand for beef and the demand for hides are shown as normally shaped demand curves. Both beef (in thousands of pounds) and hides (in unit quantities) are measured along the horizontal axis while their prices are shown along the vertical. The horizontal axis assumes that for each animal slaughtered, the firm receives 1000 pounds of beef and one hide. Because the price of a "composite animal"—that is, 1000 pounds of dressed meat and one hide—is the sum of the prices received for beef and hide, the demands for beef and for hide are *added vertically,* and the sum shows the *joint price* obtained from each processed animal. Because the monetary unit is common to both products, we may add the price of beef to the price of hide to obtain the price of beef and hide. The revenue obtained from beef and hide is the sum of the revenues from beef and from hides. If beef alone is sold, the maximum revenue (if that is the firm's goal) from beef will occur at a price of P_1 for beef with $MR_{beef} = 0$. However, corresponding to Q_1 for beef, we obtain a negative MR for hides. So, even if that many hides are available, it is unwise for the firm to sell all the hides because that will actually reduce the revenues obtained from hide sales and hence will also reduce total revenues from beef and hide sales. The most hides the firm should ever sell is where the MR_{hides} is zero. Where MR is zero, revenue is maximum. The rule then is to produce the right amount of the main product in keeping with the firm's goals and then to sell the other by-products at prices that yield the most profit (if applicable) or at least the most revenue. If there is a cost of processing the hides (or by-products) which is inseparable from the cost of processing the meat, then it is likely that the firm will end up selling fewer hides than available. We will take up this model again when we discuss the theories of profits.

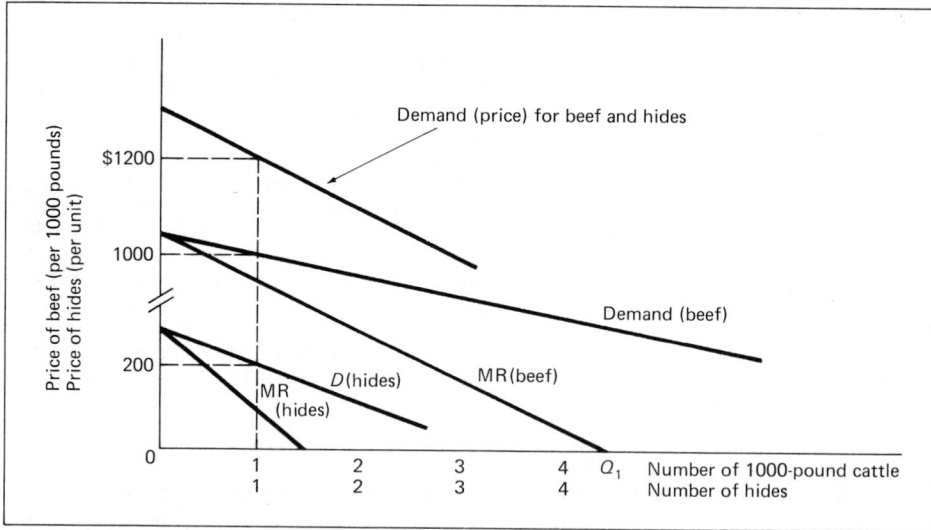

FIGURE 5-10
Firms often produce "joint" products—that is, the production of one item automatically yields another as a by-product. Thus, the meat packer not only receives beef but also hides from his cattle. Because the cost of processing beef is intertwined with part of the cost of processing hides, the firm finds it easier to compare the total cost of beef and hides to the revenues from the two products. This entails the *vertical* summation of the demands for beef and hides. Once such a joint demand function is established, the firm can derive a marginal revenue function from it and use it for profit-making decisions. In this figure, one point on the vertically summed demand curve is at quantity 1 and its joint price value is $1200—$1000 for the beef and $200 for the hide.

REVENUES AND THE PRICE ELASTICITY OF DEMAND

In discussing the theory of demand, we showed that the quantity demanded varies inversely with price. As price changes bring about changes in quantity, the revenue also changes. Because revenue is the product of price and quantity, it will rise, fall, or stay the same as price decreases bring about *proportionately* larger, smaller, or exactly equal changes in quantity demanded, ceteris paribus. If demand is price elastic, the percentage change in quantity demanded exceeds the percentage change in price. Consequently, a price reduction will increase revenues to the firm and price increases will reduce revenues. Analogously, if demand is price inelastic, price decreases will reduce revenues and price increases will increase revenues. In case of unitary price elasticity of demand, the revenues, theoretically, remain constant for both price increases and price cuts, because the percentage change in quantity equals the percentage change in price.

We can also use the very basic relationship of revenue to price and quantity to arrive at Table 5-2. Thus,

$$R = PQ$$

If P falls by $X\%$ and Q rises by more than $X\%$, then R is bound to increase

TABLE 5-2
REVENUE AND THE ELASTICITY OF DEMAND

Direction of price change	Change in price (%)	Change in quantity (%)	Elasticity conditions	Revenue
Reduced	X	More than X	Elastic	Increases
Increased	X	More than X	Elastic	Decreases
Reduced	X	Less than X	Inelastic	Decreases
Increased	X	Less than X	Inelastic	Increases
Reduced	X	Also X	Unit elastic	Stays constant
Increased	X	Also X	Unit elastic	Stays constant

because the greater proportionate change in Q will more than offset the declining percentage change in P. Because Q increases by a percentage larger than the percentage change in P, the ratio of these two percentage changes, or elasticity of demand, has to be greater than one. Similarly, if price increases, the impact of the quantity change downwards will more than offset the upward impact of price on revenues, as long as the price elasticity of demand exceeds one. Other cases can be worked out for conditions of inelastic and unit elastic demand. The basic relationship of P, Q, R, MR, and e_p is shown in Figure 5-11.

REVENUES, MARKUP, AND ELASTICITY

There is another formula that is useful in the determination of market response to prices or the appropriate "markup" required in the case of a *cost-plus* pricing situation. This formula links the price of the product to the marginal revenue as well as the price elasticity (point) of demand:

$$MR = \frac{\Delta R}{\Delta Q} = \frac{(\Delta R/\Delta P) \times (P/Q)}{(\Delta Q/\Delta P) \times (P/Q)}$$

$$= \frac{[(\Delta PQ + P\Delta Q)/\Delta P] \times (P/Q)}{e_p}$$

$$= \left(Q + \frac{P\Delta Q}{\Delta P}\right)\frac{P}{Q}$$

$$= \frac{P + e_p P}{e_p}$$

or

$$MR = P\left(1 + \frac{1}{e_p}\right)$$

where e_p includes sign, or

$$MR = P\left(1 - \frac{1}{|e_p|}\right)$$

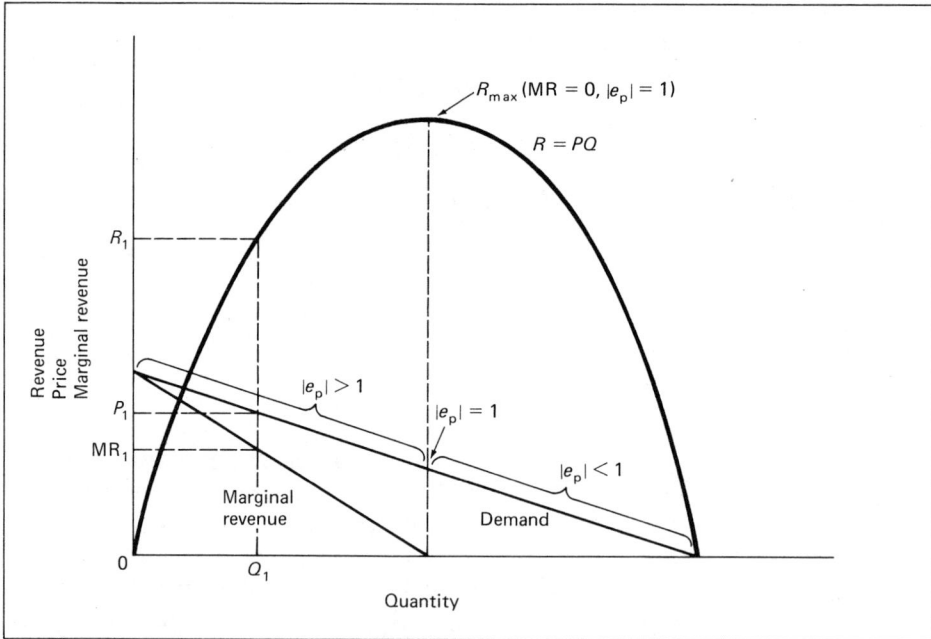

FIGURE 5-11
The elasticity of demand varies along the length of a price–quantity demand curve. In the case of linear demand functions, the upper half is elastic, and the lower half is inelastic. The midpoint is unit-elastic. In the elastic range, revenue (R) varies inversely with price and therefore, as price falls, revenues increase. Where demand is inelastic, lower prices bring forth lower revenues. Marginal revenue (MR) indicates the value of the slope of the revenue function, and in this case shows that R is maximum where its slope is zero, and where price elasticity of demand equals 1.

which may also be written as

$$e_p = \frac{P}{P - MR}$$

In business terminology the *markup* is the ratio of the *contribution profit* to the price of the product. Contribution is essentially the difference between the price of the product and its average variable cost (AVC). For example, if the AVC of a shirt is $6 and the retail price is $10, then the markup is $(10−6)/$10, or 40%. If you examine the relationship of price to cost, you will notice that the markup may be expressed as $(P-AVC)/P$. It is a standard theory of microeconomics that profits are maximized when marginal cost (MC) equals marginal revenue (MR). If the AVC of each unit is constant (and it frequently is, if the firm buys "at cost" from the wholesaler or manufacturer), then the marginal cost will also be constant and equal to the average variable cost. The markup now becomes $(P-MC)/P$ and, because for profit maximization MR must equal MC, the markup must be $(P-MR)/P$ and this expression equals $1/e_p$. Consequently, the *markup percentage* is equal to the *reciprocal* of the price elasticity of demand. The higher the elasticity, the lower the markup. If $e_p = 2$, then the markup will be 50%, and if $e_p = 10$, then the profit-maximizing markup should be 10%, and so on. This is in keeping with the basic theory of demand. The higher the price elasticity of demand, the greater the response of quantity to price changes and hence the lower the potential for high markups. You are most likely aware of the case of "perfect competition," where the demand for a typical firm's product is perfectly or absolutely elastic. In the long run, such a firm receives a price equal to the average total cost. Because all costs are variable in the long run, the price received also equals the average variable cost, and thus the markup, in essence, is zero.

REVENUES AND NONPRICE COMPETITION

A firm can employ certain strategies to improve its revenue position, among which are policies dealing with advertising and quantity and quality variation. If, for some reason, it is unwise for the firm to change the price of the product, it may increase the revenues derived from a given market via persuasive advertising. The effect of advertising is manifested, essentially, by an increase in demand. In most cases, the increases in sales revenue also bring about increased amounts of profits. There must be good reason for many large firms to publicize the amount of sales (as opposed to profits). High revenues tend to increase the credibility (saleability) of the product. The "best-selling" brand must be good! Large amounts of sales revenues also help maintain customer loyalty and constitute a form of advertising for the firm. That is to say, the sales record speaks for the product. Consumers would, most likely, be perturbed if the company boasted about its profits—more profits, in the consumer's mind, translate to price gouging or "ripoffs." The firm must compare the added cost of advertising to the additional revenues expected from advertising. A dollar of advertising must contribute at least a dollar in revenues over the additional cost of producing and selling the items. Sometimes it may be more economical to simply wait and not do anything.

In addition to advertising, the firm may also attempt to change the quality of the product. A product which is better made will no doubt cost more to make, but the additional costs of product improvement will eventually be more than offset by revenues earned from more and happier customers. Here, too, the firm must exercise caution in not "overimproving" a product such that the excessive costs of such improvements will necessitate very high prices for the product. High prices will reduce the quantity sold and may very well reduce revenues (and profits) to the company. The so-called "marginal reasoning" dictates that for added profits the firm should only spend so much on product improvements that can be easily recovered through increased sales, perhaps at higher prices. Any additional revenues above costs of production and improvement constitute profits. In many types of markets, firms engage in "nonprice competition." Advertising and product variation are two types of nonprice competition.*

---

*Product variation is often aimed at cost cutting. Thus, if a firm replaces metal parts with plastic ones or substitutes screws with rivets, the costs of production decrease. If revenues are unaffected by these changes, the firm's profits increase.

APPLICATIONS

1. The Firm and the Sales Tax

Sales taxes also affect the revenues of the firm. Usually sales taxes are imposed on an *ad valorem* basis, that is, the sales tax is some fixed percentage of the value of the item or the price of the item. Suppose the initial price of the product is $7 and Q_1 units are being bought. If a sales tax of 10% is imposed on this item the price inclusive of the tax will be $7.70. The higher effective price will discourage some buyers and the new quantity may be Q_2. Because the firm cannot keep the sales tax revenues, it receives only the price, net of the tax—that is, $7.00. The end result is that fewer units are sold due to the sales tax and the firm also receives fewer dollars in revenues and, in this case, the reduction in sales revenue equals $(Q_1 - Q_2) \times \$7.00$ (see Figure 5-12). The firm does have a choice, however. It can lower the price to $6.36, in which case the price inclusive of the tax will be $7.00. In this case, the quantity sold will remain at Q_1. Now, whether a price of $6.36, a price of $7.00, or a price in between is "optimal" depends on the cost structure of the company. As far as revenues to the government are concerned, tax revenues may rise or fall with the rate of the tax. If the sales tax rate is set too low, then tax revenues may not be very high despite large amounts of sales. If the tax rate is set too high the tax revenues may also be very low due to a decline in the quantity of sales. There is, then, an "optimal" tax rate which will maximize tax revenues for the government. (More on that in later chapters.)

2. Joe Blow's Gas Station

Every gas station usually carries more than one type of gasoline and some stock diesel fuel. Since the available space at a site obtained for the construction of the station and the erection of pumps is limited, the gas station owner must choose among the various combinations of fuel he wishes to stock. Each type of fuel must also be stored in a separate underground tank. Because the storage of one type of fuel takes up a certain amount of space both above and below the ground, less of the other types of fuel can be accommodated. Consequently, there is a trade-off among

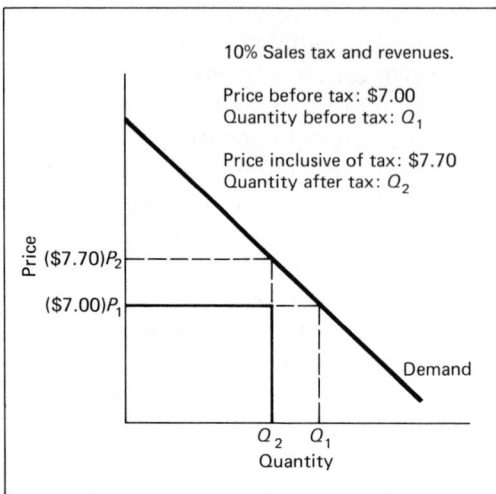

10% Sales tax and revenues.

Price before tax: $7.00
Quantity before tax: Q_1

Price inclusive of tax: $7.70
Quantity after tax: Q_2

FIGURE 5-12
Before the sales tax of 10%, the price of the product was $7, and the consumer purchased Q_1 units. A sales tax makes the price go up by 10% to $7.70, and accordingly the consumer buys a smaller quantity Q_2. The seller, however, receives the price *net* of the tax, that is $7.00. The effect of the sales tax is to reduce quantity demanded by the consumer and revenue received by the seller.

TABLE 5-3
JOE BLOW'S GAS STATION (UNLEADED GAS ONLY)

Maximum capacity of reserve tank:		5000 gallons per week
Average sales:	New car owners:	2800 gallons per week
	Older car owners:	1200 gallons per week
	Price of gasoline:	66¢ per gallon

the revenues received from the sales of the various types of fuel stored and sold. The costs of serving and storing the different types of fuel are essentially the same. Thus, the more revenues earned from sales, the more profit to the owner. The most profitable combination of fuel stock is that which produces the maximum revenue.

Revenue is the product of price and quantity. It is quite possible that the gas station owner can maximize his revenues by maintaining a very low markup on the price of each type of gasoline and thereby maximize revenues by large sales volumes. Alternatively, he can maintain high markups on the types of fuel that are in high demand and low markups on the type that are in relatively low demand. For example, if the majority of the cars in that particular neighborhood are new, then the gas station owner may very well stock only unleaded gasoline. Cars that use leaded gasoline may also use unleaded gasoline, and if there is occasional demand for fuel by the owners of older model vehicles, the gas station owner may still sell them some unleaded gasoline, thereby bringing in some additional revenue.

Consider the example given in Table 5-3. If you examine the table you will notice that, on the average, there is an idle reserve of 1000 gallons of unleaded gasoline per week. If the gas station owner can sell the idle reserve, he will make more profits. Holding idle reserves means an opportunity cost to the owner. By the law of demand, we know that lowering the price will increase the quantity demanded. If the owner lowers the price of gasoline to the owners of older cars so that the price is competitive with the price of leaded gasoline, more cars using leaded gasoline may very well use the lower-priced unleaded gasoline. Suppose Joe Blow puts up a sign that reads: *10% Discount To Customers Whose Vehicles Do Not Require Unleaded Gasoline*. At a price of approximately 60¢ per gallon, it is conceivable that 2200 gallons will be sold to the owners of older cars. The revenues from the owners of new cars will not change because they have to buy the unleaded gasoline anyway, but the gas station owner's revenues will increase from the sale of the additional 1000 gallons that previously lay idle. What will the profits be before and after such a strategy?

Before "dual pricing" scheme
Sales revenues: 4000 × $0.66 = $2640 per week
Cost of gasoline: 4000 × $0.50 = $2000 per week
Other costs (fixed) . . . = $100 per week
Idle capacity cost (1000 gallons) = $50 per week
Gross profits to owner: $490 per week

After "dual pricing" scheme
Sales Revenues:
New car owners: 2800 × $0.66 = $1848 per week
Old car owners: 2200 × $0.60 = 1320 per week
Total: $3168 per week

Cost of gasoline: $2500 per week
Other cost (fixed):   100 per week
Total cost: $2600 per week

Gross profits: $568 per week

From this very simple illustration we see that the gas station owner will add $78 per week to his gross profits by following the "dual" pricing scheme.

EXERCISES

1. Distinguish among the following.
   a. Total revenue.
   b. Average revenue.
   c. Marginal revenue.
   d. Incremental revenue.
   e. "Net" marginal revenue.

2. List as many reasons as possible why a firm might wish to maximize revenues instead of profits.

3. Establish the relationship among price, price elasticity of demand, and marginal revenue.

4. How do credit cards affect the revenues to
   a. businesses accepting such cards?
   b. companies and banks issuing such cards?

5. ABC, CBS, and NBC have competing programs ranging from news and talk shows to movies, children's programs, and "specials." How would a revenue-maximizing firm attempt to select the proper times and stations for its advertisements?

6. Many textbooks use multiple-colored diagrams and charts. Does the use of an additional color add significantly to the sales (revenues) of the book-publishing company? Should they use quite a few colors or not any? Discuss.

7. Suppose a movie theater is patronized by children, adults, and the elderly. What type of pricing strategy should the theater pursue in order to maximize its sales revenues? The theater also maintains a concession stand.

8. A multinational company has a market at home and one abroad. Show how it should sell quantity Q in either or both markets in order to maximize total revenues. Assume that the transportation cost to the foreign market is $t per unit. Both the home and the foreign markets have "ordinary" demand curves.

9. The U.S. Post Office has monopoly privileges in the area of first class mail. Should the price of first class postage stamps be raised or lowered for increased revenues? Explain.

10. High revenues may be obtained from very high prices (low quantities) or low prices (large quantities sold). What is the right price for maximum revenue from a single market?

11. State whether each of the following is generally true or false and explain why.

a. The value of the slope of the revenue function at a point is the same as the value of the marginal revenue at that point.
b. Revenues are maximized when marginal revenue equals zero.
c. If a firm has two markets it will maximize its total (joint) revenue by selling equal quantities in both markets.
d. Incremental revenue is a synonym for marginal revenue.
e. If a firm can earn revenues *either* in the present *or* in the future, the total real revenues over the life of the firm will be maximized if the firm equates the present value of future marginal revenues with the current marginal revenue from business operations.
f. A profit-seeking firm will not spend a dollar for additional advertising unless such advertising "contributes" at least a dollar in "net" additional revenue.
g. Total revenue can also be obtained by summing the area under the marginal revenue function.
h. A firm can earn more revenues from the sale of a given quantity of a product if it can charge different prices to different buyers, as opposed to charging the same price to all customers. (This practice is known as *first-degree* or *perfect* price discrimination.)
i. If 100 units may be sold at a price of $10 and 120 at a price of $9, the marginal revenue of the 20 additional units will be $80 and the *average* marginal revenue of each of the 20 additional units will be $4.
j. To earn the most income, a real estate salesman (on commission) should try to maximize the number of homes he sells by offering houses for sale at drastically reduced prices.

12. Using suitable graphs or other analyses, illustrate the case of the firm producing complementary products and maximizing total "combined" revenue from the sale of such joint products.

13. Show the effect of advertising on a firm's sales, revenues, and prices.

14. In some states grocery store owners carry soda pop in cans and bottles that require a deposit. Should the store carry bottles or cans for revenue maximization?

15. In some states many supermarkets carry their own brand of soda pop in "recyclable" bottles requiring deposits of about 20¢ per bottle. They also carry the widely distributed national brand Canada Dry, which also comes in bottles requiring deposits. Can the store charge a bigger deposit on Canada Dry? Should it? Explain.

16. Draw graphs of the following total revenue functions.
 a. $R = 100Q - 2Q^2$.
 b. $R = 100Q$.
 c. $R = 100$.

17. From the following demand functions, derive expressions for the corresponding total revenue functions.
 a. $P = 100 - 2Q$.
 b. $P = 100$.
 c. P varies from 1 to 100, and price elasticity of demand $= 1$.

18. Set up a model with a linear demand function. Assume that the government imposes an excise tax of $\$t$ per unit of output sold. Show what value of t will maximize tax revenues to the government. (Use the graphical method and employ areas to bring out the amount of tax revenue received by the government.) Use the supply and demand method.

19. Do Exercise 18 with the following information.

$$P_d = 100 - 2Q_d \quad \text{(demand)}$$
$$P_s = 40 + 2Q_s \quad \text{(supply)}$$

20. Why do some manufacturers leave out sales tax information when quoting prices?

21. Prove that if a firm sells a specific quantity between two markets, it will maximize total joint revenues by allocating quantities in the two markets such that

$$P_1\left(1 + \frac{1}{e_1}\right) = P_2\left(1 + \frac{1}{e_2}\right)$$

The prices in the two markets are P_1 and P_2 and the price elasticities of demand (inclusive of sign) are e_1 and e_2, respectively.

SUGGESTED READINGS

Baumol, W. *Business Behavior, Value and Growth.* New York: Harcourt, Brace, and Jovanovich, 1967.

Brown, R. S. "Estimating Advantages to Large-Scale Advertising." *Review of Economics and Statistics,* Volume 60, August 1978.

Cyert, R., and March, J. *A Behavioral Theory of the Firm.* Englewood Cliffs, New Jersey: Prentice-Hall, 1963.

Schmalensee, R. "A Model of Advertising and Product Quality." *Journal of Political Economy,* June, 1978.

Chapter
Six
Chapter
Six
Chapter
Six

THEORY OF PRODUCTION

Chapter 3 analyzed the utility-maximizing behavior of the consumer. This chapter focuses attention on the motivations, objectives, and decisions of the producer. The producer's primary aim is to produce (and sell) the goods and services and make profits. Although producers also have utility functions, for the moment we will separate utility considerations from production decisions.

PRODUCTION FUNCTIONS, OUTPUT, AND INPUTS

In economics terminology, the final or finished product is the *output,* while the resources used for production are the *inputs.* The production method (or combination of methods and processes) is called technology. The *production function* is a technical relationship between the output and the inputs under a specified set of conditions. More complex functions relate many different forms of output to several variables. The inputs may be classified as being either *fixed* or *variable,* depending on the circumstances. Those inputs that may be varied are usually called *variable inputs,* while those whose quantities are invariant are referred to as *fixed inputs.*

Suppose the quantity of output Q is governed by the quantities of three variable inputs, V_1, V_2, V_3, and two fixed inputs, F_1 and F_2. Then, ceteris paribus, we may express the production functions as

$$Q = f\left(\frac{V_1, V_2, V_3}{F_1, F_2, \ldots}\right) \tag{1}$$

Equation (1) suggests that, given the quantity and quality of the fixed resources (the Fs), and provided technology remains the same, Q will vary with the amounts of variable resources (the Vs). For example, in the generation of steam, the variable inputs might correspond to the quantities of fuel, water, and labor, while the fixed inputs are represented by the quantity of boilers and the number of supervisors. All other factors remaining equal, the output of steam will be affected by the amounts of fuel, water, and labor in use in conjunction with the fixed number of boilers and supervisors.

THE PRODUCTION ENVIRONMENT

Production theory is discussed in terms of either the *short run* or the *long run.* These "runs" do not necessarily imply different lengths of time, but rather the circumstances surrounding production. In almost all cases, the producer employs several inputs to produce the output. Generally speaking, the producer or the firm is restricted to very few variable inputs in the short run, while virtually all resources are allowed to vary in the long run. The short run basically refers to a production environment allowing limited variability and flexibility in resource utilization and technology of production. In contrast to the short run, the long run permits the producer to vary all the resources quantitatively as well as qualitatively. Thus, in the short run, the steam producer discussed earlier is constrained by fixed quantities of boilers as well as supervisory personnel, and the output of steam is varied by changing the quantities as well as combinations of the three variable resources—fuel, labor, and water. But, in the long run, the company cannot only vary the amounts of those resources currently variable, but also the others that are held fixed in the short run. That is, in the long run, the producer can vary the number of boilers in operation, in addition to being able to change the number of supervisors. Conceivably, the firm can also adopt newer or different technology in the long run.

PRODUCTION WITH ONE VARIABLE INPUT

Generally interpreted, a production function does not state *all* possible input–output relationships, but rather the most efficient ones—those that produce the maximum possible output from each combination of inputs. Because we assume that management usually uses the best production techniques available, the production function states the relationship of the maximum output to the inputs, which are combined in the most technically efficient proportions. The relationship between the maximum possible output and specified quantities of inputs is referred to as the *short-run production function.* In discussing short-run production theory, economists have found it convenient to combine all the fixed factors of production and call the aggregation "capital," although *capital* in itself connotes capital resources represented by the plant, equipment, and other long-term capital goods investment. In what follows, we shall refer to the fixed resources as capital and, for the sake of clarity, we will use only one variable resource—labor.

Under the conditions already stipulated, the short-run production function may be symbolically stated as

$$Q = f\left(\frac{L}{\bar{K}}\right) \tag{2}$$

Equation (2) shows the relationship between output Q and the variable resource L, given that all other resources $\bar{K}$ are held constant.

Total versus Marginal Physical Product

When the firm uses one variable resource, the output varies with the quantity of that variable input. The change in total output or *total physical product* associated with a *one-unit change* of the variable input is the *marginal physical product* of that particular variable resource. Thus, if 10 workers produce 20 units of output, while 11 workers collectively increase output to 26 units, the marginal physical product of the eleventh worker is 6 units of output. Because the variable resource may not always be changed by units, a more general definition of marginal physical product (or MPP) is shown by

$$MPP = \frac{\text{Change in total output}}{\text{Change in variable resource}} \qquad (3)$$

In our example, where labor (L) is the variable resource, the marginal physical product of labor will be

$$MPP_L = \frac{\text{Change in output } (Q)}{\text{Change in number of workers } (L)}$$

$$= \frac{\Delta Q}{\Delta L}$$

The marginal physical product of a resource may be positive, zero, or negative, and its value may or may not remain constant with changes in the quantity of the variable resource.

There is good reason to believe that the limitation on (or fixity of) certain resources and other constraints in the short run create certain hardships and inefficiencies for the producer, leading to declining marginal product of the variable input. That is, under such conditions, when more of the variable resource is utilized, each additional unit of the variable input helps produce progressively smaller quantities. Notice that we added the words "helps produce" to bring out the correct interpretation of marginal (physical) product. If three workers produce a total of 45 units and four workers produce 50, while five workers produce 52, the marginal products (*from the firm's point of view*) of the fourth and fifth workers are 5 and 2 units, respectively. This does not mean that the fourth worker is any better than the fifth worker or that the fifth worker necessarily works less than the fourth, but rather that the system gains 5 more units by employing one more worker beyond the first three, and gains an additional 2 units by hiring one extra worker beyond the fourth. We can describe such a situation as being indicative of declining marginal product. Such a phenomenon is also called the diminishing marginal productivity of the variable input, or very simply *diminishing returns*. With reference to the above example, it is quite possible that the fourth and fifth workers were not working equally hard. Such a situation would lead to similar results if the fourth worker hired is more diligent than the fifth. On the other hand, the declining efficiency of the fifth worker may very well have been brought about by the presence of the first four workers before him. Why not fire the first four in order to improve the performance of the fifth?! Whenever we encounter such diminishing returns we say that the output *increases at a decreasing rate*.

Why and how does the phenomenon of diminishing marginal physical productivity occur in the short run? Is it inevitable? These questions may be answered with the help of a simple example. Suppose an entrepreneur wants to make profits by selling hay. As such, he has to have the resources necessary to cut and tie the hay in bundles and deliver it to the market. Let us assume that he has one truck and a plot of land with hay. He wishes to keep the operation small and consequently he is the only worker. He cuts the hay, bundles it, and also delivers it. Most likely, because the owner performs all three chores, he must waste a considerable portion of his time and energy in tying the hay, in addition to driving the truck. Such a process is very inefficient. In essence, the productivity of his resources is not as high as their full potential. However, if he hires one worker, one of them can cut the hay while the other concentrates on tying and delivering it. The hiring of one worker will increase the efficiency of the operations through *specialization* and *division of labor*. An additional worker will conceivably add further efficiency to the system. As long as additional workers continue to increase the marginal efficiency of hay "production," output will *increase at an increasing rate.* This also implies that the marginal product from each additional worker is rising.

You may surmise that such a happy state of affairs, involving increasing marginal productivity, cannot continue indefinitely. Eventually, the fixed resources—one truck and a given plot of land—will have some effect on the productivity of the variable resource, labor. Beyond some point, an additional worker will add a smaller amount to the total output as compared to the already employed workers, and all other workers hired subsequently will add progressively less to total production. Such a development ordinarily describes the basic notion of diminishing marginal productivity, or simply *diminishing returns.* It is entirely possible that some workers will prove to be totally useless relative to the production of total output. From what we have just described, as more workers are employed in the hay gathering operation, output at first will tend to increase at an increasing rate and subsequently at a decreasing or diminishing rate. Thus, in the stage of increasing marginal productivity, the production function will be shown as a function concave from above. In the zone of diminishing marginal productivity, the production function will be depicted as being concave from below. Such a shape is typical of most short-run production functions employing one variable resource—at least traditionally that has been the case. However, not all short-run production functions conform to the shape suggested by the example of hay cutting shown in Figure 6-1.

Figure 6-1 illustrates the production function relating the output of bundles of hay to the number of fieldhands, including the owner himself. We see that up to point *A*, or four workers, the output is increasing at an increasing rate. The positive slope of the function indicates positive marginal physical product from the workers and the increase in the value of the slope indicates that marginal physical product is increasing up to point *A*. Beyond point *A*, we notice that the output of hay is increasing at a decreasing rate. This implies that the production function is now subject to diminishing returns. The workers in this range add some output, but each additional worker adds progressively smaller quantities, until the maximum output with the given amount of fixed resources (one truck and the same plot of land) is reached at point *B*. After point *B*, the production of hay is shown to fall, implying *negative* marginal physical product from the additional workers. Had the production function remained horizontal beyond point *B*, the slope of the function would have been zero, indicating zero marginal productivity of those employees. However, because the production function does show reduced output beyond point *B*, these workers are actually a hindrance. It is a case of too many cooks spoiling the broth. It is not very

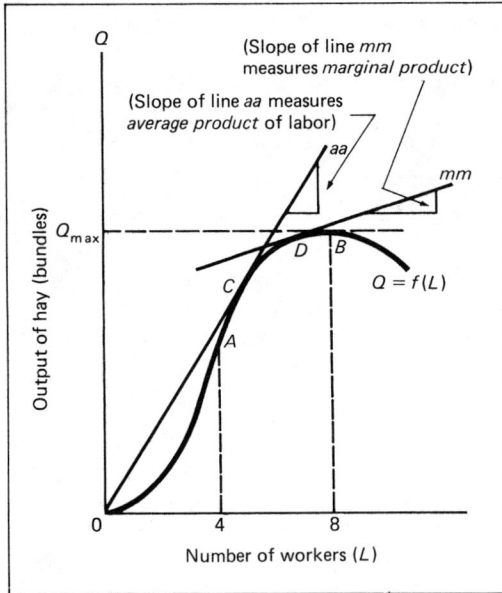

FIGURE 6-1
The diagram here shows a typical short-run production function, where output Q is related to one variable resource and other fixed resources. In this example, the workers are the variable resource, while the one and only truck and the fixed amount of land constitute the resources that are available in fixed quantities. Line aa drawn from the origin reflects the value of the average product of labor, while line mm shows the magnitude of the marginal product of labor. The higher the value of the angle subtended by the line, the higher the value of the marginal or average product. Because the production function in the region O–A is concave from above, the slope of line mm increases in this range, and the marginal product of the workers rises. Diminishing returns occur immediately past point A (the inflection point) and the function becomes concave from below. The diagram also shows that average product is highest at point C, and marginal product is zero at point B. At point C the marginal and average products of labor are equal.

difficult to visualize 40 workers getting into each other's way, probably being run over by the truck, even if they did not end up killing each other with their scythes.

The marginal product of a resource was defined as the additional output resulting from the use of one more unit of that resource. If we add the marginal product from each separate unit of the variable resource, we will obtain the total product or output from all the units working collectively. Thus, the total output equals the sum of the marginal physical products. Total output (or physical product) Q and marginal physical product (MPP) are related by equation (4):

$$Q = \sum_{}^{n} MPP_i \qquad (4)$$

Average Physical Product

The average physical product expresses the average output of each unit of a variable resource at a particular level of resource allocation. Thus if five workers collectively produce an output of one hundred bundles of hay, the average productivity will be $100 \div 5$, or 20 bundles. Analysts frequently resort to average values because they are more easily obtained and understood than the marginals. However, marginal analysis plays a very domineering role in microeconomics. The average product of a given quantity of a resource is the ratio of the total output and the total number of units of the resource. Thus, average physical product (APP) is linked to total output (Q), as shown in equation (5):

$$APP = \frac{\text{Total output}}{\text{Total quantity of resource}} \qquad (5)$$

Equation (5) may also be expressed as follows:

Total physical product (Q) = Average physical product (APP) × Total quantity of resource
For our discussion involving the bundles of hay, the total number of bundles produced can be obtained by multiplying the average product of the workers by the total number of workers, or

$$Q = (N) \times (APP_L)$$

where N represents the total number of workers on the field.

Graphically speaking, the average physical product of a variable resource is measured by the angle subtended by a straight line from the origin drawn to the production function. From Figure 6-1, we see that the slope of such a line drawn from the origin increases up to a point C and then declines, indicating that the average productivity of the workers increases up to that point and then drops. The highest average product occurs where the line from the origin is tangent to the production function, and because such a line also measures the slope of the production function at a point such as C, the average and marginal values are equal. This leads to the generalization that *the highest average physical product of a resource occurs at a level of employment that equalizes the marginal and average physical products.*

Table 6-1 illustrates a schedule of total output, the units of a variable resource, and the associated marginal and average products. The numbers are purposely chosen to reflect the S-shaped production function shown in Figure 6-1. Because we have chosen only certain discreet numbers for the first column, the average product of the variable resource is not shown to be maximum where it equals the marginal product. Had Table 6-1 employed all possible points along a continuous function, the marginal and average

TABLE 6-1

(1) Units of a variable resource	(2) Total output	(3) Marginal product $\Delta(2)/\Delta(1)$	(4) Average product (2)/(1)
0	0		
1	20	20	20
2	60	40	30
3	110	50	36.67
4	155	45	38.75
5	190	35	38
6	210	20	35
.	.	.	.
.	.	.	.
10	280	.	28
12	280	0	23.33
20	260	− 2.5	13

products would have been equal at a level of employment where the average product of the resource was maximum.

Factor Proportions and Returns from a Variable Input

Under the assumptions of a single variable input, the firm or producer cannot vary the resources available in fixed quantities, but it can alter the ratio of combinations of the variable input to the fixed. The fixed resources, which collectively have been referred to as capital, may or may not be divisible. For example, if a garage has only one hoist, and there are many cars that need to be lifted for repairs, even though there are adequate mechanics some of them will be practically useless because the hoist cannot be divided among all workers. On the other hand, the computer equipment for an airline reservation system is more divisible, because it can process many enquiries posed by the agents simultaneously, up to its capacity. In any case, as long as some resources are available in fixed quantities, the firm can alter the proportion of variable to fixed resources, and this leads to a production phenomenon generally called the *law of returns* or the *law of variable proportions.*

The firm's "return" is the output obtained from the employment of the inputs. We have already discussed the various possible outcomes due to the employment of a single variable input in combination with the fixed inputs. We will now summarize each possible case.

a. *Constant returns.* The firm's production function is subject to *constant returns* when the proportionate change in output is equal to the proportionate change in the variable input.

b. *Decreasing returns. Decreasing* or *diminishing returns* are present if the percentage change in output is less than the percentage increase in the variable input.

c. *Increasing returns.* The producer experiences *increasing returns* when a one-percent increase in the variable input leads to more than a one-percent increase in output.

The implications of these output–input relationships will become clear when we discuss the firm's cost and profit behavior. Table 6-2 shows simple illustrations of each case.

TABLE 6-2

Constant returns		Decreasing returns		Increasing returns	
Quantity of variable input	Output	Quantity of variable input	Output	Quantity of variable input	Output
1	10	1	10	1	10
2	20	2	15	2	25
4	40	4	20	4	60

The Stages of Production

Because the firm has a choice of combinations of the variable and fixed inputs, which proportion should it utilize in order to be efficient? For the moment, we are using the concept of efficiency as it is related to production and not to cost. The theory concerning the optimal combination of the resources will have to be deferred until we have had a chance to discuss the prices of the resources as well as the firm's output and its objectives. Using the "stages" approach, we can at least delineate the zone from which the efficiency-conscious firm will select its ideal combination of the variable and fixed resources.

The zones of production are divided into three stages—Stage I, Stage II, and Stage III. Very briefly, in Stage I there is too much of the fixed resource being combined with relatively small quantities of the variable resource, and such a combination proves uneconomical to the firm. For example, if the firm already has all the necessary equipment for a conveyor-belt/assembly-line setup for assembling cars, one solitary worker will prove to be most inefficient, as will two. In Stage I, the ratio of the fixed resource (F) to the variable (V) is too high and results in a negative or extremely low productivity of the fixed resource. Stage III contains exactly the opposite case—that is, such combinations involve a very high ratio of the variable resource to the fixed, and thereby cause the productivity of the variable resource to be very low or negative. Again, imagine what confusion and havoc 700 assembly line workers and one belt would cause. Consequently, the firm finds Stage II most desirable.

Stage II is generally chosen by the firm for a variety of reasons. First of all, the combinations of V and F in this stage are technically efficient. It can be shown that the marginal product of the variable resource (V) is positive throughout Stage II. As a consequence, the total output increases as it is added to the given amount of the fixed resource (F), suggesting that the ratio of V to F is not excessively high. Furthermore, because the average product of V is declining and still positive, the ratio of F to V is also not excessive in this stage. Additional considerations* of the average and marginal productivities of the fixed factor in this stage also make Stage II more acceptable than Stages I and III. Secondly, the firm's basic goal is to minimize costs and maximize profits. It will be seen that Stage II is more attractive to the firm when profits and costs are also taken into account. We summarize here the basic characteristics of the various stages.

Stage I. The marginal and average products of the variable resource are positive; productivities of the fixed resource are negative.

Stage II. The marginal and average products of the fixed as well as the variable resource are positive.

Stage III. The marginal product of the variable resource is negative, although the average product is positive. The marginal and average products of the fixed resource are positive.

Figure 6-2 shows the various stages of production. Only the variable

---

*Refer to the appendix to this chapter at the end of the book for more details.

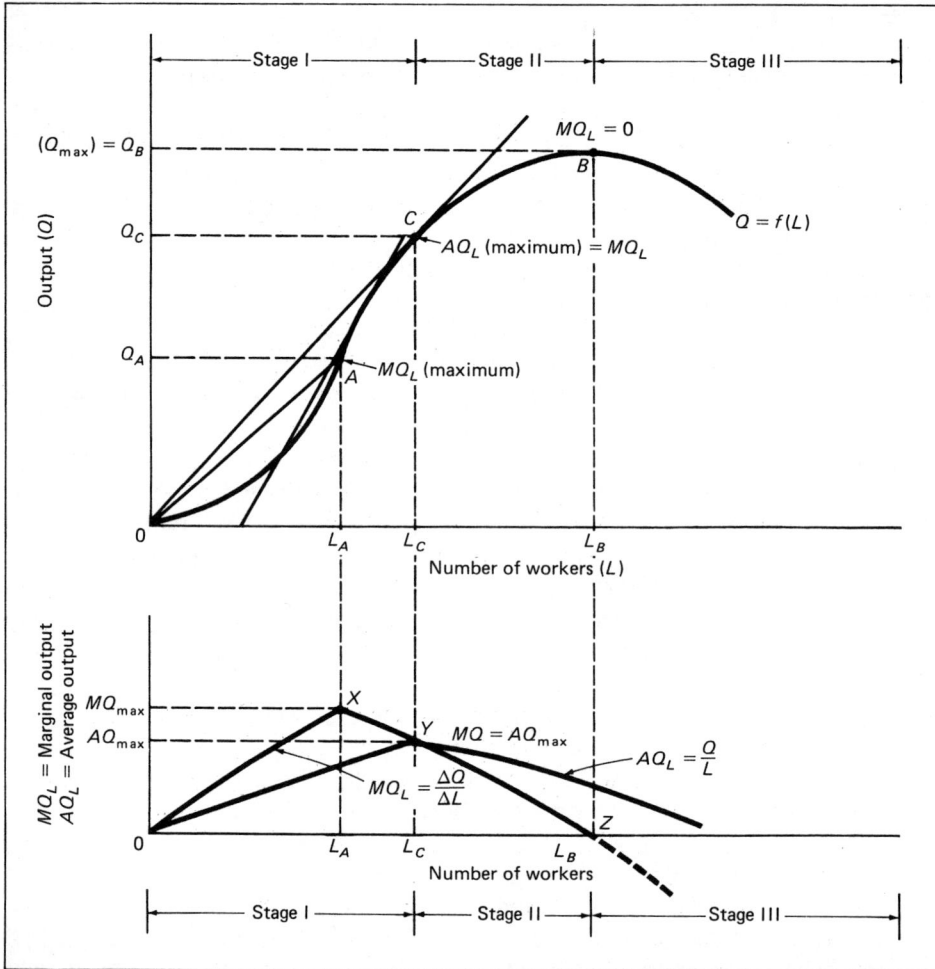

FIGURE 6-2
The upper half of the figure contains the production function $Q = f(L)$, while the lower portion shows the associated marginal and average (physical) products of the variable resource, labor (L). Due to the short-run conditions, the productivity of labor goes through various "stages." In Stage I, both marginal and average products are positive, but the productivity of the fixed resource is negative. In Stage II, all productivities are positive, even though the marginal and average products of the variable resources are declining. In Stage III, the marginal product of the variable resource is negative. Therefore, the firm or producer normally elects Stage II for production. The actual combination of the variable and fixed resources in Stage II that the firm will choose depends on the prices of the resources and the price of the output, as well as the firm's objectives. The marginal product of labor is maximum at an employment level of L_A, while the average product is maximum at L_C. The slope of the production function indicates the value of the marginal product, while the slope of the radius vector shows the magnitude of average product. The lower half of the figure further shows the various marginal and average values as well as relationships.

resource's marginal and average products are shown in the diagram. Stage II, from an efficiency point of view at least, is considered desirable because both the marginal and the average products of the variable resource (labor) are positive.

The Equimarginal Principle in Production

When we discussed the theory of utility in Chapter 2, we employed the so-called "equimarginal principle," or the Second Law of Gossen, in allocating a given amount of resources among several competing alternatives. Consumers maximized utility by allocating their income so that each product purchased yielded as much marginal utility per dollar as every other product. The producer also optimized the use of his resources. We will be discussing the theory of production involving more than one variable resource in Chapter 7. The equimarginal principle as it applies to the producer will be fully explained.

The producer's objective is to minimize the cost of producing a given volume of output or to maximize the output for a given cost outlay. Such objectives are consistent with profit-maximization goals as well. If the firm has several divisible and adaptable resources—A, B, and C—and the prices of the resources are known and positive, the most efficient combinations of these resources will result if

$$\frac{\text{Marginal product of } A}{\text{Price of } A} = \frac{\text{Marginal product of } B}{\text{Price of } B} = \frac{\text{Marginal product of } C}{\text{Price of } C} \quad (6)$$

Equation (6) is the equimarginal principle of production and is homologous to the equimarginal theory of utility.

Effect of Changes in Factor Mix

It has already been stipulated that, in the short run, the firm is limited to a given maximum amount of certain fixed resources. From this amount, the producer may choose to employ "correct" quantities of the fixed resource, provided the resources are divisible. For example, if labor is the only variable resource and capital is divisible, does the amount of capital employed affect the productivity of labor? In most cases, the marginal and average productivities of the variable resource are directly related to the amount of the fixed resource. Thus, it is generally true that the greater the amount of capital, the higher the productivity of labor.

Increments or changes in capital investment may be brought about by better use of the existing machines or through the use of newer equipment, as well as by improvements in the working conditions and increased training of the workers. There is adequate evidence to suggest that work performance is enhanced by such changes in the company's capital structure. Theoretically, revolutionary and large changes in the use of the fixed resources, as well as the incorporation of new technology, is only permissible in the long run. But, the

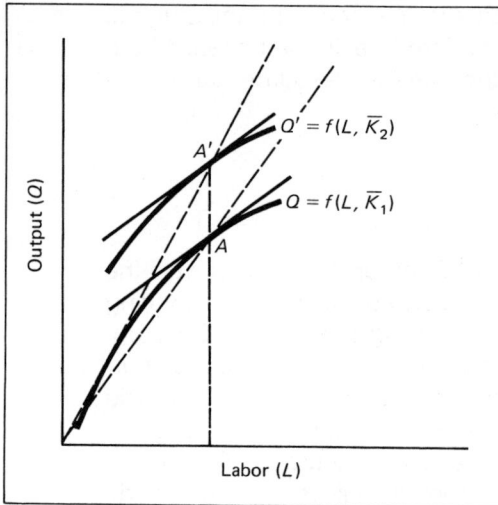

FIGURE 6-3
Tangents drawn at A and A' are parallel suggesting that the marginal product of labor is the same at both points. However, the average product of labor is higher at A' because the line from the origin to this point has a greater slope than the one drawn to point A.

many barriers to long-run adjustment notwithstanding, the firm can often make some changes in the short run.

Figure 6-3 shows the production function $Q = f(L)$, with fixed amounts of capital K_1. The production function is subject to diminishing marginal returns from the very start. If additional amounts of capital are brought into use, so that the firm now uses K_2 amount of capital, the production function will tend to shift upwards, as suggested by Q'. This new or amended production function will bring forth a larger amount of output as compared to $Q = f(L/K_1)$, although such a development may not always be possible.

Such changes in the location or configuration of the production function affect the marginal and average physical products of the variable resource as well. If the two production functions have identical slopes at points A and A', the marginal product of the L_Ath worker will not have changed, although those of the other workers may change. However, the average physical product of all the workers is shown to have increased; that is, due to the use of larger amounts of capital, on the average, each worker is more productive than before. Such an innovation should be considered efficient and economical, provided its additional usage does not bring about disproportionately large capital costs, labor wage demands, and, due to larger output, a harmful depression of market prices.

Similarity of Production and Utility Analysis

By now, you have probably recognized the obvious similarity between the discussions pertaining to consumption and production. Just as a consumption commodity can yield increasing, decreasing, or constant marginal utility, a variable productive resource in the short run can produce increasing, diminishing, or constant marginal product. The slope of the utility function measures the marginal utility of a commodity, while the inclination of the production function gives us the value of the marginal product of a variable resource under ceteris paribus conditions. The equimarginal principle is also applicable to both theories. The consumer is mainly interested in maximizing utility, while the producer is more concerned with the minimization of cost and the maximization of output, in order to make profits. Theories of utility can be used in the decision-making processes involving private or public interest, and the theories of production are also suitable for attaining private and public goals.

In Chapter 7, we will examine the adjustments of the producer in the long run. There, too, you will notice the many similarities between consumer and producer behavior.

APPLICATIONS

1. How Much Police Protection?

Governments, as well as firms, must decide among the competing uses for their funds. Take the case of a city government which must finance various types of public goods—such as police protection, fire fighting equipment, street cleaning, snow removal, and recreational activities—from its tax revenues. A good decision maker must have some idea about the benefits from each of the above-named activities that the city dwellers will receive. Such benefits must be weighed against the cost of obtaining these benefits. The total available budget should be allocated in a manner that will provide the maximum total benefit.

It is reasonable to assume that too much money allocated to a particular area will probably prove to be uneconomical, because the marginal benefit from many of the public goods mentioned decreases with their added availability. For example, how much more benefit will a 50th tennis court provide in a city of 40,000 inhabitants? These marginal benefits may be compared to or thought of as the marginal products. The city will maximize its total benefits for a given budget by following the equimarginal principle as shown here:

$$\frac{\text{Marginal benefit}_{(police)}}{\text{Price}_{(police)}} = \frac{\text{Marginal benefit}_{(parks)}}{\text{Price}_{(parks)}} = \frac{\text{Marginal benefit}_{(recreation)}}{\text{Price}_{(recreation)}}$$

This condition should be attained subject to the following budget constraint:

$\text{Expenditures}_{(police)} + \textit{Expenditures}_{(parks)} + \text{Expenditures}_{(recreation)} = \text{Total available budget}$

2. A Little Change Can Go a Long Way

Several years ago, one of the most affluent nations on earth sent a team of economics and development experts to a so-called "less developed country" to study the problems indigenous to that nation. The basic problem involved irrigation of cultivable land. Large canals with water already existed in the region, however, smaller tributaries feeding into these were necessary for transporting the water to the appropriate areas. These smaller canals were not being dug rapidly enough, because the local inhabitants possessed very crude and primitive tools.

Because the land area belonging to the average farmer was not very large, the use of heavy modern equipment was correctly ruled out by the experts. Had they recommended the use of such machinery, the marginal product of the resource would have been very minimal and the local people would have had to have been trained in their use. Instead, it was decided that the people should be given good shovels for the task. Soon after, the shovels were delivered and the experts went home.

A second (smaller) team of experts was sent to the underdeveloped region to check on the progress of the canal-digging operation. To its dismay, the team found no evidence of improvement in the pace of ditch digging. The natives did not wear shoes and it was very difficult for them to press down on the shovels with their feet—their feet hurt! Thereupon, the team was about to send for several hundred pairs of good work boots from the aid-donating country, except that an economic anthropologist came up with another idea. He suggested that all of the shovels be fitted with a small flat wooden crossbar at right angles to the base of the shovel handle. Such an addition could then be used as a pedal and the natives could use the shovels with their bare feet, which, as it turned out, they were glad to do. This simple short-run adjustment increased the productivity of the variable resource (labor) tremendously and the objective was attained at very little cost. The pedal-fitting operation also created several other jobs in the community.

EXERCISES

1. Define and explain the following terms:
   a. Production function.
   b. Total physical product.
   c. Marginal physical product.
   d. Average physical product.
   e. The slope of a function.
   f. The slope of a radius vector.
   g. Constant returns to proportion.
   h. Increasing returns to proportion.
   i. Diminishing returns to proportion.
   j. The stages in short-run production.
   k. Economic versus technical efficiency.
   l. The equimarginal principle.

2. Relate the use of production functions to each of the following:
   a. The municipal golf course.
   b. The city swimming pool.
   c. The armed forces.
   d. The learning curve.
   e. Agriculture.
   f. Graduate education.
   g. Fishing with boats in a small lake.
   h. Classroom teaching.
   i. Textbook writing.
   j. Research and development.

3. Explain the output–input relationship that prevails in each of the "stages" of short-run production.

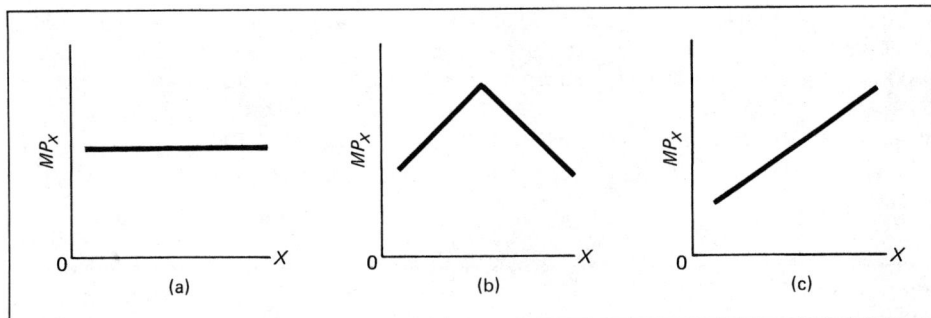

FIGURE 6-4

4. Draw representative diagrams of the short-run production function with one variable resource to exhibit the following:
   a. Constant returns throughout.
   b. Increasing returns followed by diminishing returns.
   c. Increasing returns followed by constant returns.
   d. Zero returns with each additional worker beyond the first.
   e. Constant returns followed by zero returns.
   f. Constant returns followed by negative returns.

5. Suppose a car wash hires college students as employees. Can you perceive the use of short-run production theory in such a case? Explain.

6. Suppose that the following are several short-run production functions, each a function of one variable. Make sketches of the functions and identify the nature of "returns" in each case.
   a. $Q = 20L$.
   b. $Q = 100L + L^2$.
   c. $Q = 200L^{1/2}$ (The ½ means the "square root of.").
   d. $Q = 1000\,(2-L)$.
   e. $Q = 1000$.

7. From the diagrams of marginal physical product functions in Figure 6-4, draw reasonably correct total product functions.

8. Now attempt the sketches for the production function from the average (physical) product functions in Figure 6-5.

FIGURE 6-5.

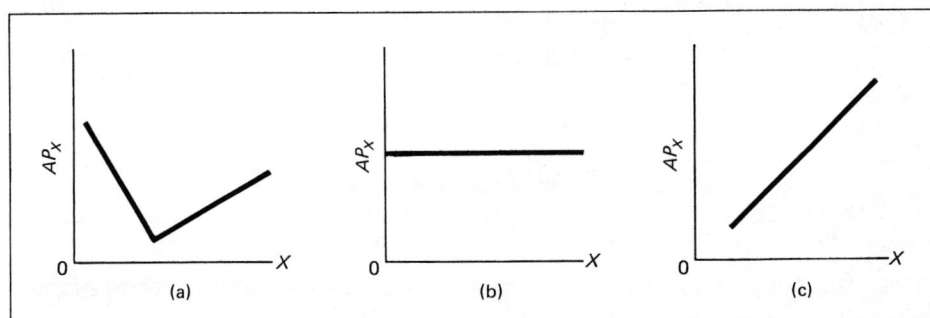

9. Shown below are the marginal productivities of the various workers employed in a cigar-manufacturing company. There are four processes—A, B, C, and D—which produce cigars. Of the 20 available workers on the company payroll, 4 are assigned to process A, 6 to B, 8 to C, and the remaining 2 to D. Each worker is paid $100 per day and the marginal product of each worker on a daily basis is as shown.

Marginal product of the ith worker	Process A	Process B	Process C	Process D
1st	12	6	9	10
2nd	10	4	8	10
3rd	8	2	7	10
4th	6	1	6	10
5th	4	1	5	6
6th	3	0	4	6
7th	2	0	3	3
8th	1	0	2	2
9th	0	0	1	2
10th	0	0	0	1

  a. What is the total combined output of all the workers under the current work assignment?
  b. What is the unit labor cost to produce a cigar?
  c. If you were given the task of reassigning the workers, would you do so? Explain.
  d. What would be the new total output of cigars? The new labor cost per unit?
  e. What principle did you use in the reassignment process?

10. How will each of the following affect the productivity of the total labor force for a company? Use the notion of average productivity.
  a. Mandatory jogging during special "breaks."
  b. Free time for exercise (optional) at a company-built health spa.
  c. More capital investment per worker.
  d. Higher wages per worker.
  e. Profit-sharing bonuses.
  f. Productivity incentive bonuses.
  g. Company-sponsored concerts.
  h. Company-provided subsidized breakfasts.
  i. Employment of more managers and foremen.
  j. Installation of a more effective air-conditioning system.
  k. Company-sponsored family picnics for employer/employee.
  l. Publication of company magazines emphasizing the "family" relationship of company and workers.

SUGGESTED READINGS

Bosworth, D. "Some Evidence on the Productivity of Qualified Manpower in Britain." *Bulletin of Economic Research*, Volume 30, May 1978.

Heady, E. *Agricultural Production Functions*. Ames, Iowa: Iowa State University Press, 1961.

Heaton, H. *Productivity in Service Organizations: Organizations for People.* New York: McGraw-Hill, 1977.

Ippolito, R. "The Division of Labor in the Firm." *Economic Inquiry,* Volume 15, October 1977.

Mahoney, T. A. "The Rearranged Work Week: Evaluation of Different Work Schedules." *California Management Review,* Volume 20, Summer 1978.

Morris, D. "Household Production Theory, the Lancaster Hypothesis and the Price–Quality Relationship." *Bulletin of Economic Research,* Volume 30, May 1978.

York, J. "Productivity and Technology in the Electric Motor Industry." *Monthly Labor Review,* August 1978.

Chapter Seven

FURTHER CONSIDERATIONS IN PRODUCTION THEORY

Chapter 6 dealt largely with the theory of short-run production, where output was generally produced with one variable input. Actually, even in the short run, a firm uses more than a single variable resource. For instance, in the production of french fries, cooks must use not only labor, but also oil and potatoes as the other variable resources. However, because the use of such raw materials is in some constant proportion to the volume of output, the theory of production with one variable input is not altered significantly with their exclusion from the model. In this chapter we will analyze the production decisions and output–input relationship when a firm uses two variable resources, such as capital and labor. We will also discuss the implications of the long run.

PRODUCTION WITH TWO VARIABLE INPUTS

We can dig ditches with shovels, machines, or a combination of the two. This suggests that, to some extent, the labor-intensive ditch-digging resource (men with shovels) is a substitute for the capital-intensive resource (machines). In the discussion to follow, the first resource is referred to as labor, and the second as capital.

When a firm uses two variable resources, such as capital and labor, the ceteris paribus production function may be stated as

$$Q = f(K,L) \qquad (1)$$

Equation (1) states that the volume of output Q is a function of capital K and labor L. It further suggests that because Q is technically related to the quantities of K and L, output will be affected by changes in K and L.

Isoquants

Equation (1) is a production function relating Q to K and L. If we select a particular volume of output, we will be able to use several combinations of the two resources that will yield the desired quantity of Q. When all such combinations of K and L are connected by a line or a curve, the resulting locus is called an *isoquant*. The prefix "iso" means equal, hence the word isoquant means "equal quantity." In essence, an isoquant shows all possible combinations of the available resources that yield a given Q. Every production function of the type described by equation (1) will generally yield an infinite number of isoquants. An isoquant in production theory is comparable to an indifference curve of utility analysis.

With reference to the digging of ditches, suppose that each and every one of the combinations of the two inputs in Table 7-1 can dig 15 ditches per day. If we plot the various combinations as points on a K–L plane, we will obtain an isoquant representing 15 ditches dug, as shown in Figure 7-1. Because we can dig either a larger or smaller number of ditches as well, the graph shows other isoquants that correspond to different quantities. Just as a utility function is shown by an indifference map, an isoquant map containing many isoquants represents a production function.

TABLE 7-1

Machines (K)		Men with shovels (L)
12	and	1
8	and	13
3	and	33
1	and	43

Isoquants also possess certain properties similar to the characteristics of indifference curves. As a matter of fact, an indifference curve is sometimes referred to as a "utility isoquant." Some of the fundamental properties of isoquants are listed here.

a. An isoquant shows the many possible combinations (usually two) of the resources that yield a unique volume of output.
b. Normally, an isoquant shows an inverse relationship between the inputs.
c. Isoquants do not intersect and are generally convex to the origin, although many shapes are possible.
d. Isoquants representing larger quantities of output lie above and to the right of those that represent smaller volumes.
e. An isoquant map is a graphical representation of a production function.

While the expression for the production function is $Q = f(K, L)$, the one for an isoquant, for a level of output such as Q_2, may be written as

$$Q_2 = f(K, L) \tag{2}$$

Because Q_2 is unique, equation (2) describes all possible ways of combining K and L that will bring forth Q_2 units of output.

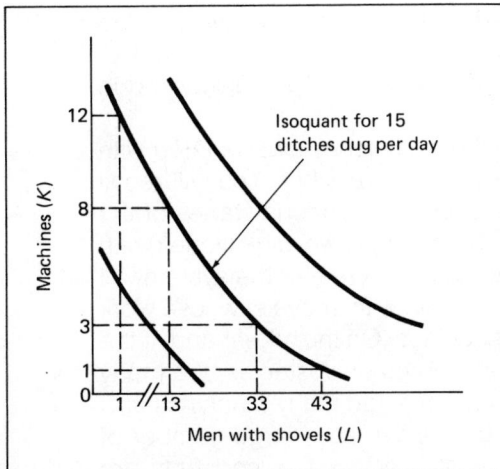

FIGURE 7-1
An isoquant shows all combinations of two resources (inputs) which produce a given or constant quantity of output. Thus, machines or men may be used to dig ditches. Twelve machines and 1 man can dig 15 ditches per day. But, 8 machines and 13 workers can also do the same amount of work.

The Marginal Rate of Technical Substitution

You have already seen that the two resources may be combined in several proportions to yield a specific volume of output along a given isoquant. Thus, one resource can replace the other to some degree. The extent to which such substitution can take place is indicated by the *marginal rate of technical substitution*. The marginal rate of substitution, or MRTS, measures the amount of one resource that can be substituted by *one unit* of the other resource, in order to maintain the same volume of output. It is easy to see that such a ratio, in effect, indicates the *slope of an isoquant*.

Take for example the combinations of K and L that can dig 15 ditches per day. These combinations, which are derived from Table 7-1, are drawn as an isoquant in Figure 7-2. Point A, with 12 units of K and 1 unit of L, produces just as much as point B, with $8K$ and $13L$. Thus, in moving from point A to point B, we see that 12 additional units of L are necessary to take the place of the 4 units of K no longer in use, which essentially suggests that (on the average) each unit of L is able to substitute ⅓ units of K. Hence the MRTS of K by L is ⅓:1, or simply 1:3. You can verify that the absolute value of the MRTS in the range B–C is 1:4 and that the MRTS between points C and D is 1:5. Because the MRTS compares the change in K to the change in L along a given isoquant, it in effect measures the value of the slope of the isoquant. Consequently, it is quite correct to state the marginal rate of substitution as the ratio of the rise to the run, or, in our case,

$$\text{MRTS} = \frac{\Delta K}{\Delta L}$$

As you can see, the isoquants are convex to the origin. If the isoquants are convex as we move down them, the absolute value of the MRTS declines. This indicates that the more we use one resource in place of the other, the less its capacity to substitute. With reference to the ditch-digging illustration, the more men we employ the less the ability of each additional worker to replace machines. Such a phenomenon is described as the principle of *diminishing marginal rate of technical substitution,* and is very similar to the concept of diminishing marginal rate of substitution in indifference analysis discussed in Chapter 3.

Diminishing MRTS largely occurs due to the inefficiencies associated with the excessive use of one productive input relative to the other. You will recall that we referred to such a case in the discussion of the various stages of the short-run production function in Chapter 6. Thus, when we dig ditches with men and machines, it is entirely possible that the output rate of the system will be less than economical if we employ too many men with shovels, whose work could have been performed better by a few machines. On the other hand, if the area of work is small or constrained by fences and other obstacles, too many machines will prove to be very inefficient. In any case, too many machines and a very few manual laborers may be just as productive as a large number of diggers and a very few machines. However, as long as the isoquants are

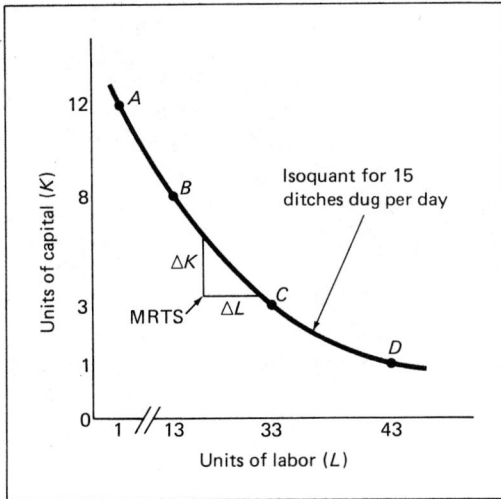

FIGURE 7-2
The rate at which one input can replace the other, along an isoquant, is known as the marginal rate of technical substitution (MRTS). The MRTS is shown by the slope of the isoquant.

convex, they suggest that each type of resource's capability to replace the other diminishes with increases in its use.

Those of us interested in body building know that many physical culturists use anabolic steroids to increase the size of their muscles. Muscles may be strengthened or enlarged by a variety of combinations of exercise and consumption of steroids. Suppose we wish to attain a unique level of muscle size. If all combinations of the two inputs, steroids and exercise, that help produce the desired state of muscular development are connected on a graph, we will have an isomuscularity curve. Such an isoquant is shown in Figure 7-3. Notice that the isoquant is drawn convex to the origin, suggesting the diminishing marginal rate of substitution between the food supplement and the exercise. Thus, an excessive amount of additional exercise will be necessary to replace a few steroid tablets as we move down; quite a few steroid tablets will be necessary to take the place of exercise when we operate in the upper corner.

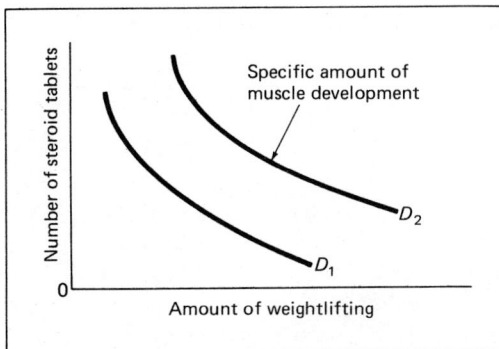

FIGURE 7-3
Either food supplements or exercise can "produce" muscles. Many combinations of the two inputs can lead to the same amount of muscle development. These combinations form "iso-development" curves labeled as D_1 and D_2, and in essence constitute production isoquants.

Marginal Physical Product and the MRTS

The marginal physical product, or simply marginal product of a resource, was described as the change in output resulting from a one-unit change in the use of that resource, all other factors remaining equal. For example, if we have two variable inputs, M and N, and if N is held constant, then the change in output associated with a unit change of M will measure the marginal product of M. In the discussion that follows, we will establish a relationship between the marginal products of the inputs and the marginal rate of technical substitution.

Suppose the production function $Q = f(M, N) = MN$. Let us further stipulate that the desired level of output equals 64 units. Thus, all possible values of M and N which, when multiplied, result in 64, form the combinations of M and N for the 64-unit isoquant. Table 7-2 shows six combinations of M and N—three of which provide the appropriate combinations for the 64-unit isoquant, and three of which reflect the volume of output if N is held constant at 1, while M is allowed to take on the suggested values.

The first three combinations of M and N yield the 64-unit isoquant shown in Figure 7-4. The second set yields points on three different isoquants, and it is to this set of combinations that we must now pay attention. Because N is held constant at 1 unit, the resulting change in output associated with changes in M alone must measure the marginal physical product of M. Thus, when M is at 16, the output with 1 unit of N equals 16 units at point Z on the 16-unit isoquant. When N holds constant at 1 unit, 32 units of M increase output to 32, suggesting that the incremental output of the 16 additional units of M is 16. Hence the marginal physical product of M in this region is 1. Similarly, 64 units of M and 1 unit of N produce an output volume of 64 units, and this implies that the 32 additional units of M produce 32 more units of output, again implying that the marginal product of M in this range is also 1. Now refer to Table 7-3. With the information about the marginal products of M and N as shown in Tables 7-2 and 7-3, we can now use Figure 7-4 to derive the relationship between these productivities and the MRTS.

In Figure 7-4, the 64-unit isoquant is labeled STU. At point S, 64 units of M are being combined with 1 unit of N and at point T the same output is produced with 32 units of M and 2 units of N. Because the volume of output along the isoquant is constant, the total productivity of the 32 units of M no longer in use must equal the total productivity of the additional unit of N. Tables 7-2 and 7-3 tell us that the marginal product of the 32 units of M—with N held constant at

TABLE 7-2
PRODUCTION FUNCTION: $Q = MN$

Units of M	Units of N	Q	MRTS $= \Delta M/\Delta N$	Units of M	Units of N	Q	Marginal product of $M = \Delta Q/\Delta M$; $N = 1$
64	1	64	32:1	64	1	64	32/32 = 1
32	2	64	16:2	32	1	32	16/16 = 1
16	4	64		16	1	16	

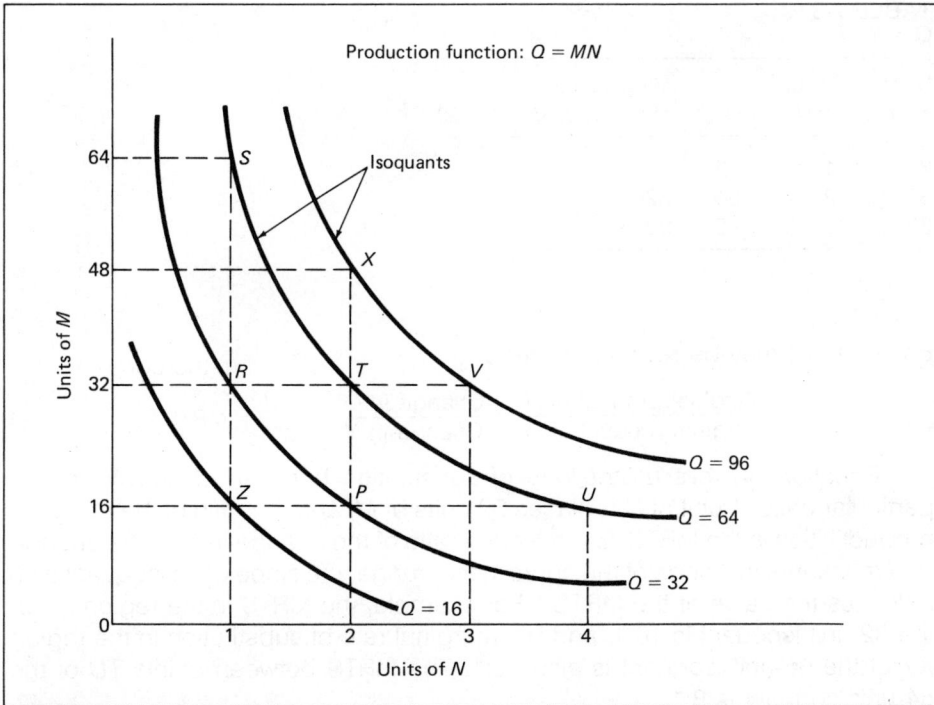

FIGURE 7-4
Point S on the 64-unit isoquant uses 64 units of M and 1 unit of N, while point T, also on the same isoquant requires 32 units of M and 2 units of N. Because both points lie on the same isoquant, output is equal at both of these points. Thus, in moving from S to T, the producer replaces 32 units of M with 1 additional unit of N; therefore, the incremental productivity of the new unit of N is exactly as much as that of the 32 units of M that it replaces. This ratio of substitutability is called the marginal rate of substitution, or MRTS. The value of the MRTS is also given by the ratio of the respective marginal physical products of the two inputs, or

$$\text{MRTS} = \frac{\Delta M}{\Delta N} = \text{Slope of isoquant}$$

$$= \frac{\text{Marginal product of } N}{\text{Marginal product of } M}$$

1—equals 32 units of output; and the marginal product of the second unit of N—with M held constant at 32 units—equals 32 units of output. Thus, the marginal product of each unit of M—where $N = 1$—equals one unit of output; and the marginal product of each unit of N—where $M = 32$—equals 32 units of output. Hence, in going from point S to point T, we replace 32 units of M with 1 unit of N, and in accordance with the marginal productivities of these two resources,

(Marginal product)$_M$ × change in M = (Marginal product)$_N$ × change in N (3)

or, in our case, between points S and R,

$$(1) \times (32) = (32) \times (1)$$

TABLE 7-3
$Q = MN$

Units of M	Units of N	Q	Marginal product of $N = \Delta Q/\Delta N$; $M = 32$
32	1	32	
32	2	64	32
32	3	96	32

Equation (3) may be rewritten to read

$$\frac{\text{Marginal product of } N}{\text{Marginal product of } M} = \frac{\text{Change in } M}{\text{Change in } N} = \frac{\Delta M}{\Delta N} = \text{MRTS} \qquad (4)$$

Equation (4) tells us the rate of substitution between M and N. In this particular case, 1 unit of N replaces 32 units of M, and the ratio of the marginal productivities is the MRTS. Because the ratio of the change in M to the change in N measures the slope of the curve in that range, the slope of an isoquant also indicates the value of the MRTS.* For example, the MRTS in the region RP of the 32-unit isoquant is 16:1, and the marginal rate of substitution in the region XV of the 96-unit isoquant is also 16:1. The MRTS between points TU of the 64-unit isoquant is 8:1.

The Economic Zone of Production

When a firm uses two variable inputs, there is a possibility that the excessive use of one relative to the other may contribute to substantial losses in overall productivity of the resource. Thus, if too many laborers are employed with only a few machines, it is entirely possible that output will be less than that possible with the same number of machines and fewer laborers. Because more workers produce less output than a smaller number, the additional workers yield *negative* marginal product. However, every isoquant must maintain a constant volume of output, and when some of the workers actually tend to reduce that volume, additional machines are necessary to offset such negative production. Hence, instead of the two resources being substitutes, they end up as *complements*. When this occurs, the isoquants become positively inclined—that is, they bend away from the respective axes. An efficiency-conscious firm will usually prefer not to produce in such a range, because not only do more resources cost more, but a negative marginal product hinders production. Therefore, the economic zone of production is limited to those portions of the isoquants where the marginal products of the resources are at least zero or positive.

Before a resource's marginal product attains negative values, it must

*This description of the measurement of the slope is only valid if the changes are infinitesimally small, since the slope of the isoquant varies over the entire length of the curve. Also, we are measuring the *absolute* value of the slope.

reach zero. Areas of positive marginal products are separated from the negative by a pair of buffer lines, each one connecting points on the various isoquants where the marginal products of the two resources are zero. These lines are called *ridge lines*. One of the lines is drawn through all points where the marginal product of A is zero; the other ridge line forms the locus of all points where the marginal product of B is zero. Figure 7-5 shows the two ridge lines and the economic zone of production, which is bounded on both sides by the pair of ridge lines. The remaining two zones, each bounded by a ridge line and the corresponding axis, may be thought of as the uneconomical Stages I and III in the theory of production discussed in Chapter 6. The marginal product of one resource is negative in each of these uneconomic zones of production.

Returns to Scale

Suppose the producer is able to vary the quantities of all resources in order to produce a larger volume of output. How much will output increase? The relative change in output depends on the conditions referred to as *returns to scale,* and such a concept is the multiple variable counterpart of *returns to proportion* discussed in Chapter 6. Returns to scale compares the ratio of the percentage change in output to the percentage change in *all* the inputs. As you might expect, the percentage change in output may be greater than, equal to, or less than the percentage change in inputs. Three different types of returns

FIGURE 7-5
As long as the isoquant is downward sloping, one input can be substituted for the other. But, when the isoquant slopes upwards, *more* of both resources must be used to keep output constant. Consequently, the area where the isoquants are upward sloping is considered uneconomical.

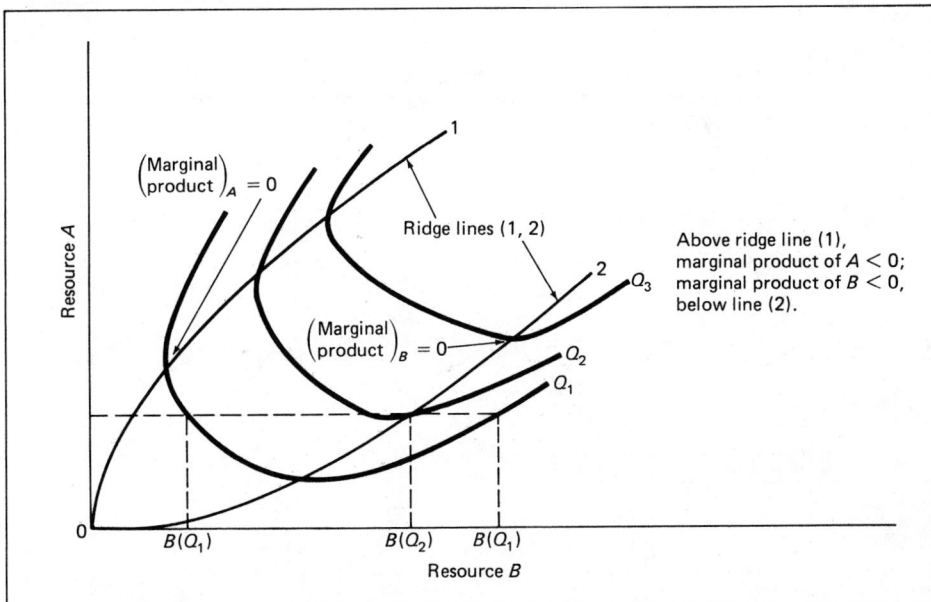

are generally encountered: *increasing, constant,* and *decreasing* returns to scale. When a company increases its "scale" of operations, such as from a small-scale enterprise to a large-scale operation, it generally means that the firm is increasing the usage of all its resources. The three types of returns to scale are listed here.

a. *Increasing returns to scale:* The percentage change in output exceeds the percentage change in inputs.
b. *Constant returns to scale:* The percentage change in output equals the percentage change in inputs.
c. *Decreasing returns to scale:* The percentage change in output is less than the percentage change in inputs.

The various returns to scale are encountered by firms in the process of enlargement of the volume of operations. If the firm can produce the output much more efficiently, with larger amounts of all resources, it experiences increasing returns. For example, an airline can enlarge its scale of operations by replacing its fleet of 707 jets with a series of 747's. The bigger planes not only allow the company to offer more seats—more than twice the number possible on the smaller aircraft—but they are technically more efficient. Such large-scale expansion permits the firm to take advantage of the economies made possible by the use of the jumbo jets, which otherwise would not have been available with the existing equipment. Thus, if the larger planes and associated supporting resources constitute a 100% increase in the use of inputs, and if the total output of revenue increases by 200%, the airline's production function will experience increasing returns to scale.

Greater efficiency is not always associated with a larger scale. For

FIGURE 7-6
In the long run, the firm moves out along its expansion path *OM.* In (a), the returns to scale are increasing because in going from *A* to *B,* the output increases by 100%, while the inputs increase by 75%.

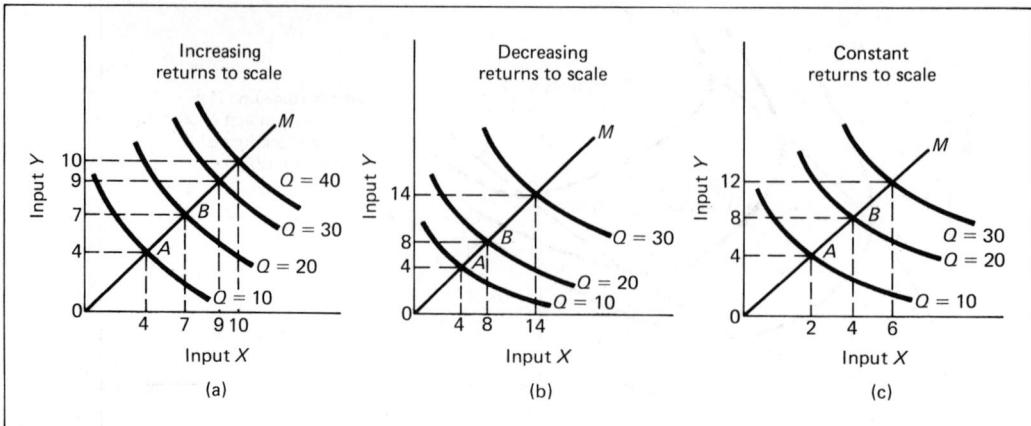

example, where the firm uses fixed proportions of all resources to produce a unit of the output, an increase in the employment of all resources will lead to an equal percentage change in the output. The case of the garment industry probably comes close to this phenomenon. If 10 workers with 10 sewing machines can sew 100 shirts per hour, then 20 workers and 20 machines can produce 200 shirts per hour. Because the percentage changes in output and input are equal, the returns to scale are constant.

Large scale operations occasionally contribute to certain inefficiencies. For example, after a certain point, increases in a city's crime-fighting resources (police, street lights, TV-monitors) bring forth a relatively small increase in benefit. Organizational problems are frequently encountered when the scale of operations becomes too large. Decreasing returns to scale is also noticeable around certain airports where the growth in passenger volume and the number of commercial as well as civilian aircraft has led to a slowdown in service by the airport's facilities. The busy skies during certain peak hours also account for part of the lost output, as do the nerves of the overworked air traffic controllers. The three isoquant maps of Figure 7-6 illustrate the different returns to scale.

ECONOMIES AND
DISECONOMIES OF SCALE

Although we will have more to say about this topic in the next chapter, a few words about the *economies* (and *diseconomies*) *of scale* are in order. The producer obviously incurs certain costs in the acquisition of the many resources. However, if economies of scale are present, expansion of scale leads to a less than proportional increase in costs, be it the cost or outlay for the purchase of resources or the production of output. Generally speaking, to determine whether a firm is beset with economies or diseconomies of scale, we compare the relative change in output to the change in cost. If there are diseconomies, the cost of production rises faster than the output.

Economies or diseconomies of large-scale operations may be attributed to production as well as pecuniary considerations. If the producer's production function is of the increasing returns-to-scale variety, then even if the resource prices do not change, the cost of producing a unit of output will fall as the firm expands its scale of operations. For example, if two workers on a small assembly line produce 100 units per hour, and if each receives $10 per hour, the labor cost per unit will be 20¢. However, if the company quadruples its production rate by hiring an extra worker and using a larger assembly line area, the labor cost per unit will drop to 7.5¢. Such a cost reduction will be due largely to the increased efficiency leading to increasing returns to scale.

Most firms qualify for substantial discounts on raw materials if such resources are purchased in large enough bulk quantities. Consequently, the cost of raw materials per unit of output also tends to fall under such circumstances, and does so if and only if the firm is operating on a large scale. Many people refer to such cost-reducing phenomena as "cost cutting through mass production."

THE FIRM'S OPTIMAL CHOICE OF INPUTS

Although a firm's eventual and final objective may be to obtain profits, its immediate goal is to produce a given volume of output of a particular quality at the least cost possible. In Chapter 3, the consumer's utility was maximized where the isocost or budget line was tangent to the highest indifference curve. In a very similar manner, the firm's cost of producing a given output with two variable inputs is minimized where its isocost line is tangent to the relevant isoquant. Alternatively, at such a point output is maximized for a given cost outlay.

Suppose a firm's production function is stated as $Q = f(X,Y)$ and the prices of the two resources are P_x and P_y, respectively. If the isoquants are convex, the production function will appear as in Figure 7-7. As long as the prices of the resources remain constant, and the budget outlay is known, the familiar isocost line will be drawn as a straight line, and its vertical and horizontal intercepts with a budget of $B will be the distances B/P_y and B/P_x. Thus, if the firm's budget is restricted to $1000 and the price per unit of X is $4, while the price of a unit of Y is $5, the Y intercept of the budget line will be at 200 and the X intercept at 250. At point M, the budget line is tangent to isoquant Q_3, and under the circumstances, Q_3 is the maximum volume that can be produced with $B. At any other point along the isocost line the output will be less, although the expenditures will still equal $B.

At the point where the isocost line is tangent to the isoquant, the slopes of the two functions are equal. The absolute value of the isocost line is given by the ratio $B/P_y \div B/P_x$, or P_x/P_y. The slope of an isoquant is the marginal rate of technical substitution or the MRTS, which in turn is the ratio of the marginal physical products of the two resources. At a point such as M, in Figure 7-7, the price ratio P_x/P_y is equal to the MRTS. This leads to the following relationship:

$$\text{MRTS} = \frac{\Delta Y}{\Delta X} = \frac{(\text{Marginal product})_x}{(\text{Marginal product})_y} = \frac{P_x}{P_y} \tag{5}$$

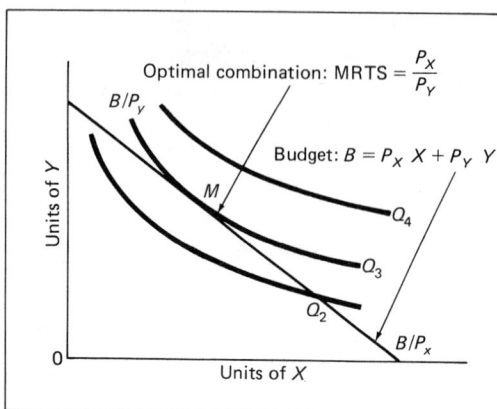

FIGURE 7-7
The optimal combination of inputs is that which minimizes the cost of producing a given output, and such a point normally occurs where the firm's budget line is tangent to an isoquant. At point M, the MRTS equals the price ratio of the inputs (P_x/P_y).

The firm's optimal choice of inputs
175

Equation (5) may also be expressed as

$$\frac{(\text{Marginal product})_x}{P_x} = \frac{(\text{Marginal product})_y}{P_y} \tag{6}$$

Either equation (5) or (6) may be used to select the cost-minimizing combination of inputs under ordinary circumstances. The ratio of marginal physical product of a resource to its resource is called (at least by this author) the *efficiency ratio*. The higher the efficiency ratio of an input, the greater its employment by a cost and efficiency-conscious producer. Where possible, the cost of producing a given volume of output will be minimized when the efficiency ratios are equal to each other.

A numerical example will be used to illustrate the point further. Let us suppose that the production function is $Q = (XY)$ and the prices of X and Y are $8 and $12, respectively. Let us further assume that we wish to produce 600 units ($Q = 600$). Table 7-4 shows a few of the combinations that will produce the desired Q and the corresponding costs of such combinations.

The least costly combinations of X and Y are 30 and 20, respectively. You will notice that the absolute values of the MRTS and P_x/P_y are not quite equal at this point. We can use mathematical techniques to determine the exact combination necessary for cost minimization. However, because the two ratios are closest with this combination, and because it also results in the lowest of all the tabulated costs, the X/Y ratio of 3:2 is considered optimal. As it happens, if we use mathematical techniques, the 3:2 ratio of X to Y will still be the least costly.

Optimal Input Ratio for Cobb–Douglas Functions

All production functions where the inputs are multiplied by each other are referred to as *multiplicative production functions*, and very often as *Cobb–Douglas functions*. For example, functions like $Q = X^2Y$, $Q = MN$, $Q = K^2L^2Z^2$, and $Q = 100\,RS^2T$ represent Cobb–Douglas production functions. The general form of the Cobb–Douglas function (C–D) is $Q = AK^aL^b$, where K and L

TABLE 7-4
$Q = XY = 600$

X	Y	MRTS	Cost	P_x/P_y	
2	300		$3616		
		75:1		.67:1	
4	150		1832		
		19:1		.67:1	
8	75		964		
		7.5:1		.67:1	
10	60		800		
		4:1		.67:1	
15	40		600		
		2:1		.67:1	
20	30		520		
		1:1		.67:1	
30	20		480		—optimal ratio: $X/Y = 3:2$.
		.5:1		.67:1	
40	15		500		
		.25:1		.67:1	
60	10		600		

represent the two resources, capital and labor, respectively; the *a* and *b* correspond to the exponents, as well as to the elasticities of output*; and *A* is a parameter for technology. If the prices of *K* and *L* are known for the C–D function, the least costly *K/L* occurs according to the following formula:

$$\text{Optimal } \frac{K}{L} = \frac{aP_L}{bP_K} \tag{7}$$

Thus, for the example discussed earlier, because $Q = XY$, the *X* and *Y* correspond to the *K* and *L* resources, respectively. According to equation (7),

$$\text{Optimal } \frac{X}{Y} = \frac{(1)(P_y)}{(1)(P_x)} = \frac{\$30}{\$20} = \frac{3}{2}$$

Because $X/Y = \frac{3}{2}$, and $Q = XY = 600$, $X = \frac{3}{2}Y$, and $Q = \frac{3}{2}Y$, $(Y) = \frac{3}{2}Y^2 = 600$. Solving for *Y*, we obtain $Y^2 = 400$ and $Y = 20$; hence $X = \frac{3}{2}Y$ or 30.

Optimal Input Ratio when Isoquants are Nonconvex

It is not always possible or necessary for the production functions to yield smooth and convex isoquants. When the isoquants are not convex, the firm minimizes costs by selecting the inputs with the highest efficiency ratios. For example, consider the linear production function in Figure 7-8, $Q = 2K + L$. If we wish to draw the 100-unit isoquant, we can do so by drawing a straight line from 50 on the *K* axis to 100 on the *L* axis. All other isoquants will also be linear and parallel to this one. The production function tells us that the marginal product of *K* is 2, while that of *L* is 1. If *K* and *L* are equally expensive, the isocost line will be a 45° line having a slope of −1:1. As shown in Figure 7-8, the optimal point occurs at one "corner"—that is, the firm hires only *K*. In this particular instance, the efficiency ratio of *K*, $(2/P_K)$, is consistently greater than that of *L*, $(1/P_L)$. For linear isoquants, the MRTS is constant.

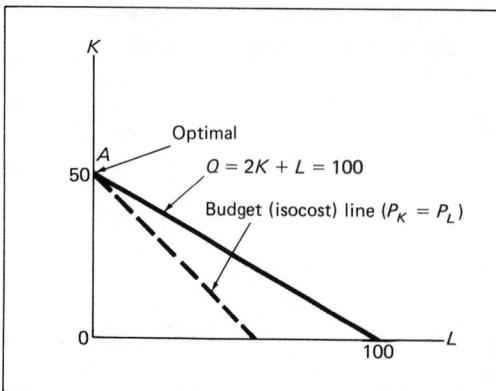

FIGURE 7-8
Some situations produce "corner" solutions to optimal combinations of inputs. In this case, the cost of producing 100 units is lowest at point *A* where the budget line (dotted) touches or intersects the 100-unit isoquant.

*The *elasticity of output* is the ratio of the percentage change in output to the percentage change in a particular input. Detailed discussion is contained in the appendix to this chapter at the end of the book.

When the isoquants are convex, the MRTS continually changes. That is why, for cost-minimization purposes, it is necessary to bring the efficiency ratios into equality. Too much of one input relative to the other reduces the former's efficiency, while an excessive use of the latter contributes to its decline in efficiency. The "best" combination is reached where each resource's marginal product per dollar of expenditure is equal to every other input's marginal product per dollar.

The Efficiency Ratio and Profit Maximization

There is a well-known proposition in economics that a firm or producer will maximize profits by equating *marginal cost* to *marginal revenue.* Marginal cost is defined as the additional cost of producing one more unit of output—in the case of two variable inputs, the marginal cost due to either resource will be the additional resource cost necessary to produce an extra unit of the output. Thus, if the marginal product of the fifth unit of labor is 10 units, and if labor receives $100, the marginal cost of production due to labor will be ($100/10), or $10. Notice that such a *marginal cost is the reciprocal of the efficiency ratio.*

In markets characterized by perfect competition, the price of the output is determined by the interaction of supply and demand. Furthermore, under such conditions, each firm accepts the market price as the only possible price. Consequently, each unit of output sold at that price adds an amount exactly equal to price to total revenues. Because marginal revenue is defined as the change in total revenues associated with the change in the sale of one unit of output, price and marginal revenue are equal. For example, if the price of a bushel of wheat is $4, the marginal revenue from each bushel of wheat sold will also equal $4.

A profit-maximizing producer will try to equate marginal revenue to marginal cost. Thus, the profit-maximizing level of employment as well as the combination of inputs may be described by the following:

$$MC = MR$$

$$\frac{\text{Price of resource } A}{\text{Marginal product } A} = \frac{\text{Price of resource } B}{\text{Marginal product } B} = \text{Price of output}$$

or, in abbreviated terms,

$$\frac{P_A}{MQ_A} = \frac{P_B}{MQ_B} = P \tag{8}$$

where the MQ represent the marginal physical products. Equation (8) can be rewritten as follows:

$$P_A = (MQ_A)P; \qquad P_B = (MQ_B)P \tag{9}$$

Either part of equation (9) fulfills the profit-maximization condition. For instance, the left-hand term of $P_A = (MQ_A)P$ represents the *marginal cost* of an additional *unit of the resource,* while the right-hand side of the equation corresponds to the additional (marginal) revenue received from employing that additional resource unit. Profit maximizers try to make these two marginal values equal. Thus, an additional unit of an input whose marginal product is expected to be 20 units, and whose price is $100, will be hired if, and only if, the price of the output is *at least* $5. If the price of the output is, say, $6, this input unit's revenue contribution will be 20 × $6, or $120, and the firm will gladly employ it if all it has to pay the resource is $100. The term obtained by multiplying the marginal product of a resource and the price of the output, such as $(MQ_A)P$, is called the *marginal revenue product of a resource.*

CHOICE OF INPUTS WITH PRICE VARIATIONS

From the preceding discussion, you can see that the employment of inputs is affected by the price of the output—the higher the price of the output, the greater the marginal revenue product of an input, and hence the higher the likelihood of its employment. In general, all other things remaining equal, the demand for inputs is positively related to the price of the output. However, if the price of the output remains the same, and the relative price of the inputs changes, will the optimal combination be affected?

Assume that the conditions of production lead to convex isoquants and the firm is maximizing the output volume for a given cost outlay at point *B,* as shown in Figure 7-9. If for some reason, such as an increase in supply, the price of wood falls, the budget line will swing outwards in a counterclockwise fashion. The new point of tangency between the budget line and the higher isoquant will be at point *C.* A greater amount of furniture can now be produced for the same budget but, as shown, the ratio of wood to plastic will be higher than before. If such changes in the composition of the finished product do not affect demand adversely, the producer will stand to make more profits than before. Whether the optimal ratio of the two inputs will change due to the price change depends on the amount of such change as well as the production function, and hence the shape and location of the isoquants. We will trace through the various effects of a price change in one resource with a worked out example and a set of calculations.

Assume that the furniture manufacturer's production function of two inputs, plastic and wood, is $Q = f(P, W) = PW^2$. Further, suppose that each unit of P can be obtained for $50, while each unit of W costs the firm $120. Using the formula of equation (7), we obtain the optimal ratio of P to W: (1 × $120) ÷ (2 × $50), or $P/W = 120/100 = 1.2$. Thus, for a maximum budget of $1800, the firm can combine 12 units of P with 10 units of W to obtain 1200 units of output. This implies that the cost of each unit of output is ($1800/1200), or $1.50.

Now suppose that the demand for wood by other users declines and the price of wood falls to $100 per unit. The new cost-minimizing ratio of P to W is now 1:1. The producer will now combine $12P$ with $12W$ for the same budget of $1800. The new volume with this combination of P and W will be 1728 units. Consequently, the cost of each unit of output will fall to ($1800/1728), or $1.04. Though less costly to manufacture, each unit of output will now contain more wood relative to plastic, and conceivably such changes may even improve the

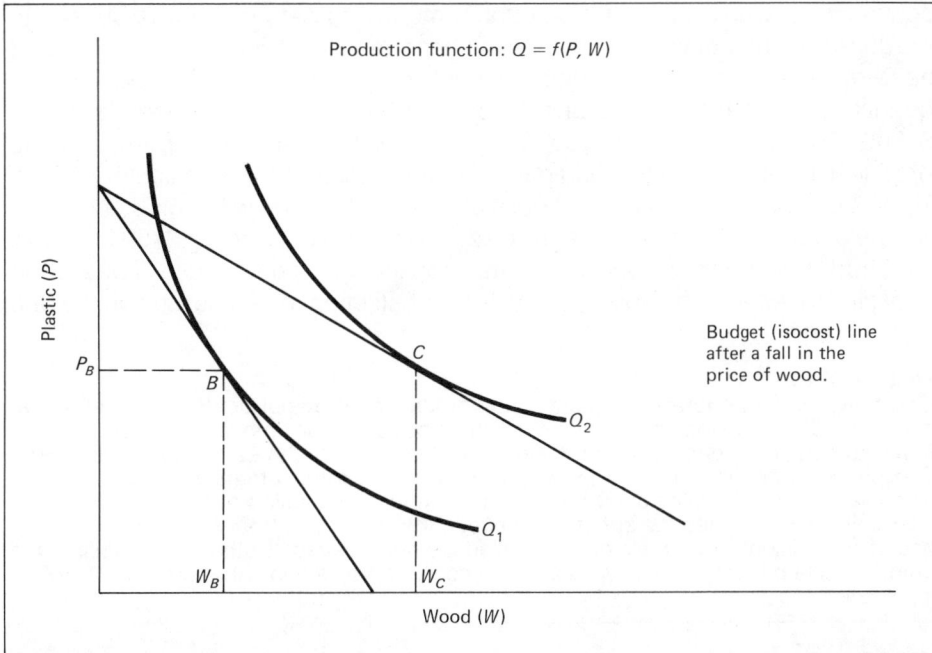

Production function: $Q = f(P, W)$

Budget (isocost) line after a fall in the price of wood.

Plastic (P)

P_B

B

C

Q_2

Q_1

W_B

W_C

Wood (W)

FIGURE 7-9
If the relative price of an input declines, the firm usually tends to employ relatively larger amounts of the resource. In this diagram, the firm was originally at point B, producing output volume Q_1. It employed W_B amount of wood in combination with P_B amount of plastic. When the price of wood fell, the same budget permitted the firm to produce a larger level of output—Q_2. The budget (isocost) line is flatter than before to indicate a decline in the relative price of W. The new optimal point of production is C, and the new level of wood usage is shown by W_C.

demand for furniture and lead to an expansion of the firm's scale of operations, in which case the choice of inputs will remain the same, but larger amounts of both inputs will be employed. Such cases will be demonstrated in the next few sections.

The Substitution and Output Effects

In Chapter 3 we showed that whenever the relative price of a consumer good changes, the consumer's utility changes, usually resulting in a move to another indifference curve. The change from the first quantity to the second was explained with the use of the substitution and real income effects. Two similar effects are also encountered in the theory of production. When the relative price of an input is altered, ceteris paribus, production occurs on a different isoquant. The change from one isoquant to another is the sum of the changes occuring due to the *substitution* and *output* effects.

In the example just discussed, the furniture manufacturer produced a larger volume of output when the price of wood declined, although he continued to spend the same amount of money as before. Had he chosen to produce the original volume despite the change in the price of wood, he would have remained on the 1200-unit isoquant, but he would have used a larger quantity of wood than before and his expenditures would have been less than $1800. The change in the use of wood, which would have permitted the producer to remain on the original isoquant, is called the substitution effect. Thus, it can be shown that 10.63 units of P in combination with 10.63 units of W will yield 1200 units of output at the least cost—the cost being $1594.50. The 0.63 additional units of wood (10.63 as opposed to 10) now in use is due to the *substitution effect*. In Figure 7-10, the substitution effect is shown by the

FIGURE 7-10
Originally, the firm operated at point A and produced an output of 1200 units at a total cost of $1800. When the price of wood fell, the production point moved to C, such that the firm was able to produce a larger volume—1728 units—for the same budget of $1800. The change from A to C was by way of point B. The movement along the *original* isoquant (1200 units) from point A to B, requiring the substitution of 1.37 units of P with 0.63 units of W, is called the *substitution effect;* the movement from B to C, requiring the use of an additional 1.37 units of W, is called the *output effect.* Both the substitution and output effects bring about a reduction in the costs of production if the relative price of an input falls.

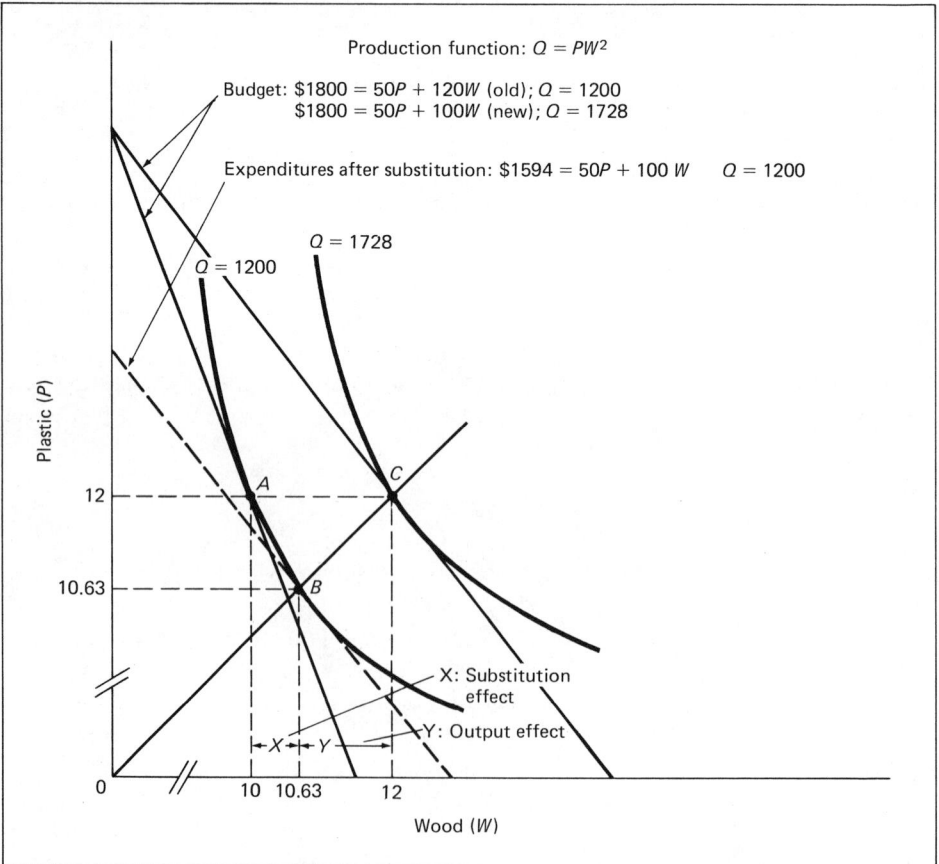

Production function: $Q = PW^2$

Budget: $1800 = 50P + 120W$ (old); $Q = 1200$
$1800 = 50P + 100W$ (new); $Q = 1728$

Expenditures after substitution: $1594 = 50P + 100 W$ $Q = 1200$

$Q = 1728$

$Q = 1200$

Plastic (P)

12

10.63

C

A

B

X: Substitution effect

Y: Output effect

0   10 10.63   12

Wood (W)

movement from point *A* to point *B*—the output volume is still 1200 units, but the cost is less.

The output effect of an input price change is comparable to the real income effect of utility theory. When the price of *W* falls, the producer can actually operate at point *C* and produce 1728 units. At point *C* we see that 12 units of *W* are in use, suggesting that the producer uses 1.37 more units of wood. This additional use of wood, which permits the producer to move to a higher isoquant, is called the *output effect*. The total change in the demand for *W* is the sum of the two effects. Such effects play an important role in the explanation of the theories related to cost and the markets for inputs.

THE FIRM'S EXPANSION PATH

Many factors are subject to change in the long-run: the firm's scale of operation, the budget, the prices of inputs, and the technology of production. It is entirely possible that some changes may bring about other changes; reduced prices of inputs and the attendant cuts in production costs often lead to declines in the prices of the output. However, the firm alone can initiate the changes in its scale of operations and the budget, even though such changes may be the result of changes occuring elsewhere. Increases in a firm's scale of operations, made possible by increases in the budget, are described by the *expansion path* in an isoquant map. We can think of such a path as being comparable to the income-consumption locus described in Chapter 3. In addition to describing the firm's returns to scale, the expansion path also provides information about the presence of economies or diseconomies of scale, as well as total and unit costs of production. Such information aids the producer in plans for future expansion and other related objectives.

We will use the isoquant map of Figure 7-11 to illustrate the expansion path. Essentially, the expansion path is the locus of all points where various budget lines are tangent to the relevant isoquants, with the assumption that the relative price of the inputs and other factors remains constant. Thus, given the knowledge about the production function and input prices, successively larger budgets will yield the correspondingly higher points on the many isoquants. When these points are joined, the resulting line becomes the expansion path. Such a path is indicated by *ABCDE* in Figure 7-11. Unless something unusual occurs, the input ratio along an expansion path is constant. Figure 7-11 shows a firm subject to decreasing returns to scale, which contributes to rising unit production cost—from $1 a unit at a volume of 1000 to $2 a unit at a volume of 2000. Such phenomena are also responsible for the rising, upward-sloping, long-run supply curves often studied in demand/supply analysis.

CHANGES IN TECHNOLOGY

One of the shortcomings of the short run is that the producers are prevented from using newer and better technology under such an environment. Whatever the short-run constraints may be, such obstacles bring about

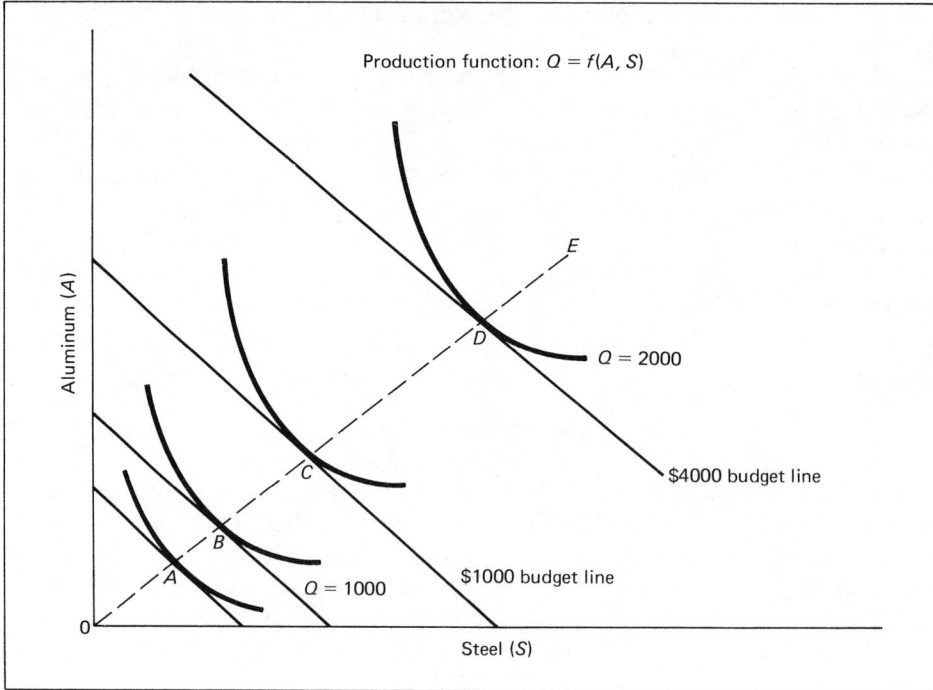

FIGURE 7-11
In the long run a firm expands output along its *expansion path* shown by *ABCDE*. Each point along this locus is formed by tangencies of the successively higher budgets and isoquants.

the usual inefficiencies and keep the firm from engaging cost-efficient methods of production. For example, in the short run, an airline company must continue to use its fleet of older and perhaps inefficient jets, although it may "retrofit" the engines and alter the fuselages of the aircraft, and retrain the crew members and ground-support personnel in order to increase the productivity of the system. However, in the long run, the firm can conceivably resort to a different technology, better airplanes, different crew sizes, revolutionary methods for takeoffs and landings, and perhaps different cruising speeds and altitudes. If we generalize the production function and assume that output Q is a function of capital K and labor L, the technology changes can be described in three separate categories—*capital using* (or *labor saving*), neutral, and *labor using* (or *capital saving*).

Capital-Using Technological Innovation

If a capital-using innovation is introduced by the firm, and if the prices of the inputs remain the same, the new optimal combination of capital and labor will require a larger amount of capital (relative to labor). Innovations may or may not be accompanied by changes in the volume of output possible for a given budget, but, generally speaking, because the firm is reluctant to use new technology unless there are concomitant gains, capital-using innovations, ceteris paribus, reduce the cost of the output. For example, the use of microwave ovens in place of conventional ones, and the employment of CTS (computerized tomographic scanners) in lieu of x-ray machines, can save restaurants and hospitals vast sums in labor and time costs. Figure 7-12a

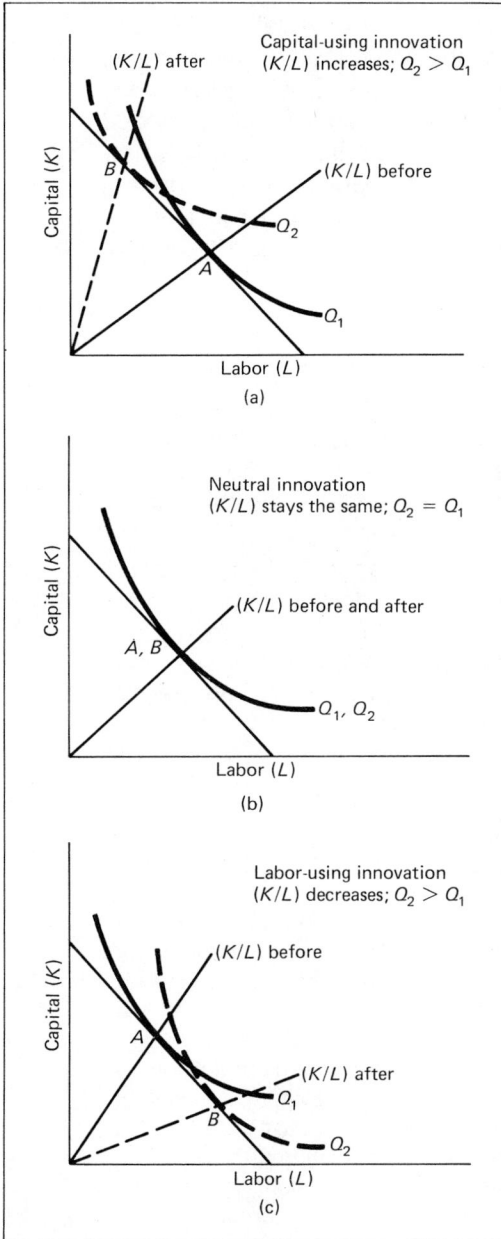

FIGURE 7-12
Innovations or changes in technology affect a firm's optimal input ratio. Panel (a) shows an increase in output (Q_2) is possible for the same budget, but at a higher capital–labor (K/L) ratio. Panel (c) indicates a lower (K/L) due to a labor-using (or capital-saving) innovation.

illustrates the change in the shape of isoquants resulting from a capital-using innovation. Thus, the new capital/labor ratio at point *B* will be higher than the previous combination shown by point *A;* the innovation has also increased the total output of the firm.

Neutral Innovation

A neutral innovation occurs when the new method or technology, ceteris paribus, requires the use of the previous optimal ratio of capital to labor. For example, if someone invents a new sewing machine that requires two workers to operate it, and the output of the machine is three times that of an ordinary machine, the combination of machine and labor will remain constant, provided the new machine is equated to two of the older machines. If the cost of this new machine is twice that of the older design, the firm's budget line will be tangent to the new isoquant at the same point as before; however, output will increase, and the cost per unit will fall. Such a development is described by Figure 7-12b.

Labor-Using Innovation

When capital is relatively expensive or scarce, firms find it advantageous to use labor-using technology. For example, it is in the interest of the People's Republic of China to invent capital-saving technologies. The introduction of a labor-using innovation, all other things remaining equal, lowers the capital/labor ratio. The isoquants change as shown in Figure 7-12c.

The introduction of such innovations and other changes in technology not only affect the input ratios, but eventually have considerable impact on the prices of the inputs as well as the price of the output. Such developments lead the firms to pursue other strategies and/or objectives, which in turn affect the rate of introduction of the innovations. The topic of innovations will be covered further in the following chapters.

APPLICATIONS

1. The Dean's Dilemma

The dean of a college is often entrusted with the task of selecting an appropriate faculty. To that effect, he or she must not only hire the correct number of people, but must also make a concerted effort to maintain the *quality* of instruction by employing suitable educators. In addition, the dean must stay within the constraints of the budget.

Suppose Dean Klutz is considering hiring only assistant and full professors. If the number of class hours taught is defined as the output of the system, the optimal combination of the two types of professors will be that which maximizes the value of output for the given budget. We must mention that the identification of output of an educational institution is not as simple as supposed for our discussion—realistically, the "output" of universities should include such factors as the quality and quantity of

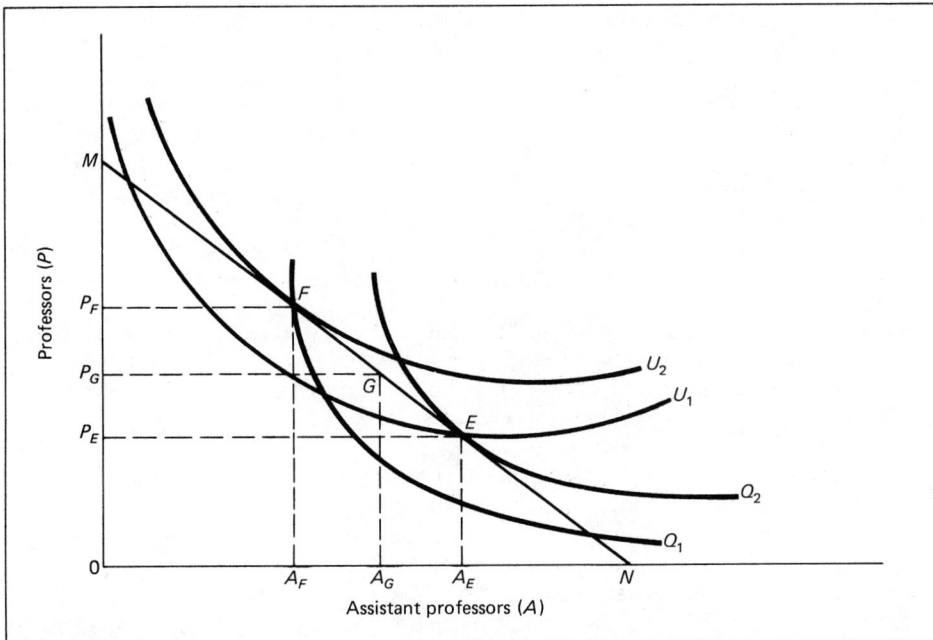

FIGURE 7-13
The dean's dilemma: more Q or U? (Tradeoff between utility and efficiency.) U—Dean's utility; Q—output of professors/assistant professors; MN: total budget.

graduating students, their success in the marketplace, the income to the university from tuition and grants, and the value of research conducted by the staff.

By making the usual assumptions concerning isoquants, we show the various combinations of professors (P) and assistant professors (A) that yield the many levels of output (Q). These output volumes are designated as Q_1, Q_2, etc., in Figure 7-13. In the same graph we also reproduce the indifference curves of the dean. After all, the dean is interested not only in the output of the institution, but in his own happiness as well. The reputation of a college, as well as its growth, is influenced by the composition of its faculty, which in turn affects the utility of the dean.

If the dean hires many professors, the outcome will presumably be more quality programs and more students, although only a small number can be hired because professors get paid considerably more than assistant professors. On the other hand, although a larger number of assistant professors can be hired for the same budget, and the *quantity* of output may be greater, such a large faculty can dilute the *quality* of the program and conceivably cause more personnel problems for the dean. In addition, a larger number of offices must be made available. The dean's utility function is shown by a few indifference curves labelled U_1, U_2, etc. The budget available to the dean is shown by the line MN.

You can see the dilemma the dean faces. Combination F maximizes his utility, while combination E promises the maximum output. At point F the quantity of output is Q_1, although utility is U_2; at point E the output is Q_2, but utility is U_1. What should Klutz do?

One solution is for him to compromise between utility and productivity and hire the combination suggested by point G. With P_G professors and A_G assistant professors the dean's utility will be between U_1 and U_2 and output between Q_1 and Q_2.

An alternative solution is to introduce a *professor-using* innovation. If the dean can somehow increase the relative productivity of the professors, the isoquants will shift upwards to the left and the U and Q curves may possibly be located so that the budget line will be tangent to both at point F. Such an innovation may be brought about by forcing the highly paid professors to do a little less "research."

2. Examination Copies or Telephone Calls?

Book companies use a variety of strategies to promote and sell the textbooks they publish. They send out free examination or preview copies of new books to potential adopters, mail out very colorful and well-laid-out brochures, and make long distance telephone calls to professors. Each of the strategies mentioned costs the book company money. If it is interested in maximizing its book sales, it should (from an economic point of view) do so at as little cost as possible. We can use the theory of production to suggest certain optimization strategies.

Assume that a book publisher can sell a specific quantity of books by sending out examination copies, making telephone calls, or by doing both. Let Figure 7-14, represent the estimated sales volumes due to the various combinations of examination copies and telephone calls. Each isoquant represents a specific volume of sales.

Suppose the company's budget for promotion is limited to $24,000 per year, that each examination copy sent out costs the firm $8, and each telephone call comes to $4. Disregarding other factors, the company can make a maximum of 6000 telephone calls per year; in the place of telephone calls, the firm can send out a maximum of 3000 examination copies. The isocost or budget line is drawn to reflect the cost ratio of telephone call to examination copy.

While the telephone calls are relatively less costly than the cost of examination copies, the "success rate" with book samples is usually much higher. Telephone calls by book company representatives are often annoying to college instructors but can be quite successful in winning orders for new books. We will assume that the book company can estimate the various combinations of the two methods by which it can hope to sell a desired number of books. The marginal rate of substitution of

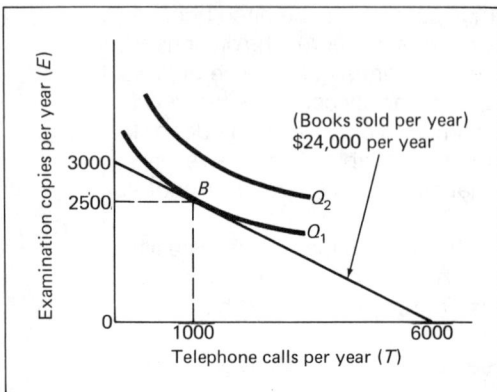

FIGURE 7-14
The book company maximizes annual sales for a given advertising budget by operating at a point such as B where the budget line is tangent to a convex isoquant.

examination copies for telephone calls diminishes with greater use of examination copies, just as the marginal rate of substitution of telephone calls for examination copies decreases with increased use of the telephone. As shown, the maximum quantity for the given budget is obtained where the marginal rate of substitution (MRTS) equals the price ratio of telephone calls to examination copies. Thus, the $24,000 is best spent in making 1000 telephone calls and sending out 2500 examination copies. If, on the average, 70% of those receiving examination copies tend to select that book, and only 40% of those receiving telephone calls are persuaded to choose a book for their classes, the combination of books and calls suggested would be *expected* to produce a sales order for 2150 books.

3. Anyone Want a Used Colonel?

Many educational institutions and private companies hire retired military officers. Most often they are employed by the firms not so much out of love for country as for pure and simple reasons of cost efficiency and reliability. The retired military officers most often are very eager workers and productive due to the new and challenging environment. Most frequently they accept tasks for relatively less money because of their supplemental retirement income. Thus, *even if* a retired military officer is half as productive as a trained professional in a particular occupation, the first is more cost effective at $15,000 per year than the second at $40,000.

EXERCISES

1. Explain and define the following:
   a. Production function and isoquants.
   b. Marginal rate of technical substitution.
   c. Ridge lines and the economic zone of production.
   d. Marginal product, average product.
   e. Diseconomies and economies of scale.
   f. Principle of diminishing MRTS.
   g. Returns to scale.
   h. Optimal combination of inputs.
   i. Capital-using technological innovation.
   j. Cobb–Douglas production function.

2. Graphically derive the short-run, one-variable production function, $Q = f(B)$, from the two-variable one, $Q = f(A,B,)$, where the quantity of input A is fixed. (Assume that the two-variable production function yields convex isoquants.)

3. Draw representative isoquants to bring out the following:
   a. Constant MRTS.
   b. Diminishing MRTS.
   c. Increasing MRTS.
   d. Unique (acceptable) combination of inputs (fixed proportions).

4. Test the following production functions for returns to scale:
   a. $Q = KL^2$.
   b. $Q = 100K + 20L$.
   c. $Q = K^2 - 2KL + 3L^2$.

d. $Q = (KL)^3$.
e. $Q = K^{1/4}L^{1/2}$.
f. $Q = K^{-1}L^2$.

5. Suppose you have a total budget of $1000 and the production function is such that $Q = KL$. If the price of each unit of K is $40 and that of L is $50, what combination of K and L will maximize output for the given budget? How large will Q be?

6. What sort of difficulties do you perceive in the construction of an *aggregate production function* for a particular industry? For a nation?

7. You wish to enclose a rectangular area containing 400 square feet; the cost of fencing is $5 per linear foot. What dimensions will minimize the cost of fencing? Will a circular area be cheaper?

8. Explain how the following pairs of inputs may be used to draw isoquants. Identify the probable output in each case, and draw some representative isoquant maps:
   a. Navy, Air Force.
   b. Jogging, swimming.
   c. Audiovisual equipment, teachers.
   d. Oil, coal.
   e. Missiles, bombers.
   f. Ground meat, beans.
   g. Polyester, cotton.
   h. Hospitals, health maintenance organizations.
   i. Government expenditures, tax cuts.
   j. Generals, soldiers.
   k. Men, women.

9. Determine the optimal input ratios for each of the following sets of conditions:
   a. $Q = KL^2$, $P_K = \$10$, $P_L = \$15$.
   b. $Q = MN$, $P_M = \$1$, $P_N = \$4$.
   c. $Q = S^{1/4}T^{1/2}$, $P_S = \$4$, $P_T = \$6$.

10. An agriculturist wishes to have her 1000-acre farm sprayed with insecticide. The spraying can be done manually, by engaging the services of an aerial crop duster, or by a combination of the two. The productivity of labor spraying the farm by hand is 10 acres per standard eight-hour day, while that of the aerial sprayer is 50 acres during the same time period. If the price of labor is $12 per hour, and the price of aerial spraying is $50 per hour, what is the least-costly combination of the two types of resources if more than one worker and aerial sprayer may be engaged simultaneously? Draw an isoquant map and show the optimal combination using an isocost line. What is the minimum level of the budget that will permit the spraying of the farm? Will your answers be any different, if the time to the agriculturist is valued at $20 per hour?

11. The production function for the annual output of electricity E, which is related to the quantities of labor L and capital K, is estimated to be $E = 100KL$. E is measured in watts and both K and L are measured in units. If the price of labor is $12,000 per year and that of capital $3000, what is the economic cost of producing a megawatt of electricity?

12. Comment on the returns-to-scale behavior of the following:
   a. If the dimensions of a cuboid are doubled, the volume enclosed increases eight times.

b. It takes less time to make the bed when two people work together than if there is only one person.

c. Increasing the diameter of an oil pipeline by 10% increases the flow of oil by more than 10%.

d. "All work and no play, makes Jack a dull boy."

13. Can you think of examples where the isoquants are either parallel (straight) or vertical lines? Points?

14. Suppose production is limited to only four combinations of the two resources A and B; the inputs may be combined only in the following proportions to yield one unit of output:

$A/B = 4:1$
$A/B = 3:2$
$A/B = 1:4$
$A/B = 2:3$

Draw these "process" rays from the origin and place points on each ray to indicate an output volume of 60 units. Connect the points by linear segments. What will you have?

15. With reference to Exercise 15, suppose the firm has 400 units of A and 200 of B. What is the maximum possible output? (Hint: You may combine several processes.)

16. Assume that a firm produces three different types of products—X, Y, and Z. Each product requires the use of two resources A and B. The firm's total budget is $100,000 and the prices of A and B are $20 and $25, respectively. Each unit of X requires 4 of A and 1 of B; each unit of Y requires 3 of A and 2 of B, and each Z needs 2 of A and 3 of B. If the profit from each unit of X, Y, and Z is $10, what is the profit-maximizing combination of output?

SUGGESTED READINGS

Barnum, H., and Squire, L. "Technology and Relative Economic Efficiency." *Oxford Economic Papers*, N. S., Volume 30, July 1978.

Burt, D. R. "On the Statistical Estimation of Isoquants and Their Role in Livestock Production Decisions." *American Journal of Agricultural Economics*, Volume 60, August 1978.

Chapman, J., Hirsch, W., and Sonenblum, S. "Crime Prevention, the Police Production Function, and Budgeting." *Public Finance*, Volume 30, No. 2, 1975.

Colenitt, D. "Economies of Scale in the United Kingdom Ordinary Life Assurance Industry." *Applied Economics*, Volume 9, September 1977.

Dahm, F., Heady, E., and Sonka, S. "Estimation of Gain Isoquants and a Decision Model Application for Swine Production." *American Journal of Agricultural Economics*, August 1976.

Enos, J., and Pearl, D. "Engineering Production Functions and Technological Progress." *The Journal of Industrial Economics*, September 1975.

Koot, R. "On Economies of Scale in Credit Unions." *Journal of Finance,* Volume 33, No. 4, September 1978.

Mansfield, E., *et al. The Production and Application of New Industrial Technology.* New York: Norton, 1977.

Passy, U. "On the Cobb–Douglas Function in Multi-Objective Optimization." *Water Resources Research,* August 1978.

Walters, A. "Production and Cost Functions: An Econometric Survey." *Econometrica,* January–April 1963.

Chapter Eight

Chapter Eight

Chapter Eight

LINEAR PROGRAMMING

In Chapter 7, we saw how the producer attempted cost optimization with a nonlinear production function and a linear isocost budget line. The objective was to either minimize the cost of producing a given output or maximize the output for a given budget outlay. Depending on which came first, either the isoquants or the budget line represented the constraint to the producer. In essence, the producer was "programmed" to abide by the constraints, and to pick the "best" of the available combinations of resources, that combination being the point of tangency between the isoquant and the budget line. Such situations, involving the maximization or minimization of a given variable subject to certain restrictions, are known as *constrained optimization* problems.

The *linear programming* approach to the solution of economic and business problems is a branch of *linear economic theory* in which all functions are assumed to be either straight lines or actually linear. In the various linear programming situations, we use linear functions to represent the *constraints* as well as the function to be optimized, the *objective function*. In Chapter 7, where the isoquants were linear, we were working with a simplified linear programming problem involving one constraint (the budget line) and one objective function (the volume of output shown by the isoquants). The objective there was to maximize the output subject to a given cost.

There is more than one method for solving simple linear programming problems: the graphical method, the algebraic method in combination with the graph, or the purely mathematical technique can be used to arrive at the optimal value. However, when the number of items contained in the objective function or the number of constraints exceeds manageable quantities, we use the computer and the large-number or preprogrammed "packages" now available for many different types of complex linear programming problems. We will first use a profit-maximization example to illustrate the fundamental techniques associated with the graphical version of the linear programming solution and subsequently explore the other methods.

SOLUTION WITH GRAPHS

Suppose a company manufactures two products, X and Y, such that each good requires specific amounts of three resources—A, B, and C. The company has limited amounts of the three resources and the profit from each unit of X and Y sold is known and constant. The objective of the firm is to maximize profits by selling the correct quantities of X and Y.

Because all relationships are linear—the input requirement and the profit per unit for each X and Y is constant and the total resource utilization, as well as the total profit, is directly proportional to the total quantities of X and Y produced—we can use the linear programming method to solve this problem. In Figure 8-1 are plotted the three linear constraints for the available amounts of A, B, and C. Because the firm knows the exact amount of each resource used by X and Y, we can plot the various combinations of X and Y that can be produced with the use of a limited amount of each resource. For example, if there are only 100 units of A and each unit of X requires 2.5 units of A, while

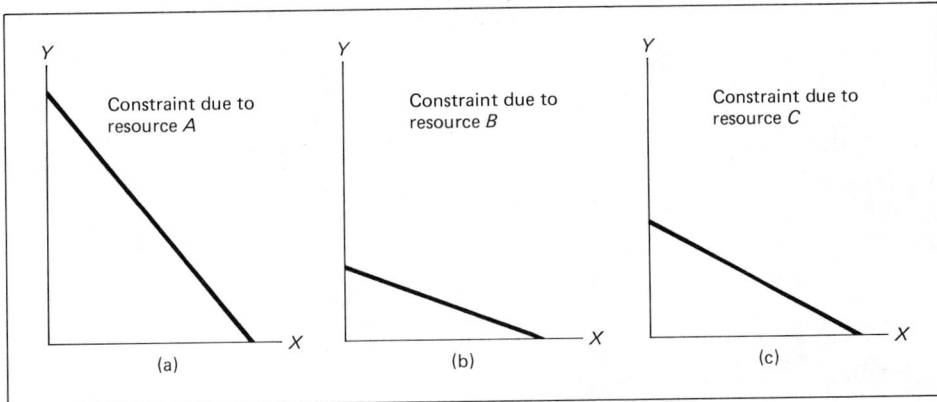

FIGURE 8-1
Since the firm's resources are limited and both X and Y require specific amounts of all three resources, there are limits to the quantities of production of X and Y. Each resource constraint is drawn as an isocost or budget line to show the feasible combinations of the two products that can be produced if that resource is the only constraint. For example, if each X requires 2.5 units of A, while each Y needs only 2 units of A, the vertical intercept of panel (a) will be 50 and the horizontal 40 if only 100 of A are available. Panels (b) and (c) show the other two resources, which have been drawn under similar assumptions. All constraints are linear because each unit of X and Y always requires the same proportion of the resources, which implies a constant trade-off ratio between X and Y in resource utilization.

each Y needs 2 units of A, then the most X that can be produced with the available A is 40, and the maximum number of Y is 50. The A constraint is plotted on the X–Y plane; it has Y and X intercepts of 50 and 40, respectively. In essence, each constraint can be drawn like a budget line. This is what has been done in the case of the other two resource constraints.

Because both X and Y require all three resources, only those combinations of the two goods that do not violate any of the resource constraints are acceptable to the producer. The *feasible combinations* of X and Y are those points which lie within or on *all three* constraints. Figure 8-2 shows how we determine the *feasible set,* or the *feasible region.*

When all three constraints are plotted on one graph, they form the relevant polygon shown by the shaded area *OJTMN* of Figure 8-2. Only those points that lie on or within a constraint boundary are actually attainable by a firm. Consequently, the feasible set is bounded by the appropriate segments of the three constraints. The polygon so formed (*OJTMN*) is comparable to a productions-possibility curve (discussed in all beginning economics classes).

Now it is time to make the decision about the best combination of X and Y that will maximize the firm's profits. To do so graphically, we first determine the shape and size of the objective function. Because the profit per unit of X and Y is positive, the total profits to the firm equal the sum of the profits from the sale of X and Y. The profit from X is the quantity of X multiplied by the profit per unit of X, and likewise for Y. Thus, we can write a profit function showing the total profit (Π) as a function of profit per unit of X (Π_x), the profit per unit of Y (Π_y), the

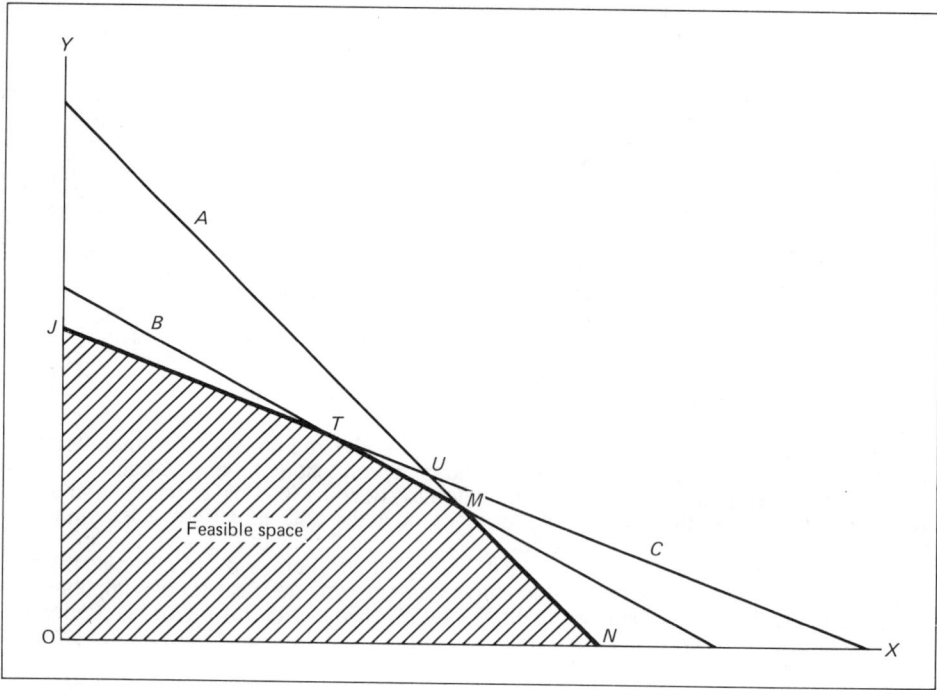

FIGURE 8-2
When we plot the three resource constraints on one graph, we obtain the "feasible space" of the firm. The firm may choose combinations of X and Y that are attainable. These combinations are shown by the shaded polygon *OJTMN*. The polygon is formed by the relevant segments of the individual constraints. No point beyond the space designated as the feasible space is attainable. If the firm selects a point that lies on one of the constraints, the resource is being fully used, and if a point occurs below the constraint line, some idle capacity or *slack* exists.

quantity of X (X), and the quantity of Y (Y). The equation for the profit function is shown by equation (1):

$$\text{Total profit} = \Pi = \Pi_X X + \Pi_Y Y \tag{1}$$

As long as the profit per unit of X and Y is constant, the profit function will be linear. For example, if the profit per unit of X is $4 and per unit of Y is $5, the total profit ($\Pi$) will equal $4X + 5Y$. This function will be linear with a slope whose absolute value is $\frac{4}{5}$, and the X and Y intercepts for this line will be governed by the amount of profits. For instance, the firm can make a $200 profit by selling only X, only Y, or some combination of both. The firm can produce a profit of $200 with 50X or 40Y. But 25X in conjunction with 20Y will also provide a $200 profit, as will 30X and 16Y. Thus, a given amount of profit can be obtained by many combinations of X and Y. When we plot a line connecting all points yielding a given amount of profit, we obtain an *isoprofit line*. The isoprofit lines that lie farther away from the origin represent greater amounts of profits. An isoprofit line is shown in Figure 8-3.

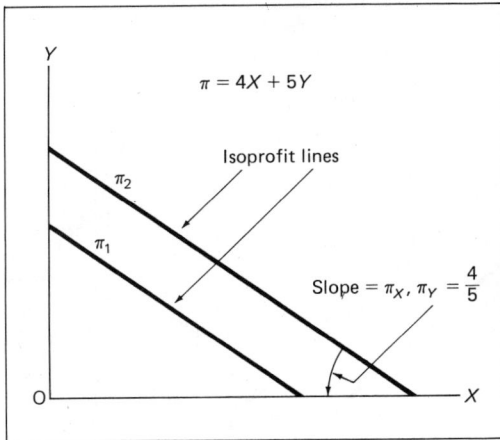

FIGURE 8-3
Isoprofit lines (Π_1, Π_2) show all combinations of the two types of output (X, Y) which yield a given or constant amount of profits. The slope of an isoprofit line reveals the profit ratio of X and Y. If unit profits are constant, isoprofit lines are linear and parallel.

The objective of the firm is to maximize profits. Thus, it will attempt to operate on that isoprofit line which is maximum under the circumstances. The firm's ability to maximize profits is constrained by the feasible polygon. Consequently, the point on this polygon which lies on the highest isoprofit line is chosen as the profit-maximizing combination of X and Y.

In Figure 8-4, we show the feasible polygon by itself in panel (a) and the objective function (isoprofit lines) in panel (b); panel (c) contains both. Point M on the feasible polygon OJTMN allows the maximum profit, since all other (higher) isoprofit lines are unattainable. At any other point on or within the polygon, the profits are less. Thus, the firm maximizes its profits by producing (and selling) X_M of X and Y_M of Y. Point M occurs where the constraints for resources A and C intersect. In such linear programming problems, the optimal point usually lies at one of the vertices of the feasible polygon.

In this particular situation, the firm is using all the available A and C at point M. However, since point M lies below or within the boundary imposed by constraint B, some of resource B is not being used. This excess amount of a resource is called *slack*.

The linear programming framework allows us to obtain so-called "optimal" points in a variety of situations. Not all problems call for profit maximization. Many of the linear programming (LP) situations require the solution to cost minimization, and others have a combination of maximization and minimization. For instance, we can formulate a cost-minimization problem involving the minimally acceptable diet for animals or humans in addition to a utility-maximizing diet. On the one hand the objective might be to obtain the least-costly mix of foods to satisfy nutritional requirements and on the other it might be to maximize utility. At times the objectives may conflict with each other. Soybeans might be an inexpensive source of protein, but they are not as palatable as filet mignon! In the section that follows, we will use a simple numerical example to illustrate the profit-maximization problem discussed earlier.

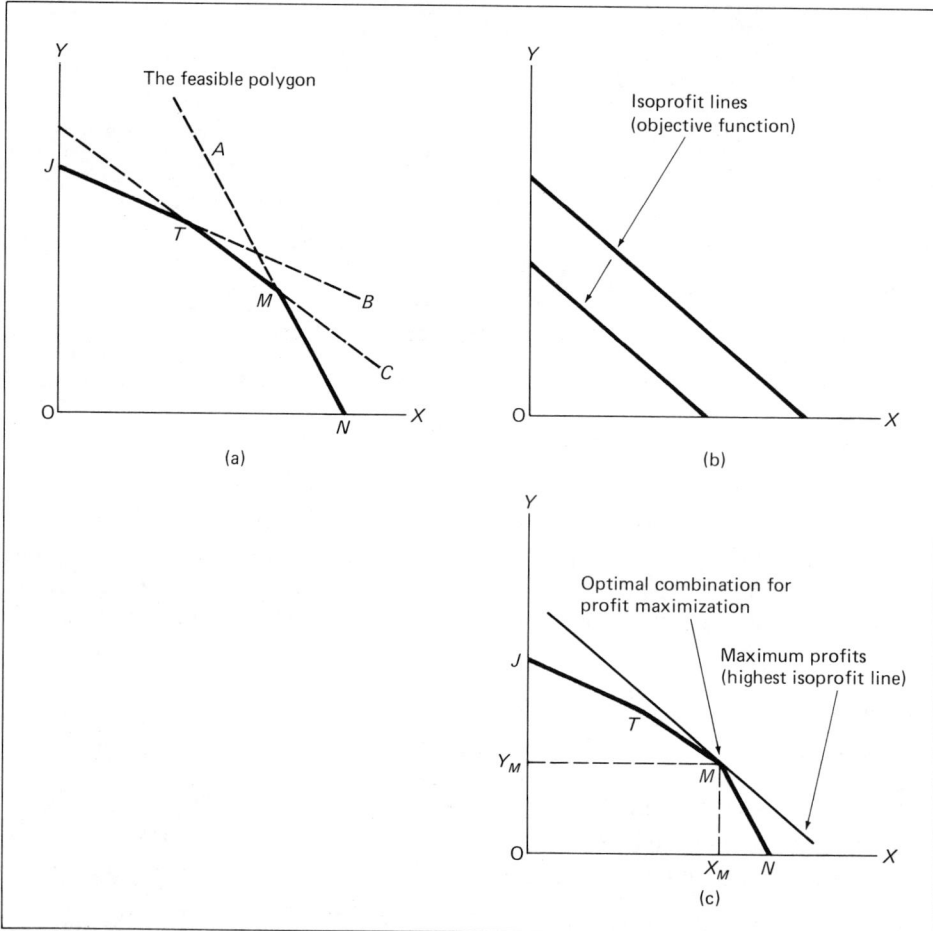

FIGURE 8-4
In selecting the best solution for LP problems, we first designate the feasible zone as shown by *OJTMN* in (a). The isoprofit lines are shown in (b). The "best" point on *OJTMN* is that which allows us to "touch" the highest isoprofit line. In (c) we see that point *M* is the most profitable.

A NUMERICAL EXAMPLE
INVOLVING PROFITS

Let us suppose that a firm has fixed quantities of three resources, *A, B,* and *C,* in the amounts of 1000, 1225, and 240 units, respectively. The production technology is such that each unit of *X* requires 10 units of *A,* 7 of *B,* and 2 of *C.* Each unit of *Y* requires 10 units of *A,* 17.5 of *B,* and 3 of *C.* The market is well established, and each unit of *X* produced (and presumably sold) yields $4 in profits and each *Y* brings in $5. What combination of *X* and *Y* should the firm produce to maximize profits?

Figure 8-5 contains the graph of the problem. If the constraints and objective function are drawn accurately, the profit-maximizing point can be determined by visual inspection. Thus, we see that point *P* on feasible polygon

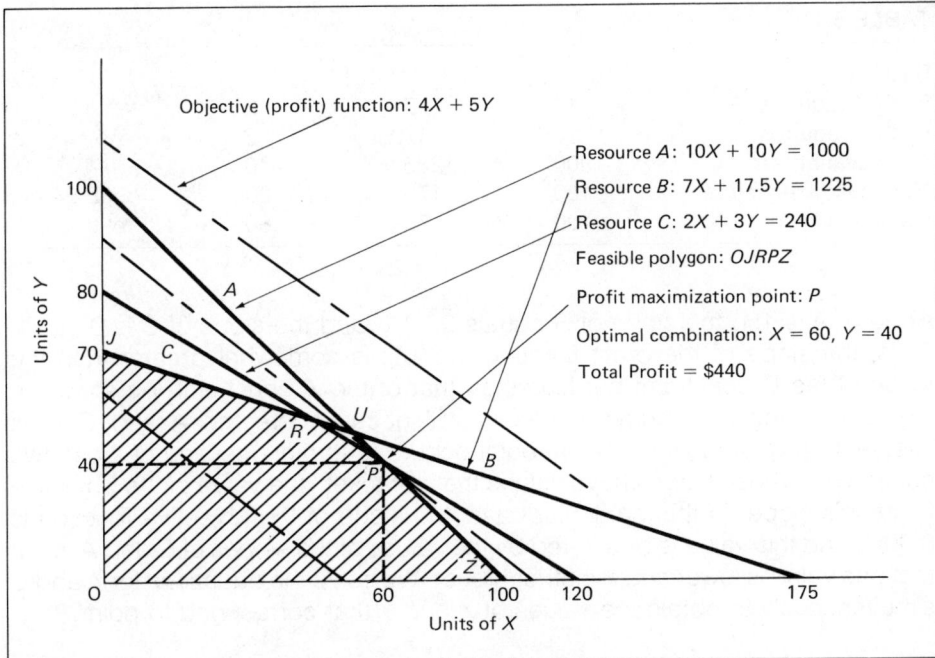

Objective (profit) function: $4X + 5Y$

Resource A: $10X + 10Y = 1000$
Resource B: $7X + 17.5Y = 1225$
Resource C: $2X + 3Y = 240$
Feasible polygon: $OJRPZ$
Profit maximization point: P
Optimal combination: $X = 60$, $Y = 40$
Total Profit = $440

FIGURE 8-5
The "feasible zone" is described by the polygon *OJRPZ*. The optimal point occurs at *P*, formed by the intersection of constraints *A* and *C*. This means that resources *A* and *C* are being used completely. Because point *P* lies below constraint *B*, that resource has some unused or idle capacity. The combination given by point *P* shows that for maximum profit, the firm should produce 60*X* and 40*Y* for a combined total profit of $440. The value of "slack" in resource *B* is $S_B = 105$. Point *P* is found by the simultaneous solution of the equations for resources *A* and *C*.

OJRPZ yields the most profit because the highest isoprofit line passes through that point. Point *P* suggests the production of 60 units of *X* and 40 units of *Y*, for a combined total profit of $440. Point *P* can also be determined by solving the equations for the *A* and *C* resource constraints simultaneously. At point *P*, resource *B* has some idle capacity, or slack.

The resource (input) requirements for *X* and *Y*, as well as the information on the constraints and profits, are shown in Table 8-1. Starting with resource *A*, of which there are only 1000 units, we see that a maximum of 100 units of *X* are possible, or in their place a maximum of 100 *Y* can be produced. Consequently, the constraint for resource *A* is drawn from 100 on the *X* axis to 100 on the *Y* axis. Similarly, constraint *B* is drawn to reflect *X* and *Y* intercepts of 175 and 70, respectively. The *C* constraint is drawn from 120 on the *X* axis to 80 on the *Y* axis. The three linear constraints form the feasible polygon *OJUPZ*. The profit function has a slope (absolute value) of 4:5. Because *Y* is more profitable than *X*, 4 units of *Y* will be just as profitable as 5 units of *X*, or 20 units of *Y* will contribute as much to profits as 25 units of *X*.

When we superimpose the profit function on the feasible polygon, we notice that each of the constraints has a different slope. In absolute terms, the

TABLE 8.1

Resource	A	B	C	
Each X requires	10	7	2	
Each Y requires	10	17.5	3	
Total available	1000	1225	240	
Maximum X possible	100	175	120	Profit: $4/unit
Maximum Y possible	100	70	80	Profit: $5/unit

slope of A is 1:1, the slope of B equals 0.40:1, and the slope of C is 0.667:1. Thus, the slope of the profit function (0.80:1) is somewhat greater than the slope of the C constraint but less than that of the A constraint. As shown in Figure 8-5, the maximum-profit point will occur where the A and C lines intersect. In general, the optimal point occurs at the intersection of those two constraints whose slopes have values that "bracket" the value of the objective function's slope. In this particular case, the slope of the objective function is 0.80:1, and this value is bracketed by the values of the slopes of C and A, such that one value is lower and the other higher. We solve the equations for A and C simultaneously to obtain the values of X and Y that correspond to point P.

THE ALGEBRAIC SOLUTION

Graphs for solving linear programming problems are neither always possible nor always desirable. The previous profit-maximization problem was solved with graphs, and it was possible to do so because we had very few constraints as well as products with which to contend. When the number of variables and constraints gets very large, the mathematical method or access to computers is desirable. We will now demonstrate the use of the algebraic method in conjunction with the graphical technique already explored.

When using the mathematical method to obtain solutions to linear programming problems, we must write all the conditions in equation format. Essentially, all the resource constraints will appear as inequalities. For example, because resource A is limited to 1000 units, its total usage for the production of X and Y may not exceed this amount. Thus we may write an expression for the A resource as $10X + 10Y \leq 1000$. The other constraints are written similarly. All the constraints, along with the objective (profit) function, are shown below:

$$\text{Resource } A: \quad 10X + 10Y \leq 1000 \qquad \text{(at most 1000 units)}$$
$$\text{Resource } B: \quad 7X + 17.5Y \leq 1225 \qquad \text{(at most 1225 units)}$$
$$\text{Resource } C: \quad 2X + 3Y \leq 240 \qquad \text{(at most 240 units)}$$
$$\text{Profit}: \quad 4X + 5Y \qquad \text{(maximize this value)}$$

After attending to certain other limitations and performing a few mathematical operations, we solve the resource equations simultaneously to obtain values for X and Y. Finally, the various combinations of X and Y so determined are substituted into the objective function, which indicates the amount of total profit from a combination. That combination which satisfies all the requirements, as well as maximizes the value of the objective function, is chosen as the optimal combination of X and Y.

To solve the problem algebraically, we must first convert the inequalities into equations. We do so by adding an artificial term to each inequality. The rationale is this: Because the total usage of each resource may be equal to or less than the available amount, we can insure equality by adding an *artificial variable*; that is, a variable whose value is just right to render the inequality an equation. These artificial variables are referred to as *slack variables*. Furthermore, in order to stay within the constraint of limited resources, the values of these slacks are restricted to either zero or positive amounts. For instance, if the slack variable for resource A or S_A turns out to be 10, it means that the combination of X and Y produced at that point is such that 10 units of resource A are being unused—that is, resource A has a slack (or idle capacity) of 10. Had the slack turned out to be negative, that particular combination of X and Y would have been unacceptable, because a negative slack implies a shortage of that particular resource. With reference to the diagram of Figure 8-5, such a point would be point U.

Now we write the entire linear programming problem as a set of linear equations:

$$\text{Resource } A: \quad 10X + 10Y + S_A = 1000 \qquad (2)$$
$$\text{Resource } B: \quad 7X + 17.5Y + S_B = 1225 \qquad (3)$$
$$\text{Resource } C: \quad 2X + 3Y + S_C = 240 \qquad (4)$$
$$\text{Profit:} \qquad 4X + 5Y \qquad (5)$$
$$X, Y, S_A, S_B, S_C \geq 0$$

We now have three independent equations (2)–(4) in five unknowns. Generally speaking, for particular and unique solutions to simultaneous equations, the number of unknowns must equal the number of independent and consistent equations. In our case, because the number of unknowns exceeds the number of equations, we may solve the set of equations by allowing two of the variables to assume zero values. Once this is done, we solve the pairs of equations using ordinary algebraic techniques to determine the values of X and Y, which in turn are tested for all the constraints to see if they satisfy the nonnegativity condition. This procedure is repeated for all possible feasible combinations of X and Y, and eventually the profit-maximizing combination is selected. We will now compute the many values of X and Y.

If we solve equations (2) and (3), in effect we will be solving for a point where the two resources A and B intersect. Note that in Figure 8-5 the point of such an intersection is shown by the letter U. Because all combinations right on a constraint line indicate 100% use of that resource, point U suggests that both A and B are being used to the available amounts. Consequently, neither A nor B has any slack. We solve the two equations by setting S_A and S_B equal to zero, or

$$10X + 10Y = 1000 \qquad (6)$$
$$7X + 17.5Y = 1,225 \qquad (7)$$

Multiplying equation (6) by 7 and equation (7) by 10 and subtracting the first from the second, we obtain

$$(70X + 175Y) - (70X + 70Y) = (12{,}250 - 7000)$$

or

$$105Y = 5250$$
$$Y = 50 \quad \text{and} \quad X = 50$$

Substituting this information into equation (4), we obtain a value for S_C of -10. Because no value may be negative, this combination of X and Y is unacceptable. Therefore, $50X$ and $50Y$ cannot be produced due to the shortage of resource C. Had there been 10 more units of C, the suggested combination of X and Y would have been feasible.

Figure 8-5 shows the feasible region ($OJRPZ$) by the shaded area as well as the objective function made up of a series of dots and dashes. The graph indicates that the objective function attains the highest value at point P. This point's coordinates can be determined by solving the equations for resources A and C simultaneously. Thus, when we solve equations (2) and (4) using techniques similar to those used for solving equations (2) and (3), we find that at point P, $X = 60$ and $Y = 40$. Furthermore, this combination satisfies all the requirements of the problem. At point P, profits are $440.

Solving equations (3) and (4) simultaneously yields the values for combination R, where $X = 37.5$ and $Y = 55$. Assuming that noninteger values are acceptable, the R combination produces $425 in profits. You can verify that point J ($X = 0$, $Y = 70$), although feasible, is not as profitable as point P. Similarly, point Z ($X = 100$, $Y = 0$) yields only a $400 profit.

Point P, which produces the most profits to the firm, indicates that resource B has some idle capacity, because such a point lies well within the resource boundary imposed by B. Substituting the values of $X = 60$ and $Y = 40$ into equation (3), we find that $S_B = 105$; that is, where the firm reaps the most profits, resource B lies idle by about 8.57%. Conceivably, the firm can take steps to get rid of unwanted resources by selling or renting them.

The calculations in the previous section no doubt appear tedious and cumbersome, but this is exactly what a computer would do when "programmed" to abide by the various constraints. Once programmed, a computer can handle many constraints, variables, and objective functions for both minimization and maximization cases. It is essentially an iterative process of solving simultaneous equations. Another method using matrix operations is very often taught by business schools and the author finds this method equally tedious although the method is called by the acronym SIMPLEX (*Simple Linear Example*)! For those who are interested, the method is explained in the appendix to this chapter contained at the end of the book.

INTEGER PROGRAMMING

There are certain qualifications that need to be made about the linear programming models that we have discussed. One concerns the values of the unknowns when they are fractions. *Integer programming* is another variation of programming which specifies that all values must be integers. For instance, a contractor cannot build and sell 9.75 Type A homes and 12.36 Type B homes even if the mathematical solutions indicate such a combination for maximum profits. Obviously the builder can build 9 Type A and 12 Type B homes and should see if 10 and 12 are possible. When integer values are specified, then we determine the optimal solution in the usual manner and select integer combinations around this point to find the best combination. Such a method has also been referred to as the *Gomory method*.

Suppose we wish to maximize profits from the sale of two products, X and Y, which are produced with limited quantities of three resources, R_1, R_2 and R_3. We can obtain the feasible polygon by drawing the linear constraints shown by *ABCD* in Figure 8-6. However, if all values have to be non-negative integers (whole numbers), not all points along *ABCD* are feasible, because some of these points may constitute fractions. To arrive at the restricted-to-integers feasible boundary, we select the integer values permissible by the feasible polygon *OABCD*. Suppose that there are no other integer values along the line segment *AB* except at point *B*. Thus, the highest integer values permissible by part of the feasible polygon will be points such as 1, 2, and 3, where the combinations of X and Y are integers. Similarly, we see that with the exception of point *B*, there are no other combinations along line segment *BC* that provide

FIGURE 8-6
Not all points along a feasible-set boundary yield integer values. In the case of integer programming, only those points which are feasible and correspond to integer values are acceptable, while *OABCD* constitutes the conventional feasible polygon, 1–2–3–4–5–6–7–8–9–10–11 is the acceptable outermost boundary for an integer programming situation.

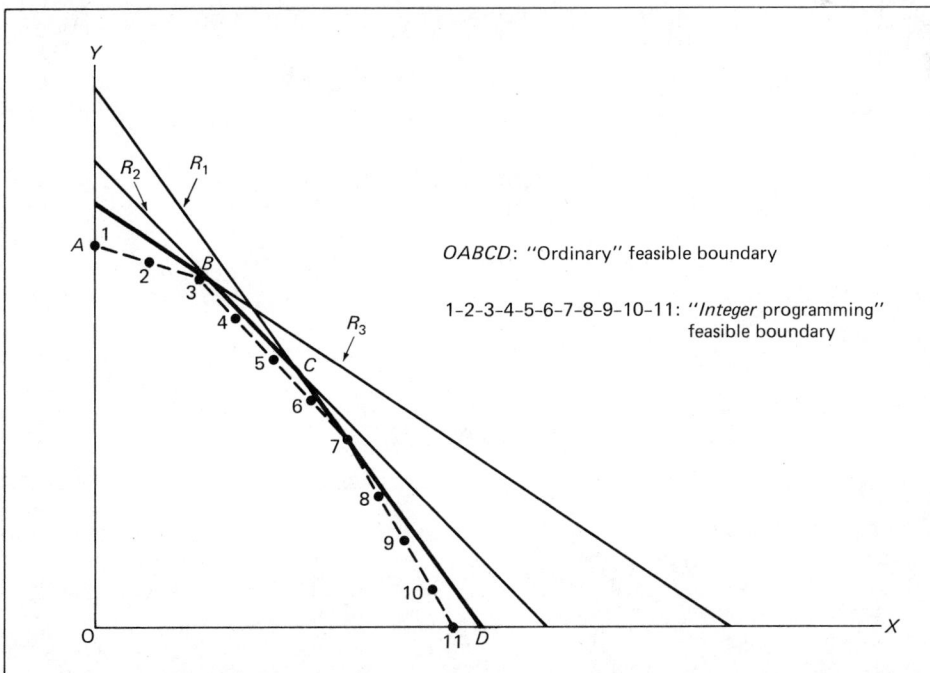

integer values for X and Y. The "best" integer values are shown by points 4 and 5. We also pick out other integer values that are feasible according to segment CD—these are points 6–11. The new boundary governed by only points and integer values is shown by the dotted-line polygon, although only the points are relevant. The feasible region formed by points 1–2–3–4–5–6–7–8–9–10–11 must be evaluated by the firm for selection of the optimal solution.

LIMITATIONS TO LINEAR PROGRAMMING

We have already pointed out one of the difficulties associated with linear programming (LP) problems—all values must be integers. This requirement makes the solution a little more involved and does not diminish the importance of the method in any manner. However, there are certain assumptions concerning LP that perhaps limit its usefulness. One of these is the assumption of strict linearity. Not all economic or technical relationships are linear. We have assumed that all functions are linear.

Another problem relates to the assumptions concerning the objective function. It is not entirely correct to assume that the profit from the cost of each unit of output of the firm remains constant. The objective function need not be linear. Furthermore, the *linear* programming version of profit maximization neglects the effects of demand and production returns to scale. A product will not sell unless the price is right and there is a right price for profit maximization. The unit cost of a product will change continuously depending on the volume of output, the prices of the resources, the rate of production, and so on.

Despite its limitations, the LP model is more useful and practical than not. It has been and is still being used in a variety of situations. The petroleum industry uses it for the economical blending of gasoline and additives; the Department of Defense has employed it to determine the optimal mix of weapons; transportation companies use it for selection of delivery routes; and even the banks use it for selection of the best portfolio. In the next section we will show how a bank uses LP in portfolio selection. Although the bank's use of LP is an isolated example, the applications are limitless. All that is required is that the constraints and the objective functions are linear. There are other forms of programming beyond the scope of this book and among them are *integer, parametric, nonlinear,* and *dynamic programming.*

APPLICATIONS

1. Bank Portfolio Management

Portfolio decisions made at any given time affect a bank's current income and profits and may very well influence the bank's future course of events. Asset selection is difficult because alternative courses of action invariably represent trade-offs between risk, profit, and liquidity. Compounding the difficulty is the pressure on commercial banks to maintain adequate profits in the face of rising competition for funds from nonbank financial institutions and other money market instruments. As a result, the commercial banking industry has begun to apply more sophisticated techniques to portfolio management. One such technique receiving much attention is linear programming.

The typical bank's balance sheet consists of a set of assets and liabilities. The first is the *bank's use of funds* and the second is the *source of funds*. The object of bank management is to achieve a proper balance among income, adequate liquidity, and the risk of default. The problem is that usually assets offering high yields, e.g., consumer installment loans, are less liquid and more risky than other assets such as short-term government securities. Government securities such as 90-day Treasury Bills, are quite liquid and reasonably risk free, but they normally offer somewhat low rates of return. Linear programming can assist the bank in selecting a sound portfolio. Although what we are going to describe is highly simplified, with the aid of adequate hardware we could extend the model to include many more variables and constraints.

Consider a hypothetical bank that holds two classes of assets, loans (L) and securities (S). Its liabilities consist of demand deposits (D) and time deposits (T). Let us further stipulate that the total funds available to the bank equal $200 million, loans earn at a rate of 12%, and securities yield 6%. All securities can be liquidated during the decision period without capital loss, and the bank does not incur costs in attracting and maintaining deposits. We now proceed to formulate the LP problem with only three constraints: the total funds constraint, the liquidity constraint, and the loan balance constraint. The objective of the bank is to maximize the total return from loans and securities.

The funds constraint. Because the total availability of funds is limited to $200 million, the total funds constraint may be written as

$$L + S \leq \$200 \text{ million} \qquad (8)$$

In Figure 8-7, this constraint is shown as a linear function having a $-1{:}1$ slope and vertical as well as horizontal intercepts of $200 million. Any point along the line will constitute the total use of the available funds.

The liquidity constraint. Some quantity of negotiable securities must be held by the bank at all times because loans may not be liquidated to meet unanticipated deposit withdrawals. Suppose the bank has decided that it must maintain a *minimum*

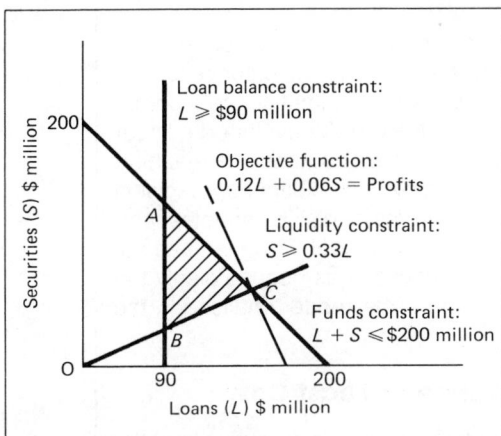

FIGURE 8-7
Because the bank has minimum as well as maximum constraints, the feasible space lies above or below these constraints. The applicable feasible area in this instance is given by triangle *ABC*, and *C* is the most profitable point.

of 25% of the available deposits $(L + S)$ in the form of negotiable securities. This constraint may be expressed mathematically as

$$S \geqslant 0.25 (L + S) \quad \text{or} \quad 0.75 S \geqslant 0.25 L \quad \text{or} \quad S \geqslant 0.33L \qquad (9)$$

Equation (9), representing the liquidity constraint, is also shown in Figure 8-7. The constraint begins at the origin and is drawn positively at an inclination of 0.33. Any point along or above this line satisfies the constraint. [By contrast, all points along the line or within the area bound by the line are feasible for constraint (8)].

The loan balance constraint. Finally, let us assume that the bank must loan *at least* $90 million, as this constitutes the average aggregate request from its principal and important loan customers. Because this is a *minimum* constraint applying only to loans, it is shown as the vertical line of Figure 8-7, and all points along this line are feasible as are points to its right. The feasible space is shown by area *ABC*.

The optimal asset portfolio. We now have all the elements relevant to the bank's portfolio decision including the objective function, $0.12L + 0.06S$, showing the relative merit of loans and securities. The bank, in attempting to maximize the net yield from L and S chooses the appropriate combination by placing the objective function at various points on the feasibility space shown by triangle *ABC* in Figure 8-7. The graphical solution indicates that the objective function will be maximized where the liquidity constraint intersects the funds constraint at point *C*. We can compute this point algebraically by equating equations (8) and (9). Thus,

$$L + S = 200$$
$$S = 0.33L$$

or

$$1.33L = 200$$

$$L = \frac{200}{1.33} = 150.38$$

and

$$S = 200 - 150.38 = 49.62$$

$$\text{total income to bank} = 0.12 (150.38) + 0.06 (49.62) = 21.02.$$

This simple illustration of the application of the LP model to the bank's portfolio selection suggests that out of the total of the $200 million in funds available to the bank, it should try to lend about $150.38 million and invest the rest in short-term securities. Once this is accomplished, it will not only satisfy the stipulated constraints but will also earn a total of $21.02 million on the total funds of $200 million, amounting to an average rate of return of 11%.

It should be mentioned that the linear programming model just described was only for the purpose of illustration. In actual use, the model is quite successful in performing analytical tasks and suggesting reasonable approximations to income-maximizing portfolios. The Bankers Trust Company in New York developed a linear programming model during the 1960s to assist the bank's management in reaching portfolio decisions. The model is quite detailed and employs a multiperiod decision framework, a large number of balance sheet categories as decision variables, and numerous constraints of the variety described earlier. The model, however, has not been a substitute for managerial judgment. Its chief function has been to clarify the many consequences of alternative decisions. In short, the model challenges the judgment in a most comprehensive manner.

2. Recommended Daily Allowance at Least Cost

Dieticians and nutritionists maintain that we should consume certain amounts of the essential vitamins and minerals present in the various food groups. Often such

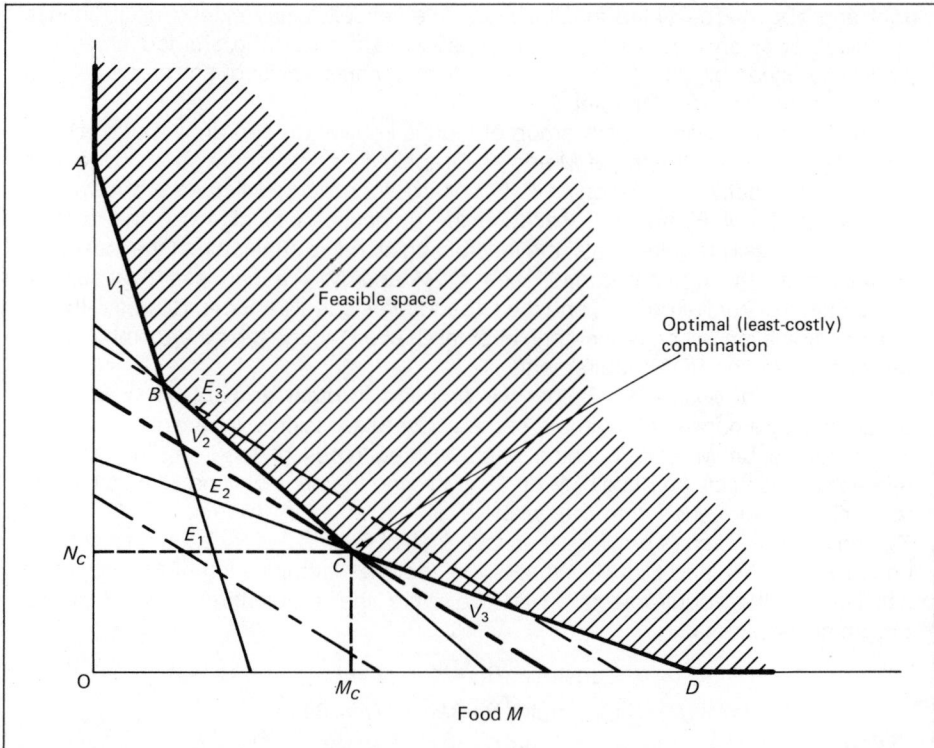

FIGURE 8-8
In general, when the linear programming constraints are stated in the "at least" or "a minimum of" format, the feasible region lies *above* the relevant portions of the constraints. Such a problem usually involves the minimization of the objective function. In the diagram above, the feasible zone is depicted by the shaded area and cost is minimized at point *C*. Point *C* indicates that consumption at that point will minimize the expenditure of purchasing the correct quantities of *M* and *N*—the quantities that also provide the recommended daily allowance of vitamins.

minimums are referred to as the recommended daily allowance (RDA). You will find these listed on most packages containing processed food. We can use the LP model to compute the consumption of various foods that will provide us with the RDA at the least cost. For the time being, we will disregard the utility derived from such a combination.

Assume that there are two groups of foods M and N that contain the three essential vitamins V_1, V_2, and V_3. Each unit of M provides certain amounts of all three vitamins, as does each unit of food group N. If we know the amounts of such vitamins contained in each food group and if the minimum requirements are stipulated, we can easily obtain the constraints necessary to incorporate them into the linear programming problem.

Figure 8-8 shows the three constraints representing the minimum necessary amounts of the three vitamins. Because the objective is to consume *at least* these *minimum* amounts, all points that lie on or beyond a particular constraint satisfy that constraint. Consequently, the feasible space contains only those combinations of M and N that lie on or beyond all three constraints. Thus, *ABCD* forms the *minimum* border of the feasible space which extends from this border to other areas to the right and above. The entire feasible area, theoretically, may extend up to infinite quantities of M and N, but for our purposes is shown as the shaded area. The piecewise linear border $ABCD$ very much resembles an isoquant of production theory, as discussed in Chapter 6.

Because the price of each group of food is known, we can draw a budget line reflecting the relative prices of M and N. Graphically speaking, such a budget line will have a negative inclination of P_M/P_N. Many such budget lines are shown and labelled as E's in Figure 8-8. Because the objective is to minimize the cost of obtaining the daily requirements, the feasible point that is attainable at the least cost is chosen as the optimal combination of M and N. We can see that such a combination occurs at point C, and the expenditures equal E_2. Expenditures with any other combination will be higher than at point C, even though the other combinations will also satisfy the RDA requirements.

A numercial illustration. Before we proceed to other applied areas of linear programming a numerical example of the above discussion will be worked. Let the two products be M and N which contain three types of food, R_1, R_2, and R_3, respectively, and let the price of M be \$2 a unit and the price of N be \$3 a unit. Other requirements are such that we wish to obtain *at least* 40 units of R_1, 60 of R_2, and 80 of R_3. Each M *provides 4 units of R_1*, 3 of R_2, and 2 of R_3. Each N provides 1 unit of R_1, 2 of R_2, and 8 of R_3. What is the "optimal" combination of M and N that satisfies all the requirements? First we write the problem in the LP (linear programming) format:

$$\text{Constraint } R_1\text{: } 4M + N \geq 40$$
$$\text{Constraint } R_2\text{: } 3M + 2N \geq 60$$
$$\text{Constraint } R_3\text{: } 2M + 8N \geq 80$$

Minimize the cost function $E = 2M + 3N$. We convert the inequalities (greater than or equal to) into exact equalities by subtracting "slack variables" S_1, S_2, and S_3 from the constraint equations R_1, R_2, and R_3, respectively, which yields:

$$4M + N - S_1 = 40 \tag{10}$$
$$3M + 2N - S_2 = 60 \tag{11}$$
$$2M + 8N - S_3 = 80 \tag{12}$$

We further stipulate that all values of M, N, R, and S have to be zero or positive, which can be described by writing,

$$M, N, S_1, S_2, S_3 \geq 0$$

If we draw the constraints with M along the horizontal and N along the vertical axis, the R_1 constraint will have N and M intercepts of 40 and 10; the R_2 constraint will have intercepts of 30 and 20; and the R_3 constraint will have intercepts of 10 along the N axis and 40 along the M axis. The constraints are shown in Figure 8-9. Point B occurs where R_1 intersects R_2, hence the amounts of M and N represented by such a point can be found by the simultaneous solution of the equations representing R_1 and R_2 or equations (10) and (11).

Similarly, point C can be found by solving equations (11) and (12). Point A is found by setting M of equation (10) equal to zero and, similarly, point D is found by setting N of equation (12) equal to zero. Point K of Figure 8-9 is found by solving equations (10) and (12), but the values of M and N at such a point will be unacceptable because it is not feasible. To find the least-costly point from the feasible set we systematically solve for all the "corners" of the feasible-set lower

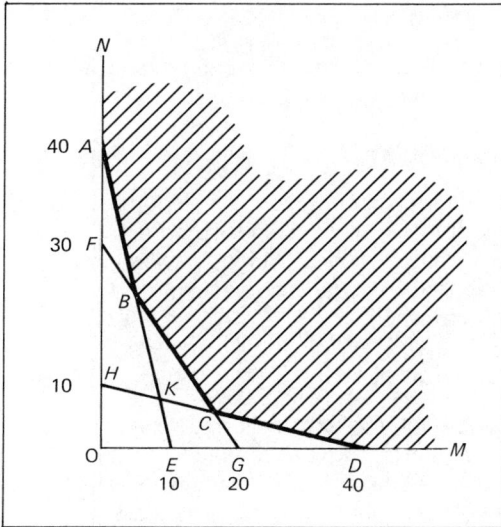

FIGURE 8-9
Note: All points shown by (**) are not feasible because at least one of the variables is negative. For example, point *F* is not acceptable because $S_1 = -10$, which means that resource R_1 is not being consumed in adequate quantities; point *F* is violating constraint R_1 by 10. Point *C* is the least costly point and is also feasible. Point *H* would have been less costly ($30), but it is not feasible. Similarly, point *K*, had it been acceptable, would have been more economical ($40).

Point	M	N	S_1	S_2	S_3	Cost: $2M + 3N$
A	0	40	0	20	240	$120
F	0	30	−10	0	160	(**)
B	4	24	0	0	120	$80
K	8	8	0	−20	0	(**)
C	16	6	30	0	0	$50 Optimal
E	10	0	0	−30	−60	(**)
G	20	0	40	0	−40	(**)
D	40	0	120	60	0	$80
H	0	10	−30	−40	0	(**)

boundary, *ABCD*. The optimal solution usually lies at one of these corner points. The procedure is to make the number of unknowns equal to the number of equations, by setting as many variables as necessary equal to zero and determining the values of *M* and *N* at each of these points. Provided the solutions are acceptable (all values zero or positive), the optimal point is chosen from all such corner points, and this combination of *M* and *N* yields the cost-minimizing solution. Now we calculate the values of *M* and *N* at points *A, B, C, D,* and *K* and tabulate the results for the selection of the optimal solution. The points that are not feasible are shown by (**), because such points violate at least one constraint.

Suggested Applications

1. Process Combination and Selection

The linear programming model can also be used to determine the optimal combination of several production processes capable of producing the output at the least cost and/or producing the best combination of products that yield the most profit.

2. Petroleum Blending

The oil industry uses one form of linear programming to combine or blend several petroleum additives with various types of gasoline in order to minimize costs.

3. The Airlines and Scheduling

Commercial airlines use several types of linear programming models to select the best operating schedules and to assign crews to particular flights. Linear programming may also be used to determine the best combination of range, payload, cruising altitude, and aircraft speed for profit maximization. It can also be employed for profitable seating configurations for particular markets.

4. The Transportation Model

The "transportation model" is a special example of the application of linear programming. This model is frequently used for minimizing transportation cost between factories and destinations or between warehouses and markets. For example, a firm may produce the item in Denver, Austin, and Los Angeles, but sell the product in Denver, Albuquerque, and Tulsa. Since the production facilities have limited capacity, and because the demand for the product is different for each city, the firm should try to minimize the total transportation cost between the supply and demand points. It does so by evaluating the transportation cost for each factory—market pair and then minimizing the sum of all transportation costs with the use of a standard linear programming routine.

EXERCISES

1. Define the following and explain where necessary:
   a. Programming.
   b. Feasible space.
   c. Objective function.
   d. Constraints.
   e. Optimal solution.
   f. Integer programming.
   g. Slack variable.
   h. Feasible solution.

2. Briefly outline how you would use the linear programming model in at least six areas other than those mentioned in this book. Elaborate upon the constraints as well as the objective function.

3. Using outside sources, explain the meanings of the following:
   a. The dual in linear programming models.
   b. Imputed values.
   c. Shadow prices.

4. Using any of the references mentioned in the text, show how you would use the linear programming model in the following:
   a. Input-output analysis.
   b. The transportation model.

5. Draw the following constraints and indicate the feasible space:

a. $6.25X + 10Y \leqslant 50$
   $200X + 100Y \leqslant 800$

b. $X + Y \leqslant 1000$
   $2X + 4Y \leqslant 3200$
   $X \leqslant 900$
   $Y \leqslant 700$

c. $500X + 300Y \geqslant 1500$
   $400X + 400Y \geqslant 1600$
   $200X + 600Y \geqslant 1200$

6. Draw the following objective functions:
   a. $5X + 3Y$
   b. $8X + 9Y$
   c. $2X + 3Y$

7. Use each of the following objective functions in Exercise 6 (one at a time) to:
   a. *maximize* their value for Exercise 5, parts (a) and (b);
   b. minimize their value for Exercise 5, part (c).

8. Willie Wonka produces and sells Reggie Bars and Chompo Bars. Each type of candy bar yields a 36¢ profit. A Reggie Bar requires 9 grams of sugar, 10 grams of nuts, and 16 grams of sunflower seeds. Each Chompo Bar requires 18 grams of sugar, 10 grams of nuts, and 8 grams of sunflower seeds. Wonka has a total availability of 16,200 grams of sugar, 10,000 grams of nuts, and 12,800 grams of sunflower seeds. Labor is free and abundant. What combination of the two types of candy should Wonka produce in order to maximize profits? Which combination will have the least opportunity cost (in terms of unused resources) while maximizing profits? The costs of the ingredients are as follows:
   sugar: 2¢ per gram
   nuts: 3¢ per gram
   seeds: 1¢ per gram

Also, compute the total amount of profit and the price of each type of candy bar.

9. A building contractor can build two types of homes—brick and frame. Each brick home requires 4000 bricks, 900 feet of lumber, and 40 bags of mortar. Each frame home requires 3000 bricks, 1200 feet of lumber, and 500 nails. The contractor's total supply of resources are shown below:
   bricks: 1.2 million
   lumber: 360,000 feet
   nails: 100,000
   mortar: 8000 bags
   Labor: unlimited

Using graphical or algebraic techniques, calculate the profit-maximizing mix of the two types of homes if profit (a) per home is equal to $8000; (b) per brick home is $9000 and per frame home is $12,000. Compute the amount of total profit in each case. All answers must be integers.

10. Bill and John work for a small manufacturing company that produces hatchets (H) and axes (A). Bill's hourly output is 6 hatchets *and* 9 axes, and John's output per hour is 9 hatchets *and* 5 axes. (The technology is such that the proportion of H to A for each person remains constant at all volumes of output.) Bill receives $12 per hour and John $10. The other requirements/constraints are as follows:

a. A minimum of 108 hatchets and 90 axes must be produced.
b. To satisfy the labor union, the total time of Bill and John must be at least 16 hours.
c. Each person may work a maximum of 15 hours.

Draw the "feasible region" and determine the optimal combination of time devoted by Bill and John and the cost of such a combination. (The answers do not have to be integers; the optimality here refers to cost minimization.)

11. The Navy is experimenting with two types of bombs, A and B. Each bomb requires three ingredients, X, Y, and Z. Bomb A requires 100 units of X, 200 of Y, and 120 of Z. Bomb B requires 150 units of X, 80 of Y, and 300 of Z. The Commander feels that *no more than* 1000 units of X, and *at least* 800 of Y should be utilized; the amount of Z utilized should be *exactly* 800. Write the constraints in algebraic format. If each bomb of type A produces a 10-ton explosion and each B bomb produces the equivalent of a 14-ton explosion, write an expression for the total explosion function. Calculate the combination of the two types of bombs which, when exploded, will produce the biggest bang.

12. Dr. Welby of the United States Department of Longevity recommends the following diet:

A *minimum of:* 180 units of Vitamin C
420 units of Vitamin D
400 units of Vitamin E
300 units of Vitamin F

The good doctor has also found that the above requirements can be very easily met through the consumption of apples (A) and/or beer (B). An apple provides 2 units of C, 6 units of D, 8 units of E, and 10 units of F. A bottle of beer contributes 6, 7, 5 and 3 units of C, D, E, and F, respectively. Dr. Welby also has certain warnings: *No more* than 80 apples; no more than 80 bottles of beer; and a *maximum* of 100 units of apples and/or beer (A + B ≤ 100).
a. If L (longevity function) = 100A + 90B, what combination will maximize L?
b. If the price of apples and beer equals $2.00 per unit, what combination will minimize costs?
c. If U (consumers' utility function) = 90A + 100B, what combination yields maximum utility?

Use the graphical and algebraic methods.

SUGGESTED READINGS

Dallenbach, H. *User's Guide to Linear Programming*. Englewood Cliffs, New Jersey: Prentice-Hall, 1970.

Loomba, N. *Applied Linear Programming for Management*. New York: Holt, Rhinehart, and Winston, 1974.

McNamara, J. "A Linear Programming Model for Long-Range Capacity Planning in an Electric Utility." *Journal of Economics and Business,* Spring/Summer 1976.

Thompson, G. "Linear Programming and Microeconomic Analysis." *Nebraska Journal of Economics and Business,* Autumn 1972.

Vandermeulen, D. *Linear Economic Theory*. Englewood Cliffs, New Jersey: Prentice-Hall, 1971.

Wicks, J. "An Alternative Solution to Linear Programming Problems with Stochastic Input–Output Coefficients." *Australian Journal of Agricultural Economics,* April 1978.

Chapter Nine

THEORY OF COSTS

In general, cost is the sacrifice necessary to obtain certain benefits. Thus, the cost of production represents the value of inputs used, as well as the opportunity cost of foregone alternatives in the production of the output. There are many types of costs in addition to production costs. For example, one may encounter cost of information, cost of transaction, acquisition cost, and cost of operation. There are also private, as opposed to social, costs. Our primary goal in this chapter is to focus attention on production costs.

In the discussion of production in Chapters 6 and 7, we saw that the firm was very careful in selecting the proper types of inputs and combining them in the most economical manner to produce the output. Such a choice of inputs was largely governed by the equimarginal principle, that is, by the productivities of the inputs in relation to their prices. When the prices of the inputs are systematically linked to the volume of output, we obtain the cost–output relationship, or the *cost function.*

COSTS OF PRODUCTION IN THE SHORT RUN

Variable Costs

Those costs that vary with the volume of output are called *variable costs.* We must be careful in maintaining the ceteris paribus assumption with such a definition of variable costs, because the costs of production also vary with the *rate* and *speed* of production. Those costs that remain constant at all levels of output are called *fixed costs.* Thus, a car wash company that uses manual methods will basically use one variable *productive* resource—labor. In addition to hiring workers, the company will also use certain other variable but *passive* inputs in the form of water and detergent. The largest percentage of variable costs will be labor costs. The cost of buildings and equipment will be largely fixed.

Productivity and Cost

Suppose, as described in the car wash example, a firm requires only one variable resource, labor. Due to such short-run constraints, the variable resource's marginal, as well as average, physical products will be subject to variation with changes in the use of such a resource. Thus, if the variable resource is very productive and efficient, and its price remains constant, the cost of acquiring output will not be as high as if the resource's productivity was low and the system was inefficient. For the discussion to follow, we will assume that the firm pays a constant price to each of its workers, and that the short-run production function is of the S-shaped variety used in Chapter 6, and the output's production goes through the various production "stages."

We will use Table 9-1 to explain how the total output curve (the production function) is related to the total variable cost function. Assume that the output, Q, is related to the only variable input, L, as shown by columns (1) and (2), and that each unit of L receives \$100.

Columns (2) and (5) contain the variable cost information. When the values of column (5) are plotted against those of column (2), we obtain a variable cost function. From column (3) we can see that the output is subject to increasing marginal returns up to the third worker—that is, the marginal physical product of L (MPP$_L$) rises up to that point, and diminishes thereafter. The rate of change of the variable cost is affected by the rate of the output as well as the rate of change of the price of the inputs. In this particular case, the price of each unit of L (labor) is constant at $100. Consequently, the variable cost is affected by the marginal physical product of labor. Whenever the output increases at an increasing rate, ceteris paribus, variable cost increases at a decreasing rate. It follows that when output increases at a decreasing rate, all other factors remaining equal, variable cost increases at an increasing rate. In general, the rate of change of variable cost is opposite to the rate of change of output.

From Table 9-1, we can see that the marginal physical product of the variable resource declines after 16 units of output are produced with 3 units of L. In the diminishing (marginal) returns stage of production, the additional variable cost of hiring an extra unit of L is still $100, but the additional benefit from hiring each additional worker is shown by the declining values of the marginal physical products. Thus, the fourth worker adds 8 more units of output and is paid $100; the fifth worker contributes 5 units of output and is also paid $100. Since the firm receives progressively less incremental output with each additional unit of L, the variable cost of production with a single variable input rises at an increasing rate. You can verify that the variable cost will rise at a decreasing rate up to 16 units of output.

Figure 9-1 shows the derivation of the variable cost function from the production function. There are four quadrants (a)–(d), and each contains part of the information contained in Table 9-1. Quadrant (a) shows the short-run ceteris paribus production function $Q = f(L)$, which is derived from columns (1) and (2). Quadrant (b) contains the information about total wages to labor for various levels of employment. Thus, if each unit of L receives $100, the equation for total wages (TW) will be TW $= 100L$. This equation is shown as a

TABLE 9-1

(1) Units of L	(2) Total output	(3) Marginal product of L (3) = $\Delta(2)/\Delta(1)$	(4) Price of L	(5) Total variable cost (due to L) (5) = (1) × (4)
1	2	2	$100	$100
2	6	4	100	200
3	16	10	100	300
4	24	8	100	400
5	29	5	100	500
6	33	4	100	600
7	35	2	100	700
8	36	1	100	800

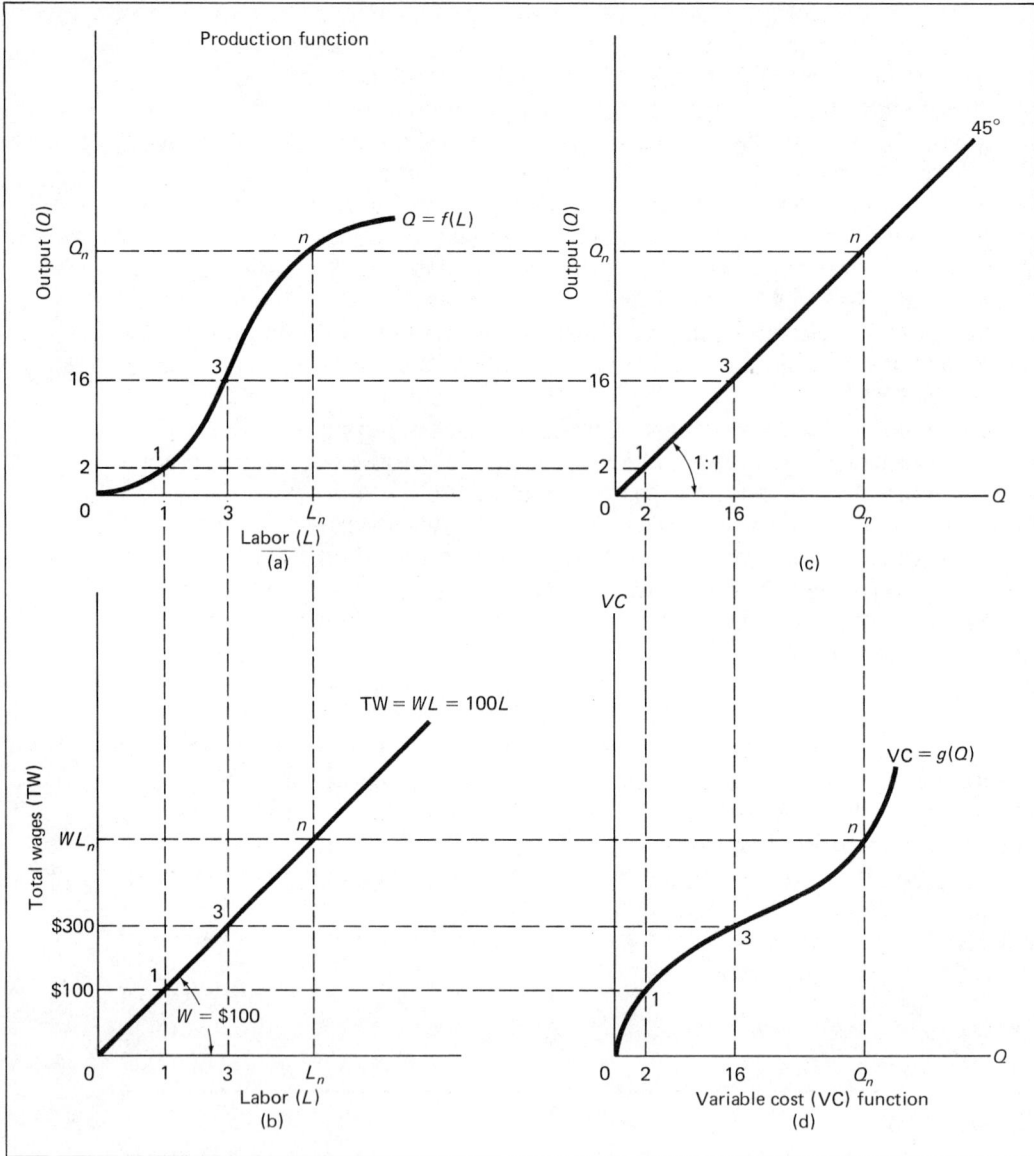

Production function

FIGURE 9-1

straight line starting at the origin. The line subtends an angle whose value is equal to the wage rate per unit of L or, in this case, $100. Quadrant (c) contains a 45° line which merely converts vertical distances into horizontal ones. Finally, quadrant (d) shows the variable cost (VC) function as derived from the other three quadrants—that is, it shows the total labor cost (total wages) as a function of output. Mathematically, we can derive a function or equation in two variables from two other equations containing the variables in question. For example, if height is related to age, and weight is related to height, then we can also derive a relationship between age and weight. Thus, if $Q = f(L)$ and TW = 100L, then VC = TW = $g(Q)$.

In quadrant (a) when $L = 1$, $Q = 2$ and total wages equal $100. Thus $100 is the total variable cost of producing 2 units of output. Point 1 on the production function shows an output of 2 units, corresponding to an employment level of 1 unit of L. This point is projected down to quadrant (b), where the total wage to the firm equals $100. This $100 figure is also shown in quadrant (d). Now we move to quadrant (c), which has a 45° line, and this converts total output from quadrant (a), which is measured vertically, into an equal distance measured horizontally. Hence when $L = 1$, $Q = 2$ as shown in quadrants (a) and (c). Projecting this output volume shown in quadrant (c) down to quadrant (d), we see that an output volume of 2 units is associated with a total wage cost of $100. Thus, the variable cost of producing 2 units is $100. Taking other points in quadrant (a), such as $L = 3$, we find that $Q = 16$, and this output level is associated with total wages of $300. We can now draw part of the variable cost function by drawing a line through points 1 and 3 showing the combinations of output and variable cost already discussed. When all the combinations of cost (total wages) are plotted against corresponding levels of output, we obtain the total variable cost as shown in quadrant (d).

We have shown a very simple version of the total variable cost function—namely, one that contains only a variable input such as labor. Realistically speaking, many resources are utilized in the production of the output, and the utilization rate of some of the other resources may or may not remain constant with output volume. However, the raw material content of each unit of output is usually consistent. For example, every cigar may require 1 gram of tobacco. Thus the variable cost function will reflect the cost of labor as well as raw material. Interestingly enough, even though the physical composition of the product may not change with volume, its cost per unit might. For instance, if the firm can obtain quantity discounts on a bulk purchase of tobacco, the raw material cost of each cigar will be lower at higher output volumes than if the company produced small quantities of cigars. Figure 9-2 shows the probable shape of a variable cost function derived from the previous variable cost function and a linear raw material cost function. The total variable cost at each level of output is the sum of the two variable costs—labor and raw material. If the raw material cost had been subject to volume discounts, its slope would have declined with increases in output.

Before we discuss other costs, notice that the total variable cost function of Figure 9-1 is S-shaped (although backwards), because the production function was also S-shaped. If the production function had been linear, ceteris paribus, the variable cost function would also have been linear. The production function is *concave from above* until the third worker, therefore the variable cost function is *concave from below* in that corresponding range up to 16 units of output and $300. Because output increases at an increasing rate, variable cost increases at a decreasing rate. After the third worker and 16 units of output, variable cost increases at an increasing rate and the function starts to rise very rapidly. Variable costs generally occur only if the output is produced or changed. Therefore, they are also called *avoidable costs*.

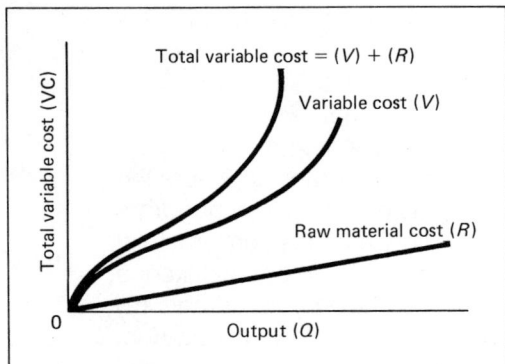

Total variable cost = (V) + (R)

Variable cost (V)

Raw material cost (R)

Total variable cost (VC)

0

Output (Q)

FIGURE 9-2
The firm's variable cost consists of all costs associated with variable resources, including the cost of raw material. Thus, the total variable cost is the sum of the cost of productive variable resources (V) and the cost of raw material (R).

Fixed Costs

Fixed costs to a firm do not vary with the level of output. Such costs include insurance premiums, property rent or mortgage payments, salaries of managerial personnel, and license fees. Regardless of the volume of output, the firm must pay these costs. Thus, whether a company produces one million cigars or none at all, as long as it is in business it must pay its fixed costs. Because the total fixed costs are invariant with the volume of output, they may be shown as a horizontal line drawn at the appropriate level, as in Figure 9-3, which also shows the *total cost* to a firm, which is the sum of its variable and fixed costs. When we add the fixed cost to the variable cost, we see that the sum reflects the shape of the variable cost. This is because the fixed cost has a slope of zero. Consequently, the total cost (TC) function has the same slope as the variable cost (VC) function but lies above it by a distance equal to total fixed cost (FC), that is, TC and VC are *vertically parallel,* and TC = VC + FC.

Sunk Costs

All the costs that have already been "sunk" into a project and are normally not recoverable or changeable, are called *sunk costs.* For example, when a bridge is partially complete, all the costs associated with labor, raw materials, and capital equipment time, as well as certain overhead costs, are already sunk and cannot be recovered. At that point in time, whether the bridge is finished or abandoned, the costs that have been incurred will not change. Consequently, sunk costs are irrelevant to economic decision making. Economic decisions are based on any change in costs due to a certain action and the corresponding benefits of such an action. Hence *incremental costs* and benefits are more important to the economist than sunk costs.

Incremental Costs

Incremental cost is the change in cost due to a new decision, including the change in cost due to changes in the quantity of output produced. Thus, the

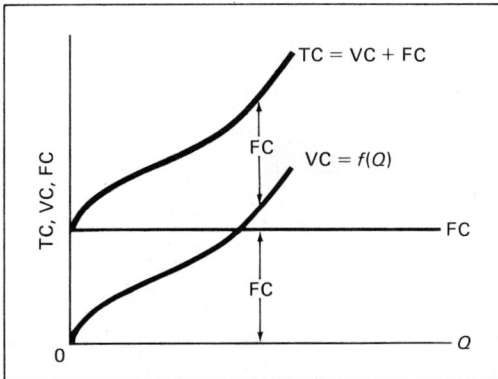

FIGURE 9-3
Total cost (TC) is the sum of total variable cost (VC) and total fixed cost (FC). In a graph, the vertical distance between the TC and the VC is constant and equal to the FC. Consequently, the TC and the VC are *vertically parallel*.

additional cost due to advertising is a type of incremental cost, just as deciding to buy equipment instead of leasing it may involve an incremental cost. The incremental cost may be negative, zero, or positive.

Marginal Costs

Marginal cost is the change in total variable cost associated with a one-unit change of output. We may also express marginal cost (MC) as the ratio of the incremental cost (IC) of output to the change in total output (ΔQ). Graphically, marginal cost is given by the slope of the variable cost function. As long as the change in output is not inordinately large, the following definition is reasonably accurate:

$$\text{Marginal cost} = \frac{\text{Change in variable cost}}{\text{Change in output}}$$

or

$$MC = \frac{\Delta VC}{\Delta Q} \tag{1}$$

Thus, if a firm's variable costs increase by $12 when output increases by one unit, the marginal cost of the additional unit will be $12. For example, suppose that a firm must hire an additional worker in order to produce more output. Let the cost of hiring the new worker be $100. Because the new worker will produce more than just one unit in most cases, we may use equation (1) to determine the *average* marginal cost of the new units of output. If the marginal physical product of the new worker is 10 units, the marginal cost of each of the 10 units will be $100/10, or $10. The $100 will be the change in the firm's variable costs due to the production of the 10 additional units. From what has been just illustrated, we can also express marginal cost (MC) by equation (2):

$$MC = \frac{\text{Price of variable resource}}{\text{Marginal product of resource}} \tag{2}$$

Marginal Cost and Variable Cost

From equation (1) one can see that marginal cost is related to variable cost. Consequently, we can rewrite equation (1) to reflect the variable cost as a function of marginal cost. Thus, from equation (1),

$$MC(\Delta Q) = \Delta VC$$

or

$$\sum MC_i = VC \tag{3}$$

Equation (3) tells us that the total variable cost (VC) is the sum of the marginal cost (MC_i) of each unit of output. For example, if the marginal cost of the first unit of output is $10, and that of the second unit is $8, then the change in total variable cost due to the production of both the units is $18. Note that the average marginal cost in this range is ($18/2), or $9. In a graph, *the total variable cost can be shown by the value of the area under the marginal cost function* (see Figure 9-4).

Average Variable Cost

The average variable cost (AVC) of the output is the ratio of the total variable cost to the total quantity of output. This ratio may be expressed as

$$AVC = \frac{\text{Total variable cost}}{\text{Total output}} = \frac{VC}{Q} \tag{4}$$

But the total output (Q) can be obtained by multiplying the average physical product (APP) of the variable resource by the quantity of the resource, and the total variable cost is the product of the price of the resource and its quantity. Hence, equation (4) may also be written as

$$AVC = \frac{VC}{Q} = \frac{(\text{Price of resource}) \times (\text{quantity of resource})}{(\text{Average product of resource}) \times (\text{quantity of resource})}$$

$$= \frac{\text{Price of resource}}{\text{Average product of resource}} = \frac{P_r}{(APP)_r} \tag{5}$$

For example, if, on the average, each unit of the variable resource produces 10 units of output, and the price of each unit of the resource is $100, the average variable cost will be ($100/10), or $10. From equation (5) it follows that the total variable cost (VC) is the product of the average variable cost (AVC) and total output (Q), or $VC = AVC \times Q$. In a graph, the AVC can be found by measuring the slope of a straight line drawn from the origin to the VC function. In Figure 9-4, the AVC, when quantity equals 100, is $7000 divided by 100, or $70. If we draw a line from the origin to point X in panel (a), its slope will be $70.

Average Fixed Cost

Average fixed cost (AFC) is equal to the total fixed cost (FC) divided by the total output (Q), or

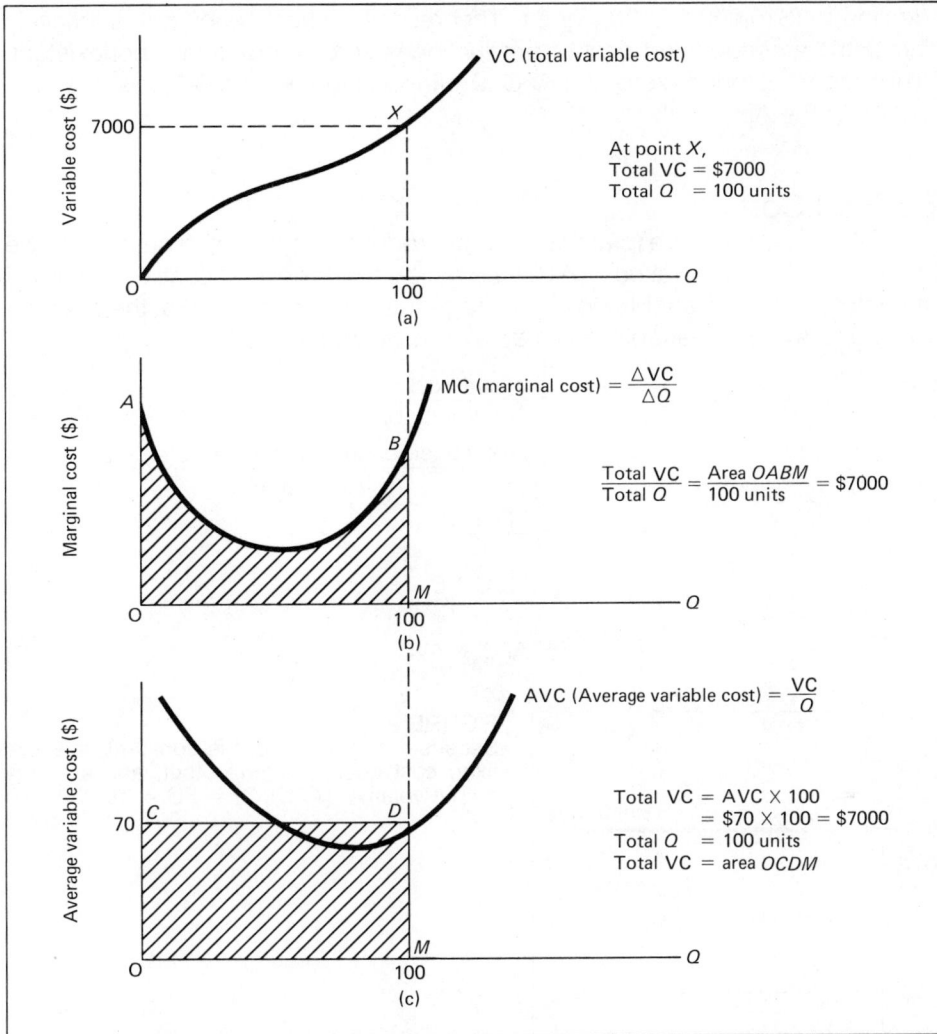

FIGURE 9-4
Total variable cost can be expressed in more than one way. In (a) we see that the variable cost of producing 100 units is $7000. (b) shows the variable cost as the area under the marginal cost curve, which also equals $7000. Finally, (c) illustrates that VC is the average variable cost (AVC) multiplied by quantity, or $70 times 100.

$$AFC = \frac{FC}{Q} \qquad (6)$$

As output increases, Q increases, and because fixed cost is constant at all levels of output, the ratio of FC to Q declines with increases in Q. For instance, if a firm's fixed costs, composed of rent, mortgage payments on machinery, and insurance, are $10,000, the average fixed cost due to these resources will decline as output increases. With output at one unit, the AFC will be ($10,000/1), or $10,000, while at an output volume of 10,000 units, the AFC will decline to ($10,000/10,000), or $1. Theoretically, when the output is infinitely large, the average fixed cost of production is zero or practically nonexistent, while for an output of zero, the AFC is infinitely high. Figure 9-5 illustrates the shape of the AFC.

Average Total Cost

When we divide the total cost (TC) of production by the total output (Q), we obtain the average total cost (ATC). However, because total cost is the sum of the total fixed and variable costs, average total cost is the sum of the average fixed and average variable costs as shown by equation (7):

$$\text{Average total cost} = \text{ATC} = \frac{\text{Total cost}}{\text{Total output}} = \frac{\text{TC}}{Q}$$

$$= \frac{(\text{Total fixed cost}) + (\text{total variable cost})}{\text{Total output}}$$

$$= \frac{\text{FC} + \text{VC}}{Q}$$

$$= \frac{\text{FC}}{Q} + \frac{\text{VC}}{Q}$$

$$= \text{AFC} + \text{AVC} \qquad (7)$$

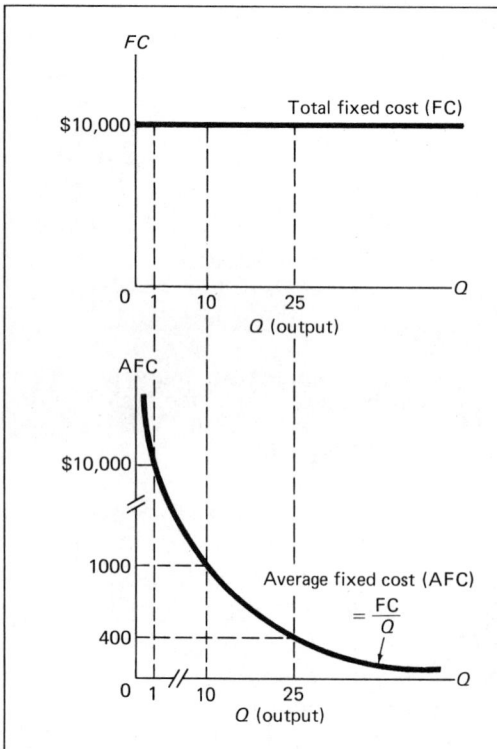

FIGURE 9-5
Because total fixed cost is constant, average fixed cost declines with output, and at every output volume, $(AFC)(Q) = FC = 10,000$.

Figure 9-6 summarizes the discussion concerning the short-run shapes of the various cost functions. Panel (a) shows the total fixed and variable costs as well as their sum, total cost. Panel (b) contains the graphs of the average fixed cost, average variable cost, average total cost, and marginal cost. Where the slope of the variable cost (or total cost) is minimum, such as at quantity Q_2 in panel (a), the marginal cost also attains its minimum value [point 1 in panel (b)]. Where the slope of the vectors to the VC and TC are minimum, the AVC and the ATC also attain their respective minima (points 2 and 3, respectively). Thus, AVC is minimum at quantity Q_3, and ATC is minimum at quantity Q_4. Furthermore, because the straight line from the origin is tangent to TC at quantity Q_4, it not only measures the magnitude of the ATC, but the MC as well. Consequently, at quantity Q_4, the marginal cost equals the lowest possible average total cost. For similar reasons, the MC equals AVC at quantity Q_3.

For an S-shaped production function of one variable input, with constant resource price, the average variable as well as the average total cost curves are normally U-shaped. The marginal cost function is also similarly shaped. The actual shapes of the various cost functions will eventually be governed by the quantity and quality of the resources, their prices, and productivities as well as the firm's fixed costs.

Before we proceed to other topics in cost analysis, one final point should be emphasized, and that is the relationship of the marginal and average costs at their minimum points to the marginal and average physical products of the variable resource. As long as all other factors remain constant, the marginal cost will be minimum where the marginal product of the variable resource is maximum, and the average variable cost will be minimum where the average product is maximum. [see Figure 9-7, panels (c) and (d)]. Necessarily, where the average and marginal products are equal, the marginal and average variable costs are also equal. From our discussion in Chapter 6, we know that the average product of a variable resource equals its marginal product, where the former is at its maximum. Consequently, the marginal cost equals the average variable cost where the latter is at its minimum.

We can see the various relationships between cost and productivity in Figure 9-7. Panel (a) contains the production function $Q = f(L)$, while panel (c) shows the corresponding marginal (MQ_L) and average (AQ_L) products of the variable resource, labor (L). Panel (b) shows the variable cost of production (VC), and panel (d) shows the corresponding marginal and average variable costs. Using the graphs of Figure 9-7, as well those of Figure 9-1, you can verify the accuracy of the above propositions.

How will the marginal and average variable costs be affected if the price of the variable resource changes with employment? All other factors remaining equal, the marginal or average variable costs will depend on the change of resource price relative to the changes in the marginal and average productivities of the resource. Thus, if every time the firm hires 10 more people, the average wage rate rises by 20%, but average productivity increases by 50%, the new average variable cost with a larger volume of labor employment will be lower than before. If the productivity rises at the same rate as the wage, the

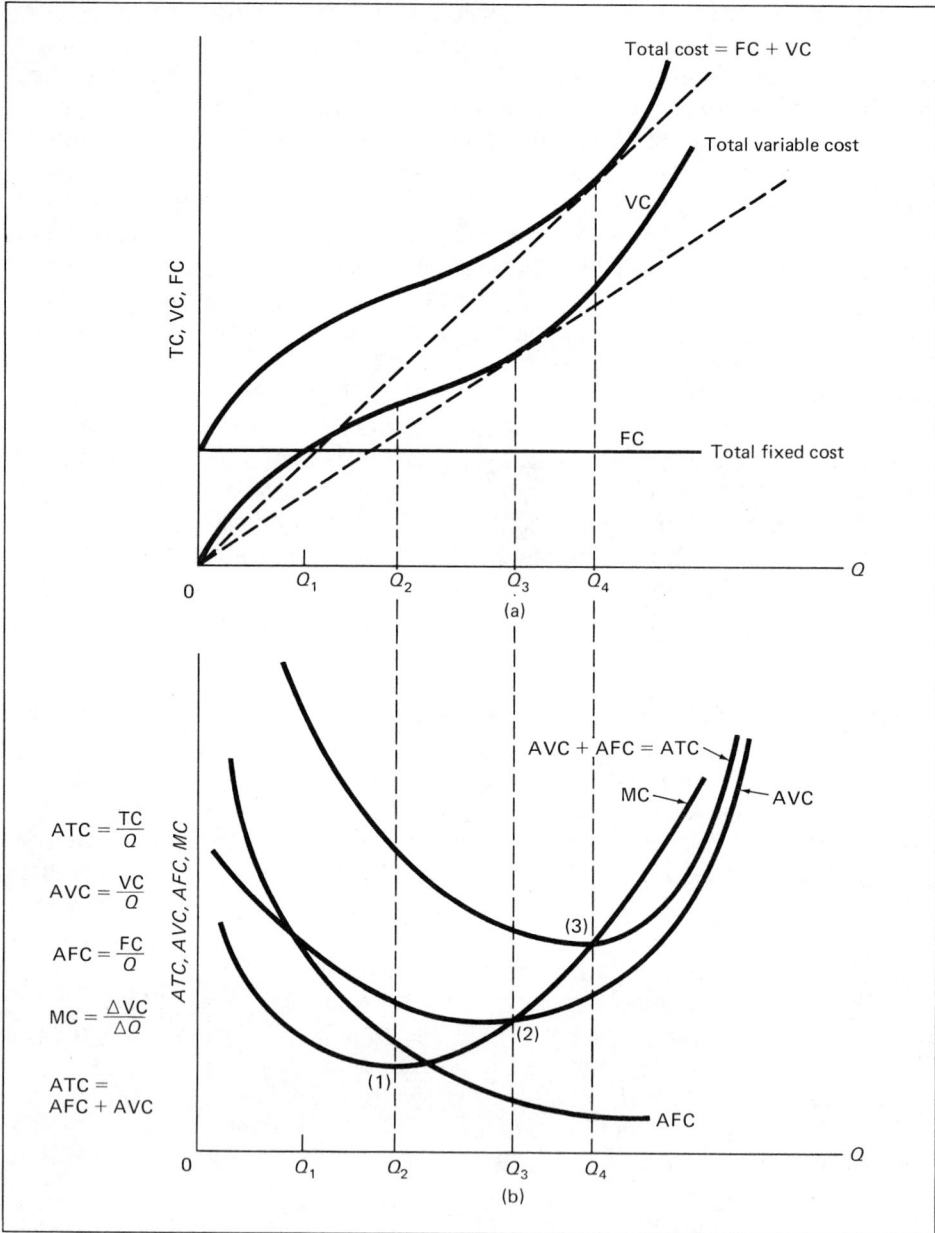

FIGURE 9-6
(a) Shows the total cost functions, while (b) contains the average and marginal cost functions derived from the total costs. At point (2), the average variable cost is minimum and equal to the marginal cost; at point (3), the average total cost is minimum and equal to the marginal cost.

new and old average variable cost will be the same. Equations (2) and (5) may be used to determine the effect of changes in the marginal product, the average product, and the price of the resource on the marginal cost and the average variable cost.

Although we have extensively discussed the case of the U-shaped marginal and average cost functions, it is not entirely correct to assume that all short-run costs are of that type. Research indicates that in many industries, the firms' short-run average and marginal cost function are L-shaped. If the greater percentage of a firm's costs are fixed, and if the average variable cost is either negligible or constant, the average total cost will fall with output. This continuous decline in average total cost will be largely due to the decrease in average fixed cost. For example, in the production of telephone services, a great percentage of total costs are fixed; each additional customer hooked up to the telephone company's lines increases variable costs very little. With a greater number of customers, the average total cost declines. Such a decline, however, may not continue forever, for sooner or later other variable costs will increase with output and cause average total cost to rise.

Technology and Cost

We mentioned earlier that technology is not permitted to change in the short run. However, even with the same technology, a firm may find ways to increase the marginal and average productivities of its resources. An improvement in the output performance of the resources will cause the production function to shift upwards and, in effect, cause the variable cost function to shift down. For example, if the introduction of piped-in music in a factory doubles the workers' output, even if the company must pay 50% more wages, the cost of production will tend to fall, as long as the cost of the music system is not prohibitively expensive.

Recall from our discussion of the average and marginal products of a variable resource in Chapter 6 that the slope of the production function measures the value of the marginal physical product, while the slope of a radius vector to the function showed the magnitude of the average physical product. The effects of changes in technology on the marginal or the average variable cost depend on whether the slope of a straight line from the origin drawn to the variable cost changes. In general, changes in the marginal value bring about changes in the average. Thus, if the marginal cost of production declines or shifts down due to the introduction of new methods of supervision, it is quite likely that the average cost will also fall. It is true, however, that whenever the marginal value exceeds the average value, the average value rises; the average falls when the marginal value is below the average.*

---

*If the marginal cost is linear, the average variable cost will also be linear. It can be shown that for upward-sloping linear functions, the MC will rise twice as fast as the AVC. Similarly, for downward-sloping linear functions, the MC will decline twice as rapidly as the AVC.

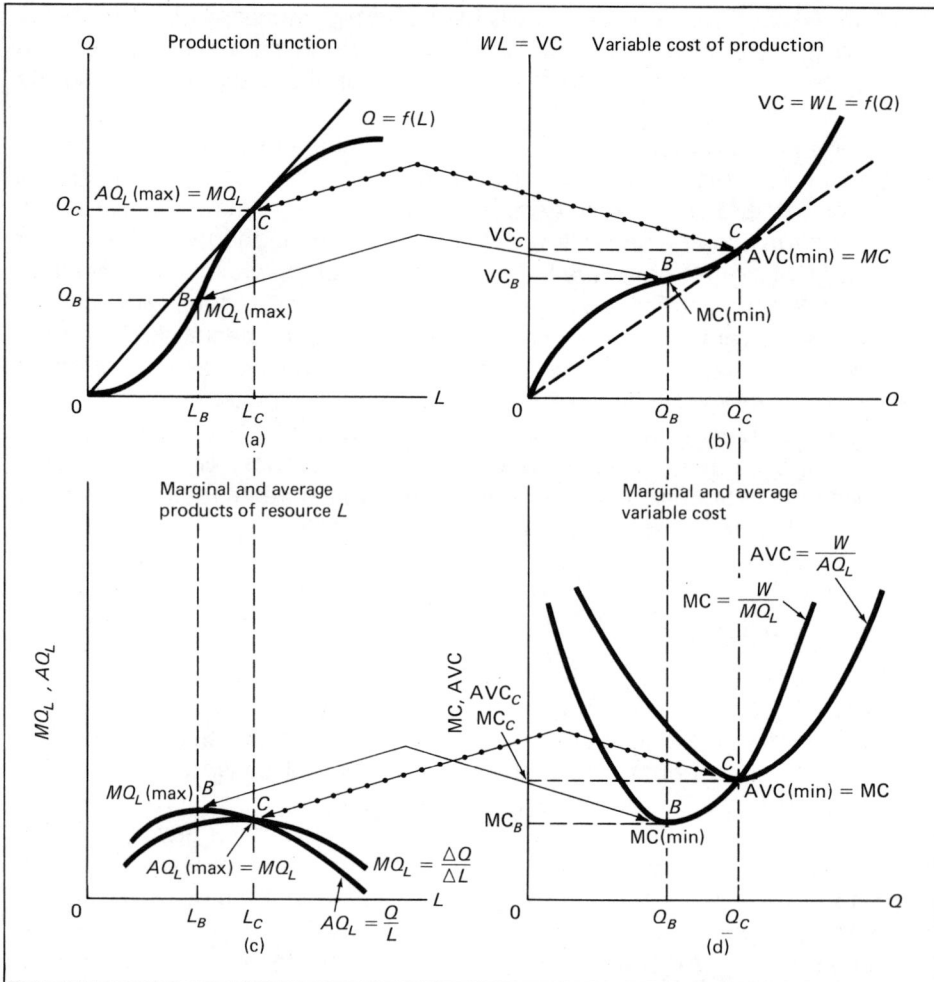

Q — Production function $WL = VC$ Variable cost of production

$Q = f(L)$

$AQ_L \text{(max)} = MQ_L$

Q_C

C

Q_B B $MQ_L \text{(max)}$

L_B L_C

(a)

$VC = WL = f(Q)$

VC_C

C

VC_B B $AVC\text{(min)} = MC$

$MC\text{(min)}$

Q_B Q_C

(b)

Marginal and average
products of resource L

Marginal and average
variable cost

MQ_L , AQ_L

$MQ_L \text{(max)}$ B

C

$AQ_L \text{(max)} = MQ_L$

$MQ_L = \dfrac{\Delta Q}{\Delta L}$

$AQ_L = \dfrac{Q}{L}$

L_B L_C

(c)

MC, AVC

$AVC = \dfrac{W}{AQ_L}$

$MC = \dfrac{W}{MQ_L}$

AVC_C
MC_C

C

$AVC\text{(min)} = MC$

MC_B B $MC\text{(min)}$

Q_B Q_C

(d)

FIGURE 9-7

Composition of Cost

We have simplified our analysis by deliberately disregarding the cost of some of the other variable but passive resources. For example, in the production of the output, the producer incurs costs of raw material. If the percentage composition of the average variable cost at each volume of output can be ascertained, we will be in a position to know the effects of changes in the productivities and/or prices of these resources on the average variable cost. For example, suppose the labor portion of the variable cost constitutes 60%, while the remaining 40% is made up of the cost of raw material. These proportions, no doubt, will change with the volume and the prices of the two variable resources. However, assume for the moment that these percentages remain constant throughout all levels of output. Then the total variable cost (VC) is

$$VC = \text{Labor cost} + \text{raw material cost}$$
$$= 0.60(VC) + 0.40(VC)$$

and average variable cost (AVC) is

$$AVC = \frac{VC}{Q} = 0.60\,(AVC) + 0.40\,(AVC)$$

Because the AVC is the ratio of the price of the resource to its average physical product, 60% of AVC will be affected by changes in the price and average productivity of labor. Similarly, 40% of the AVC will be influenced by the changes in the price of raw material and average raw material requirements. Thus, if the price of labor falls by 50% or labor's productivity rises by 100%, all other things remaining equal, the AVC will decline by only 30%.

As an example, assume that the current AVC is $20, of which labor is 60% or $12 of the cost, and raw material constitutes 40% or $8 of the AVC. If either the wages fall to half their former value, or the output of labor rises to twice its former value, the labor cost will decline to $6 per unit. If nothing else changes, the new AVC will be ($6 + $8), or $14, which is (0.60 × 0.50), or 30% less than before.

COST MINIMIZATION WITH MULTIPLE PLANTS

In the so-called "short run" environment, the producer incurs fixed and variable costs. The shorter the run, the larger the number of inputs that are held fixed, while the number of variable resources increases, as the time period increases. However, even in the short run, a firm may have more than one production facility, such as more than one plant in one or more locations. If each plant has its own cost structure, the firm should produce the desired level of output in either one or more of these plants in such a combination that the total cost of production is minimized. Under such circumstances, the firm can minimize the cost of producing a given output by following the equimarginal principle.

Suppose a firm owns two plants, and each plant has its own cost structure. Let the two cost functions be $C_1 = FC_1 + VC_1$, and $C_2 = FC_2 + VC_2$. As the firm must pay the fixed costs of both plants, regardless of the volume of output, the total cost of production will be minimized where the *total variable cost is at a minimum*. Marginal cost is the rate of change of the variable cost, or the additional variable cost of producing an additional unit. Furthermore, the total variable cost is the sum of the individual marginal costs. Consequently, the firm's total variable cost of producing a particular quantity will be minimized when each plant produces just the right amount to permit the equality of MC_1 and MC_2.

Figure 9-8 shows the total desired output as the distance OD, and the origins for plants 1 and 2 are located at points O and D, respectively. Curves MC_1 and MC_2 intersect at point X. Thus, an output volume of OZ in plant 1 will yield the same marginal cost as output DZ in plant 2. It follows that the area in $OEXFD$ is the total variable cost of producing output OD. The total cost to the

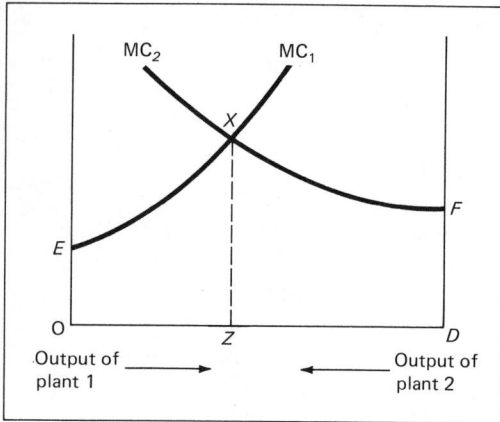

FIGURE 9-8
If a firm has more than one plant, and if each plant has rising marginal costs, the combined total variable cost is minimum if the desired output is allocated between the plants such that the marginal cost of production at each plant is the same.

firm equals the value of this area plus whatever fixed cost is associated with both the firms. The equimarginal principle of cost minimization with multiple plants suggests that the firm should allocate the total output among the plants according to their marginal costs, selecting those with the lowest marginal (and hence variable) cost first. *In the short run, decision making should be based on variable costs, not total costs.*

COST MINIMIZATION WITH SEVERAL VARIABLE INPUTS

If the firm has access to several productive variable resources, it can minimize short-run variable costs by applying a rule very similar to that employed in the case of the firm having multiple plants. Chapter 7 contains the discussion about the cost-minimizing principles involving two variable inputs and isoquants. Hence, cost will be minimum when the output is produced with the cost-minimizing combinations of the variable inputs—that is, each variable input should be employed in such quantities that the marginal cost of production with the use of one input is equal to the marginal cost of production with the use of each of the other inputs. Thus, if the firm can combine three resources—A, B, and C—to produce output Q_1, the cost-minimizing combination will occur when

$$\frac{\text{Price of } A}{(\text{Marginal product})_A} = \frac{\text{Price of } B}{(\text{Marginal product})_B} = \frac{\text{Price of } C}{(\text{Marginal product})_C}$$

COST VARIATION WITH RATE AND QUALITY OF OUTPUT

The cost of production varies directly with the *quality* as well as the *rate* of output. Better quality requires better materials, skilled workers, more watchful supervision, and a higher degree of quality control. Consequently, in most cases, the better the quality, the higher the cost. The quality aspect does permit the firm certain flexibilities in the short run so that it can conceivably lower the costs through quality variation. For example, an inferior or not-so-durable plastic component may replace a part made of steel, or skilled workers may be replaced by semiskilled ones. Such changes allow the producer to keep costs down, although before the introduction of such changes the firm is well advised to determine their adverse effects on demand.

Increases in the speed of production and the rate of output also increase the cost of producing a given volume of output. There are usually higher costs of overtime and waste associated with increases in the rate of output. Furthermore, a higher rate of output with the use of certain fixed resources brings about increases in other costs. For example, beyond normal use, if a machine is run much more frequently than before, it is liable to require greater numbers of overhauls which, if not done at the correct moment, will bring about high costs associated with down time.

AN EMPIRICAL COST FUNCTION

We have postulated that cost functions come in many sizes and shapes. Economists researching various industries have produced many types of cost functions from actual data with the use of statistical and econometric methods. One such cost function—the average total cost of a public service—was developed by W. Z. Hirsch. Professor Hirsch empirically related the average annual residential refuse collection and disposal cost per pickup to six variables. The estimated equation for the average cost (ATC) as a function of the variables (V_i) is shown below:

$$ATC = 6.16 + 0.000089V_1 - 0.000000000436V_1^2 + 3.61V_2 \\ + 3.97V_3 - 0.000611V_4 - 1.87V_5 + 3.43V_6$$

where

V_1 is the number of pickup units;
V_2 is the weekly collection frequency;
V_3 is the pickup location;
V_4 is the pickup density;
V_5 is the nature of contractual arrangements;
V_6 is the type of financing.

The signs of the coefficients, as well as their magnitudes, make economic sense. Variable V_1 is a substitute for the quantity of refuse collected, while V_2 and V_3 are essentially indicators of quality. The other V's impose certain service conditions and therefore influence the input requirements. Once the values of the V's are known, we can estimate the average total cost of this type of service.

COSTS IN THE LONG RUN

The great majority of the firm's decisions are of the short-run variety, as they are made largely in view of the fixed factors that cannot be changed appreciably. Eventually, however, the firm does make long-run plans. The long run is that period of time, or that environment, which allows the firm to vary all the factors. In the future, even after the initial variations of all the factors, the firm will once again be confronted with the short-run decisions, although the new restrictions or parameters will be influenced by earlier decisions. In essence, over the entire long-run period the firm moves from one short-run situation to another. In so doing, it is able to vary all the factors with respect to time. Thus, if the firm initially has fixed costs of $1000 and $2000 in variable costs, as long as it is operating in the first short-run period the fixed costs will remain constant with output. However, in a longer time period, if the firm is able to adjust its fixed factors to a new (and perhaps higher) level, the fixed costs will rise, say, to $3000. The firm will once again have some factors and some variable factors. Therefore, we normally assume that in the long run the firm can vary all its factors and, consequently, all costs in the long run are only variable costs.

Economies and Diseconomies of Scale Once Again

If you will recall from Chapter 7, the firm experiences various types of returns to scale when it varies all its resources. The various points of tangency between successively higher budgets (isocosts) and isoquants, when joined, form the firm's expansion path. The long-run movement of a firm is along an expansion path, an option not open to the producer in the short run. Thus, the firm's production is subject to the conventional "laws" of the short run, mainly due to the fixed factors. In the long run, however, the firm is able to avoid the negative or inefficient aspects of the short run by also being able to vary those factors that were initially fixed. It is entirely possible for a firm to experience diminishing returns to the variable factors in the short run, but increasing returns to scale in the long run. For example, when we discussed the theory of the short-run production function, we employed the illustration about a car wash. In the short run, the company can vary the number of workers, and very soon run into the zone of diminishing returns. However, in the long run, such a company can not only use more efficient equipment, but can also alter the size and shape of the buildings, thereby more than offsetting the tendency of diminishing returns to labor.

If substantial economies of scale are present, the firm's long-run average total cost declines with output. The long-run average total cost rises due to diseconomies of scale, and remains constant if the returns to scale are constant. The economies or diseconomies of scale can either be *internal* or *external* to the firm, and may or may not be pecuniary in nature. Thus, if the firm's managerial effectiveness declines with increases in scale, the firm can experience higher costs due to such internal sources. On the other hand, if the cost of transportation declines with increases in volume, the firm's long-run cost may decline due to such external and pecuniary economies of scale. A rise in factor prices due to expansion can bring about external diseconomies and cause costs to rise, unless the internal economies of scale strongly prevail.

As we have mentioned before, the short-run average total cost function is not always U-shaped. However, for the purpose of illustration, we will make use of U-shaped, short-run ATC curves. The assumption behind such a shape is that the firm's short-run production function is initially subject to increasing and then diminishing returns. As the firm increases its scale of operations let us assume that for a particular range of output it is blessed with economies of scale. We will also stipulate that the firm will experience diseconomies of scale beyond some volume of output. Under these circumstances, the firm will have two types of ATC functions—the many short-run ATC and one long-run ATC. Each of the short-run ATCs will be based on different quantities of the factors that were originally fixed, but are variable in the long run. The different ATCs may be thought of as the average total costs associated with different sizes of plants. The long-run ATC is composed of the most efficient portions of these short-run ATCs. The firm will need only one plant at a time. Thus, as it envisions future expansion, it also plans for the construction of the "optimal"-sized plant. A plant is of the optimal size when it can produce a given and required volume of output at the lowest average total cost.

Graphical Analysis of the Long Run

With the use of a few graphs and some geometry, we can see the results of the firm's long-run decisions. Figure 9-9 shows several short-run production functions. Each function is of the typical S-shape, and is related to the variable resources (V) at various levels of the fixed factor (F). Initially, in the first short-run period ($t = 1$), the firm is presumed to be operating with the smallest production function, $Q = f(V; F = F_1)$. From the radii vectors drawn to the three production functions, you can see that the average productivity of V is maximum at point 1 ($Q = Q_1$) with $F = F_1$; other such points, corresponding to different levels of F, are shown by 2 and 3. With F fixed at F_1, the firm's average variable cost will be minimized at quantity Q_1, and this production function will be superior to the other two up to volume Q_*. After this point, it will be less efficient than the production function $Q = g(V; F = F_2)$, but still better than $Q = h(V; F = F_3)$, until point 5, after which it will be worse than the other two production functions. Thus, for output volumes of Q_* or less, the smallest production function with scale F_1 will be ideal. For production volumes that range between Q_* and Q_{**}, the next larger scale ($F = F_2$), will be considered the most efficient, and for desired output levels beyond Q_{**}, the largest scale ($F = F_3$) will prove most beneficial. Thus, during each of the short-run periods, ($t = 1,2,3$), the firm is operating with one of the three production functions; in the long run, it changes the scale of operations by varying the levels of F. In effect then, in the long run the firm varies both V and F. The long-run production expansion path for this firm is 0–1–4–2–5–3. This also provides us with the proper choice of scale for each of the desired levels of output during each of the short-run periods, $t = 1,2,3$.

The two graphs drawn in Figure 9-10 also illustrate the short- and long-run cost conditions for the firm. In panel (a), we see that the firm minimizes its costs by combining V and F along the expansion path of the long run. However,

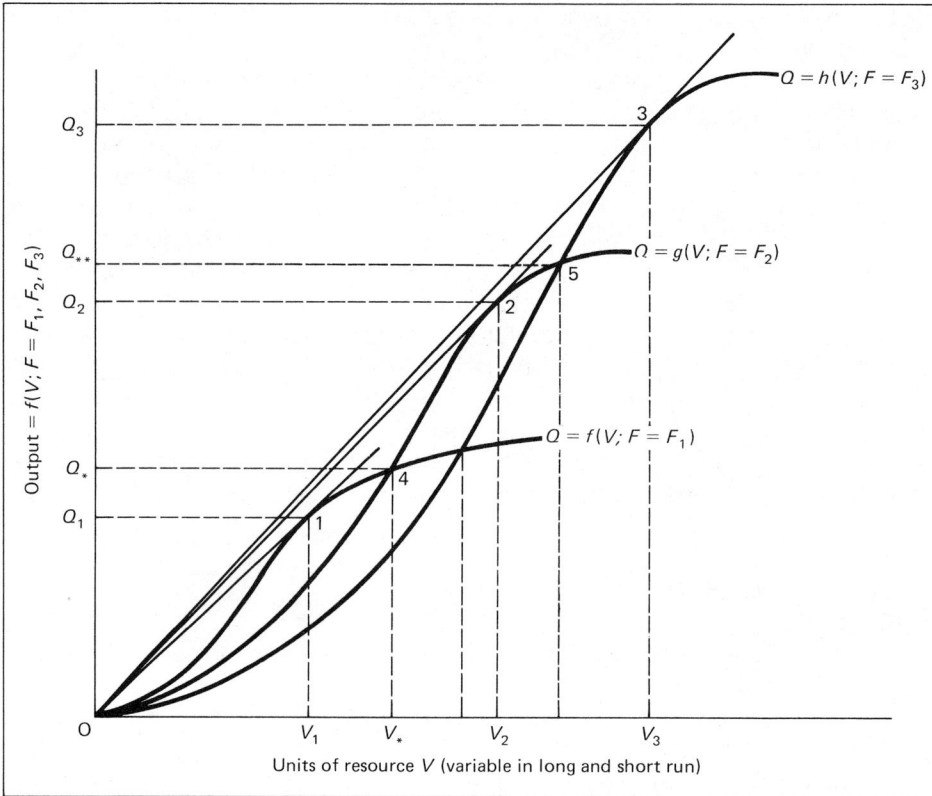

FIGURE 9-9
The three short-run production functions represent the three different scales of operation employed by the producer in his move from one time period to another. During each time period (t = 1,2,3), the level of the fixed factor F is adjusted to a particular level. Thus, F = F_1 during the initial short-run period (t = 1), and eventually F = F_3 after t = 3 has elapsed. Changing the amount of F_1 at least in this instance, caused the shifts in the production functions as shown. All factors (F and V) are variable in the long run, while only V is assumed to be flexible in the short run.

during a particular short-run period, such as t = 1 and F = F_1, the firm is temporarily prevented from varying F, a condition which results in greater costs than necessary when output expands. Thus, if the firm is initially producing quantity Q_1, during time t = 1, it will minimize its cost by combining F_1 units of F and V_1 of V. Such a combination will minimize the firm's average cost. This is shown in panel (b), where the firm's initial-period cost function is labeled ATC_1. If the firm's output is to increase, as long as F is restricted to F_1, the firm must operate at the initial scale and consequently must move horizontally. We see that for an output of Q_*, V_* of V and F_1 of F are necessary, a combination which is more costly than those that lie at points of tangency between the isocost and isoquant functions.

For output volume Q_2, ATC_2 will be optimal, because the average cost is lowest with such a cost function. If the firm cannot vary the F factor, it will be forced to stay on ATC_1, and this will cause the average cost to be much higher

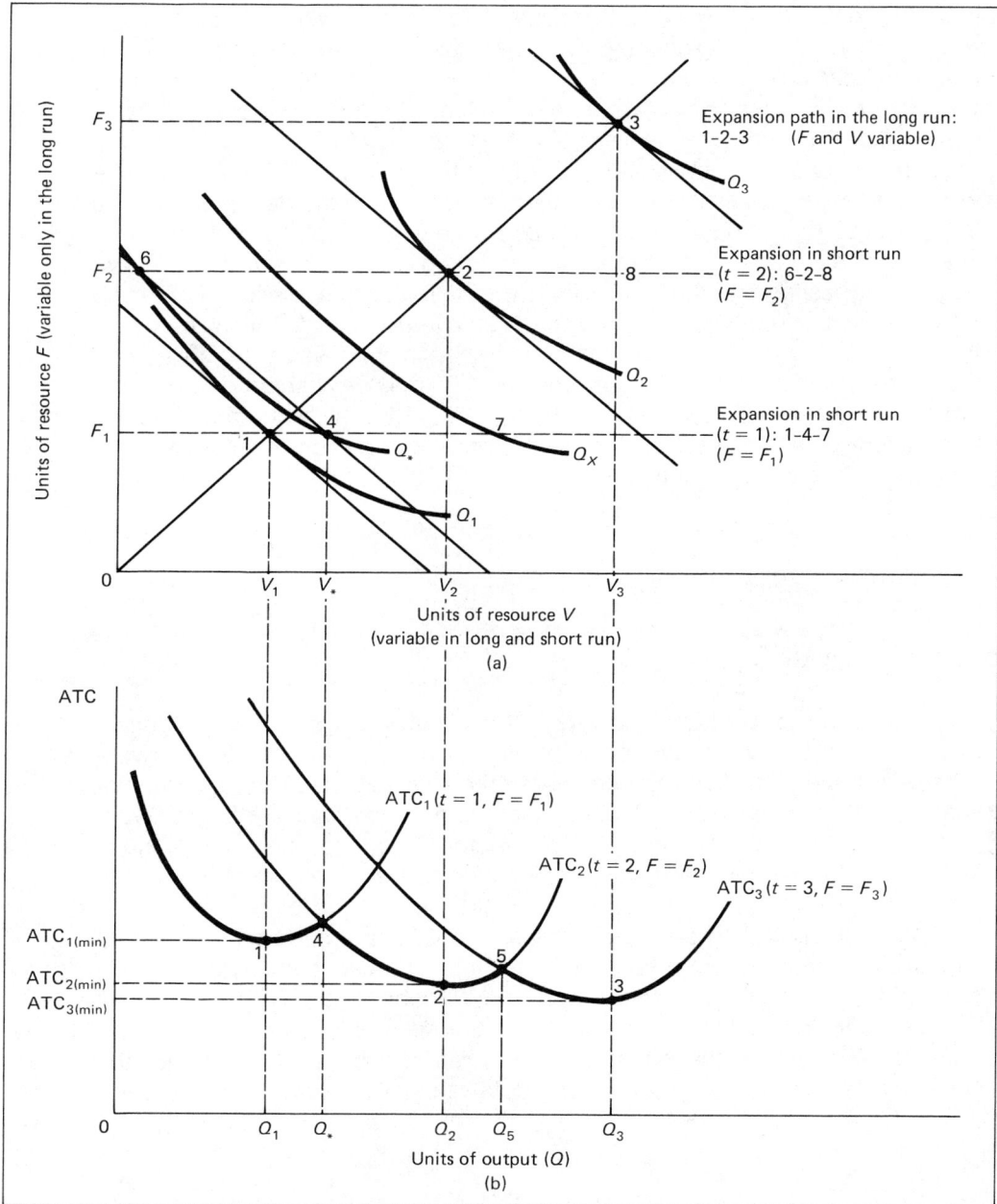

FIGURE 9-10

than necessary. However, in the initial short run ($t = 1$), the firm must put up with F_1, and hence the average total cost curve is shown to be rising beyond some point. As the time period is increased and the environment becomes more flexible, the firm is able to vary all its factors (F and V), and is able to keep its costs down to their optimal levels. We see how the firm moves from one ATC curve to another by varying its F factor in the long run. Curve ATC_1 is best for output levels up to Q_*, ATC_2 best for output volumes between Q_* and Q_5, and ATC_3 best for output exceeding Q_5. The most economical portions of the average total cost curves are shown by the boldface lines. When these portions are joined together, we obtain the firm's long-run average total cost curve. (Some authors take the kinks out of the long-run ATC by surrounding the relevant portions of the individual ATC curves by a smooth, ATC-shaped curve which forms the "envelope" for the other curves, hence the name. See Figure 9-11.) Notice that if the long-run ATC of Figure 9-10 were a smooth curve, it would indicate that the average total cost would decline with increases in output, suggesting that the firm's long-run production is subject to increasing returns to scale. Thus, although the short-run average cost functions may rise, the firm's long-run ATC can decline due to economies of scale. Regardless of the shape of the short-run ATC, the long-run ATC may be U-shaped, L-shaped, horizontal, constantly rising, or constantly falling. It is also true that where a firm's short-run ATCs equal the firm's long run ATC, the short-run marginal cost equals the long-run marginal cost.

OTHER TYPES OF COST FUNCTIONS

The Economic Order Quantity (EOQ)

In addition to the traditional fixed and variable costs, there are certain other costs that vary with the levels of production. Some of these costs vary directly with the level of production, while others vary inversely with output. For example, a firm that expects a particular volume of demand for a given year must have adequate amounts of raw materials on hand to satisfy such demand. If the rate of utilization of the raw material is known, the firm can survive by ordering only the amount necessary for production for a portion of the entire time period under consideration. Thus, a firm need not keep more than a two-months supply of raw material on hand to meet annual demand. If it were to keep the entire year's supply, it would be incurring storage costs unnecessarily in addition to losing substantial alternative uses of its capital. However, the smaller the quantity of raw materials ordered, the larger the necessary number of orders to satisfy total annual demand. Consequently,

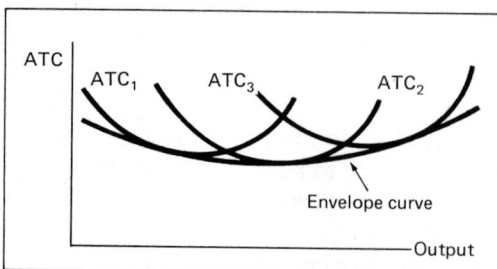

FIGURE 9-11
The long-run average total cost curve is obtained by joining together the "optimal" portions of the many short-run average total cost curves. Sometimes it is possible to draw an "envelope" around the short-run average total cost curves to obtain a generalized shape of the long-run ATC.

ordering costs vary inversely with the size of the order, while storage and inventory costs rise with the size of the order. The best size order is one which minimizes the sum of these two costs. Such an order size is referred to as the *economic order quantity* (EOQ). The EOQ model has been successfully extended to many other areas in the public as well as private sectors.

Figure 9-12 generalizes such a model with only two costs—one that varies positively (or directly) and another that varies negatively (or inversely) with the level of activity. The first is labeled DVC and the second IVC. The vertical sum of these two costs resembles a U-shaped average total cost function. The "optimum" level (corresponding to the EOQ) occurs where the total cost function's value is minimized, and in this particular instance is shown by the word "optimum."

Cost with Quantity Discount

Frequently, firms receive discounts from suppliers on the purchase of large quantities of raw material or other inputs. For example, the discount may take the form of progressively lower prices for each of the incremental units beyond certain specified minimums. If the first 100 units cost $1 per unit, the next 100 cost $0.80 per unit, and the subsequent 100 cost $0.75 per unit, the cost function will appear as shown in Figure 9-13. If the firm elects to purchase 220 units, the total cost will be $195, and the cost per unit will be $0.89.

Social Cost versus Private Cost

Social cost, as opposed to private cost, is the cost borne by society. An act of production by private parties brings about *private costs* composed of the

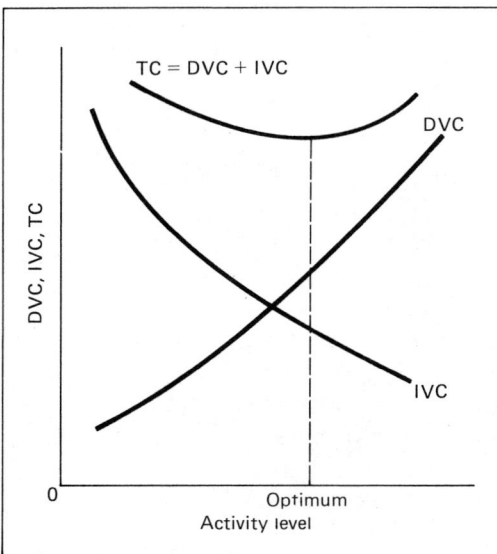

FIGURE 9-12
The "optimum" level of activity corresponds to the economic order quantity. At this level of operation, the total cost, which is the sum of the inversely varying cost (IVC) and the directly varying cost (DVC) is at its minimum.

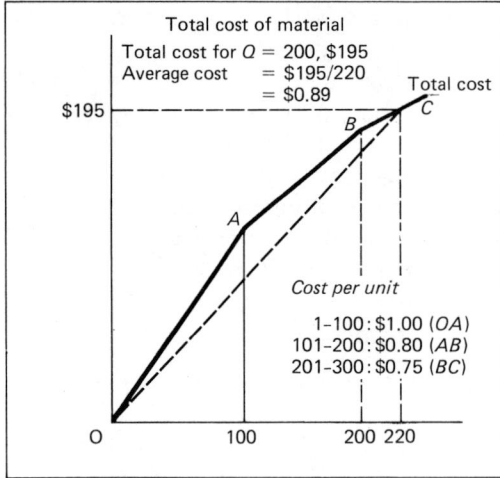

FIGURE 9-13
If a firm receives discounts on the purchase of incremental quantities of raw material, the average cost of acquiring raw material declines with volume. The successively lower *marginal* price reduces the *average* price.

costs of production and associated opportunity costs. But the private producers, in producing the output for private profit, may also create certain other costs which are "paid" by individuals and institutions other than the producers themselves. For example, if an excessive amount of air and noise pollution by aircraft contribute to the loss of health, loss of earnings, reduction in property values, and increases in the cost of keeping the house and body clean, the private act of air transportation will have forced others to bear the cost of its negative effects. In this particular instance, the social cost will exceed the private cost. The negative effects, or harmful side effects, are called *negative externalities*. Not all externalities are negative. Acts by private agents may sometimes bring benefits to others. Thus, if all the homeowners in your neighborhood keep their lawns and trees sprayed with proper insecticides, you probably will not have to bear the cost of spraying your own shrubs and yard; there will be a reduction in your normal cost of upkeep. In a situation such as this, the social cost will be less than the private cost. The social cost of production is the sum of the private and public costs. If *positive externalities* are present, the social cost will be less than the private cost.

In subsequent discussions, we will focus attention on the profit-making behavior of the firms. The producers' decisions are based on the revenue and cost considerations; however, the costs that are taken into account are largely the private costs. If firms base their decisions on social costs, and if the social costs exceed the private costs, the profit-maximizing output will tend to be less and the price higher than if they were to concentrate solely on the private costs of production. Today we see greater interest of society in forcing the private firms to recognize the existence of public costs and negative externalities. Governments have begun to impose fines on firms, and certain antipollution standards as well as laws are increasingly being put to use to halt the endless damnification of our environment. We will have more to say about this topic in later chapters dealing with the public sector and welfare economics.

APPLICATIONS

1. The Farmer's True Costs of Production

We will explore the notion of true economic costs with the use of a model suitable for production in agriculture. A rational farmer will take into account not only production costs, but also the other associated costs, including opportunity costs. In the discussion that follows:

A is the total acreage for agricultural use;
$X is the lease price per acre for agricultural use;
$Y is the price per acre for alternative use;
q is the output per acre;
Q is the output produced;
Q^* is output sold;
h is the inventory holding cost per unit;
s is the storage cost per unit;
v is the variable cost of production per unit;
F is the total fixed costs;
i is the interest rate on money (per year);
$G is the government subsidy per acre of idle land.

From the information provided, we can state that the acreage devoted to agriculture is equal to (Q/q), therefore the amount of land available for other use is $A - (Q/q)$ acres. Since land not put to agricultural use can be leased to other farmers, sold to other users, or left fallow, the farmer incurs an opportunity cost equal to the lost opportunity of an equivalent amount of money. We can use the interest rate on money, i, as the opportunity cost of idle money. Thus, any land not used for agriculture, will have a potential market value of X, Y, or G dollars per acre, and from an economic point of view the highest of these is taken into account. Consequently, the opportunity cost of idle land is the lost interest on the monetary value of $A - (Q/q)$ acres, which for a period of one year will be $(i) [A - (Q/q)]$ (the maximum of X, Y, G).

The farmer stores any output that is produced but is not sold. The quantity stored will equal $(Q - Q^*)$, and the cost of holding and storing a unit of output is $(h + s)$. The total cost of holding and storing will equal $(h + s)(Q - Q^*)$. The total variable cost of producing the output will be vQ, and the total fixed cost will remain at F. With the available amount of information, we can now write a total cost equation for the farmer as follows.

$$\text{Total cost} = F + vQ + (h + s)(Q - Q^*) + (i) [A-(Q/q)] (X, Y, \text{ or } G)$$

2. The Ideal Speed Limit

Members of the U.S. National Transportation Safety Board and others representing private interests are questioning the rationale behind the current 55 mph legal speed limit imposed on vehicle operators. Presumably many benefits have come about due to the reduction of the official speed limit from 70 to 55 mph. Statistics are cited to indicate the reduced fatality rates, the decrease in the consumption of gasoline, and the lower insurance rates as the direct result of the lower speed limit. Furthermore, the lower dependence on imported oil and the conservation of domestic oil supplies bring about substantial social benefits. On the other hand, many people feel that the slower speed limit necessitates greater amounts of travel time, and time does have value. Thus, the higher the allowable speed limit, the less the cost of time associated with travel.

As can be seen, there are two sets of costs involved in the decision on an "optimal" speed limit. On the one hand, the higher the legal speed limit, the higher the cost of gasoline and social costs. On the other hand, the lower the speed, the higher the cost of time, and perhaps a cost of loss in utility to owners of fast cars and other vehicles. The ideal speed limit is that which minimizes the sum of all the aforementioned costs. The policy implications are that society can impose sufficient fines and rewards that force the drivers to travel at a speed which minimizes their own private costs, but which also coincides with the lowest social cost.

3. A Cost Function of Hospital Services

There are numerous cost functions that have been empirically determined by economists and other reserachers. The following cost function is adapted from a study done in 1968. The inpatient costs (C) per patient-day were estimated from the study of 68 hospitals in western Pennsylvania, and were estimated to be

$$C = 29.64 - 0.0145A - 0.0721R + 0.1291E - 0.0356D$$

where

A is the number of admissions
R is the occupancy rate;
E is the patient care expenses per inpatient operating expenditures;
D is the number of pateint-days per personnel.

From our study of cost behavior, you should be able to understand why the variables affect cost in the manner suggested by the C equation. Accurate information, to the extent possible, is very important and necessary to hospital administrators as well as public bodies for correct policies toward efficient and economical allocation of health care resources.

EXERCISES

1. Describe the basic relationship of the theory of production to the theory of cost, both in the short and long runs.

2. Define and explain the following.
   a. Short-run cost.
   b. Long-run cost.
   c. Average total cost.
   d. Marginal cost.
   e. Average variable cost.
   f. Incremental cost.
   g. Sunk cost.
   h. Future cost versus present cost.
   i. Opportunity cost.
   j. Social versus private cost.
   k. Explicit versus implicit cost.

3. State the rule of "equimarginal cost" as applicable to either several variable resources or many plants. Explain how the rule works for cost minimization.

4. Is it possible for a firm to encounter diminishing marginal returns in the short run, but long-run economies of scale? Explain with illustrations.

5. Draw total cost functions from the following data:
   a. $TC = 1000 + 20Q - 5Q^2 + Q^3$
   b. $TC = 200 + 10Q$
   c. $TC = 1200 - 10Q + 2Q^2$
   d. $TC = 2000 + 100Q^{1/2}$

6. Suppose a firm owns two plants in the short run. Each of the plants has its own marginal cost structure as shown:

$$MC_1 = 100 + Q_1$$
$$MC_2 = 50 + 3Q_2$$

If the firm's desired level of output is 150, and the fixed costs of plants 1 and 2 are $600 and $400, respectively, how many units of output should be allocated to each plant?

7. Enumerate several cases from your own experience that adequately illustrate the concept of economic cost trade-offs.

8. Suppose you are given the Cobb–Douglas production function, $Q = 100K^2L^{1/2}$. If the price of a unit of $K = $20, and the price of $L = $10, compute the "optimal" K/L ratio, if both K and L are completely variable. Determine the cost per unit (of Q) when $Q = 100$; 12,800; 97,200. Do the results substantiate the "laws" of returns to scale applicable to Cobb–Douglas functions?

9. Assume that the production function is as given in Exercise 8. If the prices of the two resources stay as they are, compute the average total cost of producing 100, 200, and 400 units by varying the quantity of L, with K held fixed at various levels ranging from 1 to 4. Are there increasing or decreasing returns to L in the short run? Does the unit cost of production change with variations in scale (K)? How? Explain.

10. Suppose the marginal cost is constant at all levels of output. If the firm employs only one variable input, and also has fixed costs, draw representative diagrams of the following:
    a. Total cost.
    b. Total varible cost.
    c. Average variable cost.
    d. Average total cost.
    e. Marginal cost.

11. Under what circumstances will the average total cost be horizontal and constant? (Assume there are variable as well as fixed costs.)

12. Show how the EOQ model might be applied in the following situations:
    a. Determination of the optimal level of crime detection.
    b. Determination of the "correct" number of checkout stands at a super market.
    c. Selection of the economic life of a machine.
    d. Determination of the "best" tolerable unemployment/inflation rate for a nation.

13. Derive a total cost function from the following information:

Production function: $Q = 20L$; $P_L = \$100$
Fixed costs = $1000.
(L is the only variable input.)

14. A firm's current rate of output is 5000 units and each unit sells for a price of $10. It is believed that 12,000 units can be sold at a price of $7. The firm's capacity to produce is limited to 14,000 units. The current cost *per unit of output* is as follows:

Labor cost:	$ 6.00
Raw materials cost:	$ 2.00
Fixed overhead:	$ 2.88
Total:	$10.88

It is also recognized that, at the suggested higher output, labor's productivity will increase by 50%, and raw materials can be acquired at a 20% discount. As an economist, would you recommend the price reduction? Explain and show your calculations.

15. A firm has to pay certain penalties in the form of pollution taxes, pollution being measured by the amount of BOD dumped into a nearby river. It presently discharges four million pounds of BOD per year. The costs of installing various types of purification equipment are shown below:

Type	Percent of BOD removed per year	Cost of equipment per year
A	95	$90,000
B	90	45,000
C	85	32,000
D	80	25,000
E	75	20,000

Which type of equipment should the firm choose if the tax for polluting is (a) 5¢/lb of BOD; (b) 8¢/lb of BOD; and (c) 23¢/lb of BOD? If you were a government agency, which tax rate would you recommend for (a) maximum tax revenues and (b) least amount of pollution?

16. Draw long-run and short-run total cost curves that yield the suggested average total cost curves of Figure 9-10.

17. How will a firm's various cost functions be affected under each of the following circumstances.
   a. The firm must pay an excise tax on each unit of output.
   b. Insurance premiums increase.
   c. The city increases the firm's annual water and sewer charges.
   d. Employee retirement contributions paid by the firm increase.
   e. A pollution penalty is imposed on each unit of output.
   f. The government subsidizes the production of each unit of output.
   g. The demand for the output increases.
   h. The national currency is devalued.
   i. The firm purchases new equipment.
   j. Employees are sent to training seminars.

18. The cost of health care in the United States has been on the rise for several years. Many people feel that doctors are forced to charge high fees because of the high cost of medical education. It is suggested that if the public subsidizes medical schools or provides low cost health education loans (HEAL) to medical students, health care costs will be less in the long run. What is your opinion?

19. In what way does government regulation of industries increase costs? (Refer to regulations under CAB, OSHA, FDA, HEW, FTC, and ICC).

SUGGESTED READINGS

Anthony, R. "What Should Cost Mean?" *Harvard Business Review,* June 1970.

Christensen, L., and Greene, W. "Economies of Scale in U.S. Electric Power Generation." *Journal of Political Economy,* Volume 84, No. 4, Part 1, August 1976.

Gupta, V. "Cost Functions, Concentration, and Barriers to Entry in Twenty-Nine Manufacturing Industries in India." *Journal of Industrial Economics,* Volume 17, November 1968.

Hinton, R., and Mueller, A. "Farmer's Production Cost for Corn and Soybeans by Unit Size." *American Journal of Agricultural Economics,* December 1975.

Johnston, J. *Statistical Cost Analysis.* New York: McGraw-Hill, 1960.

Merton, R. "On the Cost of Deposit Insurance when There Are Surveillance Costs." *Journal of Business,* July 1978.

Scotton, R. "Costs and Use of Medical Services." *Australian Economic Review,* 2nd Quarter, 1978.

Stevens, B. "Scale, Market Structure, and the Cost of Refuse Collection." *Review of Economics and Statistics,* Volume 60, August 1978.

Walters, A. "Production and Cost Functions: An Econometric Survey." *Econometrica,* January–April 1963.

Chapter Ten Chapter Ten Chapter Ten

PROFITS

There can be very little doubt about the assertion that profits constitute one of the primary concerns of producers. Profits, or the excess of revenues over costs, represent a firm's return for bearing risks, for being innovative, and for producing a service to mankind. Those companies or entrepreneurs that satisfy the consumers' needs the best are rewarded the most in the form of continued success and handsome profits. Profits, on occasion, also provide certain side benefits. For instance, some of the profits are given away to charities; others are distributed as dividends. Part of the profits are plowed back into the company for expansion and research and development, which help improve the quality of the product and update the firm's capital equipment, contributing to higher productivity of the firm's resources. Higher productivity usually implies lower costs and prices. It is not "wrong" for a firm to be predominantly devoted to the accumulation of profits. Only when the excessive desire for profits results in unethical, immoral, and illegal behavior by the firm may we question its profit-pursuing tactics. It is generally believed that profits are not important in public sector enterprises, where the objective is presumably to provide good and efficient service at the least cost.

Seldom is the modern firm run entirely by one person. Usually the management decision-making process involves many types of expertise at various levels, many individuals with special interests, and varying amounts of information and authority. A behavioral scientist would analyze each unit that contributes to the firm's goals and policies, but we will adopt a more holistic approach to the theory of the firm—that is, despite the existence of the many individual decision-making units within a firm, we will use the term "firm" to connote the integration of all such units working cohesively toward a common goal.

PROFITS AND PROFIT MAXIMIZATION

The assumption that firms maximize profits has a long history; even today many economists are wrapped up in extended debates about such an assumption, and the profit maximization hypothesis has never been unambiguously disproved. After all, can you imagine a firm purposely avoiding profits under ordinary circumstances? Would you turn down the opportunity to make extra gains, if such gains did not require extraordinary sacrifices?

What exactly *are,* or *should be* the goals of a firm? As profits play a significant role in the firm's ability to provide dividends, attract capital, maintain growth, engage in research and development, provide good service to its customers, and possibly even survive, we will make the assumption that its *main* goal is to make as much profit as possible. Other related and competing objectives will fall into their proper place after we examine the basic theoretical construct underlying profit maximization. The profit maximization assumption seems intuitively reasonable and analytically productive.

The Profit Function

A firm's *profit function* shows the relationship of profits to the quantity of output produced and sold. Profits here refer to *pure* or *economic* profits, which are defined as the excess of revenues over costs, including opportunity cost. Some authors call economic profit *super-normal* or *abnormal* profit. If a firm's revenues exactly equal its economic costs, it earns *normal profits,* or *breaks even.* Generally speaking, when the output is a function of the price, and cost varies with output, the profits of the firm also vary with output, and therefore with the price of the output.

Assuming for the time being that the firm produces only one type of product for an imperfectly competitive market, its profit (Π) function may be written by subtracting the costs (C) from the revenues (R). We may express the profit function as follows:

$$\text{Profits} = \text{revenue} - \text{costs}$$
$$= (\text{price})(\text{quantity}) - (\text{fixed cost} + \text{variable cost})$$

or

$$\Pi = (PQ) - C, \quad \text{where } C = f(Q) \tag{1}$$

Equation (1) suggests that revenues (R) vary with price and quantity, and total cost (C) varies with the volume of output (Q). If the conventional "law" of demand is operating, Q will vary inversely with price (P), and R will change according to the elasticity of demand conditions discussed in Chapters 4 and 5.

Figure 10-1 shows the graphical derivation of a profit function under ordinary circumstances. The R function is illustrated as the familiar upside-down parabolic curve. The typical short-run cost curve is superimposed on R. Because profit is the difference between R and C, we can derive the profit function (Π) by plotting the vertical differences between R and C against quantity. The resulting function is labeled as the profit, or the ($R-C$), curve. Such a function starts below the origin, showing that its value is negative where C exceeds R, implying that a firm will lose money (or earn negative profits) over this range of output. At zero output, the losses are equal to the firm's fixed costs. As output increases, the revenues to the firm increase up to a point, but so do the costs. The firm breaks even where R and C are equal, such as at point Q_A. Economic profits are possible in the output range from Q_A to Q_D, and the profits to the firm are maximum where the profit function attains its peak, at quantity Q_B. A profit-maximizing company will attempt to sell this quantity at the appropriate price.

Graphically speaking, the profit-maximizing point occurs where the R and C functions are *vertically parallel;* that is, at a point where the slopes of the tangents drawn to these two functions are equal. Most often, there is more than one quantity where the R and C functions are parallel. For instance, in Figure 10-1, the revenue and total cost functions are parallel at quantity Q_J and quantity Q_B. However, at quantity Q_J, the firm's costs exceed its revenues, and the firm incurs losses. In most similar models there are usually two levels of output where the R and C functions are vertically parallel, and the "best" point

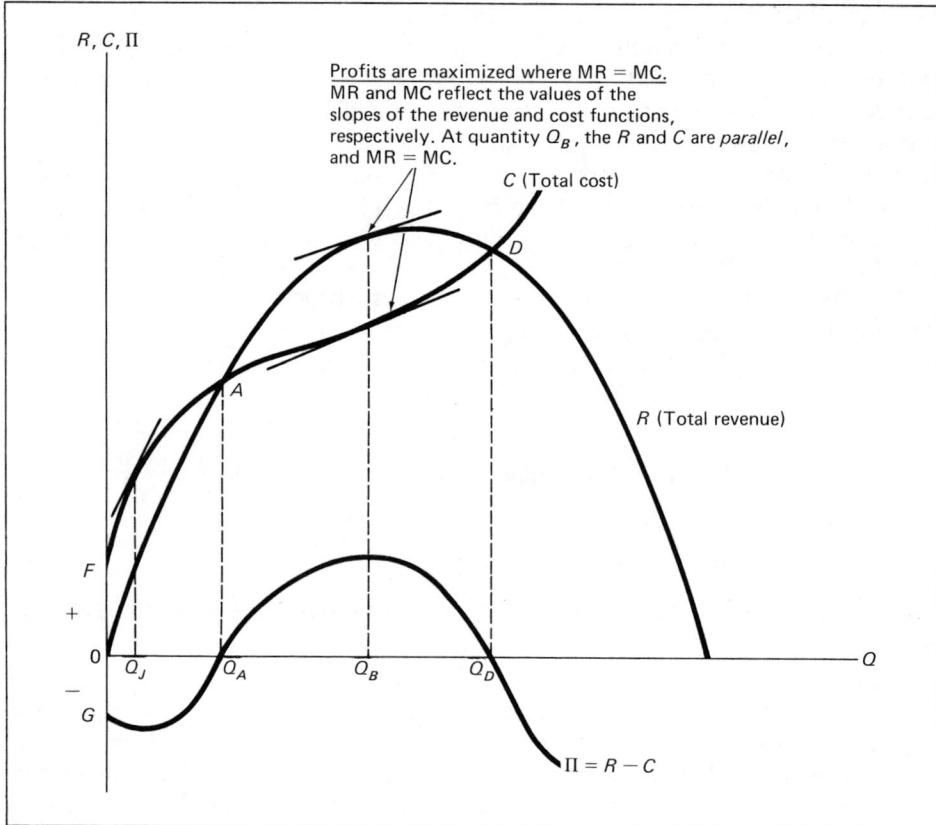

R, C, Π

Profits are maximized where MR = MC.
MR and MC reflect the values of the
slopes of the revenue and cost functions,
respectively. At quantity Q_B, the R and C are *parallel*,
and MR = MC.

C (Total cost)

R (Total revenue)

Π = R − C

FIGURE 10-1
Profit is defined as the difference between revenues and costs, and is shown by the function labeled Π, which also equals $R − C$. The profit function may be derived by plotting the vertical distances that separate the R and C functions along the quantity axis. When these points are connected, they yield the Π function. Profits are shown to be negative over the range of output, which is just short of quantity Q_A; the firm makes profits at quantities greater than Q_A but less than Q_D, and the profit function has a peak (maximum) at quantity Q_B. Because the firm's total revenues and total costs are equal at quantities Q_A and Q_D, the firm breaks even or earns zero profits at such quantities. The slopes of the R and C functions are equal at quantity Q_B, implying that MR = MC, because the marginals represent the slopes of the totals, and profits are maximized at such a quantity.

occurs at the larger of the two quantities. By "best" we mean that quantity which either maximizes profits or minimizes losses. There are situations where the cost is above revenues at all levels of output. Under those circumstances, the "better" quantity is where the R and C curves minimize losses. (See Figure 10-2.)

Marginal Revenue, Marginal Cost, and Marginal Profit

Recall that the marginal revenue is the change in revenue associated with a one-unit change in the sale of the output, while the marginal cost is the

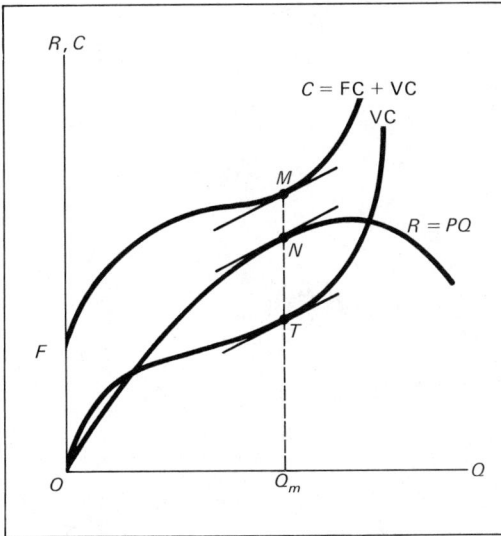

FIGURE 10-2
There is no way that this firm can make profits in the short run (with the exception of certain special pricing techniques that improve the revenue position), so it must decide between staying open and shutting down. Since revenues are adequate to more than cover variable costs, the firm would minimize its short-run losses by maximizing the difference between R and VC and using the contribution profit to pay for part of the fixed costs. Where the R and VC functions are parallel, MR = MC and we see that contribution profits at quantity Q_m equal NT, which keeps the loss down to a minimum, or amount MN. If the firm had decided to shut down, it would have incurred a much larger loss—an amount equal to the fixed costs OF. Since MN is less than OF, the firm should stay open and produce, thereby maintaining its position in the market.

change in the variable cost resulting from a one-unit change in output produced. If the R and C functions are smooth and continuous, profits are maximized (or losses minimized) where marginal revenue equals marginal cost, because the marginal values indicate the values of the slopes of the functions. Where marginal revenue equals marginal cost, the R and C functions are parallel. *Marginal profit* is the difference between marginal revenue and marginal cost, and indicates the value of the slope of the profit function. In general, a function's value is maximized (or minimized) where its slope is zero. For economic profits to be maximum, the marginal profit must equal zero, and the point of operation must occur at the peak of the profit function. This rule allows the firm to maximize profits where they are possible. Alternatively, where no profits can be made, following the rule will permit the firm to minimize its losses.

The rule of equating marginal revenue (MR) to marginal cost (MC) can be further explored with the use of Figure 10-3. Recall that the sum of the marginal costs of each unit of output equals the total variable costs to the firm. On a graph, the total variable cost is represented by the value of the area under the MC function. In Figure 10-3, the MR is derived from a normal downward-sloping demand curve. The MC is shown to be the typical U-shaped short-run function discussed in Chapter 9, and it intersects the MR at points A and B. Because the area under the MR represents the total revenue to the firm, and this area ($ORAQ_A$) is smaller than the area representing variable cost ($OCAQ_A$), the firm will lose money by producing quantity Q_A. At output level Q_A, the firm will lose not only by area RCA, but, in addition, it will lose by an amount equal to its fixed costs. The total fixed cost to the firm is shown by area $ODVQ_A$, because total fixed cost equals the average fixed cost times the quantity of output. The firm will be better off by choosing not to produce at all than to produce quantity Q_A, because in that case the firm will lose no more than the amount equal to its fixed costs.

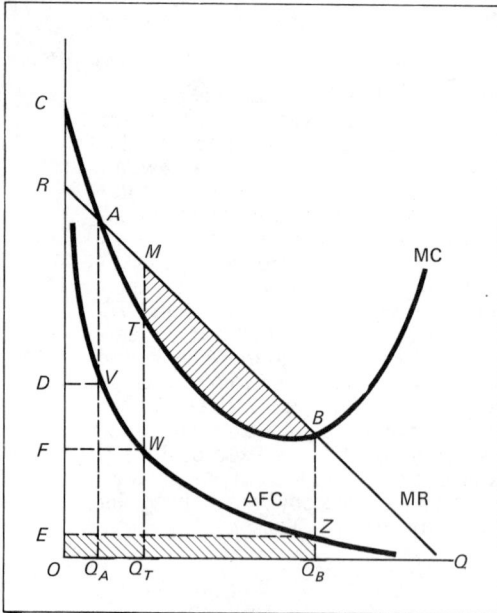

FIGURE 10-3
The firm's total variable costs are represented by the area under the marginal cost curve, while the total revenue is shown by the area under the marginal revenue function. In this figure, the firm maximizes profits by producing at a quantity where the marginal revenue equals the marginal cost. Point B satisfies the necessary as well as sufficient conditions. The excess of revenues over variable costs is referred to as contribution profits and is shown by the shaded area MTB. The fixed costs to the firm are shown by area $OEZQ_B$. If contribution profits exceed fixed costs, the firm earns pure profits.

Because MR exceeds MC at quantities beyond Q_A, it pays the firm to operate past point A. Every unit whose marginal revenue exceeds its marginal cost yields positive marginal profit, and as the total profit is the sum of all the marginal profits, a profit-maximizing firm should produce all such units. In Figure 10-3, all units that lie between quantity Q_A and quantity Q_B provide positive marginal profits. If we assume that area RCA equals area MAT, the firm's revenues will just equal total variable cost at output volume Q_T, and if the firm produces this quantity, its losses will be limited to an amount equal to its fixed costs. The MR is higher than the MC for quantities beyond Q_T, and therefore it is more profitable to produce a quantity higher than Q_T.

The marginal revenue of the units beyond Q_B is less than their marginal cost; consequently, a profit-maximizing firm does not proceed past point B. At an output volume of Q_B, the excess of revenues over variable costs is shown by area MTB. The total fixed cost, which is constant, is shown by area $OEZQ_B$. If area MTB is greater than area $OEZQ_B$, the firm earns pure profits that equal the difference between the two areas. From Figure 10-3, it seems that the firm is earning economic profits. If fixed costs had exceeded the value of area MTB, the firm would have lost money, but such losses would have been less than the amount incurred if the firm had chosen not to produce at all. Consequently, quantity Q_B, where applicable, also corresponds to the loss minimization point.

Contribution Profits and "Shutting Down"

While economic or pure profits are defined as the excess of revenues over total costs, *contribution profits* equal the difference between revenues and total variable costs. For instance, in Figure 10-3, area MTB corresponds to the contribution profits from Q_B units of output. Thus the total profits to a firm equal the difference between total contribution profits and total fixed costs. The amount by which the price of the product exceeds the average variable cost is the *average contribution* or *contribution per unit*. Some of these relationships are shown below:

Average contribution = price − average variable cost

Total contribution = revenue − total variable cost

Total profit = revenue − total cost

= total contribution − total fixed cost

In symbols,

$$A\Pi = P - AVC \tag{2}$$

$$C\Pi = (PQ) - VC \tag{3}$$

$$\Pi = (PQ) - TC = (PQ) - VC - FC$$

$$= C\Pi - FC \tag{4}$$

In the short run, the firm incurs fixed and variable costs. Because it cannot alter many of the "fixed" conditions of the short-run environment, it basically has to make two decisions: (1) to produce or not to produce, and (2) how much to produce. Will the firm be better off by not producing at all under certain circumstances? When a firm is in the industry but does not produce, it is said to have "shut down," which is not the same as going out of business. When a firm is shut down, it incurs only the fixed costs. The general rule for optimization in the short run is that a firm should shut down if, at the volume of output where marginal revenue and marginal costs are equal, the variable costs exceed the total revenues to the firm. Under such conditions, the firm will minimize its losses by shutting down. Unless there are extenuating circumstances, there is no reason for a firm to quit the industry altogether simply because the revenues are less than total costs at all levels of production.

If the revenues to the firm are greater than the variable costs but less than the total costs, the firm earns some contribution profits which reduce its losses by helping to pay for the fixed cost. However, if revenues are less than variable costs, then by staying open the firm will not only lose an amount by which variable costs exceed revenues, but it will incur added losses due to its fixed costs. Under such conditions, the firm can avoid the losses due to its inability to cover variable costs by shutting down. For this reason, variable costs are sometimes referred to as *avoidable costs*. A simple numerical example will illustrate this point.

Assume that at the quantity where marginal revenue equals marginal cost, the firm's costs and revenues are as follows:

Revenue = $2300
Total cost = 2400
Variable cost = 1800

By staying open the firm loses $100. If it shuts down, the firm's variable costs will be zero, but so will the revenues. In that case, its short-run losses will equal $600 (total cost − variable cost), which is equal to its total fixed (unavoidable) costs. By staying open, the firm's total contribution profit would have been $500 (revenue − variable cost), and losses would have equalled $100. Therefore, in this particular situation, the firm will lose less money by staying open than by shutting down. If the variable costs had exceeded $2300, the firm would have been better off by shutting down. For example, if total costs of production had been $2450, of which the variable cost was $2350, the firm would have lost $50 by not being able to cover its variable costs in addition to the loss due to the $600 of fixed costs, and total losses would have been $650. Because variable costs are avoidable, the firm can minimize its losses by shutting down. In so doing it will lose only $600 instead of $650.

Realistically, the firm should compare the *total outcomes* of all alternatives. It is not always necessary for the firm to shut down even if the revenues are not adequate to pay for all the variable costs. A firm that shuts down invariably incurs additional expenses in the form of start-up costs, costs which can be avoided by staying open. Furthermore, a firm may lose a substantial portion of its market by staying away from it, and in some industries firms must stay open for long periods of time in order to generate business and make profits. Hotels and motels in some areas stay closed during certain off-seasons, while others attract customers during slack periods by reducing their prices, largely to minimize their losses due to fixed obligations. The airlines offer special "night" rates on flights that depart after 9 P.M.

In the long run, the firm elects to either stay in the industry or exit from it. The long run is characterized by the firm's ability to vary all its factors of production in quantity as well as quality. In the long run, the firm can also hope to influence the demand for its product through advertising and by improving the product. If, after all, necessary changes have taken place and the firm's revenues are not high enough to cover total costs, it behooves the firm to leave the industry and find alternative uses for its resources. In the long run, firms must earn at least normal profits. Thus, if a hotel in existence for three years has never received enough revenues to cover all its costs, or a restaurant has been unable to break even (let alone make profits) in two years, it would be highly recommended for both of these firms to go out of business.

The Necessary and Sufficient Conditions

These two conditions of optimization are also called the *first-order* and *second-order conditions*. With reference to our discussion about the correct quantity of output for profit maximization, the necessary condition is that the marginal revenue curve intersect the marginal cost function. This condition is satisfied at points A and B of Figure 10-3. The sufficient condition is that the value of the slope of the marginal cost must be greater than the value of the slope of the marginal revenue function. This second condition is satisfied only at point B. Therefore, quantity Q_B should be chosen as the "best" level of output for profit maximization, or loss minimization. The necessary and sufficient conditions may be expressed as shown by equations (5) and (6):

Necessary (first-order) condition: MR = MC $\qquad$ (5)

Sufficient (second-order) condition: $dMR/dQ < dMC/dQ$ $\qquad$ (6)

We will now discuss a few other concepts of profit.

Average Profit

Average profit—also referred to as *profit per unit*—indicates the difference between the price of an item and its average total cost. For example, if the average total cost of producing 100 units of output is $4, and the price at which the output can be sold is $6, the average profit is $6−$4, or $2. Because different prices correspond to the various levels of output, the average profit also varies with output as well as price. Regardless of the firm's preference for

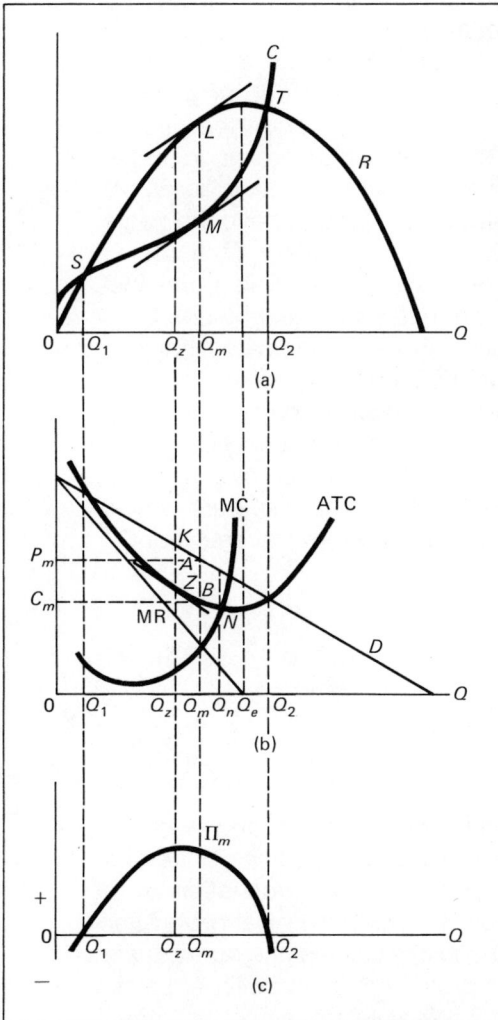

FIGURE 10-4
(a) The R and C functions are parallel at quantity Q_m. Therefore, MR = MC. (b) Profits are maximized at quantity Q_m, where MR = MC. At quantity Q_m, price is P_m and average total cost = BQ_m. Profit *per unit* = price − ATC = $P_m - BQ_m = P_m - C_m$. Total profit = $Q_m(P_mC_m)$ = area P_mC_mBA. (c) The peak for the profit function occurs at quantity Q_m, and maximum profits equal Π_m.

the magnitude of total profits, average profit must be positive before total profits can be positive. There seems to be a common misconception that a firm maximizes total profits by maximizing the profit per unit. This may be true under certain circumstances, but total profits are maximum where the marginal revenue equals the marginal cost and the second-order condition is also satisfied. For instance, if the firm can produce 100 units at an average cost of $4, and sell them at a price of $6, the average profit will be $2, and total profits will equal $200. However, if the average total cost of producing 60 units is $4.50, and these units can be sold at a price of $7.50, the average profit will be higher—$3 per unit—but total profits to the firm will be less ($180).

Figure 10-4 shows the various relationships between a firm's revenue, cost, price, output, and profit. From diagram (a) you can see that the firm is capable of earning pure profits over a range of output that lies between quantities Q_1 and Q_2, with profits being maximum at output level Q_m. Diagram (b) tells us that price P_m will enable the firm to sell the profit-maximizing quantity. At quantity Q_m, marginal revenue equals marginal cost, the marginal cost curve intersects the marginal revenue function from below, and price P_m exceeds average total cost ATC_m. The profit per unit of output, or average profit, is shown by the distance AB and total profits to the firm equal the value of the area $P_m C_m BA$. If the firm had desired to maximize the average profit, instead of total profit, it would have chosen an output level such as Q_z. At quantity Q_z, the demand and the average total cost functions have the same slope. Consequently, the difference between price and average total cost is greatest at such a quantity, as indicated by distance ZK. The price that maximizes average profit is higher than the one that maximizes total profit.

Figure 10-4 (c) shows the total profit function and again indicates that only at quantity Q_m does the firm receive maximum economic, or pure, profits. At any other quantity, the firm stands to make different levels of profits, including zero and negative profits. The two break-even points occur at quantities Q_1 and Q_2. Although the figures suggest that a firm under the described circumstances can break even at only two quantities, it will be shown that there are almost infinite break-even points. For instance, the firm can maximize revenues at Q_e, since at Q_e MR = 0.

SOME OTHER INDICATORS OF PROFITABILITY

The Net Profit-after-Tax to Sales Ratio

In addition to profit maximization, revenue maximization, and average profit maximization, firms may also seek to obtain satisfactory values for certain other types of profit indicators. One such indicator is the *net profit-after-tax to sales ratio,* which is exactly what it states. Thus, if a company's net profit after taxes is $40,000 and sales revenues are $800,000, the value of the ratio equals 5%, which indicates that the firm makes 5¢ in profit from each dollar of sales. Such a ratio may lead some managers to maximize sales revenues, because more sales imply more profits. However, such thinking is not always compatible with profit maximization, as the ratio itself is subject to change with changes in output. The ratio is probably useful to management in the planning of those sales territories that will be most profitable.

Gross Margin as a Percentage of Sales

Another commonly used measure of profitability is the *gross margin as a percentage of sales,* where gross margin equals the difference between revenues and the cost of goods sold. For example, if retailers obtain merchandise from the manufacturer at "cost" and if such cost constitutes 60% of the suggested retail price, the firm's gross profit or margin is 40%. Consequently, when sales revenues equal $500,000, the firm's gross profit is $200,000, and the gross margin as a percentage of sales will be 40%. This implies that the firm has 40¢ from each dollar of sales with which to defray the costs of selling and administration/operation, as well as to earn pure profits. Such a ratio is sometimes called the *markup,* and is useful to the firm in evaluating its profit position over a period of time.

THE FIRM'S BREAK-EVEN POINTS

Breaking Even at a Constant Price

When total revenues equal total costs, the firm *breaks even,* or *earns normal profit.* Since a firm is interested in at least recovering all its costs, break-even volumes provide it with the sales targets that are necessary for equating revenues with costs. After a firm breaks even, it is likely to be in a much stronger position to pursue profits more aggressively. For example, the publishing company incurred certain costs in publishing this book. Therefore, it should be interested in determining the number of books that must be sold such that the revenues adjusted for discounts to bookstores will be sufficient to pay for all the costs.

Because the price of the item is given or fixed in this case, the revenues to the firm can be obtained by multiplying the price by the quantity of output sold, or $R = PQ$. To break even, the firm's revenues must equal total costs (C)—costs which include the initial cost of preparing the manuscript, payments to the reviewers, and advance royalties to the author. To illustrate the computations, suppose the publishing house has "sunk" $50,000 into producing an initial printing of 8000 copies. The price of the book is set at $17 (actually $16.95!); the bookstores receive a discount of 20%, and the author receives a royalty of 12%. The company incurs a variable cost of $3.56 per book to sell and promote the work. What will be its break-even volume of sales?

Since the revenues to the company after the discount to the bookstores and the royalties to the author are only 68% of all revenues, the firm's *net revenue* function (R) may be written as $R = 0.68PQ = (0.68)(\$17)Q = \$11.56Q$. The total cost to the company equals the sum of the amounts already invested as well as the variable costs that are incurred with the sale of the book. Thus, the total cost to the company is $C = \$50,000 + 3.56Q$. Setting $R = C$, $11.56Q = \$50,000 + 3.56Q$, and we find the break-even volume Q to be 6250 books.

The company must sell 6250 books to break even. When it sells this quantity, the firm's revenues after discounts and royalties are ($17)(6250) (0.68), or $72,250. The total variable cost of selling this volume of books is ($3.56)(6250), or $22,250. Consequently, the contribution profit to the firm is $72,250 − $22,250, or $50,000, and this amount is exactly equal to the firm's initial outlay. All books sold after the original 6250 net the firm ($17)(0.68)− $3.56, or $8 on each book until the initial printing of 8000 books is exhausted. After the break-even point, the firm has 1750 books left over, which, if sold, will provide the company with a pure profit of ($8)(1750), or $14,000. A net profit of $14,000 before taxes on a $50,000 initial investment amounts to a before-tax return of ($14,000/$50,000), or 28%, assuming that all the foregoing events take place within a year.

When the firm produces the initial printing of 8000 books at a "fixed" cost of $50,000, the average fixed cost equals ($50,000/8000), or $6.25. The average variable cost of each book is $3.56, and therefore the average total cost of each book for the first 8000 copies equals $6.25 + $3.56, or $9.81. Because the book yields a *net price* of (0.68)($17), or $11.56 to the firm, the average profit per book is $11.56 − $9.81, or $1.75. Thus, the total profit on all the 8000 books is ($1.75)(8000), or $14,000. If we can assume that the firm always produces the books in printings of 8000 copies, the start-up cost of a new printing will not be as high as the original one, because the manuscript has already been typeset. Consequently, all books sold after the first printing will yield more profits.

Figure 10-5 shows the break-even point graphically. The vertical intercept of the cost function corresponds to the $50,000 the firm has already invested in the project. The slope of this cost function represents the average variable cost, or marginal cost, of selling each book, or $3.56. The revenue function is linear; it starts at the origin and has a positive slope of $11.56. These two functions intersect where the quantity equals 6250. Beyond that point, R is higher than C, and at a volume of 8000, the pure profit to the firm is $14,000.

Breaking Even when Price Varies

Since the quantity demanded usually varies inversely with price, a firm could conceivably break even at any number of units produced and sold.

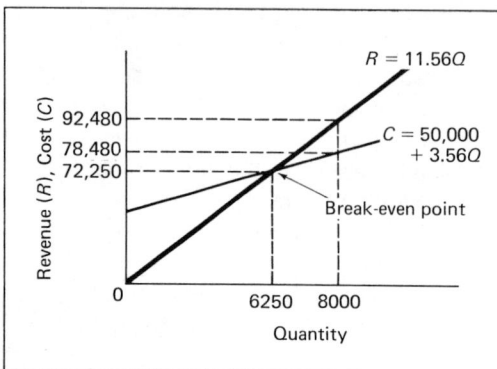

FIGURE 10-5
A firm breaks even when its total revenues are exactly equal to its total costs. Thus, the publishing firm's total costs and revenues are both equal to $72,250 at a sales volume of 6250. All books sold after that point yield pure profits to the company. Because the company has already produced the first batch of 8000 books, by selling all of them it will realize a profit of $14,000. The break-even point is computed by equating R to C.

Here, too, the objective is to equate revenues with costs. Whereas the total revenue function is linear when the price is constant, it is parabolic in Figure 10-4 when quantity varies inversely with price. In Figure 10-4, the two break even quantities were Q_1 and Q_2. We can solve for these quantities by equating the revenues with total cost. To illustrate the procedure, assume that the equations for the total revenue and total cost functions are, respectively, $R = 100Q - Q^2$ and $C = 1400 + 10Q$. By setting R equal to C, we obtain $R = C$ and $100Q - Q^2 = 1400 + 10Q$ or $Q^2 - 90Q + 1400 = 0$. When this quadratic equation is solved, we find that Q has two values—20 and 70. Thus the firm's revenues and costs will be equal if it sells either of these two quantities. At 20 units, revenues as well as costs will be $1600; at a volume of 70 units, they will be $2100.

Multiple Break-Even Points

Contrary to what the graphs suggest, a firm can actually break even at many points. Figure 10-6 contains a conventional average total-cost curve as well as a downward-sloping demand function. The ATC intersects D at points A and B. Thus, the firm can break even at a price of $100 or $32, since at either of these points, price equals average total cost. But the firm can also break even at a price of $65, provided it sells only 30 units. The total quantity demanded at a price of $65 is 100 units, implying that there will be a shortage of 70 units at that price. Similarly, the firm can lower its price to $25 and break even by selling only 140 units. Any price lower than $25 will bring about losses. Thus, a firm can pick any price–quantity combination along the portion of the ATC curve from A to B and break even. Some of these prices have important policy implications for the firms and will be covered in detail in Chapter 13, which deals with pricing strategies. For example, a firm might purposely keep its prices at a very low level to discourage entry by new firms, or even to drive some of the other existing firms out of the industry.

REVENUE MAXIMIZATION AND THE INTERNAL PROFIT CONSTRAINT

The profit-maximizing assumption permeates economic theory to a very large extent, and it is often customary for the theorist to assume that the basic driving force behind a firm's behavior is its desire to maximize profits. It is important to realize, however, that a firm may strive toward a set of goals including profits without necessarily being preoccupied with maximum profits. Certain empirical observations lead us to examine certain other alternatives to profit maximization. It is possible that, in addition to profits, a firm may be interested in sales revenues, market share, growth, and its relationship to society and the government. The firm's owner/managers may have their own set of goals which may or may not be consistent with the goals of the firm. First we will discuss the possible reasons for sales (revenues) maximization.

Many studies have been done regarding the assumptions of sales maximization, and one of these, by Baumol in 1967, provides a good summary

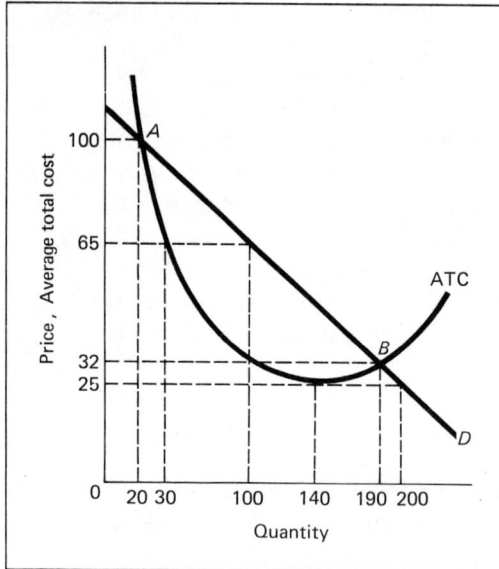

FIGURE 10-6
When the demand for the firm's product is such that the quantity demanded varies inversely with the price, there are many possible prices available to the firm. Each of these prices accomplishes a particular goal. Thus, the firm can break even at a number of prices (and corresponding quantities) that lie along the portion of the average total cost (ATC) curve from point A to point B. For instance, the firm can break even at a price of $65 if it sells only 30 units. Although the total quantity demanded at that price will be 100 units, the firm is not obligated to satisfy the total demand.

of the reasons why firms may elect sales maximization as their goal in lieu of the traditional profit maximization. A partial list of these reasons is given below.

a. Consumers usually choose a product that is popular, and this aids the firm in maintaining its share of the market.
b. The firm has an easier time obtaining more capital from various financial institutions if it maintains good sales records.
c. Increases in sales usually bring with them a more superior selling technology, which does not necessarily accompany increases in profits.
d. High and rising sales maintain good morale within the firm.
e. Executive compensation is more closely tied to sales than to profit performance.
f. Firms reluctantly abandon markets, even if they are unprofitable.
g. Separation of ownership and management in the corporation may indicate that management has a greater interest in sales than in profits.

The many proponents of the sales maximization hypothesis do not always contend that such behavior is absolutely incompatible with the basic notion of profit maximization. Empirical studies and questionnaires have revealed different results. Some seem to show that firms are interested in profits but not at the expense of sales. Others feel that profits should not be sacrificed for the sake of sales revenues. Many of the firms are probably more interested in earning a certain minimum acceptable level of profits. Once this amount is earned, the firm may very well opt for either maximum profits at the expense of maximum sales or somewhat less-than-maximum profits and maximum or more sales. Figure 10-7 shows the various possibilities associated with sales/profit maximization behavior as well as the revenue, cost, and profit functions.

Suppose the firm is operating under an internal profit constraint and must earn at least Π_1 in profits. We can see that Q_m and Q_r are the profit-maximizing and revenue-maximizing levels of output, respectively, and that producing quantity Q_r will more than satisfy the firm's internal profit constraint. Under such circumstances, it will pay the firm to produce quantity Q_r, maximize sales revenues, and still obtain sufficient profits equal to Π_4, by selling this volume of output at a price of (R_r/Q_r). No conflict between the profit and the revenue objectives occurs as long as the required minimum profit is about Π_1.

Now suppose that the firm's internal profit requirement is raised to amount Π_2. Output Q_r, which yields profits equal to amount Π_4, will no longer be acceptable, and the firm will be forced to operate at volume Q_2, which will allow the firm to satisfy its internal profit constraint but will generate less-than-maximum revenues, namely R_2. The price required to sell quantity Q_2 will be higher than the one charged to sell quantity Q_r, which maximized sales revenues. If the profit constraint is raised as high as Π_3, the quantity sold will probably be at Q_3; prices at this volume of output will still be higher, and sales revenues will be lower.

FIGURE 10-7
The revenue-maximizing firm will choose to operate at quantity Q_r, while the profit-maximizing one will select output Q_m. In addition to maintaining goals of either profit or revenue maximization, many firms have an internal profit constraint. Such a constraint specifies the minimum acceptable level of profits that a firm has to earn before attempting other collateral objectives such as more revenues, profits, or market share. Frequently such a constraint is also expressed in the form of a percentage and is referred to as the *target-rate-of-return*. If Π_1 were the profit constraint, the firm could easily maximize revenues and satisfy the profit constraint. However, if the profit constraint were increased to level Π_2, the firm would have to reduce output level to Q_2, which would not yield maximum revenues but would produce the minimum acceptable level of profits. Note that both profits and revenue, as well as market share, increase up to quantity Q_m, beyond which more revenues and a greater physical market share can be obtained at the expense of reduced profits.

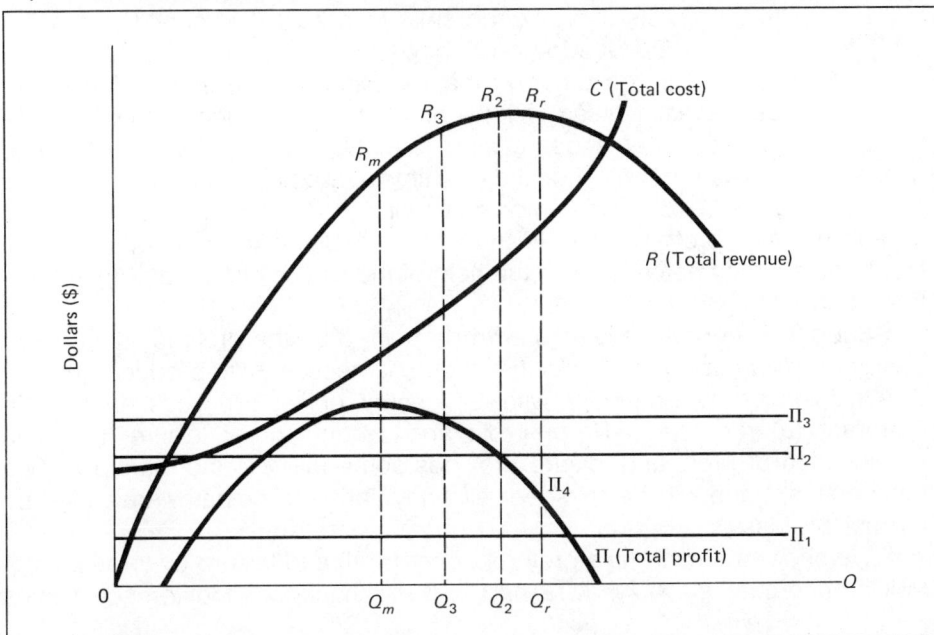

In the situation described in Figure 10-7, profits and sales revenues are complementary up to output Q_m, and competing beyond that point. It is in this range of output—where profits are sacrificed for revenues and vice versa—that the appropriate choice of price and output becomes difficult. Presumably other factors are then taken into account in arriving at the correct point of production.

PROFITS AND THE MANAGERIAL FUNCTION

Why should profits be more important than, say, fishing? Some decision makers might wish to sacrifice profits in order to attain other objectives. It was already mentioned that the firm's decisions are made by a number of managerial units, and each unit can conceivably have a definite set of personal goals. Certainly a manager must possess an objective (utility) function. We will call this function the *managerial function*. The managerial function essentially describes the variables or set of objectives that satisfy the manager's needs and hence provide him or her with utility or disutility. If the manager is rational, he or she will normally try to maximize utility subject to the constraints imposed by the firm.

Let us assume that for a given amount of time available to our manager, he or she can allocate as much time and effort (E) to profit making and other activities as desired within the time constraint. These other activities might include the pursuit of pastimes, traveling, or even promotion of certain other collateral objectives of the firm. We will integrate all the other activities, and for simplicity refer to them as leisure-time activities. As such, all time not used for managerial effort is devoted to leisure (L). Given the existence of such a managerial function, the manager will choose that combination of profit and leisure which maximizes utility.

Figure 10-8 consists of four quadrants. Quadrant (b) contains a familiar profit function $\Pi = f(Q)$. Quadrant (d) shows the relationship of output (Q) to managerial effort (E). Presumably, the *marginal effectiveness of effort* to produce output varies inversely with the amount of effort. Hence, the $Q = g(E)$ function is increasing at a decreasing rate. Quadrant (c) shows the total available time as a 45° line. Since the total time available is constant, the sum of effort (E) and leisure (L) must also be constant. Quadrant (a) shows all possible combinations of profit (Π) and leisure (L) available to the manager. We will trace one such combination with the help of the values obtained from the first three quadrants.

Suppose the profit level is shown by point 3 on the profit function. From quadrant (d) we see that an effort level of E_3 is necessary to produce quantity Q_3—this leaves the manager with L_3 amount of leisure. Thus, point 3 in quadrant (a) represents Π_3 of profit and L_3 amount of leisure, and this combination of profit and leisure provides some utility to the manager. Two other points, 1 and 2, have also been similarly derived. The paths are shown by the dotted lines.

We show the manager's preference for profit and leisure by three sets of indifference curves—X_1, X_2; Y_1, Y_2; and Z. If the manager's indifference curves

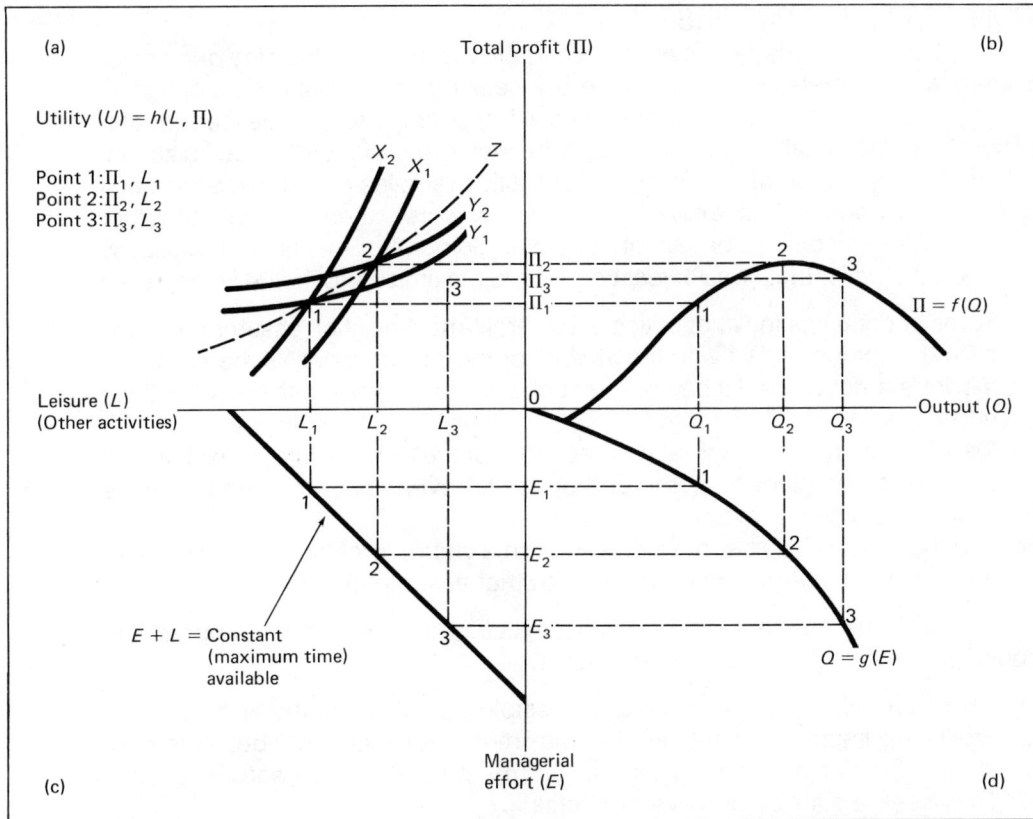

FIGURE 10-8
A manager's desire for profits is influenced by preference for profits relative to other activities, defined here as leisure. Profit is related to the volume of output and output necessitates effort. From a given amount of time, more effort implies less leisure. The decision makers's utility is assumed to be governed by the amounts of leisure (L) and profits (Π). All combinations of profit and leisure possible under the given conditions are shown in quadrant (a). The manager will choose point 1, 2, or 3 to maximize utility. The choice will depend upon the indifference curves.

are as shown by the X curves, he will choose point 1 over 2 and 3, because such a point will maximize his utility. Point 1 corresponds to a profit level of Π_1 and the consumption of leisure by an amount equal to L_1. Point 2 will be chosen over the other combinations if the manager's utility function has indifference curves shown by the Y's. In this case, the manager will favor maximizing profits. An indifference curve such as Z shows that points 1 and 2 are equally acceptable to the decision maker.

The model of Figure 10-8 suggests that analysts of the firms' profit-making behavior should pay close attention to the *set* of objectives that affect the decisions of the managers employed by the firm. It sheds light on managerial behavior and the attitude toward profit or some other objective. The level of profits, as well as revenues, employment, and prices, will be governed by the overall objectives of the manager or decision maker.

DO FIRMS MAXIMIZE PROFITS?

The point was made earlier that profitability is probably the *sine qua non* of American corporate enterprise. If we are seeking an accurate description of reality, the profit-maximizing assumption will probably prove to be inadequate. There are many other goals of the firm that preclude profit maximization. Nevertheless, the profit-maximizing assumption remains a valuable and useful tool for microeconomic analysis, and is no worse than any of the other assumptions made on behalf of the firm. Some arguments that basically support the belief that firms at least *appear* to maximize profits are listed here.

a. Some economists feel that critics of the profit-maximization assumption have been too preoccupied with the *validity* of the assumptions of the model. A model is a good one if it can predict behavior regardless of the assumptions underlying it.
b. Many economists have attempted to "prove" the profit maximization assumption empirically; some of the results reveal that firms tend to move toward maximum profits.
c. Although not all firms may strive for maximum profits, only those that presumably have goals consistent with that assumption will survive.

Those who feel that the profit maximization assumption is inappropriate point to some of the following arguments.

a. Profits are simply one of the many possible objectives of the firm.
b. Profits are important to the firm but maximum profits may not be. Instead of attempting to maximize profits, many firms pursue a *profit-satisfying* goal. They seek a satisfactory level of profits.
c. Because of uncertainty and lack of perfect information, it probably is impossible for the firm to maximize profits.
d. Some economists observe that firms are probably nonrational and may choose not to maximize the payoff from the various courses of action.

And so the debate goes on. We have analyzed the various positions that a firm may take with respect to profits. In the models that follow in the remaining part of the book, we will use the profit-maximization assumption only to illustrate the possible behavior of the firm under a set of conditions. One can easily amend the model by making suitable changes in it, including the profit-maximization assumption, to arrive at the appropriate conclusions.

APPLICATIONS

1. Denver to New York—Nonstop

There are many nonstop flights that operate between these two cities. Why don't they make intermediate stops? Can we use marginalism or, in this case, incremental reasoning, to explain such behavior? Assume that the expected load factor is 60% and the firm usually receives $18,000 in revenue per nonstop flight. The cost of each flight is $14,000. If no stops are made, the airline earns $4000 of profits per flight.

Incremental revenue and incremental cost come into play as soon as the airline considers the possibility of adding an extra city to its route. If Chicago is added, 15 additional passengers for Chicago are expected to be picked up in Denver, but the firm also expects to lose four passengers bound for New York, as they prefer to fly nonstop. The airline estimates that there will be about 10 New York-bound passengers out of Chicago. The fare from Denver to Chicago is $130 and from Chicago to New York $40, while the nonstop fare from Denver to New York is $150. Since the plane must land in Chicago and again take off, the airline will incur additional costs due to landing fees and extra fuel consumption during landing, take-off, and climbing to cruising altitude. If we disregard the additional costs of the crew working overtime and the cost of additional meals, the additional cost of stopping in Chicago will be $2000. The airline is now in a position to determine whether it will be profitable to add Chicago to its route.

The change in revenue (incremental revenue) will be the gain in revenue from the Chicago-bound passengers as well as from the Chicago–New York passengers, less the revenues lost from the four Denver–New York passengers. The net additional revenues amount to $1750. Since the incremental revenue from adding Chicago to the route will be less than the associated incremental cost, adding Chicago will prove to be unprofitable under the circumstances. The Denver–New York nonstop run yields $4000 in profit, while the same flight with an intermediate stop at Chicago will reduce the profits to $3750.

2. The Notorious Dr. Kananga

Some firms expect to lose some money initially when introducing a new product. New firms entering an industry for the first time may also expect to incur losses during the early years. Such losses may not be accidental, but seriously and deliberately perpetrated. The basic purpose behind the initial losses is to establish a market through very low prices. Eventually, it is expected that increased demand coupled with higher prices will make the enterprise profitable.

Take the case of Dr. Kananga of the James Bond movie *Live and Let Die*. The good "doctor" was planning to give away heroin, free to all users. Giving away such a product would no doubt have destroyed all other competitors while encouraging consumption. At the end, Kananga would have had monopoly power over the sale and distribution of heroin as well as control over a large number of addicts. The future (expected) profits from such operations should more than offset the current cost in losses and foregone revenues to make the plan profitable. Fortunately for mankind, Bond saved us once again by destroying Kananga and his empire.

3. The 10-Ounce Can of Soda Pop

The vending machine price for a 12-ounce can of Poka Hola has been 50¢ for a long time. Now that the prices of resources have risen, the company is considering raising the price of Pokes, which would force coin-operated machine prices to 60¢ per can. The demand for this very popular drink is rather price inelastic and, at the moment, the weekly demand at 50¢ per can is 2 million cans. It is believed that demand will be only 1.6 million at a price of 60¢. The manufacturer earns a net profit of 10¢ per can by producing the drink at 32¢ and selling to the retailer at 42¢. The new cost of the drink is expected to be 42¢ per can, and the new price to the retailer 52¢.

The manufacturer decides in favor of reducing the quantity of soda pop per can instead of raising the price, and offers a 10-ounce can for the old price of 42¢. This permits the retailer to continue charging 50¢ per can of Poke. The cost of manufacturing a 10-ounce can of Poke is estimated to be 33¢. The company feels that the demand for the new smaller can will still be 2 million at the old price of 50¢, since most people probably do not receive that much more utility from the last two ounces of a drink after they have consumed the first ten. Consequently, they would rather pay 50¢ for 10 ounces than 60¢ for 12 ounces. If the manufacturer is right, and it seems very probable that she is, profits will be higher by maintaining the old price but giving less in quantity. If the retailer is forced to raise the price to 60¢, the profits to the company will be 10¢ × 1.6 million, or $160,000. By keeping the old price, the total profits with a 10 ounce can will be 9¢ × 2 million, or $180,000. Don't be too surprised to see the 10-ounce beauties in the very near future. We already have 13-ounce cans of coffee.

EXERCISES

1. Define and explain the following.
   a. The profit function.
   b. Marginal profit versus total profit.
   c. Average profit versus total profit.
   d. Contribution profit versus total profit.
   e. Profit maximization versus loss minimization.
   f. The necessary and sufficient conditions.
   g. Pure profit versus normal profit.
   h. Net present value of profits.
   i. Break-even volume of output.
   j. The managerial function.
   k. The shut-down criterion.
   l. Satisficing profits.
   m. Markup.

2. Explain the necessary and sufficient conditions as they relate to profit maximization and loss minimization.

3. Can you think of some of the collateral (in addition to profits) objectives of a firm? Explain how these goals may or may not be tied to the profit motive.

4. What do you suppose are a nonprofit organization's objectives?

5. How do quantity and quality of advertising and promotion affect the profits of a firm?

6. Can the MR/MC model be applied to other areas besides profits? Cite examples of some activities where we may use such marginal analysis for maximizing the value of the objective function.

7. The linear programming model of profit maximization was discussed in Chapter 8. How does the marginal revenue–marginal cost rule relate to the model in linear programming?

8. Suppose a firm's average total cost (ATC) is given as

$$ATC = 15 - 0.1d$$

where d represents the *percentage deviation* from 100 units of output. Thus, when the quantity of output is 120, d equals 20, and the ATC at that volume equals $13. The demand for the product is known to be $Q = 200 - 2P$, where P stands for the price of the item. Plot graphs of the average profit, total profit, and average total cost as well as demand functions for quantities ranging from 80 to 200 in increments of 10 units.
   a. What is the profit-maximizing price?

b. What is the amount of such profits?
c. What price will yield the highest profit per unit?

9. Compute the break-even volumes for each of the following total cost functions, assuming that the price of the product is $12 per unit.
   a. $C = 2000 + 10Q$.
   b. $C = 5000 + 12Q$.
   c. $C = 1000 + 15Q$.

10. With reference to Figure 10-9 (a)–(i), indicate in each case the short-run output volume for a profit-maximizing (loss-minimizing) firm.

11. With reference to Figure 10-10, indicate the price that does the following.

FIGURE 10-9

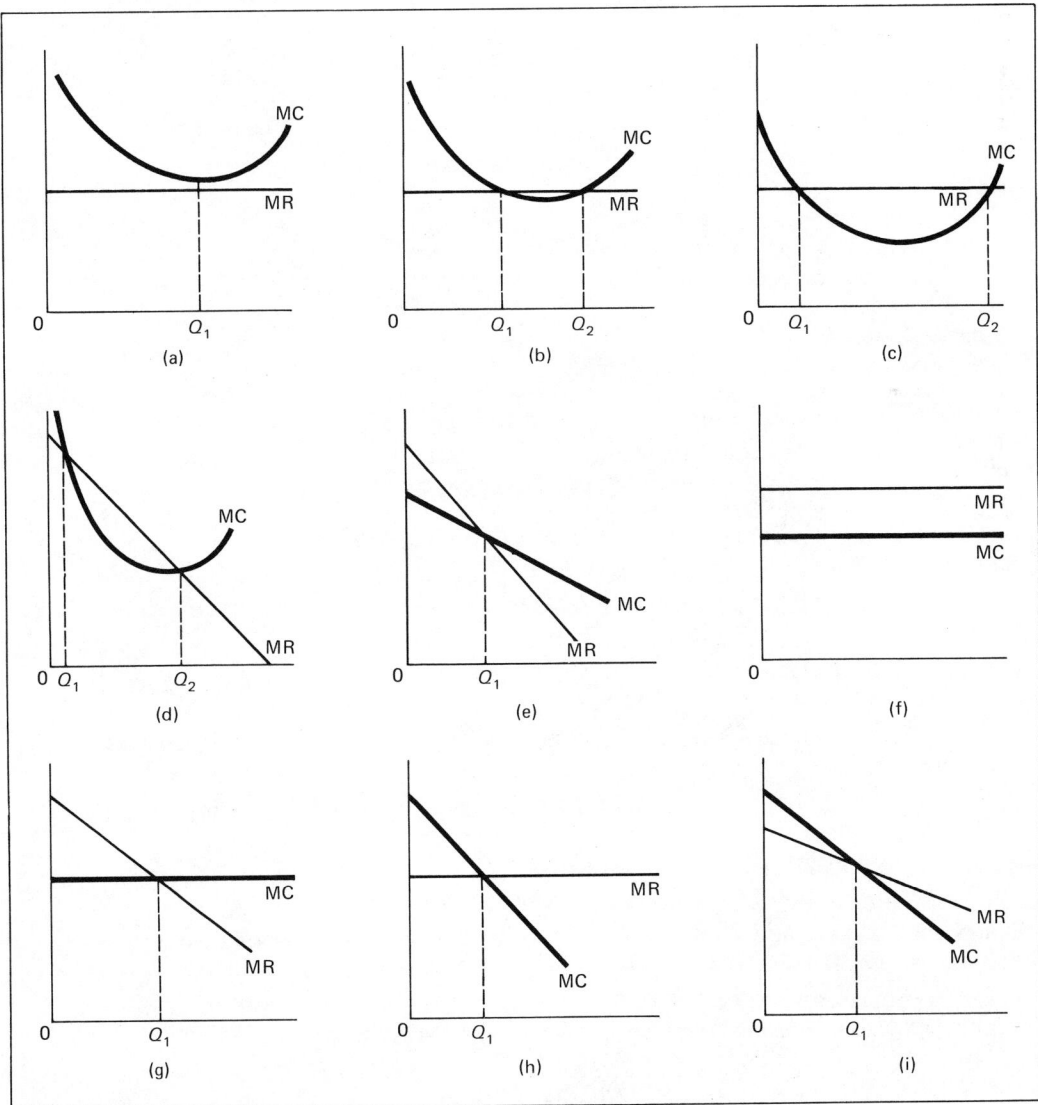

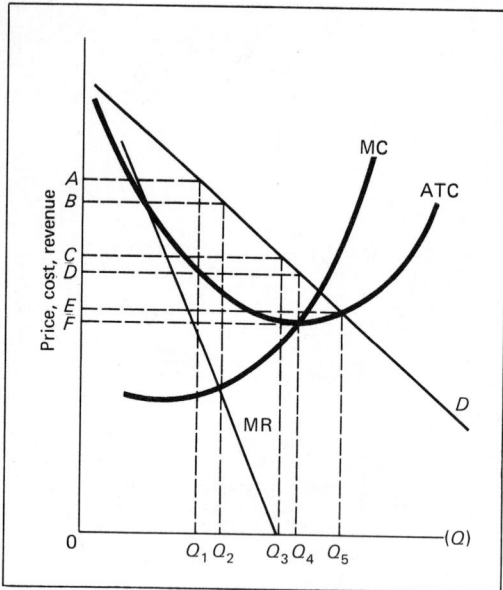

FIGURE 10-10

a. Maximizes profits.
b. Maximizes revenues.
c. Maximizes average profit.
d. Minimizes ATC.
e. Allows the firm to break even.

12. What is your definition of "fair" profits for a firm? Should firms maximize profits?

SUGGESTED READINGS

Craycroft, J., and Lackman, C. "Sales Maximization and Oligopoly: A Case Study." *Journal of Industrial Economics,* December 1974.

Hiller, J. "Long-Run Profit Maximization: An Empirical Test." *Kyklos,* Volume 31, No. 3, 1978.

Kamin, J. "The Effects of Corporate Control on Apparent Profit Performance." *Southern Economic Journal,* July 1978.

Kraus, J. "Productivity and Profit Models of the Firm." *Business Economics,* Volume 13, September 1978.

Purcell, T. "Institutionalizing Ethics on Corporate Boards." *Review of Social Economics,* April 1978.

Roth, T. "Employee Stock Ownership Trusts, Myopia and Intertemporal Profit Maximization." *Quarterly Review of Economics and Business,* Summer 1978.

Shavell, S. "Do Managers Use Their Information Efficiently?" *American Economic Review,* December 1978.

Talley, R. "The True Condition of Profits as Reflected in Stock Prices and the Rate of Capital Formation." *Business Economics,* Volume 13, September 1978.

Williamson, O. *The Economics of Discretionary Behavior: Managerial Objectives in a Theory of the Firm.* Englewood Cliffs, New Jersey: Prentice-Hall, 1964.

Chapter Eleven Chapter Eleven Chapter Eleven

PERFECT COMPETITION

Firms produce goods and services and sell them to buyers that demand them, under various conditions. Normally, sales occur in *markets* and the basic environment surrounding buyers and sellers is called the *market structure* or *market organization*. A market exists whenever and wherever buyers and sellers assemble to satisfy their mutual needs. With the immensely developed infrastructure of most advanced economies, the market is no longer restricted to a geographical location. Thus, purchasing an automobile by a long-distance telephone call is tantamount to entering the market, just as going downtown to buy a pizza is equivalent to engaging in a market transaction.

DETERMINANTS OF MARKET STRUCTURE

All industries possess certain characteristics that imply the presence of different types and degrees of competition. The relationship of buyers and sellers and the environment in which exchanges take place is usually evaluated in terms of the number of sellers in the industry as well as the relative strength of each seller; the type of product produced by each seller; the ease or difficulty with which new firms can enter the industry; and the amount of information and mobility possessed by the buyers and sellers.

In general, the market structure is divided into two broad categories: *perfect* and *imperfect competition*. Imperfect competition is further subdivided into many other industrial market structures. In this chapter, we will deal only with the models of perfect competition.

PERFECT COMPETITION

The Market Structure

An industry is classified as being perfectly competitive if it satisfies *all* of the following conditions.

a. Many sellers produce and act independently. An individual firm has the capacity to produce only an insignificant portion of the total output of the industry.
b. All firms in the industry produce a homogeneous or highly standardized product.
c. New firms have virtually no difficulty in entering the industry and competing.
d. All buyers and sellers have perfect information and possess perfect mobility.

Agricultural and some stocks and bonds markets come close to being perfectly competitive.

THE FIRM IN THE SHORT RUN

The Firm as a "Price Taker."

The typical firm under perfect competition does not have much influence over the price of its product. For example, if you are a wheat farmer who produces only a millionth of the total output of the wheat industry, it is highly unlikely that you are in a position to charge any price you desire for your wheat. This is due to the conditions of perfect competition. If the market price of wheat is $4 a bushel, you have no choice but to charge $4 or less a bushel. If you charge more than $4, no one will buy your wheat. However, the entire market will be yours if you charge $3.90 a bushel, while all the other farmers charge $4. But since you can produce only a very small percentage of the total demand, there is no need for you to charge any less than $4 a bushel. All such wheat farmers, yourself included, are known as "price takers," because you take the price given by the market. Price-taking firms must make decisions about the quantity of output, not its price.

Short-Run Price and Output

The price in a perfectly competitive industry is determined by the interaction of total industry demand and supply. A single firm in the industry then takes this price as a given constant and selects its optimal quantity of output consistent with the firm's objectives, presumably profits.

A profit-maximizing firm tends to operate where the marginal cost (MC) of the output just equals its marginal revenue (MR). In perfect competition, the price to the firm is given, therefore, the price of the product is also the marginal revenue to the firm. For example, if you are in a situation where the going price of wheat is $4 a bushel, every bushel you sell adds $4 to total revenues. Thus, the marginal revenue from each unit of output equals $4. If you are a profit maximizer, you will produce as many bushels as necessary until the marginal cost of the last additional bushel equals the price, or $4.

The market supply and demand conditions that determine the total industry price and quantity are shown in Figure 11-1. In effect, the price line becomes the "demand" for an individual firm's product. This is because each firm can sell all it wants at the market price and, under the circumstances, the same line also describes a firm's marginal revenue function. The firm's profit-maximizing level of output occurs at the point where the marginal cost (MC) equals the price (or marginal revenue, MR). Thus, as long as the price remains at level P_1, the firm will choose to sell quantity Q_1.

The Short-Run Supply of the Firm

If market conditions change such that different demand and supply functions bring about a new price, the firm's output will need to be adjusted to a new profit-maximizing volume. Since the firm does not know what the market price is likely to be, it cannot specify a quantity. However, it does know how many units it would choose to sell at each alternative price. Thus, all other things remaining equal, the firm supplies the quantity where the market price equals the marginal cost. With reference to Figure 11-2, the firm's profit-maximizing level of output for a price P_3 is Q_3, and for a price of P_1 the output volume equals Q_1. Consequently, the firm is "supplying" the quantities at which each price equals the marginal cost. In essence, the firm's supply curve is made up of its marginal cost. However, if price falls below the firm's average

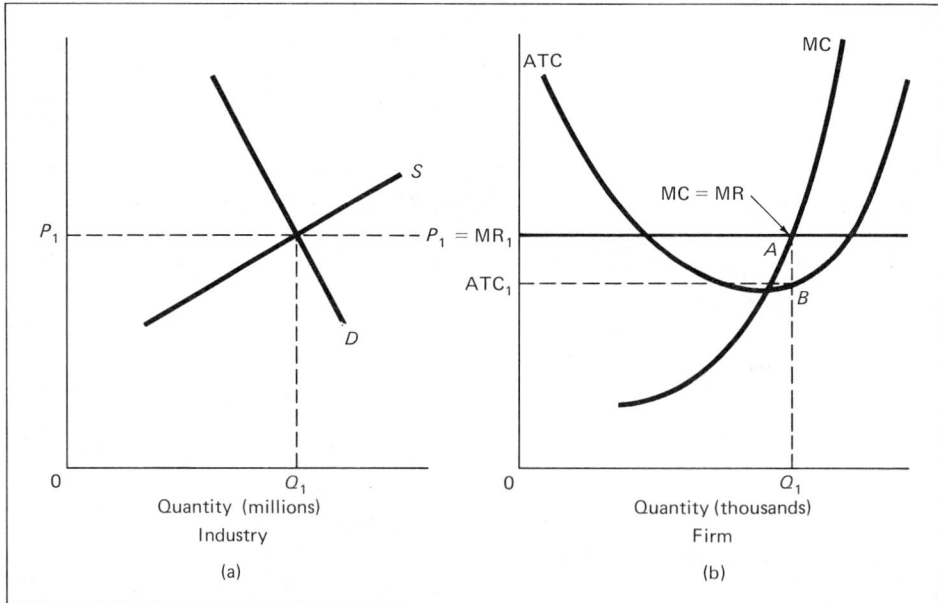

FIGURE 11-1
Price and quantity in the model of perfect competition are determined by the market demand and supply. In diagram (a), we see that the industry or market price is P_1 and the total output is Q_1 million units. The industry supply is the sum of the quantities that are supplied by each firm at each alternative price, and the demand is the sum of the quantities demanded by each buyer at each alternative price. We may add the individual demands and supplies to arrive at the aggregate values, because in such a market the product is homogeneous. Since each firm accepts the market price, it treats the price as the marginal revenue. Thus, $P_1 = MR_1$. A profit-maximizing firm operates where MR = MC, and this occurs at a volume of Q_1 thousand units (diagram (b)). This particular firm is actually earning above-normal profit, because at Q_1, price P_1 exceeds the average total cost ATC_1. The difference between price and average total cost is the profit per unit, or average profit, and is shown by distance AB, which also equals $(P_1 - ATC_1)$. The total profit to the firm is shown by the value of the area $P_1AB(ATC_1)$.

variable cost, the firm will prefer to shut down in the short run. Hence, that segment of the marginal cost function that lies above the average variable cost (AVC) constitutes the firm's short-run supply. In Figure 11-2, the perfectly competitive firm's short-run supply function is shown by the boldface portion of the MC line, designated $ABCD$.

The Short-Run Supply in Industry

The perfectly competitive industry is composed of many sellers. If each of the producers is assumed to be a profit maximizer, it will supply the quantity where marginal cost equals the market price. When all such supplies are aggregated, we obtain the industry's supply curve. In essence, the industry's short-run supply is the horizontal summation of all the individual firms' marginal cost functions that lie above the average variable cost. When the total industry demand is equated to this total supply, the market has an equilibrium price and quantity. In Figure 11-3, we have added the short-run supply functions of two

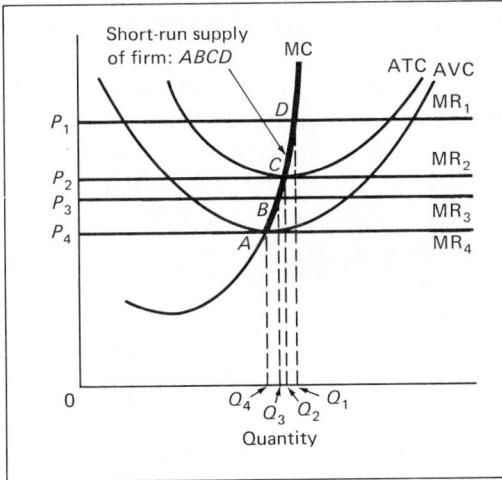

FIGURE 11-2
Profit-maximizing firms operate where MR = MC. In the short run, firms continue to operate as long as price is no less than the average variable cost. If price falls below the average variable cost, firms prefer to shut down in order to minimize their short-run losses. Since price equals marginal revenue under perfect competition, the firm will operate at points where the prevailing price equals marginal cost. As price varies from P_4 to P_1, the quantity produced changes from Q_4 to Q_1. At price P_4, the average variable cost, which is at a minimum at quantity Q_4, equals price or marginal revenue MR_4. As such, the firm will choose to supply output if and only if price is greater than or equal to P_4. Segment $ABCD$, which is the portion of MC that lies above the average variable cost, is the firm's short-run supply curve. As price moves in an upward direction, the firm will expand output along line $ABCD$.

firms that symbolically represent the entire industry. Each firm supplies 100 units of output at a price of $3, and 200 units at a price of $4. Thus, the total market supply at a price of $3 is 200 units, and at a price of $4, 400 units. If the industry equilibrium price of $5.50, and the total output of 600 units is brought about by the interaction of aggregate demand and total supply, each firm produces 300 units. Such an analysis can be extended to include a large number of similar firms.

Price Variations in the Short Run

The industry, as well as the firms, may be subject to certain pressures that may influence the short-run price, and hence the output of the firm. For

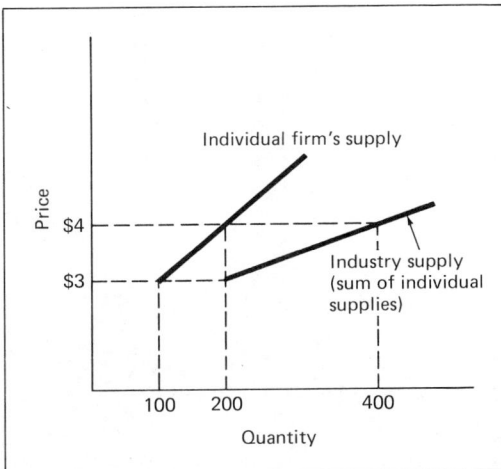

FIGURE 11-3
The industry supply function is derived by horizontally summing the individual supply curves of all the firms in the industry. Thus, if there are two firms in the industry, and if each supplies 100 units at a price of $3, and 200 units at a price of $4, the market supply at $3 will be 200 units, and at a price of $4 it will equal 400.

instance, if for some reason the variable costs of the firms increase, the marginal cost will increase. When the marginal cost shifts upward, as long as price does not change, the profit-maximizing firms will reduce their quantity of output. A reduction in the volume of output by a substantial number of firms will reduce market supply and force the price up. As the price starts to rise, the firms slow down their reduction of output. Eventually, the market is at equilibrium at a higher price and lower quantity. Whether the typical firm will earn more or less profits, as compared to before the cost and price change, will be governed by the nature and extent of the changes as well as the demand and supply price elasticities. We will use Table 11-1 to illustrate some points concerning a firm under perfect competition.

Table 11-1 shows the relevant cost and revenue information for a firm under perfect competition in the short run. The market price is $100, therefore the firm's marginal revenue is also $100 at all levels of output sold. The marginal cost of the seventh unit is $95; that of the eighth is $103. Thus, it would pay the firm to produce the seventh unit but not the eighth. The total profit to the firm, if it produces 7 units, equals $103. Although the marginal revenue from the seventh unit is not exactly equal to its marginal cost, it is the profit-maximizing level of output. The true level of profit-maximizing output lies somewhere between 7 and 8 units.

You can see from the figures in Table 11-1 that this firm can break even at 3 as well as 9 units of output, and make pure profits in the range of 3–9 units. It is possible that a few firms that are not interested in maximizing profits may elect to sell an amount different from the profit-maximizing level of output. If a substantial number choose not to maximize profits, the market supply will be less and the equilibrium price will be higher.

Elasticities of Supply and Demand

The price elasticity of demand measures the ratio of the percentage change in quantity demanded to the percentage change in price of the product. Similarly, the *price elasticity of supply* is the ratio of the percentage

TABLE 11-1

Market price	Quantity sold	Total revenue	Marginal revenue	Total cost	Marginal cost	Total profit
$100	1	$100	$100	$150	—	−$50
100	2	200	100	245	$ 95	− 45
100	3	300	100	300	55	0
100	4	400	100	350	50	50
100	5	500	100	410	60	90
100	6	600	100	502	92	98
100	7	700	100	597	95	103
100	8	800	100	700	103	100
100	9	900	100	900	200	0
100	10	1000	100	1200	300	−200

change in the quantity supplied to the percentage change in the price of the product. These elasticities determine the magnitudes of price and quantity changes brought about by changes in demand and supply. Although we can conceivably analyze all sorts of changes in demand and supply, it is sufficient for the moment to keep demand stable and change only supply in order to study the effect of such changes on price and quantity. Figure 11-4 shows some of the most probable effects.

In Figure 11-4 there are two demand curves—one relatively price elastic (D_E) and the other relatively price inelastic (D_I). There are also two supply curves—one relatively elastic (S_E) and the other relatively inelastic (S_I). The dotted supply curves (S_I' and S_E') represent the shift in supply brought about by either an excise tax or an exodus of producers. If demand is relatively price inelastic, but supply is rather elastic, the quantity change from S_E to S_E' will be very small (Q_2 to Q_1). If supply is relatively price inelastic and demand relatively

FIGURE 11-4
In perfectly competitive industries, the changes in supply bring about changes in the market equilibrium price and quantity. The magnitude of such changes due to changes in supply alone will depend largely on the relative values of the price elasticities of demand and supply. The greatest change in price will occur with very inelastic supply and demand curves—such as from P_C to P_D, while the least change in price will come about for a relatively elastic demand and rather inelastic supply. The largest change in quantity will occur when both the demand and supply functions are very price elastic.

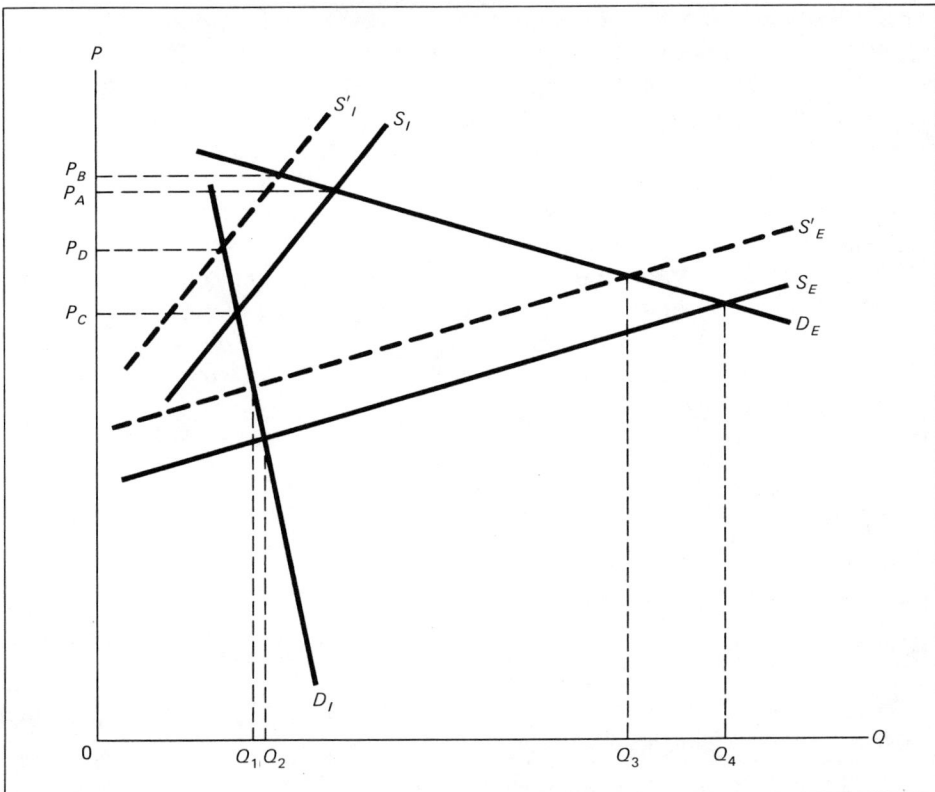

elastic, the change in price will be very minimal (P_A to P_B). The combinations of the values of the demand and supply elasticities that bring about large or small changes in price and quantity are summarized in Table 11-2.

THE FIRM IN THE LONG RUN

In the short run, the firms in an industry may prefer to shut down in order to minimize their losses, but in the long run they must earn pure or at least normal profits. Because the entry into a perfectly competitive industry is very easy, new firms enter it if they notice that other firms already in that industry are earning economic profits. When sufficient numbers enter the industry, the market supply increases. If demand and other factors remain stable, the market equilibrium price will decline. When this happens, the profits of the firms already in the industry will also decline. If the price declines below the long-run average total cost, the firm will go out of business.

From our discussion of economies and diseconomies of scale in Chapter 9, we learned that a firm's long-run average total cost may decline with output up to a point. Since all the firms in a perfectly competitive industry are relatively small, the average total cost of the long run is largely U-shaped—that is, the economies of (large) scale exist only for some volume of output. When the entry of new firms depresses prices, firms try to avoid losses or try to build up their profits by increasing their scale of operations, and operate at quantities where the long-run marginal cost equals the price. As long as economic profits exist, new firms continue to enter the industry and depress prices still further. Eventually, those firms whose long-run average total cost is higher than the market price at all levels of output exit from the industry. Their departure reduces market supply and forces the price back up, or at least the decrease in supply keeps the price from falling any further. The entry and exit in the long run allows all the firms in the industry to earn just normal profits. Such a condition is called the long-run equilibrium in the perfectly competitive industry.

Figure 11-5 illustrates the events in the long run. The market price initially was at level P_1, and at that price the firm was producing Q_1 units. Since price exceeded short-run average total cost (ATC_1), the firm was earning pure profits. Attracted by the possibility of pure profits, new firms entered the industry, and supply increased to S_2 and price fell to P_2. To survive the fall in price, the firm enlarged its scale. As long as the price exceeded the average

TABLE 11-2

Demand elasticity	Supply elasticity	Result of shift in supply
High	High	Large change in quantity
Low	High	Small change in quantity
Low	Low	Large change in price
High	Low	Small change in price

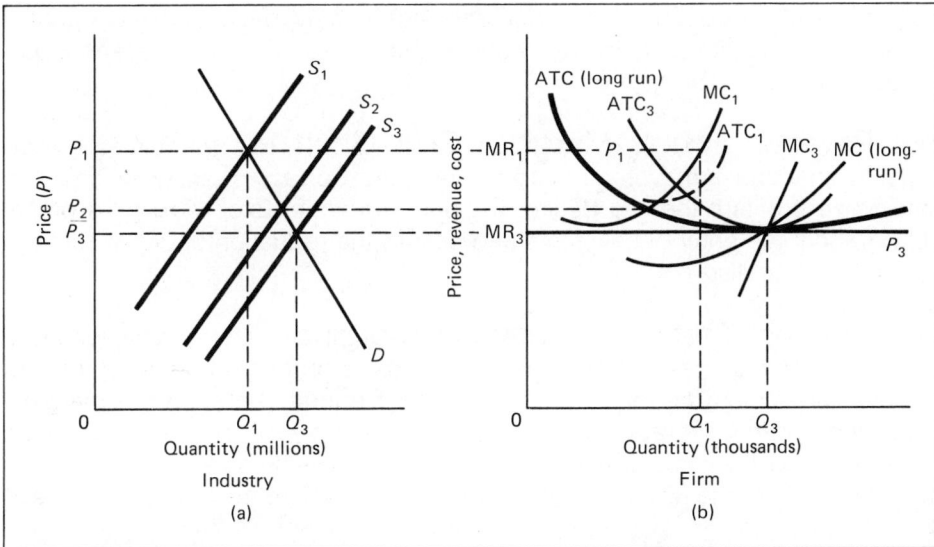

FIGURE 11-5
A firm in perfect competition is a "price taker" in the sense that it can attempt only to sell the correct quantity at the price set by the market supply and demand forces. The price in the industry is determined by the interaction of demand and supply, and is initially shown to be at P_1. Since P_1 exceeds the short-run average total cost of the firms, other firms enter the market to share in the profits. Entry of new firms causes supply to increase and price to fall to P_2, a price which is now below the original average total cost ATC_1. Firms expand their scale and move to a new average total cost ATC_2. Ultimately, all existing firms will be stabilized at price P_3 when each firm earns only normal profit and operates with the optimal-sized plant ATC_3. At the point of equilibrium for the firm, the long- and short-run marginal, as well as average total costs, are all equal to the price.

total cost (ATC), new firms continued to enter. Ultimately, price stabilized at P_3, and those firms that survived operated with plant size ATC_3 and quantity Q_3. Recall, from our discussion of costs, that the "envelope" of the many short-run ATCs constitutes a firm's long-run ATC. The typical firm, in the long run, will maximize profits and earn normal profit by equating long-run marginal cost with long-run market price. Since maximum profits can be only as high as normal profit, the price equals the firm's long-run average total cost (ATC). Thus, at quantity Q_3, the following conditions are met:

Price = Marginal revenue = Marginal cost (short run)

= Marginal cost (long run) = Long-run minimum average total cost

Economic Implications of the Long Run

Whether perfect competition is "good" or "bad" depends on the viewpoint of the analyst as well as the benefits and costs of such competition as perceived by the participants themselves. However, most economists tend to agree that a perfectly competitive system brings about a reasonably efficient allocation of resources. The arguments are largely based on the equality conditions described in the previous section. We will examine each part separately.

Marginal Revenue Equals Marginal Cost (Short Run) This condition implies that the firms are free to choose the correct quantity in order to maximize profits if they so desire, without hindrance. Excessive pure profits bring about the entry of new firms and ensure the reduction of prices through quantity competition.

Long-Run Marginal Cost Equals Short-Run Marginal Cost In the long run, the firms will change their scale of operations in order to reduce the cost of production. When the long-run marginal cost equals the short-run marginal cost, the long-run average cost also equals short-run average cost. Thus, when firms expand their scale, they operate with the "best" size plant under the circumstances. The ultimate long-run plant size is where the long-run ATC is at a minimum.

Price Equals Marginal Cost A firm minimizes the cost of production by combining resources according to the *equimarginal* principle. Under perfect competition, the marginal costs (or the ratio of the price of the resource to its marginal physical product) of all resources are equal to each other, in addition to being equal to the price of the output. Such a condition is usually not fulfilled by other types of market structures, and the failure to meet this condition presumably contributes to certain inefficiencies in those markets. Furthermore, because price equals marginal cost, perfect competition is deemed "socially desirable"—that is, the price of the good, which implicitly measures the consumer's value from that good, is no different from the true cost of the resources employed to produce it. Thus, perfectly competitive producers continue to produce the output as long as the value (to society) from an extra unit is as high as the additional cost of producing that unit. Social welfare is maximized under perfect competition.

Marginal Cost Equals Average Total Cost (Long Run) The model of perfect competition essentially suggests that only the fittest survive in the long run. Since the marginal cost equals the average total cost where the latter is at its minimum, all firms that survive in the long run are producing the output under the most efficient conditions. Because the cost of each unit of output is as low as possible, price is also low. Scarce resources are allocated economically, and the consumers benefit from low prices and, therefore, large quantities.

Price Equals Average Total Cost (Long Run) If price equals the average total cost, total revenues equal total costs. This implies that all surviving firms earn normal profit, an amount sufficient to compensate the entrepreneur for opportunity costs. Under other types of market organization, firms tend to produce a less than desirable quantity, and charge a price in excess of marginal and average total cost.

The above is not intended to imply that other types of competition are inferior to perfect competition. For one thing, even though the perfectly competitive firm operates at minimum average total cost in the long run, such a cost curve may still lie higher than one possible under a monopoly, especially if the monopolist is big and efficient. Other types of market structure with a few producers may also tend to produce the output at a lower unit cost, although not necessarily at minimum average total cost, as compared to a small firm in a perfectly competitive industry. In addition, while products in the perfectly competitive industry are highly standardized, other markets allow and encourage product differentiation. We derive much utility from having a choice, which is nonexistent under perfect competition. For example, for the garment industry to be perfectly competitive, we would all have to wear identical, navy blue, double-breasted suits with pink buttons. Finally, perfect competition encourages very little innovation on the part of the individual firm.

LONG-RUN COST (SUPPLY) IN THE INDUSTRY

New firms enter an industry under perfect competition if the demand for the product increases. The eventual market price due to the rise in demand and the subsequent increase in supply may be higher, lower, or the same as the initial equilibrium price. The actual change in price will depend on the increases in supply relative to demand. Since, in the long run, all firms must earn no higher than normal profit, the long-run price in the market is the same as the long-run average total cost of the output. This long-run average total cost of the higher volume of output may be different from the initial value of the average total cost. Thus, perfectly competitive industries may be categorized as being either *increasing-cost, constant-cost, decreasing-cost,* or *increasing-cost* industries, according to whether increases in demand and supply leave the equilibrium price unaltered, bring about a fall in prices, or contribute to higher-than-before market prices.

Constant-Cost Industry

The long-run average total cost may rise, fall, or remain the same as output expands. If the new and existing firms can maintain the previous average total cost of output at the higher level of output by increasing their scale, the market price will, in the long run, also remain at its former level. Such constancy of the average total cost will occur if the firms do not experience any *net* internal and external economies or diseconomies of scale. Thus, even if factor prices tend to rise due to increases in their demand, the firms can exactly offset such higher costs (of resources) through internal economies of scale; or, if the factor supply is *perfectly price elastic,* rising demand will not increase their prices, and if the firm's production function is subject to constant returns to scale, the average total cost of production will not change with increases in output.

In Figure 11-6a, the higher level of demand is shown by D_2 and the new supply by S_2. If these functions intersect at the old price (P_1), the industry's

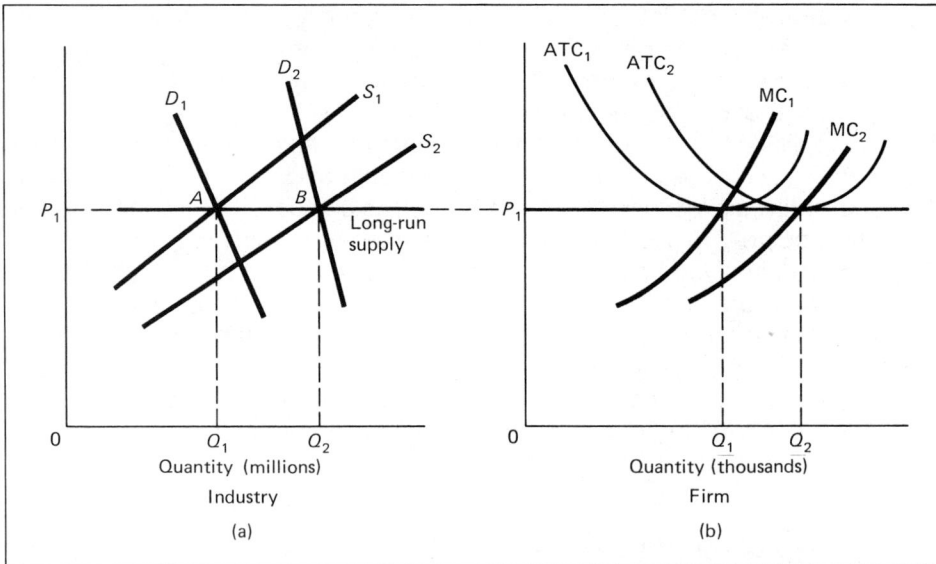

FIGURE 11-6
As demand increases, price rises and attracts other firms to enter the industry which now offers above-normal profits. Existing firms try to compete by moving to larger scales of production as shown by the various sizes of plant ATC labeled ATC_1, ATC_2. If supply changes to S_2 and demand does not increase beyond D_2, price will eventually be stabilized at the old level. Under such circumstances, all firms will again be earning normal profits, and price will equal average total cost. This type of industry is referred to as a constant-cost industry.

long-run "supply" will be the locus of points A and B. When the locus is horizontal, the industry is one of constant cost.

Decreasing-Cost Industry

When increases in demand and accompanying increases in supply bring about a decrease in the long-run equilibrium price, the industry becomes a decreasing-cost industry. Such changes in price are due to *net* economies (internal and external) of scale experienced by the firms. An example is a reduction in transportation and marketing costs due to the construction of a railroad to expanding and distant markets. If such cost-reducing external economies outweigh the probable internal diseconomies of scale, the average total cost of output will decline, as will the market price. The case of decreasing costs is shown in Figure 11-7.

Increasing-Cost Industry

Figure 11-8 illustrates an increasing-cost industry. Due to internal diseconomies of scale, rising factor prices, or both, the market price will rise in such an industry. The long-run locus of the various equilibrium points ($D_i = S_i$) is positively inclined, suggesting that the expansion of output can take place only at higher-than-before average total cost and price.

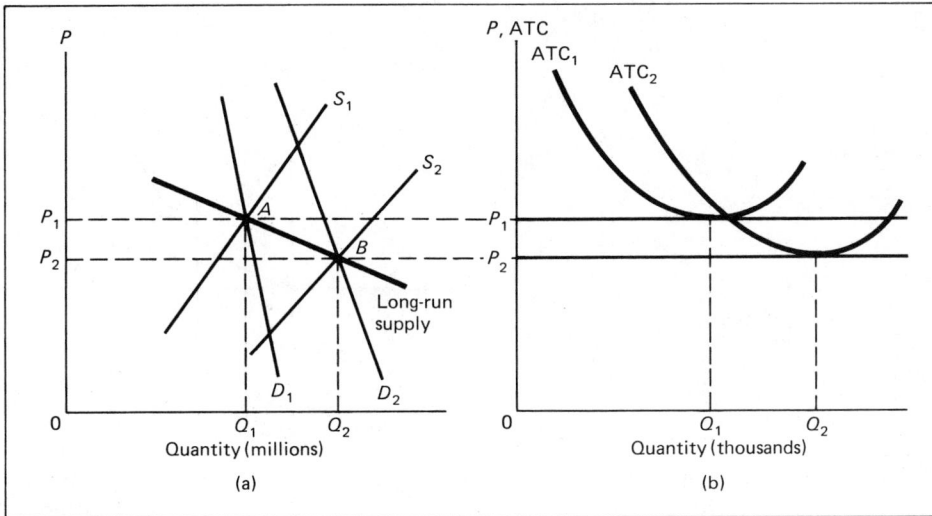

FIGURE 11-7
In the case of the decreasing-cost industry, the long-run supply is shown by the downward-sloping boldface line *AB*. Firms operate under conditions of increasing returns to scale and move from cost curve ATC_1 to ATC_2. As demand increases from D_1 to D_2, the price initially rises and leads to the usual adjustments that normally occur in perfectly competitive industries. The entry of new firms and reduction in costs of production increase supply to S_2 and this establishes a lower price, P_2. When the industry is once again in long-run equilibrium, each firm earns normal profits at a lower price and produces Q_2 thousand units of output. In decreasing-cost industries, the price falls as output increases.

PURE COMPETITION

Since it is very difficult to find industries that satisfy all the conditions required by perfect competition, economists have chosen to discuss competitive behavior by way of *pure competition.* In pure competition, the firms are basically as described under perfect competition, except that they possess neither perfect information nor perfect mobility, nor are all firms identically capable. An industry can be classified as being purely competitive if the firms produce basically standardized products and are price takers. Such a model helps explain some of the changes in the so-called "real world," in addition to showing why some firms may be better off than others even in the long run. Pure competition can explain why some producers may continue to earn super-normal profits in the long run. The pure competition model is not as restrictive as its perfect counterpart, and yet it possesses practically all its explanatory powers.

APPLICATIONS

1. The Farm Strike

The price and quantity in perfectly competitive industries are set by the interaction of supply and demand. American farmers have occasionally advocated a reduction in

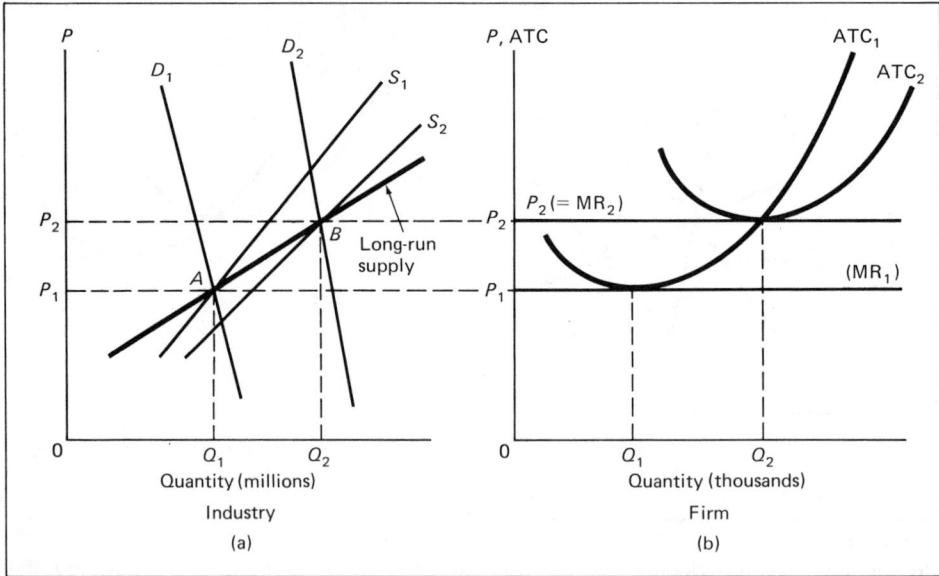

FIGURE 11-8
Under perfect competition, the price is set by industry supply and demand conditions. Initially the price is P_1, determined by the intersection of demand D_1 and supply S_1. The firm is producing quantity Q_1 in the initial phase of the long-run adjustment process in the industry. If demand increases to D_2, price will rise as long as no increase in supply takes place. As price rises above P_1, firms in the industry earn above-normal profits and attract others to enter the industry. This causes price to fall. In an increasing cost industry, the firms experience diseconomies (internal and external) of scale and the cost of production rises. The rise in unit cost with increases in output is indicated by ATC_2. The number of firms that enter and remain in the industry is automatically regulated by the market forces. Supply is stabilized at S_2 and price at P_2. All firms in the industry receive price P_2 per unit and the cost per unit is minimized at volume Q_2. Again the firms earn normal profits. The industry expands along line AB—higher prices coupled with higher quantities—and this line forms the long-run supply curve for the industry. If it is upward sloping, the industry is characterized by increasing cost.

supply to raise the price of farm products. It is true that if a reduction in supply takes place, ceteris paribus, the price of the product will rise according to the price elasticity of demand—the lower the elasticity, the higher the price increase. If each farmer produces only 50% of what he normally produces, other things being equal, the total supply in the market will also decline by a like amount. Will the individual farmer be better off? Not necessarily.

If the price elasticity of demand is sufficiently high, higher prices will bring about a decline in expenditures on such items. Furthermore, if agricultural industries are of the decreasing-cost variety, the unit cost of production will be higher at lower levels of output. If total costs of production decline less than total revenues, the farmer will end up having less net revenues (pure profits) than before.

Also, if the world market is perfectly competitive, unrestricted international trade will encourage an inflow of those agricultural products whose prices rise due to a reduction (contrived or otherwise) in supply. So even if the farmers successfully increase their profits by raising prices, they will do so for only a brief period of time. The increase in supply due to the inflow of foreign agricultural products will eventually bring down the market prices.

2. Unions and the Minimum Wage

The unskilled labor market is a good example of an industry under pure competition. The wage rate in such an industry is normally determined by supply and demand. If the going wage rate is deemed too low by societal standards, can we improve the well-being of the workers by legislating a minimum wage law?

Suppose the current equilibrium wage rate for the unskilled workers is $2.50 per hour. If the government insists that all employers pay their unskilled workers a minimum of $3.00 per hour, the supply and demand will no longer be at equilibrium, due to the $3.00-per-hour "floor." More workers will be looking for the $3.00-per-hour jobs and employers will be reluctant to hire as many workers as they did under the old equilibrium rate. Some of the workers will be laid off (*disemployed*) while others newly entering the market due to the higher wage will be unemployed. Unions presumably favor such minimum wage laws.

Most labor unions are made up of skilled or semi-skilled workers. The higher the minimum wage for the unskilled workers, the less the incentive for the employer to hire them. Instead of hiring unskilled workers at artificially higher wages, the employer may prefer hiring the semi-skilled workers at a slightly higher wage. If the productivity of the semi-skilled workers as compared to their wages is higher than the productivity of the unskilled workers relative to the minimum wage, the former type of employee will be more economical. For example, if the semi-skilled worker produces 40% more than her unskilled colleague, the employer will be willing to pay the more skilled workers no more than 40% higher wages. Suppose the semi-skilled workers now receive $3.50 per hour. When the minimum wage law goes into effect, the unskilled workers will be paid a wage of $3.00 per hour. The extra 50¢ per hour above the old wage constitutes an increase of 20%. At this point, the semi-skilled union members can very easily demand a wage rate as high as $4.19 and have more of their kind employed in place of the unskilled workers. The 69¢ per hour additional wage will make the semi-skilled wage rise by only 19.71%, and as such they will be more economical at $4.19 per hour than the unskilled workers at $3.00 per hour.

3. Markets over Time—The Futures Market

Markets may also be defined in terms of time—that is, they may be designated as being either in the present or at some time in the future. A producer can arrange to sell his output in the current market at the existing prices or agree to deliver a given quantity of the product at some future date at a price agreed upon by the buyer and seller at the time of signing such a contract. For example, a wheat farmer may agree to deliver 100,000 bushels of wheat at $4.00 per bushel, eight months from the signing of the contract.

Almost all agricultural marketing enterprises involve some degree of risk. The risk comprises losses due to storage costs, spoilage, and price changes. Producers attempt to avoid or reduce such risks by shifting them to other parties who are obviously willing and able to assume them—for a price. One method of reducing price risks is by *hedging* the current transactions in the *futures market*. The futures market consists of buying and selling contracts for the future delivery of goods. Buyers and sellers assume that the change in price of goods on hand (*spot goods*) and the agreed-upon future price will be such that the losses incurred in the spot market will be more than offset by transactions in the futures market.

The following example will illustrate how an individual may hedge against losses. Suppose a country elevator of grain goes through the following operations on the various dates stipulated:

September 30: Grain bought from farmer at $4.50 per bushel.
June futures sold at $4.55 per bushel.
November 1: Grain sold at $4.40 per bushel.
June futures bought at $4.45 per bushel.

If we disregard the costs of storage between September 30 and November 1, the reduced price of grain will bring a loss of 10¢ per bushel. However, since the elevator expects to make 10¢ profit per bushel from its June sale, the net loss for the operation is zero. If the June grain had been sold for a price higher than $4.55, ceteris paribus, the elevator would have made some profit, unless of course the costs of storage and spoilage were appreciable.

Two major groups are usually involved in the futures market—*hedgers* and *speculators*. It is erroneous to assume, as people occasionally do, that hedging is "good" while speculating is "evil." Actually, the second activity assumes the risk that the first wishes to avoid. It takes risk avoiders as well as risk takers to make the futures market operate. Both parties help stabilize the price of agricultural commodities. Thus, while we have utilized a very static or comparative-static model for the analysis of perfect competition, the introduction of the futures markets renders its explanatory powers more potent. To predict the true behavior of prices in the immediate as well as the distant future, we must understand the behavior of participants on the spot as well as futures markets.

EXERCISES

1. Define and/or explain the following:
   a. Market structure.
   b. Perfect competition.
   c. Pure competition.
   d. Nonprice competition.
   e. Price taker.
   f. Economic efficiency.
   g. Perfect mobility.
   h. Decreasing-cost industry.
   i. External economy.
   j. Internal diseconomies of scale.

2. Explain why increasing returns to scale may or may not be compatible with a stable, perfectly competitive industry.

3. Why is the demand for an individual firm's product considered to be perfectly price elastic? (The firm is under perfect competition.)

4. Under what circumstances will the firm's marginal cost curve also be its short-run supply curve? Under what circumstances will this not be true?

5. Suppose a firm's marginal cost function is negatively inclined. Using a graph, show a profit-maximizing, perfectly competitive firm's optimal level of output.

6. Will advertising by an individual firm in a perfectly competitive industry prove profitable? Will advertising by the industry be profitable?

7. Which of the following, if any, qualify to be perfectly competitive firms?

   a. Prostitutes in a large city.
   b. Automobile companies.
   c. Automobile dealers.
   d. A corporate farm that produces 30% of the industry's output.
   e. Garment manufacturers.
   f. Small feedlots.
   g. State universities.
   h. Hamburger establishments.
   i. Commercial banks.
   j. Car-rental companies.

8. Suppose the market price of the product in a perfectly competitive industry is $40. Determine the break-even quantities for the firm under each of the following cost structures:

a. Total cost (TC) = 1000 + 50Q

b. TC = 500 × 40Q

c. TC = 10,000 + 30Q

d. TC = 10,000

e. TC = 30Q

9. Determine the profit-maximizing output of the firm, if the market price is $100, and the total cost of the firm is given by the following equation. (Also show the amount of profits.)

$$TC = 100 + (1/20)\, Q^2$$

(Hint: Use calculus or a graph; profit-maximizing $Q = 1000$. Consult the appendix to this chapter at the end of the book.)

10. Find the two break-even quantities using the information of Exercise 9. (Hint: You will need the *quadratic* formula—consult the appendix to this chapter at the end of the book.)

11. Suppose that the typical firm's marginal cost (MC) in a perfectly competitive industry is given by

$$MC = 10 + (1/1000)Q$$

There are 1000 identical firms in the industry, and the demand for total industry output is known to be

$$P = 110 - (1/1,000,000)Q$$

Calculate the following:
   a. the industry price and quantity,
   b. the profit-maximizing output per firm,
   c. the amount of profits,
if each firm's fixed costs are $10,000 and the expression for the average variable cost (AVC) is known to be

$$AVC = 10Q + (1/2000)\, Q^2$$

(Hint: The short-run industry supply curve is the sum of the individual firms' short-run supply curves.)

12. In futures market terminology, a "spreader" is one who buys the commodity in one market and sells it in another to make a profit. Explain how spreading action may influence the price in each market.

13. "Arbitrageurs" are essentially spreaders of foreign exchange. Assume the following exchange rates between the various currencies as quoted in the various cities. How would you go about buying and selling the different currencies to maximize your profits, if you have $10,000 and there are no transaction or communication costs?

New York: $1 U.S. = DM 2; $1 U.S. = 0.50 U.K. Pound; $1 U.S. = 4 French Francs.
Frankfurt: DM 1 = $0.60 U.S.; DM 1 = 0.30 U.K. Pound; DM 1 = 2.20 French Francs.
Paris: 1 French Franc = $0.28 U.S.; 1 French Franc = 0.13 U.K. Pound; 1 French Franc = DM 0.50.

SUGGESTED READINGS

Blair, R. "A Survivor Analysis of Commercial Health Insurance." *Journal of Business,* July 1978.

Greenhut, M. L. "A Theoretical Mapping from Perfect Competition to Imperfect Competition." *Southern Economic Journal,* October 1975.

Mundlak, Y. "Occupational Migration Out of Agriculture—A Cross-Country Analysis." *Review of Economics and Statistics,* August 1978.

Scherer, F. *Industrial Market Structure and Economic Performance.* Chicago, Illinois: Rand McNally, 1970.

Snyder, W. W. "Horse Racing: Testing the Efficient Markets Model." *Journal of Finance,* September 1978.

Yeats, A. "Monopoly Power, Barriers to Competition and the Pattern of Price Differentials in International Trade." *Journal of Development Economics,* June 1978.

Chapter Twelve Chapter Twelve Chapter Twelve

FIRMS UNDER IMPERFECT COMPETITION

In contrast to perfect competition, many industries are classified as being under *imperfect competition.* In general, firms operating under conditions of imperfect competition have some choice about the price, whereas perfectly competitive firms do not. A firm under perfect competition takes the price in the market as given, while a firm under imperfect competition "searches" for the best price. The first is a price taker, the second a *price searcher* or *price maker.* The models of the firm most often discussed under imperfect competition include *monopolistic competition, monopoly,* and *oligopoly.* There are also other special variations of these types of market structure.

MONOPOLISTIC COMPETITION

Market Structure

Just as we described perfect competition with its market characteristics, we can also pinpoint the salient features of a monopolistically competitive industry. In such an industry: there are many sellers; the firms produce "differentiated" but close substitutes; it is usually easy for new firms to enter and compete with the existing firms; and perfect information may or may not be available to all the firms.

From the above description we can see that monopolistic competition, though imperfectly competitive, comes close to the theoretical model of perfect competition. Although each firm in such an industry is its own price maker, it is so in a restricted sense. The many firms produce products that are very close, but not perfect, substitutes. Product *differentiation* can mean anything from a different name to a substantially different product. For example, beer made by Miller may be identical in contents to beer made by Anheuser Busch. The prices of these two brands may be close, if not equal. Even if Budweiser sells for a dime less per six-pack, it is unlikely that Miller High Life will be driven out of business, because each firm has sufficiently differentiated its product, and in the process has built up a substantial and faithful following. Most beer drinkers actually prefer one brand over another either because it actually tastes different from the other brand, or because they have been persuaded to think that it is a better buy for their money. If you look around, you will find thousands of differentiated products. Is Crest toothpaste bascially the same as Aqua Fresh? Are Tide and Dash homogeneous products?

Demand and Supply in the Industry

Although we talk about demand and supply in a monopolistically competitive industry, we cannot assume that *the* price is determined by supply and demand forces. For one thing, because the firms do not produce identical products, they need not charge identical prices for their products. Furthermore, the market demand or aggregate demand is the sum of all the individual demands, and the products must all be identical in order to add the demands for the product. Thus, even if two brands of calculators are very similar, we may not add the demand for Hewlett-Packards to the demand for Texas Instruments, and call such a sum the aggregate demand for calculators. That would be like adding the demands for oranges and bananas and calling it the demand for fruit. Coincidentally, all firms may elect to charge the same price, or they may be forced by competition to charge very similar prices; but unlike perfectly competitive firms, there is no guarantee that this will occur. Similarly, since each firm makes its own decision regarding price (and hence quantity) we do not have an industry supply curve for nonhomogeneous products. In monopolistically competitive industries, there are many individual but perhaps close prices for the many close substitutes.

The Optimal Output of the Firm

A firm may have a variety of objectives. Because each firm's demand for its product is unique, and the quantity demanded varies inversely with the price, the firm has the option of charging that price which best satisfies its needs. For example, if the firm is interested in maximizing short-run profits, it will operate at the price and output level where the marginal cost of the output is equal to its marginal revenue, or where MR = MC. This is the necessary condition for profit maximization.

Figure 12-1 shows the demand for Cindy's hamburgers. Notice that it is negatively sloped in contrast to the horizontal demand facing a perfectly competitive producer. The moment a firm's demand curve becomes downward sloping, we should suspect the presence of imperfect competition. There are many prices along such a demand curve, implying the possibility of an almost infinite number of price–quantity combinations. Cindy's must select the best price consistent with its goals. Since it can choose the price, it becomes a

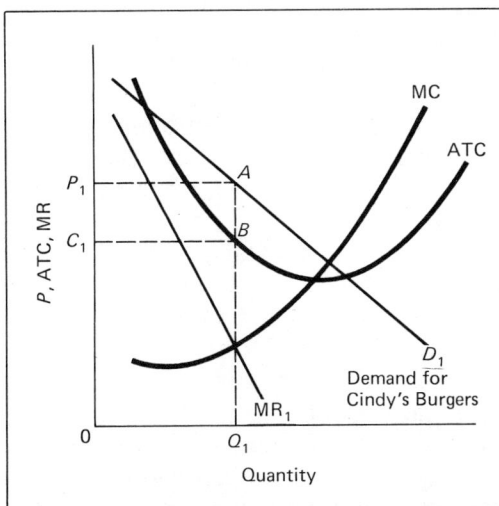

FIGURE 12-1
Cindy's Burgers is a firm operating under conditions of monopolistic competition. Monopolistically competitive firms produce very similar but "differentiated" products. Such differentiation may range from actual differences in quantity and quality to consumer-imagined differences created through color, packaging, and advertisement. Monopolistic firms are free to set their own prices, hence they are referred to as "price makers." If Cindy's is a profit-maximizing firm, the price will be set at P_1, which will lead to sales of quantity Q_1. We see that the firm's average total cost is well below the price, hence Cindy's is earning economic profits with this price–quantity combination. The profit per hamburger is $(P_1 - C_1)$ and total profits equal the value of area $P_1 C_1 BA$. Theoretically, new firms may enter such industries without much difficulty. If the majority of hamburger establishments are in Cindy's position, more firms will enter such a profitable industry. Presumably such entry will reduce the market share of each firm in the industry.

price maker. We will assume that the hamburger establishment is interested in obtaining maximum profits.

The marginal revenue (MR) function lies below the downward-sloping demand curve. The demand function (D_1) is linear, and therefore the corresponding marginal revenue (MR_1) curve is also a straight line. The cost curves are drawn as for firms under perfect competition. Consequently, the short-run average total cost (ATC) and the marginal cost (MC) are basically U-shaped. Since Cindy's is interested in maximizing profits, it produces that quantity where marginal revenue and marginal cost are equal, quantity Q_1. Given a conventional demand curve, there is only one price which will enable the firm to sell quantity Q_1, and that price is P_1. Thus, the profit-maximizing output (Q_1) determines the price, and the consumers react to such a price and, in turn, purchase the profit-maximizing output. From the firm's point of view, $P = f(Q)$, while from the consumer's standpoint, $Q = g(P)$. Since, in the case of Figure 12-1, the price of each hamburger exceeds its average total cost, Cindy's is earning pure profits in the short-run.

The Firm in the Long Run

Ordinarily, only those firms that earn profits choose to stay in the industry. However, a firm may continue to operate at a loss in the short run if it can earn adequate revenues to offset its variable costs. In the long run, the firms will operate if and only if they earn normal or economic profit. Entry into a monopolistically competitive industry is not unusually difficult. Thus, if the typical firm is earning pure profits, other firms will tend to enter the market. If the new firms bid some of the customers away from the existing firms, on the average, the market share per firm will decline. In other words, the entry of new firms will most likely reduce the demand for the other firms' products. When demand falls, the old firms must adjust to the changing conditions by seeking out new profit-maximizing prices and quantities. In general, we may conclude that almost all firms will be forced to reduce their prices due to the decline in demand.

Some firms may experience a greater decline in demand than others. However, since all firms in the industry produce very similar products, most of them will experience similar cuts in the demand for their products. If, for some reason, the demand function falls to a level below the average total cost, such a firm will lose money. To reduce the losses or even to make profits, a firm may attempt to lower its costs of production and increase the demand for its products. For example, if all hamburger producers such as Cindy's are earning profits and thus attract new firms to the industry, it is possible that Cindy's demand will fall below its average total cost. When this happens, if the conditions are suitable, Cindy's may attempt to reduce the cost of its hamburgers by introducing better methods of production, by using other relatively inexpensive ingredients, or both. It may also try to regain the lost market by advertising and promotional schemes, or by improving the quality of its hamburgers. If the net effect of these policies is to grant Cindy's at least normal profits in the long run, Cindy's will continue to sell hamburgers.

Those firms whose long-run average total costs lie above the demands for their products will go out of business, for they will not be earning even normal profits. Necessarily, we have to assume that all firms will try to improve their demand and cost positions in the long run in order to survive in a monopolistically competitive industry. When some firms leave the industry, the residual firms gain additional buyers, and this change in demand may very well increase the profit situation for some, if not all, of the firms. For example, if, for some reason, all McDonald's hamburger restaurants went out of business, the other firms such as Burger King, Whites, and Cindy's would tend to experience rising demands and perhaps profits. Again, if the firms earn economic profits, other new firms may wish to sell hamburgers, which in turn will most likely reduce the demand faced by the existing hamburger producers and the whole cycle consisting of changing prices, quantities, costs, and qualities will be repeated. Only when the firms earn normal profits is the industry in long-run equilibrium, because normal profits may not be appealing enough for the average new firm to enter the industry. The long-run model of monopolistic competition suggests that, in most cases, the firms in the industry will be earning normal profits and charging very similar prices. McDonald's would have no particular reason to charge 85¢ for its "Big Mac" just because Burger King chose to charge that price for its "Whopper." If the two products are sufficiently differentiated (and they are), McDonald's could charge a higher price without losing all of its potential customers to its competitor. Price is not the only criterion by which people judge a product's desirability.

At one time, *Life, Look,* and other magazines with similar layouts and contents had a large following, making the publication of these journals very profitable. The publishing houses also earned substantial revenues from the sale of advertising space. But as other, more "contemporary" magazines appeared on the scene, and as the taste of magazine buyers changed with the years, the demand for these two magazines declined substantially. When the revenues could no longer cover the costs of production, the magazines folded. However, with changing demand and the revival of nostalgia, *Life* started to publish again in late 1978—that is, it reentered the magazine industry as did *Look.* If all such magazines survive into the year 2000, we have to assume that they are earning at least normal profits.

Nonprice Competition

Although firms under monopolistic competition may resort to price-cutting tactics in order to improve their position in the industry, they engage in substantial amounts of *nonprice competition.* Such competition includes, but is not limited to, product variation, advertising, marketing, and promotion. All firms under monopolistic competition possess about equal amounts of market power, since they produce virtually identical products. Hence, nonprice competition gives the firm some advantage over its competitors, but, in the long run, the effectiveness of such competition may be only illusionary. For instance, if all firms attempt to enlarge their shares of the market through aggressive marketing and promotional policies, it is entirely possible that all of them will obtain some additional customers, but not necessarily at the expense of one another—the total demand for the products manufactured by all the firms will have grown. Furthermore, nonprice competition can also be costly. Thus, an additional dollar spent on this type of competition may or may not return a dollar in benefits. Allegedly, the greater the number of firms in an industry, the more the competition and hence the greater the downward pressure on the individual firm's prices. However, nonprice competition, with its associated costs, may contribute to high demand and, therefore, prices. The automobile companies, although not monopolistically competitive, illustrate this point. The prices of American automobiles have risen to higher-than-necessary levels despite keen competition, due to each firm's attempts to capture the market by offering "more" in its vehicles, albeit for higher prices. Nonprice competition can, in many instances, be wasteful.

Monopolistic Competition and Efficiency

Although the firms under monopolistic competition earn normal profits in the long run, how do they rate against perfectly competitive firms? Are these firms equally "efficient"? In the first place, the word efficiency may and does have more than one meaning. We may speak of efficiency as it relates to cost, productivity, value, equity, and utility. Thus, while a monopolistically competitive firm may produce an item at an average cost higher than that which would prevail under perfect competition, the quality and value offered by the first type may be much greater than the product manufactured by perfectly competitive firms. Since the demand facing the monopolistically competitive firm is downward sloping, in the long run the firm earns normal profit, where price is equal to average total cost. If the average total cost is U-shaped, the profit-maximization as well as the normal profit points occur where the demand curve is tangent to the average total cost curve. Consequently, such a firm would not be operating at the minimum point on its long-run average total cost, as opposed to a firm under perfect competition, which would. Thus, from one point of view, the monopolistically competitive firm is probably not as efficient as its perfectly competitive counterpart.

Figure 12-2 points out another source of inefficiency. Since the price of the output in the long run exceeds its marginal cost, the firm under monopolistic competition presumably "underproduces"—that is, it does not produce the volume of output where the price of the output is equal to its marginal cost. If this point of view is adopted, society is not as well off as it could be, since the value (as measured by price) that could have been received, had the firm produced until price equalled marginal cost, is lost. We will explore this point in more detail when we discuss welfare economics.

All conditions pertaining to monopolistic competition are neither readily observable in the marketplace nor need they all be satisfied all the time to make such competition viable. Many industries come very close to being monopolistically competitive. For example, hotels and motels, fast-food

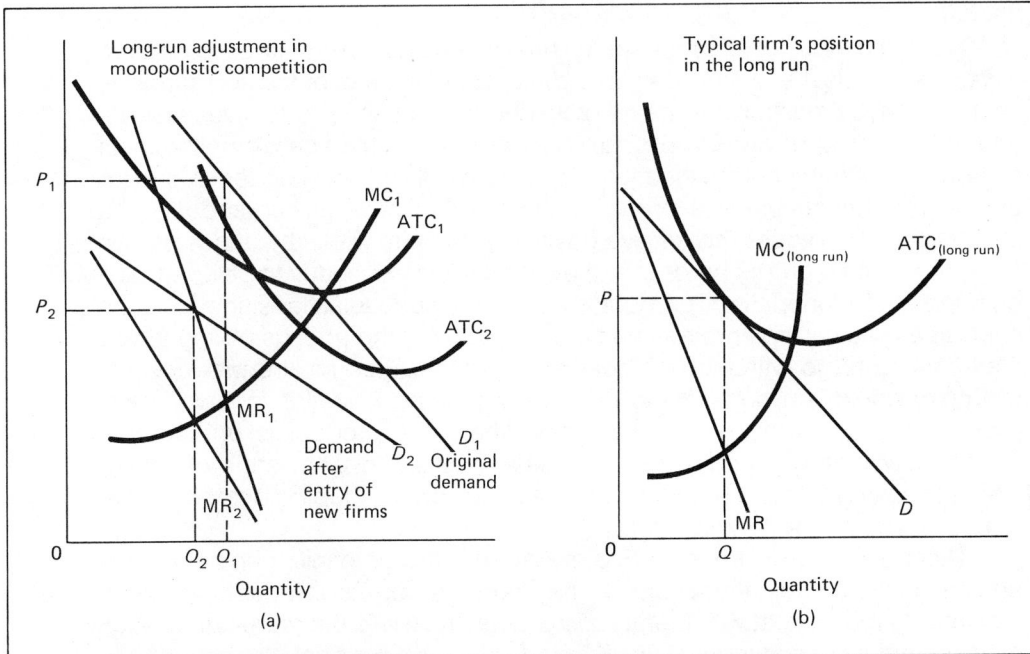

FIGURE 12-2
Entry into the monopolistically competitive industry is not difficult. In panel (a) we show that the typical firm in the industry with demand D_1 and average total cost ATC_1 is earning economic profits with price P_1 and quantity Q_1. New firms attracted by profits enter the industry and reduce the other firms' demand. The reduced demand is indicated by curve D_2. Since D_2 lies below the original average total cost, the firm expands its scale of operation, hoping, through economies of scale, to reduce its losses and, also to increase demand for its product by quality improvements and other promotional devices. If demand still lies below the best average total cost curve, such a firm will leave the industry in the long run. When unprofitable firms leave the industry, the remaining firms get a bigger percentage of the market. Panel (a) further shows that the firm will be forced to lower its prices to price P_2 because of the reduced demand. Panel (b) depicts the position of each firm in the long run. Since, in the long run, excessive profits attract new firms and losses discourage entry as well as encourage the departure of firms, the industry is stabilized when the firms earn no more than normal profits. Under such conditions, maximum profit will be no more than normal profit.

restaurants, drug stores, clothing outlets, magazine publishers, and in some instances commercial banks qualify for the monopolistic-competition market model of the firm. We repeatedly see "going out of business" signs displayed by unsuccessful haberdashers, and many doctors (specialists as well as general practitioners) move to other cities and states. No sooner do the firms leave the industry than others appear to take their place. Banks engage in many types of price as well as nonprice competition. Do you have a "free" checking account? How often have you utilized a bank's travel department? Even though not all firms earn normal profits in the long run, the model of monopolistic competition is probably more representative of the real world than the model described as perfect competition.

MONOPOLY

When the industry is a *monopoly,* there is a single seller—the monopolist. A monopoly industry is the most *concentrated* of all types of market structure. That is to say, almost all the assets of the industry, all the productive facilities, and all the market power are concentrated in one firm. In general, the theory of monopoly resembles the theories describing other firms under imperfect competition. Since there is only one firm producing a given product, it is meaningless to discuss the relative position of the firm within the industry. The consumers either buy its product or they do not. It is erroneous to believe that a demand for a monopolist's product is perfectly price inelastic, since it has no substitutes. Actually all products have substitutes. If the price is not right, you may choose to go without it, if there are no substitutes for the product. For example, would you buy a flying saucer from the only Martian in town at any price? Only under those circumstances where the product is an absolute necessity will the demand tend to be rather inelastic over a range of prices. Consequently, we may use the conventional downward-sloping demand curve to analyze monopolistic behavior.

The monopolistic firm is a price maker and has an infinite choice of price and quantity combinations along the demand for its product. A profit-maximizing monopolist will operate at the quantity where the marginal revenue of the output equals marginal cost. Figure 12-3 shows a monopolist maximizing profits at quantity Q_1 by charging price P_1. In this particular case, the monopoly

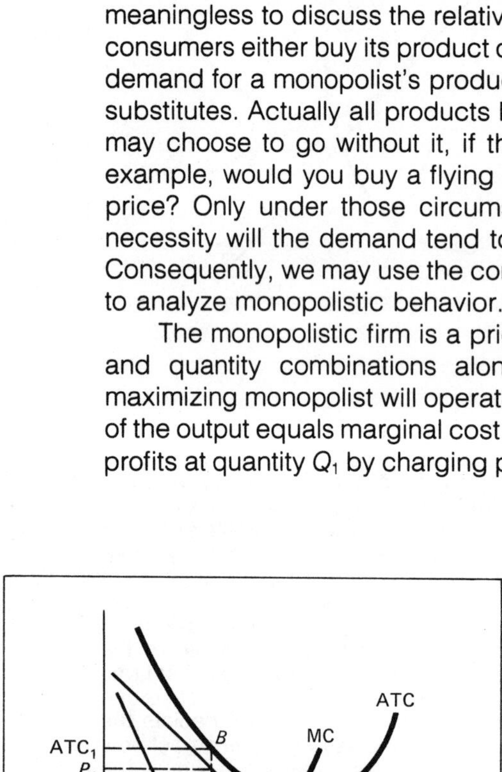

FIGURE 12-3
Dr. Fletcher Christian is a surgeon specializing in heart transplants and other cardiac surgery. Since he is the only person who can perform such operations in the small country of Gauginland, he is termed a monopolist. The demand for his services is shown as the inverse price–quantity demand curve of earlier discussions. If the surgeon is a profit maximizer (or loss minimizer), he will tend to perform Q_1 operations per year, and this quantity of operations will be demanded at a price of P_1. As shown, his average total cost of maintaining the operating theatre, paying his staff, and obtaining spare parts for the heart transplants exceeds price P_1. In the short run, this doctor will lose money equal to area $P_1(ATC_1)BC$. Conceivably, in the long run, the doctor may experience an increase in demand and/or a reduction in costs. If price then exceeds average total cost, he will earn pure or economic profit. Since Dr. Christian is a monopolist and probably possesses very special and inimitable skills, he can continue to enjoy monopoly profits in the long run by preventing entry into the industry. One way to accomplish this is not to train any other doctor to become a heart surgeon. Another is to persuade the authorities to refuse entry visas to foreign medical graduates.

is incurring losses, since the price per unit is less than the average total cost. This ought to clarify a common misconception that a monopolistic firm automatically makes profits. It can make profits if, and only if, its total revenues exceed its total costs. If this firm can eventually increase the demand for its product or reduce its costs, or resort to special pricing techniques (discussed in Chapter 13) so that price exceeds unit cost, then it will make a profit.

The Monopoly in the Long Run

A monopolistic firm earning reasonably attractive profits may draw the attention of others, and whether the industry remains a monopoly for long depends on the circumstances. A monopoly can retain its position as long as it can prevent other potential entrants from producing similar products and as long as no other firm wishes to enter the industry. If, for example, the monopolistic firm controls the patent rights to, or has special knowledge of, technical secrets, it can conceivably maintain the unique monopoly position. It is also possible that the industry's size may limit its entry desirability by other firms. A small town or city with 6000 people can perhaps support only one taxicab company. If another enters and divides the market, both duopolists will lose money, until one of the firms leaves the industry and restores it to a monopoly. A monopoly can also protect its privileged status if it can preempt the natural resources required by other interested producers. For a long time, Polaroid was the only camera of its kind. Polaroid had the patent rights to the camera as well as to the film. Kodak was prevented from bringing out similar cameras because of the limit imposed by the patent laws, and it did not even dare manufacture the instantly developing film under its own brand name even though it had been making the film for Polaroid for years. Take the case of Coca Cola. Although the industry for soft drink beverages is not a monopoly, presumably the industry for "cola" drinks is highly concentrated. Since the makers of Coke have the secret formula that makes a cola drink a Coca Cola, consumers refuse to accept substitutes. As far as they are concerned, Coca Cola is a monopoly. In any case, as long as the producers of Coca Cola can closely guard the secret to their magic formula, they can continue to dominate the market.

In the long run, even a monopolistic firm must close its doors if its total revenues do not equal its total costs. If persistent losses continue, the firm may try to do certain things in order to make profits. In the short run, if the monopolistic firm's revenues fall below its variable costs, it can shut down. Even here, there are exceptions. For example, if a new medical specialist is in town, he may have to stay open in the short run despite losses due to insufficient revenues to cover variable costs. His future revenues and profitability are contingent on his staying open in the short run, regardless of the unfortunate circumstances.

Some of the other goals of a firm are described in Chapter 13. A monopoly can also pursue other objectives in addition to, or instead of, profits. It can try to maximize profits, revenues, value of the firm, or some other argument in the managerial utility function. With the exception of "natural," "regulated," or governmental monopolies, very few true large-scale private monopolies exist in the United States today.

Even if an industry is not a true monopoly, a firm may still possess substantial monopoly power by virtue of the circumstances. For example, when the Boeing 747s first came out in the early 1970s, Pan Am was the first airline to receive delivery of its orders for these large airplanes. Until such time that some of the other carriers also obtained the superjets, Pan Am reaped substantial monopoly profits by being the sole possessor of the new-generation jets. Similarly, Coca Cola was the first soft drink company to set up distribution and marketing facilities in the Republic of China after relations between the United States and China were normalized, and needless to say was able to earn very handsome profits as a monopolist. There also are isolated instances of monopoly power in small communities where there may be one hamburger establishment, one supermarket, one commercial bank, or one automobile dealer. Such firms become true monopolies, although small in size, and are most often found in small cities far removed from any major market. Durango in the state of Colorado, for example, has only one pizzeria and a single laundromat, and since the city is far away from a major market such as Denver or Albuquerque, most of the owners of such firms enjoy substantial monopoly power.

MEASUREMENT OF MONOPOLY POWER

Perfect competition is presumably most desirable for societal welfare. Monopoly, being the furthest away from it on the spectrum of competition, represents the least desirable form of market organization, at least in the sense that a monopolist's price exceeds the marginal cost of the output. Whether a monopoly should be encouraged, destroyed, broken up, taxed, or subsidized need not concern us at the moment. However, it might be important for us to recognize the presence and magnitude of monopoly power. We will next examine some indicators of monopoly power.

The Lerner Index

We may use certain indexes to measure the degree of monopoly power possessed by a firm. One such index is the *Lerner Monopoly Index,* named after the economist Abba Lerner. The Lerner Index is equal to the price minus the marginal cost divided by the price. According to Lerner, the greater the deviation of marginal cost from price, the greater the value of the index and hence the greater the degree of monopoly power. When price equals marginal cost, the Lerner Index equals zero. A profit-maximizing monopolist equates marginal revenue (MR) to marginal cost (MC) and, at the profit-maximizing level of output, the Lerner Index becomes $(P - MR)/P$ which, in effect, is the *reciprocal of the absolute value of the point price elasticity of demand.* For example, if price and marginal revenue equal $20 and $15, respectively, the point price elasticity's absolute value will equal $20/($20 − $15), or 4. The

Lerner Index, in turn, will equal ¼. The rationale behind the use of such an index to measure the degree of monopoly power is that Professor Lerner was interested not so much in measuring the profit-making powers of a firm, as in the relative deviation from perfect competition, which provides the social optimum. Thus, such an index is only a partial indicator of a firm's true market monopoly power, because price may exceed marginal cost even under other circumstances.

The Bain Monopoly Index

Another monopoly index, named after economist J.S. Bain, uses the divergence between price and average total cost to measure monopoly power. Persistent price–average cost discrepancy probably indicates the presence of a good deal of monopoly power, even though excess economic profits are no sure indication of such market power. Thus, while the Lerner Index may indicate the presence of monopoly power, the Bain Index may not if the firm's average total cost equals the price of the output. In Figure 12-4, at quantity Q_1, and with average total cost curve ATC_2, the Bain Index is zero, while the Lerner Index is positive. As an indicator of monopoly profits and hence perhaps monopoly power, the Bain Index seems to be more suitable.

The Rothschild Monopoly Index

The *Rothschild Index* compares the slope of a firm's demand curve to that for the entire industry. Thus, when the two slopes are equal, the value of the Rothschild Index is one. The index is defined as

$$\text{Rothschild Index} = \frac{\text{Slope of firm's demand}}{\text{Slope of industry's demand}}$$

The higher the value of this index, the greater the monopoly power of the firm. Note that the value of the Rothschild Index for a perfectly competitive firm is zero.

OLIGOPOLY

Students of political science know that *oligarchy* means rule by the few. *Oligopoly* is the term reserved for an industry with few sellers. The American economy is largely dominated by oligopolistic industries. Chances are, the cigarette you smoke, the car you drive, or the airplane that you fly in, was each made by an oligopolist.

Market Structure

In an oligopoly:

a. There are a few sellers that dominate the market. More specifically, the industry is highly concentrated and the five to nine largest firms produce at least 70% of the total industry output.

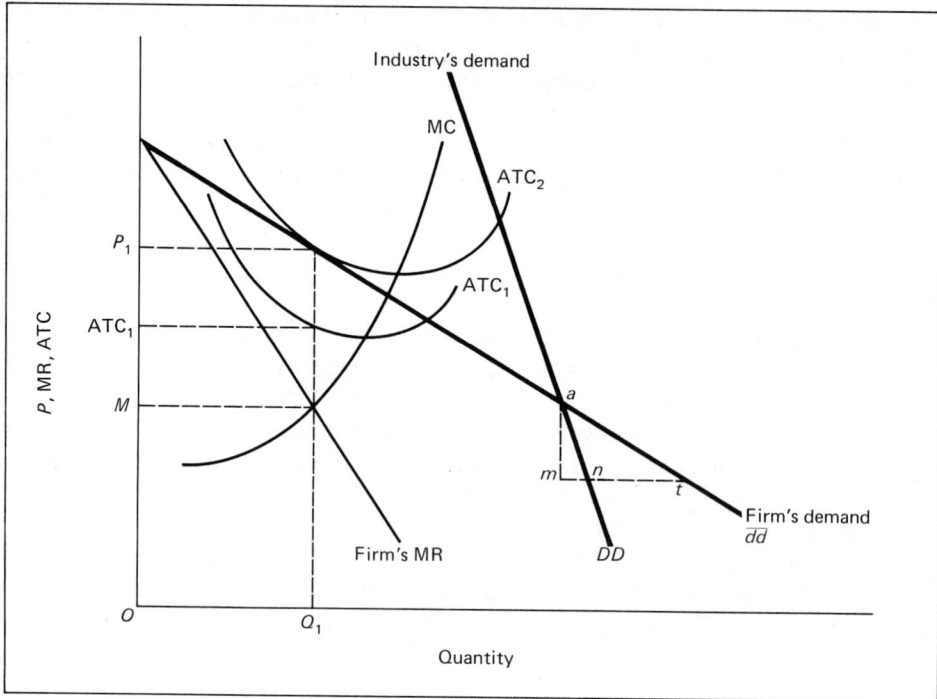

FIGURE 12-4

$$\text{Lerner Index} = \frac{\text{Price} - \text{marginal cost}}{\text{Price}}$$

$$= \frac{OP_1 - OM}{OP_1} = \frac{MP_1}{OP_1}$$

$$\text{Bain Index} = \frac{\text{Price} - \text{average cost}}{\text{Price}} = \frac{OP_1 - ATC_1 \text{ (or } ATC_2)}{OP_1}$$

$$\text{Rothschild Index} = \frac{\text{Slope of firm's demand}}{\text{Slope of industry's demand}}$$

$$= \frac{am/mt}{am/mn}$$

$$= \frac{mn}{mt}$$

In the particular situation illustrated and with cost curve ATC_1, all three indexes indicate that the firm possesses monopoly power. With ATC_2, however, the Bain Index is zero, indicating the relative absence of monopoly power, whereas the Lerner and Rothschild Indexes indicate that the firm does have monopolistic tendencies. The Lerner and Bain Indexes are measured at the profit-maximizing quantity, while the Rothschild Index may be measured anywhere for linear functions. If the firm is not a profit maximizer, the Lerner as well as the Bain Index may not yield consistent results.

b. The firms produce either homogeneous or differentiated products.

c. There are substantial barriers to entry into the industry.

d. Firms are very much aware of each other's actions, and there is quite a bit of nonprice competition.

e. The firms sometimes collude.

In the United States, oligopolies include the automobile, computer, chemical, aircraft, cement, steel, cigarette, petroleum, rubber, and appliance industries. There are also many other oligopolies in the service industries. For example, bank credit cards like Master Charge and VISA compete with those issued by American Express, Diner's Club, and Carte Blanche. Hertz, Avis, and National are the dominating oligopolists in the car rental business. Coca Cola, Pepsi Cola, and the "Un Cola" (7-Up) produce the largest share of the total output of the soft drink industry. If we use the entire world as the market region, it is possible that some of these companies will not come out as strong or big oligopolists, although American Express, General Motors, IBM, Boeing, and Coca Cola unmistakably are.

Since there are few firms in an oligopoly, and because there is keen rivalry among them, competition takes many forms. There is no single generalized model of the oligopolistic firm, as we saw under both perfect and monopolistic competition. Each model of oligopoly arises from a unique set of assumptions. We will examine a few models in this chapter. The other models are included as special topics in the theory of pricing in Chapter 13.

TWO MODELS OF OLIGOPOLY

The Kinked Demand Model

The "kinked demand" model is particularly useful in explaining the absence of price competition as well as in giving a possible explanation for price rigidities in oligopoly. In it, each firm starts out by charging the price it wants in accordance with its profit (or other) goals. If a firm wishes to increase its market share by lowering its prices, it assumes that all the other firms will do the same. On the other hand, each firm also assumes that any price increase on its part will not be matched by the other firms. If these two assumptions are maintained, we obtain the kinked demand curve in Figure 12-5. Since the demand curve is kinked (TXZ), the corresponding marginal revenue is discontinuous at quantity Q_1. The firm does not expect to gain much by lowering prices, nor does it wish to lose money by raising them. Under the assumptions of this model, the typical firm prefers to maintain its original price, though it may and does engage in nonprice competition.

Until airline deregulation, the scheduled airlines in the United States offered a good example of this type of model. For instance, United and TWA offered similar flights between Denver and New York, with the exception that United fed many domestic and international airlines, while TWA, in addition to performing the feeder function, had its own international destinations. Because the rates were largely regulated, and there was a considerable amount of travel involving interline connections, all participating airlines were charging identical and standardized fares between the same two points of travel. If TWA chose to lower its prices for competitive reasons, other airlines would have done likewise in order not to lose their customers traveling from Denver to New York. On the other hand, if the airlines did not act in collusion, and TWA alone decided to raise its fares, the other airlines would have maintained their original fares, expecting to gain business at the expense of TWA. Consequently, no airline changed its fares.

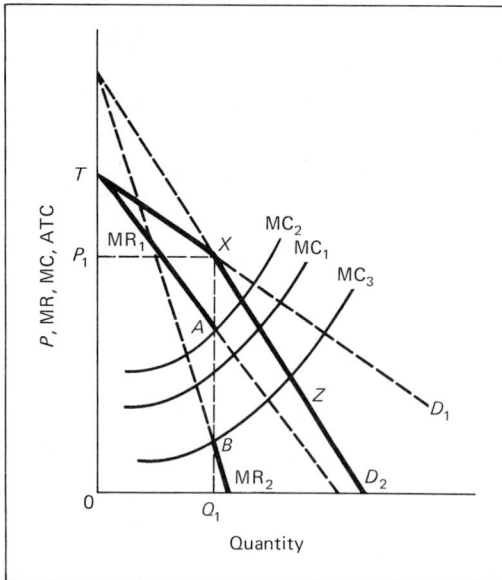

FIGURE 12-5
Rivalry is very keen in oligopolies. In the "kinked" demand version of oligopoly pricing, firms match price cuts offered by rivals but do not follow any price increases. If an oligopolist lowers his price and the others also lower their prices, he will not obtain too many additional customers. If the other firms had not followed price cuts, this firm would have expanded output along demand D_1, but such action by rivals makes its demand less price elastic, as shown by the steeper segment of demand curve D_2. Similarly, if the firm raises its prices and the others do not, it will be the only one to lose a substantial number of customers, and this makes the upper portion of the demand quite price elastic, as shown by D_1. The price kink occurs where the two demand curves intersect, or at point X. The marginal revenue curve under the circumstances is discontinuous and is shown by the appropriate segments of MR_1 and MR_2. The firm continues to produce at quantity Q_1, charging price P_1, as long as the marginal cost intersects the portion of MR that is discontinuous and indicated by distance AB. Even if marginal cost changes from level MC_2 to MC_3, the output level will remain at Q_1, and hence price will continue to be P_1. Since price is not expected to vary, this model is somewhat useful in explaining price rigidities in oligopolistic industries.

An extension of the kinked demand model is the "reversed-kink" model, where each firm's assumptions concerning the behavior of the rivals is reversed for price increases and cuts. Each firm assumes that all other firms will follow price increases by raising their prices, but they will not lower their prices if one firm lowers its prices. As a result, under the assumptions of this model, a firm's prices as well as its market share might be very volatile. Under such circumstances, there is no unique solution to the firm's profit-maximizing price.

The "Open" Oligopoly

Economist George Stigler has suggested a theory concerning an "open" oligopoly, which first appeared in his textbook in 1952. In this model, the firm is more interested in maximizing the *discounted* value of its stream of profits. The discounting technique of reducing all values from the future to the present is discussed in Chapter 3. In this model, the firm will set reasonably high prices for its products, prices that will allow other firms to gradually enter the industry. The open-oligopoly model attempts to explain why the existing firms in an oligopoly might be willing to yield part of their markets to new rivals, as opposed to keeping the entry closed by deliberately keeping prices low

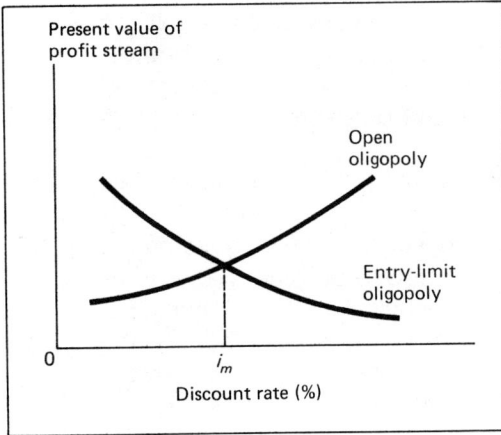

FIGURE 12-6
Oligopolies may choose to remain "open" and allow other firms to gradually enter the industry, or they may follow what is known as "entry-limit" pricing policies. Under the first choice, the existing oligopolies maintain prices high enough to allow other firms to enter the industry; under the second arrangement, the firms maintain prices low enough to discourage potential entrants. The open oligopolists initially earn high profits, which decline with the entry of new firms. The entry-limit oligopolists' profits rise with time. If a discount rate is utilized for present value calculations, a high rate will favor the open oligopoly, whereas a low rate will permit the entry-limit follower to earn more profits. Only at a rate of i_m will both strategies yield equal amounts of profits in present value terms.

enough to discourage market penetration by others. The practice of keeping prices low in the industry in order to discourage new competitors is called *entry-limit pricing* (see Figure 12-6). According to Stigler, such a model of open oligopoly correctly describes the developments of a few industries in the United States during the twentieth century; among them are the industries for steel, tin can, and corn product markets.

BARRIERS TO ENTRY IN OLIGOPOLY

Nowhere is it more difficult to enter an industry than in one dominated by oligopolists. New firms usually confront substantial barriers to their entry, some covert and others quite open. For example, the policy of maintaining low prices by existing oligopolists can very well discourage new firms from entering the market.

When undertaking a business venture, a firm requires capital in the form of plant, equipment, and inventories, as well as working capital. If the capital market is operating under imperfect competition, small firms not yet established may not be able to obtain sufficient funds or may have to pay substantially higher interest to obtain such funds. Paucity of capital and/or high interest costs may deter entry. General Motors is likely to attract capital rather easily by selling stocks to the public, but the Peabody Car Company will probably have a more difficult time in obtaining either equity or debt funds.

Cost barriers may also discourage entry. The average total cost curves of the existing oligopolists may be falling over a relatively large range of output. If newcomers enter the industry, they will reduce the market share for at least some firms and make it unprofitable for these and the new firms to stay in the industry. Such conditions imply that a particular oligopoly can support only a few firms.

Product preference of the consumers is influenced by the firm's abilities to differentiate its products. Usually in the initial stages, the cost of differentiation is high. Consumers are normally attached, rather strongly, to existing brands. New entrants to the industry must expect to spend considerable sums in promotional expenditures, without any concomitant guarantee of their products' success. Such costs to the potential entrants may prove more burdensome than they are equipped to handle. Why aren't there more automobile manufacturers in the United States?

Although technically speaking they do not constitute barriers, government procurement and contract-awarding procedures have aided the bigger firms and oligopolists by favoring them over the relatively unknown smaller firms. For example, when the United States government was experimenting with the possibilities of developing a space shuttle, it chose some of the more established firms for the project, and Rockwell International was chosen as the prime contractor. Of course, this is not to suggest that oligopolists are so favorably treated by the government in all cases. Some oligopolists genuinely deserve to be industry leaders because of their products, innovations, and pricing strategies.

In most empirical studies we find that barriers to entry may be very high or moderate. At least two or three studies maintain that the automobile industry poses very high barriers, as do the industries for aircraft, network broadcasting, precious metals, cigarettes, and electric lamps, among others. The industries with the least amount of barriers include footwear, clothing, real estate, foundries, surgical appliances and supplies, and, among others, the industry for soft-drink bottlers.

The presence of barriers does not absolutely impede entry nor prevent profitability in all cases, but it makes it difficult. An efficient firm with a highly marketable product may very well enter and stay in an oligopoly industry despite severe problems posed by barriers. The Maytag washing machine company, which is one of the smallest oligopolists in the industry, not only has survived very handsomely in the industry, but also has a very steady and loyal clientele despite the relatively high prices of its appliances.

OLIGOPOLY AND CONCENTRATION INDEXES

In an oligopoly, the competition is among the few larger firms in the industry. Since the biggest percentage of the total industry output is produced by the few, the industry is highly concentrated, and the degree of concentration increases as larger and larger quantities are produced by fewer and fewer firms. For example, in the American automobile industry, the Big Three (GM, Ford, and Chrysler) produce about 85% of all automobiles, whereas in the petroleum industry, the same percentage of output is produced by the 12 largest oil companies. In such cases, the automobile industry is said to be more concentrated than the oil industry. The degree of concentration may be measured by *oligopoly concentration indexes* not unlike the indexes used for the measurement of monopoly power. Such indexes are basically used as "competitive thermometers." The government, and particularly the Antitrust Division of the U.S. Department of Justice, has often used concentration indexes in cases involving the abuse of market power by larger companies in certain oligopolies. In general, the higher the degree of concentration, the greater the absence of "true" competition and, presumably, the greater the propensity of the firms to engage in tactics against the public interest. High concentration bestows a high degree of market power on the oligopolies. Without going into elaborate detail, we will briefly describe some of the oligopoly concentration indexes.

The Concentration Curve

A *concentration curve* shows the cumulative percentages of total employees, industry assets, and other related resources controlled or held by the leading firms in a given industry. If, for example, the cumulative assets of the four largest firms in a ten-firm industry equal 80%, the six smaller firms will have only 20% of the industry's total capacity, if we are to assume that a firm's capacity to produce and sell is proportional to the quantity of its assets. Consequently, under the circumstances, 40% of the largest firms control 80% of the industry's total output, while the remaining 60% of the firms have access to only 20% of the total output of the industry. Such an industry is highly concentrated. The concentration in the industry is shown graphically by plotting the cumulative assets of the firms against the cumulative numbers of the firms. When both values are measured in percentages, we obtain a concentration curve.

The Lorenz Curve and the Gini Coefficient

Two other concentration indexes are the *Lorenz Curve* and the *Gini Coefficient*. The first is very similar to the concentration curve in that it also shows the relative strength of the leading firms vis-à-vis the smaller ones. The Lorenz Curve has also been used by economists to show the income distribution of a nation or a region. The Gini Coefficient is derived from the Lorenz Curve, in that it measures the relative deviation of the actual distribution of the industry's assets from the line of equal distribution. The greater the deviation, the more "skewed" the distribution of industry output and capacity, and the higher the value of the coefficient.

Other measurements of concentration are the *Herfindahl Index* and the *Pietra Ratio* which are used in statistical experiments concerning the measurement of concentration. Another statistical indicator of concentration is the *Relative Mean Deviation,* which is related to the Gini Coefficient. Detailed accounts of the many indicators of concentration along with discussions of their applications can be found in books and references devoted to industry studies and antitrust economics.

We have briefly described some aspects of competition as found in various types of market structure, without giving a detailed account of the behavior of the firms, especially their strategies associated with price and nonprice competition under perfect information and uncertainty. These additional features, together with certain other models that explain other aspects of the theory of the firm, will be included in Chapters 13 and 14. Finally, the model of the firm under economic regulation—such as a "natural monopoly," which is regulated by an agency of the public sector—is covered in Chapter 18.

APPLICATIONS

1. *Wonder Woman* versus *The Six Million Dollar Man*

There are three large commercial (and one or two public service) television networks in the United States—ABC, NBC, and CBS. Strictly speaking, the network television industry is an oligopoly. Each oligopolist pursues certain strategies in order to accomplish its objectives. Networks gauge the success of their programs by the number of viewer hours. The profits of the firm, or television station, are affected by the quantity and quality of the viewers, since the networks receive substantial revenues from commercials. Competition among the networks takes the form of scheduling the "right" programs at the right time. If ABC is showing *The Six Million Dollar Man* at 7:00 P.M. EST, and if a similar audience watches *Wonder Woman,* CBS may find it more profitable to schedule *Wonder Woman* at 8:00 P.M. EST, so that both ABC and CBS can reach a substantial portion of the market. These two stations may even collude, and collusion is presumably quite common in oligopolies.

2. Why Does Diet Soft Drink Cost More?

Sugar-free foods are the current rage among health-conscious people. Sugar costs a lot more than sugar substitutes, such as saccharin and xyletol, yet, surprisingly enough, the beverages advertised as being sugar-free cost more than equal amounts of the drink made with pure sugar. Some claim that it is harder to make the sugar-free drink, and therefore the sugar-free version costs more. This is not so. The explanation lies in demand, as well as cost. It takes both to determine the market price. There are many brands of sugar-free beverages sold in the market, and their demand is much higher today than it used to be. As people began demanding more sugar-free drinks, the manufacturers were able to charge higher prices for them. Even if the cost of making sugar-free drinks is only half as much as the cost of producing sugar-containing ones, it is not incompatible for the first to be priced higher than the second. Remember "pet" rocks?

3. Don't Leave Home Without It

That is the message that has been preached by American Express for years. The powerful force of advertising cannot be overstated. Although there are comparable credit cards competing with American Express, they somehow have not managed to attain the same stature. American Express also charges more in annual membership fees than its competitors, and yet has more customers than they do. One reason for this large enrollment is the continued emphasis on service brought out by American Express advertisements. In addition to this, the company has built up a superb reputation about its sound financial position. The company often suggests that you keep some of the travellers' checks for future use; if you do, you are contributing to the firm's profits. As long as people do not cash the checks, American Express can use the money tied up in checks. The more you charge with your credit card, the more the company makes in commissions. The famous, the rich, and the jet-setters tell you not to leave home without it. Charles Prost tries very hard to differentiate its service from its rivals.

EXERCISES

1. Define and explain the following:
   a. Imperfect competition.
   b. Monopolistic competition.
   c. Differentiated versus homogeneous oligopoly.
   d. Monopoly.
   e. Concentration.
   f. Monopoly power.
   g. Monopoly index.
   h. Nonprice competition.

2. Suppose the demand for a monopolist's product is perfectly (infinitely) price elastic. Will this firm fulfill all the "desirable" features of a perfectly competitive industry? Explain, using graphs.

3. Some writers distinguish between perfect and imperfect monopolistic competition, in that the first type of industry provides perfect knowledge to all firms, while the second does not. What are the most probable long-run positions of the firms, if
   a. All firms have perfect knowledge?
   b. Some firms have perfect information?
   c. No firm has perfect information?

4. To the best of your knowledge, what type of market structure do the following goods and services industries fall under?
   a. Video recorders.
   b. Scheduled airlines.
   c. State universities.
   d. Professional football teams.
   e. College bookstores.
   f. Microeconomics textbooks.
   g. Professional boxers.
   h. Car-rental companies.
   i. Postal services.
   j. City police.

5. Assume that a monopolist faces the following demand for his product:

$$P = 100 - 2Q$$

If the monopolist's marginal cost of production (MC) is known to be

$$MC = 4 + 4Q$$

calculate the following:
   a. The firm's profit-maximizing quantity and price.
   b. The total economic profits to the firm, if total fixed costs equal $50.

(Hint: The demand function is linear, as is the marginal cost function. Under conditions of linearity, the absolute value of the marginal is twice that of the absolute value of the average.)

6. Draw a suitable diagram of an oligopolist's demand and cost curves under assumptions of the "reverse kink." What pricing strategy do you suppose the firm will follow under the circumstances?

7. Is monopoly bad? Explain.

8. Provide local examples of industries that fall under the various types of market structure.

9. Why do some professionals receive substantially higher pay than their colleagues?

10. Why doesn't a large company such as General Motors attempt to capture 100% of the automobile market?

11. What type of market organization does the automobile industry in the United States, inclusive of all foreign makes, fall under?

12. How would the restriction of foreign trade (such as through tariffs and quotas) affect domestic competition and prices?

13. Compute the break-even volume(s) and price(s) for the firm described in Exercise 5.

14. Assume that an oligopoly is made up of only two firms—that is, the industry is a duopoly. If each firm has identical initial demand, but different marginal costs, will they tend to charge different profit-maximizing prices? Explain.

15. Suppose everything remains the same as described in Exercise 14, with the exception that the firm with the lower marginal cost has the higher average total cost. Which firm will tend to have the greater power to set industry prices? What, do you suppose, will happen eventually? Use diagrams.

SUGGESTED READINGS

Aduddell, R. "Remarks on Elasticity, Product Differentiation, and Market Structure." *Rivista Internazionale de Scienze Economiche e Commerciali,* June 1978.

Baumol, W. "Cost-Minimizing Number of Firms and Determination of Industry Structure. " *Quarterly Journal of Economics,* August 1978.

Bonham, J. "An Empirical Analysis of Industrial Concentration in the Electronic Data Processing Industry, 1952–1970." *Antitrust Bulletin,* Summer 1978.

Caves, R. "Market Structure, Oligopoly and Stability of Market Shares." *Journal of Industrial Economics,* June 1978.

Leffler, K. B. "Physician Licensure: Competition and Monopoly in American Medicine." *Journal of Law and Economics,* April 1978.

Marfels, C. "The Structure of the Military–Industrial Complex in the United States and Its Impact on Industrial Concentration." *Kyklos,* 1978.

Stevens, B. "Scale, Market Structure and the Cost of Refuse Collection." *Review of Economics and Statistics,* August 1978.

Chapter
Thirteen Chapter
Thirteen Chapter
Thirteen

PRICING TOPICS

Perfectly competitive firms usually have no appreciable influence over price, whereas the firms under imperfect competition are able to select the prices most consistent with their goals, at least most of the time. Consequently, monopolistic and oligopolistic firms generally possess a greater degree of market power and price-setting ability than their counterparts operating under conditions of perfect competition. We will now examine some additional pricing policies of price-making, or price-searching, firms.

PRICE DISCRIMINATION

Imperfectly competitive firms tend to set price according to the MR = MC rule. Thus, a profit-maximizing monopolist will sell a volume of output which permits the equality of marginal revenue and marginal cost, and all consumers will pay that price which corresponds to this output. However, in some instances, not all consumers pay the same price for a product. *Price discrimination* occurs when either individuals or groups are charged different prices for the same product, and there is good reason to believe that a firm's profits are greater with price discrimination than without it.

First-Degree Price Discrimination

A firm is said to be engaging in *first-degree* or *perfect* price discrimination if it charges a different (unique) price to each customer. For example, if a car dealer can extract a different price from each buyer, but all buyers receive the same automobile, the dealer will have succeeded in discriminating among the buyers. In spite of the "sticker price" displayed on a new car, car buyers almost always bargain with the seller in order to reduce the actual sales price. Consequently, the ultimate price of the product is decided by the relative bargaining strengths of the buyer and seller. It follows that such price discrimination is possible if the seller can segregate the buyers from each other, and provided such discrimination is not considered illegal, price discrimination can very easily occur in the open.

What advantages are there to such price discrimination? For one thing, it permits the firm to earn more profits than possible under a single price system. Consider a surgeon, for example, who can conceivably charge different fees to his patients even though he or she performs identical operations on them. In medicine, and especially surgery, it is very difficult to bring price discrimination charges against doctors, since they can very easily defend themselves by claiming that not all operations are alike. If you were the patient, you probably would not ask your surgeon to provide services not to exceed $300, since your neighbor paid that price for a similar operation. If you pay $500 for your operation, the total revenue from you and your neighbor will be $800. On the other hand, if the surgeon charges $300 per person, he will obtain only $600 for the two patients. Because you needed the surgery, and were willing to pay the $500, the surgeon was able to charge you the higher price.

In Figure 13-1, the demand for a firm's product is shown as *D*. If the firm wishes to maximize profits by charging a single price to all buyers, it will

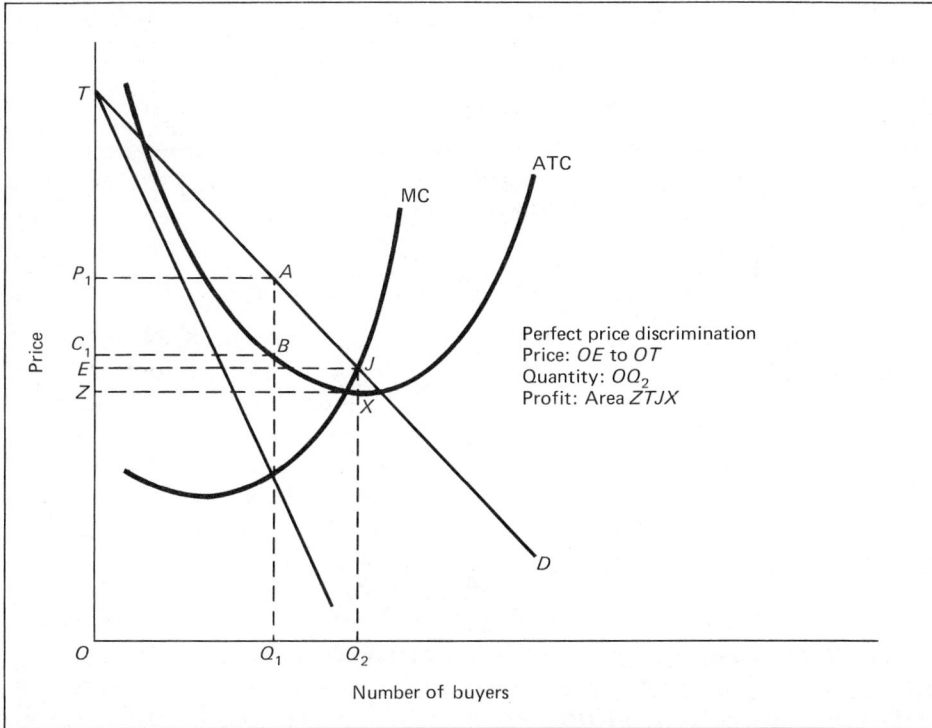

FIGURE 13-1
The profit-maximizing firm has a choice of many prices as long as these prices lie on the demand curve. Where MR = MC, the firm maximizes its profits if it charges the same price to everyone. At price P_1, the quantity demanded is Q_1 and the profit to the firm is given by area P_1ABC_1. However, the firm will make more profit by charging different prices to its customers. As long as a customer is willing to pay a price above the marginal cost of the good, the firm will make a profit. Under perfect discrimination, price effectively becomes the marginal revenue to the firm. The firm will continue to sell at successively lower prices along its demand curve (marginal revenue, in effect) until marginal cost equals price. The highest price, under the circumstances, will be OT and the lowest OE. The total revenue to the firm will be the area under the demand curve, to quantity Q_2, or area $OTJQ_2$. The total cost is the product of the average total cost and the quantity, or area $OEJQ_2$, and total profits to the firm are given by area $ZTJX$. Output, as well as profits to the firm, will be greater with first-degree discrimination.

charge price P_1 and sell Q_1 units, and the profit will be shown by area P_1ABC_1. Now suppose the firm decides to employ a discriminatory pricing system. Any price along the demand curve is available to the firm. If the firm can isolate those buyers who are willing to pay high prices from those who will buy only at lower prices, it can extract different prices from different customers for the same product. Because each buyer pays a unique price, the price, in effect, constitutes the firm's marginal revenue and the demand curve now becomes the firm's marginal revenue function. The discriminating firm that wishes to maximize profits will sell the product as long as the price paid by the buyer is at least as high as the marginal cost. For example, if the 100th patient's marginal cost to the surgeon is $356, and the surgeon is a profit maximizer, he will

TABLE 13-1

(1) Price	(2) Quantity	(3) Revenue	(4) Marginal revenue	(5) Marginal cost	(6) Revenue with discrimination	(7) Marginal revenue with discrimination
$10	1	$10	$10	$16	$10	$10
9	2	18	8	8	19	9
8	3	24	6	5	27	8
7	4	28	4	3.75	34	7
6	5	30	2	3.80	40	6
5	6	30	0	3.90	45	5
4	7	28	−2	4.00	49	4
3	8	24	−4	6.00	52	3

consent to operate if the patient is willing to pay at least $356. In Figure 13-1, we see that the profit-maximizing firm will produce Q_2 units of output, and price will vary from *OE* to *OT*.

Suppose the demand for a product is as shown by the first two columns of Table 13-1. The firm can sell 1 unit at $10 and 2 at $9. It follows that the person who is willing to pay the $10 price should also be willing to pay $9. Thus, if two people will buy the product at a price of $9, but only one will buy if the price is $10, the firm can charge $10 to one customer and $9 to the other. In so doing, the total revenue from the two customers will be $19, whereas if both pay a price of $9, the total revenue will be only $18. By using a discriminatory-pricing policy the firm can obtain more revenues, and therefore more profits. Because each customer pays a unique price, the total revenue to the firm is the sum of these individual prices, and each new price constitutes the marginal revenue to the firm. The firm then uses this marginal revenue function, which in effect is the demand curve, and the marginal cost information to arrive at the profit-maximizing level of output. In Table 13-1, columns (1) and (2) contain demand information, while (3) is the total revenue if the firm charges the same price to all buyers. Column (4) is the marginal revenue derived from (3), and (5) shows the values for the marginal cost of output. Under the single price scheme, the firm will maximize profits by producing approximately 4 units of output at a cost of $7 to each buyer, because the marginal revenue almost equals the marginal cost at this output volume.

As you can see from column (6), the total revenues obtained by charging different prices for the units are higher than those obtained under the single-price scheme. Column (7) is the marginal revenue from perfect price discrimination and, in essence, shows the demand prices paid by the many different consumers. Under these circumstances, the firm maximizes profit by equating marginal cost to price and, in this particular case, profits will be maximum at 7 units of output, because the marginal revenue (price) of the seventh unit is just equal to its marginal cost ($4). Revenue with discrimination is $49. If the firm had sold all 7 units at the same price, total revenues would have been only $28. Discrimination or no discrimination, the cost of producing the 7 units is the same, and therefore more revenues mean more profits.

In addition to making more profits, the discriminating monopolist presumably provides a service to society. Whereas only Q_1 buyers (in Figure 13-1) will have been served without price discrimination, a larger number (Q_2) will now have access to the product. The price will range from OT down to OE. Furthermore, since the customers are actually willing to pay the higher prices, it is not exactly immoral to charge them. In effect, price discrimination causes some buyers to subsidize the price to the others. Since the firm also makes more profits, we can hope that it will use part of the proceeds to fulfill its corporate social responsibility more thoroughly.

Second-Degree Price Discrimination

Another form of price discrimination is a diluted version of perfect price discrimination. Under second-degree price discrimination, or quantity-discount pricing, the firm charges successively lower prices for each additional range of output purchased. Thus a firm offering a price of $1 a unit for the first 100 units and 90¢ a unit for the following 100 units is, in effect, practicing second-degree price discrimination. Utility companies often use such pricing,

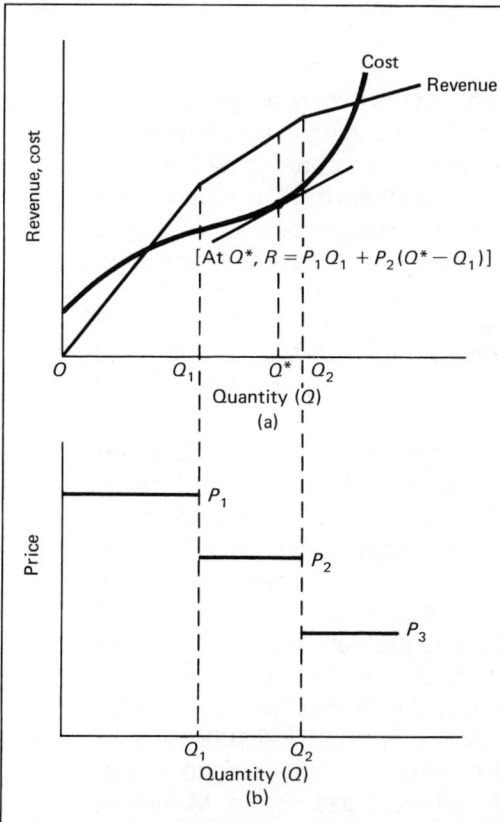

FIGURE 13-2
Second-degree price discrimination involves charging different prices over different incremental ranges of output. In this case, the firm's prices are shown by the segments labelled P_1, P_2, and P_3 [diagram (b)]. Only after purchasing the first Q_1 units will the consumer be able to obtain the subsequent units up to Q_2 at a lower price P_2. Since price varies over ranges of output, the total revenue curve has different slopes over the entire range of output [diagram (a)]. The most profitable volume of output is at quantity Q^*. Utility companies often practice second-degree discrimination and such discrimination favors buyers or users of large quantities and penalizes those that use less.

as do many retail outlets. Consider the following price schedule:

1 for $1.00
2 for $1.98
3 for $2.94

If a consumer buys only one unit, he or she will pay $1.00, whereas the person wanting two units will pay an *incremental* price of only 98¢ for the second unit, and the *average* price of the two units will be 99¢. Figure 13-2 illustrates the prices in effect under such a scheme. Diagram (b) shows the applicable prices for the different ranges of output. The price is P_1 for from 1 to Q_1 units; P_2 for units above Q_1 up to and including Q_2 units; and P_3 for quantities in excess of Q_2. The total revenue (R) function is shown in diagram (a). Its slope declines as price declines, because the slope of the R shows the marginal revenue to the firm. The average price at a given volume of output is shown by the angle subtended by a line drawn from the origin to the R function.

A profit-maximizing firm produces and sells that volume of output where the marginal cost and marginal revenue are equal. Thus, at output level Q^*, where the slopes of the revenue and cost functions are equal, the total profits to the firm are also greatest. Most regulated utilities are permitted to use this type of pricing schedule because it enables them to collect adequate revenues to cover all their costs and provide service to all customers at reasonable charges.

Third-Degree Price Discrimination

Yet another type of price discrimination occurs when a firm charges varying prices to different groups of customers. Such pricing is also referred to as multiple-market price discrimination. Thus, when Hertz charges $20 per day to business users of rental cars and $26 per day to other users, it is practicing *third-degree price discrimination.* Markets may be categorized according to age, race, income, time, or other common group characteristics. In essence, third-degree discrimination involves charging different prices in different markets. Commercial banks charge different rates to different groups of borrowers, who are presumably graded according to risk. Whatever the real reason, discriminatory pricing offers more profits to a firm if it has several different types of markets.

In Figure 13-3, the firm has two markets—market 1 and market 2. Each market has its own demand and the total demand for this firm's products is obtained by the horizontal summation of demands D_1 and D_2. This is shown in diagram (c). Similarly, we can also derive the total marginal revenue to the firm, shown as $MR_1 + MR_2$. The firm's total profit from both markets will be maximized where its marginal cost equals its aggregate marginal revenue, and this occurs at an output volume of 1000 units. The problem now is to allocate the 1000 units between the two markets so that total profits are maximized.

Once the firm elects to sell the 1000 units, the production cost will be determined. In order to maximize profits, the firm should sell the 1000 units to obtain maximum total (combined) revenue. Maximum revenue from the sale of a given output (and hence for a given cost) will maximize profits. Maximum

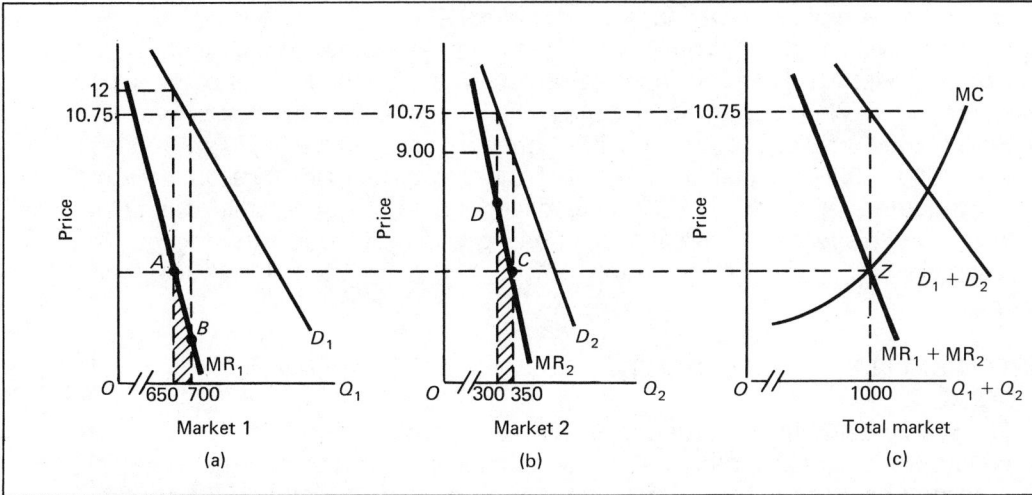

FIGURE 13-3
If a firm has many markets, it can either charge the same price in all of them or elect to charge different prices. The act of charging different prices is called third-degree price discrimination. The firm's total profits from all markets are maximized at the quantity where its aggregate marginal revenue equals its marginal cost. This total quantity is then allocated between the two markets such that the maximum combined total revenue is obtained from its sale. Since the cost of a given volume of output is predetermined, maximizing revenue is tantamount to maximizing profit. Using the equimarginal principle, the firm allocates the total output between the two markets until $MR_1 = MR_2$. This brings about the sale of 650 units in market 1 and 350 in market 2, where the prices have to be $12 and $9 respectively. Revenue to the firm is $10,950. The firm can also sell the 1000 units by charging $10.75 per unit in each market, but the profits will be less since the revenues will be only $10,750. The price ratio of P_1 to P_2 is determined by the value of the price elasticity of demand in each market. In general, the market with the higher price elasticity will have the lower price.

revenues can be earned by selling the 1000 units so that MR_1 equals MR_2. By selling 650 units in market 1 and 350 units in market 2, the two marginal revenues can be equated. The points of equal marginal revenue are determined by moving horizontally from point Z [diagram (c)] to the intersection of the individual marginal revenue lines at points C and A in markets 2 and 1, respectively. The price for the 650 units in market 1 is $12, and that in the second market for the 350 units is $9. Total revenues to the firm equal $10,950. This is a form of price discrimination, since the prices in the two markets are not equal. A supermarket does not have to charge the same prices in its stores on the east and the west sides of town. Would the firm have profited more by charging identical prices in both markets?

From Figure 13-3, we can see that the entire 1000 units can also be sold at a single price of $10.75 in both markets. If each market charges $10.75, market 1 will sell 700 units, while market 2 will sell 300 units. Even though the total quantity sold is still 1000, the marginal revenue from each market will not be equal. Market 1's marginal revenue will drop from point A to point B, and the marginal revenue of the second market will rise from C to point D. By selling 50 more units in the first market (and therefore selling 50 fewer in market 2), the firm will receive less additional revenue for the 50 units than it would have by selling them in market 2. The shaded area under section *AB* will be the gain in total revenue, while the shaded area under *CD* will be the loss, and since the second area is larger than the first, the firm will incur net losses in total revenue. Selling 1000 units at $10.75 per unit will bring revenues of $10,750, and such a sum will be $200 less than the amount obtainable under discriminatory pricing. Third-degree price discrimination is based on the *equimarginal principle*, which was discussed in the sections dealing with utility, cost, and revenue in Chapters 3, 5, and 8.

Discrimination and Price Elasticity of Demand

We just saw how a firm can maximize its profits by selling its output at different prices in different markets. To do so, the firm equates the marginal revenue from each market. Since marginal revenue is related to price and the elasticity of demand, we will derive the ratio of the prices in each market as a function of the price elasticity of demand in each market. The price elasticity of demand in absolute terms is (Price)/(Price−marginal revenue), or $e = P/(P-MR)$. If the firm engages in third-degree price discrimination, $MR_1 = MR_2$. Denoting the price elasticities of demand in the two markets as e_1 and e_2, respectively, the marginal revenue can be written as

$$MR = P\frac{e - 1}{e} \tag{1}$$

Since $MR_1 = MR_2$,

$$P_1\frac{e_1 - 1}{e_1} = P_2\frac{e_2 - 1}{e_2} \tag{2}$$

or

$$\frac{P_1}{P_2} = \frac{\dfrac{(e_2 - 1)}{e_2}}{\dfrac{(e_1 - 1)}{e_1}} \tag{3}$$

Equation (3) suggests that the market with the higher price elasticity of demand will have the lower price.

PROFIT MAXIMIZATION WITH MULTIPLE PRODUCTS

Joint Products

Firms often produce more than one product, and sometimes these become complements in the supply sense. For example, in the lumber industry, the extraction of two-by-fours also yields wood pulp, plywood, roofing shingles, and lumber for building homes. Such products are often called "joint" products, and in many cases the costs of producing the many items are thoroughly intertwined and rather inseparable. We can use Figure 13-4 to illustrate the behavior of the profit-maximizing firm that produces two products, beef and hides.

The demands for beef carcasses and hides are shown by lines D_B and D_H, respectively. If the firm wishes to maximize profits, it has to accurately compare its total joint revenues from the sale of beef and hides to their joint costs of production. We cannot add the demand for beef to the demand for hides horizontally as we did when we aggregated the total market demand under third-degree discrimination. After all, what would you get if you added 10 hides to 6 carcasses? In this particular situation of beef and hides, we measure the number of processed cattle (one carcass and one hide for each) along the

FIGURE 13-4
Joint products are essentially the main product and its by-products. In this case, the firm sells beef carcasses and hides, where the first constitute the main product and the second the complementary product. To arrive at the profit-maximizing combination of beef and/or hides, we first add the demands for beef and hides *vertically*. The vertical summation shows the combined price of beef and hide at every alternative level of output. Where the vertically summed marginal revenue equals the joint marginal cost of beef and hides processing, the firm maximizes profits. This quantity occurs at Q_B amount of beef carcasses which equals the number of hides Q_H. Once the quantities of the products are known, the prices are determined from the individual demand functions. The graph shows the price of beef and hides to be P_B and P_H, respectively.

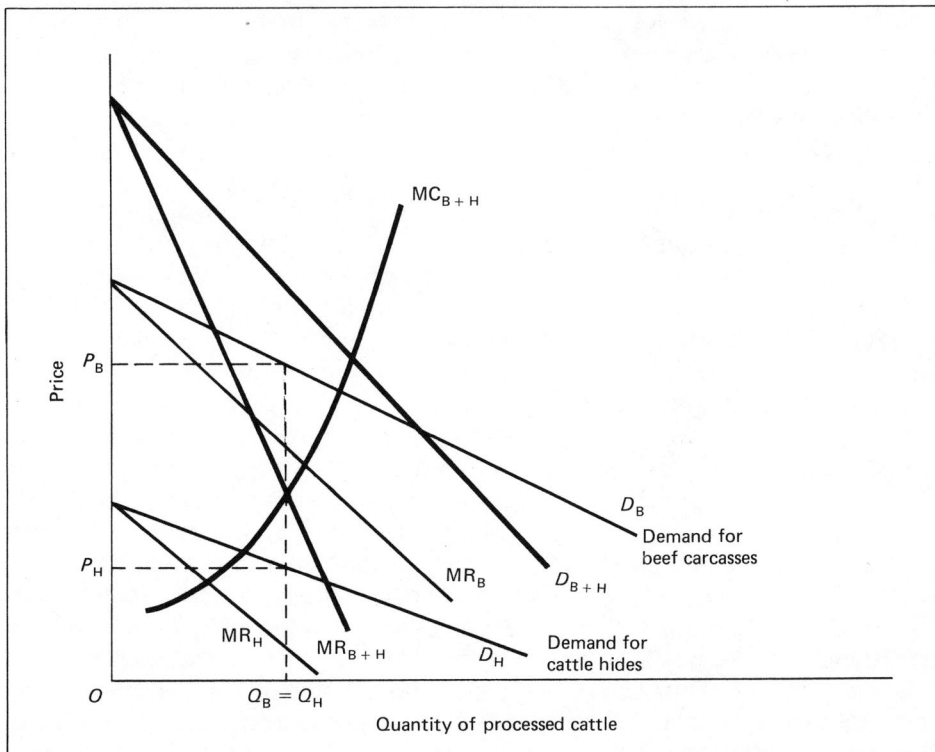

quantity axis. We add the two demands by adding the demand prices at each volume of output of beef carcass and hide. Since the vertical axis measures price and cost in monetary units, we can add the prices without problem. Thus, if the first carcass can be sold at $1000 and the first hide at $300, the combined price of this animal will be $1300. Lowering the price of beef carcass will lead to greater quantities demanded, as will lowering the price of hides. Suppose that four carcasses will be demanded at $900 and the same number of hides will be bought at $250. The combined demand price per animal will then be $1150. Using such price–quantity combinations, we can draw the combined demand curve for beef and hides shown as D_{B+H}. The firm's profits are maximized where its joint marginal cost of producing beef and hides equals its joint marginal revenue from selling them. This occurs at quantity Q_B for beef and Q_H for hides, which are equal. The price for each item is determined from the individual demand curves—P_B for beef carcasses and P_H for hides.

In our discussion of beef and hides, hides are treated as the by-product. In Figure 13-4, at the quantity for profit maximization, the marginal revenue from hides is still positive. In some instances, however, it is quite possible that the marginal revenue from hides will be negative. For example, if the firm decides to slaughter 1000 cattle, it will have 1000 hides. The marginal revenue from the 900th to the 1000th hide can, conceivably, be negative. In such cases, the firm will be better off to simply sell 899 hides, or at least no more than necessary to maximize revenues from the sale of hides. Negative marginal revenue implies less than maximum revenue, hence less than maximum profit. What will be done with the extra hides will depend on the firm's policies. It can choose to store them (provided the benefits from storage exceed the costs of storage), sell them in a faraway market, or simply destroy them.

Competing Products

Firms also produce items which literally compete with each other. For example, a farmer raising a herd of cattle can prepare the animals for beef, veal, or both. However, producing more beef means less veal. Airlines offering more first-class seats have fewer coach-class seats as long as fleet size and the capacity of the aircraft are not altered. In such situations, the firm must produce the right combination of the products in order to maximize its profits.

Figure 13-5 shows a production-possibilities frontier (PP) for a firm with a given amount of resources. The firm produces two competing products, Gogomobiles (G) and Deloreans (D). We are using the word "competing" in the sense that more of one type of vehicle can only be produced at the expense of the other. Similar to the linear programming situation, the object here is to determine the profit-maximizing combination of the two types of cars.

Under assumptions of constant average variable cost (and therefore constant marginal cost), and perfect competition, the contribution per unit is also constant, contribution profit being the difference between price and average variable cost. Suppose that the contribution profit per unit of Gogomobile is R_G and for each unit of Delorean, R_D. The total contribution (C)

FIGURE 13-5
A firm produces two competing products, Gogomobiles and Deloreans. Since the firm's resources are limited, only certain combinations of the two products are feasible and the many available combinations are shown by the production-possibilities curve PXP. The object is to maximize profits by selecting the "best" combination of D and G. Under assumptions of perfect competition and constant average variable cost, the contribution per unit of either D or G is constant. Maximum total contribution revenue will maximize the profits of the firm. The total net revenue (contribution) function R is the sum of the total contributions from the sales of D and/or G, or $C = R_G G + R_D D$. This isorevenue function is shown as a straight line because the ratio of contributions is constant. Any point along the revenue line represents a specific amount of revenue and the farther out the point is on the revenue line, the greater amount of revenue and hence profit. The maximum revenue will occur with the combination suggested by point X, because no other revenue line representing a greater amount of revenues can be drawn without violating the constraint imposed by the production possibilities curve. At point X, the slope of the revenue line equals the slope of the production boundary, and the ratio of individual contribution is equal to the marginal rate of transformation.

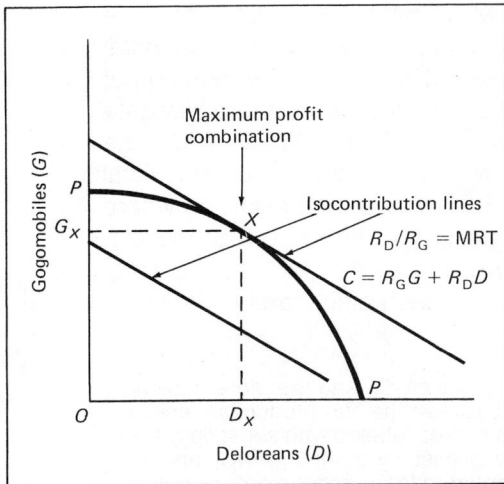

will then be $C = R_G G + R_D D$. The firm earns maximum profit where the value of C is maximized and the production boundary is not violated. Such a point generally occurs where the linear contribution line is tangent to the production-possibilities boundary, for example, at point X. In economic terms, point X is where the ratio of contributions equals the ratio of production tradeoff between G and D, $\Delta G/\Delta D = R_D/R_G = $ MRT, where MRT stands for the marginal rate of transformation (or substitution) of D for G. Thus, profits are maximum at point X, and the firm should produce G_X Gogomobiles and D_X Deloreans.

PROFIT MAXIMIZATION AND COST CONSIDERATIONS

Profit Maximization and Multiple Plants

The discussion about third-degree discrimination involved differential pricing in multiple markets. In this section, we will analyze the profit-maximizing implications of multiple plants. If a firm has several plants for producing output, it should attempt to use them in a cost-efficient manner. Since fixed costs to the firm are unavoidable in the short run, costs of production will be minimized through the minimization of total variable costs. The firm should use the plants in that proportion which minimizes the total variable cost arising from their use. In the discussion of costs in Chapter 9, we saw that the firm can minimize the cost of producing a given quantity by allocating output among the many plants according to the equimarginal principle. In other words, the total variable cost will be at a minimum if the output is distributed so that the marginal costs of the plants involved are equal.

Figure 13-6c shows a firm under imperfect competition with demand D and marginal revenue MR. The firm has two plants whose individual cost curves are shown as ATC_1, MC_1 and ATC_2, MC_2 [diagrams (a) and (b)]. The total cost–output relationship with multiple plants is shown by the *horizontal summation* of the marginal cost curves, labeled $MC_1 + MC_2$. The total output necessary for profit maximization occurs at a quantity where the aggregate marginal cost equals the marginal revenue function, or quantity $Q_1 + Q_2$. The firm is required to charge price P in order to sell this output volume. Total revenue to the firm will equal $P(Q_1 + Q_2)$, and profits will be maximized where this quantity can be produced for the least cost. In order to do this, the firm allocates the total quantity between the two plants so that MC_1 equals MC_2. Once Q_1 and Q_2 are determined, the total cost in each plant can be shown by

FIGURE 13-6
A monopolist that maintains two plants can minimize its costs, and therefore maximize profits by appropriately allocating the total output between the two production facilities. Each plant has its own cost structure shown by the curves labeled with subscripts 1 and 2. The firm first determines its aggregate marginal cost by summing MC_1 and MC_2 horizontally. This aggregate marginal cost is then equated to the firm's marginal revenue MR, which yields the profit maximizing quantity $Q_1 + Q_2$ and the corresponding price P. Revenues to the firm then become $P(Q_1 + Q_2)$. To maximize profits, the firm must produce the total quantity at the least cost, since minimizing cost subject to the given revenue will maximize profits. Costs are minimized according to the equimarginal principle, which requires that the marginal cost of plant 1 equals the marginal cost of plant 2. The firm allocates the total quantity so that $MC_1 = MC_2$. The total cost of producing quantity Q_1 in the first plant is shown by area $OABQ_1$ and that in plant 2 by area $OCDQ_2$. The joint total cost to the firm is the sum of the two areas.

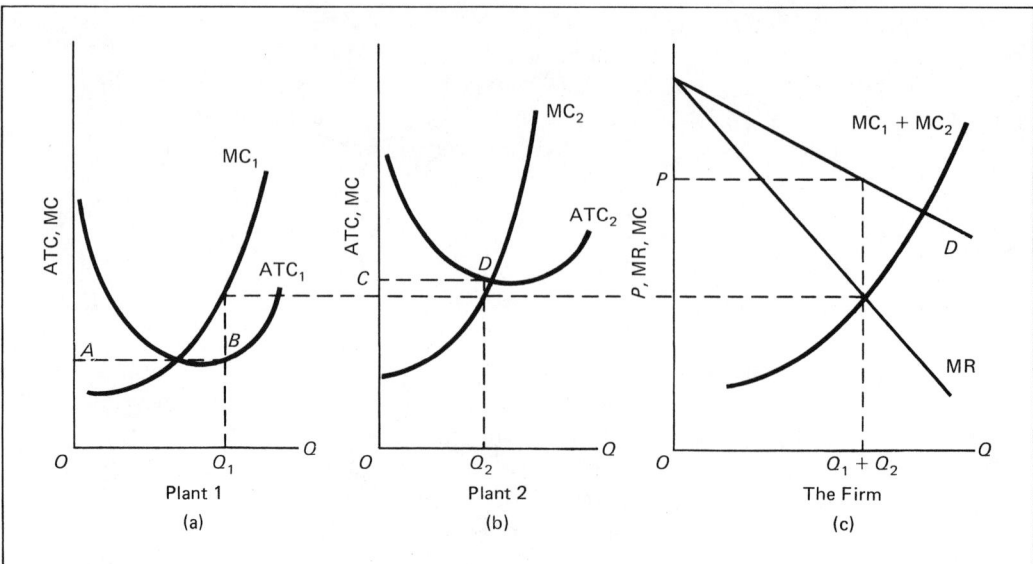

Plant 1
(a)

Plant 2
(b)

The Firm
(c)

the area obtained by multiplying quantity and average total cost. The total cost of producing Q_1 in plant 1 is given by the area ABQ_1O and that of quantity Q_2 in plant 2 by area $OCDQ_2$.

Profit Maximization and Transportation Cost

We have purposely avoided the question of transportation cost until now. The cost of transportation can have a significant impact on the firm's territory and its pricing policies. For this discussion we have chosen a monopoly with multiple markets but a single plant. Assume that the firm wishes to maximize profits as under the model of third-degree price discrimination and that it must pay a transportation cost of t per unit transported from the plant to market 2. Market 1 is located very near the plant, and therefore no transportation cost is associated with it.

Figure 13-7 shows the necessary changes required in the model. Since the firm pays a transportation cost of t per unit shipped to market 2, its *net*

FIGURE 13-7
The firm practicing third-degree discrimination may have to adjust its price and quantity due to the transportation cost incurred in supplying goods to the distant market. Here we see that the firm has two markets, one of which (market 2) is distant and requires a transportation cost of t per unit sold in that market. The home market, market 1, does not incur any transportation cost. To allow for the cost of transportation, the firm subtracts t from MR_2 to arrive at the *net marginal revenue* ($MR_2 - t$). The two marginal revenue curves are summed horizontally and equated to the firm's marginal cost. The profit maximization quantity occurs where ($MR_1 + MR_2 - t$) = MC. This quantity is then allocated between the two markets such that $MR_1 = (MR_2 - t)$, and the prices in the two markets are shown as P_1 and P_2. Total production cost to the firm is shown by area $OABQ_T$ and cost of transportation by area $EFGH$. Total revenue to the firm is the sum of areas OP_2ZQ_2 and OP_1NQ_1.

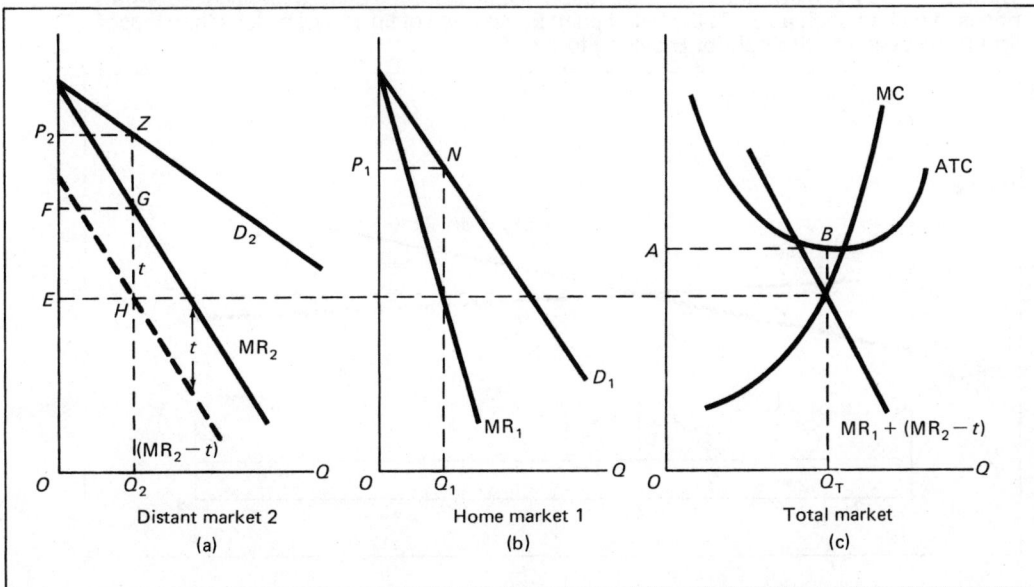

Distant market 2   Home market 1   Total market
     (a)   (b)   (c)

marginal revenue can be determined by subtracting $\$t$ from MR_2. This net marginal revenue (MR_2-t) is then added to MR_1 to arrive at the total market's marginal revenue, which is then equated to the marginal cost of the firm to arrive at the total profit-maximizing level of output. After that, the total is allocated between the markets as before, and $MR_1 = (MR_2-t)$. Prices are determined by the quantities sold in each market. The total cost to the firm is the sum of the production and transportation costs, which, in this case, happens to be $\$(tQ_2)$. Using this model, we can understand how high transportation costs can very easily keep the firm from supplying distant markets.

Transportation Cost and the Extent of Market

Several early models of the firm have used the cost of transportation to explain the prices prevailing in many markets as well as to define the potential limits for a firm's competitive ability. In Figure 13-8, we show two firms, 1 and 2, located at points A and B. If the transportation cost is $\$a$ per unit for firm 1 and $\$b$ per unit for firm 2, the supply price of the products produced by the two firms will be $(P_1 + ad_1)$ and $(P_2 + bd_2)$, where d is the distance of the market from the plant, and the P's represent the prices at the plant locations. Both

FIGURE 13-8
If two firms are located at sufficient distances from each other as well as from the market, the prices charged by them will be affected by the distance as well as the transportation cost per unit of output. Firm 1 is located at A, where the price is P_A, and it pays $\$a$ for transporting each unit of output. Similarly, the other firm pays a transportation cost of $\$b$ per unit. The distance for firm 1 from point A is shown as d_1 and that for plant 2 from point B is indicated by distance d_2. The delivered price at any point away from the home base is the price at the plant plus the price of transportation. Thus the delivered prices for firms 1 and 2 will be $P_A + ad_1$ and $P_B + bd_2$, respectively. Both will charge identical delivered prices at a point such as E. To the left of point E, the price of firm 1 will be less than that of firm 2. All points to the right of E belong to firm 2.

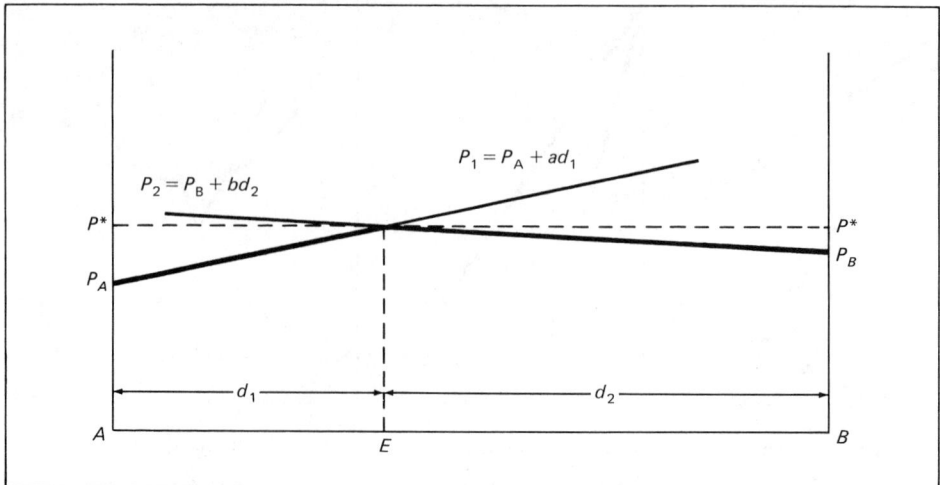

firms will charge identical prices for their product if the distance from the plant to the market is appropriately short or long enough to make the sum of price and transportation cost equal for each firm. This occurs where the delivered price line for firm 1 equals that of firm 2, or where $(P_1 + ad_1) = (P_2 + bd_2)$. We have assumed that transportation cost varies linearly with distance, which may not be so in all cases. There are more elaborate models dealing with the economic theory of location which make use of nonlinear models, and with their help we can establish the economically competitive sales territory of firms whose market areas may be elliptical, circular, or rectangular. Volkswagen decided to locate one of its plants in the United States partly because of lower transportation costs and largely due to favorable labor, material, and import-duty costs.

OLIGOPOLY BEHAVIOR MODELS

The Cartel

It seems as though the firms manufacturing important products around the world belong to *cartels*. Cartels are formed by producers who enter into certain collusive agreements for their mutual benefit. United States laws consider cartels operating in the country as illegal, but presumably many domestic producers get around the illegality by avoiding formal collusions and resorting to "gentlemen's agreements." Cartel activities can include price fixing, market sharing, and, in general, agreements for the benefit of the cartel. The rule among the cartel members is to agree to avoid competition between the members. The Three Musketeers' motto—one for all and all for one—seems appropriate also for the cartel.

Suppose there are two oligopolists who wish to form a cartel. Their objective is to charge the same price and maximize the total profits of the cartel. Once a cartel has been formed, we can think of it as a monopoly having multiple plants. The firm (cartel) charges the profit-maximizing price and produces the correct quantity in each plant, the plant being the cartel member. Prior to the formation of the cartel, each oligopolist was competing against the other and charging a price consistent with profit maximization. In Figure 13-9, the two cartel members were initially charging prices P_1 and P_2, and each firm sold the appropriate quantity for individual profit maximization. When a cartel is formed, both firms add their demands to arrive at the total market demand. The total cost of production to the cartel is found by summing the marginal cost curves of the two firms horizontally. The quantity that maximizes cartel profit is given by the intersection of the total marginal revenue and total marginal cost functions. This total quantity $(Q_{C-1} + Q_{C-2})$ can be sold for price P_C, and each cartel member charges this price to its customers. To maximize profits, a multiplant monopolist allocates the total output according to marginal cost so that MC_1 will equal MC_2. Cartel member 1 produces Q_{C-1} units at an average cost of C_1, and member 2 produces Q_{C-2} units at an average cost of C_2. Before the cartel came into effect, member 1 was producing fewer units and charging a lower price than the cartel price P_C and was just breaking even.

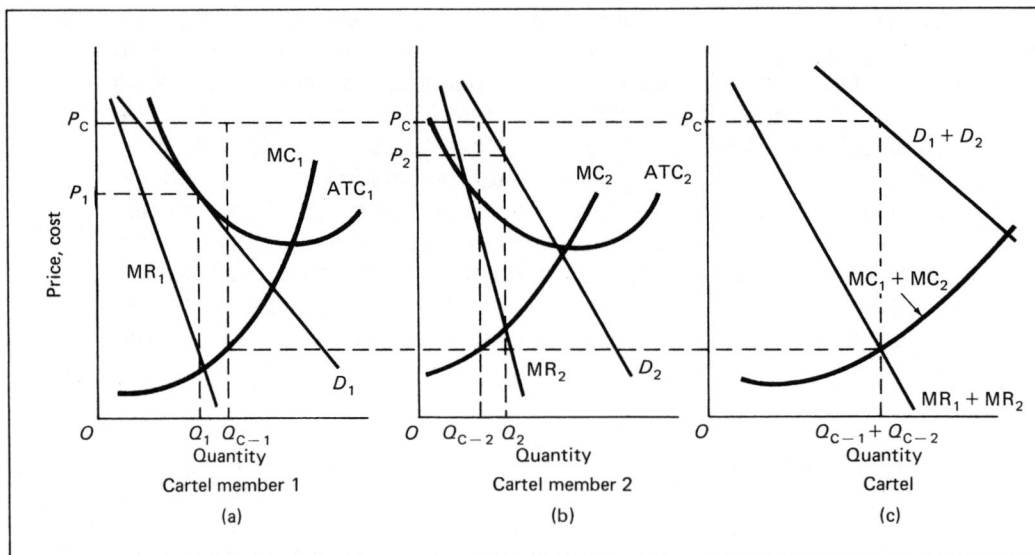

FIGURE 13-9
A cartel is a formal union among producers, particularly oligopolists, who band together to determine the best price for maximizing joint profits for the industry. Such collusion not only restricts the total industry output, but also results in higher prices to the consumer and more profits for the cartel members. In effect, the cartel operates like a monopoly with multiple plants, where each firm within the cartel becomes a plant for the monopoly (cartel). Initially, each firm was maximizing its own profits and charging the price where its marginal cost equalled its marginal revenue. Firm 1 charged P_1 and firm 2, P_2. From the diagram we can see that 1 was breaking even while 2 was earning profits. After the formation of the cartel, the total demand, total marginal revenue, and total marginal cost are used to determine the optimal cartel price, P_C. Each cartel member produces the amount dictated by marginal cost considerations. Firm 1 produces quantity Q_{C-1} and firm 2, quantity Q_{C-2}, and all charge price P_C. At this new price, both members are earning profits. Occasionally, the firms share the profits according to some prearranged formula.

Now it will earn economic profits. Member 2's output decreased after the formation of the cartel, and profits appear to be somewhat less than what they were. Firm 1 might share part of the excess profits with firm 2 in order to persuade the latter to stay in the cartel. For example, if firm 1 made $100 more profits and firm 2 $40 less, firm 1 might give $70 to firm 2 so that both would be $30 ahead.

Governments are usually concerned about cartels, and occasionally something happens which breaks them up. Thus, Iran, prior to the deposition of the Shah, threatened to shake up the OPEC (Organization of Petroleum Exporting Countries) oil cartel by not raising oil prices as much as other cartel members, and Alitalia did break the IATA (International Air Transport Association) cartel by lowering its fares, just as action by Laker Airways ruined the organization. In most cartels, there is a strong temptation to "chisel" or sell more than one's fair share. Once the cartel price is established, it is to the advantage of the individual firm to expand production up to the quantity where the cartel price equals the marginal cost. If all the firms start doing this, however, the cartel breaks down due to an overabundance of supply. The cartel's profitability depends, in part, on the artificial restriction of supply. Some people envision a world of global cartels some day, and it may not be surprising to read about beef, coffee, nuclear fuel, wheat, and weapons cartels in the future.

The Dominant Firm Model

Price fixing is illegal in the United States. However, we may surmise by observing price behavior that some sort of collusive agreement is probably in effect among the producers. Even if the agreement is not formal, there are some firms that are recognized as being the "leader," and they exert considerable influence on the prices in the industries. One such model of leadership has a large firm within the industry as the "dominant" firm, which presumably has enough market power to dictate the general level of prices to the other producers. Dominance comes from being large. For example, General Motors is most likely the dominant firm in the passenger car industry, and IBM in the computer industry. Supposedly, the leader sets the general level of prices in keeping with its own profit goals, and the others sell any quantity they wish at the industry price. This is not to suggest that all producers in the industry charge the same price, but rather in the general vicinity of that price. Thus, when General Motors charges $5600 for its Pontiac Sunbird, Ford will probably charge around $5300 for its Mustang.

Figure 13-10 shows the market demand for a particular type of car such as a compact. Since the dominant firm will set the price and then allow the others to sell all they can at this price, the amount still demanded by the market but not supplied by the smaller firms will be sold by the large firm. To work this model, we derive the "residual demand" for the dominant firm's products. If the dominant firm sets the price as high as P_H, the smaller firms will be able to supply the entire Q_H units demanded in the market and consequently there will be fewer sales for the dominant firm. On the other hand, if the large firm sets the price at P_L or lower, the other firms will not be able to supply even a single unit, leaving the entire market to the dominant firm. Both the dominant firm and the smaller firms will be able to sell some units if the industry price is set somewhere between price P_H and price P_L. The dominant firm's quantity demanded is found by subtracting the quantity supplied by the smaller firms from the total market demand at each alternative price level. As we have already seen, such demand will be zero at P_H and equal to market demand at P_L, and therefore the heavy line connecting P_H to point T forms the so-called demand for the dominant firm's products.

Once we have a demand curve for the large firm, we can also establish the position of the marginal revenue curve. Profits are maximized where the firm's marginal revenue equals its marginal cost. This quantity is Q_D, and in order to sell this output the firm charges a price of P, as do all the other firms. At a price of P per unit, the total quantity demanded in the industry equals OQ_T, of which the dominant firm sells quantity OQ_D. The difference, or quantity Q_DQ_T, (which equals quantity OQ_S) is supplied by the other firms.

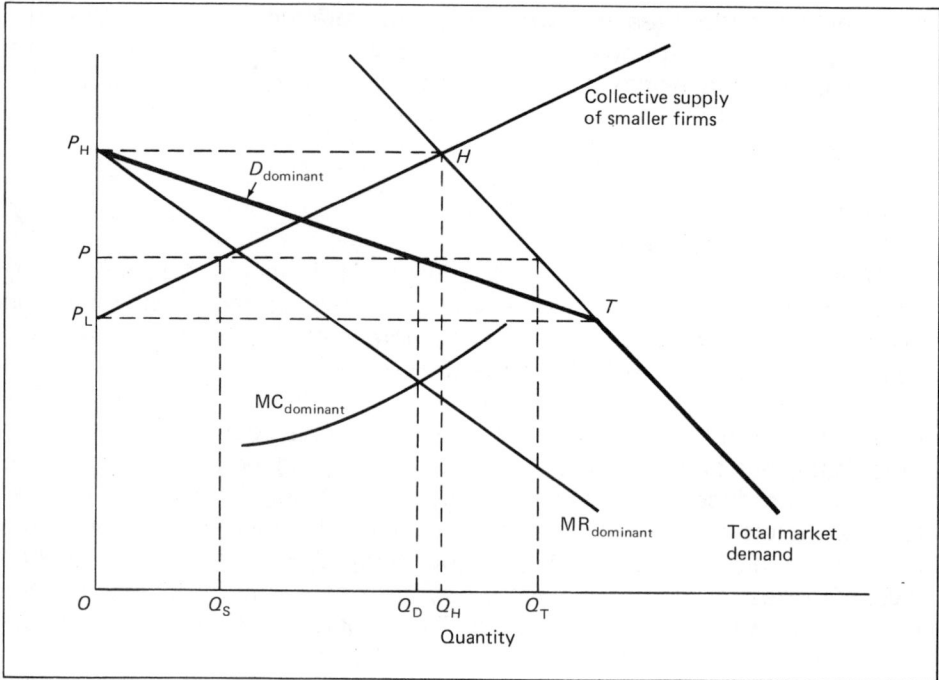

FIGURE 13-10

In the dominant-firm model of oligopoly pricing, the large firm selects the best price according to its needs and allows the smaller firms to sell all they wish at this price. Effectively, the smaller firms become pricetakers. The larger firm's residual demand is found by subtracting the quantity supplied by the small firms from the total market demand at each price. At price P_H, the total supply of the small firms equals the total demand, and therefore there is no demand for the dominant firm's products at this price. At a price P_L, small firms cannot afford to sell and the entire market belongs to the large firm. The heavy line labeled $P_H T$ forms the demand for the dominant firm. The large firm maximizes its profits by equating its marginal cost with its marginal revenue and produces quantity Q_D and charges price P. All firms charge prices in the general vicinity of P. At this price, the total market demand equals Q_T, the small firms supply is OQ_S ($= OQ_T - OQ_D$) and the dominant firm sells OQ_D units.

Another Price Leadership Model

The power to set prices for an industry can come from being large, efficient, or popular with certain groups. Frequently, oligopolists are able to become price leaders by virtue of their low costs of operation, specifically low marginal costs. To prove the point, let us consider the two oligopolists illustrated in Figure 13-11. For the sake of argument, let us assume that both firms can expect to have the same demand, hence $D_1 = D_2$ and $MR_1 = MR_2$. Since each firm is expected to maximize profits, the quantities offered by them occur at a level where the marginal cost equals the marginal revenue. Firm 1 has the higher marginal cost (MC_1), and its profit-maximizing price and quantity are P_1 and Q_1, respectively. Firm 2 tends to charge a lower price and sells a greater quantity. If both firms offer almost identical products, it is conceivable that firm 1 will be forced to lower its price to P_2 so as not to lose all business to firm 2. For example, if there are two gasoline stations located on opposite sides of the same highway, it is reasonable to assume that each will

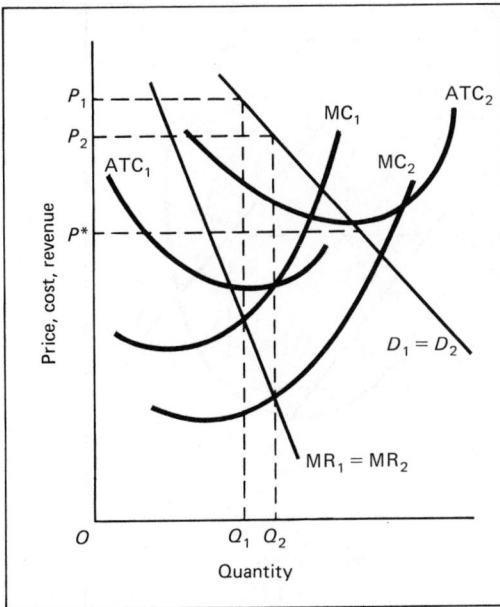

FIGURE 13-11
Some firms may become price leaders by virtue of higher efficiency, especially by having lower marginal costs of production. In the situation here we have two oligopolists, each having identical potential demand. Firm 1 has a lower ATC but higher MC than firm 2. Since firm 2 has the lower marginal cost, it will tend to charge price P_2, where firm 1 will charge P_1 for maximum profits. If both firms sell very similar products, such as two brands of regular gasoline, firm 1 must lower its prices to P_2 in order to compete. This action, in effect, makes firm 2 the price leader. However, since firm 1 has the lower average total cost, it could conceivably lower its prices to P^* and drive firm 2 out of business. Such pricing tactics are in keeping with the entry-limit model.

receive one half of the motorists. If the drivers notice that firm 1 charges 62¢ per gallon for regular, while firm 2 charges 60¢ per gallon, it is unlikely that firm 1 will attract many customers. In such a case, firm 2 *may* become a price leader by virtue of its lower marginal cost. However, it is possible for the high cost (marginal cost) firm to maintain the price differential by resorting to nonprice competition. For example, firm 1 could give away Green Stamps or glass tumblers. Occasionally, the name of the brand also helps maintain customer loyalty. There is a possibility that firm 1 can exert substantial pressure on firm 2 by setting prices as low as price P^*, a price level which is well below firm 2's average total cost. This type of entry-limit pricing can force firm 2 out of business or propagate a price war.

SOME SPECIAL MODELS

The Loss-Leader Model

This model is used to explain the pricing strategies of a firm that produces or sells several products. It deliberately keeps the price of one item very low in order to increase the demand for the complement. Figure 13-12 shows the initial prices of electric cars and the cables used for charging the vehicles as P_1, and profits to the firm are shown by the sum of the areas labeled A. If the firm follows loss-leader pricing, it will lower the price of the cars to P_2 (below cost) and thereby increase the demand for the charging cables to D_2. The loss in one area hopefully will now be more than offset by additional profits from the sale of the other product. Thus, by selling cars below cost, the firm loses amount CP_2XY, but gains a greater amount of profits from the sale of the electric cables, as shown by area $MNUP_2$. As long as the sum of the new profit and loss exceeds the sum of the two areas labeled A, the firm will increase its

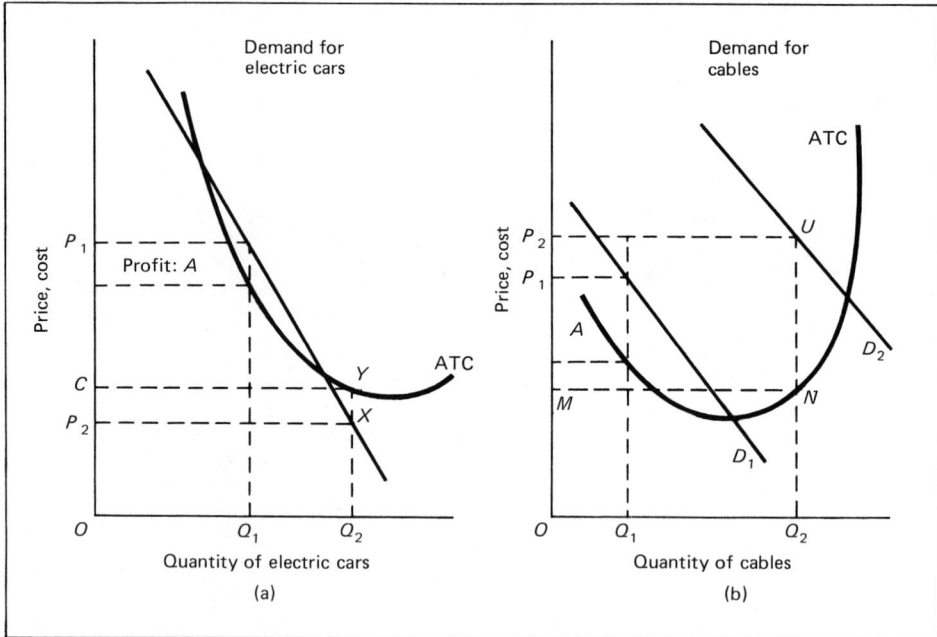

FIGURE 13-12
The firm is interested in profits and if it sells more than one item, it attempts to obtain as much combined total profit as possible. The company that manufactures electric cars knows that the car buyer must also have a cable to go with the car. It can keep car prices very low in order to sell a lot of cars and therefore a lot of cables. If it prices cars below cost, it loses money, but the demand for cables increases and brings in additional profit. If the additional profit from cable sales is greater than the loss incurred in the sale of cars, the profits to the firm increase. The company used to charge price P_1 and made a profit equal to the sum of the areas labelled A. Then the firm lowered the price of the car to P_2 and this increased the demand for the complementary product to D_2 and enabled the firm to charge P_2 for the cables. The total profit to the firm is now the difference between areas P_2UNM and $CYXP_2$.

profits. The appropriate combination of prices in the two markets will have to be determined by the firm. Clothing stores often engage in this sort of pricing by offering a dress at a very attractive price to bring in many customers with a hope of selling them the additional required "accessories" at high markups. Automobile dealers often have very high markups on accessories. The base price of a "stripped down" version may be as low as $3000, but after all the extras are added, the price approaches $6000. Movie theatres charge $1.00 admission to children for Saturday matinees, but sock it to the accompanying adults by charging them $3.00. The price of popcorn and candy is also appreciably marked up.

Price Skimming

Many firms introduce the most expensive and luxurious models of their product before they bring out the "cheapies." After the expensive models have been sold, the less expensive models are introduced to induce other buyers to enter the market. In this manner, the firm "skims" the profits from each successive model, starting with the most profitable models of the product. The Polaroid camera offers a good illustration of such skimming. The lower-priced version of the instant-photo camera was introduced only after satisfactory sales of the luxurious model SX-70. Book publishers first introduce the hardcover version before they bring out the softcover editions. Since the latter are usually less expensive, if both editions were brought out together, the cheaper editions would reduce the sale of the more profitable hardcover books. Movies are first shown in theatres, then on television, followed by reappearances in movie theatres, reruns on television, and finally as premiere showings in the student unions of some impoverished educational institutions. Other facilities show old movies in the interests of art.

Quality Variation and Pricing

Consumers are often very sensitive to prices, but not as much to variation in quality. For example, if you are buying scotch, you may have a choice of paying $8.95 a fifth for 86.8 proof whisky or $7.99 a fifth for the 80 proof version. You may very well be satisfied with the second combination, which is what the seller probably wants you to buy. Some restaurants brag about their ability to maintain the same price for their meals over the years despite inflation. Thus, if a dinner consisting of a filet mignon and lobster tail cost $8.95 in 1978, and it still costs the same to buy the dinner in 1979, we do not suspect that the *quality* of the meal has deteriorated. For one thing, the size of the piece of meat may not be as big; or the filet mignon may have been replaced by an adequately tenderized and properly shaped piece of roundsteak. Giving less, quantitatively or qualitatively, is tantamount to raising prices and most likely is adding to the firm's profits.

The "Free Gift" Model

At this point, it is wise to remember that the first lesson in economics is that there is no such thing as a free lunch. Consequently, when firms offer "free" gifts to buyers of certain merchandise, and the consumers buy the items, they help pay for the product as well as the gift. Consider the case of the manufacturer who sells detergent and offers free towels inside the box. The towel itself comes packaged in a special cardboard box (to keep it from getting soiled by the detergent) which is then placed inside the box of detergent. The towel takes up 15% of the room that could have held detergent. Furthermore, because this brand of detergent contains the added prize, it can be sold for a higher price than comparable brands offering no premiums. You will notice that those companies that offer towels or dishes with their detergent urge the buyers to collect matching sets! Such pricing policies are very profitable.

Prestige Pricing

This pricing tactic should be self explanatory. Here the seller prices his or her products by persuading the buyer to indulge in a little bit of "conspicuous consumption." Extremely high-priced products do not go unwanted. Some people wish to buy very expensive things because they derive tremendous utility from their possession. You will hardly expect a Pierre Cardin silk tie to be less than $17.00, or an Yves St. Laurent bikini to sell for less than $60.00. Wearing a shirt with the Bill Blass symbol will no doubt increase your station in life and therefore you may be willing to pay $45.00 for it. Others feel that quality is positively correlated with the price of the product, and it may very well be that the higher-priced item is, in fact, of superior quality. But often, the quality difference alleged to be present is in the consumer's mind. Is Bayer aspirin, which sells for $2.95 a bottle, really that much better than a generic brand which sells for $1.25 a bottle?

Psychological Pricing

Some firms resort to pricing strategies employing subtle consumer psychology. One price may appear more attractive than another, without actually being so. I once saw some recording tape for sale at a drug store, where the consumer had the choice of buying one for 99¢ or two for $1.99, and at first glance the second price seemed to be the better one. Almost all products in the United States are priced according to the "95" rule. Televisions sell for $299.95 and sofas for $365.95, while an automobile tire sells for $42.95. The use of the 95¢ figure keeps the manufacturer from quoting the next higher round dollar figure and thereby provides the illusion of low prices. Lately, the automobile manufacturers have been experimenting with prices like $6913 and $4992. Occasionally we see advertisements for high-priced items written, for example, as "$10,256 plus tax."

We have now examined some of the models of the firm and the associated behavior patterns with the hope of providing you with a set of tools and concepts which may be used in the exploration of firm theory.

APPLICATIONS

1. Buy Three and Get One Free

Tire sales are often advertised in this manner, where the seller offers an extra tire as an incentive to buy the first three. This probably is an example of good psychological pricing, because the average consumer may think that he is actually receiving a free tire. Receiving a free tire is no different than receiving a 25% discount, yet the wording of the tire sale including the "free" has more appeal to the customer than the percentage figure. Consider the following offers from a tire company.

a. Buy three for $120 and receive a free tire.
b. Buy the first pair at the regular price of $80 and receive a 50% discount on the second pair.
c. 25% off the regular price ($40) if bought in sets of four.

Any of these prices will result in the customer paying $120 for a set of four tires, yet one combination may appear more attractive than another.

2. A Pack of Five Sticks of Gum for 35¢?

The price you will pay for a small pack of Spearmint gum if you buy it at a dispenser is 35¢. If you buy the same package of gum at a supermarket, chances are you will receive seven sticks of gum for about 17¢. It is a matter of price elasticity. When you need chewing gum, and the dispenser is conveniently located in the lobby, you will be willing to pay the higher price. The alternative to buying it at the dispenser is to go without sweet breath or to run out to the city shopping center. Your price elasticity of demand for gum when you are going to a class is less than the price elasticity of demand when you are downtown. According to our discussion of third-degree price discrimination, the higher the price elasticity of demand in a market, the lower the price of the product.

3. *Passionate Storm* versus *Gray's Anatomy*

Both titles belong to books—the first represents a best-seller in fiction and light reading, whereas the second is a required textbook for aspiring students of medicine. Both books are published by the same company. The novel contains 1200 pages, is hardbound, and is priced at $9.95, whereas the textbook has only 600 pages, also is hardbound, and sells for $19.95. How come? Here, too, we must examine the types of markets aimed at by the seller. Novels are read by thousands of people if the price is right, and they are purchased by libraries in communities showing interest in such novels. Textbooks, or special references, are bought mostly by students. Readers of novels do not have to buy a particular book if they can acquire it at the library, whereas the medical student cannot afford not to have a textbook for a long period of time, even if the local libraries keep books on medicine.

4. A Rose by Any Other Name

Many firms are now marketing generic brands. In essence, the generic brands do not come under the firm's original brand name, but merely indicate the general name of the product. For example, in medicine, a druggist may label the container with the patented name Ampicillin or with its generic name penicillin. Some liquor distributors are marketing many alcoholic beverages under the broad name of bourbon, scotch, gin, and vodka. Generic brands are supposed to give the consumer quality products at lower prices. Since all products are labeled generically, no one brand has any distinct advantage over another and, as a result, the company can very easily reduce some of its promotional and packaging expenses. But, does the consumer actually receive the same product quality for a lower price? Since there are no specific brands involved, it is unlikely that the customer will remember to reject a certain product the next time, if the first purchase was not satisfactory. This might induce producers to package inferior products. Secondly, the firms at the retail level may still advertise and compete with each other vigorously enough to make some generic brands sell at higher prices than others. In the end, the consumer may not be any better off, except in limited situations.

5. Passengers and Cargo

When an airline offers a flight, it generally carries passengers and cargo. Usually, the lower part of the aircraft is designated as cargo space, and in that sense the space available for passengers does not compete with the space reserved for cargo. Every flight generates "joint" products—passengers and cargo. The revenue from passengers plus the revenue from cargo is compared with the cost of carrying cargo and passengers, and the optimal combination of the two is determined for profit maximization. While cargo and passengers are joint or complementary (on the supply side), first-class and coach passengers are competing products. More first-class seats imply fewer coach and economy class seats. Here, too, the company must weigh the benefits and costs of carrying first-class versus coach passengers. This can be analyzed by the multiple product model discussed earlier.

6. Price of a Ticket from London to Bombay

If you buy a roundtrip ticket from London to Bombay in London, you will pay approximately $475, whereas the same ticket bought in New York will run you at least $800. This type of pricing structure can be explained by the logic of price discrimination. The travelers in England have different abilities to pay than the ones in the United States. There is more competition among airlines offering flights out of London to Bombay, and these airlines do not offer sales facilities in the United States. The price elasticity of demand for air travel to Bombay is higher in London than it is in New York. As long as the airline can segment its markets and prevent the sale of tickets between markets, the company can make more profits through price discrimination.

EXERCISES

1. Define and explain the following.
   a. Price discrimination.
   b. Market segmentation.
   c. Collusion.
   d. Cartel.
   e. Price leadership.
   f. Psychological pricing.
   g. Prestige pricing.
   h. The loss–leader model.

2. What type of products do stores like Seven-Eleven carry? Why?

3. Discuss some of the strategies employed by these types of firms:
   a. Hallmark Card Company.
   b. Chanel perfumes.
   c. General Motors.
   d. Maytag.
   e. Steinway pianos.
   f. Baskin-Robbins ice cream.
   g. Hilton hotels.
   h. Adidas shoes.
   i. Hewlett-Packard computers.
   j. IBM.
   k. Pan Am.
   l. Charmin toilet tissue.
   m. Harvard Business School.
   n. Phillips Petroleum.
   o. McDonald's hamburgers.
   p. Coca-Cola Company.

4. Suppose a monopolist's demand is estimated to be $P = 120 - 3Q$. If the firm's marginal and average variable costs are constant at \$4, what will be the profit-maximizing price and quantity? If this monopolist successfully employs first-degree price discrimination, compute the profit-maximizing quantity as well as the maximum and minimum prices. (Assume that $Q \geq 1$.) How much profit does the firm earn if the total fixed costs equal \$40?

5. What type of pricing policy is suggested by each of the following situations?
   a. A hotel offers two days and one night's accomodation for \$24.95, double occupancy
   b. A restaurant advertises all you can eat for \$4.95.
   c. A second dinner is free at a restaurant if you pay full price for the first one.
   d. A cosmetic manufacturer offers you a \$35 "value" as bonus for buying a \$10 jar of makeup cream.
   e. A long-knitted scarf sells easily for \$12.95.

6. Which of the following is a "good buy"? Explain.
   a. A Lincoln Versailles for \$10,780.
   b. A Cadillac Seville for \$12,200.
   c. A Chrysler Le Baron for \$11,300.

7. How is "planned obsolescense" economically justifiable?

8. Suppose a firm's average total cost (ATC) is given by the expression: $ATC = 10 + \frac{1}{2}Q + (50/Q)$. If the firm desires to earn 10% above average cost, write an expression for the "cost plus" price function. What weakness, if any, do you see in pricing products in this manner?

SUGGESTED READINGS

Collin, M. "The Possible Effects of Exchange Rates Upon Domestic Price." *Business Economics,* Vol. 13, May 1978.

Dornstein, M. "Managerial Theories, Social Responsibility, and Goal Orientation of Top-Level Management in State-Owned Enterprise." *Journal of Behavioral Economics,* Vol. 5, Winter 1976.

Kushman, J. "Pricing Health Services: Verification of a Monopoly Price Model for Dentistry." *Journal of Human Resources,* Vol. 13, Summer 1978.

Monroe, K., and Della Bitta, A. "Models for Pricing Decisions." *Journal of Marketing Research,* August 1978.

Rubin, P. "The Theory of the Firm and the Structure of the Franchise Contract." *Journal of Law and Economics,* April 1978.

Schmitz, A. "Semi-Price Discrimination." *Economic Review,* December 1977.

Swan, P. "Product Durability under Monopoly and Competition." *Econometrica,* January 1977.

Touruk, K. "The OPEC Cartel: A Revival of the 'Dominant-Firm' Theory." *Journal of Energy and Development,* Spring 1977.

Young, "Some Practical Considerations in Market Segmentation." *Journal of Marketing Research,* Vol. 15, No. 3, August 1978.

Chapter Fourteen

Chapter Fourteen

Chapter Fourteen

DECISIONS UNDER UNCERTAINTY

Very rarely do we have perfect knowledge or information about future outcomes. Firms often make decisions with limited information. Sometimes the decisions are made under conditions of known probabilities—that is, they are made under *risk;* at other times the results or events of the future are completely unknown. Under such circumstances, we use *probabilistic* and *Bayesian* models in the decision-making process. Probability is the chance that a given event will occur. Thus, when you toss a coin, there is a 50% chance that the coin will turn up heads. In what follows, we will discuss certain models that make use of probability information.

THEORY OF GAMES

One category of decision making under conditions of chance is the *theory of games.* The tactics suggested by such theories are not unlike those employed, for example, in chess where each player analyzes several possible moves (based on the anticipated moves of the opponent), before he or she actually makes a move. Former U.S. Defense Secretary McNamara was one of the first to introduce game theory in war strategies. Under conditions of war, where neither country is fully aware of the other's intentions or schemes, the prudent use of game theory advice could be quite effective. In such games, the countries involved in the war become the "players" and each player then makes the appropriate "moves" to defeat or bluff the enemy. There are many types of games and, as you will see, each one has a special application.

The Payoff Function and Game Types

In simple terms, a game can be described as a competitive situation in which two or more participants are involved. Each player is assumed to have some knowledge of the consequences of his or her actions, known as the *payoff function,* which is determined by the combination of strategies employed by all the players. So we may have *two-person, three-person,* and *N-person* games. Games can further be classified according to the amount of payoff, such as constant-sum and nonconstant-sum games. When the payoff (the reward or loss due a particular action) is such that the gains and/or losses add up to a constant value, we have a constant-sum game. Thus, when one person's gains are another's losses, we have the special case of the constant sum, called the *zero-sum* game. For example, if you shoot dice with a friend, his losses are your gains, and vice versa. However, if you both must pay a third person to be on the lookout for the law, not all gains to one person are losses to the other player, for some of the gains must be paid to the observer. In such an event we have a *nonzero-but-constant-sum game.* When the sum of gains and losses varies, a nonconstant sum game occurs. In almost all games, the players either compete or cooperate. Generally speaking, cooperation is advantageous in nonconstant games.

Two-Person Constant-Sum Game

Suppose there are two producers in a market, competing for various percentages of the market share. Since the total market amount is 100%, the sum of the percentages obtained by both producers must add to 100%. Hence the name constant-sum game. Here we illustrate a case in which each player's gain is the other's loss. We will designate the two firms A and B and their strategies 1 and 2—that is, each firm has two possible strategies. Table 14-1 contains the payoff matrices and strategies of each firm.

Firm A's strategies are shown by the two rows labeled A_1 and A_2, while those of B are indicated by the columns labeled B_1 and B_2. Firm A's payoff matrix tells us that if A selects strategy A_1, and B chooses B_2, A's share of the market will be 60%, leaving 40% to B. Similarly, if we observe B's payoff matrix, cell A_1–B_2 indicates that B expects to obtain 40% of the market by employing strategy B_2, provided A chooses A_1. The sum of the corresponding cells in the two payoff matrices must add to 100%. The exact choice of strategy will be governed by certain decision rules or criteria, including *maximax, maximin, La Place, Hurwicz, minimax,* and *Bayesian*.

Maximax

Maximax policy is decision making under conditions of optimism. If a firm follows a maximax strategy, it is out to get all it can regardless of the outcome. With reference to the payoff matrix for A in Table 14-1, A should follow that strategy which maximizes its potential share of the market, *regardless of what B might do*. The best outcome possible under A_1 is 60%, and the highest market share possible with A_2 is 50%. Since strategy A_1 offers the chance of the higher of the two maximums (maximum of the maximums), A will select A_1 under a maximax strategy. Such a decision implies that A's decision makers are aggressive and optimistic. The selection of strategy A_1, however, does not

TABLE 14-1

A's payoff matrix

		B selects strategy:	
		B_1	B_2
If A selects strategy:	A_1	40%	60%
	A_2	50%	30%

B's payoff matrix

		If B selects strategy:	
		B_1	B_2
and A selects strategy:	A_1	60%	40%
	A_2	50%	70%

guarantee A the 60%, which will come about if, and only if, B chooses strategy B_2.

Maximin

The maximin criterion places emphasis on some gain but not the highest payoff. Here the player wants to ensure that he or she receives at least some gains with certainty. For example, if A chooses strategy A_1, the least he can expect is 40% of the market; and if he chooses the other strategy, the minimum share of the market will be 30%. Since 40% is the highest of all minimums, or the *maximum of the minimums,* firm A should employ strategy A_1 under the maximin criterion. Such policies are relatively "safe" and more conservative when compared to the maximax ones.

Minimax

Minimax policy making is best when a player is trying to minimize her losses. Under this criterion, the player chooses that strategy which *minimizes the maximum possible loss.* We will illustrate the minimax strategy using Table 14-2. Assume that both firms A and B wish to employ their minimax strategies. Since B's gains are A's losses, the percentage figures shown in B's payoff matrix (Table 14-1) may be used to represent A's losses. Similarly, B's losses may be shown by the payoffs for A. First each firm selects the values of the highest possible losses associated with each strategy and then selects that strategy which provides the lowest loss. For A, the minimum of the maximum losses is A_1, while that for B is B_1. A can expect to lose no more than 60% to B, and B can expect to lose a maximum of 50% of the market to A. Thus, if both firms choose their number 1 strategies, A will capture 40% of the market, leaving B with the remaining 60% (see Table 14-1).

The firm playing the minimax game is pessimistic in the sense that it expects its rivals to follow policies which are harmful to it. Consequently, the least the firm can do is to minimize the worst of all possible outcomes.

The minimax criterion can also be explained by the *minimax regret principle.* This essentially implies that a firm "regrets" not having made the correct decision, since it possesses no knowledge about its rivals' strategies. The values for regrets are found by subtracting the value earned from a particular strategy from the (best) value that *could have resulted had the firm made the correct decision.* The "regret matrix" for A, shown in Table 14-3, was derived from Table 14-1. If A selects A_1, and B decides to employ B_1, A's regret will be 10%, since A can obtain 50% (as opposed to 40%) of the market if it

TABLE 14-2

Maximum loss for A	Maximum loss for B
A_1: 60%	B_1: 50%
A_2: 70%	B_1: 60%

Theory of games
331

TABLE 14-3
A'S "REGRET" MATRIX

	B_1	B_2
A_1	10%	0
A_2	0	30%

chooses strategy A_2. We determine the other values of the regrets similarly. The maximum regret for A in selecting A_1 is 10%, while the maximum regret associated with strategy A_2 is 30%. Thus, under the principles of minimax, A should select A_1, because it will minimize the worst of the regrets.

Probability-Associated Criteria

The LaPlace, Hurwicz, and Bayesian criteria use probability information in the strategy-selection process. The first two methods employ known and conventional probability distributions, while the Bayesian method uses "revised" probability information. Instead of discussing each one separately, we will use an example to illustrate probability in decision-making processes first.

Suppose we have the situation shown in Table 14-4, which gives us A's payoff matrix. As before, we have two firms, A and B, and the game is a zero-sum game. The positive numbers show gains to A, and hence losses to B. The negative numbers indicate the amount of gain to B or loss to A. Assume that each firm has three strategies.

The payoff matrix reveals that some strategies are better than others. For example, if you are firm A, you will almost always pick strategy A_1 over A_2, since the first promises relatively better gains (and losses) on the whole. Similarly, A_3 is also "better" than A_2. In the event that one strategy has advantages over another, it is reasonable to suppose that the firm will be no worse off by cancelling the inferior strategies. The superior strategies *dominate* the undesirable ones. In any case, let us assume that A reduces the strategies to the two best—A_1 and A_3. Firm B also keeps the dominating strategies and plans to use either B_1 or B_2. Thus the "reduced matrix" for A is shown in Table 14-5, which also shows the probabilities (p) with which B is expected to employ the two strategies. For example, if firm A expects firm B to use B_1 60% of the time, A also expects B to use B_2 40% of the time. Firm A must now compute the

TABLE 14-4
A'S PAYOFF MATRIX

	B_1	B_2	B_3
A_1	2	−1	1
A_2	−1	2	−2
A_3	1	−2	4

TABLE 14-5

	B_1	B_2
P:	0.60	0.40
A_1	2	−1
A_3	1	−2

expected value of each strategy before deciding to act. The expected value of a strategy is the average winnings or losses from that strategy given the weights of the various probabilities. Thus, if you were playing a heads-or-tails game, and won $2 for a correct guess and paid $1 for an incorrect one, the expected value of each guess would be ($2)(½) + (−$1)(½) or $0.50, since the probability of guessing correctly is ½. We may define the expected value of a strategy as the *probability-weighted sum of all the payoffs along a given row or column*. Thus, the expected value for A's strategies will be computed as follows:

$$\text{Expected value } (E(A_i)) = \Sigma V_i p_i$$

where the V_i and p_i represent the payoff values and the probabilities of their occurrence, respectively. Since A has two possible strategies, the individual expected values will be

$$E(A_1) = 0.60(2) + 0.40(-1) = 1.2 - 0.40 = 0.80$$
$$E(A_3) = 0.60(1) + 0.40(-2) = 0.60 - 0.80 = -0.20$$

Since the expected value of strategy A_1 is greater than the expected value of A_3, A would be wise to select A_1 as its strategy most of the time. In essence, the expected value reveals which strategy will be the most profitable (or least harmful) for a firm in the long run if the probabilities assigned are predictable and stable. The strategy selection will be different if we also assign the probabilities chosen by firm B to A's strategy selection.

Nonconstant-Sum Games

Occasionally, we encounter situations where the sum of the gains and/or losses to all of the players is not constant. This occurs when the payoffs of each player are not equal in magnitude, or have identical signs, or have some combination of magnitude and sign such that the sums of the values in the payoff matrix are never constant. For example, consider the payoff matrices of A and B shown in Table 14-6. As before, let the positive values indicate profits, and the negative ones show losses. If both A and B play the maximax game, A will select A_2, while B will select strategy B_1. The outcome will be that A will win 30, while B will lose 10. This suggests that A's gains are not necessarily B's losses in their entirety. For example, if A and B are two firms in the automobile industry, and A lowers the price of its automobiles while B concentrates on advertisement, A might make more profits due to increased sales, while B

TABLE 14-6

Player A's payoff matrix

	B_1	B_2
A_1	20	0
A_2	30	-10

Player B's payoff matrix

	B_1	B_2
A_1	20	-5
A_2	-10	10

might lose money by incurring substantial advertising adventures without appreciable increases in demand. Under the circumstances, since B is aware of the potential losses, it might wish to play a more conservative game in order to minimize its risk. A better solution might be to come to an agreement with A—that is, to *collude* with A—so that both A and B will use their number 1 strategies. If such an agreement between the firms is possible, the result will yield gains of 20 to both, and there will not be any need for wasteful competition. An oligopolistic *cartel* might use such a model, where all the members of the cartel benefit from collusion.

Mixed-Strategy Models

The above games were *strictly determined;* that is, we can predict the moves of the players quite consistently. When the moves or strategies of the participants cannot be prognosticated with any degree of certainty or consistency, we have *nonstrictly determined* conditions. For instance, if after A selects its "best" strategy, B chooses a strategy which makes A's selection no longer its best, A will have to revise its alternatives. If B selects a strategy first and A follows, *after* learning about B's choice, the outcome can conceivably be very pleasing to A, *provided* B does not change its initial strategy. In the kinked-demand model of oligopoly, if all other firms maintain rigid prices, then a single firm lowering its prices will possibly attract a large number of new customers. However, once a firm lowers its prices, the others may very easily follow suit and the expected benefits of price reduction will no longer be the same. Under such conditions, a firm may choose to play a *mixed-strategy game,* where it employs the various strategies in some optimal mix. The mix of strategies is based on the players' abilities to compute the probabilities of occurrence of the strategies.

Let us assume that instead of two players, we have two parties to a game—the workers and the management. The workers' future is shaped by their union and the employer's interest is represented by its management. The union wants high wages, while management wishes to give as small a wage increase as necessary. The payoff matrix of the union for a wage increase,

TABLE 14-7
PAYOFF MATRIX FOR UNION

| | | Management strategies | |
		M_1	M_2
Union strategies	U_1	50¢/hr	30¢/hr
	U_2	20¢/hr	40¢/hr

expressed in cents per hour, is shown in Table 14-7. The union's problem is to determine the optimum mix of its strategies. Suppose that the union employs strategy U_1, P% of the time. Then strategy U_2 will be employed (100−P)% of the time. If management pursues strategy M_1, the expected payoff to the union will be

$$E_{1-u} = P\% \ (50¢) + (100-P)\%(20¢) \tag{1}$$

and if management selects strategy M_2, the expected payoff to the union will be

$$E_{2-u} = P\%(30¢) + (100-P)\%(40¢) \tag{2}$$

Since the union is interested in maximizing its gain, and since either payoff could be attractive under the appropriate conditions, it attempts to determine that value of P, which makes either E value equally desirable. This optimum value of P is found by equating expressions (1) and (2). Thus,

$$P\%(50¢) + (100-P)\%(20¢) = P\%(30¢) + (100-P)\%(40¢) \tag{3}$$

When we solve for P, using equation (3), we obtain a value of 50. Hence, the union should employ strategy U_1 50% of the time and strategy U_2 50% of the time. The expected values of the payoffs under these circumstances [equations (1) and (2)], will both equal 35¢ per hour.

We can compute the optimal mix for management in a similar manner. Let the management's frequency for employing M_1 be R%, making the frequency with which M_2 will be employed (100−R)%. Since management loses by paying higher wages, we show the expected loss functions for management. The first function is under the assumption that the union selects strategy U_1, and the second function represents the company's expected losses if the union selects strategy U_2. Using the union's payoff matrix shown in Table 14-7, we obtain the following expected values for the management's losses:

$$E_{1-m} = R\% \ (50¢) + (100-R)\%(30¢) \tag{4}$$
$$E_{2-m} = R\% \ (20¢) + (100-R)\%(40¢) \tag{5}$$

Solving equations (4) and (5) simultaneously by setting E_{1-m} equal to E_{2-m}, we obtain an R value of 25. Thus, management should choose strategy M_1 25% of the time and strategy M_2 75% of the time. The expected values for both loss equations are 35¢ per hour, which was the expected value of the union's winnings. When both parties select their number 1 strategies, the union will receive a wage increase of 50¢ per hour. If both choose the number 2 strategies, the union's gain will amount to 40¢ per hour. Other combinations of wage increases to the union are shown by the original payoff matrix. The graphical solution to mixed-strategy game theory models is illustrated in Figure 14-1.

DECISION TREE ANALYSIS

Another approach to decision making with partial information is *decision-tree analysis*. When using this method, the decision maker lays down all the possible outcomes in the future as consequences of certain actions at various stages. Once finished, the diagram resembles a tree with many branches, lying on its side.

All firms must make decisions at some time during the life of a project. Once the firm makes a decision and carries out certain strategies, the

FIGURE 14-1
This figure illustrates the graphical technique of solving a mixed-strategy game. For the union, we plot the two expected payoff functions represented by equations (1) and (2); the two management payoffs described by equations (4) and (5) are plotted adjacent to the union's. P represents the frequency with which the union picks strategy U_1, which makes $(100-P)$ the frequency it selects U_2. Line E_1 shows the expected payoff for the union under these circumstances if management selects strategy M_1, and line E_2 corresponds to the union's expected payoff when management selects strategy M_2. The two lines intersect at point X, where $P = 50\%$. Thus, the union should employ U_1 only 50% of the time. If it employs U_1 any more than 50% of the time, the expected value will be higher if and only if management pursues strategy M_1. But the management would not do this, since its objective is to grant as little a wage increase as necessary. The union would be wise to pursue a maximin criterion, and the minimum expected payoffs are shown by the kinked line AXZ. Similarly, management employs strategy M_1 with frequency $R\%$, and M_2 with $(100-R)\%$. Since it wants to minimize the wage increase granted to the union, it plays a minimax game—that is, it grants the lowest of all highest possible wage demands. This upper limit is shown by the kinked line KLV. Of these wage combinations, the minimum expected value occurs at point L, where $R = 25\%$.

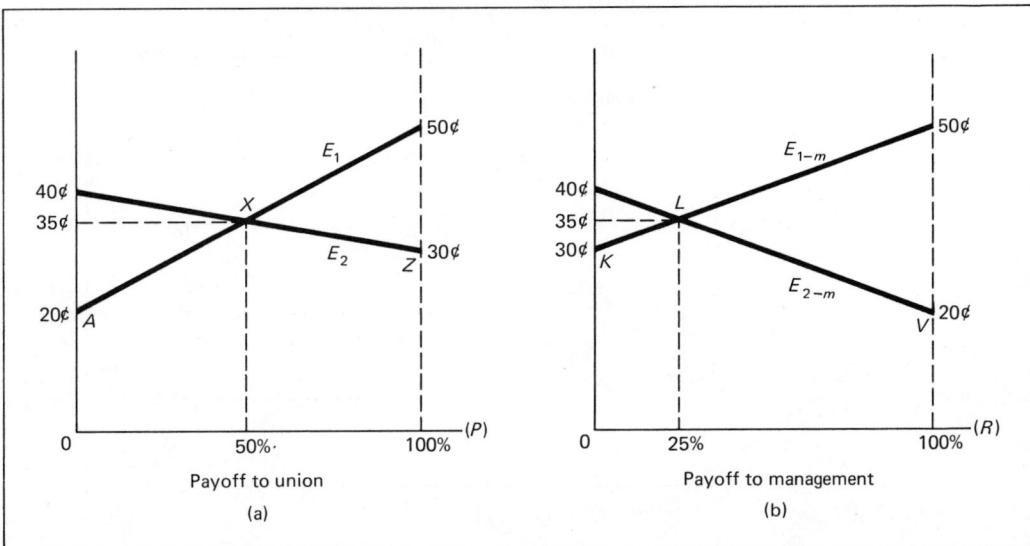

outcomes may or may not be satisfactory. In essence, the results are a matter of chance. Usually the firm has some knowledge of the various outcomes that might result from a given action. If the probabilities of the outcomes are known, the firm can estimate the payoffs associated with its actions and accordingly can attempt to minimize the damages and/or maximize its gains.

We will use Figure 14-2 and some other assumed information to illustrate the decision-tree technique. In the diagram, the circles represent *chance occurrences*—that is, the outcome at those points are beyond the firm's control. The hexagonal figures represent *deliberate decisions* on the part of the firm. The firm takes an action at such points, and the action may very well be one of not doing anything. In decision-tree terminology, the points of chance

FIGURE 14-2
At some point in the decision-making process, the firm takes deliberate action, and at other points the events are controlled by nature. The decision points are shown by hexagonal decision nodes such as A, D, and C. The circles represent chance outcomes that are beyond the control of the firm. The tips of the tree branches show the net payoffs which have been adjusted for the initial marketing cost where applicable. After rolling back the tree from right to left, the firm chooses the most attractive action to take at point A. The tree shows the possible outcomes of certain decisions and chance events and provides the firm with a guide to selecting the optimal combination of decisions/actions that will lead to a desirable objective. After all information provided by the tree is analyzed, the firm may wish to spend additional sums to obtain more information. The probable additional value due to knowledge that eliminates uncertainties is the expected value of perfect information. If the cost of such information is less than the value, the firm would be wise to obtain such information.

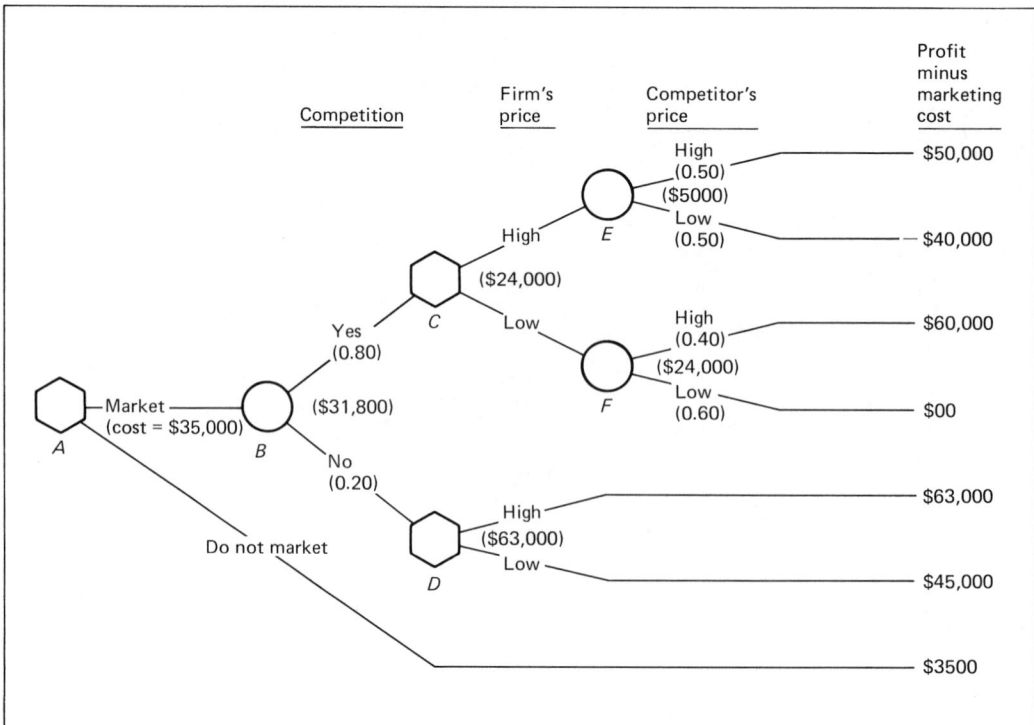

occurrences are called *chance nodes* (knots), and those associated with decisions are the *decision nodes*. The objective of the firm is always to proceed along the "best" branch and attain the best possible results under conditions of chance.

Assume that a firm is contemplating marketing a totally new product. The firm estimates that its marketing costs will be $35,000. If such a product is not produced, an alternative investment will bring $3500 to the firm. The firm's experts feel that there exists an 80% probability that a competitor will market a very similar product. If the firm charges a high price, there is a 50% chance that the competitor will do likewise; and if both parties charge high prices, the firm expects to make a profit of $85,000. On the other hand, if the competitor charges a lower price, the firm stands to incur economic losses of $5000.

The firm also has the option of charging relatively low prices for its product, and if it does, there is a 60% chance that the competitor will also charge low prices, in which case the firm expects to make economic profits of $35,000. However, if the competitor charges a high price, the firm stands to earn profits in the amount of $95,000.

If there is no competition, and there is a 20% chance that there will be no competition, the firm expects to earn $98,000 in profits by charging a high price, and $80,000 by charging a low price. Under these circumstances, what should be the firm's profit-maximizing strategy?

In Figure 14-2 we have a decision tree. Examining the tree from left to right, we see that the firm has to make decisions at three points. Each of these is shown as a decision node and is so indicated by the hexagons *A, C,* and *D.* After the decisions have been made, the firm has to contend with certain chance occurrences, shown by the chance nodes indicated by circles. Under each branch following a chance node, we indicate the probability of occurrence of an event (due to chance) by the percentage figures in parentheses. The last column shows the net payoffs to the firm, adjusted for the marketing cost of $35,000. Before we analyze the optimal strategy for the firm, let us follow a branch of the tree to verify the facts.

Starting at point *A,* we see that the firm faces a choice of either marketing or not marketing the product; hence, a decision node. If it is decided not to market the item, the alternative investment will bring $3500, since no marketing cost is involved. On the other hand, if the firm decides to market the product, it will proceed to point *B.* There is an 80% chance that a competitor will emerge. If there is a competitor and our firm charges a high price, it will be at point *E.* Beyond point *E,* you can see that there are two branches corresponding to the two possibilities concerning the competitor's pricing policy. There is a 50% probability that the competitor will also charge a high price and, if this happens, our firm expects to make profits of $85,000, which, when adjusted for the marketing cost of $35,000, means a net payoff of $50,000. Thus, the firm will make $50,000 by following branch *ABCE,* if, and only if, all the events shown along this branch actually occur. All the net payoffs for the other branches are similarly calculated.

Although we have shown only two possibilities after each chance node, in reality a firm can be faced with multiple random events, and the greater the number of different possible events, the larger the number of branches following each node. Similarly, following each decision node, we have usually shown two choices open to the firm. Again, in reality as well as in theory, the decision maker could very well have more than two options from which to make a selection. For example, right after point A the firm would have a choice of three options: market the product, do not market the product, or invest in an alternative project and make a marketing survey about the product. Under such conditions, there would be three branches coming from decision node A.

We use the expected value concept discussed earlier to determine the value of a decision. Once the expected values of the various branches have been calculated, the firm will decide on the best course of action. The ultimate selection is made after the "rollback" process. Rolling back a tree implies moving from the right to the left, and in so doing we determine the expected value (weighted value of the payoffs) of a decision at each point.

The expected value at point E is the weighted sum of the payoffs expected from each branch leading out of E. This value equals (0.50)($50,000) + (0.50)(−$40,000), or $5000, which is indicated in parentheses adjacent to node E. The expected value at point F equals $24,000. Going back to point C, we notice that the firm must make a decision. Since the firm is after maximum profits, it should choose to earn $24,000 instead of $5000, and consequently the higher of the two expected values is written next to node C. Similarly, $63,000 is the better of the two values shown by the branches leading from node D, and this sum is indicated adjacent to the decision node.

The next point in the rollback procedure is node B. You can calculate the expected value at point B by using the two probability values, and this amounts to $31,800 [$E(B) = 0.80(24,000) + 0.20(63,000) = 31,800$]. Now the firm has to step back to point A. At point A, the firm is faced with a choice of two options—market the product or invest elsewhere. The first decision has an *expected value* of $31,800, and the second is *certain to yield* $3500. Since the expected value of marketing the product is unusually higher than the amount to be gained with certainty by not marketing it, an optimistic firm may very well decide to market the product. However, whether the decision maker actually chooses to market the product under the given conditions will depend on whether he or she prefers one outcome to the other—that is, on the indifference curves or utility function describing the trade-offs between chance gains and guaranteed profits.

Expected Value of Perfect Information

After determining the expected value of marketing the product, the firm may decide to conduct a market survey. Whether such a survey, probably at considerable cost, is worth it to the firm will depend on the improvements that may be expected due to additional information. To decide on the desirability of obtaining such information, the firm computes the *expected value of perfect information*.

With reference to Figure 14-2, it would pay the firm to charge a low price for its products, *if it knows* that the competitor will charge a high price for his, for under these circumstances the payoff to our firm will be maximized at $60,000. Similarly, if the firm knows that there will not be any competition, a high price will bring about the greatest payoff. Since the probability of there being competition is 80%, and of there being no competition 20%, the expected value of the strategies with perfect information is (80%)($60,000) + (20%)($63,000), or $60,600. This expected value (with more information) will improve the earlier expected value by ($60,600 − $31,800), or $28,800. In other words, the incremental benefit of additional information will be expected to equal this amount. Since the firm stands to gain $28,800 with the use of more information, the acquisition of information at a cost will be profitable provided the cost of information does not exceed $28,800. Such reasoning is an extension of incremental (or marginal) analysis. If the marginal gain from a decision is expected to exceed the marginal cost of the decision, the decision is considered profitable. Thus, our firm can expect to make $15,800 in extra net income if, ceteris paribus, the cost of information is $13,000.

APPLICATIONS

1. Derivation of Utility Functions

We can use probability information to derive an individual's utility function under some circumstances. Thus, depending on the preferences of the individual under discussion, an opportunity to earn $10,000 with a probability of 60%, combined with the possibility of a loss of $6000, may bring as much, more, or less happiness (utility) as receiving $2000 with certainty. Given the odds of winning (and losing) the amounts stipulated, a person will "reveal" his preferences by selecting either the *chance* of winning $10,000 or accepting a *guaranteed* sum of $2000. The expected value of the gamble is (60%)($10,000) + (40%)(−$6000), or $3600. If the person is a risk taker, he may gamble for the larger sum and take the chance of losing $6000, which, incidentally, means a "regret" of $8000 as compared to accepting the guaranteed cash sum of $2000. A risk avoider will probably choose the $2000. The expected value of the gamble is determined by the probability values assigned to winnings (and losses.)

Let us suppose we find a person who is willing to tell us his preferences for winning $10,000 with various probabilities, over certain guaranteed cash sums. We will also assume that if he loses, he will lose $6000. Table 14-8 shows the expected values of the gamble associated with various probabilities (p) of winning $10,000 and the probabilities ($1-p$) of losing $6000.

Having established the expected values, we can now ask this person what amount of guaranteed cash will be equivalent to a given expected value—that is, we ask him to tell us how much money he will accept *in lieu* of an expected value, and be as satisfied as if he had gambled. Assume that the person's taste is such that he indicates the amount of guaranteed cash equivalent (GCE) which, when given to him, will make him indifferent between the two options—guaranteed cash versus the corresponding expected value of the winnings, as shown by Table 14-9.

Since this individual is indifferent between the guaranteed cash equivalent and the corresponding expected value, the utility of the guaranteed cash equivalent will equal the utility of the expected value. For example, the utility from receiving $1000

TABLE 14-8

(p) Probability of winning	(1 − p) Probability of losing	Amount won	Amount lost	Expected value
0.00	1.00	$10,000	$6000	−$6000
0.10	0.90	10,000	6000	−$4400
0.20	0.80	10,000	6000	−$2800
0.30	0.70	10,000	6000	−$1200
0.40	0.60	10,000	6000	$ 400
0.50	0.50	10,000	6000	$2000
0.60	0.40	10,000	6000	$3600
0.70	0.30	10,000	6000	$5200
0.80	0.20	10,000	6000	$6800
0.90	0.10	10,000	6000	$8400
1.00	0.00	10,000	6000	$10,000

with certainty will equal the utility from winning $10,000 with a probability of 0.50 coupled with losing $6000 also with a probability of 0.50; or taking a guaranteed loss of $2000 will bring as much disutility as expecting to lose $1200. It is reasonable to assume that a person attaches greater importance to guaranteed income as compared to expected income. Consequently, as Table 14-9 reveals, our consumer is willing to accept a smaller guaranteed cash amount in place of a relatively larger *expected* winning, in order to remain equally satisfied. Recall that each of the expected values of Table 14-9 corresponds to a unique value of *p*.

If we assign certain arbitrary values to utility from guaranteed income, we can draw a utility function relating utility to expected income. Suppose the utility index associated with guaranteed income is such that the utility (U) of $10,000 is 100. Given the utility of guaranteed income, and the person's indifference between pairs of guaranteed income and expected income, we can draw a utility function linking utility to the various probability values. (See Figure 14-3.)

Since it is possible to be indifferent between a certain amount of expected income and the corresponding amount of guaranteed cash, it is also possible to

TABLE 14-9

Guaranteed cash equivalent	Expected value
−$6000	−$6000
− 5000	− 4400
− 4000	− 2800
− 2000	− 1200
0	400
1000	2000
2000	3600
3500	5200
4000	6800
6000	8400
10,000	10,000

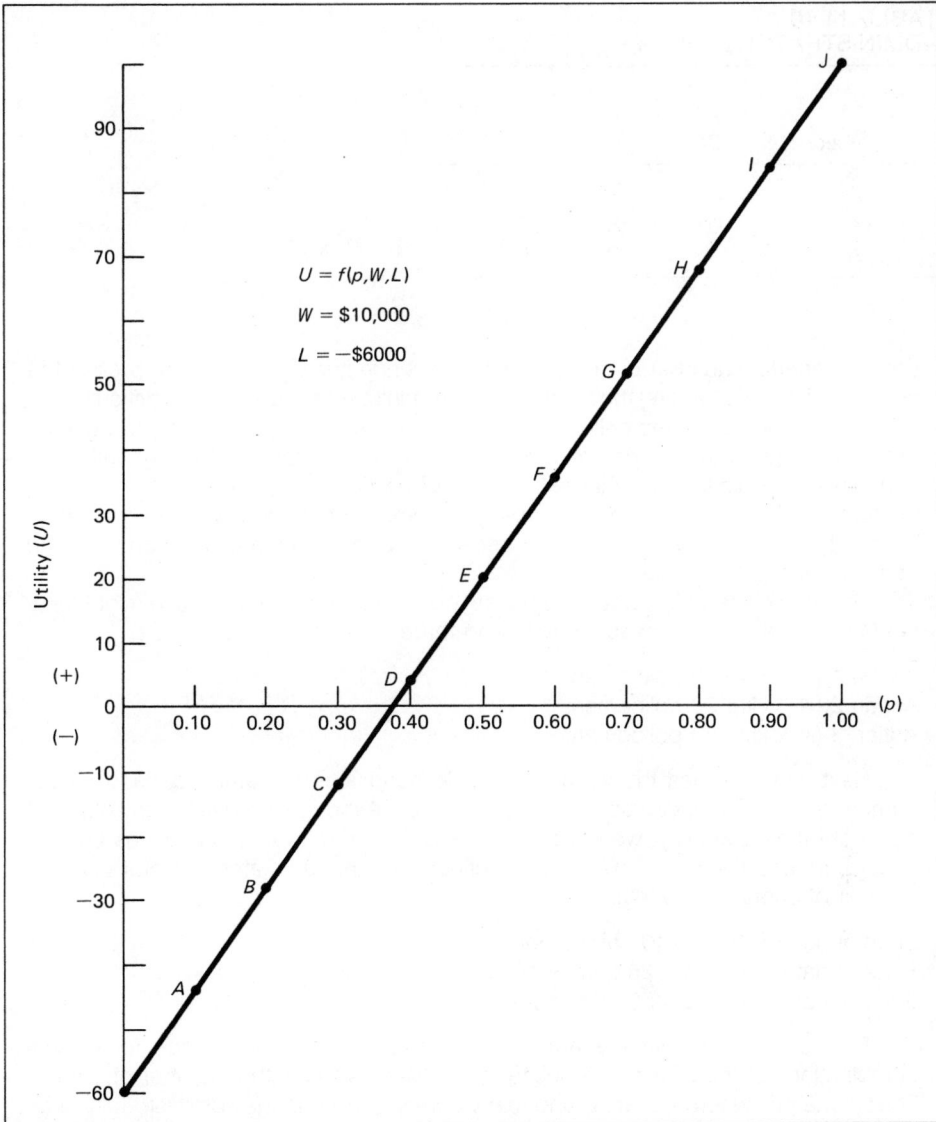

FIGURE 14-3
Each point (A, B, . . .) represents a unique level of utility which is linked to the expected
value of the outcome at that point. Thus, the expected value at E is (0.50)($10,000) +
(0.50)(−$6000) = $2000. The $2000 is assumed to yield 20 units of utility (U).

determine the trade-offs between guaranteed and expected income; that is, in
addition to being able to derive utility functions, we can also derive indifference
curves showing the rates of substitution between the two types of income. Such
information may be of help in predicting behavior under conditions of chance.

2. How Many Policemen?

Police protection is a public good produced by the city government. This law
enforcement agency of the municipality should be large enough to handle and

TABLE 14-10
ADMINISTRATOR'S UTILITY

	States of nature		
Actions	S_1	S_2	S_3
A_1	40	35	15
A_2	20	38	22
A_3	5	10	50

prevent a certain number of crimes. However, since it is very difficult to predict the number of crimes before they occur, the administrator may have a difficult time deciding on the size of the police force. If the force is too large, and very few crimes are committed (independent of the size of the police force), the city will incur unnecessary costs in paying large numbers of police officers. On the other hand, if the force is very small, and large numbers of crimes occur, there will be a great cost to society. Can the administrator use certain probability information to arrive at the optimal-sized police force?

The administrator first specifies the several possible actions that she might take. Let us assume she proposes the following three alternative actions:

Action 1 (A_1): Hire 20 policemen.
Action 2 (A_2): Hire 30 policemen.
Action 3 (A_3): Hire 50 policemen.

Next she specifies the various possible conditions of nature, defined as the number of crimes that can occur in any one week. Although there are many different types of criminal activity, we will generalize by referring to them simply as crimes. Thus, suppose the city administrator defines the various states of nature by the number of crimes per week:

State of nature$_1$ (S_1): 0–10 crimes per week.
State of nature$_2$ (S_2): 11–25 crimes per week.
State of nature$_3$ (S_3): 25–50 crimes per week.

Let us suppose that the administrator has her own preference for certain combinations of the size of the police force vis-a-vis the actual number of crimes. Thus, if the police force is large, and many crimes do occur, the administrator will be happier than if there are very few crimes and the police force is very large. In Table

TABLE 14-11

Probability of occurrence	State of nature
(p_i)	(S_i)
0.50	S_1
0.20	S_2
0.30	S_3

TABLE 14-12

Actions (A_i)	Probabilities of S_i			Expected value
	0.50	0.20	0.30	
A_1	40	35	15	31.50
A_2	20	38	22	24.20
A_3	5	10	50	19.50

14-10 we have assigned certain values representing the amount of utility experienced by the administrator for each combination of action (A_i) and state of nature (S_i).

Since the administrator is experienced in city matters, she also has certain subjective probabilities for the occurrence of the number of crimes. Suppose she assigns probabilities for the occurrence of the various numbers of crimes per week—probabilities associated with the various likely states of nature (S_i), as shown in Table 14-11.

Although there are more sophisticated techniques for arriving at the correct decision (i.e., the Bayesian technique), we will use the expected value criterion for selecting the optimal strategy. Thus, for each action (A_i), there is a corresponding expected value (EV_i), which equals the sum of each cell's utility value multiplied by the appropriate probability of occurrence of that state of nature (S_i),

$$EV_i = \Sigma(U_i)p(S_i) \tag{6}$$

Table 14-12 shows the computed expected values.

Since action A_1 promises the largest expected utility, the administrator should decide to hire a small police force. To obtain an extra margin of safety, she could hire a little larger crew than suggested by A_1. For example, it is reasonable for her to hire a 20-person police force for most of the time but reinforce it with additional help during certain times of the week, or at special times of the day, when most crimes are likely to be committed.

EXERCISES

1. Define and explain the following:
   a. Risk.
   b. Uncertainty.
   c. Expected value.
   d. Probability.
   e. Cash equivalent.
   f. Maximax.
   g. Minimax regret.
   h. Decision versus chance node.

2. Are game theory models the same as decision-tree models? Explain.

3. Economists often use the ratio of the mean income of a project to its variance as a measure of risk associated with a project. Explain.

4. Assume that a drilling firm has the option to drill for oil wells. If it does not drill, it can sell the option for $1 million. Before drilling, the company can perform certain geological tests at a cost of $100,000. Generally speaking, the tests reveal the presence of oil, or gas and oil, as well as the complete absence of either. In the past, actual drillings have produced wells containing oil and gas 40% of the time, oil alone 30% of the time, and dry wells the rest of the time. If oil is discovered, the gross revenues to the firm will be $5 million, and oil and gas will bring $7 million. The cost of drilling is estimated to be $2 million. Geological tests performed on nearby locations have indicated the presence of oil 50% of the time, gas and oil 30% of the time, and neither the remaining 20% of the time. If these tests are performed by this company, it is probable that they will also indicate the same frequencies for the existence of the minerals. But to confirm its suspicions, the firm must spend the $100,000. Under these conditions, what should the firm do? Draw a decision tree to analyze the situation.

5. How would you go about reducing expected values to cash equivalents? Would such conversion be useful in
   a. postponing a trip?
   b. buying out a contract?
   c. selling a home?
   d. resigning from a job?
   e. hiring new football players?
   f. purchasing automobile insurance?
   g. studying for advanced degrees?
   h. forecasting the effect of national policies?
   i. drawing up strategies for war?
   j. pricing a book?

6. Look up any reference or textbook that explains the so-called "Prisoners' Dilemma." Explain the use of game theory with such a theme.

7. Provide examples of situations and/or games where the probability of winning is: 1, ½, ⅓, ¼, ⅕, and ⅙.

8. Suppose you can enter a contest where every contestant buys one or more $1 tickets. The winner receives the entire amount of ticket money as the prize. For the sake of simplicity, assume that 200 tickets are sold for each contest. What will be the expected value of such a game if you purchase 1 ticket, 2 tickets, 10 tickets, 100 tickets? (Hint: If you purchase 1 ticket, you may expect to lose $1 or gain $199.)

9. Assume that you have an opportunity to go into a certain business where, if the conditions are right, you will make a profit of $10,000. If conditions are unfavorable, you will lose $4,000. Prepare a table of expected values of going into this business, if the probability of making a profit is: 0.10, 0.20, 0.30, 0.40, 0.50, 0.60, 0.70, 0.80, 0.90, and 1.00.

10. With reference to Exercise 9, list the amount of guaranteed income you will accept in place of each of the expected values. Is there any evidence of diminishing marginal rate of substitution between expected income and guaranteed income?

11. Actuarial tables provide information about the various risks that an insurance company may face in enrolling different types of clients. Can probability information about longevity be used to compute life insurance premiums? Explain.

12. With reference to Exercise 11, assume that the following probabilities are associated with a normal, healthy person:

Probability	Age at death
0.60	70 years
0.20	65 years
0.10	60 years
0.05	55 years
0.04	50 years
0.01	45 years

The person's present age is 40 years and her beneficiary(ies) will collect $50,000 if she dies before she reaches the age of 70. If she lives to be 70, she will collect the $50,000 herself. Disregarding the time value of money, and using only the 5-year periods, compute the average annual premium that she should pay to obtain this life insurance. (Hint: The insurance company expects to pay the $50,000 after 5 years with a 1% probability, after 10 years with a 4% probability, . . . , and after 25 years with a 60% probability.)

13. Now compute the average annual premium for a relatively sick person with the following probabilities:

Probability	Age at death
0.01	70 years
0.05	65 years
0.50	60 years
0.24	55 years
0.15	50 years
0.05	45 years

14. With reference to the two exercises dealing with life insurance premiums, why do some companies require medical histories of clients?

15. If the insurance company were to chart a decision tree before signing up a client, how would the medical checkup of the client fit into the tree? How much should the insurance company pay the doctor, if it were to pay the examination fees?

16. Assume that you have enough time left to study either for economics finals or the final in biology. Your current average grade in economics is 66, and in biology, 72. The final course grade is determined by the arithmetic average of the present grade and the final examination grade. The instructors in the two courses use the following grading scale:

Economics	Grade points	Biology
0–54 F	0	0–44 F
55–62 D	1	45–60 D
63–71 C	2	61–70 C
72–83 B	3	71–80 B
84–100 A	4	81–100 A

If you study economics, and the questions in economics as well as in biology are easy, you expect to get a 78 in economics and a 90 in biology. If the questions are hard, you expect to get a 58 in economics and a 70 in biology. If you decide to study biology, instead, and the questions in both subjects are easy, you will receive a 56 in economics and a 100 in biology; if the questions are hard, you expect to earn a 50 in economics and a 74 in biology. The economics instructor gives hard finals three out of four times, and the biology instructor gives easy finals seven out of ten times. What should be your decision to maximize your grade point average?

SUGGESTED READINGS

Brown, R., Kahr, A., and Peterson, C. *Decision Analysis for the Manager.* New York: Holt, Rinehart and Winston, 1974.

Carlton, D. "Market Behavior with Demand Uncertainty and Price Inflexibility." *American Economic Review,* September 1978.

Dean, G., and Halter, A. *Decisions under Uncertainty.* Cincinnati, Ohio: South-Western Publishing Company, 1971.

Horowitz, I. *Decision Making and the Theory of the Firm.* New York: Holt, Rinehart and Winston, 1970.

Raiffa, H. *Decision Analysis: Introductory Lectures on Choices under Uncertainty.* Reading, Mass.: Addison-Wesley, 1970.

Thompson, G. *Statistics for Decisions.* Boston, Mass.: Little, Brown and Company, 1972.

Weller, P. "Consistent Intertemporal Decision-Making under Uncertainty." *Review of Economic Studies,* Vol. 45, June 1978.

Chapter Fifteen

Chapter Fifteen

Chapter Fifteen

THE MARKET FOR RESOURCES

To produce potato chips you need potatoes, labor, equipment, raw materials, and a place to work. The inputs are necessary for the production of the output. Just as we have markets for goods and services, we also have markets for production resources. The markets dealing with the resources may be under either perfect or imperfect competition. The objectives of the producers of the output influence the demand for the inputs, and the goals of the owners of the resources affect the quantity and quality of the inputs supplied to the demanders. For example, a hotel needs employees in order to cater to the tourists. The demand for hotel services (the output) will be affected by a variety of factors. The demand for employees (the labor resource) in turn will be influenced by the hotel's decisions regarding the prices for hotel rooms. Consequently, once the demand for employees is known, the owners of labor resources (the employees, or their unions) will decide whether they wish to work for the hotel. Depending on the circumstances, the price of the resource may or may not be set by the owners of the resource. Thus, if all the employees under question are unskilled labor, it is very unlikely that they will be in a position to dictate their wages. They will be "price takers," as were the perfectly competitive firms.

THE FACTORS OF PRODUCTION

All resources are generally called the *factors of production*. There are four broad categories of resources: *land, labor, capital,* and *entrepreneur*. All raw materials or, essentially, all resources that are in fixed supply are usually called land resources. Thus, lumber is a land resource, just as are water, iron ore, and land itself. The resource which supplies human productive effort is called a labor resource. There are obviously different qualities of labor resources. A factory supervisor is a labor resource, as is a hired hand at a farm. Capital resources include all the producer's goods, plant, equipment, and invested capital that are necessary to produce the final product or output. A six-ton truck becomes capital to the trucker; a shovel is a piece of capital equipment to the gardener; money borrowed by companies is invested in physical capital and, therefore, is also a form of capital resources. Remember that there is a distinction between physical and monetary capital. Each type of capital has its own market. Thus, there are markets for tractors (physical capital or capital good) and markets for investment funds (monetary capital). The price in the first market is usually quoted in dollars and cents and in the second in percentages as the interest rate on capital. Finally, the enterprise is provided by entrepreneurs. They come up with the ideas and bear the risks. For example, the owner of a corner grocery store is an entrepreneur, although he may also be the sole labor resource. Generally speaking, entrepreneurs combine and use the other three resources to attain the objectives of the firms.

The many theories of the firm that we explored earlier explained the behavior of the output-producing firms. In studying the market for resources, we will examine the theory and practice of goal achievement by the sellers of the inputs. When you examine the models that explain the behavior of the variables, you will notice many similarities in the markets for resources. We will start our discussion with a simple model of a resource bought in a perfectly competitive input market.

MARKET STRUCTURE AND INPUT PRICE

Firms purchase resources to produce and sell the output in order to attain their objectives, such as to maximize profits. In this particular discussion we will assume that the resource-purchasing firms are operating under perfect competition and therefore the price of the output is fixed or given. Consequently, a profit-maximizing firm will demand that quantity of resources which will permit it to equate the marginal cost to the marginal revenue. Thus, the demand for a resource is a *derived demand*. If the resource market is also under perfect competition, the price of the resource is determined by the demand and supply forces in the resource market.

Marginal Revenue Product

The marginal revenue product of a resource is the change in total revenue associated with a one-unit change in the number of units of the resource employed by a firm, all other factors remaining equal. For example, if an additional worker will produce 10 more units of output, and the price of the output in the perfectly competitive market is $6.30, the marginal revenue product (MRP) of this worker will be the change in total revenues to the firm, (10 × $6.30), or $63. The marginal revenue product is the resource's marginal physical product (MQ) multiplied by the price of the output (P). More correctly, the MRP is the product of the marginal revenue (MR) of the output and the marginal product of the input. Because the marginal revenue and price are the same under perfect competition, they can be used interchangeably, as in equation (1).

$$\text{Marginal revenue product (MRP)} = \text{Marginal revenue} \times \text{Marginal product}$$
$$= \text{Price of output} \times \text{Marginal product}$$
$$MRP = MR \times MQ = P \times MQ \tag{1}$$

Table 15-1 illustrates the derivation of the marginal revenue product of a variable resource (labor) at a car wash, where the price of each wash is $2.

The last column of Table 15-1 shows the change in total revenue resulting from the employment of an additional worker. The car wash will use the information contained in this column to decide on the "correct" number of employees for its operations. For instance, a profit-maximizing car wash will tend to hire an extra employee so long as the employee's marginal revenue product is at least as high as the wages paid to the employee.

Under perfectly competitive conditions, the price of the resource is given or fixed and, therefore, the price of the resource becomes the marginal cost (of hiring) to the resource-purchasing firm.

TABLE 15-1

(1) Number of employees	(2) Number of cars washed	(3) Price of a wash	(4) Total revenue (2) × (3)	(5) Marginal product Δ(2)/Δ(1)	(6) Marginal revenue product (3) × (5) or Δ(4)/Δ(1)
1	180	$2	$ 360	180	$360
2	450	2	900	270	540
3	850	2	1700	400	800
4	1080	2	2160	230	460
5	1285	2	2570	205	410
6	1385	2	2770	100	200
7	1400	2	2800	15	30
8	1410	2	2820	10	20

The Demand for the Resource

The demand for a resource is essentially "derived" from the demand for the output. Table 15-2 shows the relationship between a resource's marginal revenue product and its price, as well as its employment level and the marginal resource cost to the firm. Marginal resource cost is the change in cost associated with a one-unit change in the quantity of the variable resource. In our situation, because we have assumed that the resource is being sold under perfect competition, and its price is $400, the firm is free to choose any number of workers at this price. If the car wash is a profit-maximizing firm, it will employ as many workers as necessary to equate the marginal income (MRP) of each worker to his or her marginal cost (MRC). Thus, if each employee can be hired for $400, this firm, if it wishes to maximize its profits, and provided no other variable resource is involved, will hire no more than five full-time workers, because the benefit from hiring the sixth worker (the MRP) is only $200, while the extra cost of hiring the worker is $400.

Figure 15-1 shows a resource's MRP and MRC under conditions of perfect

TABLE 15-2

(1) Number of employees	(2) Marginal revenue product	(3) Price of resource	(4) Total cost of resource (3) × (1)	(5) Marginal cost of resource Δ(4)/Δ(1)
1	$360	$400	$ 400	$400
2	540	400	800	400
3	800	400	1200	400
4	460	400	1600	400
5	410	400	2000	400
6	200	400	2400	400
7	30	400	2800	400
8	20	400	3200	400

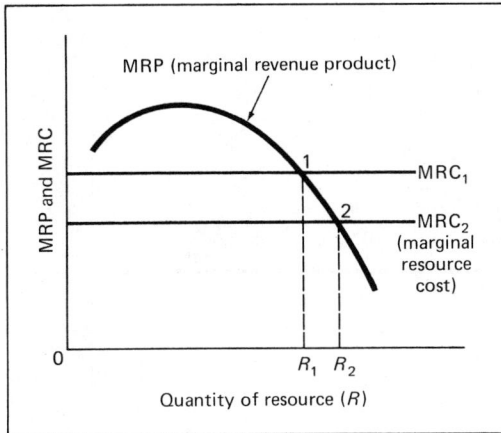

FIGURE 15-1
A profit-maximizing firm equates the marginal
revenue product of the resource to the marginal
resource cost. If marginal resource cost is
MRC_1, the firm will hire R_1 units of the resource,
and if it is MRC_2, the firm will employ R_2 units of
this resource.

competition in output as well as resource markets. The profit-maximizing levels
of employment or purchase occur where the MRC equals the MRP, therefore all
such points lie along the MRP. As a result, ceteris paribus, *the MRP becomes
the profit-maximizing firm's demand for a single variable resource.*

Resource Pricing in a Competitive Market

The total supply of resources is the sum of all supplies offered at various
alternate prices. Thus, if R is an unskilled labor resource, the various numbers
of workers that will be looking for employment at the various wage rates will
make up the supply function. In general, the higher the market price of a
resource, the higher the quantity of that resource supplied. When the
aggregate supply of the resource is matched against the aggregate demand,
we obtain the equilibrium price and quantity of a resource in a perfectly
competitive market. This is shown in Figure 15-2.

The equilibrium price of $400 per person per week is viewed as the
marginal resource cost by the firm. Figure 15-2 also shows that the total
demand for labor (L) will be 2000 workers, and each firm will pay $400 to each
worker and hire as many as necessary to equate labor's marginal revenue
product to its marginal resource cost. If we assume that all the buyers (the
firms) use identical technology, have identical and perfect information, and
produce the same product, we can conclude that each firm will use the same
number of workers. If there is a total of 50 firms in the industry, each will use 40
workers.

Under any type of competition in product and resource markets, the
profit-maximizing firm follows the basic rule of equating the marginal revenue
from hiring a unit of the resource to the resource's marginal cost, or:

Marginal revenue of resource = Marginal cost of resource
Marginal revenue product = Marginal resource cost

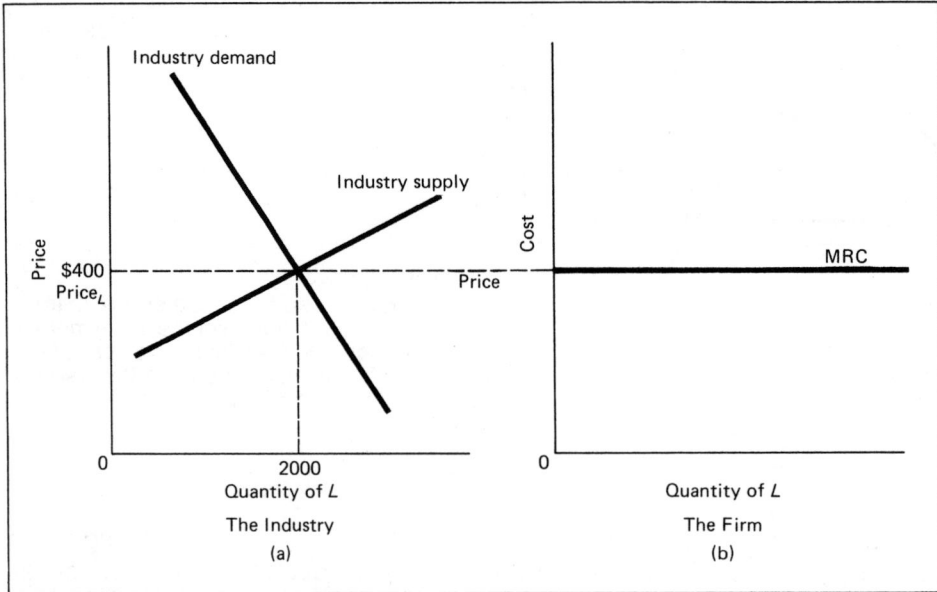

FIGURE 15-2
The price of a resource, when the resource market is perfectly competitive, is determined by the forces of supply and demand. This price then becomes the marginal resource cost (MRC) to the firm hiring the resource.

However, when both the output and input markets are under perfect competition, the profit-maximizing rule becomes

$$(MR)_{resource} = (MC)_{resource}$$
$$MRP = MRC$$
$$(MQ)_{resource} \times (MR)_{output} = MRC$$
$$(MQ) \times (P)_{output} = (P)_{input} \qquad (2)$$

Equation (2) is the profit-maximizing condition in the input market which can be transformed to reflect the conditions for profit maximization in the output market under perfect competition. In Chapter 9, we developed the relationship of the firm's marginal cost (MC) to the variable resource's price (P_r) and its marginal product (MQ). Furthermore, we also know that a profit-maximizer equates the marginal cost of the output to the output's marginal revenue. Thus, from equation (2),

$$(MQ)(P)_{output} = P_{input}$$
$$(P)_{output} = \frac{(P)_{input}}{(MQ)} = (MC)_{output}$$
$$(MR)_{output} = (MC)_{output} \qquad (3)$$

Equation (3) shows the profit-maximization condition in terms of the output, whereas equation (2) shows it in the resource market. If the firm hires the profit-maximizing quantity of the resource, it will also be able to produce the profit-maximizing quantity of output.

Marginal Revenue Product with Raw Material

Most often, firms use other variable inputs in addition to labor, such as raw material. To keep the analysis simple, we will assume that a firm uses a specific quantity of raw material for each unit of output. If we introduce the presence of this second variable, will the employment decisions of the firm be affected? The answer most often is yes, unless, of course, the second input is free.

The presence of other inputs increases the marginal cost of production, or, in essence, reduces the "net" value of the main variable resource's marginal revenue product. For example, in the case of the car wash, labor was the primary productive variable resource. If we assume that each car requires 50¢ in soap, water, and energy resources, the net marginal revenue from each car washed will be only $1.50, and this in turn will reduce the value of labor's marginal product. Thus, with reference to Table 15-2, the values of the marginal revenue product will decline by 25%. The first worker, even if he can wash 180 cars, will now contribute only (180 × $1.50), or $270. This modification is logical because if the company had not chosen to wash a particular car, it would not have to incur the cost of the nonlabor resources, but it would not have to pay for the labor resource either. Consequently, when the firm compares the benefits from an extra worker to his or her costs, the benefits are computed on a net basis. Table 15-3 contains the modified version of the marginal revenue products. Figure 15-3 summarizes the relationship of the input and output markets and the profit-maximizing firm's decision concerning input purchases.

Table 15-3 very definitely indicates the influence of the cost of raw material on the profit-maximizing level of employment. Whereas the firm initially hired five workers, it will now hire only three. The marginal cost of hiring the fourth worker will be higher than the net marginal revenue product. The higher the cost of the other inputs, the less the demand for the specific variable input. You can verify that if the raw material cost increases to $1.00 per car, the profit-maximizing level of labor employment will be affected. Similarly, if the firm has to pay an excise tax (a tax on each unit of output), it will also decide to reduce the purchase of the input.

TABLE 15-3

(1) Number of employees	(2) Number of cars washed	(3) Marginal product	(4) Net price of car wash	(5) Net marginal revenue product	(6) Marginal resource cost
1	180	180	$1.50	$270	$400
2	450	270	1.50	405	400
3	850	400	1.50	600	400
4	1080	230	1.50	345	400
5	1285	205	1.50	307.5	400
6	1385	100	1.50	150	400
7	1400	15	1.50	22.50	400
8	1410	10	1.50	15	400

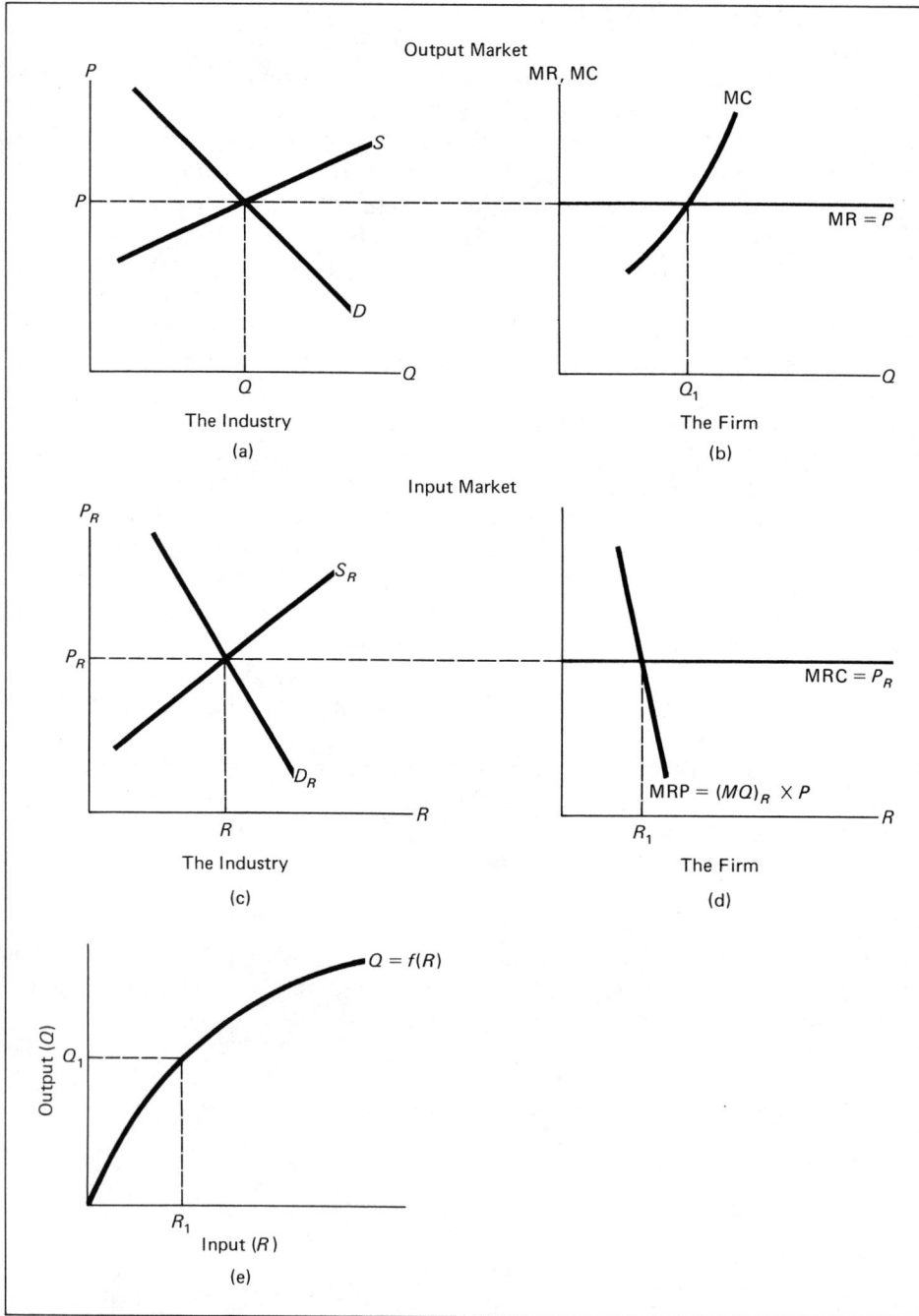

FIGURE 15-3
The profit-maximizing level of employment of a resource (R) produces the profit-maximizing level of output. The firm hires R_1 units of the variable resource and produces Q_1 units of output as shown in (e). This volume of output also corresponds to the point where MR equals MC for the firm in (b). Panel (d) shows that the resources's marginal revenue product equals the resource's marginal cost at R_1. Figures in (c) and (a) indicate that the resource as well as product markets are perfectly competitive.

DEMAND FOR VARIABLE INPUTS
WITH EXOGENOUS CHANGES

The profit-maximizing firm's input–purchase decisions are guided by the marginal revenue product and the marginal resource cost. If the *price of the output increases,* the MRP rises and, ceteris paribus, the demand for the resource increases along with it. In a graph, rising output prices shift the MRP curve upwards, and in the case of a decline in the price of the output, the MRP of the resource shifts inwards toward the origin.

In a perfectly competitive framework, a *change in the supply* of the inputs affects its market price and therefore the marginal resource cost to the firm. For instance, if the labor market is perfectly competitive, and more workers desire to enter the market to look for jobs, the equilibrium wage rate will fall. A reduced wage will lower the MRC to the firms, and the profit-maximizing firms will find it profitable to hire more workers.

Changes in technology largely affect the productivities of the resources. All other factors remaining equal, if newer methods of production increase the marginal product of a resource, its marginal revenue product will increase. Again, profit maximizers will hire more of such a resource in order to earn more profits. The net increase in profits will be the gross profits minus the added cost of the improvements. The firm can use marginal or incremental reasoning to justify the installation of newer (or technologically superior) machines and the adoption of different methods of production.

Many other changes can affect the marginal revenue product or the marginal resource cost of the input. So far we have allowed only one thing at a time to change in order to determine the effects of that change alone on the demand for the input. But one change can and does lead to other changes. For example, if the price of the resource falls, the firm's marginal resource cost will also decline, and the firm will hire more of the resource. In so doing it will also expand output. An increase in the supply of the output—provided the increase is appreciable due to larger output volumes of all the firms—will invariably depress the market price of the output. When the price of the output falls, the resource's marginal revenue product also declines and the profit-maximizing firms reduce their purchase of the input. Thus, although the price reduction of the resource may lead the firms to purchase more of the resource, in the long run, the firms may not desire such a large increase in the demand for that resource. Figure 15-4 illustrates the case of the change in demand for a resource after the output price has been affected.

Substitution and Output Effects

In Chapter 3 we discussed the substitution and income effects of a price change. There are also similar effects associated with a change in the price of an input. Suppose the firm uses two variable inputs, capital (K) and labor (L). If the price of L falls, the firm will tend to substitute labor for capital in order to produce a given volume of output. This is the *substitution effect,* and essentially involves the movement from one point to another along a *given* isoquant. But, since the firm's *real* budget outlay is higher (due to lower prices of the input), it moves to a higher isoquant and operates at a point where the

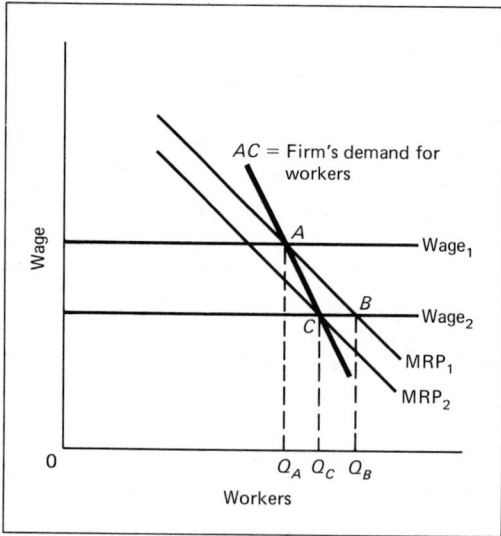

FIGURE 15-4
Initially the firm hired Q_A workers at wage W_1. When the wage rate fell to W_2, the firm increased its use of workers by moving to point *B*. However, when more workers were employed, the output of all such firms increased and depressed the price of the output, which in turn lowered the workers' marginal revenue product, causing the firm to hire only Q_C workers. In effect, the firm's demand for labor is shown by *AC* if the price of the output varies with employment.

isocost (budget) line is tangent to the isoquant. Depending on the rate of substitution between capital and labor, the amount of the relative price change, and the size of the initial budget as well as the initial input–price ratio, the firm may hire more capital in addition to hiring more labor. The movement from the original isoquant to the new isoquant is the *output effect* of the input–price change, and is very similar to the real income effect of consumer-utility theory.

Production theory suggests that the marginal product of each input is determined not only by the quantity of that input, but also by the quantities of the other productive inputs. Thus, the marginal product of labor is influenced by the quantity of capital, just as the marginal product of capital is affected by the quantity of labor employed with it. If this is true, the price change of one of the inputs will affect the demand for all the other inputs. Thus, a decline in the price of labor will lead the firm to alter not only its purchase of labor, but also the acquisition of capital, as shown in Figure 15-5.

Diagram (b) of Figure 15-5 shows that the firm is initially employing L_1 units of labor along with K_1 quantity of capital, and producing Q_1 units of output at point 1, where the budget line is tangent to isoquant Q_1. Diagram (a) shows that the firm is maximizing its profits by equating labor's marginal revenue product to its price at point *A* with L_1 units of labor. Diagram (c) shows that the firm is maximizing profits at point *D* by equating the marginal revenue product to the price. The firm is following the optimization rule (the equimarginal principle) developed in the chapters dealing with production and cost, where the costs to the firm were minimized when the ratio of the marginal products of the resources equalled the ratio of their prices. Since the firm is a profit maximizer, $(MRP)_L = P_L$ and $(MRP)_K = P_K$; or $(MQ)_L \times MR = P_L$ and $(MQ)_K \times MR = P_K$. Since the output is being produced and sold in perfectly competitive markets, the MR is constant and is the same when applied to purchase decisions concerning capital or labor. Therefore, in hiring K_1 of capital and L_1 of labor, the

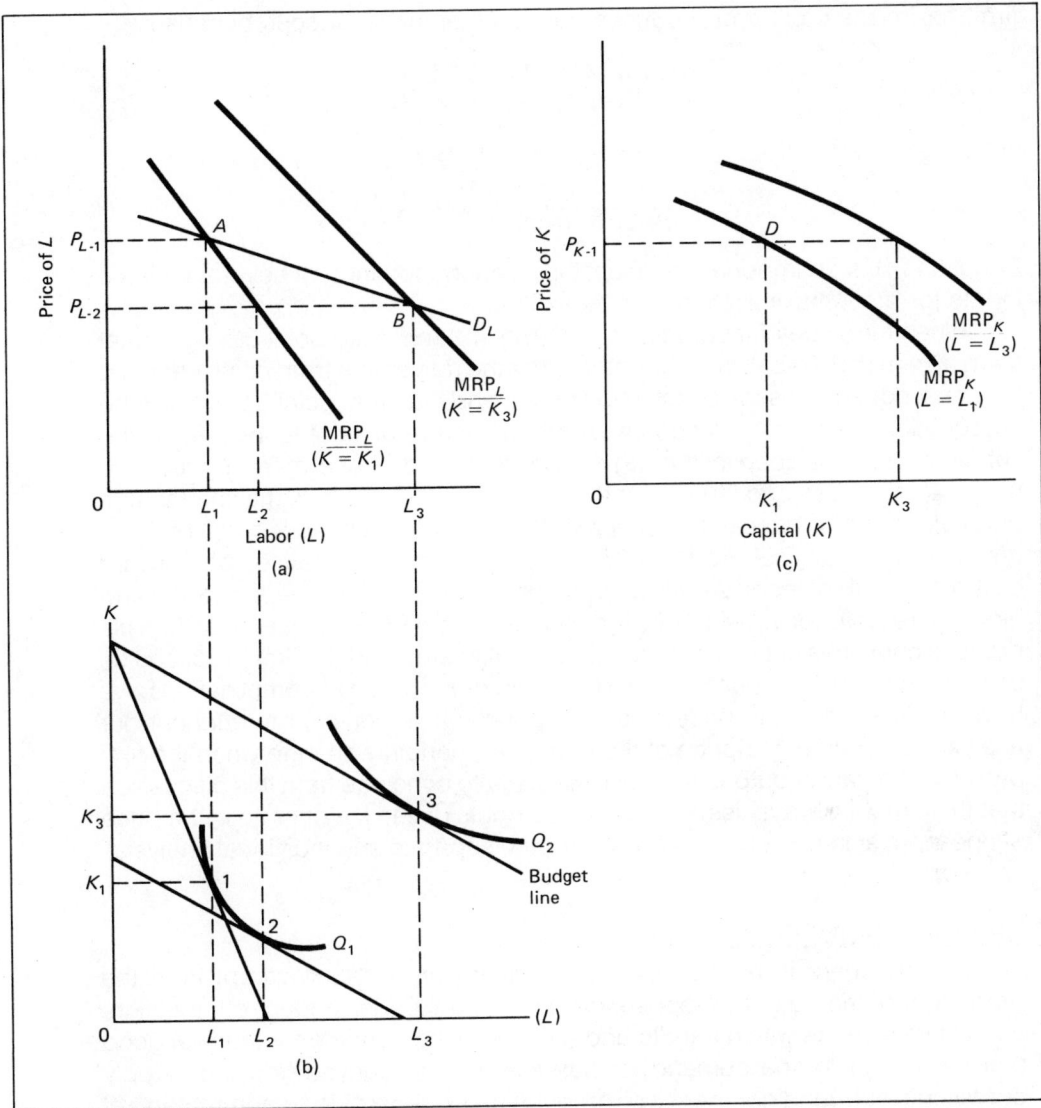

FIGURE 15-5
As the price of labor declines, the firm uses more L and more K as shown in (b), and
moves from point 1 on isoquant Q_1 to point 3 on isoquant Q_2. More K also implies higher
marginal productivity of L, and the use of more L raises the marginal product of K.
Because the marginal product of K goes up, the firm's demand for K, and hence the
MRP_K increases in (c). Panel (a) indicates that the demand for L is not only a function of
its price but also of the quantity of the other resource(s), in addition to being dependent
on the price of the output as shown in Figure 15-4.

firm maximizes profit and produces output Q_1 at the least cost, because

$$\frac{(MQ)_L \times MR}{(MQ)_K \times MR} = \frac{P_L}{P_K} = \frac{(MQ)_L}{(MQ)_K}$$

and

$$\frac{P_L}{(MQ)_L} = \frac{P_K}{(MQ)_K} = MR \tag{4}$$

Equation (4) is an important relationship used in the hiring of several variable inputs for profit maximization.

When the price of labor falls to P_{L-2}, the firm moves to point 3 on isoquant Q_2 [diagram (b)]. Recall from Chapter 7 that the movement from point 1 to point 2 along isoquant Q_1 is the substitution effect, and that from point 2 to point 3 the output effect. However, as soon as the firm hires L_2 units of labor (due to the substitution effect), capital's marginal product (and hence marginal revenue product) increases and the demand for capital shifts outward, making the firm purchase more of the capital resource. When the firm employs more of the K resource, the marginal product of L is increased and this causes an outward shift of the MRP of labor, as shown in diagram (a). When this happens, the firm hires more units of L, which in turn affects the MRP and usage of K. This process continues until the budget is totally allocated and the firm produces Q_2 units of output with L_3 units of L and K_3 units of K. To avoid complications, we have assumed that the price of the output remains constant throughout our analysis. Of course, the price of the output will certainly change when the firm produces the larger output. It is not necessary to conclude from this discussion that the firm will always use more of all the inputs due to the change in the price of one input alone. Each situation will require separate and individual analysis.

A MODEL OF DERIVED DEMAND

Usually, there is no autonomous demand for an input except from the producers of the output. Suppose knives are sold under perfect competition. Each knife is made with a handle and a blade. If the demand for the final good (knives) is known, the demand for handles can be derived from the supply conditions surrounding the sale of blades. Disregarding other factors of production, the knife manufacturer should be willing to buy handles at a price which is equal to the difference between the price of knives and the price of blades. Thus, if each knife can be sold for $12, and each blade can be purchased for $4, the knife manufacturer will pay a *maximum* of $8 for each of the handles.

Figure 15-6 describes the derivation of the demand for blades from the information provided by the demand for knives and the supply of handles. To obtain the derived demand for blades, we subtract the supply price of handles from the demand price of knives at each quantity. The demand function so derived may be used by the seller of blades for the selection of the "best" price for blades, provided the blade seller can set his own prices.

In this chapter we examined some of the basic principles that underlie the

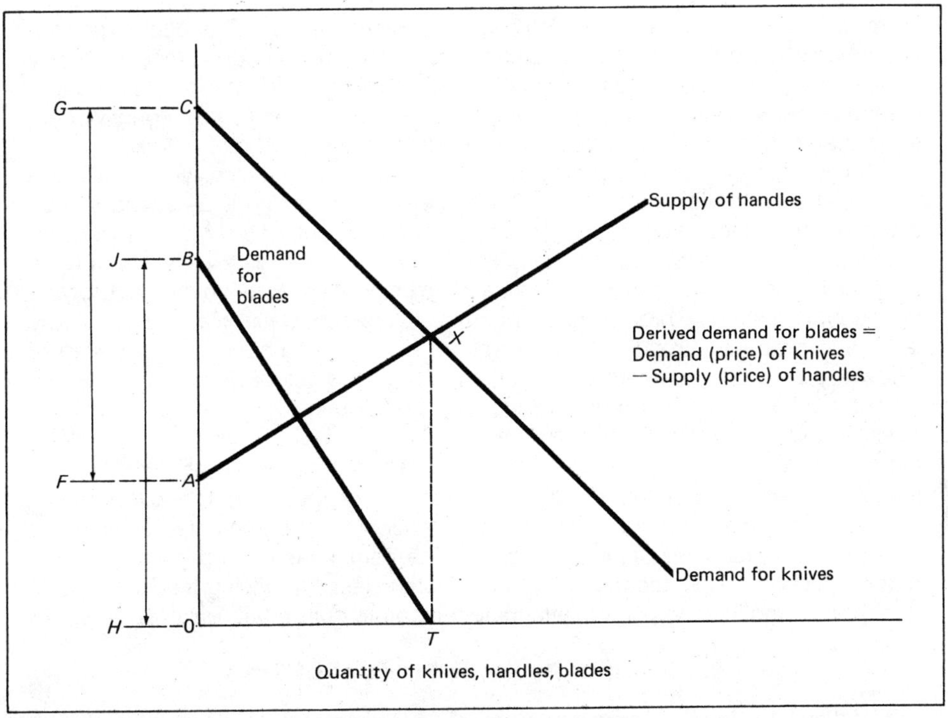

FIGURE 15-6
The "derived demand" for a resource can be obtained by subtracting the supply price of the other resource from the demand price of the product. Thus, we can derive the demand for blades by subtracting the supply price of handles from the demand price for knives at each corresponding price. The graph shows that distances *OB*, *HJ*, and *FG* are the same and form the intercept for the demand for blades. At point *T*, the demand price for blades is zero because at this quantity the supply price of handles exactly equals the demand price of knives. Line *BT* represents the derived demand for blades.

profit-maximizing firm's decisions to hire inputs. The models were based on perfectly competitive markets both in the industries selling the output and those selling the resources. To illustrate the concepts we employed only a few resources, such as labor and capital. Realistically speaking, there are many types of resources and varieties of competition and market structure in the output as well as the input markets. There are also many special models describing certain unique features of resources and market powers possessed by the buyers and sellers of resources. We will explore some of these, as well as models of land and entrepreneurial resources, in Chapter 16.

APPLICATIONS

1. Cesar Chavez in Hollywood

As you are probably aware, there has always been some unrest between the lettuce growers and their employees who have great admiration for the advice and wisdom of Mexican-American labor leader Cesar Chavez. The laborers have been uniting in order to force the lettuce growers to pay them higher wages. The lettuce growers presumably cannot afford to do so, because the market for lettuce is highly competitive (hence the price of lettuce is set by supply and demand), implying that the growers would either lose money or make less profit if they did pay higher wages, since they cannot push the cost on to consumers in the short run.

Some agronomists and engineers are working on a machine that will replace human labor in the lettuce fields almost 100%. If the machine is as successful as claimed, the lettuce growers will fire the workers and rely solely on mechanized equipment, that is, highly capital-intensive technology. In the meanwhile, the workers will have all the more reason to unite into a large union in order to prevent the growers from adopting the new production techniques. In the end, California will have a very large and probably strong labor union of lettuce workers under the leadership of Chavez, but all the members will be unemployed. This will probably lead to some violent confrontations between the workers and the growers, and it is entirely possible that the union members will attack the machines to destroy or sabotage them. The law will move in to handle the mess and Hollywood will have another theme for a movie about human foibles, the vagaries of Nature, and the ever-present battle between man and machine. Ironically enough, most of the research on these lettuce-farming machines is being done on the campuses of land-grant colleges, and it has been suggested that the inventors of the labor-replacing machines ought to subsidize the incomes of the lettuce-field laborers out of their royalties.

2. Marginal Revenue Product of Stars

It is difficult to conceptualize the "output" of movie stars, unless you adopt a particular point of view. For instance, a good movie may have many socially desirable features ("redeeming social virtues") predominantly due to the convincing acting of the movie stars. Some stars are very popular because of the image they exude. Popular stars who are good box-office attractions provide high sales revenues for the theatre owners. If you are a movie producer, you will be more interested in the movie's success with bookings and perhaps with your image as the producer of good films. If you are the owner of a theatre, your primary concern will rest with the movie's ability to attract customers.

In essence, the demand for a movie star's services is a derived demand. The movie producer will accordingly attempt to calculate the star's marginal revenue product before offering him or her a contract. The marginal revenue product of a star is the additional revenue associated with his or her presence in a movie. Thus, if the inclusion of Sigmund Arafat in *Camels in Germany* will add $3 million to revenues, Arafat's marginal revenue product will be about that. If the movie producer can obtain Sigmund's services for $1 million, she will do so in the interest of profits. As a matter of fact, the producer should be willing to hire any movie actor or actress whose market price is no greater than his or her marginal revenue product. One can apply the same principles to the calculation of payments to football players, boxers, and business consultants.

3. Should You Buy an Extra Iron?

We are referring to golf irons, which are occasionally helpful in executing a perfect shot onto the green. Not all golfers have a complete set of woods, irons, and wedges. Suppose your best score for a standard 18-hole course (par 72) is 100. You feel that if you buy a Number 3 iron, which you do not have now, your score will improve by 20 strokes. If you play for money, such an improvement could amount to sizeable winnings (or savings!) over the life of the iron. As a rational profit maximizer (and utility seeker), you should purchase the iron if its price (marginal resource cost) is no higher than the expected monetary value (marginal revenue product) due to the improvement in your game. Thus, if you feel that you will be 50¢ per game better off, you normally play 30 games per year, and the expected life of the iron is five years, you should pay (neglecting the opportunity cost of money) no more than $75 for the iron.

EXERCISES

1. Define and explain the following:
   a. Marginal product.
   b. Marginal revenue product.
   c. Marginal resource cost.
   d. Profit-maximizing level of employment.
   e. Input.
   f. Output.
   g. Perfectly competitive resource market.
   h. Net marginal revenue product.

2. How will each of the following affect a resource's net marginal revenue product? Explain.
   a. The cost of raw materials increases.
   b. The price of the output falls.
   c. The firm must now pay an exicse tax.
   d. The transportation cost per unit of output increases.
   e. The demand for the output increases.
   f. The industry supply of the input decreases.
   g. The firms switch to a new technology, which uses more of the other resources.
   h. The government puts a price ceiling on the price of the input.

3. Provide examples for (a)–(h) in Exercise 2.

4. Suppose the San Diego Zoo is interested in adding a new exhibit in the form of an Indian white tiger. Identify the relevant criteria that should be used in the decision to acquire the feline.

5. Assume that the output market is under perfect competition with the demand and supply functions:

$$\text{Demand: } P = 100 - 0.002Q$$
$$\text{Supply: } P = 40 + 0.004Q$$

   a. What will be the equilibrium price of the output?
   b. How many units of output will be produced by the entire industry?
   c. If the marginal product of the variable resource R is known to be

$$(MQ)_R = 20 - 1.25R$$

   what will be the equation for the resource's marginal revenue product?
   d. If the demand and supply conditions in the R market are

$$\text{Demand: } P_R = 733.33 - 0.01R$$
$$\text{Supply: } P_R = 466.67 + 0.01R$$

   what is the equilibrium market price of R? Equilibrium quantity?

e. Write an expression for the firm's marginal resource cost as obtained from (d).

f. How many units of R will a profit-maximizing firm hire? [See part (c) above.]

g. Approximately how many firms are there in the industry (for output) if each firm buys an equal quantity of R?

h. What is the output of each firm?

i. What is the profit per firm if there are no costs other than the cost of R?

j. What will happen to the quantity of R purchased by each firm if the demand for the output increases?

6. How would you attempt to measure the marginal revenue product of a resource employed in the public sector?

7. Do university teachers and professors, as well as administrators, have any marginal revenue products? Identify them.

8. Can a firm use marginal productivity theory to arrive at the "optimal" quantity of advertising on television?

9. Explain, with the use of the discussions contained in this chapter, whether you should go after a Ph.D. degree.

10. How would a book-publishing company make use of the theories explained?

SUGGESTED READINGS

Bell, C. "Working Women's Contribution to Family Income." *Eastern Economic Journal,* Vol. 1, 1974.

Brown, S., *et al. Regimes for the Ocean, Outer Space and Weather.* Washington, D.C.: Brookings Institution, 1977.

Feitelman, N. "Economic Stimulation of the Rational Utilization of Minerals." *Problems in Economics,* April 1978.

Flanagan, R. "Discrimination Theory, Labor Turnover and Racial Unemployment Differentials." *Journal of Human Resource,* Spring 1978.

Frank, R. "Why Women Earn Less: The Theory and Estimation of Differential Overqualification." *American Economic Review,* June 1978.

Mitchell, C. "The 200-Mile Limit: New Issues, Old Problems for Canada's East Coast Fisheries." *Canadian Public Policy,* Spring 1978.

Negatani, K. "Substitution and Scale Effects in Factor Demands." *Canadian Journal of Economics,* August 1978.

Randall, A. "Contemporary Issues in Natural Resource Economics: Discussion." *American Journal of Agricultural Economics,* May 1978.

Chapter Sixteen Chapter Sixteen Chapter Sixteen

MORE ABOUT RESOURCES

In Chapter 15, we discussed the behavior of profit-maximizing firms when the output and input markets operate under conditions of perfect competition. The price of the output is determined by supply and demand, and each firm accepts the price of the output as given. Similarly, in a perfectly competitive resource market, each resource's price is also determined by the interaction of market demand and supply and, consequently, each resource unit also accepts the going price. Both the buyers of resources (the firms) and the sellers of resources are pricetakers. In this chapter, we will examine the consequences of imperfectly competitive resource and output markets and their effects on the price and quantity purchased of the resources.

IMPERFECT COMPETITION IN THE RESOURCE MARKET

Perfectly Competitive Output Market

Producers often purchase resources in markets that are not perfectly competitive. Under such circumstances, the quantity of a resource supplied varies with its price. An example is a labor union that controls the quantity of labor supplied to a firm at various wage rates.

Assume that the firm sells its output in perfectly competitive markets. As a result, the firm's marginal revenue, which is equal to the price of the output, is constant. The marginal revenue product of the resource is the marginal revenue of the output multiplied by the resource's marginal product. If the firm purchases the resource under conditions of imperfect competition, it faces two resource cost curves in making decisions about the level of input purchase. One is the marginal resource cost (MRC) function discussed in Chapter 15, and the other is the average resource cost (ARC). The firm will still follow the rules for profit maximization, but the price of the resource will not equal the firm's marginal resource cost.

Table 16-1 shows the derivation of the various revenue and cost values the

TABLE 16-1

(1) Price of resource	(2) Units supplied	(3) Total output of resource	(4) Total cost of resource $(1) \times (2)$	(5) Average resource cost $(3)/(2)$	(6) Marginal resource cost $\triangle(3)/\triangle(2)$	(7) Price of output	(8) Marginal revenue product $\triangle(3) \times (7)/\triangle(2)$
$ 9	0	0	$ 0	—	—	$0.10	—
10	1	340	10	$10	$10	0.10	$34
11	2	620	22	11	12	0.10	28
12	3	840	36	12	14	0.10	22
13	4	1030	52	13	16	0.10	19
14	5	1215	70	14	18	0.10	18.50
15	6	1385	90	15	20	0.10	17
16	7	1400	112	16	22	0.10	1.50

firm requires to arrive at the optimal level of input purchase. The firm's output sells for 10¢ per unit, and we are assuming that the variable resource's marginal physical product declines as the firm increases the use of the resource. Additionally, the quantity of the resource supplied varies directly with its price. The firm's profit-maximizing level of input purchase occurs where the marginal resource cost equals the marginal revenue product of the resource, that is, when the firm purchases 5 units of the resource. Although the marginal revenue product is not exactly equal to the marginal resource cost, the firm will find it unprofitable to hire 6 units, because the marginal cost of the sixth unit ($20) exceeds its marginal revenue product ($17). Notice also that five units of this resource can be purchased at a price of $14 per unit. Thus the average cost of the resource to the firm is also $14, while the marginal resource cost is $18. It is the marginal resource cost that the firm takes into account in making decisions about the quantity of a resource to be purchased or hired.

Table 16-1 shows that when the supply of a resource varies with its price, the average resource cost (ARC) and marginal resource cost (MRC) are no longer equal. In the case of the perfectly competitive resource market, because the price of each unit of the resource is constant, the MRC equals the ARC. However, in the case just discussed, the MRC is higher than the ARC, for the same reason that the average variable cost of production is influenced by the marginal cost. When the marginal cost of the output production exceeds the average variable cost, the AVC increases. Thus, with reference to Table 16-1, both the MRC and the ARC will rise as the number of units of the resource increases.

Figure 16-1 illustrates the relative positions of the MRC and the ARC in the case of a firm that is selling its output competitively, but purchasing labor under conditions where the MRC is higher than the ARC. Because a supply curve relates the quantity supplied to the price, the ARC function is also the supply curve of labor S_L. Curve S_L shows that the quantity of workers "offered" by the

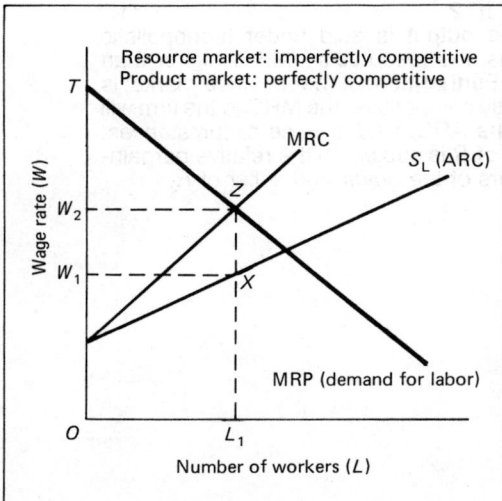

FIGURE 16-1
If the resource market is imperfectly competitive, the firm faces a marginal cost of labor different from the supply curve of labor. Since each additional worker hired contributes to an additional variable cost greater than the higher wage itself, the MRC function lies above the S function. This is because not only is a higher wage necessary to attract a larger number of workers, but all workers receive the higher wage in the absence of wage discrimination. This firm would hire L_1 workers and pay them a wage of only W_1, since at that wage rate they would voluntarily "supply" their labor in the quantities shown.

labor union is positively related to their price (or wage) W. Thus, the S_L is the average resource cost (average variable labor cost) to the firm. The marginal resource cost above the ARC represents the change in the total cost of labor resulting from a one-unit change in the level of input purchase. If this firm is a profit maximizer, it will equate the MRP (the short-run demand for labor) function with the MRC, and hire L_1 employees at a wage rate of W_1. The total cost to the firm will equal area OW_1XL_1. Because the total revenue due to the utilization of L_1 units of labor is given by the area under the MRP function, area W_1TZX represents the total revenue contribution of labor to the firm. Furthermore, because the marginal revenue product of the workers exceeds the wage rate, according to some, the worker is being *exploited*. Note that even if the labor union is successful in demanding a wage rate of W_2, the firm will still hire L_1 workers. Although its profits will not be as much as before, they will be maximum under the circumstances.

Imperfectly Competitive Output Market

When the firm that buys the resources sells its output in markets that are under imperfect competition, the marginal revenue from the sale of the output is not equal to the price of the output. Under such circumstances, the demand for the firm's output lies higher than the corresponding marginal revenue function, and both curves are negatively sloped. Consequently, the marginal revenue product of a resource—the product of the resource's marginal product and the marginal revenue of the output—declines very rapidly with the use of additional units of resource. It declines first of all because the marginal revenue declines with increases in output; and second because of the assumptions concerning the diminishing marginal productivity of the resource.

When the price of the output exceeds the marginal revenue, the monetary

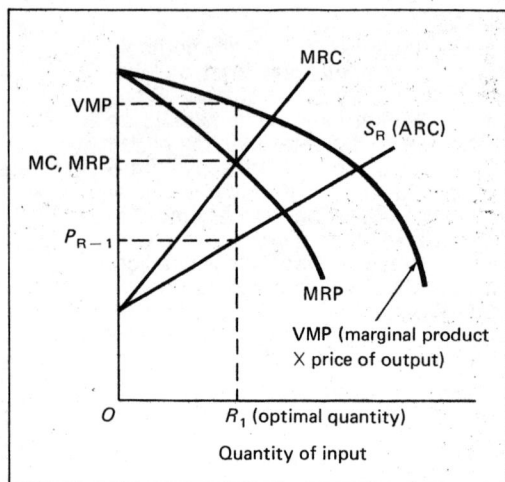

FIGURE 16-2
When the output is sold under monopolistic conditions, the resource's VMP is higher than its MRP. Furthermore, if the resource market is imperfectly competitive, the MRC to the firm will exceed the ARC. Under these circumstances, the price of R is subject to the relative bargaining powers of the buyer and seller of R.

value of the marginal product of the resource, known as the value of the marginal product (VMP), is different from the resources marginal revenue product (MRP). The VMP function lies above the MRP, just as the demand (average revenue) function lies above the marginal revenue. The profit-maximizing firm chooses that quantity of resource which equates its MRP with its MRC.

In Figure 16-2, the firm maximizes profits by hiring R_1 units of resource at a price of P_{R-1}. Notice, however, that the MRP of the R_1th unit of the resource is higher than its price, which results in some "exploitation" referred to earlier, and also that the VMP exceeds its MRP as well as price. This is another form of exploitation, since the firm receives a value higher than what the resource receives in payment. It is generally acknowledged that a resource will be exploited somewhat if its price is below its marginal revenue product. But the exploitation will be greater if the firm that purchases the resource sells its output in a monopolistic market.

Monopsony

We discussed the theory of monopoly under imperfectly competitive output market models. *Monopsony* refers to a resource market in which there is a single buyer of the resource. For example, in a small town, the local mining company may be the sole employer of the town's inhabitants. In the antebellum South, some large plantations were monopsonistic employers of slaves. In professional football, the AFL or the NFL has considerable influence over the employment status of the players. Just as a monopolist in the output market has considerable market power, a monopsonist also wields substantial power in the input market. However, a monopsonist has an additional power over the resource market—its ability to engage in *price discrimination* in the purchase of the resource.

If the monopsonist is the only purchaser of a resource, such as labor, it can conceivably offer different prices for different units of the resource. As long as each worker receives a price which is at least as high as the supply price, the workers will agree to be hired by the monopsonist. Thus, if the supply of the resource is positively related to its price, the monopsonist can offer the progressively higher prices to each additional unit of the resource, where each new price corresponds to a given level of resource supply shown by an S or ARC function. Since each new unit of the resource receives a unique price for services, the S function is the firm's MRC.

Figure 16-3 shows how a firm may buy a given resource. We will use labor as our resource, although we could use this model for any type of production factor. Assume that a university is a monopsonist. If the institution is a profit maximizer and can pay prices suggested by first-degree price discrimination in the theory of the firm, it can hire teachers along the supply curve S. Since each additional worker is paid the wage which urges him or her to offer employment, the price on the S function constitutes the MRC for the firm. For example, at an annual salary of $12,000, only one teacher may want a job and,

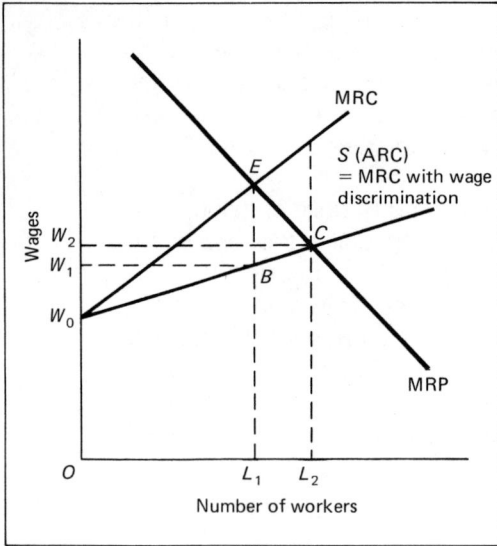

FIGURE 16-3
If the firm can hire each worker at a unique wage rate, the supply function (of labor) is the effective MRC. Consequently, the profit-maximizing firm will employ L_2 workers and pay them wages ranging from W_0 to W_2.

at an annual salary of $13,000, another teacher may also be interested in a teaching position. If the university pays both teachers $13,000, the total cost will be $26,000, or $14,000 above the cost to employ a single teacher at $12,000. However, since the first person will work at the $12,000 salary and the second one will not, the university can hire the first and second at $12,000 and $13,000, respectively, thereby saving $1000.

In Figure 16-3, the firm would ordinarily hire L_1 teachers and pay each a wage of W_1. However, if the firm can pay each worker a different wage, and each additional worker can be attracted with a slightly different wage, the effective marginal cost of hiring the workers will be given by the resource's supply curve, labeled S. Consequently, the profit-maximizing level of employment will occur where the resource's marginal revenue product equals its *marginal* price (or wage), which is given on the supply curve. In Figure 16-3, the MRP equals the ARC at an employment level of L_2. The workers now receive wages ranging from W_0 to W_2, and the total labor cost to the firm is given by the sum of all the individual wages, shown by area OW_0CL_2.

SUPPLY OF INPUTS

Firms purchase a supply of inputs to produce goods and services. The resources are supplied under a variety of conditions, just as the output is sold under many different market structures. There are four broad categories of factor inputs—land, labor, capital, and entrepreneur. Instead of analyzing the supply conditions surrounding each type of resource, we will examine a few models as they apply to some of the factors of production. We will also explore a few empirical models and evaluate the findings in relation to the theories of the resource market.

THE LABOR MARKET

The Individual Supply of Labor

The elementary model of the supply of labor effort assumes that all the time available to a worker is allocated between work and leisure. Work (and hence income) allows the worker to purchase goods and services which provide utility, and leisure (or nonmarketable time) yields satisfaction obtained from leisure-time activities. The utility-maximizing consumer (worker) therefore budgets his or her total time so that the ratio of the marginal utility of income to the marginal utility of leisure equals the price of income divided by the price of leisure. If we divide the available time into hours, the price of an hour's worth of work is equal to the wage rate, while the price of an hour of leisure is the value of the goods and services that the worker sacrifices during each hour of leisure. Consequently, the ratio of the price of work and the price of leisure equals (W/P_G), which equals the *real wage* per hour. Thus, the rational worker, if he or she faces no other constraints, will allocate the total available time according to equation (1):

$$\frac{\text{Marginal utility of income}}{\text{Marginal utility of leisure}} = \frac{W}{P_G} \tag{1}$$

Figure 16-4 shows the indifference curves for a worker whose utility is a function of goods (G) and leisure (L). The object is to attain a combination of G and L which lies on the highest possible indifference curve. Such a point normally occurs where the budget line is tangent to the indifference curve. In this situation, the budget line is restrained by the maximum total time available

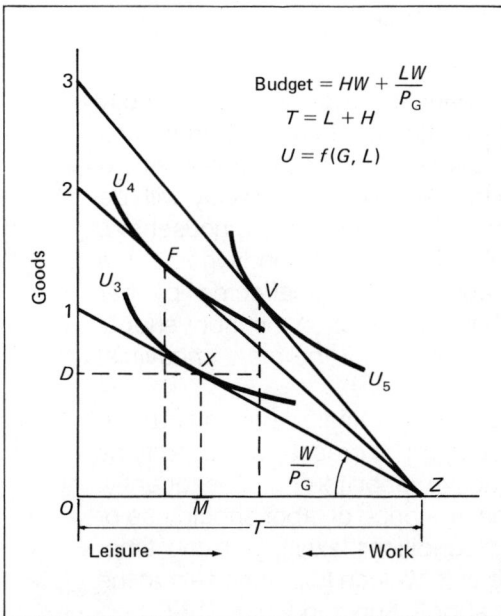

FIGURE 16-4
A utility maximizing individual will operate at a point where the budget line is tangent to an indifference curve. Initially she is at point X, but as the real wage rate (W/P_G) increases, she moves to point F and then subsequently to V. At V, she prefers to work less than at points F or X.

(*T*), the price of goods, and the nominal wage rate. The time available for work (*H*) and leisure (*L*) is measured along the horizontal axis, and the vertical axis measures the quantity of goods (and services). Given the values of *W* and P_G, we can draw an income budget constraint having a slope of (W/P_G). This line is tangent to indifference curve U_3 at point *X*. The worker maximizes utility by working *ZM* hours, and devoting *MO* hours to leisure. The *ZM* hours of work provide the worker with *OD* quantity of goods, an amount purchased with (W/P_G) × *OD* amount of real income. We are assuming here that the consumer spends all of his or her income.

If the utility function of the worker is stable, and the total time available remains the same, a change in either P_G or *W*, or both, may cause the ratio (W/P_G) to change. The slope of the budget line will also change, and the worker will maximize utility at a different point on another indifference curve. What can we hypothesize about the amount of work that he or she will now offer if the real wage changes?

Assume that the real wage rises because *W* rises proportionately more than P_G. When the real wage increases, the budget line for this worker is tangent to indifference curve U_4 at point *F*. This particular worker will offer more work for higher real wages. It is possible, however, that a worker will offer less hours of work, if allowed, when the real wages rise. For instance, if the new budget line is tangent to U_5 at point *V*, less work will be supplied. This type of behavior is called the "backward bending supply" of labor. This type of behavior is possibly true of some of the underdeveloped or developing economies, but is seldom applicable to advanced economies like that of the United States, where the workers (wage earners and salaried) do not have that much control over the hours of work they would like to offer.

Household Supply of Labor

The labor supply decision of an individual cannot be considered as strictly isolated, because the decisions about work are often made according to their effects on other members of the household, as well as sociocultural household priorities. Thus, a decision to work an extra ten hours per week will be governed by such factors as whether the worker is the head of the household, whether there is more than one earning member in the family, and whether the group has very small children. A wife's labor supply is affected by her husband's earnings, yet the wife's earnings have no effect on the labor supply of the husband. Some authors have called this behavior the *male chauvinist* model of labor supply.

As long as industry is willing to substitute male for female workers and vice versa, the supply of labor should decrease or increase as conditions encourage *net* entry into, or exit from, the active labor force. Consequently, under perfectly competitive market conditions, the price of labor should rise or fall depending on the demand and supply conditions existing at the time. Taking the household as the decision-making unit, we can hypothesize that the supply of labor will be similar to the secular supply curve in Figure 16-5.

In Figure 16-5, segment *FG* is the range in which all members of the

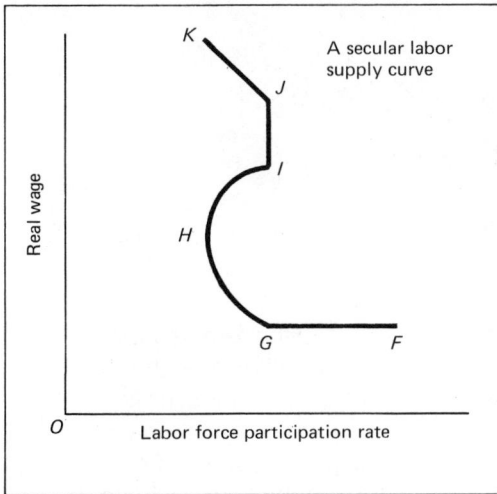

FIGURE 16-5
A secular labor supply curve.

population must work in order to subsist. Segment *GH* constitutes the backward-rising portion and is probably typical of countries in the early stages of industrial development and rising real incomes. In portion *HI,* the increase in real income is accompanied by an increase in the participation rate, because the new level of income affects the group's tastes and consumption patterns. The higher the level of income, the greater the demand for income-elastic goods and services and, therefore, the higher the offer of labor effort. Section *IJ* may be more characteristic of highly developed or fully industrialized economies. Here, the tendency to retire early or to pursue educational careers depresses the rates of participation, although in many cases this is partially offset by increases in the participation rate by females. The more advanced the economy, the less time required to produce "home goods," and consequently the greater the availability of time for work by the domestic spouse. Lastly, portion *JK* may be reflective of highly advanced postindustrial societies, where the citizens may offer very little labor for appreciable periods of their working life.

An Empirical Participation Model

Empirical studies show that the labor force participation rates in the United States and England have been remarkably stable from the late nineteenth to the mid-twentieth century. This apparently corroborates the participation behavior alluded to in Figure 16-5, and corresponds to section *IJ* of the secular supply curve. During the period under investigation, the participation rates of males declined, while that of females increased. One of the more famous empirical models examining participation phenomena is that offered by Mincer. Mincer estimated an equation of labor force participation rates of married females ($LFPR_{mf}$) from data for 57 standard metropolitan areas in 1950:

$$LFPR_{mf} = a - 0.62H_p + 1.33P_L + 0.12E - 0.41U - 0.24C$$

where

a is a constant;
H_p is the median income of male heads (with wife) in 1949;
P_L is the median income of females in 1949;
E is the percent of population aged 25 and over with at least a high school education;
U is the percentage male unemployment rate;
C is the percent of families with children under six years of age.
(All income is measured in thousands of dollars.)

Mincer's equation explained about 60% of the variation in the female labor participation rate as a function of the variables. The equation suggests that a $1000 increase in the husbands' incomes tends to reduce the participation rate of the wives by 0.62 percentage points. However, for an identical increase in the wives' incomes, ceteris paribus, the labor force participation rate of husbands increases by 1.33 percentage points. More recent studies have found the wage response of married women to be greater than the response of married men, due to the income of the household supported by a male head. We can explain this large response by females if we assume that women have a better alternative to work (in the market) in housework than do men, although this may no longer be true with economies and social structures like those of the United States. Presumably such an alternative increases the women's elasticity of labor supply to the market.

Many other empirical investigations have been conducted by economists and other social scientists. Some of these studies concentrate on the characteristics of the supply of hours of work, while others focus attention on labor force participation rates by age, sex, and ethnic background. Econometricians have attempted time-series as well as cross-section analysis to formulate the quantitative model of labor supply. Work is continuously going on in the area of model building as it applies particularly to women and other "disadvantaged" segments of the labor force.

Bilateral Monopoly

When a single buyer (monopsonist) of an input confronts a single seller (monopolist) of this input bilateral monopoly occurs. For example, if the school district is the sole employer of teachers, and the teachers negotiate terms through their union, we have a case of bilateral monopoly. Another instance of bilateral monopoly involves the federal government and the postal union. For the following discussion, we will simply label the two parties as firm's management and union. We will further assume that the monopsonist sells his or her output in a perfectly competitive market.

Figure 16-6 shows the respective curves representing the revenues and costs to the monopsonist and the union monopolist. In this case, the union is the "seller" of labor. The profit-maximizing firm's short-run demand for the input is given by the MRP function. If management sets the wages of the employees, the level of employment will be at L_1 and the wage rate per person will equal

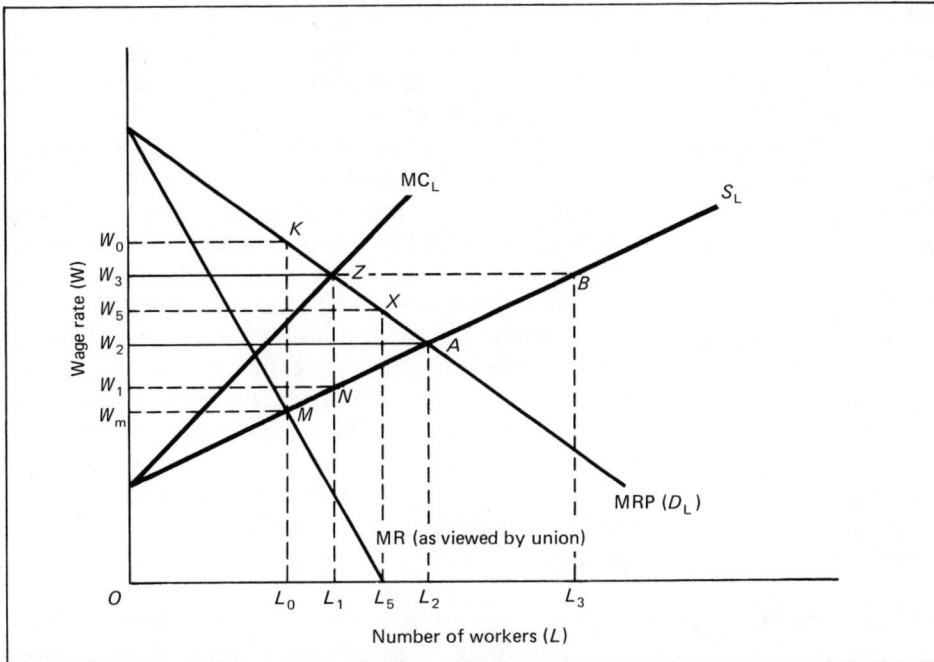

FIGURE 16-6
Different wage demands bring about different results. The union can demand a wage as high as W_3 without affecting the volume of employment chosen by a firm that maximizes profits. But a wage rate of W_2 will maximize employment. The total maximum wages will come from a wage rate of W_5. Each wage rate has a unique level of employment associated with it. The union's "profits" are maximized if it obtains W_0 at employment L_0 and pays each worker his or her supply price W_m. The two possible extremes that can occur are management's demand for L_1 at W_1 and the union's proposal for L_0 at W_0. The actual wage and employment combination depends on the relative strengths of the monopsonist and the monopolist. Some have suggested that the two will set that level of wages and employment which will maximize their joint gains.

W_1. The total income to the working members of the union will amount to area OW_1NL_1. Now the union can attempt to do any one or a combination, of the following:

1. Maximize the wage rate without affecting employment.
2. Maximize the level of employment.
3. Maximize the total wage bill.
4. Maximize the union's "profits."

1. Maximization of the Wage Rate
The profit-maximizing firm will hire quantity L_1 of labor and pay wage W_1. However, the union realizes that the MRP of labor at L_1 is as high as W_3. If the union sets wages at W_3, the horizontal line W_3Z will be the effective marginal cost to the firm and it will hire the same number of people L_1 but pay them wage W_3. The total income to the worker is now OW_3ZL_1. Here, the union prevents the exploitation profit from going to the firm and keeps it for the workers. The firm has no reason to hire any fewer than L_1 workers if it is interested in maximizing profits.

2. Maximization of Employment

The union can get its members to work for management if and only if the wages are no less than the prices shown along the labor supply curve. Consequently, the maximum level of employment occurs at an employment level of L_2 and at wage rate W_2. The firm will hire more workers at a wage less than W_2, but the workers will need to be paid a higher wage (as shown by the S_L) in order to be persuaded to work. In order to maximize the number of working members, the union demands wage W_2 per person. Under the circumstances, the effective marginal cost to the company is the horizontal line W_2A. The profit-maximizing firm, considering this to be its marginal cost, will hire L_2 workers at wage W_2. The total number working will have increased by $(L_2 - L_1)$ and the total wage to all workers (L_2) will be OW_2AL_2. Notice that under conditions of maximum employment, the union is not able to secure the maximum wage. Presumably, the entire union membership is better off, since the wages are higher than they would have been (W_1) without union efforts, and employment is greater than it would have been (L_1). In this particular case, as far as the total income of workers goes, the maximum wage and L_1 level of employment will bring less total income than the maximum employment and W_2 combination. (Why?)

3. Maximization of Total Wages

Most often, unions receive a percentage of the total income of workers as their "fees." Furthermore, members who are laid off or those on strike have to be supported by certain funds maintained by the union. These funds are maximized if the union secures the maximum total wages from the firm. A firm earns maximum total revenues by pricing its product at the point on the demand curve where the price elasticity of demand is 1 (absolute value.) This, for linear demand curves, occurs at the midpoint and at a quantity where the marginal revenue equals zero. Think of the union as the seller. It has a demand for its product (labor) shown by the MRP curve (D_L). The marginal revenue curve for the demand curve D_L is shown by the thin line labelled MR, which crosses the L axis at an employment level of L_5. The "price" corresponding to L_5, is wage rate W_5. Thus, if the union is successful in demanding and obtaining wage W_5, the firm will employ L_5 and the total wages to all the workers will be given by area OW_5XL_5, and this will constitute the largest possible level of total wages to union members. Since this area is greater than area OW_2AL_2, if the union is truly interested in the well-being of its members, it can distribute the total wages among the unemployed members. Those not working will presumably be satisfied if they receive, say, 80% of their "normal" wages. In essence, the union will have employed more people at higher wages than was the case initially with wage rate W_1.

4. Maximization of Union's "Profit"

If the union is a profit-maximizing monopoly seller of labor, it will demand a wage rate and level of employment that equates its marginal revenue and marginal cost. Since each worker would be happy to receive a wage along the S_L line, the union considers it to be its marginal cost. When this marginal cost is equated to the marginal revenue, we have the wage rate and employment combination that maximizes the union leader's net return, or "profits." Such a combination comes about if the union selects wage rate W_0

and employment level L_0. If the firm buys L_0 workers at a wage of W_0, the total income to the union will be OW_0KL_0. However, L_0 workers will be willing to work at a wage of W_m and the union can pay amount OW_mML_0 toward labor "cost" and retain the residual of revenues (W_mW_0KM) for itself.

We have broadly outlined the many possibilities that can occur within a bilateral monopoly. Two conflicting but extreme cases are where the management hires L_1 workers at a wage of W_1 in order to maximize its profits, and where the union demands a wage of W_0 and employment of L_0 workers to maximize its net return. The monopsonist buyer can no more force the monopolist seller to behave as under perfect competition than the monopolist seller of labor can force the firm to be a pricetaker. The actual wage and employment levels will occur at a level which *maximizes the joint return* of both parties. From Figure 16-6, we can surmise that the ultimate wage will be less than W_0 but greater than W_1, and employment more than L_0. The utility of the union decision makers will be maximized where the "budget line" formed by the demand for labor is tangent to the highest indifference curve of the union. Such a development is shown by Figure 16-7.

THE CAPITAL MARKET

We have already examined the importance of capital in production as well as its contribution to the productivity of the other resources, particularly that of labor. The discussion of capital can be centered around the demand and supply of capital goods, such as machines; or the analysis can be carried out with the notion of monetary capital, where the money invested in productive resources forms a firm's capital stock. In cases where we choose to employ the first definition of capital, the price of capital is expressed in terms of a "rental rate" (per unit of time) of capital, such as $100 per hour per machine, and if we use the monetary definition of investment capital, the "cost" of capital is usually

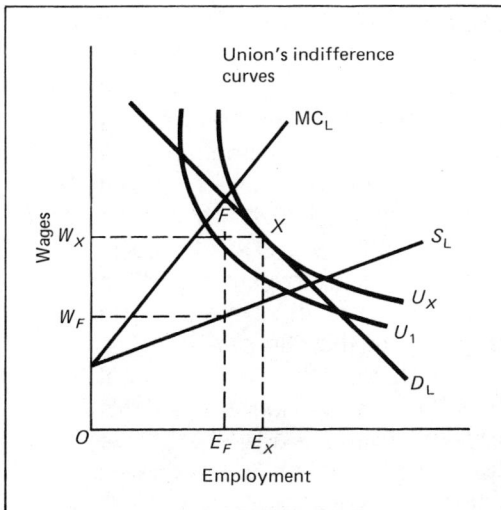

FIGURE 16-7
The union is happy to either secure high wages (and fringe benefits) for its employee–members or provide more employment. The management wishes to keep wages down and hire no more than the profit-maximizing level. The demand for labor is shown by its marginal revenue product and indicated by D_L. Given the wage rate, the firm will employ the corresponding number of workers along this line. The union's indifference map suggests that it will be happiest with a combination of wage rate W_X and employment level E_X. The management, on the other hand, prefers to hire E_F workers at a wage of W_F, which leads to a lower level of utility for the union.

measured in percentages such as 8% per annum. Although the two ideas are quite different, we can nevertheless discuss the theory of capital using either definition. In the following section we will use the monetary version of capital to illustrate the market characteristics and phenomena of the capital market.

The Supply of Capital

Firms have more than one source of capital for their expansion and production plans, and these sources may be either *internal, external,* or a combination of both. Basically speaking, retained earnings provide the biggest source of capital from internal sources. Alternatively, a firm can also draw upon its savings, or liquidate certain assets (real or other) in order to raise capital. If the firm's sources of capital are internal, the cost of such capital is the foregone earnings on such capital in their best alternative use. Thus, if a firm's own funds could have been invested at 9% per annum, the opportunity cost of those funds equals 9%. The firm also has two external sources of capital—*debt capital* and *equity capital.*

When the firm borrows money, it incurs a debt, hence the name given to capital acquired by this method. The larger firms are usually able to borrow money at very favorable rates. Since the cost to borrow money is higher than the opportunity cost of holding internal funds idle, the supply of debt capital is shown to be coming forth at a higher cost of funds. Finally, a firm may be able to raise equity capital by issuing new ownership shares (such as stocks). Because dividends are taxable, while interest expense is not, the cost of obtaining equity funds is higher than that of debt funds. Furthermore, in many cases, the risk taken by the purchaser of stock is greater than that normally faced by the lender of funds, who is usually covered by some sort of collateral. Figure 16-8 shows the basic supply function for capital as discussed. It also shows a demand function for capital which is an inverse function of the interest rate.

The Demand for Capital

Whenever a certain amount of capital is invested, the investor or firm is interested in obtaining a rate of return from its use. Consequently, a profit-maximizing firm will weigh an additional dollar's worth of capital investment in terms of its benefits and costs, or revenues and costs. Thus, if the firm can expect to earn 8% by adding an additional $10,000 of capital equipment to its plant, the marginal return of this incremental investment will be 8¢ on the dollar. Therefore, in order for the additional investment to be profitable, the cost of these funds should be no higher than 8¢ per dollar, or 8%. In Figure 16-8, the marginal return from each dollar of additional investment and the corresponding level of total investment forms the firm's demand for capital. When the demand for capital of all firms is aggregated, we obtain the total demand for capital. When the demand for capital is equated with the supply of capital, we arrive at the market rate for capital.

The demand for capital is influenced by the productivity and revenue-

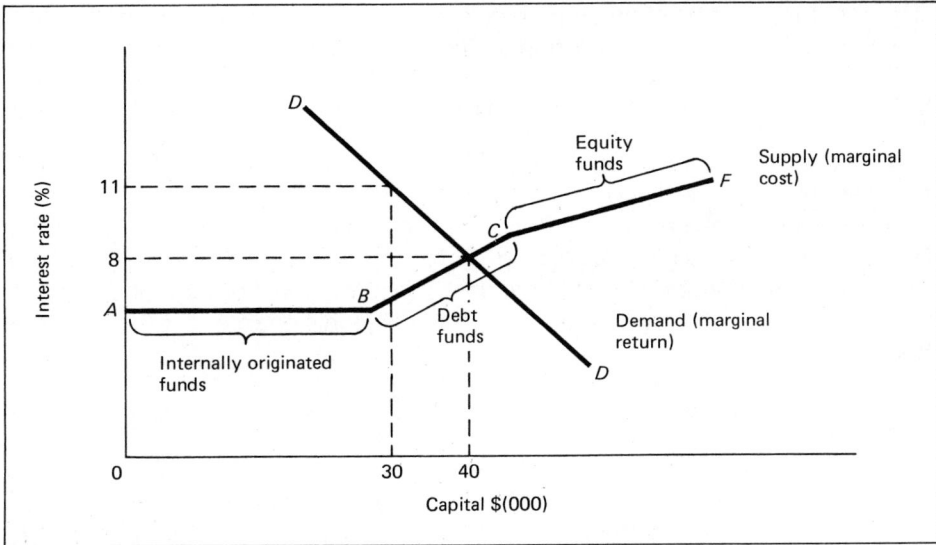

FIGURE 16-8
A firm can obtain funds from internal or external sources. Retained earnings of the firm may be invested by the firm or used for expansion, and consequently, there is an opportunity cost associated with such funds. Portion *BC* shows the supply price of borrowed capital, and *CF* the cost of raising money by issuing stocks.

creating capacity of the projects into which the capital is poured. The revenue and the productivity are also influenced by the market conditions in the output market as well as by the conditions surrounding the other resources. All investments that promise at least a positive rate of return are considered by the firm, and those whose marginal return exceeds their marginal cost are generally selected by profit-conscious firms.

DISTRIBUTION OF INCOME AND FACTOR PRICES

In each category of resources, there are different types of markets, and resource market conditions in conjunction with those of the output market and the goals of the firm influence the price of a factor of production. The price of a resource and the quantities of that resource employed affect the total income of that resource. Changes that affect any of the variables that influence the values of the resource market variables also affect the income of a resource and perhaps the distribution of income between different resources. We will use a simple Cobb–Douglas production function to elaborate on a model of income distribution.

A Model of Income Distribution

In a Cobb–Douglas production function, the quantity of output (Q) is a function of two inputs (K and L), such that

$$Q = K^a L^b \tag{2}$$

The "optimal" combination of the two resources under these conditions is that which minimizes the cost of producing the output given the prices of the inputs. This ratio is

$$\frac{K}{L} = \frac{aP_L}{bP_K} \quad \text{or} \quad L = \frac{bKP_K}{aP_L} \tag{3}$$

where P_L and P_K represent the prices of L and K, respectively. Because the firm is also interested in maximizing profits, it equates the marginal revenue product of a resource to its marginal cost. The profit-maximizing condition can be satisfied by the following (see the appendix to this chapter at the end of the book):

Marginal resource cost of labor = Marginal revenue product of labor

or

$$P_L = (P_{output}) \times (\text{Marginal product of labor})$$
$$= (P_0) \times (bL^{b-1}K^a) \tag{4}$$

Similarly,

$$P_K = (P_0) \times (aK^{a-1}L^b) \tag{5}$$

Substituting equation (5) into equation (3), we get

$$L = \frac{bKP_K}{aP_L}$$
$$= \frac{bKP_0 \, aK^{a-1}L^b}{aP_L} = \frac{bK^a L^b P_0}{P_L}$$
$$= \frac{bQP_0}{P_L} \tag{6}$$

In equation (6), QP_0 represents the total revenue to the firm, and labor receives $P_L L$ of that. Thus, the income to L equals $P_L L$, and from equation (6),

$$P_L L = bQP_0 \tag{7}$$

Similarly, the other resource, capital (K), receives ($P_K K$) from the total revenue, which equals

$$P_K K = aQP_0 \tag{8}$$

The total income to L and K then equals $bQP_0 + aQP_0$, or $(a + b)QP_0$.

Realistically, under the model of perfect competition, if firms maximize profits (and minimize production costs), $(a + b)$ cannot exceed 1. The marginal productivity theory suggests that under conditions of perfect competition, each resource is paid the value of the marginal product, and if $(a + b)$ exceeds 1, the payments to the factors of production will exceed the revenues to the firm. If $(a + b)$ does exceed 1, the firm's revenues must at least be as great as the payments to K and L. This can happen if the output market is under imperfect competition, and the marginal product exceeds the resource's marginal revenue product.

In the special case where $a + b = 1$, a represents the share of income (or revenue) received by K, and b the share of income going to L. Equation (6) may be thought of as the profit-maximizing demand function for labor, and a similar expression ($K = aQP_0/P_K$) may be treated as the profit-maximizing demand for the resource K. The share of income going to L and K will be influenced by the production function, the relative price of the inputs, the price of the output, and the market structures in the output and input markets.

So far we have concentrated on two resources—labor and capital. It is understood that firms require more than just these two resources. For instance, almost all goods or services produced require *land resources*. Although there are many definitions of land, it is basically a natural resource, available either in fixed supply and inexhaustible, or in variable quantities and reproducible in nature. The available acreage suitable for agriculture or real estate development near a city is usually limited. If more space is desired, the builders must either build vertically, or eliminate some of the existing structures. Consequently, the supply of land is normally shown as a positive function of its price, implying that higher prices may bring forth larger amounts of land into a particular use. In economics terminology, a factor of production available only in limited quantities receives *economic rent*. Rent is the payment made to a production factor which is in excess of the price that would have brought forth its supply. This type of excess payment generally occurs because of the factor's scarcity.

In Figure 16-9, the demand for and supply of a land resource are shown to determine the price of the resource. Since price P_1 will purchase the entire supply of this resource, and because the market price happens to be P_m, the resource receives an excess payment of $P_m - P_1$ on each unit. The total rent received by this resource equals $P_m P_1 AB$. Notice that if the demand for this

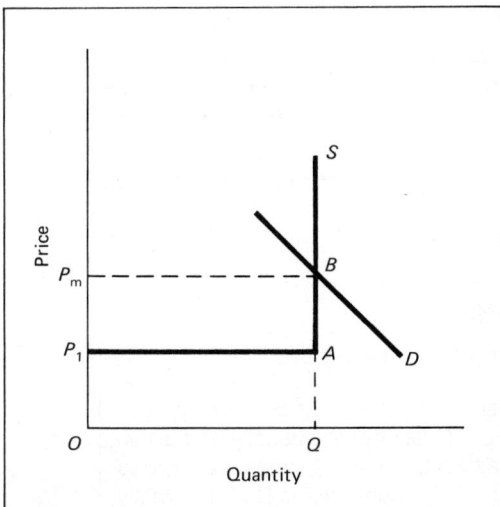

FIGURE 16-9
Line P_1AS shows the supply function of a resource such as land. The price of such a resource is determined by demand and supply forces, and is shown to be P_m. Because the minimum supply price of this resource is P_1, the excess payment shown by area P_1P_mBA constitutes economic rent. If rent is taxed away from the seller, the after-tax price will be P_1.

resource intersected the supply at point *A*, the payments to this would be OP_1AQ, and the resource's income would not have included any rent.

Practically the entire core of the theory of the firm is based on profit-maximizing behavior, and this presupposes that the firm's decision makers (including the original entrepreneurs) are very much interested in profits and therefore "optimizing." Consequently, we can use one or several of the models already discussed in analyzing the probable consequences of external and internal changes on the price and use of a resource. We can employ models of utility, production, profit, and programming to explain the behavior of the entrepreneurs as well.

There are four broad categories of resources—land, labor, capital, and entrepreneur—and each type of input receives income from the users of the resources. The producers or firms demand the use of the resources because the consumers demand the output produced with these resources. Hence, the demand for an input is largely a derived demand. Just as the output market can have a variety of competition, so can the market for inputs. The objectives of the firms, along with the demand for the output and productivity of the resource, influence the demand for that resource. The firms then compare the benefit from using the resource to its cost of acquisition, basically governed by the price of the resource. The "best" quantity of input use is then determined by the firms.

Given the market structure of the resource market, we can determine the income earned by a particular type of input. In some cases, the resource supplier can "dictate" its price and control supply; in others it is relegated to the role of a "price taker." In general, more of a resource is utilized when the output market is perfectly competitive than when it is operating under conditions of imperfect competition. Again, in general, more of an input is used if the resource market is under perfect competition than when it is subject to market "imperfections" such as monopsony. Presumably, the resource is "exploited" when the output or the input markets are imperfect.

The income of resources, as well as the distribution of income among them, is influenced by conditions of production, technology, the output and input markets, other external factors, and the objectives of the users (firms) and the owners of the resources. In macroeconomic terms, the usage of a resource produces income and output, which in turn influences the income and income distribution of the resources, and these again affect the output as well as input markets. We will have more to say about the interdependence of input and output markets in Chapter 17.

APPLICATIONS

1. Is a Ph.D. "Worth" $30,000 a Year?

A Ph.D. (Doctor of Philosophy) degree is considered the ultimate of achievements in formal academic training. Most of the holders of doctoral degrees usually end up on university or college campuses. Although not all Ph.D.s earn salaries as high as $30,000 for an academic year at the start of their career, some do. Is Dr. Fudd really worth $30,000 a year?

If the university is rational, it should pay a resource no higher than what the resource "contributes" to the university. The contribution of a resource in the marketplace is measured by its marginal revenue product. A private university is more likely to use the hard-nosed "incremental" point of view in its decision to hire or not hire an individual. What, then, is a university professor's output, and for that matter his or her marginal revenue product?

The output of a college professor is not any single product or service, although he or she is primarily engaged to teach. A reasonably conscientious teacher also attempts to publish articles in scholarly journals and books, and takes part in job-related professional activities. In most cases, such efforts pay off in a better reputation for the institution, a higher caliber of teachers, more research funds for the university, and, most important, more and better students. If a particular Ph.D. is expected to provide the university an additional $100,000 a year in one form or another, he or she should be paid at least $30,000.

Why only $30,000 and not $60,000? That is a good question. The ultimate salary of a new faculty member depends on the university's estimate of his or her marginal revenue product, as well as the conditions of the resource market. If the professor in question is very unique to a discipline and highly sought after by many universities, he or she may very well command a high salary. On the other hand, no matter how brilliant he or she is, if there are 3000 other equally able teachers applying for the same job, this professor may be forced to accept a lot less than the true worth of his or her contribution. Of course, if it "costs" a lot more to "produce" a Ph.D. than it does a teacher with a Master's degree, the demand price of the first has to be higher than the second. But, then again, a university may decide to hire M.A.s in place of Ph.D.s; or it may be forced to hire doctorates because of job descriptions or state laws.

2. The Demand for Capital and the NPV

If you recall, the profit-maximizing firm will use a dollar of additional capital if and only if the marginal benefit of that dollar is at least as great as its marginal cost. In most capital-intensive projects, the capital outlays occur first and the benefits or revenues follow. To decide on the profitability of a project, we can use the net present value (NPV) criterion.

The net present value of a project is the difference between present value (PV) of all revenues (R) and the present value of all costs (C). Because most revenues accrue to the firm in the future, we can obtain their present value by discounting them with an appropriate rate of interest. For example, if the opportunity cost of capital is 10%, $110 a year from now is worth only $100 today. Similarly, if there are any costs, or reductions in costs that occur in the future, their present value can also be obtained by the discounting process. There are many tables available to us that make discounting easier. We used one such table of interest rate factors in Chapter 3.

Why do we discount the future flows of revenues and costs? If we do not discount these values, we will, in effect, be ignoring the cost of money or capital. For example, if you can receive $1000 ten years from today by investing $500 today, it does not mean that you are receiving a 100% return on your investment, nor are you receiving 10% a year. The use of the discounting process takes exclusive recognition of the opportunity cost of money. After all, if the costs and revenues are brought to their present values and the net present values are calculated, the project with the highest NPV is the most profitable.

Consider the following situation, where a student has just finished his first four years of college and is not sure whether to go on in a five-year Ph.D. program. Although he realizes that his future income will most probably be a lot higher with a Ph.D. than with a B.S., he also knows that he could be working and earning an attractive income right away by not going to graduate school. He has compiled the following information:

Incremental benefits from a Ph.D.: An extra $X in income per year
Incremental cost of a Ph.D. (five years after B.A.): Opportunity cost in lost earnings—$12,000 per year; cost of schooling—$6,000 per year.

The student feels that at most he can work for the next 35 years, and that there is a considerable amount of "intangible benefits" associated with the advanced degree, but does not know their monetary value. He is interested in finding out what the minimum $X needs to be before he should go on for the Ph.D. If he does not go on for any more education, he can earn 10% on his money.

Essentially the problem calls for evaluating additional future benefits ($X) which would justify the expenditure of $18,000 a year for the next five years, money which could have earned him 10% interest. Using the 10% table provided in Chapter 3, we find that if the student had invested $18,000 per year for five years, he would have accumulated 5.867 × $18,000, or $105,606 at the end of the five-year period. After that time, he expects to receive the benefits in the form of additional compensation. Thus, after the five-year education the student will have invested $105,606, whose present value is precisely that amount at that moment in time. Now the student should be interested in determining the future annual benefits in the form of the additional annual pay ($X), which would pay for an initial investment of $105,606. The annual additional pay will last for 30 years from the time that the student receives the Ph.D. degree.

To find the future annual benefit which is necessary to "recover" the investment of $105,606, we use the (A/P) factor for 30 years and notice that its value is 0.0888. When this number is multiplied by $105,606 (P), we obtain the annual value (A) necessary. This annual value, or the unknown $X, now equals 0.0888 × $105,606, or $9,377.81. Thus, if the student expects to receive at least $9,377.81 more per year than he or she would receive with just a B.A., the pursuit of the Ph.D. would be justified. You can verify that the PV of $9,377.81 per year at 10% for 30 years is exactly $105,606, hence the net present value of the entire investment is zero. When a project's NPV is 0, the project earns the stipulated rate of return; when it is less than 0, the project is earning less than the opportunity cost of capital, and when NPV exceeds 0, the project is profitable.

EXERCISES

1. Define and explain the following:
   a. Marginal product.
   b. Average product.
   c. Marginal revenue product.
   d. Marginal resource cost.
   e. Value of marginal product.
   f. Average resource cost.
   g. Monopsony.
   h. Monopoly.

i. Derived demand.
j. Net present value.
k. Economic rent.

2. We have discussed monopsony. Explain *oligopsony*.

3. Assume there are only a few buyers of a resource. Develop a "kinked demand" model for the resource.

4. Suppose a firm produces cigars that are sold at 10¢ each in a perfectly competitive market. Each cigar requires 2¢ of raw material, and there are no costs other than the cost of labor, which is $100 per week. The productivity of the labor force is such that during a week, the marginal product of labor (L) is

$$(MQ)_L = 11,250 - 2L$$

where L represents the number of workers employed. How many workers should the firm hire in order to maximize profits? What amount of profits will it make?

5. Repeat Exercise 4 with the price of labor (P_L) equal to

$$P_L = 50 + 0.00L$$

6. Using suitable graphical analysis, show that in the long run a greater level of employment will result if the output market is purely competitive than if it is under imperfect competition.

7. Why is it that some elementary education teachers with Ph.D. degrees earn only $14,000 per year, while others with no graduate education earn much more than twice that amount?

8. Explain why labor unions might be very much in favor of minimum wage laws for nonunion employees.

9. How does legislation that places a "ceiling" on the price of the output affect the income and price of the resources used in the production of the output. Provide examples.

10. Suppose you wish to produce 100 units of output by using two resources A and B using a method which produces output (Q) according to the formula $Q = AB$. Select several sets of prices for A and B and compute the optimal combinations of A and B that will yield the desired output. What is the least costly ratio of A to B? Will you always select this ratio? Why or why not? What factors determine the prices of A and B?

11. Compute the NPV of the following project. Use the 10% table.
    Initial outlay = $200,000
    Additional outlay after 10 years = $100,000
    Annual cost of upkeep = $2000
    Salvage value of assets = $50,000
    Life of project = 20 years
    Annual gross receipts = $20,000

Is this project profitable?

12. Why do universities grant sabbatical leaves to faculty?

13. Assume that a firm's production function of one variable L is

$$Q = 100L - \tfrac{1}{2}L^2$$

and the demand for the firm's product is

$$P = 50 - \tfrac{1}{10}Q.$$

Compute the profit maximizing level of demand for L for each of the prices of L: $500, $300, $200, $100, $50. Also determine the corresponding volumes of output and output prices. (Hint: $MQ_L = dQ/dL$. Consult the Appendixes to Chapters 15 and 16 at the end of the book if necessary.)

14. Suppose the demand for knives (K) is

$$P_K = 10 - \tfrac{1}{10}Q_K$$

If the supply of handles (H) is

$$P_H = 2 + \tfrac{1}{20}H$$

derive an expression for the derived demand for blades (B) if each knife uses one handle and one blade.

15. How would you "measure" the marginal revenue product of a new airplane? Elaborate upon all issues to be taken into account.

SUGGESTED READINGS

Barron, J., and McCafferty, S. "Job Search, Labor Supply, and the Quit Decision: Theory and Evidence." *American Economic Review,* September 1977.

Bigman, D. "Derived Demand and Distributive Shares in a Multifactor, Multisector Model." *American Economic Review,* December 1978.

Brown, C., and Medoff, J. "Trade Unions in the Production Process." *Journal of Political Economy,* June 1978.

Greenhalgh, C. "A Labor Supply Function for Married Women in Great Britain." *Economica,* August 1977.

Hansen, W., and Weisbrod, B. "Modeling the Earnings and Research Productivity of Academic Economists." *Journal of Political Economy,* August 1978.

Perry, M. "Vertical Integration: The Monopsony Case." *American Economic Review,* September 1978.

Reder, M. "An Analysis of a Small, Closely Observed Labor Market: Starting Salaries for University of Chicago M.B.A.'s." *Journal of Business,* April 1978.

Warren-Boulton, F. "Vertical Control by Labor Unions." *American Economic Review,* June 1977.

Chapter Seventeen

GENERAL EQUILIBRIUM AND WELFARE ECONOMICS

Through *partial equilibrium* analysis, we have examined consumer models in a particular market and profit-maximizing decisions in a perfectly competitive industry, but we have ignored the consequences of one party's actions. We will now introduce *general equilibrium* analysis, which will permit us to evaluate the possible results due to the interdependence of the various economic units. It will help us determine the outcomes of change as it affects the consumers, the producers, and the resources.

To illustrate the basic nature of the interdependence among the economic agents, suppose all markets are perfectly competitive, the producers maximize profits, and consumers maximize utility. If the demand for a consumer good, such as beef, is influenced by an increase in consumer income, the effects of the change in beef consumption will be felt by all parties involved with the beef industry. For example, a rising demand for beef, ceteris paribus, will decrease the demand for chicken, and the price of beef will rise, while the price of chicken will tend to fall. Fewer chickens will bring forth a smaller quantity of feathers, while the increase in cattle slaughters will provide more hides. Chicken feathers are often used by manufacturers of "goose-down" jackets, and hides are mainly used for the production of shoes. If we assume that the hides are purchased largely by domestic shoe manufacturers, the cost of shoes will decline due to the reduction in the price of hides, while the cost and price of feather jackets will rise. A decline in the price of domestic shoes may very well decrease the demand for imported shoes. The changes in price and quantity in each of the output markets will affect the consumers' utility.

The changes described will also affect the producers' profits and the income of the resources employed in the production of the output. For example, the quantity of beef produced will increase, hence more of the resources (K,L) employed in beef production will be required. On the other hand, since the production of chicken will fall, less of the resources will be employed. Whether the price and quantity of the resources will be affected will eventually be decided by the *net* effect of all the changes. The changes, in turn, will influence the resources' incomes as well as the shares of their incomes out of the total income of all resources.

Figure 17-1 shows some of the probable outcomes of the rising demand for beef. Diagram (a) indicates the price change in the beef industry and diagram (b) shows the effects of price and quantity changes on the chicken industry. Diagram (c) shows that the price of feathers has risen, and diagram (d) tells us that the price of domestic shoes has gone down. The declining demand for imported shoes is shown by diagram (e), and the rising price of feather jackets by diagram (f). In diagram (g) we see the increase in the output of beef, and in diagram (h) the decrease in the production of chicken. Diagram (i) shows the consumers' increase in income accompanied by a decline in the price of domestic shoes which produces an increase in the consumers' utility.

A Simple General Equilibrium Model

Suppose we have an economic system which produces only two goods X and Y with the use of two resources K and L. The total quantity of K and L are

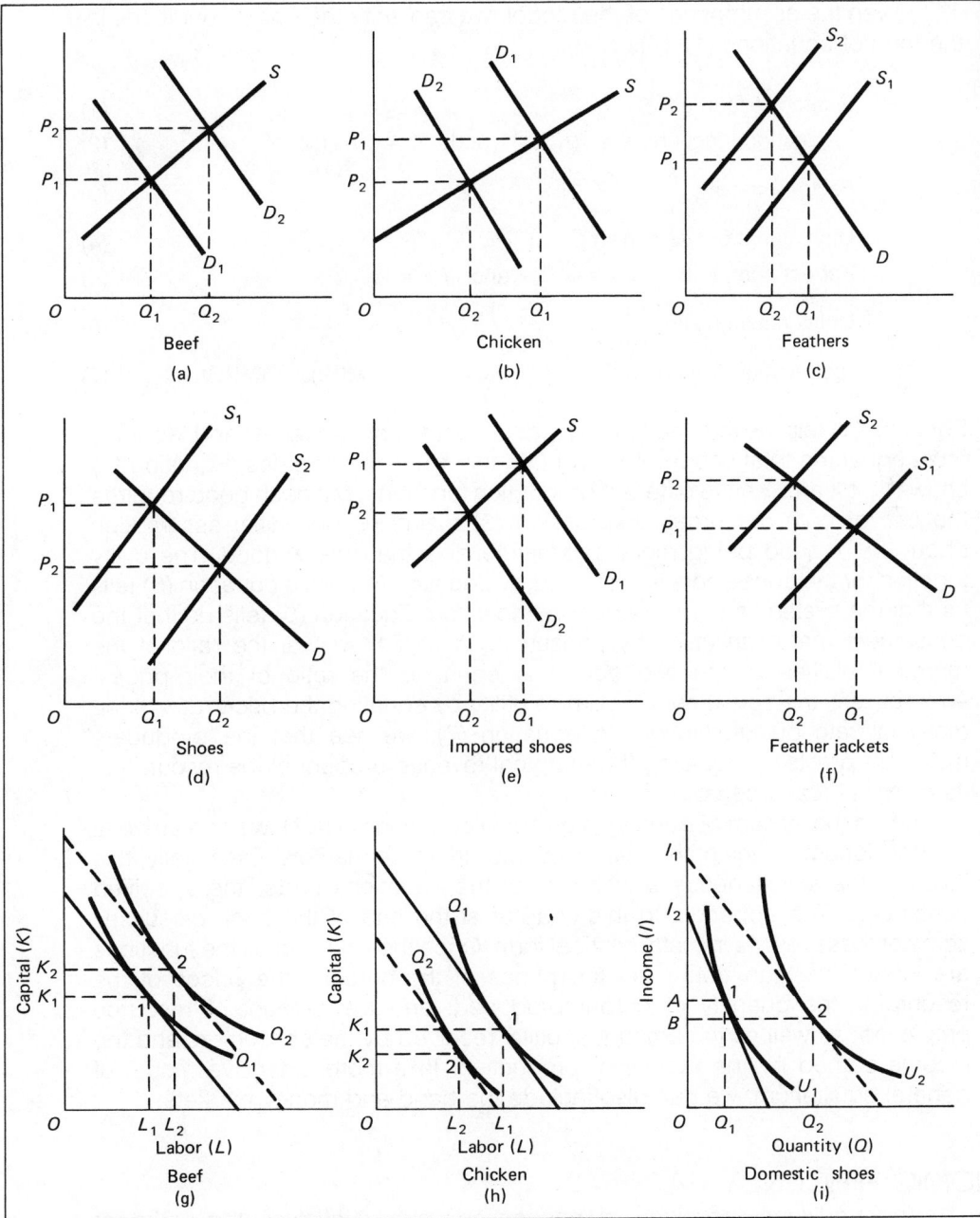

FIGURE 17-1

fixed, the output markets are under perfect competition, the producers maximize profits, and the consumers maximize utility. Furthermore, assume that the Y good is capital-intensive and the X good is labor-intensive. A capital-intensive good requires relatively more capital per unit of labor in production, while the opposite holds true for the labor-intensive good.

Given the assumptions of the model, we can write the basic conditions in the form of equations (1)–(7):

Limited resources: $K_x + K_y = K,$ $\quad L_x + L_y = L$ (1)

Production function: $X = f(K_x, L_x)$ and $Y = g(K_y, L_y)$ (2)

Factor intensity: $\dfrac{K_y}{L_y} > \dfrac{K_x}{L_x}$ (3)

Utility function: $U = f(X, Y)$ (4)

Perfect competition: $P_x = MC_x$ and $P_y = MC_y$ (5)

Utility maximization: $\dfrac{MU_x}{MU_y} = \dfrac{P_x}{P_y}$ (6)

Profit maximization: $(MRP)_L = (MRC)_L$ and $(MRP)_K = (MRC)_K$ (7)

Equation (1) tells us that the total available quantity of capital (K) and labor (L) must equal the total usage of K and L in the X and Y industries. Equation (2) shows that X and Y have different production functions, but each good requires the use of both resources. Expression (3) maintains our initial assumption about the Y good being more capital-intensive than the X good. The utility function for the consumers is indicated by equation (4), while equation (5) tells us that the system is under perfect competition. Equation (6) tells us that the consumers maximize utility by consuming X and Y so that the ratio of the marginal utilities of the two goods is equal to the ratio of their prices. Alternatively, the consumers maximize utility by equating the price ratio to the marginal rate of substitution. In equation (7), we see that the producers maximize profits by equating the marginal revenue product of the resource to its marginal resource cost.

Using the system of equations given by equations (1)–(7), we can arrive at the equilibrium values of the many variables in all the markets. Essentially, this involves the simultaneous solution of all the equations under the specified constraints. The appendix to this chapter at the end of the book discusses some of these results in mathematical form. Once the values of all the functions are known, we can determine the prices of the outputs, the prices of the resources, the quantity of output produced, and the amount of resource employed, as well as the amount of utility received by the consumers and the income earned by the factors of production. In a more extensive model of general equilibrium, we can also include the bond and money markets.

ECONOMIC EFFICIENCY

The traditional definition of economics usually involves the "efficient allocation of resources." This allocation process is carried out through decisions concerning production and consumption. What, then, is economic efficiency in a general equilibrium sense? We will first state the necessary conditions that, in general, contribute to economic efficiency. When these conditions are met, we have the *Pareto optimality,* named after the late Vilfredo Pareto. The basic tenet of Pareto optimality is that a situation is efficient if an attempt to improve one part leads to the deterioration of another.

Pareto Conditions in Production

Producers minimize the cost of producing a given volume of output by equating the ratio of the marginal products of the resources to the ratio of their prices. Continuing our example, since we have only two resources, K and L, they will be used by the X and Y industries in the appropriate combinations. Because the system is perfectly competitive, both industries will pay the same prices for capital (K) as they will for labor (L). Furthermore, because the total quantity of K and L is fixed, the greater the amount of a resource allocated to one industry, the less the availability for the other.

In Figure 17-2, the prices of L and K are w and r, respectively, and diagram (a) shows the optimal capital/labor ratio in the Y industry for the given resource price ratio (w/r) as $(K/L)_Y$, while the cost-minimizing capital/labor ratio in industry X is shown as $(K/L)_X$. The (K/L) ratio for the Y industry is higher than that of the X industry, since Y is a capital-intensive good and X is labor-intensive.

Diagram (b) shows an *Edgeworth–Bowley box*. The height of the box represents the total available quantity of capital, and the width corresponds to the total availability of labor. Thus, the total production of X and Y must be limited to the amounts possible with these resources. The origin for the X isoquants is located at the southwestern corner O_X. As we move from this point to higher isoquants, the quantity of X produced increases. Because more X implies less Y under ordinary circumstances, the origin for the Y isoquants is located at the competing northeastern corner, O_Y. Moving in a southwesterly direction we can get on higher isoquants for Y. Any point inside the box is feasible, but, as we will see, not all points are efficient.

FIGURE 17-2
For any given ratio of resource prices (w/r), Y will use a higher (K/L) than X, as shown by diagram (a). Diagram (b) shows all combinations of X and Y that allow the X and Y isoquants to be tangent to each other. The locus of all these points is called the *efficiency locus*, and is shown by O_XABCO_Y.

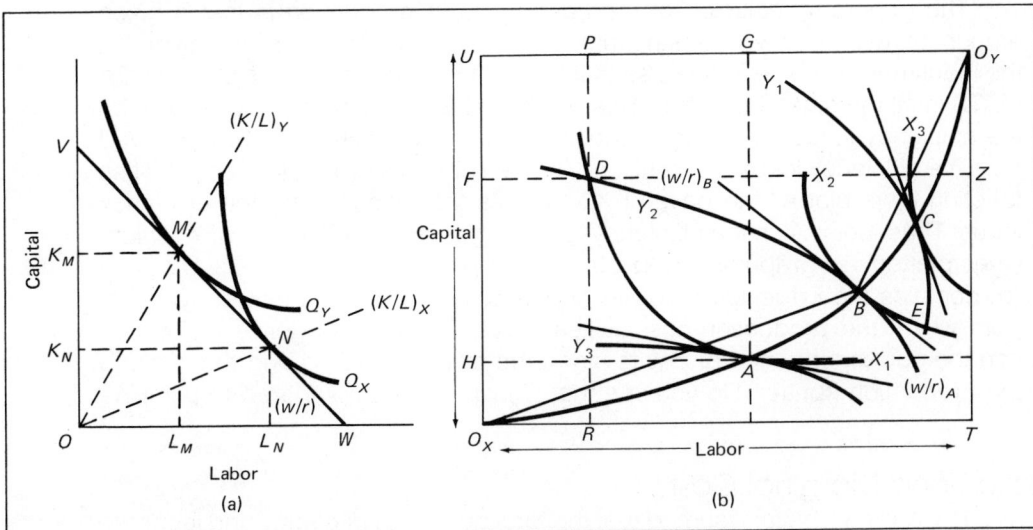

Suppose production occurs at point D, which is at the intersection of isoquants X_1 and Y_2. At that output combination, O_XF of capital, and O_XR of labor are used for the output of X_1 units of X. The remaining amounts of capital (O_{YZ}) and labor (O_YP) are allocated to the Y industry for the production of Y_2 units of Y. Is point D efficient from a production point of view? Can we produce more of either X or Y by moving to another point? Points A and B are certainly more efficient than D. At these points, the X and Y isoquants are tangent to each other. In general, this situation is more efficient than one in which the isoquants intersect.

You probably recognize why A is better than D. At A, we have more Y (Y_3) and the same amount of X (X_1). Similarly, point B yields as much Y as point D, but more X (X_2). When two isoquants are tangent to each other, their slopes are equal, which implies that the marginal rate of technical substitution in each industry is equal. Furthermore, each industry faces the same resource price ratio (w/r), which is also equal to the marginal rate of substitution at such a point of tangency. Notice that the isoquants intersect at point D, consequently the MRTS in each industry is not the same. Under conditions of perfect competition, production will occur only at points where the isoquants are tangent to each other. When all points of tangency are joined together by a line, an *efficiency locus* results. Thus, in Figure 17-2b, the locus of all efficient points is given by the line O_XABCO_Y. At point A, the price ratio of the resources is indicated by the slope of the tangent drawn to both isoquants and labeled $(w/r)_A$.

For the factor-intensity assumptions to be valid, the efficiency locus has to be drawn the way it is—that is, it has been purposely drawn concave from above. No matter where you measure the capital/labor (factor-intensity) ratio along this path, the (K/L) for Y will always be higher than for the X industry. For instance, at point B, the angle subtended by line O_XB and the horizontal line is smaller than the angle formed by line O_YB and the horizontal. What happens to the (w/r) value as we move along this efficiency locus?

The general conclusion of the Pareto rule in production is that a given amount of resources will yield the maximum possible output of Y for a given X if the industries combine X and L so that the MRTS in one industry is equal to the MRTS in all the other industries. This results in the production points shown by the efficiency locus. The much-used production-possibilities curve is derived from the efficiency locus just analyzed. We will obtain a production-possibilities function if we plot all the pairs of X, Y values that occur along the efficiency locus. Thus, point A on the efficiency locus suggests X_1 of X and Y_3 of Y, which, when plotted in a graph on the XY plane, yield point A in Figure 17-3a. Diagram (b) contains the Edgeworth–Bowley box and the associated efficiency locus, from which the production-possibilities curve O_XABCO_Y is derived. You can see the correspondence of points along the efficiency locus and those along the production frontier. Do you see that D is inefficient compared to point A?

Production and Marginal Cost

Because we have assumed that the total quantities of capital and labor are fixed, their "costs" to society are also fixed. Thus, any point along the

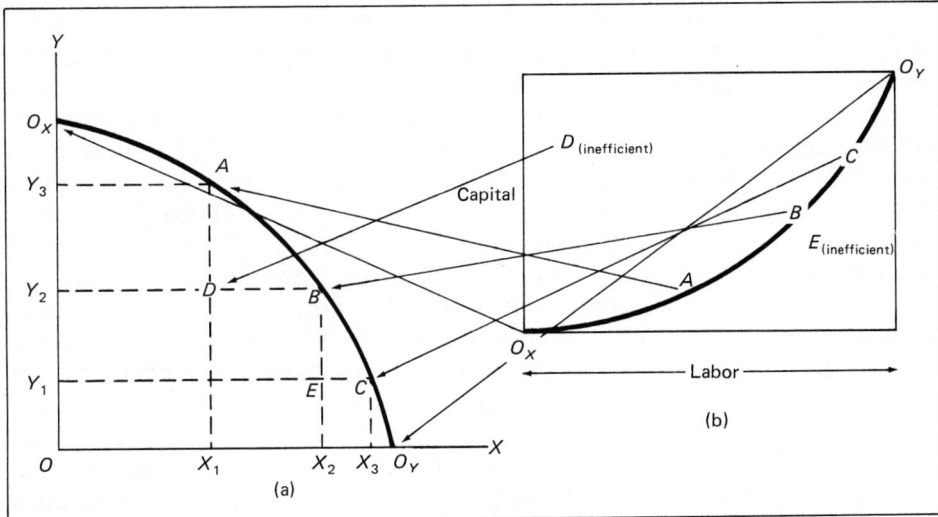

FIGURE 17-3
When the various combinations of the output of *X* and *Y* that lie along the efficiency locus (in diagram (b)), are plotted on the *XY* plane, the production-possibilities curve of diagram (a) emerges.

production frontier involves the same total quantity of resources and hence the same cost. In Figure 17-3, for instance, in moving from point *A* to point *B*, society produces more *X* for less *Y*. Thus, the opportunity cost of each additional *X* is measured by the quantity of *Y* sacrificed. The total additional cost of producing more *X* is offset by an equal decline in the cost of producing *Y*. The total incremental cost of the new *X* is equal to the marginal cost (MC_X) of each new *X* times the number of new *X*, while the cost reduction in the production of *Y* is equal to the marginal cost of $Y(MC_Y)$. While this is not entirely accurate from a mathematical point of view, it will suffice at this point. We may state the preceding discussion as:

$$MC_Y \Delta Y = MC_X \Delta X \tag{8}$$

or

$$\frac{\Delta Y}{\Delta X} = \frac{MC_X}{MC_Y} \tag{9}$$

Equation (9) tells us that the slope of the production-possibilities function ($\Delta Y / \Delta X$) is equal to the ratio of the marginal cost of *X* to the marginal cost of *Y*, (MC_X/MC_Y). This slope is called the *marginal rate of product transformation* (MRPT), or simply the marginal rate of transformation (MRT).

EFFICIENCY IN CONSUMPTION

The efficiency propositions concerning consumption in a general equilibrium context are similar to those of the Pareto criteria for efficiency in production. A consumption point along a production frontier is considered efficient if moving to another point makes at least one person better off, without making another worse off. All points along a production frontier are efficient as far as production is concerned, but not all points are efficient from the point of view of utility to consumers. To analyze the implications of efficiency in consumption, we will use the Edgeworth–Bowley diagram.

In Figure 17-4, we see a production-possibilities curve in diagram (a). Under conditions of perfect competition, the price of a good equals its marginal cost. Thus, if X and Y are produced under perfectly competitive conditions, the ratio (P_X/P_Y) must equal the ratio (MC_X/MC_Y). At point 1, the price ratio (P_X/P_Y) is given by the angle of the tangent drawn at that point. If production occurs at point 1, the total output of X and Y will be X_1 and Y_1, respectively. These quantities of X and Y will form the dimensions of the Edgeworth–Bowley (E–B) diagram in Figure 17-4b $(OY_1 1 X_1)$. Similarly, if the price ratio of P_X to P_Y had been given by the angle of the tangent shown at point 2, the dimensions of the E–B box would have been $OY_2 2 X_2$. Whether point 1 is better than point 2 or some other point depends on the utility provided to the consumers by the quantities of goods produced and distributed at these points. If we can say that point 2 yields more utility to the consumers than point 1, point 2 will be considered more efficient, although both points are Pareto-efficient in production.

For the sake of argument, assume that the economic system's conditions are such that production takes place at point 2. Accordingly, the E–B box's dimensions will be OY_2 in height, and OX_2 in width. We will also assume that the goods are consumed by the two individuals denoted A and B. Person A's indifference curves are drawn with O_A as the origin in the XY box of Figure 17-5. The "competing" individual's indifference curves originate from the opposite

FIGURE 17-4
A production-possibilities curve can yield infinite combinations of the two products X and Y. Consequently, each combination of X and Y taken from diagram (a) will produce an Edgeworth–Bowley box of unique dimensions as illustrated in diagram (b).

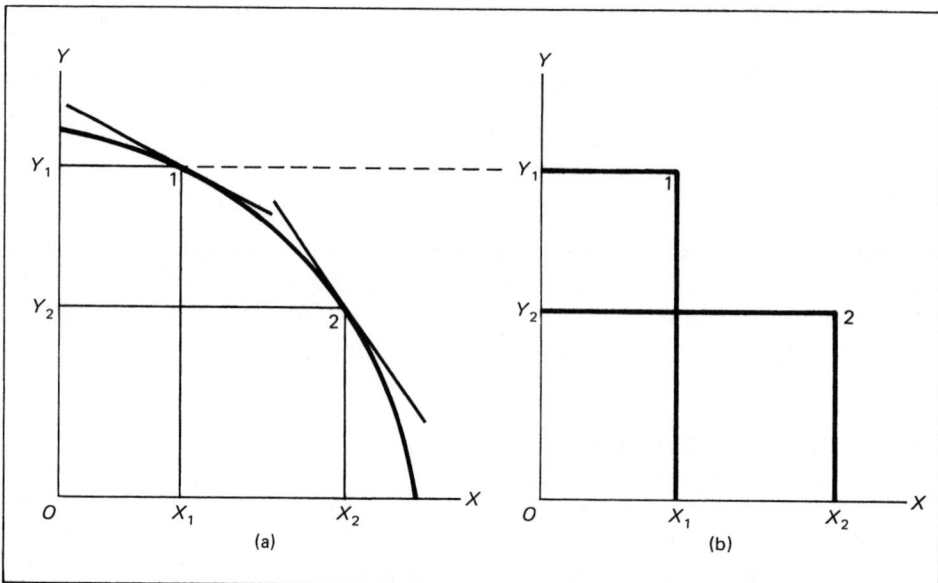

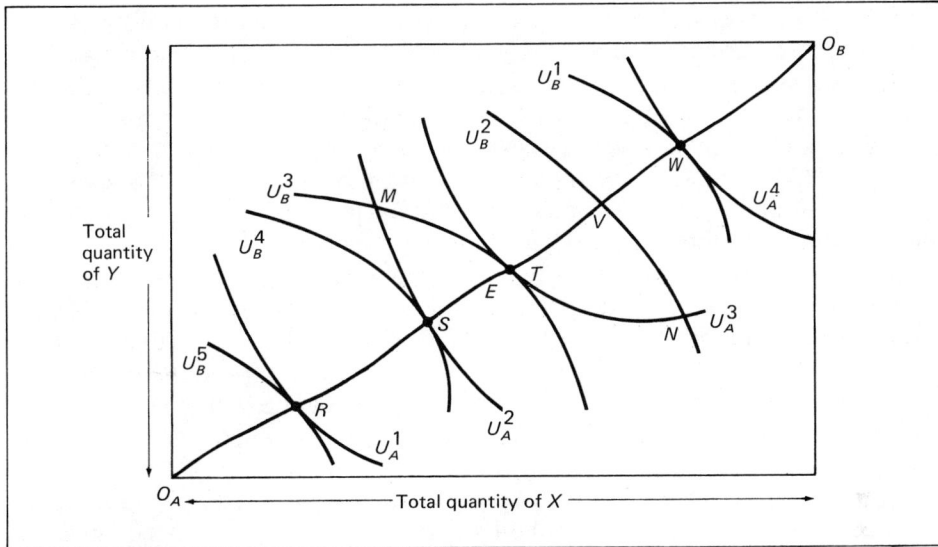

FIGURE 17-5
Just as the efficiency locus in production was derived from production isoquants, the *contract curve* can be similarly derived from the tangency points of the two sets of indifference curves. The locus of these points is shown as $O_A RSETVWO_B$.

corner, labeled O_B. All points within or along the perimeter of the box are feasible, and more of one good allocated to one person implies less for the other. Without going into too much detail, you can verify that all points formed by the tangencies of the two sets of indifference curves are more efficient than those formed by the intersections of the indifference curves. For instance, point S is more efficient than point M, because at point S B's utility increases, while A's utility remains the same. Similarly, point E is more efficient than point M, because it increases the utility for both A and B. Under perfectly competitive conditions, the two individuals will always prefer to operate at a point of tangency. The locus of all such points of tangency is called the *contract* or *conflict curve*. The contract curve in consumption theory is the counterpart of the efficiency locus in the theory of production efficiency.

All points along the contract curve are Pareto-efficient in consumption. In Figure 17-5, the contract is the line $O_A RSTVWO_B$. Because we cannot compare the utility of one person to that received by another, it is difficult to tell which point is "best" for society, unless we have an indicator of societal utility. For example, what is the best combination of food and automobiles for a society that is made up of just men and women? Should we produce more food or more cars? Some groups prefer cars to food, while others prefer food. The further the point is from O_A along the contract curve of Figure 17-5, the higher the utility of A, therefore the less the utility of B.

Consumers maximize utility by equating the marginal rate of substitution (MRS) between the two goods to the ratio of the price of the two goods. Thus, under perfect competition, both A and B will face the same price ratio (P_X/P_Y).

The MRS is the ratio of the marginal utility of X to the marginal utility of Y, or simply the slope of an indifference curve which, when the consumers maximize utility, equals the ratio of the prices of the two goods. Consequently, A and B will consume those quantities of X and Y shown by a point on the contract curve, where the slope of each indifference curve is exactly equal to the price ratio (P_X/P_Y). Because we have specified that the output of X and Y is shown by point 2 of Figure 17-4, we must assume that the price ratio shown by that point also equals the slope of the indifference curves for A and B at a point such as S in the E–B diagram of Figure 17-5. At that point, A's utility is given by U_A^2, and B's by U_B^4. If we had chosen point 1 of Figure 17-4, more Y and less X would have been produced, and the ratio (P_X/P_Y) would have been smaller than that at point 2. (Why?) As a result, the price of X at point 1 would have been lower and the price of Y would have been higher, and we would have had an E–B box of different dimensions, and probably a different allocation of X and Y for consumers A and B.

Pareto optimality in consumption requires that the ratio of the marginal utilities of the goods be equal to the ratio of their prices. Since this condition is true at all points along a contract or conflict curve, from a purely consumption and utility-maximization point of view, all such points are efficient, although from society's point of view one point may be "better" than another. Now we will look at society's choices.

WELFARE ECONOMICS

Welfare economics deals with the otpimal allocation of resources in an economic society using a set of propositions suggested for the maximization of societal utility or welfare. Since society consists of many individuals, and usually no two are alike, it is very difficult to arrive at a societal utility function. Conceptually, however, we might think of a benevolent dictator making allocation decisions in the best interests of society. We will assume that he has perfect or correct information about the likes and dislikes of the country's or community's citizens as well as the benefits and costs of the decisions. In a democracy, the decisions are presumably made collectively by the chosen representatives of the people. If these people agree on the decisions unanimously, we will come close to a surrogate for the people's utility function, or the *social welfare function*. For the time being, let us assume that we have such a function at our disposal.

Societal Utility Maximization

Suppose that the economy can produce the two goods shown in Figure 17-6, food and education. Since the total available supplies of these two utility-creating products are limited by the quantity and quality of resources, the decision maker must produce and distribute them in the "correct" mix that maximizes the utility for society.

We have assumed that a social welfare function exists. The utility function for society is shown by a few indifference curves that have the same basic shape as those associated with individual utility functions. In Figure 17-6, M will

FIGURE 17-6

Society's production-possibilities curve is shown by function ZZ, and its social welfare function is indicated by the set of indifference curves U_1, U_2, U_3 . . . , U_n. Maximum utility occurs at point M, where E_m of education and F_m of food are produced and consumed. While point M is efficient from consumption and production points of view, not all points qualify for such distinction. For example, point K is efficient as far as production goes, but point N is more acceptable from the consumption and utility points of view. Society, at times, must make a choice between more efficiency and greater utility. Point T, on the other hand, is preferred to point K or N, since it provides the same level of utility as point N (U_2), but it is also efficient in production. Utility level U_n is unattainable under the circumstances due to the limits of production. Conceivably, with proper economic growth fostered by correct economic policies, the economy could increase its societal utility to level U_n. Points that lie within the production-possibilities boundary are caused by a variety of factors, such as imperfect competition, taxes and/or subsidies, and externalities in consumption and production.

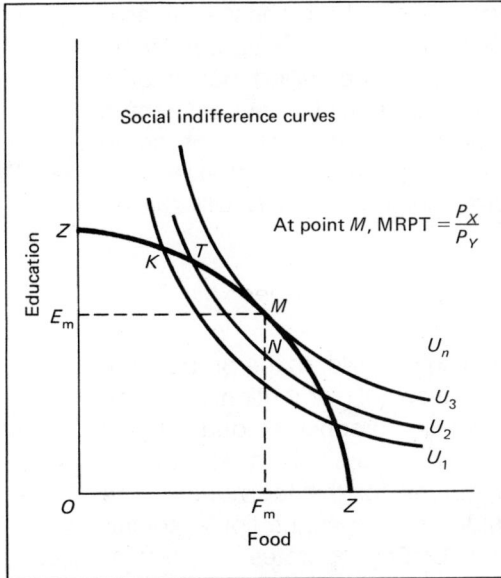

Social indifference curves

At point M, MRPT $= \dfrac{P_X}{P_Y}$

permit society to attain the highest level of satisfaction. At this point, the economy will produce E_m education and F_m food. When we say that society will produce these quantities, we mean that the market structure *ought* to be such that it will bring forth these correct quantities of the two goods. If the market structure fails, the decision makers (presumably the citizens and/or the government) should take action in order to persuade the system to produce the best output mix. Notice that we have used the words "should" and "ought" to bring out the normative nature of welfare economics. What may be considered as a "fact" by one group may only be an "opinion" to the others.

The elected representatives of the people try to bring about the proper output mix of goods and services through legislation, taxation, subsidies, regulation, and other forms of market intervention. The "free market" theoretically provides a very powerful mechanism by which the economic system produces the correct amounts of goods in keeping with the consumers' tastes. But remember that what the free market produces may or may not be for the ultimate well being of society. For example, are cigarettes good for society? Should firms be allowed to remain as price makers? Are there any advantages to government regulation? Some of these questions will be tackled presently in the context of public-sector efficiency.

Consumptive versus Productive Efficiency

We have seen that certain conditions have to be met before the economy can produce efficiently. This occurs when the marginal rate of substitution of labor for capital is equal in all industries. The points on the efficiency locus correspond to the many points along the production possibilities boundary, and society maximizes its welfare when it operates on the highest attainable indifference curve. Point M of Figure 17-6 is called an *allocative efficiency*, while all other points along the production frontier are called points of X *efficiency*. When we compare points K and N, K is certainly more efficient in production than N. On the other hand, N yields more utility although some resources will either not be employed or will be "underemployed," that is, used inefficiently. If utility is of prime importance to society, point N will still be considered more desirable.

Utility-Possibility-Frontier

We will use the *utility-possibility frontier*, which is similar to the production-possibilities curve, to examine the welfare implications of distribution. Suppose society is composed of individuals A and B who like to consume quantities of food and housing produced by the economy. Figure 17-7a shows the production frontier PP and the indifference curves for the individuals. The indifference curves for B have the normal upside-down configuration associated with the Edgeworth–Bowley box. If the economy operates at point 1, rectangle $OM1N$ serves as the box, and the relevant price ratio of the two goods is given by the value of the slope of the production-possibilities curve under perfect competition. The two individuals move along the contract curve $OT1$, and the distribution of housing and food is given by point T, since the indifference curves are tangent to each other, and the value of the common tangent equals the value of the price ratio of the two goods being produced. At point T the utility of A is given by curve U_{A_1} and of B by U_{B_1}. Similarly, if the production point were at point 3, the E–B box would be rectangle $OD3E$, and the commodity price ratio would be higher than at point 1. Such a development would lead A and B to operate at point U on the new contract curve $OU3$. The indifference curves for B will "shift" each time we have a new origin for it, and the different locations of these curves will cause the sets of indifference curves to intersect.

The various combinations of food and housing produced will yield different levels of satisfaction for A and B. If we plot the many combinations of utility received by A and B on a *utility possibility frontier*, we will see the highest utility possible for one individual, given a certain level of utility for the other. The utility frontier is shown in Figure 17-7b.

The Social Welfare Function

It is very difficult to derive an aggregate utility or welfare function for a society composed of many heterogeneous elements. Nevertheless, decisions are made on the basis of imperfect information and some value judgment to bring about results which seem to be in the best interests of society. Naturally, all of us are somewhat selfish, and therfore it is quite probable that a public servant will select an option which may not be in the public interest. However,

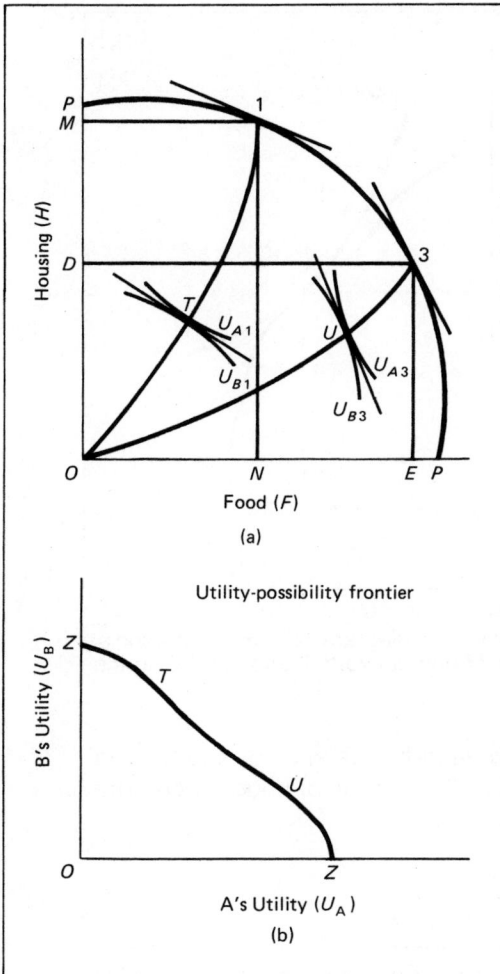

FIGURE 17-7

given the limitations of group decision making, if we have some sort of agreement about what is "good" and what is "bad" we can attempt to obtain the utility-maximizing combination of goods and services for society at large. Figure 17-8 contains two versions of utility or welfare maximization. Diagram (a) shows the utility-maximizing point at M. Diagram (b) uses the utility-possibility frontier. Here we see that the maximum utility for society occurs at point 4.

Arrow's Impossibility Theorem

Nobel laureate Kenneth Arrow thinks that it is impossible to construct a social welfare function by aggregating individual preference functions, even if the tastes of all individuals in society are very similar. This "impossibility" theorem also states that majority voting does not necessarily reflect the true tastes of society. We will use a simple example to illustrate this idea.

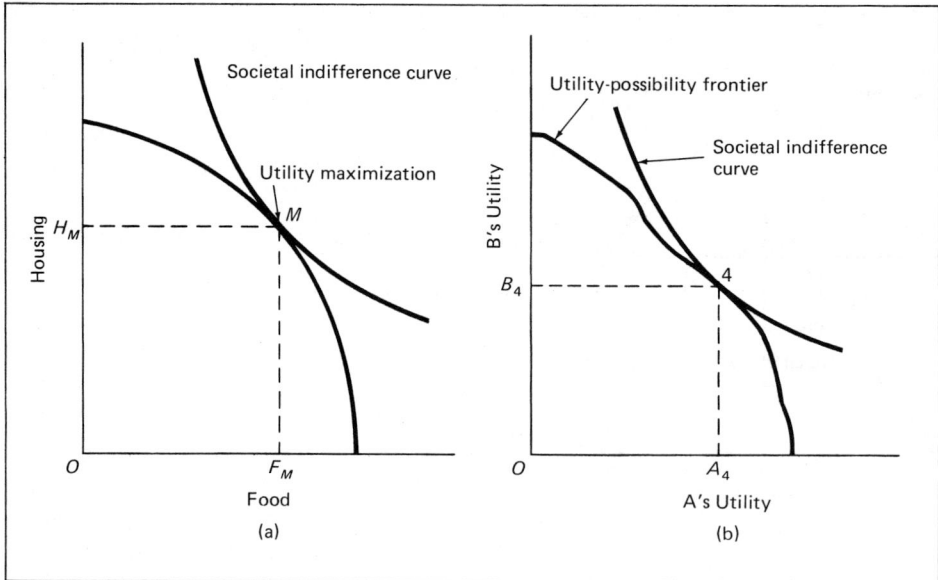

FIGURE 17-8
If we use a production-possibilities curve as shown by diagram (a), maximum social utility occurs at point *M*. Diagram (b) takes point *M* and converts it into point 4 on the utility-possibility frontier.

Suppose that society is composed of three individuals, A, B, and C, who are asked to rank three proposals, *X*, *Y*, and *Z*, in order of importance. The following is a possibility.

	Proposal		
Individual	*X*	*Y*	*Z*
A	1	2	3
B	3	1	2
C	2	3	1

Citizen A likes *X* the best and *Z* the least, while B rates *Y* as the highest and *X* as the lowest in priority. Citizen C finds *Z* the most and *Y* the least attractive. If the criterion for project selection calls for that project with the greatest number of 1 and 2 votes, all projects will qualify. The original version of Arrow's theorem is more detailed, but this example makes the point. Since the rule of majority voting is bound to yield ambiguous and indeterminate results, it is probably meaningless for politicians to talk about the "common" good.

The Theory of the Second Best

Given the type of social welfare function that we have employed, societal utility is maximized when all the Pareto or "marginal" conditions of efficiency in production and consumption are satisfied. However, occasionally all these conditions are difficult to satisfy due to a variety of market imperfections and constraints. For example, if all industries, except one, are perfectly competitive, the marginal conditions will not be met. Since the price ratio will no longer be equal to the marginal cost ratio, the price line will intersect the production-possibilities curve instead of being tangent to it, and output will be less. Is it better, under these circumstances, to move to another point which is at least efficient in production? If all the marginal conditions cannot be satisfied at a point, is it always desirable to move to a more satisfying point? The answer seems to be that the "second best" choice should be to stay where you are and not look for any other solution that would yield a result "closer" to some of the Pareto conditions.

In Figure 17-9, the economy is operating at point 1, where the social indifference curve U_1 is tangent to the existing price-ratio line. We have assumed that (P_X/P_Y) exceeds (MC_X/MC_Y) due to imperfect competition in the X industry, and therefore the overall output of X and the total utility of society are less than possible. Would it be better to move to point 2, which is at least more efficient than 1 in production? Here, the answer is no. Moving to point 2 will reduce the utility of society. Point 3 may be realized through suitable intervention by the government or lawmakers in the form of regulations, taxes, and subsidies. Without the use of some of these policies, however, moving to another point which satisfies X efficiency, will make the situation worse.

WELFARE CRITERIA

Economists and politicians have attempted to "improve" a given situation by suggesting certain changes. Such proposals include everything from health maintenance organizations for preventive medicine to sending astronauts into space in a reusable space shuttle instead of conventional methods. When is a

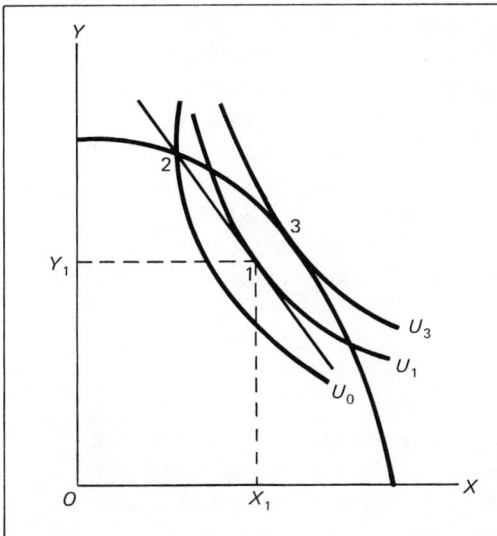

FIGURE 17-9
Point 2 is efficient in production, while point 1, which is not efficient in production, yields more utility and is, therefore, efficient in consumption. Point 3 is considered more efficient than points 1 and 2 because it provides the maximum possible utility and is also efficient in production.

change an improvement? We have already discussed Pareto's general principles for resource allocation, but there are other types of criteria that can be used in judging the desirability of the proposed changes, including the criteria of Scitovsky, Hicks, Kaldor, and Bergson.

Scitovsky Criterion

According to Scitovsky, a proposed change is considered worthwhile if the gainers can somehow persuade the losers to voluntarily accept the change, and if the losers cannot bribe the gainers to resist the change. For example, if higher import duties are charged for imported shoes, the price of and demand for domestic shoes will increase. Shoe consumers, as well as foreign shoe producers, will be the primary losers, while the domestic shoe manufacturers will be the gainers. In this case, if the domestic shoe manufacturers can somehow persuade the domestic consumers to go along with the suggested higher tariffs on imports, and if the manufacturers cannot be "bribed" to resist the new tariffs, the policy calling for higher import duties will be socially desirable.

Hicks Criterion

According to Hicks, a change from A to B is socially desirable if the losers from the change cannot bribe the gainers to avoid the change. The implication of this criterion is that the change is desirable if the cost of the change is less than the benefits accruing from the change. Thus, the move from A to B is desirable if the gain to the winners is higher than the loss to the losers.

Kaldor Criterion

Kaldor's criterion stipulates that a change is socially desirable or beneficial if the winners can compensate the losers and are still better off with the change than without it. For example, if a city builds a new airport adjacent to a residential area, the values of some of the properties will go down. Furthermore, the residents will be exposed to more atmospheric and noise pollution. The winners will be those who use the airport, and the city and businesses that receive revenues from air traffic and passengers. If some of these gainers are willing to pay for the losses suffered by the residents, such as through the payment of taxes and license fees, and still feel that they are better off with the airport than without it, the move to build the airport and locate it in that particular area will be socially desirable.

The Bergson Criterion

This criterion is somewhat complex, although not difficult. Use of this criterion requires the construction of a *Bergson contour,* which is an envelope curve derived in the fashion of the utility-possibility frontier. Given the Bergson contour and a social welfare function, any change that reduces utility is undesirable.

You can see the applicability of some of these criteria to real-life situations of the very recent past and the immediate future. For instance, after the Three-Mile Island fiasco of early 1979, were the authorities correct to encourage the production of nuclear energy? What happened when some of the water projects were cancelled by the Carter administration in 1979? Was that a good move?

BENEFIT–COST ANALYSIS

This criterion is widely used by practitioners to evaluate the desirability of a project or a change. A project is worthwhile if its benefits are at least as great as its costs. The trouble with most benefit–cost studies is the difficulty of accurately measuring *all* benefits and *all* costs associated with a project or proposed change. Another problem is that of time. Most costs occur at the beginning and during the life of a project, while the benefits are usually reaped only in the future. Because knowledge about the future is imperfect, and because the factors affecting the success or failure of a project are uncertain, it is again somewhat difficult to estimate the future benefits and costs. Some feel that the determination of the "correct social" rate of discount for the time value of money is yet another problem, since we cannot know for sure what the productivity of capital funds should be. In spite of some of these drawbacks, benefit–cost analysis is still a very valuable tool for organizing our thoughts and comparing the advantages of a proposal with its disadvantages. After all the possible benefits and costs are evaluated and discounted with an appropriate interest rate, a project should be considered if its benefits equal or outweigh its costs. Alternatively, only those projects whose benefits B equal or exceed their costs C and yield a B/C ratio of 1 or higher should be considered. If $B/C \geq 1$, then $B - C \geq 0$.

The Benefit–Cost Ratio

In computing the benefit–cost ratio, we have to make certain adjustments to future benefits and costs to reflect the changes in the existing benefits and costs due to the proposed change. Thus, the adjusted B/C is defined as

$$\frac{B}{C} = \frac{\text{Total benefit} - \text{total disbenefit}}{\text{Total cost} - \text{cost reductions}}$$
$$= \frac{\text{Adjusted total benefit}}{\text{Adjusted total cost}}$$

This adjustment is necessary because most proposed new projects affect the existing cost and benefit structure. For example, in changing the highway system from an ordinary two-lane to a very sophisticated six-lane super highway system with its attendant cloverleaves, overpasses, underpasses, and other improvements, entails a very large cost outlay. The major benefits accrue to the users of the highway in the form of reduced travel time, less wear and tear on vehicles, fewer accidents, and so on. However, there is a substantial cost reduction to society in the form of the reduced necessity to patrol the better highway. Although there is a very fine line of distinction between a benefit and a cost reduction, in this particular case the reduction in the cost of policing the highway is a reduction in the cost of producing highway safety. However, if the new highway swallows up valuable agricultural property, or destroys the scenic beauty of the countryside, it is *nonbeneficial*. At times it may be difficult to compute some of the benefits as well as the nonbenefits, because there are many unquantifiable "intangibles" or "irreducibles." We will now illustrate the computation of the B/C with an example.

Suppose the State of Colorado is considering upgrading a stretch of highway U.S. 85 between Greeley and Denver. The following data is provided by the Department of Highways:

Under present system

Number of vehicles using the highway (each way): 1 million per year
Number of nonfatal accidents: 20 per year
Number of fatal accidents: 6 per year

Proposed system

Expected number of vehicles (each way): 1.5 million per year
Expected number of nonfatal accidents: 5 per year
Expected number of fatal accidents: 1 per year
Reduction in patrolling cost: $1200 per day
Savings to each vehicle: $10 per year
Cost outlay for new highway: $200 million
Increases in upkeep cost: $30,000 per year
Life of the new highway: 50 years
"Cost" per nonfatal accident: $3000
"Cost" per fatal accident: $150,000
Reduction in property value, loss in agricultural output, destruction to environment: $500 per day
Opportunity cost of capital: 10%

The governor is interested in the annual benefit–cost (B/C) ratio of the proposed highway system.

In computing the annual B/C ratio, we must first reduce those costs and benefits that occur once to their annual equivalent with the use of the 10% cost-of-money tables, like those in Chapter 3. We have one cost item—the initial cost outlay for the new highway. Using the 10% discount rate, we amortize the $200 million to be equivalent to $[200 million × (A/P, 10%, 50 years)], or $(200 million × 0.1009) = $20.2 million per year. Now we collect all the annual cost items, annual benefits, and nonbenefits, and adjust them for any reductions in costs. The last step is to divide the total adjusted benefit by the total adjusted cost and recommend the project if the B/C ratio is equal to or greater than 1.

Benefits

Savings to vehicles: (1.5 million)(2)($10) = $ 30 million per year
Reduction in accidents: 15 nonfatal, 5 fatal = $ 0.795 million per year

Nonbenefits

Losses to property owners, damage to environment at $500 per day, which is equivalent to (approximately) $500 × 365 + opportunity cost of money = $0.20 million per year

Adjusted total benefit = $30.59 million per year

Costs

Capital outlay for new highway: $20.2 million per year
Increase in upkeep costs: $0.03 million per year

Cost reductions

Reduced cost of highway patrol at $1200 per day + opportunity cost: $0.48 million per year

Adjusted total cost = $19.75 million per year

B/C = 30.59/19.75 = 1.55, and $B-C$ = $10.84 million per year.

Because the project is expected to yield a *positive net benefit* of $10.84 million per year, and B/C is greater than 1, it deserves further consideration.

Incremental *B/C* Ratio

When we are faced with the selection of a project from several different proposals, and there is a known opportunity cost of capital, we must compute the *incremental benefit/cost ratio* as well as the B/C ratio. An additional dollar of investment expenditure is justifiable if and only if it contributes at least an additional dollar in benefits or revenues. Consider the following *mutually exclusive* proposals:

Proposal:	1	2	3
Discounted benefit	$10 million	$25 million	$36 million
Discounted cost	$ 9 million	$23 million	$35 million

If we use the B/C ratio to evaluate the project, the following ratios will result:

$$(B/C)_1 = (10/9) = 1.11$$
$$(B/C)_2 = (25/23) = 1.09$$
$$(B/C)_3 = (36/35) = 1.03$$

Since all the proposals have a B/C exceeding 1, they all qualify. Which, then, is the "best" proposal?

To answer that question, we use the same logic we employed in the theories of profit maximization. Starting with proposal 1, we ask ourselves whether the extra investment is desirable considering the added benefits, especially when the extra money not tied up in a project can be used to earn a

10% return. The incremental cost of project 2 over 1 is $14 million, while the incremental benefit of 2 over 1 is $15 million. Therefore, 2 is "better" than 1. Is proposal 3 even better? The incremental cost of 3 over 2 is $12 million, but the incremental benefit of 3 over 2 is only $11 million. Hence, it is uneconomical to build 3, even if its total benefits are higher than the other two proposals. The rule here is to continue to increase the size of the investment as long as the incremental benefits exceed the incremental costs. This is equivalent to the profit-maximization rule of MR = MC.

Thus, the incremental benefit/cost ratios are computed as follows.

$$(B/C)_{2-1} = (15/14) = 1.07 \quad \text{(O.K.)}$$
$$(B/C)_{3-2} = (11/12) = 0.91 \quad \text{(not O.K.)}$$

Recommendation: Select project 2.

We can also use the value of $(B-C)$ to arrive at the "best" proposal. The one with the highest $(B-C)$ or net benefit, is the one that should be chosen, and in this example project 2 yields the highest $(B-C)$ of $2 million.

THE PUBLIC SECTOR

The public sector's presence is due mostly to society's normative perceptions about the utility function of society. Society is not a single person, nor is it any unique economic or political entity. It is composed of individuals, institutions, and systems. When something is done for the social good, it does not mean that everyone is better off. For example, if the United States opens its borders completely in order to enhance international trade, will everyone be better off? Most likely, you will find the domestic producers complaining about unimpeded trade, while the consumers will be overjoyed. Now whether free trade is good or bad depends on the net effect of such a policy. On the whole, if we can somehow prove that the benefits of a policy outweigh the costs, the policy is desirable. The calculus of benefit–cost analysis suggests that the public sector is responsible for *market failure*.

Market Failure

The market "fails" when the quantity and quality of goods and services produced are not in the best interest of society. Problems arise because the markets do not operate under perfect competition and the side effects of consumption and production are not recognized or their effects felt by the producers and consumers.

In earlier chapters we focused on the decisions of economic entitites as related to their private needs. The consumers opted for actions that maximized utility, and the producers favored those decisions which presumably increased their profits or helped them with their true objectives. However, in pursuing their private goals, consumers and producers do not necessarily bring about the production and consumption of the "appropriate" quantity and quality of goods at the "correct" prices in the best interests of society. The free market system is fine up to the point where it begins to bring about more harm than good.

Furthermore, if left to the private decisions of the market and its participants, some goods and services that are very desirable will probably not be forthcoming. For example, why would anyone purchase an F-115 fighter plane to protect himself, knowing that others would benefit from this purchase without having to pay for it? If everyone thought in this manner, we would have no national defense, unless provided by the people, for the people. Because of this "free-rider" problem associated with goods and services that yield benefits to all, regardless of whether all pay for it, some valuable goods and services are provided by the public sector and are called *public goods*. Most public goods are also *collective goods* in the sense that no matter how much of such a good a person consumes, he or she will not deprive others from consuming as much of it as they wish. The national highway system is a good example of a collective public good.

Efficiency and Perfect Competition

Theoretically speaking, perfect competition brings about a higher level of societal utility than imperfect market structures. When markets are imperfectly competitive, the prices paid for resources do not equal their marginal revenue product and the price of the output exceeds its marginal cost. In addition, if the prices of resources are different in different industries, the conditions for production efficiency will be in violation. The basic underlying philosophy of *supporting perfect competition* is probably highly normative. Who is to say that we would be happier driving the same type of automobiles and wearing identical clothes. Chances are, we would not want to be lost in total anonymity due to such equalities brought about by perfect competition. Furthermore, if returns to scale are taken into account, a monopoly could conceivably produce consumer products at a considerably lower cost than possible by an atomistic number of perfectly competitive firms.

Part of the argument against imperfect competition is summarized in Figure 17-10. If all markets operate under perfect competition and firms are profit maximizers, the price will equal marginal cost. If price equals marginal cost, the ratio of the prices of the two goods will also equal the ratio of their marginal costs. The marginal rate of product transformation, which equals the ratio of marginal costs, will also equal the slope of society's indifference curve, since for utility maximization, the price ratio must equal the marginal rate of substitution. At point 2, the social indifference curve U_2 is tangent to the production possibilities curve and the following conditions are observed:

$$(P_E/P_F)_2 = MRS_{E/F} = \frac{MC_E}{MC_F} = MRPT$$

Now suppose that the economy is not characterized by perfect competition in all the markets. For the sake of argument, let us assume that the market for entertainment is imperfectly competitive and the market for food operates under perfect competition. We have already discussed that profit-maximizing firms produce at the point where the marginal cost equals the marginal

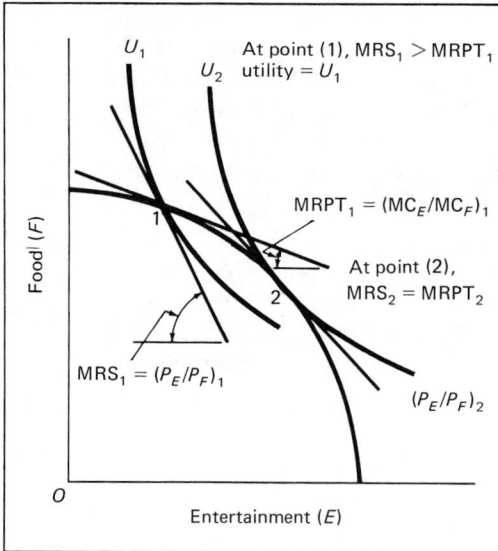

FIGURE 17-10

revenue. Thus, for perfectly competitive firms, price, which is marginal revenue, equals marginal cost. However, whenever the firms become price-makers, price exceeds the marginal revenue and at the point of profit maximization it also exceeds the marginal cost. In our example of the markets for food and entertainment:

$$P_F = MC_F \quad \text{(Perfect competition)} \tag{10}$$

$$P_E > MC_E \quad \text{(Monopolistic competition)} \tag{11}$$

In general, the monopolistic firm will charge a higher price than a competitive firm under similar circumstances. Using equations (10) and (11), and assuming that $P_E > P_F$, we may state:

$$\frac{P_E}{P_F} > \frac{MC_E}{MC_F} \tag{12}$$

Equation (12) suggests that the MRPT is not equal to the MRS, and whenever this is the case, the slope of the indifference curve is not equal to the slope of the production-possibilities curve at productively efficient points. Since the MRS is greater than the MRPT, point 1 is the economy's position. From a utility standpoint, society is consuming too much food and not enough entertainment. However, since the price ratio line is tangent to the indifference curve U_1, consumers are maximizing their utility, but this level of utility is not as high as at point 2. If the entertainment industry can be separated into a perfectly competitive industry, profit-maximizing firms will equate price with marginal cost. Since both industries will now be perfectly competitive, the price ratio, the marginal rate of substitution, and the marginal rate of product transformation will all be equal, and the economy will operate at point 2. Utility will increase—the citizens will eat less food and partake of more entertainment.

Taxes and subsidies can also help bring about perfect competition. For example, a subsidy to the producer usually results in lower prices and encourages consumption. An excise or production tax has opposite effects. In the situation just discussed, we want the price of entertainment to fall and the quantity consumed to increase. However, more entertainment can be produced if and only if the quantity of food produced is reduced. So we have to accomplish several things. First, the firms prices should equal the marginal costs. Second, the MRS must equal the price ratio P_E/P_F. Finally, the MRS must equal the MRPT.

If the demand for entertainment is increased through advertising, more of it will be demanded and its price will increase. But as long as price exceeds marginal cost, the MRPT will not equal the MRS; also, the price ratio P_E/P_F will be greater than it was and will deviate further from the price ratio necessary to bring about point 2 in Figure 17-10. But the change in price alone will not be sufficient. The producers of food must be willing to reduce production to allow more entertainment to be produced. So an increase in the demand for entertainment alone will do more harm than good.

Would it be better to subsidize the producers of entertainment? Figure 17-11 shows that a per-unit subsidy will lower the cost and price of entertainment. On the other hand, a per-unit tax on food will increase its price and bring forth a smaller quantity of output. This combination of policies, taxing food and subsidizing entertainment, perhaps with the tax revenue proceeds from the food industry, will cause a more favorable result. The price of food increases and therefore reduces consumption, whereas the price of entertainment falls and encourages a larger quantity to be demanded. Furthermore, the price ratio P_E/P_F will be brought into closer alignment with the "ideal" price ratio and the economy will move toward point 2.

But there is a hitch. Whenever such tax and subsidy policies are put into effect, the quantities and price are altered, but there is no guarantee that the price of each good will equal its marginal cost. If, in spite of the tax/subsidy policy just mentioned, the price of entertainment exceeds its marginal cost, we will be somewhat better off than we were at point 1, but not as well off as we were at point 2. Figure 17-10 shows why the price of the product will still exceed its marginal cost in the entertainment industry.

We can also regulate the entertainment industry to operate where price equals marginal cost. This will bring prices down and cause the quantity demanded and produced to increase. This type of marginal cost pricing regulation, coupled with taxation of the food industry, will probably be the most effective. The price of entertainment will decline, while that of food will rise. In addition to changes in prices, the quantities of entertainment and food produced will also change, with the output of the first increasing and the second decreasing. Whether such a policy is truly worthwhile depends on the set of welfare criteria we use. Presumably, according to the social welfare standard, such a policy will be recommended.

We have already shown one instance of "market failure" in the sense that the existing conditions do not bring about the optimal allocation of results. For instance, the discussion concerning the output of entertainment and food explained the reason for the misallocation due largely to the presence of

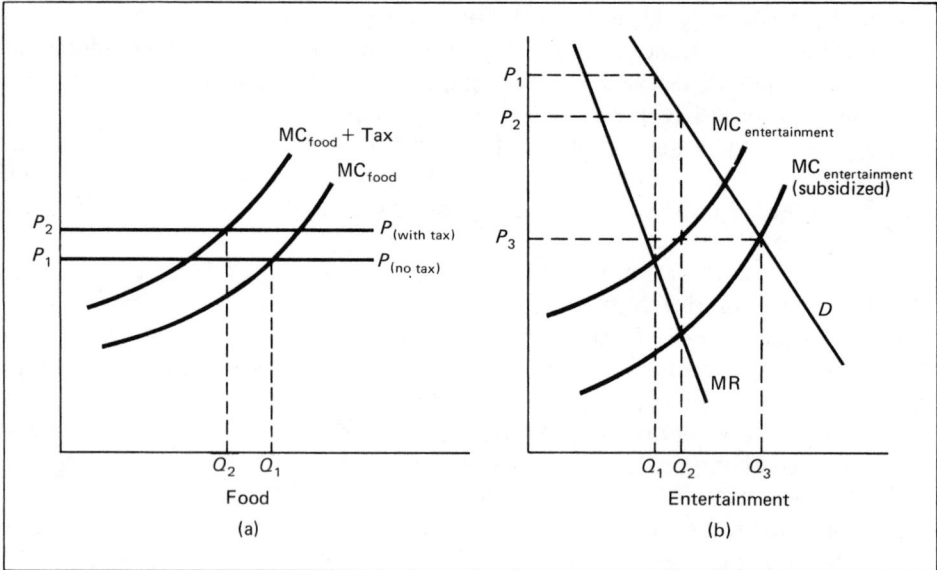

FIGURE 17-11
In Figure 17-10, the economy was at point 1, since the food industry was perfectly competitive and the entertainment industry was not. The societal indifference curve was tangent to the price ratio of entertainment to food but not to the marginal cost ratio. As a result, MRS > MRPT and society did not maximize its utility. Point 2 was a more desirable point. In order to bring about maximum utility for society, we have to reduce the price of entertainment and/or increase the price of food while ensuring that more entertainment and less food is being produced by the system. We can tax the production of food and subsidize the cost of entertainment. Diagram (a) shows that a tax on the production of food increases its market price and reduces its output. Diagram (b) suggests that a subsidy to firms in the entertainment industry brings forth a larger quantity at a lower price. Ideally speaking, price should equal marginal cost. If we subsidize the entertainment industry and regulate it to charge price P_3, it will produce output Q_3. Since price equals marginal cost in each industry, we approach the maximum utility point, such as point 2 of Figure 17-10.

imperfect competition in the entertainment industry. Markets may also fail to provide the correct quantities of the goods necessary for a social optimum due to *externalities* or *spillover effects*. Essentially, an externality is the side effect due to the consumption or production decisions of economic units within a society. Externalities can be positive or negative. For example, if the city decides to spray all the trees along the streets with certain pesticides, you stand to gain from such an action. Presumably, your own trees have a better chance of survival if the city trees are sprayed with bug killers. However, it is equally likely that such spraying will have harmful side effects. For example, the birds that perch on these trees may be poisoned and the ecological balance may be upset. Birds also eat bugs and thereby preclude the necessity of spraying the trees in your yard. Since the winged creatures will no longer be there, certain types of vermin will continue to infest your trees.

When private parties create externalities and do not recognize them, the quantity of output produced and consumed is not socially optimal. For example, there is substantial negative externality associated with automobile production. Because of the lack of adequate pollution and safety standards, automobiles contribute to the destruction of the environment as well as to a large number of dangerous accidents. Automobile companies seldom pay for the costs of cleaning up the environment, and they are rarely held liable for highway fatalities due to faulty equipment. Furthermore, the companies, in producing automobiles, frequently release considerable amounts of effluents into the atmosphere, rivers, and soil. Others have to incur private costs in order to stay healthy and clean. Therefore, the true *social cost* of producing automobiles is in excess of the private cost. Since the profit-maximizing firms do not pay for the additional costs borne by society, they tend to operate where the private marginal cost equals the marginal revenue. If they are forced to recognize the costs due to the negative externalities, their marginal cost will have to be adjusted to show the true cost to society. The total output of such products will be less and the price will be higher.

Figure 17-12 shows the output of a firm that is maximizing profits by producing quantity Q_P and charging price P_P. However, the social marginal cost, which is the sum of the private marginal cost and the cost due to the externalities, is above the private marginal cost. If the firm uses the social MC as its guide, it will tend to produce quantity Q_S and charge price P_S. The government can bring about the production of Q_S and the associated price by imposing a tax equal to the difference between the social and private costs. Alternatively, it can set certain standards of safety and air quality, which will also increase the costs of the firm. In general, if a product produces negative externalities and private firms choose to ignore them, society will have "too much" of these goods and/or services.

Some goods and services consumed by people and firms have positive benefits. For example, if you choose to be vaccinated against a contagious disease, not only will you be more healthy, but those around you will also

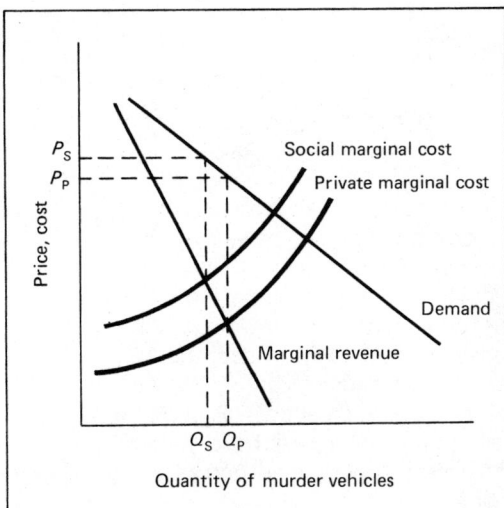

FIGURE 17-12
The profit-maximizing firm, if it chooses to ignore the social costs associated with dangerous and polluting vehicles, produces amount Q_P and charges price P_p. If it uses the social marginal cost for making decisions, the output will be Q_S and the price P_S. Presumably, the public sector can force the firm to *internalize* the externalities or force them to recognize the social marginal cost by imposing a tax equal to the difference between the private and social marginal costs and thereby bring about the socially optimum quantity and price.

benefit from your action. However, you will probably not be rewarded for your decision to be vaccinated. The private parties that gain from your vaccination do not wish to recognize your contribution to their health. As a result, "not enough" of such a socially desirable product as vaccinations is consumed. If the government subsidizes the cost of vaccinations and/or increases the value of the vaccinations through public education, the correct quantity of vaccinations will be consumed.

The general method of dealing with externalities seems to be by "rewarding the good and punishing the bad." Once the decision makers have decided on the good and the bad guys, they should have sufficient information to assess the correct amount of punishment or reward. Ultimately, all actions for controlling externalities must be weighed against one or more welfare criteria.

The Coase Theorem

Economist Ronald Coase maintains that even if there are significant externalities in private transactions, and there is sufficient reason to condemn the market, there is no reason for the government to intervene to correct the market failure. According to this theorem, the so-called "invisible hand" does not go astray due to externalities. The market is still one of the best means of attaining socially desirable quantities of goods and services, since the parties to the transactions take the costs and benefits of externalities into account when calculating for making decisions. Thus, a landlord can very easily ask for a higher rent if the next-door neighbors happen to be attractive, sociable, and helpful, and the area where the property is located is considered very desirable. An identical house under less attractive circumstances will bring a much lower rent.

APPLICATIONS

1. Meat for Peaches

You are probably aware of the effects of international trade on the prices and quantities of traded and nontraded goods, and the resulting changes in a country's welfare. We can use a general equilibrium model to explore the influences of international trade on the important variables.

Assume there are two countries, A and B, that are capable of producing meat (M) and peaches (P). Their production-possibilities curves are shown in Figure 17-13: AA for country A, and BB for country B. Before trade, country A maximizes social welfare by producing and consuming at point X, where the highest possible social indifference curve is tangent to its production frontier. Similarily, country B's optimum is at point R. The price ratio of peaches to meat P_P/P_M in each country equals the slope of the production frontier. Thus, at point X for country A, the MRT, which equals P_P/P_M, is higher than the MRT in country B, shown at point R, implying that each country faces a different price ratio. From what we have already discovered about Pareto optimality, gain to both parties is possible as long as each party's MRS and MRT are different than the other's.

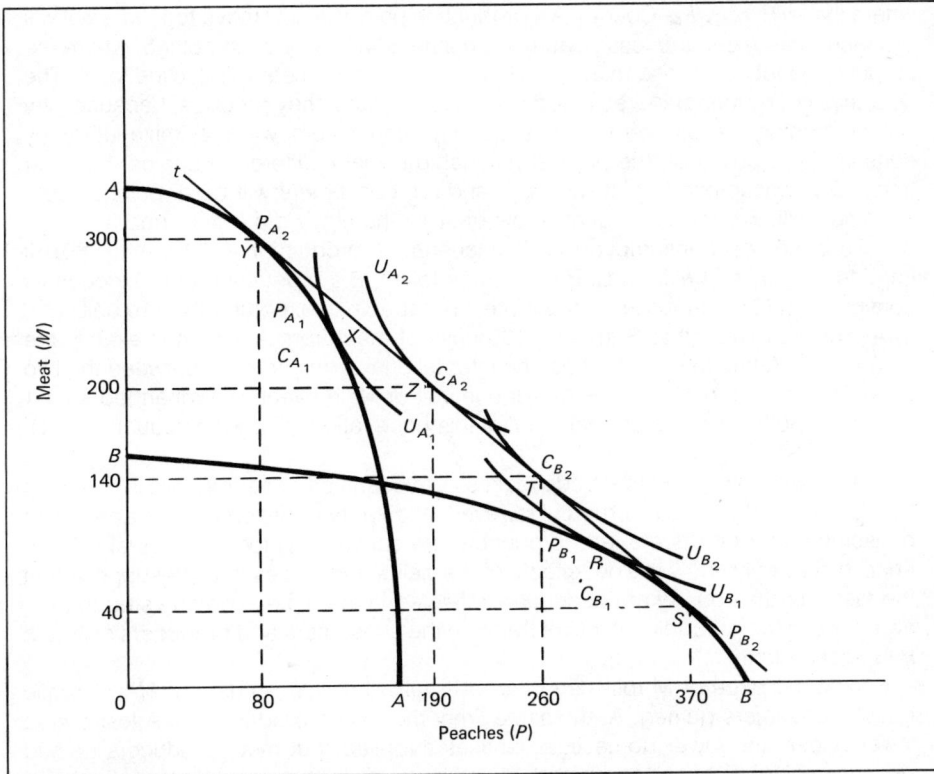

FIGURE 17-13
Before trade, countries A and B were at points *X* and *R,* respectively. After trade, *A* moved to *Z, B* moved to *T,* and both countries enjoyed a higher level of utility. Furthermore, free trade equalized the prices of meat and peaches prevailing in each country.

Country A has *comparative advantage* in the production of meat. This means that A is *relatively better* than B in producing meat. Country B's comparative advantage lies in the production of peaches. It follows, then, that the price of meat in A is lower than in B, and the price of peaches in B is lower than in A. Thus,

$$\left(\frac{P_P}{P_M}\right)_A > \left(\frac{P_P}{P_M}\right)_B$$

which is what we assumed. Because the price of meat is lower in A than in B, B will find it advantageous to import some meat. Country A will be better off by importing peaches from B up to the point where the domestic peach producers can compete with imports and also offer the same prices. If and when trade is stabilized, the price of peaches to consumers in A will fall due to added supplies through imports, but the price of meat in A will rise because of meat exports to country B. The direction of price changes in country B will be opposite to those in country A. At equilibrium, both countries will have the same price ratio P_P/P_M. Of course, we are assuming we have a free market, perfect competition, no transportation costs, and no international trade barriers or tariffs on traded goods.

The posttrade common price ratio is shown by line *tt.* Reacting to this price ratio, producers in each country operate at points on the production-possibilities curves where the MRT = P_P/P_M. Country A's production point will now move to Y, where it will produce more meat and less peaches. Country B will produce at point S, where the output of peaches will rise to 370, and the production of meat will decline to 40. The countries will no longer be restricted to consuming what they produce, because they will be trading certain items. Consequently, consumers will maximize utility by consuming at points on the highest attainable social indifference curves. So, after trade, B's consumption point will be T, and A's consumers will be at point Z. Both countries will now receive higher levels of utility than they did before trade.

Because A's consumption of P exceeds its production (190 versus 80), it imports 110 units of P from B. By the same token, B's production of P exceeds its consumption (370 versus 260), therefore it is capable of exporting the 110 units of P to A. You can verify that B imports 100 units of meat from A, which is exactly the amount that A has to export. Thus, the international *terms of trade* between the two countries amount to $100M = 110P$, or one unit of M, in effect, is exchanged for 1.1 units of P. Both countries are better off at this price ratio P_P/P_M, which equals (1/1.1), or 0.909. (Why?)

We have maintained that trade makes both countries better off. This is true in so far as the model is concerned. However, a country's citizens are made up of consumers and producers, and producers are consumers, too. The social indifference curves only show the net effects of the gains and losses and presuppose that the tastes of the country are accurately reflected in them. Let's go one step further, and analyze the probable effects of trade on the consumers and producers of M and P in each country.

In A, the price of M rose, and that of P fell. Thus, consumers of M lost, while peach consumers gained. At the same time, the peach producers of A lost due to lower prices and lower domestic quantities supplied, but meat producers gained because of higher prices and higher quantities sold. To the extent that we disregard all secondary effects, and the impact of trade on the distribution of income as well as the income of the resources, country A will be better off from trade if the gain to consumers and producers is higher than the loss.

In country B, the peach producers will gain and peach consumers will lose, while meat consumers will gain and the producers of meat will lose. Again, the gain to the involved parties exceeds the losses, and country B is better off than before, as shown by consumption point T.

2. Net Benefit of a Waterway

We have discussed the method of evaluating a project's desirability by determining its net benefits. The U.S. Army Corps of Engineers uses a similar system to obtain the net benefits of certain inland waterways. What follows is based on the model reported by Herfindahl and Kneese.

The net benefit B of a proposed waterway can be described by:

$$B = C_a - C_w - C_P + \Delta D$$

where

C_a is the cost of the alternative method of transporting a given amount of freight;

C_w is the waterway cost for that amount of freight;

C_p is the premium which shippers who use the waterway would have paid to use the alternative mode; and

ΔD is the net increase in the willingness to pay for the waterway transport for freight that would not have moved on the alternative mode.

The transportation specialists take the railway as the alternative mode of transporting freight, and the cost of the alternative mode is obtained from the published railway rates. Once the other costs and D are determined, B can be calculated. If B is positive, the waterway is considered economically sound. The model discussed is in Figure 17-14.

Many criticisms have been aimed at this model of evaluating the net benefits of a proposed waterway. Some feel that the estimation of C_a with the use of railroad rates is inaccurate because railroads are good examples of decreasing cost industries. Thus, historical costs (as reflected by the railroad rates) are not proper equivalents of economic costs. A second problem concerns the estimation of demand curve ZZ and the associated area MRX measuring ΔD. An additional difficulty is the estimation of *future* traffic on the waterway based on *current* railroad rates, which estimates are likely to exaggerate the shift of traffic.

Most critics feel that this model overestimates the benefits of the waterway. However, in spite of the apparent shortcomings, the model does suggest one approach to estimating the net benefits of a project.

3. Tax or Subsidy?

Economic activity in the private sector can be "controlled" by taxation and subsidies. Students of public finance are often exposed to a very basic theorem concerning taxation/subsidy in the public interest. A move either to increase or decrease taxes, or to subsidize an industry, is optimal if the gains at least equal or outweigh the costs. Let us examine this proposition in light of decreasing and increasing cost industries with no known externalities.

Suppose the demand and supply conditions for the industry are as shown in Figure 17-15a. Since this is a decreasing cost industry, the supply function is negatively sloped. The original equilibrium price is at P_1, and equilibrium quantity

FIGURE 17-14

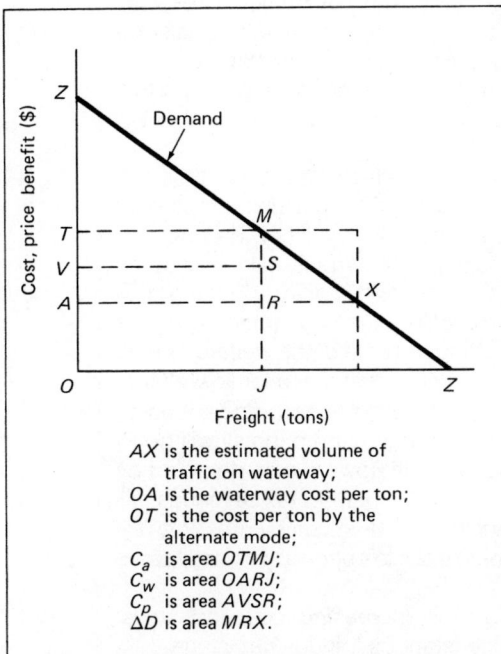

AX is the estimated volume of
   traffic on waterway;
OA is the waterway cost per ton;
OT is the cost per ton by the
   alternate mode;
C_a is area $OTMJ$;
C_w is area $OARJ$;
C_p is area $AVSR$;
ΔD is area MRX.

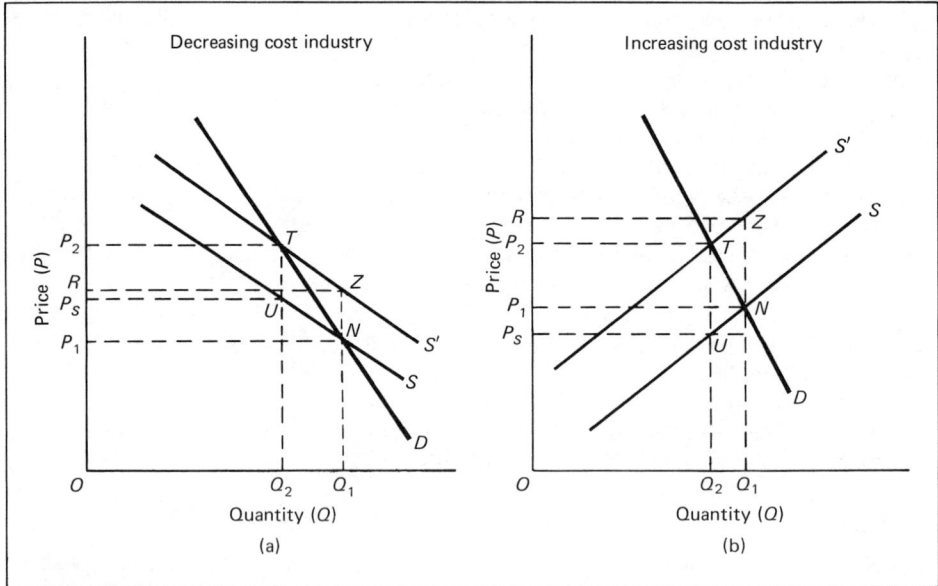

FIGURE 17-15
When the industry has decreasing costs, as in diagram (a), a subsidy to the producers reduces market price and brings about a net increase in welfare. In the case of the increasing cost industry, as in diagram (b), the producers should be taxed.

equals Q_1. If we impose a specific tax on supply, the new equilibrium price and quantity will be P_2 and Q_2. The loss to consumers will be represented by the reduction in the consumers' surplus, or by area P_1NTP_2. The government's revenue will equal the tax per unit (TU) times the quantity of goods sold, which equals the value of area UTP_2P_s. If we think of tax revenues as "gains" for society, and the reduction in the consumers' surplus as the loss, the loss will exceed the gains. In this instance, a tax on this industry's output will not be a good policy. What about a subsidy?

We can use the same graph to show the probable effects of a subsidy to the industry. Just switch S with S', because with a subsidy of TU per unit, the supply curve will shift down by that amount at all points. The new price will now be where P_1 is, since price will fall due to the subsidy. The consumers' surplus will increase by area P_2TNP_1. The cost of the subsidy will equal area ZNP_1R, where ZN = TU = subsidy per unit of output. A subsidy policy will most likely increase the consumer's surplus by a larger amount than it will cost. According to some of the welfare criteria discussed in this chapter, a subsidy to this industry will increase economic welfare.

In Figure 17-15b, we show the supply and demand conditions in an increasing cost industry. As before, with supply S, the equilibrium price and quantity will be P_1 and Q_1, respectively. With a tax, the supply curve will shift upwards, as depicted by S'. The new price will be higher, and quantity lower. The gain in tax revenues will equal area P_sUTP_2, and the loss in consumers' surplus will be given by area P_1NTP_2. Because the area of gain exceeds the area of loss, a tax is needed. You can prove that a subsidy will be uneconomical.

The general rule for these models is: Tax the increasing cost industries, subsidize the decreasing cost ones, and leave constant cost industries alone.

EXERCISES

1. Define and briefly explain the following.
   a. Partial equilibrium.
   b. General equilibrium.
   c. Marginal rate of transformation.
   d. Marginal rate of substitution.
   e. Marginal rate of technical substitution.
   f. Social welfare function.
   g. *X* efficiency versus allocative efficiency.
   h. Market failure.
   i. Externalities.
   j. Public good.
   k. Collective good.
   l. The free-rider problem.

2. Enumerate as many "marginal conditions" as you feel are necessary for Pareto equilibrium under the following circumstances: two goods (X, Y), two inputs (K,L), two consumers (A,B), perfect competition in the input and output markets, and no other constraints.

3. In the discussion about taxes and subsidies in Application 3, can you demonstrate why neither a tax nor a subsidy is called for in the case of a constant cost industry?

4. Calculate the benefit/cost ratio of owning a telephone in your home. Make appropriate assumptions about the costs and benefits.

5. Compare the economic value of adding an automatic sprinkler system to the city golf course in light of the Hicks, Scitovsky, and Kaldor welfare criteria.

6. Cite examples demonstrating the general applicability of the Theory of the Second Best.

7. Set up a model of an activity that also contributes significant amounts of environmental pollution. Determine the "optimal" level of permissible pollution. (Hint: You may use a marginal benefit–marginal cost model, or an EOQ model, or some model of your own.)

8. Analysis of accidents in a state indicates that increasing the width of the highways by 30 feet may decrease the accident rate from 800 to 290 per 100 million vehicle miles. What should be the average daily number of vehicles using the "improved" highway to justify widening on the basis of the following estimates? Average loss per accident—$3000; per mile cost of widening highway—$90,000; useful life of improvement—30 years; annual maintenance cost—5% of first cost. (Assume there is no opportunity cost of money.)

9. Suppose you have to select one of the following mutually exclusive projects, whose estimated total benefits and costs are shown.

Project:	A	B	C
Benefit	$100M	$180M	$320M
Cost	$ 80M	$150M	$315M

If money has an opportunity cost of 12%, which project is *most economical*? Which project will you select if you are interested in the maximum *absolute return*? If the money has no opportunity cost, which project will be the best for society?

10. Outline the function of government and the general nature of public activities.

11. Do a benefit–cost study of a Ph.D. degree in English literature. Include any "intangible" or "immeasureable" aspects if deemed appropriate.

12. Will Arrow's Impossibility Theorem always hold if there are three proposals (X,Y,Z) and three voters (A,B,C)?

13. State your opinions and the alleged advantages and disadvantages of:
a. pornographic material sold publicly.
b. the consumption of alcohol.
c. nuclear energy.
d. gasoline rationing.
e. wage and price controls.
f. advertising.
g. fuel standards for automobiles.
h. currency devaluation.

SUGGESTED READINGS

Besen S. M., and Manning W. G. "Copyright Liability for Cable Television: Compulsory Licensing and the Coase Theorem." *Journal of International Business Studies*, Vol. 9, No. 1, Spring 1978.

Borcherding T. E. "Competition, Exclusion, and the Optimal Supply of Public Goods." *Journal of International Business Studies*, Vol. 9, No. 1, Spring 1978.

Ellickson, B. "Public Goods and Joint Supply." *Journal of Public Economics*, Vol. 9, No. 3, June 1978.

Grout P. "On Minimax Regret and Welfare Economics." *Journal of Public Economics*, Vol. 9, No. 3, June 1978.

Jhun U. J., and Yoo, J. H. "The Public Good Demand Function: Tax Share as a Dependent Variable." *Problems of Economics*, Vol. 21, No. 2, June 1978.

Leven, C. L. *The Mature Metropolis*. Lexington, Mass.: Heath Lexington Books, 1978.

McEachern W. A. "Collective Decision Rules and Local Debt Choice: A Test of the Median–Voter Hypothesis." *National Institute Economic Review*, No. 85, August 1978.

Mishan E. *Cost–Benefit Analysis*. New York: Praeger, 1976.

Morici, P. "The Benefits and Costs of Crude Oil Price Regulations." *Journal of Energy Development*, Vol. 3, No. 2, Spring 1978.

Orr, D. *Property, Markets, and Government Intervention*. Pacific Palisades: Goodyear Publishing Company, 1976.

Simon, J. L. "Interpersonal Welfare Comparisons: A Reply." *Kyklos*, Vol. 31, No. 2, 1978.

Stokey, E., and Zeckhauser, R. *A Primer for Policy Analysis*. New York: Norton, 1978.

Sugden, R., and Williams, A. *The Principles of Practical Cost–Benefit Analysis*. Oxford, New York and Melbourne: Oxford University Press, 1978.

Veljanovski, C. G. "The Coase Theorem—The Says Law of Welfare Economics?" *Economic Record*, Vol. 53, No. 144, December 1977.

Weidenbaum M. L. *Business, Government and the Public*. Englewood Cliffs, New Jersey: Prentice–Hall, 1977.

Whitbred M. "Measuring the Costs of Noise Nuisance from Aircraft: A Review Article." *Journal of Transport Economics and Policy*, Vol. 12, No. 2, May 1978.

Chapter
Eighteen
Chapter
Eighteen
Chapter
Eighteen

ECONOMIC REGULATION

We have discussed the theory of public intervention in economic matters as they affect producers and consumers. The public sector's regulatory agencies can intervene in the decisions of the private sector by using subsidies and taxes. They can also set standards of performance and quality of service and restrict quantities of output. A third method to bring about either allocative or productive efficiency is to regulate the price of the product or limit the firm's earnings. We will examine different types of regulation and their probable effects on the price, quantity, and quality of the output. In the United States we have many agencies which either monitor or enforce standards and regulate prices of goods and services. For example, the Civil Aeronautics Board (CAB) is heavily involved in route awarding and rate setting for the airlines, while the Occupational Safety and Health Administration (OSHA) tries to make sure that factories are equipped with adequate safety measures. The Federal Aviation Administration (FAA) is concerned with the safety of flying operations, and the Public Utility Commission (PUC) of a state sets the rates for the public utility companies that provide water, electricity, and telephone services. The idea behind each type of regulation is to bring about a higher level of utility for society, largely in accordance with the Pareto criteria discussed in Chapter 17.

REGULATION OF PRICE

The price of a product is determined by the demand as well as the cost conditions in an industry, and can be influenced by changes in either demand or cost conditions or both. According to the propositions of welfare economics, the ideal situation is achieved when the price of a good or service equals its marginal cost. When the output markets are imperfectly competitive, the demand function is above the marginal revenue function, and consequently the profit-maximizing firm selects a price which is higher than the marginal cost. This unhappy state of affairs can be corrected if the firm is forced to charge a price which equals the marginal cost of the output. Presumably, perfect competition brings about the ideal conditions sought by Pareto, because in the long run, a perfectly competitive firm's price equals the marginal cost.

The general feeling is that industries that permit increases of output at successively lower unit costs should be regulated in this manner. Utility companies' production functions exhibit substantial economies of scale, and since the demand for a utility is reasonably price inelastic, if the firm charges the profit-maximizing price, the price to the consumer will be high, as will the cost of production. In addition, the natural advantages of increasing returns to scale will be sacrificed if too many firms are allowed to compete in the same market, because in that case, each firm will operate on a scale smaller than necessary to bring about the advantages of economies of scale. Duplication of production facilities is not only wasteful, but is downright unsound from an environmentalist's point of view.

The regulated company is protected from competition in the sense that the regulatory agency grants exclusive license to the firm to produce, market, and sell the product in a given area, with the proviso that the firm charges the price suggested by the regulators. This ideal price is where the marginal cost of the output equals the price. The difficulty with such a policy is that in the case of a decreasing cost firm, the average total cost falls as the output volume increases. This implies that the marginal cost lies below the average cost. If the firm selects a price which equals the marginal cost, the average total cost of production will exceed the price, and the firm will lose money. Thus, if the firm is required to charge a price equal to the marginal cost, it must be subsidized by an amount equal to its losses, so that the firm earns at least a normal profit. Of course, the cost of the subsidy should be no greater than the added benefits to the consumers.

Figure 18-1 shows a regulated monopoly with a decreasing average total cost function indicating economies of scale. The marginal cost is below the average total cost, and intersects the demand curve at price P_2 and quantity Q_2. At such a quantity, the ATC exceeds the price. If the firm is allowed to select its own price, it will probably choose a price close to P_1, since that is the profit-maximizing price, and in this case guarantees substantial pure profits to the firm. If this firm agrees to be regulated, its average total cost will be ATC_2 and the average loss will equal $ATC_2 - P_2$. The total loss to the firm will be (OQ_2) $(ATC_2 - P_2)$. If the firm receives exactly this amount in a subsidy, it will break

FIGURE 18-1
The socially optimal price-quantity combination occurs when the regulated price equals marginal cost, such as price P_2. However, at that price, the firm's ATC is higher than P_2. Consequently, for the firm to break even at price P_2, it must receive a subsidy of RT per unit of output.

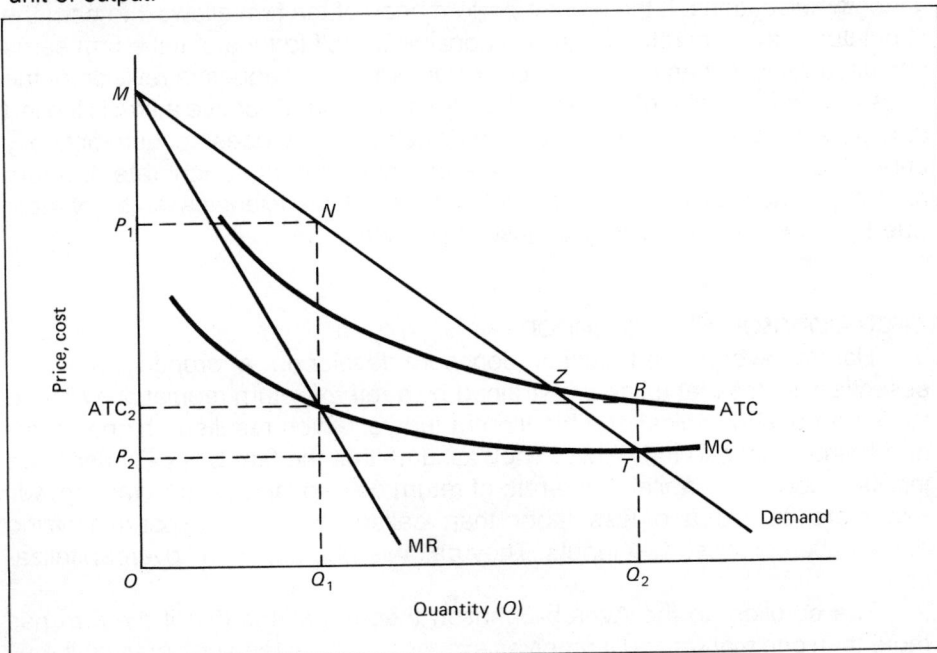

even or earn a normal profit. Furthermore, the price will equal marginal cost, and societal utility will be maximized.

The benefit to the users is often measured by the price they are willing to pay for a unit of the service. It is common practice to measure the total value to the consumers by measuring the area under the demand curve up to the quantity consumed at the prevailing price P_2. In our case, this area is $OMTQ_2$, which is an increase equivalent to area Q_1NTQ_2 over what would have prevailed if the firm had maximized profits with price P_1. The area representing the total subsidy "cost" to the government is $P_2(ATC_2)RT$. Because the area representing the gain to consumers increased by a larger amount than the area representing the value of the subsidy to the firm, price regulation accompanied by the subsidy is economical. The end results of this type of regulation are that the price to the consumer is low, the unit of service is provided at very low cost, and price equals marginal cost. Although the regulated price was set below the firm's original price choice, this is not always the case. For example, if the output contributes to substantial social marginal cost, in spite of economies of scale, the eventual price may be higher than the free market price.

REGULATION OF THE RATE OF RETURN

Instead of actually setting a price for the firm, the regulating agency can restrict profits by limiting earning to a certain rate of return on investment (ROI) which is carefully calculated to permit the firm to earn a fair return. This type of regulation is prevalent in industries involving transportation, electricity, and telecommunications. If the market performance of the firm allows it to earn the stipulated maximum rate of return, it considers itself fortunate. If the firm earns substantially less than the stipulated maximum, it can request a revision of the price or reexamination of the rate-of-return constraint. Because a firm is limited to a certain maximum rate of return on investment, this does not automatically imply that the firm will necessarily earn that amount. Such rate-of-return regulation has presumably led to certain types of inefficiencies, some of them due to the so-called "Averch–Johnson" phenomenon.

The Averch–Johnson Phenomenon

Harvey Averch and Leland Johnson developed a proposition which essentially states that a firm constrained by a rate-of-return regulation will tend to use an uneconomical combination of inputs, which results in higher costs and higher prices to the public. They assume that the firm basically uses two inputs—labor and capital. If the rate of return on capital is limited, the firm will use more capital and less labor than called for by the cost-minimizing combination of these two inputs. They call this phenomenon "overcapitalization."

The corollary to the Averch–Johnson theorem states that if the firm has more than one market and it receives excessive profits from one market, it may have to deliberately lose money in the other markets to satisfy the regulatory constraint. For the firm to lose money in the secondary market, it must price its product below the average cost of production. In so doing, not only does the firm adhere to the "law," but it also keeps competition from the market, for who can compete with a firm that sells a product at a price below cost? If this is true, such behavior by the firm is definitely a form of predatory price competition.

To explain the Averch–Johnson proposition, suppose the firm uses two inputs, capital K and labor L, to produce the output Q. The price of each unit of K is r, and the price of each unit of L is w. Under these conditions, the firm's profits equal the excess of total revenue R over total cost C. Total cost is the sum of labor and capital cost, or $C = wL + rK$. For purposes of rate-of-return regulation, the return to capital is defined as the ratio of the excess of revenues over labor costs to the total stock of capital. Thus, the rate of return on capital or rate of return on investment (ROI) may be stated as

$$\text{ROI} = \frac{R - wL}{K}$$

and if the rate is restricted to a certain maximum percentage, s, the regulatory constraint may be written as

$$\text{ROI} = \frac{R - wL}{K} \leq s \tag{1}$$

Total profit (Π) may be expressed as $R - wL - rK$, from which we can obtain

$$\Pi + rK = R - wL \tag{2}$$

Substituting equation (2) into the regulatory constraint given by equation (1), we have the ratio of allowed profits to the rate of return on capital. Equation (3) shows this relationship:

$$\frac{R - wL}{K} \leq s, \quad \text{or} \quad \Pi + rK \leq s, \quad \text{or} \quad \Pi \leq (s - r)K \tag{3}$$

The regulatory constraint shown by equation (3) suggests that if the allowed rate of return is higher than the cost of capital, s will exceed r, and $s-r$ will be positive. In all probability, the regulatory agency will set s at least as high as r, and probably higher, which implies that the firm's allowable absolute profit level will increase with K if the market conditions are right.

Given the usual assumptions of the production function and the price–quantity demand curve, profits to the firm as a function of K will appear as shown in Figure 18-2. The regulatory constraint $\Pi \leq (s-r)K$ is represented as a straight line from the origin having a positive slope equal to $s-r$. All points along or below this line are acceptable to the regulators. If the firm is a profit maximizer, it will operate at a point where the value of the profit function is maximum. Profits are maximum when $K = K^*$. However, maximum profits exceed the allowable profits under the constraint. Thus, the firm selects the "next best" level of profits at point B, where the quantity of capital is equal to K_B. When the firm's unconstrained maximum profits exceed the maximum permissible under the constraint, the constraint is said to be "binding." If the constraint had been the dotted line, it would not have been binding, and the

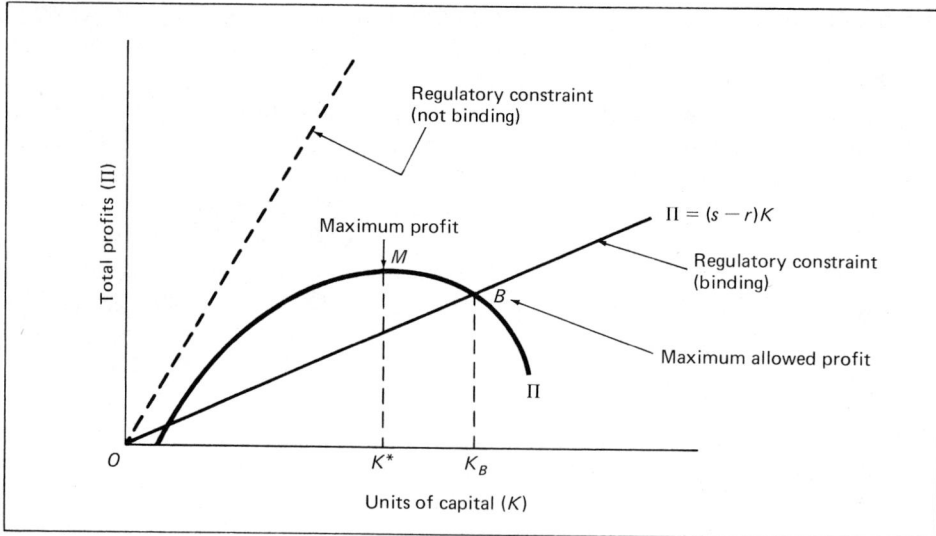

FIGURE 18-2
The firm's unconstrained profits are maximized with K* quantity of capital. If the constraint is binding, it intersects the Π function and limits the firm's profits. In this case, the firm's constrained maximum profit occurs at point B, and the firm uses much more capital (K_B) as compared to point M.

firm would have been free to maximize profits with $K = K^*$. From this illustration, we can see that the firm uses more units of K (K_B) than it would without the constraint. Hence the alleged notion of "overcapitalization." Why is the use of "excess" capital necessarily uneconomical?

According to the theory of production, a profit-maximizing firm combines resources in quantities which allow the marginal revenue products of the resources to be equal to their marginal resource costs. Thus, if the firm uses the two resources discussed, and if the price of the output is P_0,

$$\frac{(MRP)_K}{(MRP)_L} = \frac{r}{w} \quad \text{or} \quad \frac{(MQ)_K \times P_0}{(MQ)_L \times P_0} = \frac{r}{w}$$

$$\frac{(MQ)_K}{(MQ)_L} = \frac{r}{w} \tag{4}$$

Equation (4) is the cost-minimizing combination of K and L, which is employed by a profit-maximizing firm. Thus, capital in the amount K^* with the appropriate amount of L will minimize the cost of producing the output. However, in Figure 18-2, the firm uses more K than is considered optimal, hence the cost of production is higher than necessary. This is inefficient from society's point of view and represents a misallocation of resources, because condition (4) is violated.

It can be shown (with a little bit of calculus) that a profit-maximizing firm will tend to behave in the manner suggested. We can approximate the mathematical techniques of Averch and Johnson by resorting to an alternative explanation of the firm's behavior. When the allowed rate of return exceeds the cost of capital, the firm views the real cost of capital to be less than it is. Crudely stated, if s, the allowed rate of return, is 12%, and the cost of capital r is 10%, the firm will tend to think of the cost of capital as $10 - (s-r)$. Thus, in our case, the firm will tend to think of the cost of capital as 8% and will combine capital with labor according to the cost-minimization formula. Since the firm views the cost of capital as 8%, while it is really 10%, it will use a higher K/L ratio than is socially desirable.

In Figure 18-3, we have a familiar isoquant Q_1. With the costs of labor and capital measured at their real rates, the cost-minimizing combination of K and L occurs at point A. But, because the firm's estimate of the cost of capital is less than society's, it will tend to think of point B as the cost-minimizing combination of the two resources. When we measure the cost of producing at point B with the use of the real prices of K and L, the social cost of producing at point B is higher than that at point A. It is alleged that this form of inefficiency, due to the rate-of-return regulation, keeps the cost of production high, encourages firms to use more capital than necessary, and brings about higher prices.

While the Averch–Johnson theorem has much appeal, several empirical studies of the regulated industries did not reveal the presence of the A–J phenomenon to any marked degree. The industries themselves were in a state of flux during the time of the studies, and technology was undergoing significant changes. When adjusted for these changes along with inflation,

FIGURE 18-3
This regulated firm perceives the cost of capital to be less than its true cost, and, therefore, feels that point B is optimal for producing output Q_1 with budget MN. However, line FG shows the real relative price of capital and A to be the best point. Measured at true prices, the cost of production at point B is higher than at point A. Point B also uses more capital than point A.

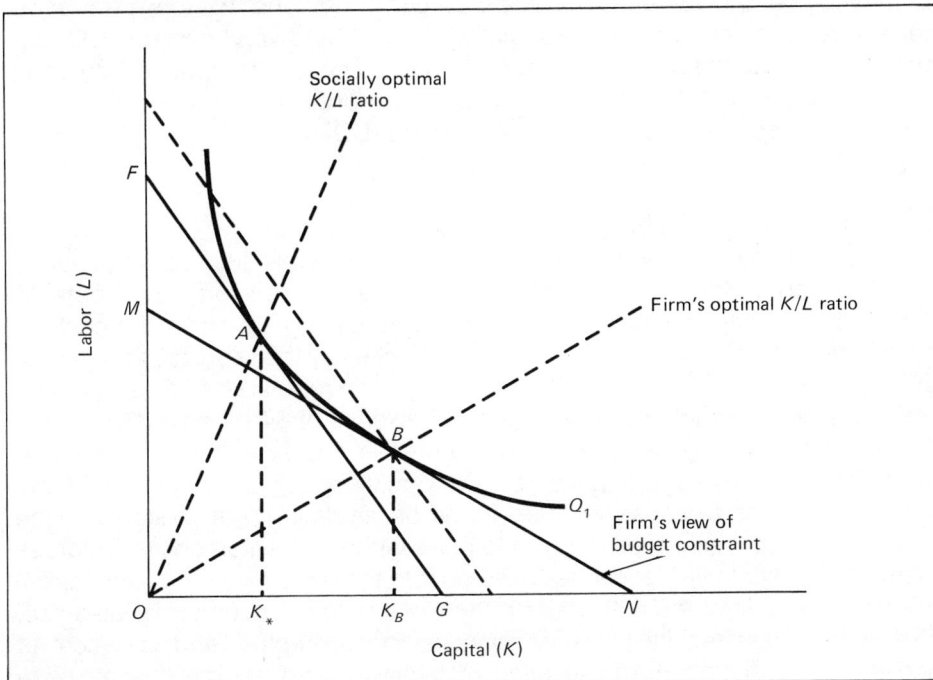

some of the data revealed a minute presence of the A–J behavior. It is entirely possible that the behavior suggested by the A–J proposition exists in more subtle forms, or that it can under certain circumstances.

THE RAMSEY PRICING AND INVERSE ELASTICITY RULE

Ramsey-optimal pricing and the *inverse elasticity rule* are often used by economists to recommend various optimal prices for regulated industries and various types of users. The Ramsey pricing scheme basically evolved from Ramsey's contributions to the study of public finance some 60 years ago. He maintained that the optimal tax rate is one that minimizes the welfare cost of meeting the state revenue requirement constraint. In terms of a regulated industry, the optimal price of the service is that which reduces the consumer's welfare the least while meeting the budget constraint of the enterprise.

The Ramsey pricing model is linked to a *Ramsey number*, which is the ratio of the difference in price and marginal cost to the price multiplied by the price elasticity of demand for the product or service. Thus, for the regulated price to be optimal, the Ramsey number should be the same for all services. The Ramsey number can be expressed as

$$\text{Ramsey number} = R = \frac{(P - MC)}{P} e \tag{5}$$

From the "Ramsey rule" we can obtain the *inverse elasticity rule*. If all services must have the same R value and the MC is the same for all services, then the higher the value of the price elasticity of demand, the lower the price necessary. In other words, the regulated price should vary inversely with the absolute value of the price elasticity of demand. The Bell Telephone Company has attempted to use Ramsey analysis to compute optimal charges for its services, especially for direct-distance-dialing (DDD).

THE COST OF REGULATION

While the intent of the regulators may be in the public interest, regulations cost the public billions of dollars each year. These costs are largely attributable to the administrative costs of maintaining the regulating agencies, the costs of monitoring the performance of the parties affected by the regulations, the cost due to higher prices, and the cost of enforcing the regulations. In 1976 alone, several federal agencies were budgeted in excess of $4 billion.

The price-setting regulations may increase social welfare, however, in those markets where the price is not regulated, we may find the firms increasing prices because of other forms of regulation. For example, if the government requires car companies to put seat belts in automobiles, or forces them to install catalytic converters, the cost to the manufacturers rises, and if the marginal cost of the output rises, the price to the consumer will also rise. The higher price results in a loss of consumer's surplus, and is a cost to society, even though the prevention of fatalities from accidents may be a benefit. While the government insists on seat belts in cars, the reduction of the speed limits has reduced the potential benefits of the belts. This phenomenon accentuates higher car prices.

Consider the regulation concerning minimum wages. When the government insists that employers pay a wage above the "natural" rate, the supply of workers exceeds the demand, causing severe unemployment and bringing about the associated social costs. Costs also increase when manufacturers are required to follow certain rigid safety codes, which in many instances cause the employers unnecessary headaches without many commensurate benefits. As a result, the employer's productivity is less than best, and the prices of products are higher than necessary.

Regulations concerning food additives are again meant to protect us from dangerous chemicals and carcinogens. For example, nitrites added to canned foods keep us from botulism poisoning; yet nitrites have been found to cause cancer. Take your choice—eat food without nitrites and risk botulism, or consume food with nitrites and die from cancer. Of course, there is a third choice—don't eat!

Cattle feeders at one time added small amounts of DES to the animal feed to increase cattle weight. A few milligrams of this additive added 20% more weight at 10% less cost. The result was that DES-fed cattle were less costly to raise, which contributed to lower beef prices. But the moment it was discovered that DES may cause cancer, the government almost totally banned its use, which may have caused a substantial increase in beef prices.

Automobile emission standards are designed to improve the quality of the air and to reduce the pollutants discharged into the atmosphere. The standards require additional gadgets, which usually reduce gas mileage. So while the air is less polluted, the cost to the owner of such a car goes up twice—first because of the higher price, and second because of poorer mileage.

We have pinpointed some of the costs of regulation. There are many other forms of regulation with attendant positive and negative effects. The basic intent of regulation is to improve life and increase social utility. However, there is a possibility of overregulation of the economic system. Decision makers must heed their own advice in the regulatory arena. A regulation is good if and only if its total benefits outweigh its total costs.

EXERCISES

1. Define and explain the following:
   a. Economic regulation.
   b. Rate-of-return regulation.
   c. Regulation for minimum standards.
   d. Quotas on imports.
   e. Ramsey pricing.
   f. Inverse elasticity rule.
   g. Averch–Johnson phenomenon.
   h. Cost of regulation.

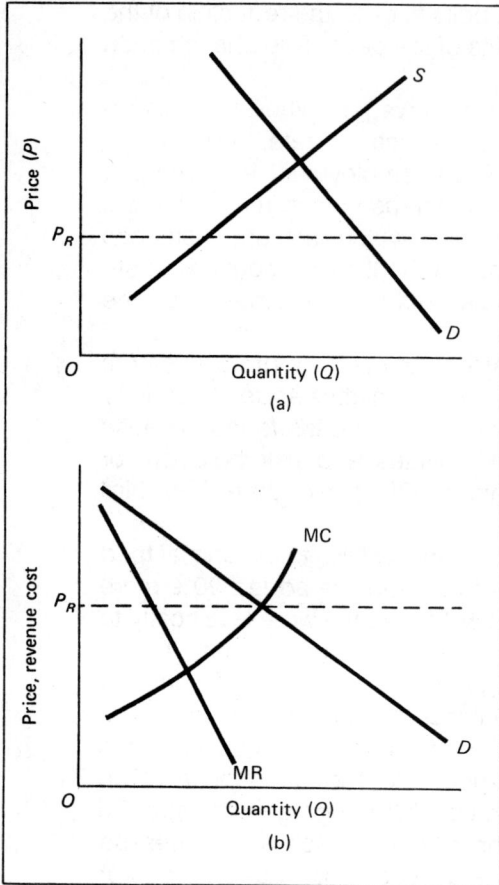

FIGURE 18-4

2. Provide examples of agencies at the local, state, and national levels that regulate some part of your life.

3. Suppose the regulated firm's production function is $Q = K^{1/2}L^{1/2}$ and the price of the output is $100. If the price of each unit of L is $100 and of each unit of K is $25, find the cost-minimizing combination of K and L for any given level of output. (Let $Q = 50$.)

4. Using the information from Exercise 3, assume that the firm is regulated to earn no more than $30 per unit of capital. If all other factors remain equal, calculate the firm's optimal capital/labor ratio according to the Averch–Johnson hypothesis. If the real cost of capital is $25, what is the true cost of producing the output? Is it higher or lower than the amount involved in Exercise 3?

5. Enumerate some benefits of regulation, citing specific examples.

6. State the costs and benefits of the following:
   a. the motorcycle helmet law.
   b. food-contents labeling.
   c. a ban on certain food additives.
   d. price regulations.
   e. minimum wage laws.

7. In Figure 18-4, P_R is the regulated price. Describe in some detail the effect of this regulated price on the quantity and price of the product, as well as on the welfare of the consumers and producers.

8. Assume that a firm's demand and marginal cost functions are, respectively,

$$P = 100 - \tfrac{1}{10}Q$$
$$MC = 10 + \tfrac{1}{20}Q$$

 a. How many units of output will this profit-maximizing firm produce at a regulated price of $50?
 b. Prove that a regulated price of $28 will lead the firm to produce the same level of output as it would produce without regulation.
 c. What price level (regulated) will bring forth the most output?

9. Suppose a country's demand and supply functions are known to be:

$$P_D = 100 - Q_D$$
$$P_S = 10 + 2Q_S$$

What will be the equilibrium price and quantity in the market? If this nation wished to import exactly 20 units, what price must it pay for the import if the foreign supply is given by $P_{S(f)} = 10 + 2Q_{S(f)}$? Now suppose that the government wishes to regulate the price of all output such that domestically made goods are priced at the same level as the imported ones. At what price will the *excess* domestic demand be exactly satisfied through imports?

SUGGESTED READINGS

American Enterprise Institute for Public Policy Research. *Proposals for the Regulation of Hospital Costs.* Washington, D.C.: 1978.

Bailey, E. E. *Economic Theory of the Regulatory Constraint.* Lexington, Mass.: D.C. Heath, 1977.

Copeland, B. L. "Alternative Cost–of–Capital Concepts of Regulation." *Land Economics*, Vol. 54, No. 3, August 1978.

Erickson, E., and Spann, R. M. "Supply Price in a Regulated Industry: The Case of Natural Gas." *Bell Journal of Economics and Management Science*, Vol. 2, No. 1, Spring 1971.

Griliches, Z. "Cost Allocation in Railroad Regulation." *Bell Journal of Economics and Management Science*, Vol. 3, No. 1, Spring 1972.

Ippolito, R. A., and Masson, R. T. "The Social Cost of Government Regulation of Milk." *Journal of Law and Economics*, Vol. 21, No. 1, April 1978.

Kahn, A. E. *The Economics of Regulation*, Vol. II. New York: John Wiley, 1971.

"Airline Deregulation: Getting from Here to There." *Policy Review*, No. 3, Winter 1978.

Levy, R. E. "Fair Return on Equity for Public Utilities." *Business Economics,* Vol. 13, No. 4, September 1978.

Mitchell, B. M. "Optimal Pricing of Local Telephone Service." *American Economic Review*, Vol. 68, No. 4, September, 1978.

Mitnick, B. M. "The Concept of Regulation." *Ohio State University Bulletin of Business Research*, Vol. 53, August 1978.

Scherer, F. M. *Industrial Market Structure and Economic Performance.* Chicago: Rand McNally, 1973.

Sherman, R. *Antitrust Policies and Issues.* Reading, Mass.: 1978.

CHAPTER 1 APPENDIX

You don't have to be a cerebral giant to understand economic phenomena. Similarly, mathematical wizardry is not a prerequisite for understanding the economic relationships and functions discussed in this textbook or in economics literature. However, some understanding of the mathematical tools employed makes life a lot easier and helps us to analyze economic models. Most microeconomic models lend themselves to the use of algebra, analytical geometry, calculus, and, of course, plain arithmetic.

ALGEBRA

Algebra permits us to express relationships among variables with the use of letters which correspond to the many values that the variables can assume. For example, we can write an algebraic statement linking the number of cents (C) to the number of dollars (D). Because each and every dollar equals 100 cents, the number of cents is 100 times the number of dollars, or

$$C = 100D$$

Similarly, the temperature in degrees Fahrenheit (F) can be equated to its Celsius equivalent (C) by using

$$F = \frac{9}{5}C + 32$$

To illustrate the use of algebra in economics, suppose we have a product whose quantity demanded depends inversely on its price. Assume that demand is zero at a price of $100 and that an additional unit is demanded for each $2 reduction in the price of the product. We can write a general expression for the demand for this product in terms of its price (P) and quantity demanded (Q):

$$P = 100 - 2Q$$

or

$$Q = 50 - \tfrac{1}{2}P$$

You can verify that Q will be zero when $P = \$100$, and $Q = 50$ when $P = \$0$.

ANALYTICAL GEOMETRY

Analytical geometry is that branch of mathematics which deals with the equations of algebraic functions. Thus, we may have equations that represent straight lines, circles, parabolas, hyperbolas, ellipses, and other forms or shapes. Some of the equations are used more than others. For instance, we use many linear (straight line) relationships in discussing demand and price functions. There are also many nonlinear (or curvilinear) functions employed in microeconomics. The average total cost function, for example, is nonlinear, as is the production-possibilities curve. We will examine some of the conventional forms of functions often found in economics models.

The Straight Line

A linear function of two variables can be expressed with an *intercept* and a *slope*. The intercept (either X or Y), is a point along the X or Y axis where the line intersects that particular axis. The slope of a function is the function's inclination to a particular axis, normally the X axis. Thus, if the straight line is such that the Y intercept is 100 and its slope is -2, the line will be drawn to reflect a vertical intercept of 100 and a negative slope (rise over run) of 2. Consequently, the X intercept has to be 50, because then and only then will the line have a slope of 100/50, or 2, and more precisely -2, because Y varies inversely with X. When Y decreases as X increases, Y is said to be *inversely* (or negatively) related to X. Such functions are downward sloping. The demand function, where Q is inversely related to P, is a good example of a downward sloping linear function. If we replace Y with P, and X with Q, we will have a price–quantity demand function as shown in Figure A1-1.

The equation for a straight line is most simply expressed as

$$Y = b + mX \tag{1}$$

where b corresponds to the vertical intercept, m represents the slope of the line, and X is the independent variable. Thus, if we write a linear equation such as $Y = 200 - 2X$, it will have a vertical or Y intercept of 200 and a slope of -2. If we convert equation (1) into a total cost (TC) equation, it might look like

$$TC = 100 + 10Q$$

Here total cost is measured along the Y axis and quantity (Q) along the X axis. This function has a positive vertical intercept equal to 100 (corresponding to fixed costs), and a positive or upwards slope of 10 (corresponding to average variable and marginal cost).

Demand and supply functions are often represented as linear functions, although they are not always straight lines. We will use one set of linear

FIGURE A1-1

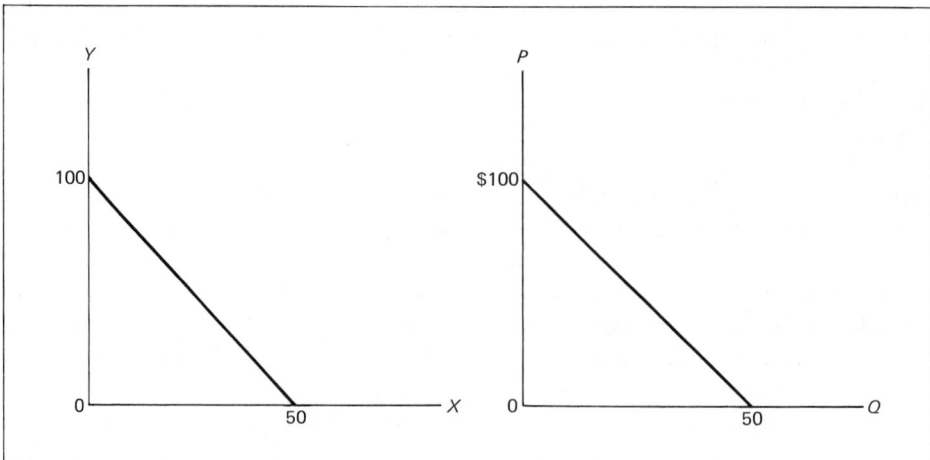

functions to solve for equilibrium price and quantity. Assume that the demand and supply functions are

$$\text{Demand: } P = 100 - 2Q$$
$$\text{Supply: } P = 10 + Q$$

Equilibrium occurs when demand equals supply, or $100 - 2Q = 10 + Q$. Solving for Q, we obtain $3Q = 90$, or $Q = 30$. Hence equilibrium price, P, is $100 - 2Q = 100 - 2(30) = \$40 = 10 + Q$.

The Slope of a Function

The *slope* measures the inclination of a function and is commonly referred to as the value of the *rise over the run*. In conventional notation, the slope is shown as $\Delta Y/\Delta X$, where ΔY is the change in the vertical direction corresponding to ΔX, the change in the horizontal direction. If the function is nonlinear, its slope at any point can be measured by the slope of the *tangent* drawn at that point.

Marginal and Average Values

In microeconomics we encounter many variables expressed as marginals or averages, for example, marginal product, average variable cost, and marginal revenue. Graphically speaking, the value of the slope is given by the value of the marginal. Thus, the slope of the total revenue function is indicated by the value of the marginal revenue function. The average value of a function is the ratio of the dependent variable to the independent variable. For example, if $Y = 20X + 2X^2$, the average Y is Y/X, or $20 + 2X$; or, if total cost $TC = 100 + 10Q - 2Q^2$, the average total cost $ATC = 100/Q + 10 - 2Q$. In a graph, the average value at a point is indicated by the slope of a straight line drawn from the origin to that point. Figure A1-2 shows the marginal and average measurements. The diagram shown could just as easily be a production function $Q = f(L)$, where Q is measured along the vertical axis and L along the horizontal. Thus, the average value of Q, or Q/L, will correspond to the average physical product of L, and the marginal value will represent the marginal product.

Maxima and Minima of Functions

The literature of microeconomics is replete with maximization and minimization problems. In many cases, the minimum and maximum values occur at the beginning or end of a function. For example, total cost is minimum when quantity is zero, and cost increases as quantity increases. On the other hand, when the marginal product of a resource is a decreasing function of the quantity of that resource, the maximum marginal product will occur at the beginning and the minimum will occur at the end.

There are other functions encountered in microeconomics, however, where the minimum or maximum values are found somewhere between the

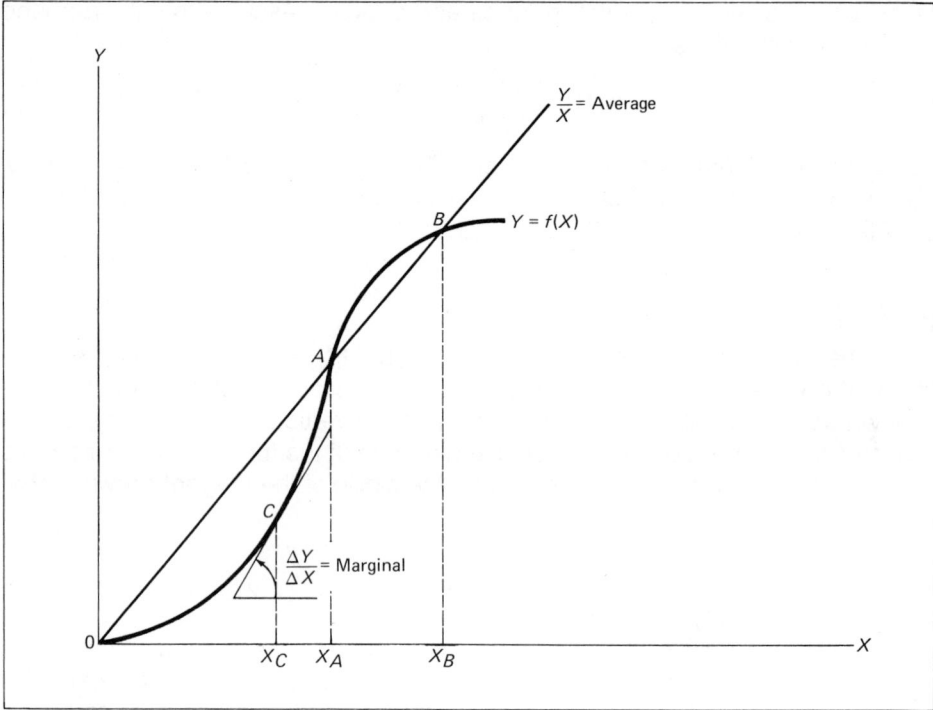

FIGURE A1-2
The angle subtended by line *OAB* measures the average values of $Y = f(X)$ at points *A* and *B*. Consequently, the averages at *A* and *B* are equal. The angle or slope of the tangent drawn at point *C* measures the marginal value of the function at that point. You can verify that the average of *Y* will be less than the marginal at point *C*.

beginning and the end; that is, if we disregard or disallow negative values of the independent variable, the maximum or minimum values occur at some finite positive quantity. Thus, in the case of the conventional U-shaped average total cost function, the minimum ATC occurs at the bottom of the U. For a total revenue function shown by an upside-down U, the maximum occurs at the peak. For all such functions, the minimum or maximum values of functions coincide with the point where the slope of the function is 0; that is, where the marginal value of the function is zero. A function may have two or more points where its slope attains zero value. To solve for minimum or maximum values of functions of this type, equate the marginal value of the function to zero and solve for the unknown quantity. (See Figure A1-3.)

Suppose we wish to find the quantity and price that will maximize the revenues to a firm. The demand for the product is $P = 100 - 2Q$ and the marginal revenue corresponding to this demand function is $MR = 100 - 4Q$. Equating MR to zero, we obtain

$$MR = 100 - 4Q = 0$$
$$Q = 25$$

from which we find that the price $P = 100 - (2)(25) = \$50$. Total revenue, $R = PQ = (100 - 2Q)(Q) = 100Q - 2Q^2 = \$1250$, is maximum at $Q = 25$.

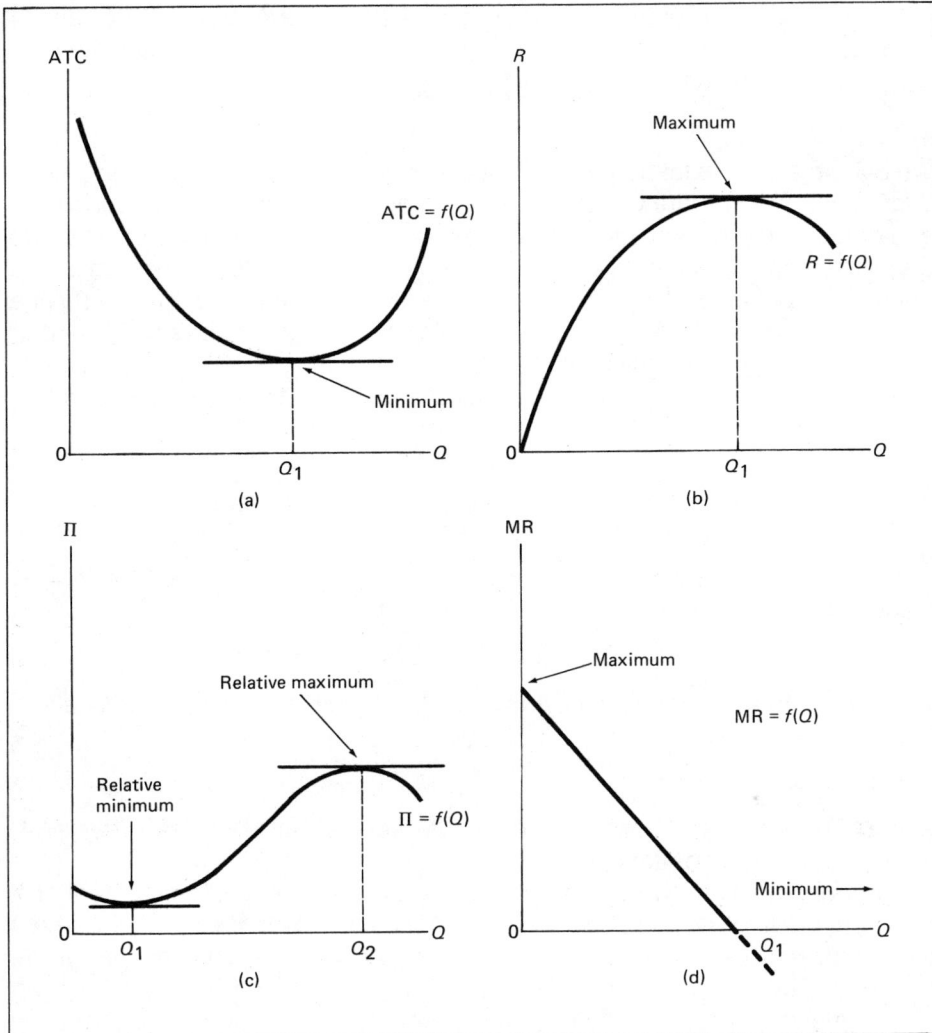

FIGURE A1-3
The ATC of (a) shows that the slope of the function is zero at quantity Q_1, and hence the ATC is minimum at that quantity. In (b), revenue (R) is maximized at output level Q_1. In (c), the profit function's slope is zero at two places—Q_1 and Q_2. At Q_1, the profits are minimum, and at Q_2 maximum. Of course, it is entirely possible for a function to have a slope of zero at more than two locations. Panel (d) shows the marginal revenue function, whose maximum value occurs at 0. The lowest value will occur at the highest possible quantity. For such functions, the slope is not zero when the function attains its maximum or minimum values.

Summation of Functions

In some models discussed in the text we had to add certain functions. For instance, in the discussion of total market demand, we added the individual demand functions to get the aggregated market demand. This was a *horizontal* summation of the quantities, because we added the quantities demanded by each consumer at each price to get the *total* quantity demanded at each price.

Suppose a firm sells its wares in two markets, and the demands in markets 1 and 2 are

$$P_1 = 12 - 0.80Q_1$$
$$P_2 = 80 - 4Q_2$$

We can obtain the total demand for the firm's products by adding Q_1 and Q_2 at each price. We can draw this function graphically by choosing the price level and determining the two quantities corresponding to that price. We add the two quantities and plot the sum against the chosen price levels. For example, at a price of \$4, Q_1 will be 10, and Q_2 19. Hence the total demand will equal 29 at a price of \$4. We can find other points in a similar manner. Algebraically, we can derive the equation for this sum.

Because we are adding the quantities, we first convert the demand functions to express Q in terms of P. Thus,

$$-0.80Q_1 = P_1 - 12 \quad \text{and} \quad -4Q_2 = P_2 - 80$$
$$Q_1 = 15 - 1.25P_1, \quad Q_2 = 20 - 0.25P_2$$
$$Q = Q_1 + Q_2 = 15 - 1.25P_1 + 20 - 0.25P_2$$

The demand functions are being added horizontally, and hence, $P_1 = P_2 = P$. Consequently,

$$Q = 35 - 1.5P$$

which is the total demand for the firm's product, and may also be expressed as

$$P = \frac{70}{3} - \frac{2}{3}Q$$

Using either of the total demand equations, we see that when the price is \$4, the total quantity Q equals 29.

In general, when we add functions horizontally, we hold the vertical or Y value constant for all functions and add all the individual X. Likewise, we hold the X value constant and add the Y values to obtain the vertical sum of the functions. Such a technique is employed if we must add the demand for two complementary products that are by-products. For example, a firm may produce beef and hides from its cattle herd. Thus, each animal slaughtered produces one carcass and one hide. Assume that the demand for carcasses is

$$P_C = 2000 - 2C$$

and the demand for hides is

$$P_H = 200 - H$$

The vertical sum constitutes the total demand price per carcass (C) and hide (H) at various levels of C and H. In this case, let's assume that $C = H = 100$. The vertical sum is equal to

$$P_C + P_H = 2200 - 3C$$
$$P_C + P_H = 2200 - 3(100)$$
$$= \$1900$$

Thus, the firm can expect 100 carcasses and hides to be demanded at a joint price of $1900; $1800 is the price of each carcass, and $100 the price of each hide:

$$P_C = 2000 - 2C$$
$$= 2000 - 2(100)$$
$$= \$1800$$
$$P_H = 200 - H$$
$$= 200 - 100$$
$$= \$100$$

The total revenue to the company will be (100)($1900) = $190,000. The firm can use such information to obtain the optimal number of animals to be slaughtered.

Sums and Areas

The sum of a set of values is shown by areas in a graph. Thus, the sum of the individual marginal costs of each unit of output equals the total variable cost which can be measured by the area under the marginal cost curve. For example, suppose the marginal cost of the firm is

$$MC = 10 + 10Q$$

If we wish to find the total variable cost for two units, we can do so by adding the marginal cost associated with each Q from 0 to 2, or by finding the area under the MC function up to quantity $Q = 2$. In Figure A1-4a, we show the linear marginal cost function. Area $OABC$ represents the total variable cost. This area is trapezoidal, and the area of a trapezoid is equal to the sum of the two parallel sides multiplied by half the distance between the sides. The two vertical and parallel sides are 10 and 30, respectively, and the distance between them is 2. Therefore, the area of trapezoid $OABC$ is

$$(10 + 30)(\tfrac{1}{2})(2) = 40$$

or the total variable cost of producing two units of output is $40. Figure A1-4b shows the area for the firm's revenue. Using the general formula for the area of a triangle, we can find area OAB.

$$OAB = \tfrac{1}{2}(2)(44)$$
$$= \$44$$

The total revenue from producing two units of output is $44, which is $4 more than the total variable cost. The general formulas for finding area are

$Circle$: Area $= \pi r^2 = \pi \dfrac{D^2}{4}$ (r is the radius; D is the diameter)

$Triangle$: Area $= \left(\dfrac{1}{2}\right)$(base)(height)

$Rectangle$: Area $=$ (length)(width)

$Trapezoid$: Area $= \left(\dfrac{1}{2}\right)$(sum of parallel sides)(distance between sides)

Area of $OABC = (\frac{1}{2})(30 + 10)(2)$

$= 40$ = variable cost

MC = 10 + 10Q

30

B

A

10

O C Q

2

Marginal cost

(a)

MR = 44 − 22Q

44 A

Area of $OAB = (\frac{1}{2})(2)(44)$

$= 44$ = revenue

Marginal revenue

O B Q

2

(b)

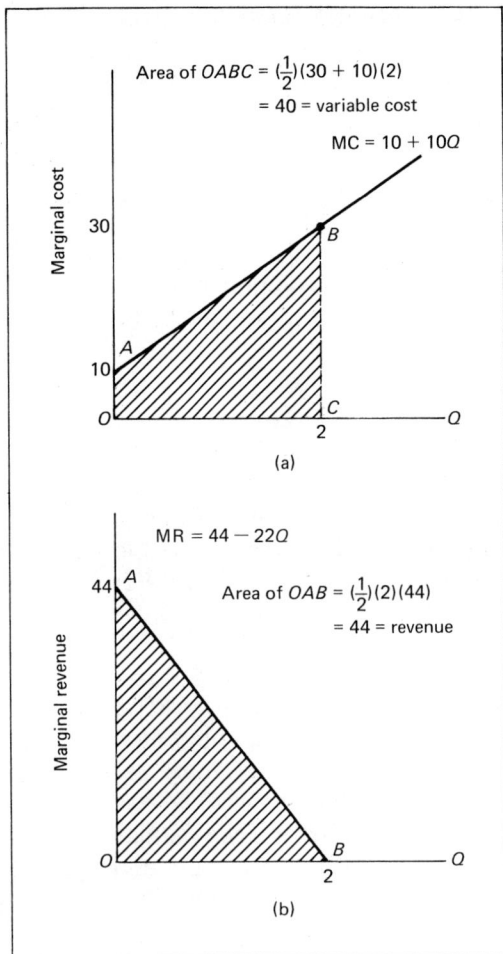

FIGURE A1-4
In (a) we have a trapezoid whose area represents the value of total variable cost. In (b) the triangular area under the marginal revenue function equals the total revenue. If these functions belong to the same firm and apply to the same product, when $Q = 2$, the firm's revenues exceed its variable costs by $4.

CALCULUS

In most microeconomic models, we are involved with slopes, or maximum and minimum values of functions. At times we also deal with the rates of change of variables. When the functions are linear, the slopes or extreme values are easily found by observation. When the functions are nonlinear, however, we must use calculus. This book is not intended as a treatise on mathematical economics, and hence we will explore only a few basics of calculus.

The Derivative

The derivative of a function is the rate of change of the dependent variable with respect to the rate of change of the independent variable. Thus, in the function $Y = f(X) = 20X - 2X^2$, the dependent variable Y will change as the independent variable X changes. The derivative compares the change in Y to small changes in X, and is written as dY/dX. In essence, the derivative of a function measures its slope. In the expression described, Y will increase as X increases from 0 to 5, and decrease as X takes on values larger than 5. Consequently, the maximum value of Y occurs at $X = 5$, and the slope of Y at that point is zero.

The most widely used "formula" for determining slopes or derivatives of simple polynomial functions is

$$\text{Function } Y = CX^n$$

$$\text{Slope} = \frac{dY}{dX} = nCX^{n-1}$$

In the expression $Y = CX^n$, C is a constant and n is the exponent of X. Thus, if $Y = 20X^2$, the 20 corresponds to C and the 2 represents n. The slope of this function will then equal $(2)(20)(X^{2-1})$, or $40X$. Because the slope increases with X, the function will increase at an increasing rate. The derivative of a sum or a difference is equal to the sum or difference of the derivatives of the individual terms. Thus, if $Y = 20X - 2X^2$, $dY/dX = 20 - 4X$. Some examples of the use of derivatives in economics are

a. Total cost $= TC = 1000 + 10Q + Q^2$;
   Marginal cost $= dTC/dQ = 10 + 2Q$.
b. Total revenue $= R = 100Q - 5Q^2$;
   Marginal revenue $= MR = dR/dQ = 100 - 10Q$.
c. Total product $= Q = 200L - \frac{1}{2}L^2$;
   Marginal product of $L = dQ/dL = 200 - L$.

Finding Relative Extremum Values
with Calculus

Because the slope of a function is zero where the maximum occurs, we can obtain the value of the independent variable that maximizes a function. Consider the revenue function $R = 20Q - 2Q^2$, whose slope (dR/dQ) is the marginal revenue (MR) and equals MR $= 20 - 4Q$. When MR $= 0$, $Q = 5$. Thus the maximum value of R occurs when $Q = 5$.

We also know that the minimum value of a function occurs where the slope is zero. For instance, the minimum average total cost occurs where the slope of the ATC is zero. Suppose a firm's average total cost is given by

$$\text{ATC} = \frac{100}{Q} + 10 + \frac{1}{4}Q$$

$$= 100Q^{-1} + 10 + \frac{1}{4}Q$$

The slope of the ATC is

$$\frac{d\text{ATC}}{dQ} = -100Q^{-2} + \frac{1}{4}$$

$$= -\frac{100}{Q^2} + \frac{1}{4}$$

For the ATC to be minimum, $dATC/dQ = 0$, or

$$\frac{100}{Q^2} = \frac{1}{4}$$

$$Q = 20$$

To make sure that the minimum can be distinguished from the maximum, we use a second set of rules; that is, for a function to have a maximum, the first derivative must equal zero, and the second derivative (derivative of the derivative) must be negative. For a true minimum, the first derivative must equal zero, and the second must be positive. The second derivative of $Y = f(X)$ is written as d^2Y/dX^2. Thus, if $Y = 20X - 2X^2$, $dY/dX = 20 - 4X$, and $d(dY/dX)/dX = d^2Y/dX^2 = -4$. Suppose we want to find the value of Q for which the revenue R is maximized:

$$R = 20Q - 2Q^2$$

$$\frac{dR}{dQ} = 20 - 4Q = 0, \qquad \text{or } Q = 5$$

$$\frac{d^2R}{dQ^2} = -4$$

R is maximum at $Q = 5$.

For the average total cost problem,

$$ATC = 100Q^{-1} + 10 + \tfrac{1}{4}Q$$

$$\frac{dATC}{dQ} = -\frac{100}{Q^2} + \frac{1}{4}$$

$$Q = 20$$

$$\frac{d^2ATC}{dQ^2} = \frac{200}{Q^3}$$

ATC is minimum at $Q = 20$

Partial Derivatives

Economics functions are frequently related to more than one variable. For example, a utility function $U = f(X, Y)$ is a function of X and Y. Under these circumstances, if we wish to determine the rate of change of U with respect to only one of the variables, we must use partial derivatives. This derivative formula assumes that all other variables remain constant. Thus, the process of taking derivatives is the same as before, except that the other variables are treated as constants. A partial derivative uses the symbol ∂ instead of d. Thus, if $Y = f(X, Z)$, the two partial derivatives will be $\partial Y/\partial X$ and $\partial Y/\partial Z$. To illustrate, suppose $Y = 2X^2Z + 3X - Z^2X + 10Z$. Then

$$\frac{\partial Y}{\partial X} = 4XZ + 3 - Z^2$$

$$\frac{\partial Y}{\partial X} = 2X^2 - 2ZX + 10$$

Partial derivatives are often used in the models of utility, revenue, and cost.

The Total Derivative or the Differential

The total change in the value of a function resulting from changes in more than one variable is written as a total derivative or a differential. The general formula for a differential of a function $Y = f(X, Z)$ is

$$dY = \frac{\partial Y}{\partial X} dX + \frac{\partial Y}{\partial Z} dZ$$

For example, take the utility function $U = f(X, Y) = X^2 Y$. The change in utility, U, is

$$dU = \frac{\partial U}{\partial X} dX + \frac{\partial U}{\partial Y} dY$$

If U is constant, as in the case of an indifference curve, $dU = 0$ and

$$\frac{\partial U}{\partial X} dX = -\frac{\partial U}{\partial Y} dY$$

$$\frac{dY}{dX} = -\frac{\partial U / \partial X}{\partial U / \partial Y} = \text{marginal rate of substitution}$$

The $\partial U / \partial X$ and $\partial U / \partial Y$ are generally interpreted as the marginal utilities of X and Y, respectively.

CHAPTER 2 APPENDIX

UTILITY FUNCTIONS

Cardinal utility functions may be written in the form $U = f(X)$, and the function will indicate whether utility is increasing or decreasing with X. It will also tell us the rate of change of utility (U) with respect to the products consumed. The utility function can also show the impact of constraints.

MARGINAL AND TOTAL UTILITY

Suppose Ann's utility function is such that her utility (U) is governed by the amount of apples (A) she buys, given the quantity of cheese (C) in her possession. Let $U = f(A) = 2C + 100A - 2A^2$. We will assume that her initial endowment of cheese is 10. Consequently, the marginal utility of apples can be found by taking the first derivative of U with respect to A:

$$\text{Marginal utility of } A = \frac{\partial U}{\partial A} = 100 - 4A$$

If Ann wants to maximize her utility, she will equate MU_A to zero. Thus, the maximum total utility occurs when $MU_A = 100 - 4A = 0$, or $A = 25$. Her total utility, when $A = 25$ and $C = 10$, is $U = 2(10) + 100(25) - 2(25)^2$, or 1270. If each apple costs 33¢, Ann will have to spend $8.25 to maximize her utility, provided cheese is free. In essence, marginal utility corresponds to the slope of the total utility function, and because the slope of a function is zero where the function acquires its maximum (or minimum) value, we maximize utility by equating marginal utility to zero.

UTILITY MAXIMIZATION UNDER CONSTRAINTS

We will now assume that Ann's utility is governed by the amount of X, Y, and Z in her possession. Let's further suppose that the utility from each product is independent of the amounts of the other product, and that total utility is the sum of the utilities produced from the possession of X, Y, and Z. Thus, $U = U_X + U_Y + U_Z$.

Assume that

$$U_X = 100X - X^2$$
$$U_Y = 200Y - \tfrac{1}{2}Y^2$$
$$U_Z = 50Z$$

If money is no object, maximum utility will occur with 50 of X, 200 of Y, and unlimited amounts of Z, or simply unlimited quantities of Z. Realistically speaking, the amount of income available for the purchase of X, Y, and Z is limited. Assume that the prices per unit of X, Y, and Z are

$$X: \$1$$
$$Y: \$2$$
$$Z: \$5$$

and that Ann's budget is limited to $1000. What combination of X, Y, and Z will maximize utility?

Total utility is maximized if Ann allocates her income according to the following rule:

$$\frac{MU_X}{P_X} = \frac{MU_Y}{P_Y} = \frac{MU_Z}{P_Z}$$

The marginal utilities of X, Y, and Z are

$$MU_X = \frac{dU}{dX} = 100 - 2X$$

$$MU_Y = \frac{dU}{dY} = 200 - Y$$

$$MU_Z = \frac{dU}{dZ} = 50$$

$$\frac{MU_X}{P_X} = \frac{100 - 2X}{1} = 100 - 2X$$

$$\frac{MU_Y}{P_Y} = \frac{200 - Y}{2} = 100 - \frac{1}{2}Y$$

$$\frac{MU_Z}{P_Z} = \frac{50}{5} = 10$$

The optimal combination occurs when all the MU/P ratios are equal, in this case at 10. Thus, $X = 45$ and $Y = 180$. The purchase of X and Y will require ($1)(45) + ($2)(180), or $405, leaving $595 for the purchase of Z. So Z must equal 595/5, or 119 units. The total utility to Ann will be

$$U = U_X + U_Y + U_Z$$
$$= 100(45) - 45^2 + 200(180) - \frac{1}{2}(180)^2 + 50(119)$$
$$= 28225.$$

Note that both X and Y are subject to diminishing marginal utility, while Z has constant marginal utility. Consequently, Ann could have acquired the same amount of utility by purchasing 28225/50, or 564.50 units of Z and none of X and Y. However, that amount of Z would necessitate a budget of $2822.50. You can verify that with the suggested combination of X, Y, and Z, Ann will receive equal marginal utility *per dollar* from each item.

THE PRINCIPLE OF DIMINISHING MARGINAL UTILITY

When utility increases at a decreasing rate, the consumer experiences "diminishing returns." Let's look at an example of a utility function that illustrates diminishing marginal utility.

Assume the utility function is $U = 100X + 10X^{1/2}$. To determine what might happen to marginal utility, we take the first derivative of the utility function. Thus,

$$\text{Marginal utility} = \frac{dU}{dX} = 100 + \frac{5}{X^{-1/2}}$$

You can see that MU_X *will decline as* X increases. In other words, as X increases, U will increase at a decreasing rate.

CONSTANT MARGINAL UTILITY

A function whose slope is always constant will exhibit a constant marginal value. Thus, a linear utility function will have constant marginal utility associated with it. For example, if $U = 200X$, the marginal utility of X will always be 200.

CONSTANT UTILITY

When the utility is not affected by the quantity of the product, the utility is constant, and therefore the marginal utility is zero. For example, suppose the utility function is $U = 1000$. Because X is not even in the function, U is independent of X and hence changes in X will not affect U. As a result, $MU_x = 0$.

INCREASING MARGINAL UTILITY

If the marginal utility function is positively related to the quantity of the product, total utility will increase at an increasing rate. For example, if $U = 100X + 2X^2$, the marginal utility of X will be

$$MU_x = \frac{dU}{dX} = 100 + 4X$$

and MU_x will increase as X increases.

CHAPTER 3 APPENDIX

Suppose the utility function is $U = f(X, Y) = 100XY$. From this function we can construct an indifference map by plotting the many points made up of X and Y values which, when substituted into the above function, provide certain chosen values for U. Thus, 1 unit of X and 16 units of Y will provide a value of 1600 for U, just as 2 units of X and 8 units of Y will also make U equal 1600. All combinations of X and Y, such that $XY = 16$ and $U = 100XY$, will automatically produce an indifference curve whose utility value (U) will equal 1600.

Let a given indifference curve having the utility level U_1 be written as

$$U_1 = f(X,Y)$$

Taking the total differential of U_1 with respect to X and Y, we have

$$dU_1 = \frac{\partial U}{\partial X} dX + \frac{\partial U}{\partial Y} dY = 0 \tag{1}$$

Because U_1 is constant, $dU_1 = 0$.
From equation (1) we see that

$$\frac{\partial U}{\partial X} dX = -\frac{\partial U}{\partial Y} dY$$

or

$$\frac{dY}{dX} = -\frac{\partial U/\partial X}{\partial U/\partial Y} \tag{2}$$

where the right-hand term of equation (2) is the marginal rate of substitution. The partial derivatives ($\partial U/\partial X$, $\partial U/\partial Y$) correspond to the marginal utilities of X and Y, respectively. In the case of the above utility function, the marginal utility of X is $100Y$ and the marginal utility of Y is $100X$. Therefore,

$$\frac{\partial U}{\partial X} = 100Y$$

$$\frac{\partial U}{\partial Y} = 100X$$

and

$$\frac{dY}{dX} = -\frac{\partial U/\partial X}{\partial U/\partial Y} = -\frac{100Y}{100X} = -\frac{Y}{X}$$

Thus the marginal rate of substitution equals $-Y/X$.

A consumer maximizes utility by equating the marginal rate of substitution to the ratio of the prices of the two commodities. Thus, if the budget equation is

$$B = P_X X + P_Y Y \tag{3}$$

the utility maximization point will occur where

$$MRS = \frac{\partial U/\partial X}{\partial U/\partial Y} = \frac{P_x}{P_y} \tag{4}$$

With reference to the utility function $U = 100XY$, if the prices of X and Y are \$10 and \$8, respectively, the optimal combination will occur where $Y/X = 10/8$.

(Since the minus sign indicates a negative slope, we can omit it in our calculations.) What is the utility maximizing bundle of X and Y for a budget of $6400?

Because $Y/X = 10/8$, $10X = 8Y$ and $10X - 8Y = 0$. Furthermore, due to the budget constraint, $10X + 8Y = 6400$. Solving these two conditions simultaneously, we obtain $X = 320$ and $Y = 400$, for a utility of $U = 100 (320)(400) = 12,800,000$. This example is shown in Figure A3-1.

Alternatively, you can solve this problem by substituting the budget constraint into the utility function and maximizing the value of the amended utility function. Thus, from the budget constraint, $X = (6400 - 8Y)/10$, and $U = (100)(XY) = (100)[(6400 - 8Y)/10](Y) = 64,000Y - 80Y^2$. Taking the first derivative of U with respect to Y and setting it equal to 0, we obtain

$$\frac{dU}{dY} = 64000 - 160Y = 0$$

and $Y = 400$. Consequently, $X = 320$.

DERIVING A DEMAND FUNCTION FROM A UTILITY FUNCTION

Suppose Sam's utility function is $U = f(X,Y)$ and he maximizes utility subject to a budget constraint $I = P_X X + P_Y Y$. We already know that maximum utility occurs where $MU_X/MU_Y = P_X/P_Y$. The marginal rate of substitution is given by $(\partial U/\partial X)/(\partial U/\partial Y)$.

For utility to be maximum,

$$MRS = \frac{\partial U/\partial X}{\partial U/\partial Y} = \frac{P_x}{P_y} \tag{5}$$

Because the quantity of X and Y that Sam can purchase is constrained by the amount of income I, we can derive the demand for X as a function of P_X from the utility-maximization equation shown by equation (5).

For the sake of example, suppose $U = 2X^2Y$, and $I = P_X X + P_Y Y$.

For maximum utility,

$$\frac{\partial U/\partial X}{\partial U/\partial Y} = \frac{P_x}{P_y}$$

$$\frac{4XY}{2X^2} = \frac{P_x}{P_y}$$

$$\frac{2Y}{X} = \frac{P_x}{P_y}$$

$$X = \frac{2YP_y}{P_x}$$

$$X = \frac{2Y}{P_x/P_y} \tag{6}$$

From the equation for the budget line, $Y = (I - P_X X)/P_Y$, and when this value of Y is substituted in (6), we have

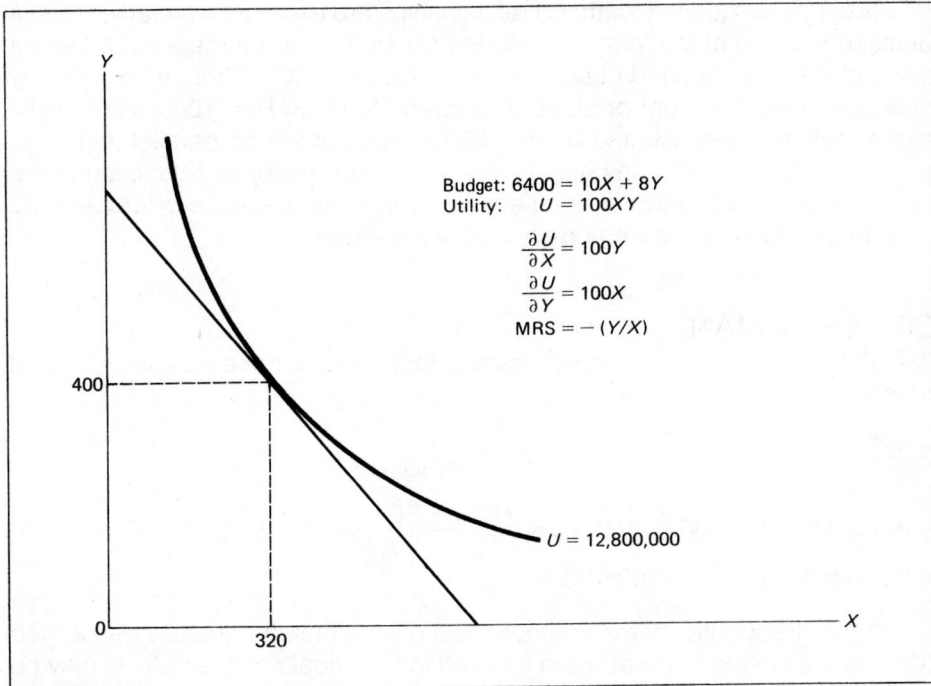

FIGURE A3-1

$$X = \frac{2(I - P_xX)/P_Y}{P_x/P_Y}$$

$$X = \frac{2(I - P_xX)}{P_x}$$

$$P_xX = 2I - 2P_xX$$

$$3P_xX = 2I$$

$$X = \frac{2I}{3P_x} \tag{7}$$

Equation (7) shows the demand for X as a function of income (I) and its own price, P_x. Thus, if I = \$1500, and P_x = \$100, X = (2)(1500)/(3)(100), or 10. Therefore, 10 units of X will cost \$1000, and the remaining \$500 will be spent for Y.

CHAPTER 4 APPENDIX

Many price–quantity demand relationships are expressed linearly. Thus, a demand function of the form $P = 200 - 2Q$ has a price intercept of 200 and a slope of -2. The demand curve may be made to "shift" or "rotate" or both, by changes in the intercept or slope. A demand function $P = 1000 - 2Q$ will lie higher than that represented by $P = 200 - 2Q$, but will be parallel to it.

Demand functions may also be nonlinear. For example, a function of the type $P = 100 - 2Q^2$ decreases at an increasing rate, because $dP/dQ = -4Q$ and dP/dQ becomes more negative as Q increases.

ELASTICITY OF DEMAND

The elasticity of demand with respect to price for a price–quantity demand function is

$$e_P = \frac{P/Q}{dP/dQ}$$

If demand is $P = 100 - 2Q^2$, $e_P = \frac{100 - 2Q^2}{(Q)(-4Q)}$. At $P = \$50$, $Q = 5$, and $e_P = (100 - 50)/-4(25) = -50/100 = -\frac{1}{2}$.

All too frequently, demand functions are such that the quantity demanded (Q) is related to many variables in addition to the price. For example, Q may be a function of price P and advertising A. Suppose the demand function is

$$Q = 100 - 2P + 10A^2$$

In this case, the price elasticity of demand is $\frac{P/Q}{\partial P/\partial Q}$, or $(P/Q)(\partial Q/\partial P)$. Similarly, the advertising elasticity of demand is

$$e_A = \frac{A}{Q}\frac{\partial Q}{\partial A}$$

For the demand function given above,

$$e_P = -2\frac{P}{Q} = \frac{-2P}{100 - 2P + 10A^2}$$

$$e_A = 20A\frac{A}{Q} = \frac{20A^2}{100 - 2P + 10A^2}$$

From these expressions, when $P = \$20$ and $A = \$1000$, the e_P and e_A are -0.0000040 and 2, respectively.

REVENUE AND DEMAND

Revenue is the product of price times the quantity. If the demand function is strictly of the price–quantity variety, revenue can be expressed in terms of either P or Q. For example, if $P = 200 - Q$, revenue (R), is PQ, or $R = 200Q - Q^2$. Alternatively, $Q = 200 - P$, and $R = (QP) = 200P - P^2$. We can also derive the revenue function if the demand is a function of more than one variable. Thus, if $Q = 100 - 2P + 10A^2$, $R = PQ = 100P - 2P^2 + 10A^2P$.

MARGINAL REVENUE

Marginal revenue is the slope of the total revenue function with respect to the independent variable in question. Traditionally, marginal revenue is defined as dR/dQ. However, in situations where $Q = f(P, A)$, and R is also a function of P and A, marginal revenue can be either $\partial R/\partial P$ or $\partial R/\partial A$. Starting with the demand function $Q = 100 - 2P + 10A^2$,

$$P = \frac{100 + 10A^2 - Q}{2}$$

$$R = PQ = \frac{100Q + 10A^2Q - Q^2}{2}$$

$$\frac{\partial R}{\partial Q} = \frac{100 + 10A^2 - 2Q}{2}$$

$$\frac{\partial R}{\partial A} = \frac{20AQ}{2} = 10AQ$$

$$\frac{\partial R}{\partial P} = 100 - 4P + 10A^2$$

THE MULTIVARIATE DEMAND FUNCTION

Frequently, researchers employ a multiplicative demand function consisting of many variables. One such form, known as the Cobb–Douglas function, shows the quantity demanded (Q) as a function of many prices and other variables. For example, the demand for X is shown as

$$Q_X = KP_X^a P_Y^b A_X^c I^d i^e$$

where the prices P_X and P_Y correspond to the price of products X and Y, respectively, and A_X represents the amount of advertising by the producer of X. I is a measure of the buyers' income, and i an index of prevailing interest rates. The letters a, b, c, d, and e are exponents of these variables, and K is a constant.

Assume that the demand function is estimated to be

$$Q_X = 100 P_X^{-2.5} P_Y^{1.2} A_X^{1.6} I^{.84} i^{-3.8}$$

The point price elasticity of demand is defined as

$$e_{P_X} = \frac{P_X}{Q_X}\left(\frac{\partial Q_X}{\partial P_X}\right)$$

$$= \frac{P_X}{Q_X}(-2.5)(100 P_X^{-3.5})(P_Y^{1.2} A_X^{1.6} I^{.84} i^{-3.8})$$

$$= \frac{P_X}{Q_X}\frac{(-2.5)(100 P_X^{-2.5} P_Y^{1.2} A_X^{1.6} I^{.84} i^{-3.8})}{P_X}$$

$$= \frac{P_X}{Q_X}\frac{(-2.5)(Q_X)}{P_X}$$

$$= -2.5$$

You can verify that the cross price elasticity of demand (with respect to the price of Y), which is $e_{P_Y} = (P_Y/Q_X)(\partial Q_X/\partial P_Y)$, is 1.2. Similarly, the income elasticity of demand is 0.84, the advertising elasticity is 1.6, and the interest elasticity is -3.8.

ESTIMATION OF DEMAND FUNCTIONS

Econometrics deals with the measurement and testing of economic phenomena. We will not go into the details of the study and the methods employed in the estimation of economic relationships, but will simply refer the reader to some research results found in a demand study, namely the demand for beef, as carried out by Professor F. E. Walters and his associates at Colorado State University (Department of Economics, Colorado State University, Fort Collins).

CHAPTER 5 APPENDIX

Total revenue (R) is the price times the quantity of the product, or $R = PQ$. Thus, if $P = 100 - 2Q$, $R = Q(100-2Q) = 100Q-2Q^2$. Because marginal revenue is the slope of R, the first derivative of R with respect to Q is the MR; or $MR = dTR/dQ = 100 - 4Q$. Note that both the demand and MR functions are linear and that both have vertical intercepts of $100. The only difference is that the P function has a slope of -2, while the MR has a slope of -4, hence the generalization that if the demand function is linear, the MR is also linear and its negative slope is twice that of the negatively inclined demand function. The MR corresponding to a nonlinear P function can also be determined in a similar manner.

REVENUE MAXIMIZATION

Where R is maximum, MR $= 0$ in most basic microeconomic models. To find the quantity of output that must be sold, we set $dR/dQ = 0$. For the revenue function $R = 100Q-2Q^2$, the MR is $100 - 4Q$. When MR $= 0$, $Q = 25$. For Q to be 25, $P = 100 - 2(25) = \$50$. Thus the revenue-maximizing price and quantity are $50 and 25, respectively, for a total revenue of ($50)(25), or $1250.

REVENUE MAXIMIZATION WITH MULTIPLE MARKETS

Suppose a firm has two markets, each having its own demand, and the firm wishes to maximize sales revenues by selling exactly 1000 items. Assume that demand in market 1 is $P_1 = 1200 - 3Q_1$, and in market 2, $P_2 = 1500 - (\frac{3}{2})Q_2$.

From discussions in Chapter 5 we know that a firm can maximize revenues for a specific quantity by equating the two marginal revenues. Thus, we have two conditions to satisfy:

$$MR_1 = MR_2$$

and

$$Q_1 + Q_2 = 1000$$

From the two demand equations we can obtain the two MR equations. (Remember that the rate of descent of the marginal revenue is twice that of the demand function.)

$$MR_1 = 1200 - 6Q_1 \qquad MR_2 = 1500 - 3Q_2$$

Equating MR_1 to MR_2, we have

$$1200 - 6Q_1 = 1500 - 3Q_2$$
$$3Q_2 - 6Q_1 = 300$$

Solving the equation simultaneously with $(Q_1 + Q_2) = 1000$, we find

$$Q_1 = 300$$
$$Q_2 = 700$$

Now we can determine the two prices:

$$P_1 = 1200 - 3Q_1$$
$$= 1200 - 3(300)$$
$$= \$300$$

and

$$P_2 = 1500 - (\tfrac{3}{2})Q_2$$
$$= 1500 = \tfrac{3}{2}(700)$$
$$= \$450$$

Combined revenues to the firm will be

$$(P_1Q_1) + (P_2Q_2) = (300)(300) + (450)(700)$$
$$= \$405,000$$

PRICE ELASTICITY OF REVENUE

Price elasticity of revenue is the ratio of the percentage change in revenue to the percentage change in price. Because revenues are important to the firm, we should note that there is a relationship between the price elasticity of revenue (e_R) and the price elasticity of demand (e_P).

Since $R = PQ$,

$$dR = \frac{\partial R}{\partial Q}dQ + \frac{\partial P}{\partial Q}dP = PdQ + QdP$$

Thus the percentage change in revenue is

$$\frac{dR}{R} = \frac{PdQ + QdP}{PQ}$$
$$= \frac{PdQ}{PQ} + \frac{QdP}{PQ}$$
$$= \frac{dQ}{Q} + \frac{dP}{P}$$

If we want to divide both sides of the equation by dP/P, we get

$$\frac{dR/R}{dP/P} = \frac{dQ/Q}{dP/P} = \frac{dP/P}{dP/P}$$

or

$$e_R = e_P + 1 \tag{1}$$

Suppose the price is currently \$10 and the firm is contemplating raising it to \$10.50. Present sales volume stands at 15,000 units and the firm estimates the price elasticity of demand to be -0.6667. Find the resulting change in revenues due to the change in price.

Because $e_P = -0.6667$, $e_R = 1 - 0.6667 = 0.3333$. The percentage change in price is 0.50/10, or 5%. So we should expect revenue to rise by (5%)(0.3333), or 1.67%. Currently, revenues equal \$150,000. The new revenues should equal \$152,505 [\$150,000 + (1.67%)(150,000)].

CHAPTER 6 APPENDIX

The short-run production function is usually shown as a function of one variable input. Although the production function may have any shape, we traditionally use the S-shaped function. Assume that the firm's short-run production function, $Q = f(N)$, is

$$Q = 50N^2 - \frac{1}{3}N^3$$

the marginal product of N is

$$\frac{dQ}{dN} = 100N - N^2$$

and the average product of N is

$$\frac{Q}{N} = 50N - \frac{1}{3}N^2$$

The total output Q is maximum where $dQ/dN = 0$, the marginal product is maximum when $d^2Q/dN^2 = 0$, and the average product is maximum where $d(Q/N)/dN = 0$.

Thus,

$$\frac{dQ}{dN} = 100N - N^2 = 0$$

$$N = 100$$
$$Q = 50(100)^2 - \frac{1}{3}(100)^3$$
$$Q = 166{,}667 \quad \text{(for maximum } Q\text{)}$$

$$\frac{d^2Q}{dN^2} = 100 - 2N = 0$$

$$N = 50$$
$$Q = 50(50)^2 - \frac{1}{3}(50)^3$$
$$Q = 83{,}333 \quad \text{(for maximum marginal product)}$$

$$\frac{d(Q/N)}{dN} = 50 - \frac{2}{3}N = 0$$

$$N = 75$$
$$Q = 50(75)^2 - \frac{1}{3}(75)^3$$
$$Q = 140{,}625 \quad \text{(for maximum average product)}$$

When the average product is maximum, it is equal to the marginal product, and

$$N = 75$$
$$\frac{Q}{N} = \frac{dQ}{dN}$$
$$= 100(75) - (75)^2$$
$$= 1875$$

The preceding computations are in agreement with our discussion about the Stage theory of short-run production.

RETURNS TO THE VARIABLE RESOURCE

The notion of "returns" to the variable resource is explored with the nature of the resource's marginal product. Recall that a production function can exhibit increasing, diminishing, or constant returns. A falling marginal product schedule is associated with diminishing returns, whereas a rising marginal product function indicates increasing returns.

Assume that the short-run production function of the firm is

$$Q = 100N^2 - 20N^3$$

and the marginal product is

$$\frac{dQ}{dN} = 200N - 60N^2$$

The marginal product will rise as N increases up to a point, and thereafter it will fall as N increases. Consequently, the returns to production will be initially increasing and subsequently decreasing.

Constant returns will occur for a production function of the type $Q = 20N$, because here the marginal product will remain constant at 20.

TECHNOLOGICAL INNOVATION AND PRODUCTIVITY

The output from a given quantity of resources will increase if suitable technological innovations can be introduced by the firm. While the newer technology can be instrumental in increasing the total output of the firm, it may or may not affect the marginal product of the variable resources.

Suppose that the initial production function of the firm is

$$Q = 50L - \tfrac{1}{2}L^2 \tag{1}$$

the marginal product of L is

$$\frac{dQ}{dL} = 50 - L$$

and the output is maximized when $L = 50$. Now assume that the firm introduces a new machine in the production process, and the new production function is

$$Q = 100L - L^2 \tag{2}$$

You can see that equation (2) is twice equation (1). The marginal product with the new production innovation is

$$\frac{dQ}{dL} = 100 - 2L.$$

Thus, the marginal product of L is now twice as great as the original marginal product. For example, when $L = 1$, originally, the marginal product was 49. The new marginal product will be 98. Despite the higher marginal product of L, output will still be maximized when $L = 50$. You can verify that the maximum output under equation (1) is 1250, and with equation (2) the maximum output is 2500.

The average product of equation (1) is $Q/L = 50 - \frac{1}{2}L$, and the average product of equation (2) is $100 - L$. This implies that the L resource is, on the average, twice as productive as before.

Figure A6-1 illustrates both production functions. The new production function is higher than the old, and it is also steeper, suggesting the new higher marginal product of L.

Now suppose the production for the firm is

$$Q = 10 + 2L$$

from which we derive the marginal product to be 2. If technological innovation or increases in the other variable resources change the production function to

$$Q = 20 + 2L$$

the marginal product of L will remain unchanged at 2, although the total output will be higher than before. The new average product will be $(20 + 2L)/L$, which will be higher than the previous average product, $(10 + 2L)/L$. Under such circumstances, the linear production function will shift upwards by 10.

OUTPUT MAXIMIZATION WITH TWO PRODUCTION FUNCTIONS

Suppose a firm has a given quantity of a variable resource, L, but two production functions, $Q_1 = f(L)$ and $Q_2 = g(L)$. The object is to maximize total

FIGURE A6-1

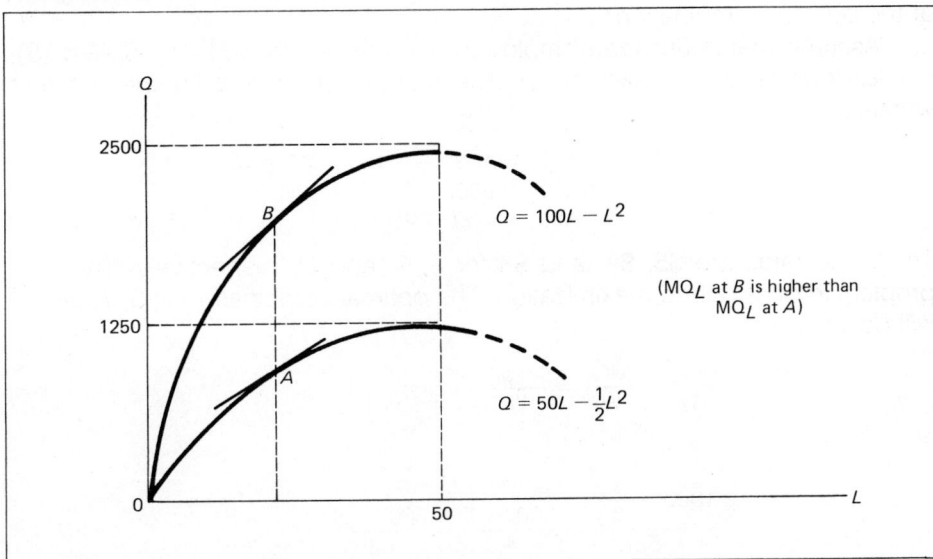

output $Q = Q_1 + Q_2$ with the given quantity of $L = L_1 + L_2$. Let total $L = 100$, and let the two production functions be

$$Q_1 = 100L_1 - L_1^2$$
$$Q_2 = 150L_2 - \tfrac{1}{4}L_2^2$$

Recall that according to the Second Law of Gossen, the total output is maximized when the marginal product of L with the first production function is equal to the marginal product of L with the second. The two marginal product expressions are

$$\frac{dQ_1}{dL_1} = 100 - 2L_1$$

$$\frac{dQ_2}{dL_2} = 150 - \frac{1}{2}L_2$$

Equating dQ_1/dL_1 to dQ_2/dL_2, and observing the constraint $L_1 + L_2 = 100$, we obtain

$$\tfrac{1}{2}L_2 - 2L_1 = 50$$
$$L_2 + L_1 = 100$$

When these two equations are solved simultaneously, we get:

$$L_1 = 0, \ L_2 = 100, \ Q_1 = 0, \text{ and } Q_2 = 12,500.$$

OUTPUT MAXIMIZATION WITH THE OPTIMAL COMBINATION OF RESOURCES

There are situations where a firm is able to combine several different types of resources to produce a given output at the lowest cost, or maximize output for a given amount of money. In either case, we follow the same rules to arrive at the optimal combination.

Assume that a firm can employ three varieties of workers—skilled (S), semiskilled (T), and unskilled (U). The marginal products for the different workers are

$$MQ_S = 1000 - \tfrac{1}{2}S$$
$$MQ_T = 800 - T$$
$$MQ_U = 600 - 2U$$

The wage rates are \$5, \$4, and \$3 for S, T, and U, respectively. This is a problem in constrained maximization. The optimal combination of S, T, and U will occur when

$$\frac{MQ_S}{W_S} = \frac{MQ_T}{W_T} = \frac{MQ_U}{W_U}$$

or

$$\frac{1000 - \frac{1}{2}S}{5} = \frac{800 - T}{4} = \frac{600 - 2U}{3}$$

Furthermore, the budget constraint $7050 = 5S + 4T + 3U$ also has to be satisfied. When we solve the two conditions simultaneously, we obtain

$$S = 1000, \quad T = 400, \quad U = 150$$

You can verify that each type of worker will provide the same marginal product per dollar, or

$$\frac{MQ_S}{W_S} = \frac{MQ_T}{W_T} = \frac{MQ_U}{W_U} = 100$$

CHAPTER 7 APPENDIX

CONSTRAINED OPTIMIZATION

Firms produce output under various conditions and restrictions or constraints. The most widely discussed constraint is the budget or cost constraint. Given the budget constraint or the limit on expenditures, a firm must combine the inputs in a manner consistent with the objectives. Here the objective is to minimize the cost of producing a given quantity, or conversely, to maximize the output for a given outlay.

COST MINIMIZATION

Assume that the firm's production function is of the standard Cobb–Douglas variety: $Q = f(K, L) = KL$. Let the price of each unit of K be \$100 and the price per unit of L be \$300. The desired level of Q is 1200.

Recall that the cost-minimizing (K/L) ratio for the Cobb–Douglas production function, $Q = AK^aL^b$, is

$$\frac{K}{L} = \frac{aP_L}{bP_K}$$

which for this particular set of numbers is

$$\frac{K}{L} = \frac{(1)(\$300)}{(1)(\$100)} = \frac{3}{1}$$

$$K = 3L$$

Because $Q = 1200$,

$$KL = 1200$$
$$(3L)(L) = 1200$$
$$3L^2 = 1200$$
$$L^2 = 400$$
$$L = 20$$

Using $K = 3L$, we find

$$K = 3(20) = 60$$

Thus the cost-minimizing combination of K and L to produce 1200 units is $60K$ and $20L$ for a total cost of \$12,000 [$(20 \times 300) + (60 \times 100)$].

OUTPUT MAXIMIZATION

The cost-minimizing combination of resources subject to an output constraint is the same as the combination that results from maximizing output for a budget contraint.

Let the firm's production function be $Q = 100K^2L^3$, with $P_L = \$300$ and $P_K = \$200$, and let the total available funds be restricted to \$60,000. What is the maximum output under the circumstances?

The output-maximizing combination of K and L is given by

$$\frac{K}{L} = \frac{(2)(\$300)}{(3)(\$200)} = 1{:}1$$
$$K = L$$

The equation for the budget constraint is $60{,}000 = 200K + 300L$. Substituting $(K = L)$ in this equation, we obtain

$$200K + 300K = 60{,}000$$
$$500K = 60{,}000$$
$$K = 120$$
$$L = 120$$

The total output of the firm will be

$$Q = 100K^2L^3 = 100\,(120)^5$$
$$= 24{,}883{,}200{,}000 \text{ units}$$

ELASTICITY OF OUTPUT

The elasticity of output of a resource is the ratio of the percent change of the output to the percent change of that resource. In the case of a Cobb–Douglas production function, the exponents represent the elasticities. These values are fairly accurate as long as the changes are not very great.

To illustrate, let $Q = 10K^{1/2}L^{1/2}$. If the initial combination of the resources is 16 units of K with 64 units of L, the original output will be $Q = 10\,(16)^{1/2}(64)^{1/2} = 320$ units. Now let us increase K by 5% and hold other factors at their former values. The new output volume will be higher and equal to $Q = 10\,(1.05 \times 16)^{1/2}(64)^{1/2} = 328$ units. The additional 8 units represent a 2.5% increase in output, resulting from a 5% increase in input K. Therefore, the elasticity of output of K is (2.5%)/(5%), or ½. This analysis also suggests that if K and L are both increased by 5%, output will rise by 5%. You can verify that if L also increases by 5%, the new Q will be 336 units.

In general, if the Cobb–Douglas function has many variables, such as $Q = AK^aL^bR^cM^d$, we can derive a relationship between Q and the resources K, L, R, and M. First we convert the production function to logarithmic form. Taking natural logs (ln) of both sides,

$$\ln Q = \ln A + a \ln K + b \ln L + c \ln R + d \ln M$$

and taking derivatives of both sides of the equation we obtain

$$\frac{dQ}{Q} = \frac{dA}{A} + a\frac{dK}{K} + b\frac{dL}{L} + c\frac{dR}{R} + d\frac{dM}{M}$$

which is the same thing as saying

% in Q = (% in A) + a(% in K) + b(% in L) + c(% in R) + d(% in M).

MARGINAL AND AVERAGE PRODUCT

The marginal product of a resource can be determined by taking the partial derivative of Q with respect to that resource. Thus, if the production function is $Q = f(K, L, M)$, the marginal product of K will be

$$MQ_K = \frac{\partial Q}{\partial K}$$

The average product of a resource is the ratio of Q to the quantity of that resource. Thus, the average product of K equals Q/K, and the average product of M is Q/M, and so on.

Assume that the production function is $Q = 100K^2LM$.

$$MQ_K = \frac{\partial Q}{\partial K} = 2(100)(K)(LM) = 200KLM$$

$$MQ_L = \frac{\partial Q}{\partial L} = 100K^2M$$

$$MQ_M = \frac{\partial Q}{\partial M} = 100K^2L$$

$$AQ_K = \frac{Q}{K} = 100KLM$$

$$AQ_L = \frac{Q}{L} = 100K^2M$$

$$AQ_M = \frac{Q}{M} = 100K^2L$$

MARGINAL RATE OF TECHNICAL SUBSTITUTION

The MRTS for a production function of two inputs is the ratio of the marginal products of the two resources. For a production function $Q = K^aL^b$, the marginal rate of technical substitution will be

$$MRTS = \frac{MQ_L}{MQ_K} = \frac{K^abL^{b-1}}{a\,K^{a-1}L^b} = \frac{bK}{aL}$$

For the cost-minimizing combination of K and L, we equate MRTS to P_L/P_K:

$$MRTS = \frac{bK}{aL} = \frac{P_L}{P_K}$$

$$\left(\frac{K}{L}\right)_{optimal} = \frac{aP_L}{bP_K} \tag{1}$$

Recall that we have often used equation (1) in solving production problems.

CHAPTER 8 APPENDIX

All of the analysis involving linear programming is basically couched in terms of linear relationships and, hence, linear algebra. In addition to solving the usual maximization/minimization problems, linear programming models also allow for the computations regarding process combinations and other related phenomena.

PROCESS ANALYSIS

Assume that a firm can produce an output using any or all of the following processes:

Process 1: One unit of output is produced with 3 units of K and 1 of L.
Process 2: One unit of output is produced with 2 units of K and 1 of L.
Process 3: One unit of output is produced with 1 unit of K and 2 units of L.

The firm has a maximum of 120 units of K, and 80 of L. Which process or processes should it use to maximize output?

In these situations, we cannot use the Second Law of Gossen, because the notion of the marginal product of K and L is not applicable. The best output results when the firm uses those two processes whose K/L ratios lie on either side of the firm's K/L availability ratio. For instance, the firm's available K and L produce a ratio of $K/L = 120{:}80$, or 1.5:1. Process 1 has a K-to-L ratio of 3:1, (K/L) of process 2 is 2:1, and Process 3 has a K/L of 1:2. Thus, the firm can maximize output with the available K and L by combining Processes 2 and 3. It can be shown that any other combination will yield much less output.

In Figure A8-1, we show the $Q = 20$ isoquant with three points, A, B, and C. The points lie along the rays corresponding to the three processes. The firm's endowment of resources (K and L) is indicated by the rectangle $OMND$, and point N lies on one of the isoquants. Because N lies on an isoquant, it is possible for the firm to produce that level of output. However, the firm does not have a process that allows it to combine the K and the L in a ratio of 1.5:1. Therefore, it should combine the methods represented by processes 2 and 3.

If the firm uses Process 1 exclusively, it will use the 120 units of K entirely, but only 40 units of L will be used along with K, resulting in the waste of 40 units of L, and only 40 units of output will be possible. Similarly, the use of Process 2 alone will result in a maximum output of 60 units and a waste of 20 units of L. Finally, Process 3 alone will provide a maximum of 40 units of output, and will leave 80 units of K unused.

To solve the problem graphically, we draw two lines from N in a southwesterly direction, one parallel to one of the process rays, and the other parallel to the remaining one. This results in parallelogram $OSNT$. The isoquant passing through point S tells us the quantity produced with Process 2, and the isoquant on which point T lies indicates the volume of output produced with Process 3. The sum of these two quantities of output equals the value of the output shown at point N.

Algebraically, we can solve the problem as follows:

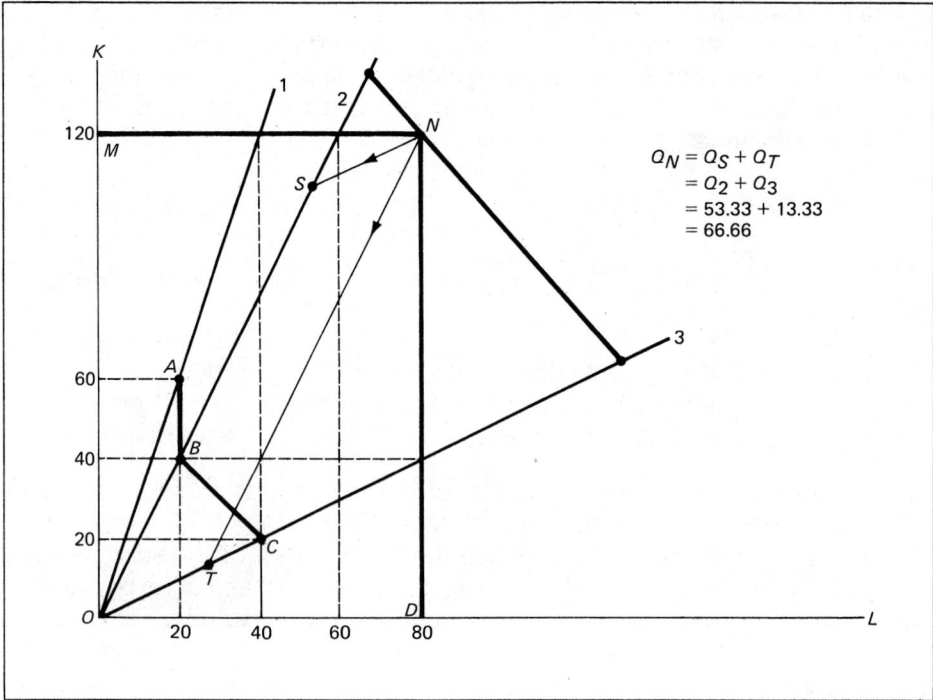

FIGURE A8-1

From Process 2:

$$\frac{K_2}{L_2} = \frac{2}{1}, \qquad K_2 = 2L_2$$

From Process 3:

$$\frac{K_3}{L_3} = \frac{1}{2}, \qquad \frac{K_3 = \frac{1}{2}L_3}{K_2 + K_3 = 2L_2 + \frac{1}{2}L_3} \tag{1}$$

The firm's available resources dictate that $L_2 + L_3 = 80$ and $K_2 + K_3 = 120$. When we substitute this condition in equation (1), we obtain

$$K_2 + K_3 = 2L_2 + \tfrac{1}{2}L_3 = 120 \tag{2}$$
$$L_2 + L_3 = 80 \tag{3}$$

When we solve equations (2) and (3) simultaneously, the results are

$$L_2 = \frac{160}{3}, \qquad K_2 = 2L_2 = \frac{320}{3}$$

$$L_3 = \frac{80}{3}, \qquad K_3 = \tfrac{1}{2}L_3 = \frac{40}{3}$$

Thus the output with Process 2 will be 160/3, and with Process 3, 40/3, for a combined total output of 200/3, or 66.66 units. You can verify that if the firm uses processes 1 and 3, the output will be only 56 units, with Process 1 producing 32 units, and Process 3 producing 24 units.

PROFIT MAXIMIZATION WITH THE PROCESS RAY METHOD

We can use the process diagram to solve profit-maximization problems involving more than two outputs, as long as only two resources are used to produce the output. In the illustration that follows, the firm uses two resources, K and L, to produce any combination of three products, A, B, and C. Resource K is limited to a total of 40 units, while L is fixed at 80 units. Profit from each item is $2 a unit. The input–output matrix below shows the production needs per unit for each of the three items. The firm's objective is to maximize profits.

	K	L
A:	3	1.5
B:	2	2
C:	1	4

In Figure A8-2 we show the requirements for the three products labeled as rays A, B, and C. Rectangle $ODEI$ represents the total available quantities of K and L. Because we know the profit per unit of each item, and the amount of K and L necessary to produce a unit, we can derive equal-profit, or profit,

FIGURE A8-2

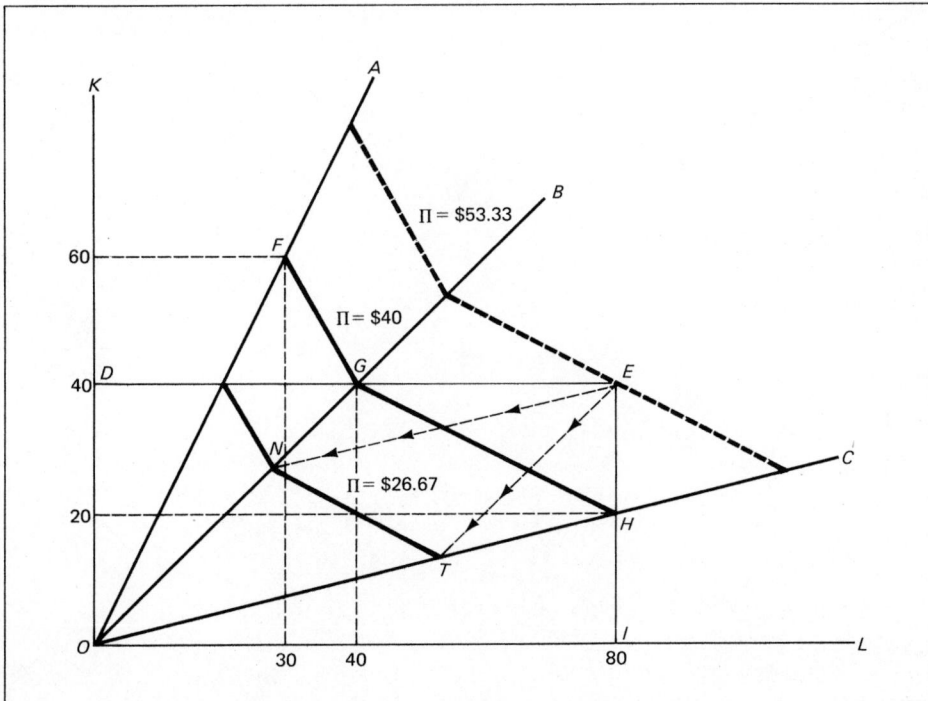

isoquants. For example, 20 units of either A, B, or C will yield the same amount of profit—$40. To produce 20 units of A, the firm needs 60 units of K and 30 of L, as shown by point F. Point G tells us that the firm requires 40 units of K and 40 of L to produce 20 units of B. Similarly, the firm can produce 20 units of C with 20 units of K and 80 units of L. Thus, FGH constitutes the $40-profit line. Other lines representing different values for profit can be similarly derived.

Point E gives the coordinates for the firm's maximum available K and L, and because point E is "bracketed" by rays B and C, the company will accrue the most profits if it produces only B and C. You can verify that the total profit to the firm will be $53.33. Points N and T both lie on the $26.67 profit line, implying that equal quantities of B and C should be produced. Thus, the firm will maximize profits by producing 13.33 units of B and an equal quantity of C.

CHAPTER 9 APPENDIX

DERIVATION OF COST FUNCTIONS (ONE VARIABLE INPUT)

Variable Cost

Assume that the firm's short-run production function of a single variable input L is $Q = f(L) = 100L - L^2$ and that the price of L is \$100. Fixed costs are \$300. The total cost to the firm is the sum of the fixed and variable costs. The total variable cost in this instance is the total cost of purchasing the variable resource, or $VC = 100L$, and total cost $TC = 300 + 100L$.

From the equation for variable cost, $L = VC/100$, and when this value of L is substituted for L in the equation for Q, we obtain:

$$Q = 100L - L^2 = 100\frac{VC}{100} - \left(\frac{VC}{100}\right)^2 \tag{1}$$

Equation (1) is a quadratic equation and can be rewritten as

$$\left(\frac{VC}{100}\right)^2 - 100\frac{VC}{100} + Q = 0$$

or

$$\frac{1}{10000}VC^2 - VC + Q = 0$$

We can use the quadratic formula to solve this equation for VC in terms of Q.

$$VC = \frac{1 \pm [1 - 4(1/10000)Q]^{1/2}}{2(1/10000)}$$

$$= \frac{1 \pm [1 - (4Q/10000)]^{1/2}}{1/5000} \tag{2}$$

From (2) we can obtain the two values of VC:

$$VC = 5000 + 5000\sqrt{1 - (1/2500)Q} \tag{3}$$

and

$$VC = 5000 - 5000\sqrt{1 - (1/2500)Q} \tag{4}$$

From the production function, Q is maximum when $L = 50$. When $L = 50$, $Q = 2500$, and $VC = 5000$. We can show that expression (4) is the correct version of the equation for the VC function. Figure A9-1 shows that equation (3) yields the upper portion of the VC function, and the lower portion is brought about by equation (4). Because VC varies positively with Q in the lower portion, up to $Q = 2500$, and thereafter "bends backwards," we can select equation (4) as the variable cost function. Hence the total cost to the firm is given by equation (5):

$$TC = 300 + 5000 - 5000[1 - (1/2500)Q]^{1/2}$$
$$= 5300 - 5000[1 - (1/2500)Q]^{1/2} \tag{5}$$

Equation (5) yields the following representative values for total cost:

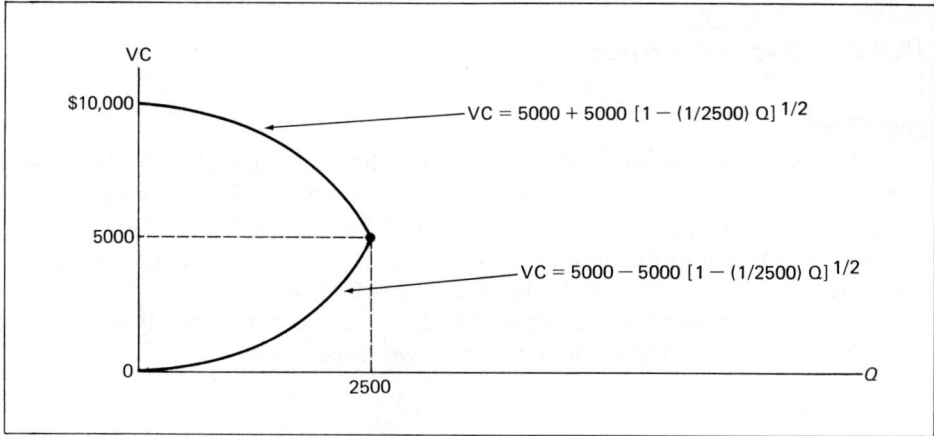

Plotted curves:
$$VC = 5000 + 5000 \left[1 - (1/2500)\, Q\right]^{1/2}$$
$$VC = 5000 - 5000 \left[1 - (1/2500)\, Q\right]^{1/2}$$

FIGURE A9-1

L	Q	VC	TC
·	0	0	300
·	10	10	310
·	20	20	320
·	30	30	330
1	99	100	400
2	196	200	500
3	291	300	600
4	384	400	700

We can also determine the average variable cost and the marginal cost:

$$AVC = \frac{\text{Price of variable resource}}{\text{Average product of resource}}$$

$$MC = \frac{\text{Price of variable resource}}{\text{Marginal product of resource}}$$

In the example illustrating the derivation of the cost curves, the production function was $Q = 100L - L^2$. The average product of L is the ratio of Q to L, and the marginal product of L is the derivative of Q with respect to L. Thus,

$$AQ_L = \frac{Q}{L} = 100 - L$$

$$MQ_L = \frac{dQ}{dL} = 100 - 2L$$

Because the price of L is \$100, the average variable cost and marginal cost will be

$$AVC = \frac{100}{100 - L}$$

$$MC = \frac{100}{100 - 2L}$$

where $L = [100-(100^2-4Q)^{1/2}]/2$ (from the quadratic equation $L^2 - 100L + Q = 0$). You can verify that as L increases positively, the denominator of the AVC as well as the MC will decline, and the AVC and the MC will take on higher values. For example, when $L = 1$, AVC = 100/99 and MC = 100/98. When $L = 10$, AVC = 100/90 and MC = 100/80.

MARGINAL COST

Marginal cost is defined as dVC/dQ. From equation (4), the equation for marginal cost (MC) is

$$MC = \frac{dVC}{dQ} = \frac{1}{[1 - (1/2500)Q]^{1/2}} \quad (6)$$

Equation (6) shows us that MC is a positive function Q as long as Q is less than 2500. Because marginal cost measures the slope of the variable cost function, the VC function is shown to be increasing at an increasing rate.

AVERAGE VARIABLE COST

Average variable cost is the ratio of total variable cost to total output, or

$$AVC = \frac{VC}{Q} = \frac{5000 - 5000[1 - (1/2500)Q]^{1/2}}{Q} \quad (7)$$

AVERAGE TOTAL COST

Average total cost is the sum of the average variable cost (AVC) and the average fixed cost (AFC). In this particular case,

$$ATC = \frac{5000 - 5000[1 - (1/2500)Q]^{1/2}}{Q} + \frac{300}{Q} \quad (8)$$

COST FUNCTIONS WITH TWO VARIABLE INPUTS

Variable Cost

Let the firm's production function be $Q = f(K, L) = 100K^2L$, and the price of L and K be \$100 and \$200, respectively. The firm minimizes the cost of producing a given output by equating the marginal rate of technical substitution to the ratio of input prices. Recall that in the case of a Cobb–Douglas production function, $Q = AK^aL^b$, the optimal combination of K and L is given by

$$\left(\frac{K}{L}\right)_{optimal} = \frac{aP_L}{bP_K} \quad (9)$$

For the situation described, the cost-minimizing (K/L) will be (2)(100)/(1)(200) = 1:1, or $K = L$.

The equation for the budget constraint is $P_LL + P_KK$, and because K and L are variable resources, the variable cost to the firm is

$$VC = P_LL + P_KK = 100L + 200K \quad (10)$$

From equation (9) we have $K = L$, or $K - L = 0$. Solving this equation and equation (10) simultaneously we can obtain the cost-minimizing levels of K and L. Thus,

$$VC = 100L + 200K \tag{11}$$
$$0 = L - K \tag{12}$$

Multiplying equation (12) by 100,

$$0 = 100L - 100K \tag{13}$$

Subtracting equation (13) from equation (11) yields $300K = VC$, or $K = (VC/300)$. Hence, L is also equal to $(VC/300)$. Now we substitute these values of K and L into the production function $Q = 100K^2L$ to obtain:

$$Q = 100 \left(\frac{VC}{300}\right)^2 \frac{VC}{300} = 100 \left(\frac{VC}{300}\right)^3 \tag{14}$$

When equation (14) is written in the form $VC = f(Q)$, we have the variable cost function $VC^3 = (300)^3 Q/100 = 270000Q$. Consequently,

$$VC = 64.63 \, (Q)^{1/3} \tag{15}$$

Equation (15) reveals that VC is positively related to Q and that as Q increases, VC increases at a decreasing rate. If total fixed cost of the firm equals \$300, the total cost to the firm will be

$$TC = 300 + 64.63Q^{1/3}$$

The marginal, average variable, and average total costs can be computed as in the previous section.

In general, for Cobb–Douglas functions of the type $Q = AK^aL^b$, with the price of L equal to w and the price of capital equal to r, the variable cost function may be shown to equal:

$$VC = (a + b) \left[\frac{(r/a)^a (w/b)^b}{A}\right]^{1/(a+b)} Q^{1/(a+b)}$$

Thus, with reference to our problem,

$$VC = (2 + 1) \left[\frac{(200/2)^2 (100/1)^1}{(100)}\right]^{1/(2+1)} Q^{1/(2+1)}$$
$$= 64.63 \, Q^{1/3}$$

THE ECONOMIC ORDER QUANTITY

The economic order quantity (EOQ) model illustrates the case of cost minimization for a firm that must place a certain number of orders with its suppliers during a given period of time. Suppose a car dealer needs D cars per year to meet annual demand. The dealer does not order all the cars at once because of the high cost associated with unwanted inventory. But there is also a cost for placing orders. The firm's objective is to minimize the sum of the ordering and holding (inventory) costs.

Let the cost per order be \$$X$ and the cost of holding inventory be \$$Y$ per unit per year. The economic order quantity is designated as Q, and we are looking for that Q which minimizes total cost. If the annual demand is D, then the number of orders equals D/Q. Thus the total cost of all the orders will be $(D/Q)(\$X)$.

For our problem, we may safely assume that the car dealer carries $Q/2$ units in inventory. This is especially true if the rate of depletion of inventory is uniform and linear over time. Thus, the cost of holding inventory is $(Q/2)(\$Y)$.

The total cost to the car dealer is the sum of the two costs described, or

$$TC = \text{ordering cost} + \text{inventory cost}$$

$$= \frac{D}{Q}X + \frac{Q}{2}Y \tag{16}$$

We minimize the value of this cost by taking the derivative of equation (16) and equating it to zero:

$$\frac{dTC}{dQ} = -\frac{DX}{Q^2} + \frac{Y}{2} = 0$$

$$Q^2 = \frac{DX}{Y/2}$$

$$Q = (2DX/Y)^{1/2} \tag{17}$$

Equation (17) is the "formula" for the economic order quantity Q.

To illustrate the use of this formula, assume that the car dealer has an annual demand for 4000 cars, the cost of placing an order is $500, and the cost of holding inventory is $100 per car. According to equation (17), the EOQ is

$$Q = [(2)(4000)(500)/100]^{1/2} = 200 \text{ cars}$$

Hence the dealer should place 20 orders of 200 cars. This works out to an order every 365/20, or about every 18 days.

CHAPTER 10 APPENDIX

A firm's profit function may be derived by subtracting the cost from revenues, or $\Pi = R - C$. If profit-maximization is desired, the firm must maximize the value of this function.

PROFIT MAXIMIZATION

Suppose the demand for the firm's product is $P = 15 - (1/20)Q$, and the total cost of production is $C = 55 + 5Q + (1/20)Q^2$. The firm's revenue (R) is the product of price times quantity, or PQ. The profit function then is

$$\Pi = R - C = \left[Q(15 - \frac{1}{20}Q) \right] - \left[55 + 5Q + \frac{1}{20}Q^2 \right]$$

$$= 15Q - \frac{1}{20}Q^2 - 55 - 5Q - \frac{1}{20}Q^2$$

$$= -\frac{1}{10}Q^2 + 10Q - 55$$

For profits to be maximum, $d\Pi/dQ = 0$ and $d^2\Pi/dQ^2 = 0$. Thus,

$$\frac{d\Pi}{dQ} = -\frac{1}{5}Q + 10 = 0 \quad \text{or} \quad Q = 50 \qquad \frac{d^2\Pi}{dQ^2} = -\frac{1}{5}$$

Total profit to the firm $= -(1/10)(50)^2 + (10)(50) - 55 = \$195$. The profit-maximizing price is $P = 15 - (1/20)(50) = \$12.50$

We can also solve this problem another way. For profits to be maximum, MR = MC. MR is dR/dQ and MC is dC/dQ.

$$MR = 15 - \frac{1}{10}Q$$

$$MC = 5 + \frac{1}{10}Q$$

Setting MR = MC,

$$15 - \frac{1}{10}Q = 5 + \frac{1}{10}Q$$

$$Q = 50$$

$$P = 12.50$$

$$ATC = \frac{C}{Q} = \frac{55}{Q} + 5 + \frac{1}{20}Q = 8.60$$

The firm's average profit or profit per unit is

$$A\Pi = P - ATC, \text{ or } 12.50 - 8.60 = 3.90$$

Hence the total profit is $(A\Pi)(Q) = (3.90)(50) = 195$.

BREAK-EVEN ANALYSIS

To break even, the firm or producer equates its revenues and costs. For example, let the firm's revenue function be $R = 200Q - 2Q^2$, and its total cost be $C = 1000 + 50Q + 3Q^2$. To find the break-even quantity or quantities, we set $R = C$. Thus,

$$200Q - 2Q^2 = 1000 + 50Q + 3Q^2$$
$$Q^2 - 30Q + 200 = 0$$

Solving the quadratic equation for Q, we get:

$$Q = \frac{30 \pm [(30)^2 - 4(200)]^{1/2}}{2}$$
$$= \frac{30 \pm 10}{2}$$
$$= 10 \text{ or } 20$$

This firm can break even at either one of these quantities. The price corresponding to the lower quantity will be higher than the one that corresponds to the larger volume.

The firm's demand function can be obtained from its revenue function, because $P = R/Q = (200Q - 2Q^2)/Q = 200 - 2Q$. Hence, when output is 10, price is $180, and when $Q = 20$, $P = \$160$. When $Q = 10$, R and C are both equal to $1800 and, at a price of $160 (or $Q = 20$), revenue and cost both equal $3200.

When a firm breaks even, its profits are zero. Consequently, the break-even points can also be found by equating the profit function to zero. In this case, the profit function is $Q^2 - 30Q + 200$. When this equation is solved for Q, we will have the answers already shown.

EARNING A SPECIFIC AMOUNT OF PROFITS

Instead of either maximizing profits or breaking even, a firm may wish to earn a certain amount of profit. Suppose the same firm that we discussed in analyzing break-even points wishes to earn exactly $45 in profit. From the revenue and cost functions we obtain the firm's profit function.

$$\Pi = R - C = -5Q^2 + 150Q - 1000$$

which must equal 45. Thus,

$$\Pi = -5Q^2 + 150Q - 1000 = 45$$
$$Q^2 - 30Q + 200 = -9$$
$$Q^2 - 30Q + 209 = 0$$

When we solve this quadratic equation for Q, we find that $Q = 11$ or 19. Hence the firm can earn $45 in profit by selling either 11 or 19 units. Because $P = 200 - 2Q$, the price will have to be $200 - 2(11)$, or $178 if the firm sells 11 units. It can sell 19 units at a price of $200 - 2(19)$, or $162. The firm will probably choose the higher quantity of 19 units in order to have a larger market share. You can verify that the firm's maximum profit will occur at an output volume of 15 units at a price of $170, and a total profit of $125.

OBTAINING A UNIQUE
PROFIT-TO-SALES RATIO

Suppose the firm wishes to maintain a unique ratio of profits-to-sales-revenues. For example, a company may wish to earn enough profits such that the ratio of total profit to total revenue is 3%. Under these circumstances

$$\frac{\Pi}{R} = 0.03$$

$$\frac{R - C}{R} = 1 - \frac{C}{R} = 0.03$$

$$\frac{C}{R} = 0.97$$

$$C = 0.97R \tag{1}$$

We can use equation (1) to determine the quantity or quantities where the firm's profits will be exactly 3% of the revenue. In our example, equation (1) will yield

$$1000 + 50Q + 3Q^2 = 0.97(200Q - 2Q^2)$$

Solving for Q, we find that at $Q = 18$ or 11 the profits will be exactly 3% of the revenue. You can verify that at the profit-maximizing quantity, the firm's profit-to-sales ratio is \$125/\$2550, or 4.9%.

CHAPTER 11 APPENDIX

The model of perfect competition assumes that all firms operate with basically the same or similar production functions, and that the marginal cost of the firm is its supply curve. Assume that there are 1000 identical firms, each with the following marginal cost function.

$$MC = 10 + 2Q$$

If we add 1000 of these MC functions horizontally, we will have the industry supply function

$$MC = 10 + \frac{2}{1000}Q \tag{1}$$

which will have the same price (cost) intercept as the individual marginal cost function, but its positive slope will be 1/1000 of the slope of the individual firm's MC. The equilibrium industry price results when the market supply is equated to the market demand.

Assume that the total demand for the product is

$$P = 190 - \frac{1}{1000}Q \tag{2}$$

Equating equations (1) and (2), we obtain

$$10 + \frac{2}{1000}Q = 190 - \frac{1}{1000}Q$$

$$\frac{3}{1000}Q = 180$$

$$Q = 60,000$$

$$P = 190 - \frac{60,000}{1000} = 130$$

Because individual firms treat the market price as their marginal revenue, the equilibrium price of \$130 = MR. A firm maximizes profits by equating its MR to its MC, or

$$MC = 10 + 2Q = 130$$

$$Q = 60$$

Thus, the total output of 1000 firms equals (60)(1000), or 60,000.

The Long-Run Price in the Perfectly Competitive Industry

In the long run, all firms under perfect competition break even, or earn normal profit. This occurs when the price line (or the MR) is tangent to the average total cost, that is, where the ATC is at its minimum.

Suppose the typical long-run average total cost of a firm is

$$ATC = Q^2 - 200Q + 10100 \tag{3}$$

When equation (3) is drawn, it will result in a U-shaped curve. Because long-run price is stabilized at the lowest ATC, we need to find the output at which the firm's ATC is lowest. To do so we take the first derivative of (3), equate it to 0, and solve for Q. Finally we solve for ATC. Thus,

$$\frac{d\text{ATC}}{dQ} = 2Q - 200 = 0$$

$$Q = 100$$
$$ATC = (100)^2 - 200\,(100) + 10100$$
$$ATC = \$100$$

Consequently, the long-run price will also be $100, and if there are still the 1000 firms, the total output of the industry will be 100,000, with each firm breaking even at an output of 100 units. The total revenue to each firm will be ($100)(100), or $10,000, and the total cost for each firm will also equal $10,000. The total cost is the product of ATC times Q, or $TC = Q^3 - 200\,Q^2 + 10,100Q$.

Calculating Economic Profits in the Short Run

If the revenues to the firm exceed the total cost of production, the firm earns economic profit. Assume that the firm's average total cost is

$$ATC = \frac{1800}{Q} + 10 + Q$$

If the market price is $130, the firm will maximize profit by either equating MR to MC, or by simply maximizing the profit function. The profit function is

$$\Pi = R - TC = 130Q - (1800 + 10Q + Q^2)$$
$$\frac{d\Pi}{dQ} = 120 - 2Q = 0$$
$$Q = 60$$

At an output volume of 60 units, the ATC will be $100, and the profit per unit will be ($130 − $100), or $30. The total profit for the firm will then equal ($30)(60), or $1800. You can verify that each firm will break even at about eight units, provided the price remains at $130.

It must be noted that once the market price is determined, the price becomes the marginal revenue. Consequently, the equation for the marginal revenue is simply

$$MR = P.$$

CHAPTER 12 APPENDIX

PROFIT MAXIMIZATION UNDER IMPERFECT COMPETITION

In general, when the market is not perfectly competitive, the price is greater than the marginal revenue. Thus, if the demand for a firm's product is

$$P = 120 - \tfrac{1}{2}Q,$$

the marginal revenue is

$$\frac{dR}{dQ} = \frac{d(120Q - \tfrac{1}{2}Q^2)}{dQ} = 120 - Q \qquad (1)$$

The firm maximizes profit by equating its MR to its MC. For the purpose of illustration, let's suppose that the firm's marginal cost is

$$MC = 20 + Q$$

which, when equated to equation (1), yields

$$20 + Q = 120 - Q$$
$$2Q = 100$$
$$Q = 50$$

When we substitute this value of Q in the demand equation, the profit-maximizing price becomes $120 - \tfrac{1}{2}(50)$, or $95.

THE NECESSARY AND SUFFICIENT CONDITIONS

In order for the firm to select the true profit-maximizing quantity, the MR must equal the MC *and* the slope of the MC must be greater than the slope of the MR. With reference to the illustration discussed, before we can declare that $Q = 50$ is the appropriate profit-maximizing quantity, we must show that

$$MR = MC$$
$$\frac{dMR}{dQ} < \frac{dMC}{dQ}$$

The slope of MR is -1, and the slope of MC is 1. Thus, the sufficient conditions for profit-maximization are satisfied.

COMPUTATION OF PROFIT

The total profit of the firm is the product of the average profit times the total output. Average profit is the excess of price over average total cost. Alternatively, total profits equal total revenue minus total cost. For the firm just discussed, the average variable cost is

$$AVC = 20 + \tfrac{1}{2}Q$$

and consequently, total variable cost is $Q(20 + \tfrac{1}{2}Q) = 20Q + \tfrac{1}{2}Q^2$. Assuming that the fixed costs of the firm are $500, the total profit at $Q = 50$ will be:

$$Q(P - AVC) - FC = 50(95 - 45) - 500 = 2000.$$

We can also compute the profits (or losses) of the firm by subtracting total cost from total revenue. Thus, profits $\Pi = PQ - TC = (95)(50) - (500 + 20Q + \frac{1}{2}Q^2) = 2000$.

TAXES AND THE MONOPOLIST

Suppose the government wishes to collect revenues by taxing a monopolist. Three possible types of tax are being considered: A lump-sum tax, a specific (or per-unit) tax, and a tax as a percentage of profits. Consider the lump-sum tax first.

Assume that the monopolist's total cost function and the demand for its product are given as shown:

$$TC = 200 + 20Q + \frac{1}{10}Q^2 \tag{2}$$

$$P = 100 - \frac{1}{10}Q \tag{3}$$

From equations (2) and (3) we obtain the MC and MR, and equate them for maximum profits to the monopolist. Thus,

$$MC = \frac{dTC}{dQ} = 20 + \frac{1}{5}Q$$

$$MR = \frac{dR}{dQ} = 100 - \frac{1}{5}Q$$

$$MC = MR$$

$$20 + \tfrac{1}{5}Q = 100 - \tfrac{1}{5}Q$$

$$\tfrac{2}{5}Q = 80$$

$$Q = 200 \quad \text{and} \quad P = \$80$$

When a lump-sum (or fixed) tax of $600 is imposed on the firm, the only thing that is affected is the total cost of the firm, which now reads

$$TC = 800 + 20Q + \frac{1}{10}Q^2$$

The marginal cost is not changed. The result is that the price of $80 and quantity of 200 are unaltered, but the firm earns $600 less in profits.

Now suppose that the firm must pay a profit tax of 10%. This implies that the firm's net profit will be 10% less than the before-tax profits, and the firm will obviously wish to maximize net profit. From the original demand and cost functions given by equations (2) and (1), we can derive the profit and the after-tax profit functions. Hence.

$$\Pi = R - TC$$

$$= \left(100Q - \frac{1}{10}Q^2\right) - \left(200 + 20Q + \frac{1}{10}Q^2\right)$$

$$= 80Q - \tfrac{1}{5}Q^2 - 200$$

Recall that when this profit function is maximized, $Q = 200$. However, after the 10% tax, the net profit will be 90% of the old profit, or

$$\text{Net } \Pi = 0.90(80Q - \tfrac{1}{5}Q^2 - 200)$$

$$= 72Q - 0.18Q^2 - 180 \tag{4}$$

To maximize equation (4), $d(\text{Net } \Pi)/dQ = 0$. Therefore,

$$\frac{dN\Pi}{dQ} = 72 - 0.36Q = 0$$

$$Q = 200$$
$$P = \$80$$

You can verify that the firm's net profit will equal $7020.

Let's suppose that the firm must pay a tax of $8 per unit of output. Since this is a variable cost to the firm, the firm's cost function inclusive of the tax becomes

$$TC = 200 + 20Q + \frac{1}{10}Q^2 + 8Q$$

$$= 200 + 28Q + \frac{1}{10}Q^2$$

$$MC = 28 + \tfrac{1}{5}Q \qquad\qquad (5)$$

Equation (5) shows that the new MC will be $8 (the amount of tax) higher than the original (before-tax) MC. As long as the demand function remains the same, the firm's profit-maximizing quantity and price are determined in the usual manner. Consequently,

$$MC = MR$$
$$28 + \tfrac{1}{5}Q = 100 - \tfrac{1}{5}Q$$
$$Q = 180$$
$$P = \$82$$

The calculations show that the firm's price rises by $2, and quantity falls by 20 units. You can verify that the firm's after-tax profits will equal $6280, and the total tax revenue for the government will equal $1440. Under the circumstances, the government will get the most revenues with a specific tax, although higher tax revenues are perhaps possible with a different value of the tax. We will now calculate the tax per unit which will maximize the government's tax revenue.

MAXIMIZATION OF MONOPOLY TAX REVENUE

The government's objective is to maximize the total tax revenue T, where $T = tQ$, and t is the unknown tax per unit. Assuming the same demand and cost functions, the monopolist will maximize profits as shown. Thus,

$$R = 100Q - \frac{1}{10}Q^2$$

$$TC = 20Q + tQ + 200 + \frac{1}{10}Q^2$$

and profits are maximized when

$$\Pi = 100Q - \frac{1}{10}Q^2 - \left(20Q + tQ + 200 + \frac{1}{10}Q^2\right)$$

$$= 80Q - \frac{1}{5}Q^2 - tQ - 200$$

$$\frac{d\Pi}{dQ} = 80 - \frac{2}{5}Q - t$$

$$80 - \frac{2}{5}Q - t = 0$$

$$Q = \frac{5(80 - t)}{2}$$

$$= 200 - 2.5t$$

The tax revenue to the government, $T = tQ$, equals

$$T = t(200 - 2.5t)$$
$$= 200t - 2.5t^2$$

When we maximize T with respect to t, we obtain

$$\frac{dT}{dt} = 200 - 5t = 0$$

$$t = 40$$

Thus a tax of $40 per unit of output will maximize revenues to the government.

With the $40 tax, the firm's profit-maximizing quantity and price are 100 and $90, respectively, as computed with the usual MC = MR rule. The government's revenue comes to ($40)(100), or $4000. Notice again that the price rises by a percentage of the tax. For this particular problem, the price due to a specific tax will rise by 25% of the tax. Thus, an $8 tax raised the price by $2, and the $40 tax forced the price up by $10. This is because

$$P = 100 - \frac{1}{10}Q = 100 - \frac{1}{10}(200 - 2.5t)$$

$$= 80 + 0.25t$$

and without t, the price is $80.

CHAPTER 13 APPENDIX

PROFIT MAXIMIZATION WITH MULTIPLE MARKETS

When a firm or a monopolist segments its markets and charges a different price in each market, we have third-degree discrimination. Usually, the firm's profits are higher with discrimination than without it. Assume that the firm has two markets, 1 and 2, such that the demands for the firm's product in these markets are

$$P_1 = 100 - 2Q_1$$
$$P_2 = 80 - Q_2.$$

The cost function for the firm is

$$C = 10 + 40Q + 2Q^2, \quad \text{where } Q = (Q_1 + Q_2).$$

The firm's profits will be maximized when the slope of the total profit function is zero. The firm's profits may be written as

$$\begin{aligned}
\Pi &= R_1 + R_2 - C \\
&= P_1 Q_1 + P_2 Q_2 - C \\
&= 100Q_1 - 2Q_1^2 + 80Q_2 - Q_2^2 - [10 + 40(Q_1 + Q_2) + 2(Q_1 + Q_2)^2] \\
&= 60Q_1 + 40Q_2 - 4Q_1^2 - 3Q_2^2 - 4Q_1 Q_2 - 10
\end{aligned}$$

To maximize Π, $\partial\Pi/\partial Q_1 = 0$, and $\partial\Pi/\partial Q_2 = 0$, or

$$\frac{\partial\Pi}{\partial Q_1} = 60 - 8Q_1 - 4Q_2 = 0 \tag{1}$$

$$\frac{\partial\Pi}{\partial Q_2} = 40 - 4Q_1 - 6Q_2 = 0 \tag{2}$$

Solving equations (1) and (2) simultaneously yields $Q_1 = 6.25$ and $Q_2 = 2.50$. To find the price for each market, we substitute the values of Q_1 and Q_2 in the demand functions. Thus, the price in market 1 will be

$$P_1 = 100 - 2(6.25) = 87.50$$

and in market 2, the price will be

$$P_2 = 80 - 2.50 = 77.50$$

We can solve this problem by using the model discussed in the book, which in effect was derived from the one above. For third-degree discrimination and profit-maximization, the following must hold true:

$$MR_1 = MR_2 = MC$$

or

$$100 - 4Q_1 = 80 - 2Q_2 = 40 + 4Q \tag{3}$$

When we solve the system of equations shown by (3), we will obtain the same results as above.

FIRST-DEGREE PRICE DISCRIMINATION

Under this type of pricing scheme the seller produces and sells the output as long as the price paid by the individual consumer is at least as high as the marginal cost of the output. Consider the demand for a monopolist's services, which is known to be

$$P = 1000 - 10Q$$

The firm's total cost is

$$TC = 600 + 100Q + 5Q^2$$

Maximum profits will accrue to the firm if it produces and sells the output up to the point where $P = MC$. Thus, the optimal quantity occurs when

$$1000 - 10Q = 100 + 10Q$$
$$Q = 45$$

Because the firm will charge a different price for each unit of output, the total revenue is the sum of all the prices paid for the 45 units. In a graph this revenue is shown by the area under the demand curve—$OABC$ in Figure A13-1. If we assume that all values of Q must lie between 1 and 45 inclusive, the price will

FIGURE A13-1

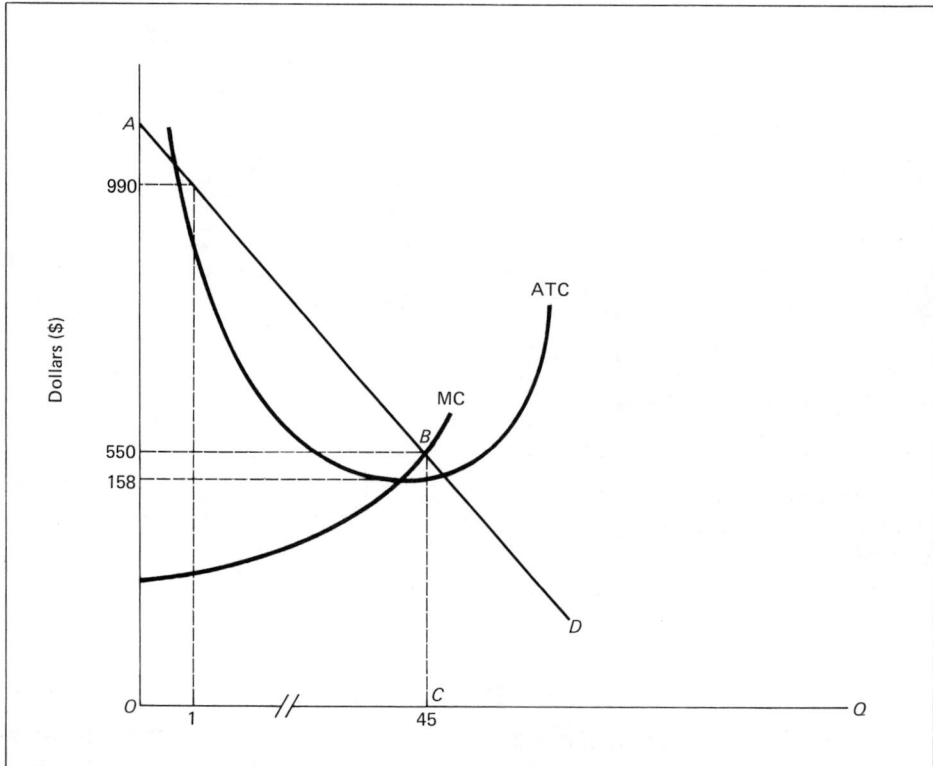

range from [$1000 − $10(45)] = $550, to [$1000 − $10(1)] = $990. The area of the trapezoid with vertical (and parallel) sides of 990 and 550, with the distance separating them equal to 44, corresponds to the total revenue of the firm, or (½)($990 + $550)(44) = $33,880. The total cost to the firm will be $600 + $100(45) + $5(45)^2, or $7125. The firm therefore earns profits equalling $26,755.

If the firm had chosen not to discriminate, it would have maximized available profits by charging the price that results from equating MR with MC. Under these circumstances the price will be $700, and the quantity will equal 30.

PROFIT MAXIMIZATION AND JOINT PRODUCTS

Some firms produce joint products in the sense that the products are produced in some fixed proportion to each other. For example, in the case of the beef producer, each animal slaughtered and processed yields one carcass and one hide. It is understood that the number of hides produced must equal the number of carcasses, but the firm does not have to sell all the hides. In what follows, we will assume that the firm produces two products, beef (B) and hides (H), and that the quantity of H sold is equal to or less than the amount of B, and that B is the main provider of profits.

Let the demands for beef and hides be

$$P_B = 2000 - 2B$$
$$P_H = 200 - \tfrac{1}{5}H$$

The total cost of producing B and H is

$$C = 10000 + 80B + 20H + \tfrac{1}{2}B^2 + \tfrac{1}{5}BH + \tfrac{1}{10}H^2$$

The profits to the firm may be expressed as the difference between the revenue from B and H and the cost producing them, or

$$\Pi = (P_B B + P_H H) - (10000 + 80B + 20H + \tfrac{1}{2}B^2 + \tfrac{1}{5}BH + \tfrac{1}{10}H^2)$$
$$= 1920B + 180H - \tfrac{5}{2}B^2 - \tfrac{3}{10}H^2 - \tfrac{1}{5}BH - 10000$$

For profits to be maximum,

$$\frac{\partial \Pi}{\partial B} = 1920 - 5B - \tfrac{1}{5}H = 0$$

$$\frac{\partial \Pi}{\partial H} = 180 - \tfrac{3}{5}H - \tfrac{1}{5}B = 0$$

When these two equations are solved simultaneously, we obtain

$$B = 377.03, \quad H = 174.32, \quad \text{and } P_B = \$1245.94, \quad P_H = \$165.14$$

for a total profit of $367,635.

The firm may also insist on selling all beef and hides, that is, $B = H$. In that case, the firm will maximize profits by producing 350 carcasses and hides. The price of B will be $1300, and the price of H will be $130, and the firm's profits will total $357,500. To obtain these results, just substitute B for H in the Π function and maximize it.

THE DOMINANT FIRM PRICE LEADERSHIP MODEL

In the case of the large (or dominant) firm which sets the price for the industry, the followers are allowed to sell as many units of output as they wish, with the leader selling the remaining units demanded at that price.

Suppose the total demand for a given product which is produced by the dominant firm, as well as the others, is

$$Q = 100000 - 10P$$

and the aggregate supply of all firms except the dominant one is

$$Q_s = -20000 + 10P$$

In this model, the demand for the dominant firm's product is derived by subtracting Q_s from Q. Thus, the demand for the dominant firm is

$$Q_D = Q - Q_s = 100000 - 10P - (-20000 + 10P)$$
$$= 120000 - 20P_D$$

or

$$P_D = 6000 - 1/20 \, Q_D$$

and

$$MR_D = 6000 - \tfrac{1}{10}Q_D$$

The dominant firm's total cost is assumed to be

$$TC = 100000 + 1000Q_D + \frac{1}{20}Q_D^2$$

from which the marginal cost is found to be

$$MC_D = 1000 + \tfrac{1}{10}Q_D$$

We find the profit-maximizing level of output for the dominant firm by equating MR_D and MC_D, which yields $Q_D = 25000$. Consequently, the price (P_D) for the industry is set at

$$P_D = 6000 - \frac{1}{20}(25,000) = \$4750$$

At this price, the other firms collectively supply 27,500 units. The total profits for the dominant firm amount to \$62.4 million, and the market share of the dominant firm is (25000/52,500), or 47.62%. The total demand at a price of \$4750 is 52,500 units.

THE CARTEL

Assume that firms 1 and 2 make up the entire industry. Each one has a demand for its product as:

$$P_1 = 100 - 2Q_1 \quad \text{and} \quad P_2 = 90 - 2Q_2$$

The total cost functions are:

$$C_1 = 110 + 20Q_1 + \tfrac{1}{2}Q_1^2$$
$$C_2 = 150 + 18Q_2 + Q_2^2$$

When each firm selects its own profit-maximizing price, the price and quantities will be:

$$P_1 = \$68, \quad Q_1 = 16, \quad P_2 = \$66, \quad Q_2 = 12$$

The total profits for the firms are:

$$\Pi_1 = \$530, \quad \Pi_2 = 282.$$

When the firms form a cartel, the total cartel output is determined by equating the sum of the MC to the sum of the MR of the cartel members, and the cartel price is obtained from the aggregate demand function. We obtain the aggregate MC from C_1 and C_2 as follows.

$$MC_1 = 20 + Q_1 \quad \text{or} \quad Q_1 = MC_1 - 20$$
$$MC_2 = 18 + 2Q_2 \quad \text{or} \quad Q_2 = \tfrac{1}{2}MC_2 - 9$$

Because we are adding the MC's horizontally, $MC_1 = MC_2$, and $Q = Q_1 + Q_2$, or

$$Q = \tfrac{3}{2}MC - 29 \quad \text{or} \quad MC = \frac{58}{3} + \frac{2}{3}Q.$$

Similarly, the aggregate MR function can be shown to equal

$$MR_1 + MR_2 = MR = 95 - 2Q$$

The cartel maximizes total profit by equating MR to MC, or

$$95 - 2Q = \frac{58}{3} + \frac{2}{3}Q$$
$$Q = 28.38$$
$$P = 66.62$$

At $Q = 28.38$, $MC = 38.25$, and because $MC = MC_1 = MC_2$, $Q_1 = 18.25$ and $Q_2 = 10.13$.

When each firm charges the cartel price of \$66.62, profits for firm 1 will increase by \$44.29. Profits for firm 2 will decrease by \$42.10. Thus, if firm 1 gives 43.195 of its new profits to firm 2, both parties will increase their profits by 1.095, or \$1.095 million, if Q is measured in millions of units. The 43.195 was determined by dividing the difference in the change in profits of firms 1 and 2 equally. After the redistribution of profits, $\Pi_1 = 531.095$ and $\Pi_2 = 283.095$. The total industry (cartel) output will remain essentially the same as before the formation of the cartel.

CHAPTER 14 APPENDIX

PROBABILISTIC DEMAND FUNCTIONS

Because firms do not have perfect information about the nature of demand for their products, they often rely on information about probabilities to make decisions. For example, it was shown in the text that with the use of probability information a firm can reduce complete uncertainty into chance certainty through expected value criteria. The probability information is obtained from the probability function, which in turn is derived from the distribution of all possible values that are likely to occur. One such probability function (or probability density function) is the famous normal curve, or the bell-shaped curve. If the firm believes that the demand for its product is normally distributed for each possible price, it can compute the probabilities that demand will equal certain values.

Without going into the elaborate description of these probability functions, let's assume that a firm believes that the following probabilities are associated with each of the quantities corresponding to each price level.

Price	Probability	Quantity demanded
	0.60	100
$10	0.30	150
	0.10	90
	0.75	200
9	0.20	220
	0.05	170
	0.55	400
8	0.30	360
	0.15	450

From the given information, we can reduce the various probable quantities to the equivalent expected values as:

Price	Expected value of Q
$10	114
9	202.5
8	395.5

The firm is now in a position to decide which quantity it should expect to sell at each possible price, and therefore be prepared to produce that quantity. Before doing so, it can also calculate the consequences of producing a certain quantity and not selling that exact quantity. For example, in case of the price of $10, the expected value of quantity is 114, although the probability is high (0.60) that only 100 units will be demanded at that price. Consequently, if the firm produces 114 and sells 100, it will suffer the consequences (if any) of producing the 14 extra units. On the other hand, if it produces 100 units and demand is 150 at that price, the firm will again face the burden or opportunity loss from the shortage of the 50 units. Under the circumstances, the firm may elect to produce 120 units as a compromise.

There are many probability models which are used by operations researchers in dealing with uncertainty. Among the widely used ones are the gamma, the chi square, the binomial, the Poisson, and the F and T distributions.

CHAPTER 15 APPENDIX

DEMAND FOR A FACTOR

Recall that a profit-maximizing firm hires a resource after comparing its cost to its marginal revenue product. Assume that the firm sells its output in a perfectly competitive market, and also purchases the single-variable resource (R) in a perfectly competitive resource market. The marginal physical product of the resource (MQ_R) and the price of the output (P) are known, such that

$$MQ_R = 100 - 2R \qquad (1)$$
$$P = \$20 \qquad (2)$$

How many units of R should the firm employ in order to maximize its profits, if the price of the resource (P_R) is $160?

From equations (1) and (2), we obtain the resource's marginal revenue product, which is the product of the marginal product times the output's marginal revenue. Because marginal revenue and price are one and the same under perfect competition, the resource's marginal revenue product (MRQ_R) is

$$MRQ_R = (MQ_R)(MR) = 20(100 - 2R) = 2000 - 40R \qquad (3)$$

The marginal resource cost (MRC) is the price of the resource, or

$$MRC = 160 \qquad (4)$$

Equating (3) to (4), we obtain the profit-maximizing level of R. Thus,

$$2000 - 40R = 160$$
$$R = 46$$

It can be shown that the total output function, or the production function $Q = f(R)$, for the MQ_R function given by equation (1) is

$$Q = 100R - R^2 \qquad (5)$$

You can check this, because $dQ/dR = MQ_R = 100 - 2R$. From equation (5) we can derive a total revenue function (PQ), which will be

$$\text{Total revenue} = PQ = 20(100R - R^2)$$
$$= 2000R - 20R^2 \qquad (6)$$

The total cost of purchasing R is

$$\text{Total cost} = (P_R)(R) = 160R \qquad (7)$$

Consequently, the total profit to the firm may be written as the difference between equations (6) and (7), or

$$\Pi = 2000R - 20R^2 - 160R \qquad (8)$$

To maximize (8), we obtain $d\Pi/dR$ and equate it to 0:

$$\frac{d\Pi}{dR} = 2000 - 40R - 160 = 0$$
$$R = 46$$

From equation (5), the total output when $R = 46$ is

$$Q = 100(46) - (46)^2 = 2484$$

and total revenue to the firm equals

$$\text{Revenue} = (20)(2484) = 49680$$

Because the cost of purchasing 46 units of R is

$$\text{Cost} = (46)(160) = 7360$$

the firm's contribution profit produced by R is 42320.

You can verify that if the price of R rises, the firm will hire fewer units of R, and if it falls, the firm will acquire more units of R. The ceteris paribus demand for R, then, is given by equation (3). No matter how low the price of R, the firm will hire at most 50 units of R, because beyond that level of employment the marginal product of R is negative. Show that if the price of R remains at \$160, but the price of the output rises to \$30, the firm will hire 47.33 units of R, and that if all other factors remain constant (i.e., $P = \$20$, $P_R = \$160$), and the MQ_R doubles to $200 - 4R$, the profit-maximizing firm will engage 48 units of R.

When the firm sells its output under monopolistic conditions, the marginal revenue of the output is less than its price. Even so, the computation of the profit-maximizing level of employment of a resource is essentially the same.

Assume that the firm's production function is $Q = 20R$, and the demand for the output is $P = 1000 - Q$. Under the circumstances, the marginal revenue of the output, and hence the marginal revenue product of R will be

$$\begin{aligned} MRQ_R = MQ_R(MR) &= 20\,(1000-2Q) \\ &= 20(1000-40R) \\ &= 20000 - 800R. \end{aligned}$$

If the price of R is 1600, the profit-maximizing level of R will be where MRQ_R equals 1600, or at $R = 23$. With 23 units of R, the output will be $(20)(23)$, or 460 units, and each of the 460 units can be sold for a price of $(\$1000 - \$460)$ or \$540. The total revenue to the firm will then equal \$248,400. The total cost of buying R (\$36,800) provides the firm with excess revenues of \$211,600.

CHAPTER 16 APPENDIX

TWO VARIABLE FACTORS OF PRODUCTION

We have already discussed some aspects of profit maximization, in the context of more than one variable resource, in the appendices to Chapters 6 and 7. In what follows we will mathematically illustrate the firm's demand for two factors of production, A and B, where the output is produced by these two resources independent of their quantities.

Assume that the firm has two production functions at its disposal such that

$$Q_A = 100A - A^2 \tag{1}$$
$$Q_B = 150B - 1.5B^2 \tag{2}$$

The output is sold under perfect competition at a market price of $10, and the two resources are also purchased competitively at $2 per unit of A and $6 per unit of B. If there are no other constraints, the firm will maximize profits by hiring quantities of A and B so that each resource's marginal revenue product equals its price.

From equations (1) and (2), and the output price information,

$$MRQ_A = 10(100 - 2A) = 1000 - 20A \tag{3}$$
$$MRQ_B = 10(150 - 3B) = 1500 - 30B \tag{4}$$

Equating (3) to the marginal cost of A (or P_A), and (4) to the marginal cost of B (or P_B), we have

$$1000 - 20A = 2$$
$$A = 49.90$$
$$1500 - 30B = 6$$
$$B = 49.80$$

The total output to the firm will be the sum of Q_A and Q_B, which in this case will equal 2500 + 3750, or 6250 units. The cost of acquiring the two resources in the quantities shown will be $399, and the total revenue to the firm will equal $62,500, resulting in a total profit (before fixed cost) of $62,101.

When $A = 49.90$, $MQ_A = 0.2$, and hence the marginal cost of the output (P_A/MQ_A) equals $2/0.2, or $10. Similarly, the marginal cost of the output when $B = 49.80$ is also $10. The firm maximizes profit by equating the marginal cost of the output to the marginal revenue of the output, which in this case is $10. If the output of the firm is produced with a production function that relates output to all variables, we can proceed in a similar fashion with the use of partial derivatives, as shown in the Appendix to Chapter 7.

BILATERAL MONOPOLY

Recall that this is the model which involves a single buyer and a single seller of the resource, such as the case involving a labor union and a monopsonist firm. We will assume that the firm sells its output under perfect competition and purchases the single-variable resource L under the conditions specified.

Let the firm's production function of a single-variable labor resource (L) be

$$Q = 100L - L^2, \tag{5}$$

and the price of the output be $10. The supply of labor is given by

$$P_L = 100 + 5L \tag{6}$$

From equation (5) and the price of the output, the demand for labor, which is the marginal revenue product of L, is

$$D_L = MRQ_L = 1000 - 20L, \tag{7}$$

and from equation (6), the total variable cost due to the purchase of L is $(P_L)(L)$, or

$$VC_L = 100L + 5L^2 \tag{8}$$

From equation (8), the marginal cost of L is

$$MC_L = \frac{dVC_L}{dL} = 100 + 10L \tag{9}$$

Thus the profit-maximizing level of L is obtained when equation (7) is equated to (9), from which we have $L = 30$.

If the firm hires the 30 units of L at the supply price shown by equation (6), it will pay a wage of $[100 + 5(30)]$ or $250 to each of the workers. However, the MRQ_L, when $L = 30$, is $400, which implies that the firm should be willing to pay a wage as high as $400 in order to hire the 30 workers and still maximize available profits.

THE MAXIMUM WAGE RATE

We have already seen that the firm should be willing to pay each worker a wage as high as $400, without hiring any less than 30 workers. Thus the union can set the wage rate at $400 and ask the firm to hire any number of workers it desires at that wage. When this takes place, the artificial supply of labor function becomes

$$P_L = 400 = MC_L \tag{10}$$

The profit-maximizing firm uses (10) and (7) to compute the optimal level of L which, as you can verify, is $L = 30$.

MAXIMUM LEVEL OF EMPLOYMENT

The maximum level of employment occurs when the firm hires that quantity of L where the demand for L equals the supply of L. When we equate (6) and (7), we obtain

$$100 + 5L = 1000 - 20L$$
$$L = 36$$

Therefore, 36 units of L will be supplied if $P_L = [100 + 5(36)]$, or $280. If the labor union sets the wage rate at $280, the firm will use this as a basis for hiring the profit-maximizing quantity of L. Thus, the marginal cost of labor to the firm now becomes

$$MC_L = 280 \tag{11}$$

and when the firm equates (11) to equation (7), $L = 36$.

MAXIMUM TOTAL WAGES

If the labor union simply wishes to maximize the total combined wages of labor, it will maximize the function $(L)(D_L)$, where the asking wage will be determined by the union, and obtained from the firm's labor demand (D_L). The total revenue to the union in this case is

$$\text{Total wages} = TW = (L)(D_L) = 1000L - 20L^2 \tag{12}$$

To maximize (12), we follow the usual procedures, where $dTW/dL = 0$, or

$$\frac{dTW}{dL} = 1000 - 40L$$

$$L = 25$$

From equation (7), the demand price of L corresponding to this level of L is $500, therefore the total wages amount to $12500. However, from (6), the supply price for 25 workers is only $225, consequently, if each of the 25 workers donates to the "cause" $275 from earnings of $500, the union will have $6875 to distribute to the unemployed members as well as to the union officials!

CHAPTER 17 APPENDIX

DERIVATION OF THE PRODUCTION-POSSIBILITIES FRONTIER

The traditional production-possibilities function is derived under the assumption that the country maximizes the output of the two goods with the available resources. Consequently, the "best" combination of the two goods (X,Y) results when, for each given level of possible X, the country produces the corresponding maximum of Y. Efficiency is maximized when all the appropriate marginal conditions of production are fulfilled.

Assume that the country produces two goods, X and Y, and has a limited amount of resources designated by K and L. The markets are all under perfect competition, and each product is produced with a production function that employs both the resources. Specifically,

$$X = f(K_X, L_X)$$
$$Y = g(K_Y, L_Y)$$
$$K = K_X + K_Y$$
$$L = L_X + L_Y$$

From these conditions, we can obtain the marginal rates of technical substitution of K for L in each industry. All combinations of X and Y that allow the MRTS in each industry to be equal, subject to the K and L constraints, are chosen. When these resulting combinations of X and Y are plotted, the production-possibilities curve emerges.

To illustrate the procedure, suppose the country under question has a total K of 100, and total $L = 200$. Furthermore, the production functions are such that

$$X = 10K_x^{1/4}L_x^{3/4} \tag{1}$$
$$Y = 20K_y^{1/2}L_y^{1/2} \tag{2}$$

From equations (1) and (2),

$$\text{MRTS}_x = \frac{\partial X/\partial L_x}{\partial X/\partial K_x} = \frac{7.5K_x^{1/4}L_x^{-1/4}}{2.5K_x^{-3/4}L_x^{3/4}} = 3\frac{K_x}{L_x} \tag{3}$$

$$\text{MRTS}_y = \frac{\partial Y/\partial L_y}{\partial Y/\partial K_y} = \frac{10K_y^{1/2}L_y^{-1/2}}{10K_y^{-1/2}L_y^{1/2}} \tag{4}$$

$$= \frac{K_y}{L_y}$$

For maximum efficiency, equation (3) must equal (4). Thus,

$$3\frac{K_x}{L_x} = \frac{K_y}{L_y} \tag{5}$$

When equation (5) is solved simultaneously with the K and L constraints of $K_x + K_y = 100$, and $L_x + L_y = 200$, we obtain many possible distributions of K and L among the X and Y industries. When these values of K_x, L_x and K_y, L_y are substituted into equations (1) and (2), we obtain values of X and Y to draw the production frontier.

SOCIAL UTILITY MAXIMIZATION

Once we obtain the production frontier, we can derive the utility-maximizing combination of X and Y with the use of equations (6) and (7). Equation (6) is the implicit function representing the production possibilities frontier, and (7) corresponds to the social welfare function. Thus,

$$f(X, Y) = 0 \qquad (6)$$

$$U = f(X, Y) \qquad (7)$$

Equation (6) serves as the constraint subject to which equation (7) is maximized. When the optimal combination of X and Y is determined, the prices of X and Y are also simultaneously determined, as are the prices of K and L. The utility maximizing combination of X and Y occurs where the slope of the U function is equal to the slope of the production-possibilities curve, or where the highest utility curve is tangent to equation (6). At that point, the marginal rate of product transformation (the slope of the production-possibilities curve) equals the marginal rate of substitution (the slope of the social indifference curve).

When the quantities of X and Y are determined, the amount of K and L to be allocated to each industry is also determined, which in turn decides the relative prices of K and L.

GLOSSARY

APPRECIATION OF CURRENCY Increase in value of a currency relative to another currency.

ARBITRAGE Speculation in the foreign exchange market.

AVERAGE CONTRIBUTION The amount by which the price of a product exceeds the average variable cost. Also called *contribution per unit*.

AVERAGE FIXED COST Cost that is equal to the total fixed cost divided by the total output.

AVERAGE PHYSICAL PRODUCT Expression of the average output of each unit of a variable resource at a particular level of resource allocation.

AVERAGE PROFIT The difference between the price of an item and its average total cost. Also called *profit per unit*.

AVERAGE REVENUE The ratio of total revenue to total quantity, which is, in most cases, not different from the price of the product.

AVERAGE TOTAL COST Cost obtained by dividing the total cost of production by the total output *or* the sum of the average fixed and average variable costs.

AVERAGE VARIABLE COST The ratio of the total variable cost to the quantity of output *or* variable cost per unit.

AVERCH–JOHNSON PHENOMENON Proposition that essentially states that a firm constrained by a rate-of-return regulation will tend to use an uneconomical combination of inputs, which results in higher costs and higher prices to the public.

BAIN INDEX Indicator using the divergence between price and average total cost to measure monopoly power.

BALANCE OF PAYMENTS Record of a country's transactions with other nations including transactions in goods, services, capital, and gold movement.

BALANCE OF TRADE The value of exports less the value of imports *or* the difference between receipts and expenditures in international trade.

BARTER ECONOMY Economy in which trade is accomplished by an exchange of one commodity for another (as opposed to a money economy).

BERGSON CRITERION Criterion holding that any change that reduces utility is undesirable.

BILATERAL MONOPOLY Situation brought about when a single buyer (monopsonist) of an input confronts a single seller (monopolist) of this input.

BREAK EVEN POINT The point where a firm operates without either profit or loss. Graphically, the point where total revenues equal total costs.

BUDGET CONSTRAINT The limitation of the choice of goods that can be purchased in various combinations as determined by the amount of the budget.

CAPITAL A resource, either physical or monetary, that includes all the producer's goods, plant, equipment, and invested capital necessary to produce the final product or output.

CARTEL Combination of producers who enter into certain collusive agreements for their mutual benefit. Cartel activities can include price fixing, market sharing, and other agreements beneficial to the cartel, such as avoiding competition with each other.

CETERIS PARIBUS Latin for "other things being equal."

CHANCE NODES In decision-tree terminology, points of chance occurrences.

COASE THEOREM Maintains that even if there are significant externalities in private transactions, and there is sufficient reason to condemn the market, the government should not intervene to correct the market failure.

COBB–DOUGLAS PRODUCTION FUNCTION Relationship obtained by multiplying inputs by each other. Also called *multiplicative production function*.

COLLECTIVE GOODS Public goods that a person can use at will without depriving others of their use. An example is the national highway system.

COLLUSION Secret agreement, often of a fraudulent, deceitful, or illegal nature, entered into, for example, by cartels.

COMPETING PRODUCTS Items produced from the same source that compete with each other in the market, such as beef and veal from cattle.

COMPLEMENT An item that is normally consumed or bought along with another product.

CONCENTRATION CURVE Curve that shows the cumulative percentages of total employees, industry assets, and other related resources controlled or held by the leading firms in a given industry.

CONSPICUOUS CONSUMPTION Profuse or excessive spending for the purpose of elevating one's position or reputation.

CONSTANT Something that does not change in value in a given situation, as opposed to a variable.

CONSTANT-COST INDUSTRY Industry in which, if the new and existing firms can maintain the previous average total cost of output at a new and higher level of output by increasing their scale, the market price will, in the long run, also remain at its former level.

CONSTANT-SUM GAME Game in which the gains and/or losses add up to a constant value.

CONSTRAINT Limiting or restricting factor.

CONSUMPTION The use of goods to fulfill needs or to produce (for example, manufacture) other goods.

CONTRIBUTION PROFIT The difference between revenues and total variable costs.

COST The sacrifice necessary to obtain certain benefits.

COST FUNCTION The cost–output relationship obtained when the prices of inputs are systematically linked to the volume of output.

CROSS-PRICE ELASTICITY OF DEMAND The elasticity that compares the demand for one product to the price of a related product.

DECISION NODES In decision-tree terminology, points associated with decisions.

DECISION-TREE ANALYSIS Method by which the decision maker lays down all the possible outcomes in the future as consequences of certain actions at various stages, producing a diagram that resembles a tree with branches, lying on its side.

DECREASING-COST INDUSTRY An industry in which increases in demand and accompanying increases in supply bring about a decrease in the long-run equilibrium price.

DEFICIT The result when expenditures are greater than income.

DEMAND The willingness and the ability of the consumer to acquire goods and services at various prices under the prevailing circumstances.

DEMAND, LAW OF Economic law stating that, when all other variables are assumed to be constant, the quantity demanded varies inversely with the price of the good. In other words, other things being equal, the lower the price of the product, the higher the quantity demanded by the consumers.

DEPRECIATION OF CURRENCY Decrease in the value of one currency relative to another currency.

DERIVED DEMAND Demand for a resource that results or develops from the demand for the output.

DIMINISHING MARGINAL UTILITY Increasingly lowered satisfaction provided by the consumption of additional items.

DIMINISHING MARGINAL VALUATION, LAW OF Principle stating that if a consumer has more of one good than another, he or she tends to value the good that is rare more than the abundant one.

DIMINISHING RETURNS, LAW OF Principle stating that increasing such factors of production as capital or labor will fail, at a certain point, to result in a corresponding increase in production.

DISECONOMIES OF SCALE Factors resulting in the rise of the cost of production at a quicker rate than the rise of output.

DISTRIBUTION Apportionment or allotment, as of goods and services, among consumers.

DISUTILITY Absence or lack of happiness, satisfaction of wants, and well-being with reference to consumers.

DIVISION OF LABOR The separation of labor into various components or processes to increase efficiency in production.

DOMINANT FIRM Large firm within an industry that presumably has enough market power to dictate the general level of prices to the other producers.

ECONOMETRICS The use of mathematics and statistics to measure, interpret, and verify economic phenomena.

ECONOMIC EFFICIENCY State which exists when the benefits of an activity exceed the costs.

ECONOMIC ORDER QUANTITY An order size that minimizes the sum of both the ordering costs (which vary inversely with the size of the order) and the storage and inventory costs (which rise with the size of the order).

ECONOMIC RENT The payment made to a production factor that is in excess of the price that would have brought forth its supply owing to the factor's scarcity.

ECONOMICS The study of the production, distribution, and consumption of goods.

ECONOMIES OF SCALE Factors that, when present, cause an expansion of scale to lead to a less than proportional increase in costs.

EDGEWORTH–BOWLEY BOX A graphical representation of pareto conditions in production. The height of the box represents total available capital and the width corresponds to the available labor.

EFFICIENCY RATIO The ratio of the marginal physical product of a resource to its resource.

ELASTICITY OF DEMAND The ratio of the percent change in quantity demanded to the percent change in the variable under question.

EMPIRICAL Based on facts, observation, or experiment, in contrast with a theoretical approach.

ENGEL CURVE A demand curve showing quantity purchased and income level. Also called *income–quantity demand curve*.

ENTREPRENEUR One who supplies the ideas, bears the risks, and also combines land, labor, and capital resources to attain the objectives of his or her business venture.

ENTRY-LIMIT PRICING The practice of keeping prices low in the industry in order to discourage new competitors.

EQUILIBRIUM State that results when the demand equals the supply.

EQUIMARGINAL PRINCIPLE The law that states that, whenever possible, the marginal values received from alternative uses should be made equal to each other in order to maximize total value from all sources. Also called the *Second Law of Gossen*.

EXPANSION PATH Path (in an isoquant map) of the increases in a firm's scale of operations. Also provides information about the presence of economies or diseconomies of scale and total and unit costs of production.

EXPECTED VALUE Average winnings or losses from a strategy, given the weights of the various probabilities *or* the probability-weighted sum of all the payoffs along a given row or column.

EXTERNALITY A side or spillover effect due to the consumption or production decisions of economic units within a society. It can be either positive (beneficial) or negative (harmful).

FIAT MONEY Money without gold or silver backing that depends on government decree for its value and acceptance in exchange.

FIRST-DEGREE PRICE DISCRIMINATION The charging of a different (unique) price to each customer. Also called *perfect price discrimination*.

FIXED COSTS Costs that remain constant at all levels of output.

FIXED INPUTS Those inputs whose quantities do not change.

FOREIGN EXCHANGE Foreign currencies, that is, all foreign money.

FOREIGN EXCHANGE RATE Ratio of exchange between one type of money and another.

FREE MARKET Economic market characterized by free competition or by unlimited buying and selling.

FREE RIDER One who tries to benefit or succeeds in benefiting at another's expense with no cost to himself or herself.

FUTURES MARKET Market in which contracts for the future delivery of goods are bought and sold.

GENERAL EQUILIBRIUM ANALYSIS Analysis that evaluates the possible results due to the interdependence of the various economic units. Helps determine the outcomes of change as it affects consumers, producers, and resources.

GIFFEN EFFECT Phenomenon where quantities bought vary positively with price, that is, as the price of relatively inexpensive goods increases, so does the demand for these goods. Concurrently, the demand for more expensive goods decreases.

GINI COEFFICIENT Measurement of the relative deviation of the actual distribution of an industry's assets from the line of equal distribution.

HEDGER One who avoids risks.

HICKS CRITERION Criterion holding that a change from A to B is socially desirable if the losers from the change cannot bribe the gainers to avoid the change, implying that the change is desirable if the cost of the change is less than the benefits accruing from the change. Thus, the move from A to B is desirable if the gain to the winners is higher than the loss to the losers.

IMPERFECT COMPETITION Competition in which the operating firms have some choice about the price.

INCOME ELASTICITY OF DEMAND The ratio of the percentage change in quantity demanded to the percentage change in income *or* the sensitivity of demand to income.

INCOME-INDUCED CONSUMPTION LOCUS A curve drawn by connecting the various points where the indifference curves are tangent to the budget lines. The various quantities are induced by changes in income alone.

INCREASING COST INDUSTRY Industry in which, owing to internal diseconomies of scale, rising factor prices, or both, the market price will rise with the expansion of output.

INCREMENTAL COST The change in cost due to a new decision, including the change in cost due to changes in the quantity of output produced.

INCREMENTAL REVENUE The change in total revenue associated with the change in another variable (instead of price).

INCREMENTAL UTILITY The additional utility brought about by adding other sources to the original source causing marginal utility.

INDIFFERENCE Attitude of liking two or more goods equally well.

INDIFFERENCE CURVE A curve that represents a person's tastes and preferences. Any point along the curve represents a unique level of satisfaction, and the higher the curve, the higher the satisfaction level.

INELASTIC DEMAND Demand whereby expenditures vary directly or positively with price.

INFERIOR GOODS Those products whose consumption declines at higher incomes.

INFLATION A condition characterized by rising prices and a resulting decline in the value and purchasing power of money.

INPUTS The resources used for production.

INTEGER PROGRAMMING A variation of linear programming that specifies that all values must be integers.

INVERSE ELASTICITY RULE Rule holding that the regulated price should vary inversely with the absolute value of the price elasticity of demand—that is, the higher the value of the price elasticity of demand, the lower the price that is necessary.

ISOCOST LINE A graphical representation of an equation in which all points on the line are equally costly. Also called a *budget equation*.

ISOPROFIT LINE A line connecting all points yielding a given amount of profit.

ISOQUANT Locus resulting from the connection of all combinations of capital and labor of a given firm by a line or curve, which shows all possible combinations of the available resources that yield a given volume of output.

JOINT PRODUCTS Products produced as complements from a single source, as beef and hides from cattle.

KALDOR CRITERION Criterion holding that a change is socially desirable or beneficial if the winners can compensate the losers and are still better off with the change than without it.

KINKED DEMAND MODEL A version of oligopoly pricing in which firms match price cuts offered by rivals but do not follow any price increases.

LABOR A resource that supplies human productive effort.

LAND RESOURCES All raw materials that are in fixed supply, as lumber, water, iron ore, and land itself.

LERNER INDEX Monopoly indicator computed by subtracting the marginal cost from the price and dividing the difference by the price.

LINEAR PROGRAMMING A branch of linear economic theory in which all functions are assumed to be either straight lines or actually linear.

LONG RUN A time period characterized by circumstances in which virtually all the resources are allowed to vary.

LORENZ CURVE A curve that shows the relative strength of the leading firms vis-à-vis the smaller ones.

LOSS-LEADER PRICING Tactic of deliberately keeping the price of one item very low in order to increase the demand for its complement.

MACROECONOMICS The detailed economic analysis of society as a whole, as with reference to the aggregate values of the nation's income, employment, and price level.

MANAGERIAL FUNCTION Function describing the variables or set of objectives that satisfy the manager's needs and hence provide him or her with utility or disutility.

MARGINAL COST The change in total variable cost associated with a one-unit change of output produced *or* the ratio of the incremental cost of output to the change in total output.

MARGINAL PHYSICAL PRODUCT The change in total output resulting from a one-unit change of variable input, all other factors remaining equal. Also called *marginal product*.

MARGINAL PROFIT The difference between marginal revenue and marginal cost. Indicates the value of the slope of the profit function.

MARGINAL RATE OF SUBSTITUTION A number that indicates a consumer's relative valuation of one additional unit of a good in terms of other goods.

MARGINAL RATE OF TECHNICAL SUBSTITUTION A ratio that measures the amount of one resource that can be substituted by *one unit* of another resource, in order to maintain the same volume of output (where two resources are combined).

MARGINAL REVENUE The change in revenue associated with a one-unit change in the sale of the output.

MARGINAL REVENUE PRODUCT The change in total revenue associated with a one-unit change in the number of units of a given resource employed by a firm, all other factors being equal.

MARGINAL UTILITY The change in utility resulting from a one-unit change in consumption.

MARKET That which comes into being whenever and wherever buyers and sellers assemble to satisfy their mutual needs.

MARKET FAILURE What occurs when the quantity and quality of goods and services produced are not in the best interests of society.

MARKET STRUCTURE The basic environment surrounding buyers and sellers. Also called *market organization*.

MARKUP The ratio of the contribution profit to the price of the product.

MAXIMAX POLICY Decision making under conditions of optimism.

MAXIMIN POLICY Decision based on some gain but not the highest payoff.

MICROECONOMICS The detailed economic analysis of individual components of a society. The focus is on price, output, and equilibrium.

MINIMAX POLICY Choice of a strategy that minimizes the maximum possible loss.

MIXED-STRATEGY GAME Game in which various possible strategies are employed in some optimal mix that is based on the players' abilities to compute the probabilities of occurrence of the strategies.

MONEY A medium of exchange that is used, for example, to buy goods and services, and whose value depends on general acceptance and official sanction.

MONOPOLISTIC COMPETITION Competition in which there are many sellers, each producing differentiated but close substitutes. Entry is usually easy for new firms and perfect information may or may not be available to all firms.

MONOPOLY Exclusive control by one group of the production and sales of a commodity or service.

MONOPOLY INDEX Indicator computed to show the presence and magnitude of a firm's monopoly power.

MONOPSONY Resource market situation in which there is a single buyer of the resource.

MULTIVARIATE DEMAND FUNCTION A comprehensive demand function that includes as many variables as possible or necessary.

NECESSARY AND SUFFICIENT CONDITIONS Two conditions of optimization. A necessary condition requires that the marginal revenue curve intersect the marginal cost function. A sufficient condition requires that the value of the slope of the marginal cost must be greater than the value of the slope of the marginal revenue function. Also called *first-order* and *second-order conditions*.

NEGATIVE EXTERNALITIES The harmful side effects of acts by private agents.

NET REVENUE Revenue reduced by the amount paid out, as for commissions, transportation costs, and taxes.

NEUTRAL TECHNOLOGICAL INNOVATION New method or technology that requires the use of the previous optimal ratio of capital to labor.

NONCONSTANT-SUM GAME Game in which the sum of the gains and/or losses to all of the players is not constant.

NONPRICE COMPETITION Selling tactics used by firms under monopolistic competition that include product variation, advertising, marketing, and promotion.

NORMAL PROFIT Profit obtained when a firm's revenues exactly equal its economic costs.

OLIGOPOLY An industry in which (1) a few sellers dominate the market, (2) firms produce homogeneous or differentiated products, (3) there are substantial entry barriers, (4) the firms are aware of each other's actions, and (5) the firms sometimes collude.

OPPORTUNITY COST The sacrifice made owing to the choice to buy or produce one thing instead of another.

OUTPUT The final or finished product.

PARETO OPTIMALITY Basic tenet holding that a situation is efficient if an attempt to improve one part leads to the deterioration of another part.

PARTIAL EQUILIBRIUM ANALYSIS Analysis that examines certain factors and outcomes in a particular market but ignores the effects of the decisions made by the participants in this market on the rest of the economy.

PAYOFF The reward or loss due to a particular action.

PEG Hold at a constant level, as price.

PERFECT COMPETITION The operation of the market when equilibrium price and quantity are determined by the fundamental laws of supply, demand, and equilibrium. It requires that (1) many sellers produce and act independently, (2) all firms in the industry produce a homogeneous or highly standardized product, (3) new firms have virtually no difficulty in entering the industry and competing, and (4) all buyers and sellers have perfect information and possess perfect mobility.

POSITIVE EXTERNALITIES The beneficial side effects of acts by private agents.

PRESTIGE PRICING Tactic of charging high prices by persuading the buyer to indulge in some conspicuous consumption.

PRICE The value of a good in terms of other goods.

PRICE DISCRIMINATION Charging individuals or groups different prices for the same product.

PRICE ELASTICITY OF DEMAND The ratio of the percentage change in quantity demanded to the percentage change in price of the product, all other factors remaining equal.

PRICE ELASTICITY OF REVENUE The ratio of the percentage change in revenue to the percentage change in price.

PRICE ELASTICITY OF SUPPLY The ratio of the percentage change in the quantity supplied to the percentage change in the price of the product.

PRICE-INDUCED CONSUMPTION LOCUS A curve drawn by connecting the various points where the indifference curves are tangent to the budget lines. The various quantities are induced by price changes alone.

PRICE LEADERSHIP Setting prices for an industry as a result of being large, efficient, or popular with certain groups or by virtue of low cost of operation.

PRICE SKIMMING Practice of taking the profits from each successive model, starting with the most expensive models of the product, a practice illustrated by the offering of the hardcover version of a book before its softcover edition.

PRICE TAKER One who takes the price given by the market in order to sell.

PRIVATE COST An act of production by private parties that is composed of the costs of production and associated opportunity costs.

PROBABILITY The chance that a given event will occur.

PRODUCTION The act of making or creating goods to satisfy human needs and wants.

PRODUCTION-POSSIBILITIES CURVE A curve showing the maximum possible output combinations with reference to producing various goods and services, given the quantity and quality of the economic resources of a society.

PROFIT FUNCTION Expression of the relationship of pure profits to the quantity of output produced and sold.

PROFITEER One who makes excessive profits on commodities in short supply.

PROGRESSIVE INCOME TAX Tax on income whose rate rises as the income increases.

PSYCHOLOGICAL PRICING Tactic of using pricing startegies that employ subtle consumer psychology in that one price may appear more attractive than another without actually being so.

PUBLIC GOODS Valuable goods and services provided by the public sector and consumed by all, for example, our legal and monetary systems and our national defense.

PURE COMPETITION Competition in which the firms produce basically standardized products and are price takers. They possess neither perfect information nor perfect mobility, nor are they all identically capable.

PURE PROFIT Economic profits *or* the excess of revenue over total costs, including opportunity cost. Also called *super-normal* or *abnormal profit.*

RAMSEY NUMBER The ratio of the difference in price and marginal cost to the price multiplied by the price elasticity of demand for the product or service.

RAMSEY OPTIMAL PRICING Scheme maintaining that the optimal tax rate is the lowest one that minimizes the welfare cost of meeting the state revenue requirement constraint.

RATE-OF-RETURN REGULATION Restriction of profits by limiting earning to a certain rate of return on investment, which is carefully calculated to permit the firm to earn a fair return.

REAL INCOME Purchasing power adjusted for changes in prices.

RECTANGULAR HYPERBOLA A curve with the characteristic that, no matter which point is picked, the values along the vertical and horizontal axes, when multiplied, always yield a constant.

RELATIVE PRICE The value of a good in terms of other goods.

RESOURCES Factors of production that include land, labor, capital, and the entrepreneur.

RETURNS TO SCALE Conditions depending on comparison of the ratio of the percentage change in output to the percentage change in *all* the inputs. The percentage change in output may be greater than (increasing returns to scale), equal to (constant returns to scale), or less than (decreasing returns to scale) the percentage change in inputs.

REVENUE The amount of sales receipts obtained from buyers *or* the product of price times the quantity.

ROTHSCHILD INDEX Monopoly indicator which compares the slope of a firm's demand curve to the slope of the demand curve for the entire industry. The higher the index, the higher the monopoly power of the firm.

SCALPING The practice of reselling admission tickets to theaters and sports events at prices above the official level charged by the issuer.

SCITOVSKY CRITERION Criterion holding that a proposed change is considered worthwhile if the gainers can somehow persuade the losers to accept the change voluntarily and if the losers cannot bribe the gainers to resist the change.

SECOND-DEGREE PRICE DISCRIMINATION Charging successively lower prices for each additional range of output purchased. Also called *quantity-discount pricing*.

SHORT RUN Time period characterized by circumstances in which the firm is unable to vary some of its production factors.

SLACK VARIABLE An artificial variable that is added to an inequality to make it an equation. The value of the variable is restricted to zero or positive amounts.

SOCIAL COST The cost borne by society for production by private industry; for example, air and noise pollution.

SPECIALIZATION The restriction of activity to a single area, which results in increased productivity and efficiency.

SPECULATION The act of engaging in ventures of more than ordinary risk in the hope of making greater than ordinary gains.

SPECULATOR One who takes greater than ordinary risks in business ventures in the hope of realizing greater than ordinary gains.

SUBSTITUTES Products that are so related that an increase in the price of one will cause an increased demand for another. One example is margarine and butter.

SUBSTITUTION EFFECT The change in quantity resulting from a price change, such that the new quantity in combination with the other goods yields as much utility as before. The substitution effect is related to the willingness of the consumer to substitute relatively less expensive goods for those that are dearer.

SUNK COSTS All the costs that have already been invested in a project and that are normally not recoverable or changeable.

SUPPLY The amounts of goods and services that are available for purchase at various prices.

SUPPLY, LAW OF The direct or positive relationship of quantity supplied to price.

SURPLUS Excess, as of receipts over expenditures, or the amount left over after the satisfaction of a need.

TECHNOLOGY All available technical knowledge and knowhow that is available at any one time.

THIRD-DEGREE PRICE DISCRIMINATION Charging varying prices to different groups of customers. Also called *multiple-market price discrimination*.

TOTAL COST The sum of the variable and fixed costs.

UNCERTAINTY Condition of imperfect knowledge or information about future outcomes.

UTILITY Happiness, satisfaction of wants, and well-being with reference to consumers.

UTILITY FUNCTION Expression of the relationship of a person's utility to the quantity and quality of goods and services that he or she consumes.

UTILITY-POSSIBILITY FRONTIER A graphical representation that shows the highest utility possible for one individual, given a certain level of utility for another person.

VALUE JUDGMENT An evaluation of something on the basis of personal standards.

VARIABLE A quantity capable of assuming any of a set of values.

VARIABLE COSTS Costs that vary with the volume of output.

VEBLEN EFFECT Phenomenon where the demand for very expensive items increases as the price increases.

WAGE EARNER One who is paid wages or a salary for his or her work.

WELFARE ECONOMICS Study of the optimal allocation of resources in an economic society.

ZERO-SUM GAME Game in which one person's gains are another's losses.

INDEX